Proceedings

FIFTH INTERNATIONAL WORKSHOP ON SOFTWARE SPECIFICATION AND DESIGN

MAY 19-20, 1989
PITTSBURGH, PENNSYLVANIA, USA

Sponsored by:
IEEE Computer Society
ACM SIGSOFT

ACM SIGSOFT Engineering Notes
Volume 14, Number 3 May 1989

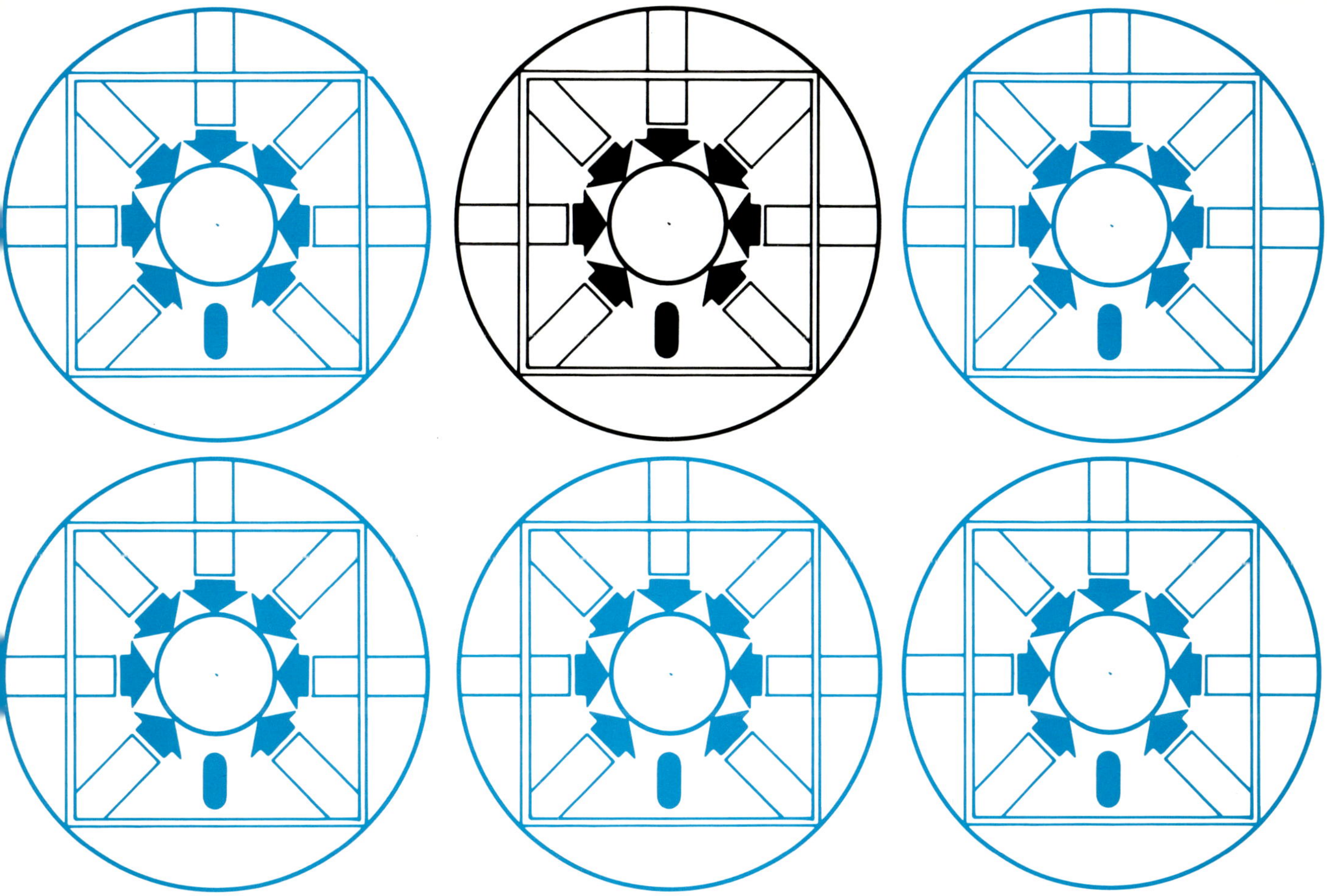

IEEE COMPUTER SOCIETY

THE INSTITUTE OF ELECTRICAL AND ELECTRONICS ENGINEERS, INC.

Fifth International Workshop on Software Specification and Design

Proceedings

FIFTH INTERNATIONAL WORKSHOP ON SOFTWARE SPECIFICATION AND DESIGN

ACM SIGSOFT Engineering Notes
Volume 14, Number 3 May 1989

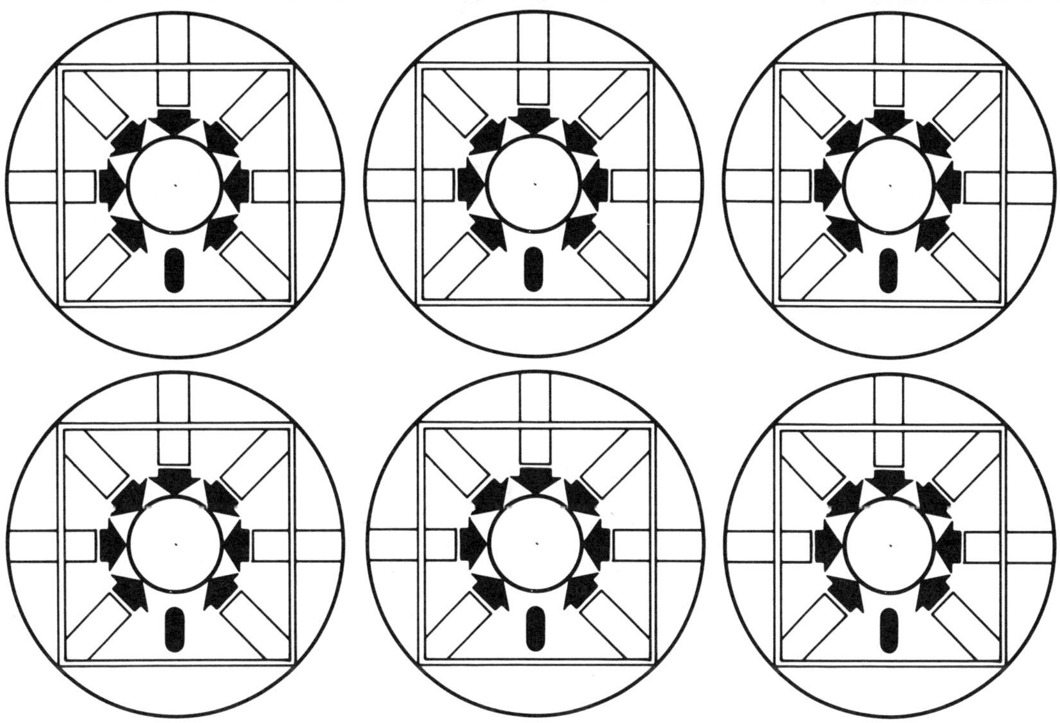

IEEE Computer Society Press
Washington ● Los Alamitos ● Brussels ● Tokyo

Published by

IEEE Computer Society Press
1730 Massachusetts Avenue, N.W.
Washington, D.C. 20036-1903

Cover design by Jack I. Ballestero

IEEE Computer Society Order Number 1942
Library of Congress Number 89-80097
ISBN 0-8186-1942-2 (paper)
ISBN 0-8186-5942-4 (microfiche)
ISBN 0-8186-8942-0 (case)
IEEE Catalog Number 89CH2717-7
ACM Order Number 592891
ISBN 0-89791-305-1
SAN 264-620X

Additional copies of the 1989 Proceedings may be ordered from:

IEEE Computer Society
Order Department
10662 Los Vaqueros Circle
Los Alamitos, CA 90720-2578

ACM
Order Department
P.O. Box 64145
Baltimore, MD 21264

IEEE Service Center
445 Hoes Lane
P.O. Box 1331
Piscataway, NJ 08855-1331

IEEE Computer Society
13, Avenue de l'Aquilon
B-1200 Brussels
BELGIUM

IEEE Computer Society
Ooshima Building
2-19-1 Minami-Aoyama
Minato-ku, Tokyo 107, JAPAN

IEEE THE INSTITUTE OF ELECTRICAL AND ELECTRONICS ENGINEERS, INC.

General Chair's Message

In September of 1982, I attended a delightful symposium in Kyoto, Japan, following the 6th International Conference on Software Engineering (ICSE-6) in Tokyo. That was the International Symposium on Current Issues of Requirements Engineering Environments, organized by the Liaison Committee on Requirements Specification Techniques (LCRST) of Japan. In Kyoto, enthusiastic participants conspired to make such a meeting a regular ICSE accompaniment.

The successor was called the International Workshop on Models and Languages for Software Specification and Design, which accompanied ICSE-7 in Orlando, Florida in 1984. A post-workshop planning meeting succeeded in shortening the workshop name to the title for which IWSSD stands today, and IWSSD-3 was held in conjunction with ICSE-8 in London in 1985 followed by IWSSD-4 in conjunction with ICSE-9 in Monterey in 1987. No IWSSD was planned to accompany ICSE-10 in Singapore, due to the new annual schedule for ICSE, which was considered too frequent for IWSSDs. This brings us to IWSSD-5, to which I welcome you today.

The purpose of this workshop, as for previous ones in the series, is to explore major trends and key issues in the specification and design of software. The workshop differs from larger conferences (e.g., ICSE) by providing a forum in which theorists and practitioners can interact in an informal yet focused setting. Approximately 80 attendees will spend most of their two days in one of five small parallel working groups where relatively specific topics can be discussed. The rest of the time will be spent in plenary sessions in which the various groups will share their progress and conclusions.

To encourage strong technical content and personal involvement, participation in the workshop is based on submissions reviewed by the program committee. Many of these submissions have been captured in the workshop proceedings, which will serve as a valuable and informative record of current work in the field.

The success of the workshop depends on many individuals and organizations who have contributed their effort and enthusiasm. First and foremost, Dr. Colin Potts has been the force behind the technical organization of the workshop. He has led a superbly well-organized and efficient review process, and we are all beneficiaries of his personal commitment to the quality of the program and of the proceedings. Members of the program committee are to be thanked for their efforts in faithfully reviewing papers and contributing to workshop planning. Indicative of the cooperation and effort put forth is the fact that virtually 100% of the referees' reports came back on time, and a large majority of program committee members attended the subsequent planning meeting in Boston. Special appreciation is due to Dr. Jeannette Wing, who was responsible for local arrangements, and Dr. Ruben Prieto-Diaz, who took care of budgetary matters. I would also like to acknowledge a generous contribution by GTE Laboratories to help support the workshop.

Finally, I would like to thank all of you who submitted papers: your ideas and accomplishments lay the groundwork for our discussions and for progress in the field.

A Steering Committee (chaired by Robert Babb) has been formed to plan the fate of future IWSSD workshops. This committee is entrusted with the task of planning the time and place of future workshops, preserving its international flavor, and maintaining its quality. Riding on the coattails of ICSE has had its advantages, but the steering committee will now consider other alternatives.

Sol Greenspan

Program Chair's Message

Welcome to the 5th International Workshop on Software Specification and Design.

IWSSD is unusual for meetings of its size, because it is arranged around focused discussions instead of formal presentations. To provide focus for IWSSD-5, we have done several things. First, full and short papers were solicited about a number of themes. 120 papers were submitted this year, and those published here represent those judged best by the Programme Committee. On the basis of the accepted submissions, the tracks of the workshop were determined. There are five of these:

Concurrency, Coordination and Distribution
Real-time, Embedded and Reactive Systems
Abstraction and Structure
Requirements Elicitation, Analysis and Formalization
Formal Techniques and Operational Specification.

Once the themes of the tracks had been identified, the chairs of the tracks went to work to familiarize themselves with the work of the participants and identify the key questions that they felt should be addressed during the two days of the workshop. The workshop itself, like its predecessors, will be conducted informally with researchers and practitioners exchanging results and experiences. By breaking down the distinction between presenter and audience, we encourage all participants to take an active role. At the end of the workshop, each track chair will report the conclusions of his or her track. Given that the tracks overlap considerably, it will be interesting to see what points of technical consensus and disagreement emerge.

Judging by the papers in this volume, several trends seem to be emerging in the field. First, there is the growing realization of the theoretical and practical importance of reasoning about concurrent and real-time behaviour. Secondly, and this is a prerequisite for a mature engineering discipline, there is a continuing emphasis on formally sound representations and analyses. Although there is a track largely devoted to formal methods, formality is a theme that cuts across all of the tracks. Another important preoccupation of an engineering approach must be the application of its techniques to large-scale and structurally complex problems. This is only just starting to be addressed systematically. (Perhaps we can look forward to scale and complexity being *the* unifying themes of IWSSD-6). Finally, specification is receiving much more attention than design. It is reassuring to see the very earliest phases of development, where errors are costliest and most difficult to detect, being given the most scrutiny. Let's not forget, though, that a specified system is considerably less useful than an implemented one.

Because of IWSSD's emphasis on discussion in place of formal presentations, this volume is not the IWSSD-5 'Proceedings' at all: it really contains detailed background material, most of which will be discussed or presented informally during the workshop. Noting that 'Proceedings was somewhat of a misnomer, the Programme Committee almost persuaded me to use the term 'Precedings' instead, but I decided that computer science is already responsible for too much violence to the language. A summary of the workshop will be printed subsequently in a professional publication, and that could well be appear as the workshop 'Succeedings'.

In closing, I would like to thank all those who have contributed to the programme of IWSSD-5: the members of the Programme Committee, each of whom contributed to the structure and vision of the workshop, and, without complaint, reviewed about twenty papers in one month; the track chairs, for their preparation and organization; and the participants, whose contributions succeeded, in my opinion, in bringing about the strongest IWSSD yet.

Colin Potts

Workshop Committee

General Chair:	Sol J. Greenspan (USA)
Program Chair:	Colin Potts (USA)
Publicity and Finance:	Ruben Prieto-Diaz (USA)
Local Arrangements:	Jeannette Wing (USA)
Programme Committee:	R. Babb (USA)
	J. Cameron (UK)
	M. Feather (USA)
	S. Fickas (USA)
	J.-P. Finance (France)
	P. Freeman (USA)
	C. Green (USA)
	M. Harandi (USA)
	D. Harel (Israel)
	J. Z. Lavi (Israel)
	D. Marca (USA)
	R. Mittermeir (Austria)
	D. Perry (USA)
	S. Prehn (Denmark)
	R. Prieto-Diaz (USA)
	G.-C. Roman (USA)
	A. van Lamsweerde (Belgium)
	J. Wileden (USA)
	J. Wing (USA)
	J. Woodcock (UK)
	A. Yonezawa (Japan)
	P. Zave (USA)

Flaws in Specifications and What to Do About Them

Peter G. Neumann
Computer Science Laboratory, SRI International
Menlo Park, CA 94025-3493

INTRODUCTION

In this brief introductory statement for the workshop,

A *system* is a coherent collection of computer hardware, software, communications, and possibly other components, as in a process-control system. For generality, subsystems and networks of systems may both be considered as systems.

A *specification* is an abstract representation of a system (or subsystem). Specifications may exist for each of various layers of functional abstraction (as opposed to refinement abstraction), e.g., in defining the desired behavior of an overall application system, or a software subsystem, or hardware. In secure systems, for example, there might be a kernel layer, a trusted computing base layer, a database layer, and an application layer. At each layer of functional abstraction, the specification characterizes (at least) the client interface(s) for that layer. There may be various types of specifications for any given layer, e.g., a requirements specification (see below), a functional specification, and a performance specification. Specifications may be formal or informal, and may differ in their degrees of specificity, explicitly or implicitly characterizing the expected behavior. They may also address interdependencies and mappings among the representations of different layers of abstraction.

Requirements are specific properties (e.g., constraints) that a system or a particular layer of abstraction must satisfy, e.g., concerning reliability, availability, security, integrity, and real-time performance. Different requirements may exist at each layer of abstraction. Further, the requirements at the various layers may be formal or informal, may have differing degrees of specificity, and differing relationships with the reality they are intended to describe. (Examples of critical requirements at different hierarchical layers are given in Neumann [86].)

• An *implementation* is the realization of a specification, in software, hardware, physical processes, etc.

The distinctions among requirements, specifications, and implementations are intended to be intuitive rather than precise, and in some cases may be only a matter of perspective. Besides, in the literature we find 'requirements specifications' (e.g., Jaffe and Leveson [89]), which bridge the requirement-specification boundary, and 'executable specifications', which bridge the specification-implementation boundary.

The stated requirements (or requirements specifications, if you wish) are in general only an approximation to what would really be required, if it were fully understood. An obvious design goal is that requirements should be made sufficiently close to the real world, complete, and precise, so that the specifications can be evaluated for consistency with those requirements; to this end, it is vital that both requirements and specifications be subjected to extensive reality checks, particularly at any exported system interface layers. As we are reminded below, software specifications must not be considered in isolation, but rather in the context of the entire system.

A subsequent implementation goal is that the implemented system should be consistent with its specifications. With requirements such as the absence of side-effects caused by Trojan horses, the consistency must be bidirectional -- the system should do no more and no less than specified. However, because most requirements and specifications are incomplete in some sense (e.g., with respect to performance and certain unstated assumptions), the concept of 'no more and no less' is subject to interpretation.

There is a wide range of problems attributable to specifications. Generic types of problems include

©1989 ACM 0-89791-305-1/89/0500/000XI$00.75

• specifications based on faulty, inadequate, imprecise, incomplete, or absent requirements,

• specifications that are inconsistent with their requirements (often resulting in design flaws),

• specifications that appear to be consistent with their requirements, but that are nevertheless incomplete (again possibly resulting in design flaws),

• specifications whose rigidity unduly constrains the implementation (e.g., premature bindings, inadequate generality, or forced selection of inappropriate hardware and operating systems).

Examination of a recent index of computer-related fiascos discussed in *Software Engineering Notes* (Neumann [89]) indicates that each of the first three types has occurred on many occasions, often with deleterious effects resulting from system or human misbehavior. The fourth type has been attributed to a few efforts, such as the PL/I and Ada programming language specifications, and identified as a contributing cause in some system development fiascos. Overall, a majority of the cited cases involved flaws in system concept, requirements, design, or specification. Furthermore, many problems commonly blamed on improper implementation are actually the result of mistakes or omissions in the earlier stages of development -- as are problems with poorly designed human interfaces and user malpractice. Thus, good specifications are really the key to software development.

A FEW EXAMPLES OF SPECIFICATION PROBLEMS

It is illustrative to review a few of the diverse specification problems that have been experienced. (References to cases not explicitly cited here can be found in Neumann [89].)

Human Safety

A fundamental flaw in the software controlling the Therac 25 therapeutic radiation device was responsible for at least three separate deaths and other injuries. There are two settings for the linear accelerator, a high-intensity X-ray mode and a low-intensity electron-beam mode. The X-ray mode was supposed to be accompanied by the placement of a movable filter (called a 'target') that diffuses the X-rays. The X-ray mode and the presence of the filter should have been linked indivisibly, but were not, resulting in an unsafe state. In general, the lack of atomicity often appears to be an implementation glitch; however, in this case the system and software requirements/specifications were incomplete in that they did not address the safety issues. Irrespective of whether my terminology is consistent with anyone else's, the source of the problem can be shared among the requirements, the specifications, and the implementation.

Other examples of incomplete system requirements and specifications (i.e., transcending just the software and hardware) are given by several instances of electromagnetic interference on systems. At least two cases of deaths have resulted from the microprocessor memory of heart pacemakers being altered by stray signals accidentally emulating the external reprogramming facility. Similar problems have been noted in external interference acting unpredictably upon microprocessor-controlled car engines. Interference is an excellent example of a problem that must be addressed by system requirements and system specifications.

Reliability

The October 1980 ARPANET collapse is one of the most dramatic examples of a distributed system problem that had remained undetected for many years. A flaw in the garbage collection algorithm was accidentally revealed by an unexpected and undetected hardware bit loss in a highest-priority network-node status message (Rosen [81]). The resulting network-wide propagation of three versions of the same status word resulted in the failure of garbage collection, the saturation of the memory of each node, and the total clogging of the ARPANET. This is an example of inadequate requirements and specifications, and illustrates some of the intrinsic difficulties in specifying distributed systems.

Even the constructive use of redundancy to improve reliability may suffer from a variety of design flaws. Anticipated fault modes may exceed the coverage of the redundancy, especially if the requirements are inadequate. There may be unexpected common-mode failures, where the same fault adversely affects each redundant instance. The specification of separate entities must be accompanied by explicit constraints that the implementation will not compromise the intent of the specification, for example, by using a common implementation for an inadequately specified function. Numerous examples of this phenomenon have been observed, including the seven separate trunk lines connecting New England with the rest of the ARPANET -- nicely redundant except that all seven were housed in the same fiber-optic cable, which was accidentally severed in December 1986. Another curious case was that of the Handley Page Victor aircraft, where three supposedly independent tests all erroneously led to the conclusion that there was no tailplane flutter problem at any attainable speed. Indeed, they all came up with roughly the same numbers -- each wrong, but for a different reason. Unfortunately, the tailplane broke off during the flight test of the first prototype, killing the crew.

Security

The recent Internet Worm is an illustration of some computer security problems. The exploited vulnerabilities -- in the *sendmail* program and the user-status query *finger* -- were directly attributable to a lack of proper attention to sound design. The *sendmail* flaw stemmed from an operating system that did not permit sufficiently selective allocation of privileges (cf. Multics' use of append-only privileges to mailboxes, restricted just to the mail handlers), the use of an 'easy' design alternative without encapsulation, and the existence of an overly powerful and widely accessible interface. The *fingerd* flaw resulted from the invocation of another program, *gets*, whose lack of bounds checking permitted the clandestine manipulation of the stack. (For detailed examinations of the worm software and its effects, see the cited reports by Eichin and Rochlis [89], Seeley [89], and Spafford [89].)

Numerous other security flaws have resulted from fundamental mistakes in specifications, or even from the absence of specifications (''just write the code''). Common cases include problems with initialization and termination, modularization and encapsulation, argument validation, user identification and authentication, and supposedly indivisible operations, to name just a few. (Many other security flaws result from sloppy implementation of specifications and from improper maintenance, but they are not considered here.)

User Interfaces

Perhaps the most neglected aspect of system development involves the choice of the human interfaces. Even the best designed hardware and software systems can be rendered ineffective by inappropriate user interfaces. The Vincennes' shootdown of an Iranian Airbus was blamed on human error, and the computer system was officially vindicated. It is apparently true that the Aegis did indicate the Airbus' altitude correctly, from which the operators should have been able to ascertain that the plane was ascending. However, the altitude data was not conveniently displayed, and there was no explicit indication over time as to whether the would-be target was ascending, descending, or flying level. There was also no indication that the target whose transponder signal was being received (a plane still on the airport runway) was a *different* plane from the one whose flight was being tracked. Thus, some blame must be placed on the specification of the human interface.

The Therac 25 design provides another example of an unfortunate user interface, in which safety-critical error messages could be overridden and the complex control commands could be edited without the integrity of any contextual abstraction, thus permitting access to an unsafe state.

ABSTRACTION AND GOOD SOFTWARE ENGINEERING PRACTICE

There are many contributions that good software engineering practice could have made to the prevention or minimization of these and many other problems. In particular, the sound use of system structuring, specification languages capable of meaningful abstraction, and rigorous analysis of specifications could all have had significant effects. For example, the use throughout design and specification of meaningful software structuring techniques following Dijkstra, Parnas, and others (such as modularization, compartmentation, layers of abstraction, encapsulation, information hiding, hierarchical or other structured locking, strict transaction protocols, protection domains, and enforcement of separation of duties) and supporting programming languages would have avoided many of the flaws noted here and in Neumann [89] generally. Emphasis on 'complete, robust and safe' requirements (Jaffe and Leveson [89]) is altogether vital. The analytic work of Leveson [86] is also appropriate, directed explicitly at software safety.

Careful structuring is especially important in supposedly secure systems, in which good specification practice can eliminate or minimize many of the commonly made errors in design, such as missing exception conditions, lack of bounds checking, type mismatching and other forms of improper argument validation, as well as overreliance on omnipotent access mechanisms (such as superuser mechanisms) and intrinsically weak protection mechanisms -- all of which have been linked with system penetrations and internal frauds. With respect to security problems, the use of mandatory controls for secrecy and integrity can add significantly to the ability to structure an application. (For example, see Lipner [82] and Clark and Wilson [87].) Layers of trusted computing bases are becoming more common, such as successively higher layers enforcing mandatory security, mandatory integrity, application security, application integrity, application correctness, etc. (e.g., the SeaView database management system described in Lunt [88]).

Many methodologies for software development have emerged in recent years, some of which contribute constructively to avoiding the most flagrant specification flaws -- such as hierarchical unsoundness, lack of encapsulation, lack of type safety, storage residues, etc. (I admit to a particular affinity for concepts found in the mid-70s in SRI's Hierarchical Development Methodology, HDM, and in its current successor Extended HDM, EHDM (von Henke et al. [88]), both of which attempt to encourage the specifier toward good practice.)

Formal verification has often been talked about as a technique for demonstrating consistency between code and assertions about that code, in some cases between code and specifications. Somewhat less popular has been the easier notion of using formal verification to demonstrate that a set of formal specifications is consistent with its formally axiomatized requirements, i.e., carrying out *design verification*. Some interesting successes have been observed in proving that specifications for kernels and trusted computing bases satisfy certain multilevel security properties (e.g., Honeywell's Secure Communications Processor, SCOMP, Silverman [83], Benzel and Tavilla [85]), or that a small system design satisfies certain reliability properties (SRI's ultrareliable flight-control Software Implemented Fault Tolerant system, SIFT). More recently, the Viper effort is aimed at proving the correctness of the hardware design and its realization (Cohn [88]). In principle, such approaches have extraordinary potential, but still remain rather unapproachable for most developers. Nevertheless, the potential of design verification in increasing assurance seems considerable and realistically more attainable than the formal verification of code and hardware. (The National Computer Security Center's 'Orange Book', TCSEC [85], is a proponent of the design verification approach for the so-called 'A1' rating. However, the existence of the 'Red Book', TNI [87], demonstrates the incompleteness of the current Orange Book requirements, especially for networks and distributed systems.)

CONCLUSIONS

Theories, methodologies, models, techniques, and tools for software specification have advanced significantly in recent years. Unfortunately, the general practice is still lagging, particularly in the development of applications that must satisfy particularly stringent requirements. Casual practice in establishing requirements and in writing specifications supposedly to meet those requirements -- or worse yet, designing systems without much attention to requirements and specifications -- remains widespread. For systems that must behave dependably with respect to critical requirements, such practice is dangerous.

Specifications must generally be considered in the context of the entire system. For example, writing specifications only for a visible software interface generally leaves many unanswered questions that when ignored can dramatically undermine system behavior -- at both higher and lower layers of abstraction. Furthermore, in those applications in which computer software and hardware represents only a portion of the overall system, *system specifications* must transcend the computer software. Specification languages should be sufficiently powerful to represent entire system designs (including but not limited to computer hardware and software) -- and necessary constraints on people. Carefully defined hierarchical abstraction is then important to structure the design and to be able to relate the various layers of abstraction to one another. Hierarchical abstraction can greatly improve the understandability of the system, as well as clearly delineating the context of the software. It can thereby facilitate the rectification of the software specifications with the system specifications. Such an approach can greatly reduce the number and effects of design flaws.

Even the best specifications can be improperly implemented. However, a demonstrably sound set of specifications can greatly increase the soundness of the development effort.

Human interfaces should be treated with the utmost care, with at least as much attention paid to good software engineering practice as to the system itself. For example, suitable use of abstraction and information hiding is vital.

As we increasingly rely on computers, the stakes are growing greater. We all recognize that the payoffs resulting from sound system design and careful specification can be very significant, throughout the ubsequent development and evolution. However, we ıust further advance the solidity and cohesiveness of he specification field, and further stimulate its lisciplined use in practical applications. Not until here are demonstrated economic advantages will the ıeeded advances occur in anything other than the nost critical applications.

ACKNOWLEDGMENT

'his note was prepared with some support from Vational Science Foundation Grant CCR-8715419.

REFERENCES

.C.V. Benzel and D.A. Tavilla [85], "Trusted ;oftware Verification: A Case Study", *Proc. 1985 EEE Symposium on Security and Privacy*, April 985, pp. 14-31.

). Clark and D. Wilson [87], "A Comparison of Commercial and Military Computer Security Policies", *Proc. 1987 IEEE Symposium on Security and Privacy*, Oakland, California, April 1987, pp. 84-194.

\. Cohn, "Correctness Properties of the Viper Block Model: The Second Level", Computer Laboratory, Cambridge University, Cambridge, England, 1988.

M. Eichin and J. Rochlis [89], "With Microscope and Tweezers: An Analysis of the Internet Virus of November 1988", MIT Project Athena report, Cambridge MA 02139, January 1989.

M.S. Jaffe and N.G. Leveson [89], "Completeness, Robustness, and Safety in Real-Time Software Requirements Specification", University of California at Irvine Technical Report 89-01, 15 February 1989. (A shortened version is included in the 1989 ICSE-11 Proceedings.)

N.G. Leveson [86], "Software Safety: What, Why, and How", *ACM Computer Surveys*, vol. 18, no. 2, June 1986, pp. 125-164.

S.B. Lipner [82], "Non-Discretionary Controls for Commercial Applications", Proc. IEEE Symposium on Security and Privacy, 26-28 April 1982, pp. 2-10.

T.F. Lunt, R.R. Schell, W.R. Shockley, M. Heckman, D. Warren [88], "A Near-Term Design for the SeaView Multilevel Database System", *Proc. 1988 IEEE Symposium on Security and Privacy*, April 1988, pp. 234-244.

P.G. Neumann [86], "On Hierarchical Design of Computer Systems for Critical Applications", *IEEE Trans. Software Engineering* vol. SE-12, no. 9, September 1986, pp. 905-920.

P.G. Neumann [89], "Risks: Cumulative Index of Software Engineering Notes -- Illustrative Risks to the Public", ACM *Software Engineering Notes*, vol. 14, no. 1, pp. 22-26, January 1989. (This index contains references to many cases discussed in ***SEN***, including highlights from the on-line ACM Forum on Risks to the Public in the Use of Computers and Related Systems.)

E. Rosen [81], "Vulnerabilities of Network Control Protocols", ACM *Software Engineering Notes* vol 6, no 1, January 1981, pp. 6-8.

D. Seeley [89], "A Tour of the Worm", Computer Science Department, U. of Utah, November 1988. In USENIX proceedings, San Diego CA, 2 February, 1989.

J.M. Silverman [83], "Reflections on the Verification of the Security of an Operating System", *Proc. 9th ACM Symposium on Operating System Principles*, October 1983, pp. 143-154.

E.H. Spafford [89], "The Internet Worm Program: An Analysis", ACM SIGCOMM Computer Communication Review 19 1, January 1989, pp. 18-57.

TCSEC [85], "Department of Defense Trusted Computer System Evaluation Criteria", DOD 5200.28-STD, December 1985.

TNI [87], "Trusted Network Interpretation of the Trusted Computer System Evaluation Criteria", NCSC-TG-005 Version-1, 31 July 1987.

F.W. von Henke, J.S. Crow, R. Lee, J.M. Rushby, and R.A. Whitehurst [88], "The EHDM verification environment: an overview", *Proc. 11th National Computer Security Conference*, Baltimore MD, October 1988.

Table of Contents

Requirements Elicitation, Analysis and Formalization

Formal Techniques and Operational Specification

†This paper will appear in the July 1989 issue (Volume 14, Number 5) of *ACM SIGSOFT Software Engineering Notes.*

CONCURRENCY, COORDINATION, AND DISTRIBUTION

Design by Decomposition of Multiparty Interactions in Raddle87

Ira R. Forman

Microelectronics and Computer Technology Corporation
Austin, Texas 78759

ABSTRACT

Synchronous multiparty interactions are becoming an increasingly important abstraction for the design of distributed systems. A method of design for multiparty interactions is described whereby large interactions are decomposed into groups of smaller interactions. The method is illustrated with the Lift Problem from the Fourth International Workshop on Software Specification and Design. The paper presents an abstract solution in which the lifts both cooperate and have distributed control. The abstract solution is then decomposed to a design for a unidirectional message-passing ring. The decomposition process is effective but informal.

1. Introduction

Synchronous multiparty interactions are becoming an increasingly important abstraction for the design of distributed systems. Multiparty interaction covers the synchronous communication of CSP (with output guards) [1], where all the interactions are two-partied. It covers the synchronous broadcast of CIRCAL [2], where one party broadcasts a value to the others. It covers the synchronous value matching of CSPS [3], where data can flow freely between the parties. There are also two proposals to add a multiparty interaction construct to Ada [4, 5]. Recently there have been two other proposals for multiparty interactions: shared actions [6] and joint actions [7]. This paper presents a method of design for multiparty interactions whereby large interactions are decomposed into groups of smaller interactions. The Lift Problem is used to illustrate the design method.

The Lift Problem was one of three used at the Fourth International Workshop on Software Specification and Design [8]. Some solutions featured centralized control with cooperative lifts; others featured distributed control with competitive lifts (that is, the lifts race against each other to satisfy passenger requests). There were, however, no solutions that featured both distributed control and cooperative lifts. This is not to suggest that these solutions are wrong, but rather that there is a portion of the solution space that is still uncovered. Design using multiparty interactions has clearly helped us to achieve a solution in this remaining part of the solution space.

In this paper, we revisit the Lift Problem to produce an abstract solution that has both distributed control and cooperative lifts. The design is expressed in Raddle87 [9, 10], which has its own form of multiparty interaction. The abstract solution is then decomposed into a design for a unidirectional message-passing ring. The decomposition process is effective but informal. It is effective in that during design the objectives are clear. The informality becomes an issue to the extent that the correctness of each decomposition is established with insufficient aid from the previous step. We conclude that the design method needs to be formalized so that decompositions preserve correctness properties.

2. A Short Introduction to Raddle87

The basic semantic concepts of Raddle are: *team, role, behavioral expressions*, and *N-party interaction*. The following informal discussion of Raddle87 provides sufficient information for understanding the examples presented in this paper. Readers interested in a more detailed discussion of Raddle87 should consult [10].

A Raddle program comprises a set of *teams*. A team is composed of a set of *roles*, of which there are two kinds, *processes* and *procedures*. When a team is instantiated, its processes begin execution. Procedures are reentrant; they are available to be entered by any process that knows the team address and role name. Roles are composed of *variables* and *behavioral expressions*. A role repeatedly executes its behavioral expression until a **return** is encountered (i.e., a role implicitly defines a loop). The variables are containers of values; the behavioral expressions describe how roles interact and alter variables.

Last, but most importantly, the *N-party interaction* (which we shorten to interaction) is the communication and synchronization mechanism of Raddle. *Interactions* can take place between any number of roles, but only when all participating roles are ready.

Figure 1 depicts a team for a bounded buffer; the bounded buffer is used to explain the syntax and semantics of Raddle87.

```
team Bounded_buffer(bound)
        integer bound;

send (pstuff)
        untyped  pstuff;

  produce[[ ]] ⟶ return
||
process buffer
        integer current := 0
        list    bqueue := nil;

  current < bound &
          produce[[ current := current + 1,
                        bqueue := append(bqueue,list(pstuff)) ]]
  []
  current > 0 & consume[[ current := current - 1,
                          bqueue := cdr(bqueue) ]]
||
receive(cstuff)
        untyped  cstuff;

  consume[[ cstuff := car(bqueue) ]] ⟶ return
end
```

Figure 1. The bounded buffer team.

Three roles are declared in Figure 1; *send* and *receive* are procedures, while *buffer* is a process. Roles are separated by "||". The procedures provide the interface for higher levels of the system, which is much like the interface provided by the operations of an abstract data type. For example, *send* has a formal parameter (*pstuff*), which is the value placed in the buffer; *receive* has a formal parameter (*cstuff*), which is the value taken from the buffer and returned to the calling role. The variables of a procedure are allocated on the stack of its caller and disappear after each call. Processes such as *buffer*, on the other hand, start execution when the team is instantiated. The processes of a team are encapsulated and interact only with the other roles of the team. The **return** action returns control to the calling role.

Teams are definitions stored in a library. Teams are instantiated with the **new** command, which returns the address of the team instance. The address is just a unique name of the instance of the team. The syntax of the **new** command is illustrated in Figure 2. In this example, the buffer size is fixed at instantiation time with the value of a formal parameter of the team. Note that the formal parameters are declared at the team level. One can also declare other identifiers and assign values to them; these identifiers are constants that represent knowledge common to all roles at the time the team is instantiated (i.e., assignment to identifiers declared at the team level by roles is not allowed).

Raddle87 is a design language; it borrows types, values, and expressions from another notation. In Figure 1, we use a generic language that borrows functions from LISP. Several interesting designs have been done, including a debit card system [11], a competitive lift system [12], and a cooperative lift system [13], which is further discussed in Section 3. Raddle87 has been given a graphical syntax by Graf [14, 15] in building VERDI (Visual Environment for Raddle Design and Investigation). VERDI also has a simulation capability that is attained by adding an embedded language for types, values, and expressions.

2.1 N-party Interactions

A labeled pair of brackets of the form

$$label\ [\![\ldots]\!]$$

is called a *box*. The set of similarly labeled boxes within a team is called an *interaction*. Interactions are the way roles synchronize and communicate. The interaction *produce* is between the roles *send* and *buffer* and the interaction *consume* is between the roles *receive* and *buffer*.

Once all the partners have synchronized, the interior of the interaction begins. The interior is a set of assignment statements. During interactions a role has access to the variables of its partners. Thus, the scope of a variable is the role and the interior of all the boxes of all the interactions in which the role participates. The partners are known at compile-time because the box labels are not storable values. The assignments are concurrent assignments. The value of a variable referenced in an expression is the value at the beginning of the interaction. The variable on the left side of the assignment must be a variable of the role in which the assignment appears. Thus one role cannot change the value of another role's variables. In Figure 1, the interiors of the interactions involve the manipulation of the variables to achieve the transfer and queuing of *pstuff* and *cstuff*. Note that the *produce* box in *buffer* references the variable *pstuff* and that the *consume* box in *receive* references the variable *bqueue*.

Boxes need not be labeled, nor does a labeled box need to have partners. These are one-party interactions. Simple assignments like $x := x+1$ can be written with the meaning

$$[\![\ x := x+1\ ]\!]$$

(the reason for this convention becomes clear when conflict resolution is discussed in Section 2.2).

A construct of the form

$$guard\ \&\ action$$

is called a *guarded action*, where a guard is a boolean-valued expression and an action is either a box (i.e., *label* $[\![\ldots]\!]$), a **return**, or a role invocation (which is explained later). The behavior of a role is described by composing guarded actions with the operators [] (choice) and ⟶ (sequence). Roles are implicitly loops in that roles execute the behavioral expression until a **return** is encountered.

In Figure 1 the *send* and *receive* have simple behaviors; they interact and return. Interacting means readying the box; when all the boxes are ready for an interaction, then it is said to be *enabled* and may "fire" (start execution). The *buffer* is a little more complex in that it contains a choice that is determined both by its state (the status of *bqueue*) and by its environment (the *send* and *receive*). When faced with a set of choices, the predicates are evaluated and then the actions for only the true guards are readied. The *buffer* can ready two interactions *produce* (if the buffer is not full) and *consume* (if the buffer is not empty). If more than one interaction is enabled, a nondeterministic choice is made. Note that if the predicate of a guarded action is not written, it is the constant predicate *true*.

In forming behavioral expressions, ⟶ has precedence over []. Parentheses may be used to override the precedence. It should be noted that [] is associative, i.e.,

$$g_1 \,[]\, (g_2 \,[]\, g_3)$$

has the same behavior in all contexts as

$$(g_1 \,[]\, g_2) \,[]\, g_3$$

where the g_i's are behavioral expressions.

2.2 Conflict and Coordination

A conflict occurs whenever one role may participate in more than one enabled interaction. In such cases the semantics of Raddle require that a nondeterministic choice be made by a coordination algorithm. Chandy and Misra [16] have invented a coordination algorithm for asynchronous message-passing networks. Back and Kurki-Suonio [17] present a method for doing this when all processes share a broadcast medium (such as Ethernet). A survey of coordination algorithms can be found in [18].

In addition, the semantics of Raddle assure weak fairness, but not strong fairness (see [19], Section 5.2). Weak fairness means that an interaction, once enabled, will fire if it is never disabled. Strong fairness means that an interaction will fire, if it is enabled infinitely often. Note that an enabled interaction is disabled if it is in conflict with another interaction and that other interaction fires.

2.3 Hierarchy

It was stated earlier that procedures can be entered by other roles. This is called *role invocation* and the syntax for it is as follows:

team_address @ *role_name* (*parameters*)

Now let us continue our example by considering a team with two roles *R1* and *R2* that wish to communicate. However, *R1* and *R2* do not want to be tightly coupled with synchronous communication, but rather want asynchronous communication. They may do this with bounded buffers. Rather than programming two bounded buffers, we can reuse the one we have already built (Figure 1) as shown in the Raddle fragment in Figure 2. The **new** command creates two new instances of the bounded buffer and assigns them to the appropriate variables in the team (remember that these variables may not be changed after the team is instantiated). Once this is accomplished *R1* and *R2* can play the *send* and *receive* roles in the bounded buffer to communicate. (Note that once one has the address of a team instance, one can play any of the procedures in the team. This is a security issue that may be taken up in later versions of Raddle, depending on whether the issue is as serious for design languages as it is for programming languages.)

```
team Buffer_users
        team     buffer1 := new Bounded_buffer(10),
                 buffer2 := new Bounded_buffer(10);

process R1
    real stuff1;
         :
    buffer1@send(stuff1)
         :
    buffer2@receive(stuff1)
         :
||
process R2
    real stuff2;
         :
    buffer2@send(stuff2)
         :
    buffer1@receive(stuff2)
         :
end
```

Figure 2. Example of creating teams and invoking roles.

The parameter-passing mechanism for Raddle is call-by-value-result. This convention was chosen because it supports the substitution of teams for interactions (as shown in Section 4.2.4).

Role invocation is an action. As such it may appear in guarded actions with the syntax

guard & team_address@role_name(parameters)

with no restriction. Consider a behavioral expression of the form

$$g_1 \,[]\, T@R$$

This expresses a choice between executing g_1 or invoking role R in team T. The choice is resolved by readying both g_1 and the behavioral expression of $T@R$. If an interaction of $T@R$ is fired, then the execution is committed to invoking $T@R$. If an interaction in g_1 is fired, then execution continues without role invocation (and with no side-effects to worry about). The semantics of invocation in Raddle87 (which are fully explained in [10]) are quite different from those of other languages. Usually, invocation of a procedure implies a commitment to its execution; this is obviously not the case in Raddle. The advantage of this decision is that syntactically teams may be viewed as expansions of interactions. This enables a method of design in which interactions may be refined. One cannot substitute teams for interactions with impunity (as described in Section 4), but we have created the framework in which to address the problem.

2.4 Replicators

One more syntactic notion is needed before we consider a larger example. Replicators are written in the following form

$$< \textit{separator variable\_list} : \textit{predicate} :: \textit{element} >$$

The *predicate* represents a set over which the variables range; the set defined by the *predicate* must be computed at instantiation time. The *element* is any syntactic element of Raddle that may be separated by the *separator*. In effect the replicator is a macro that replicates the *element* once for each member of the set defined by the *predicate*, substituting the member for the variables and inserting the separator between each replicated element. If one wants to declare an integer array, it can be done with

$$\textit{integer} <, i : 0 \leq i \leq 9 :: x_i >$$

and if one wants to sum the array, it can be done with

$$sum := <+\ i : 0 \leq i \leq 9 :: x_i >$$

The legal separators are: $[\!]$ $\longrightarrow$ $\|$, + * **and** **or** . The replicator does not specify an ordering; when using $\longrightarrow$ as a separator, one must take care that every ordering is satisfactory.

In addition, the replicator can be used in functions with a variable number of parameters. For example,

$$maximum := max(<, i : 0 \leq i \leq 9 :: x_i >)$$

Finally, if the x_i's are booleans, their conjunction is written as

$$conj := <\textbf{and}\ i : 0 \leq i \leq 9 :: x_i >$$

3. The Lift System

This section provides an overview of our solution to the Lift Problem. The statement of the Lift Problem is attributed to Neil Davis and appears in the Proceedings of the Fourth International Workshop on Software Specification and Design [8]. See Appendix A the statement of the Lift Problem. Figure 3 shows an abstraction of the design of the lift system; the full design can be found in [13]. Our design specifies a process for each lift, each button panel inside the lift, and each floor button. The lift processes coordinate with each other to schedule their movements using information from the panel- and floor-button processes. Specifically, each lift process maintains a list of floor requests that it must answer. The list is sorted according to the lift's direction of travel. A panel-button push causes a request to be entered into the list at the proper place. A floor-button push is broadcast to all lift processes through an interaction. Each lift process computes its cost for servicing the request (based on direction of travel and distance from the floor). Another interaction determines a minimal-cost lift. The request is then entered into the schedule for that lift.[1] Figure 3 shows a segment of the Raddle design that includes only a floor-button process and a lift process.

```
team Lift_system(N,F)
  integer N,F;

  process floor_button_i
    integer r := i
    boolean on,entered;
      :
    []
    on and not entered ⟶ broadcast_i[[entered := true]]
    []  :
        :
||
  process lift_j
    integer request, mycost_j
    boolean mine
    list schedule;
      :
    []
    broadcast_i[[ request := r ]]
        ⟶ mycost_j := cost(schedule, request)
        ⟶ elect [[ mine := (mycost_j = min (mycost_1, ..., mycost_N)) ]]
        ⟶ (mine ⟶ schedule := insert(schedule, request)
              || not mine ⟶ skip)
    []  :
        :
end
```

Figure 3. A segment of the lift design.

The lift system in Figure 3 supports N lifts and F floors, where N and F are integers set at team-instantiation time. In the complete design, we replicate the *lift* process N times, using j as the index. Since each floor, except top and bottom, has two buttons, we replicate the *floor_button* process $2{\times}(F-1)$ times, so that the index i encodes both the floor and the direction. The segment beginning with $broadcast_i$ in the *lift* process is replicated $2{\times}(F-1)$ times for each j. In the figure, we omit the *panel_button* processes for simplicity.

When a floor button is on and the request is not yet entered into the schedule of any lift, the *floor_button* process broadcasts the request to all the *lift* processes. Other choices at this point (not shown) include the maintenance of waiting status and the cancellation of the request after a lift going in the right direction stops at the floor.

1. We are making a powerful but reasonable assumption that desirable lift scheduling policies can be obtained for a floor-button request by each lift computing a cost that is independent of the status of the other lifts and then assigning the request to the minimum-cost lift.

The *lift* process requires the use of two external functions: the *cost* procedure that computes the cost of servicing the new request by this lift and the *insert* procedure that inserts the request at the proper place in the schedule. The *elect* interaction sets the boolean variable *mine* to **true** for the lift that has the least cost in servicing the request and **false** otherwise. The last event in this sequence is another choice: the request gets inserted into the schedule in the lift with least cost. This assumes that the *cost* function returns unique values; unique values can be achieved by multiplying the cost by the number of lifts and adding the lift index.

We have outlined a distributed and coordinated design to the Lift Problem (again, a complete solution can be found in [13]). In the design two major separations of concern can be seen. The first is the familiar one; procedural abstraction separates the finding of an appropriate cost function for lift scheduling. The second is the abstraction of the communication network from the design, which requires the multiparty interaction. That is, we have achieved a high-level solution that separates the problem of constructing networks and algorithms for the *broadcast* and *elect* interactions. At this stage a team of designers could spilt into two groups.

One group could attack the problem of how the cost of a request is computed for an individual lift. Prototyping is probably the way to identify a proper cost function. (Chandrasekharan and McGowan [20] use simulation to show that coordinated lifts dominate competitive lifts with respect to minimum waiting time.) The important point is that the N-party interaction does not interfere with early prototyping to find a proper cost function before having to solve the problem of how to implement the *elect* interaction.

A second group could address the problem of broadcasting the floor-button requests to the lifts and coordinating the lifts to find the minimum of the individual costs and select a server. The subproblem of finding minima is interesting by itself. In the next section, we address the job of decomposing the interaction *elect* when a particular network architecture is chosen.

4. Decomposing the Election Interaction

In this section, we demonstrate the separation of concerns described above by focusing on the decomposition of the *elect* interaction when a undirectional ring is chosen as the network architecture. The problem is to construct a team with N procedures, $elector_0, elector_1, \cdots, elector_{N-1}$, (which are to be used by the lifts) that are invoked with two parameters *id* and *im_leader* (which correspond to *my_cost* and *mine*). The following specification must be met: if all roles are invoked with a unique positive value *id,* then the one with the minimum value returns with *im_leader* set true and all the others return with *im_leader* set false. (Note: Raddle allows procedures to be multiply invoked. Because there is a one-to-one correspondence of lifts to elector procedures and the interaction *broadcast* forces a synchronization, multiple invocations are not a problem.)

4.1 An Abstract Solution

Figure 4 contains a first step in the solution process; it encapsulates the interaction *elect* into its own team. This team and its decompositions are solutions to the Leader Election Problem. Note that no information about the architecture needs to be included in this solution.

```
team Leader0(N)
   integer N;

<|| i : 0≤i≤N-1 ::
elector_i(id_i, im_leader)
   integer id_i
   boolean im_leader;

   elect[[ im_leader := (id_i = min(<, j : 0≤j≤N-1 :: id_j>)) ]]
      → return
>
end
```

Figure 4. Abstract solution for leader election.

4.2 Solution by Decomposition

In this section we present a message passing solution to the Leader Election Problem for a unidirectional ring. (This decision is made to demonstrate the design technique and is not indicative of any special knowledge of the lift problem domain.) Starting with the abstract solution, the large N-party interaction is decomposed into smaller interactions.

4.2.1 Leader1 The first step is to decompose the interaction such that the algorithm operates in N rounds, which is done in Figure 5. In each round all roles synchronously pass their current minimum value to the left neighbor, who computes a new minimum. We adopt the convention that the neighbor to the left is the next higher numbered role. The following invariant holds:[2]

I1 $\quad minid_i = minimum(\{id_j \mid j=i, i-1, \ldots, i-round_i+1\})$

That is, $minid_i$ is the minimum of the id_i's over the roles i to $i-round_i+1$. The invariant can be established by induction on $round_i$. It holds prior to the first round because $minid_i$ is initialized to id_i. It holds thereafter because on each round the assignment

$$minid_i := min(minid_i, minid_{(i-1) \bmod N})$$

causes $minid_i$ to be the minimum over one more role while concurrently $round_i$ is incremented by one. Using this invariant a proof of correctness is a trivial matter. The

2. Invariants hold when interactions are not executing. In all discussions of algorithms throughout this report, subscripts are computed modulo N. Statements in which the index i is free hold for all i such that $0 \le i \le N-1$.

next decomposition is proved correct.

It should be noted that it is in this step that the decision to use a unidirectional ring is made. Other architectures could also be obtained.

```
team Leader1(N)
   integer N ;

< || i : 0≤i≤N-1 ::
elector_i(id_i, im_leader)
   integer id_i,
      minid_i := id_i,
      round_i := 1
   boolean im_leader;

   round_i < N &
         pass [[ minid_i := min(minid_i, minid_(i-1)mod N),
                 round_i := round_i + 1
              ]]
   []
   round_i = N
      --> im_leader := (id_i = minid_i)
      --> return
>
end
```

Figure 5. Leader1 - first decomposition.

4.2.2 Leader2 The next step is to decompose the interaction into two-party interactions $pass_i$ between $elector_i$ and $elector_{i+1}$. In Figure 6 each role is always ready to receive a new minimum and send a minimum when it has received at least one new minimum. The state space of the roles is expanded with the variable $given_i$, which tracks the amount of information passed to the left. Invariant I1 still holds for *Leader*2 for the same reason it holds for *Leader*1. In addition the following invariants hold for $given_i$:

I2 $given_i \leq round_i$

I3 if $round_i < N$ then $given_{i-1}+1 = round_i$.

Invariant I2 holds because $given_i$ is modified only by setting it equal to $round_i$, which never decreases.

I3 is shown to be invariant as follows. First note that

$round_i = minimum(round_{i-1}+1, N)$ and $given_{i-1} = round_{i-1}$

is a postcondition of $pass_{i-1}$, which implies

$$(\text{if } round_i < N \text{ then } round_i = round_{i-1}+1) \\ \text{and } (given_{i-1} = round_{i-1})$$

which in turn implies I3. Thus, $pass_{i-1}$ is the only interaction to modify $given_{i-1}$ and $round_i$ and $pass_{i-1}$ leaves I3 true. By further noting that I3 holds initially, we conclude that I3 is an invariant.

One more invariant is important:

I4 $round_{i+1} \leq given_i + 1$

To show that invariant I4 holds, we first note that I4 holds initially. Now if $round_i < N$ when $pass_i$ executes, then by the assignments in $pass_i$

$$round_{i+1} = given_i + 1$$

If $round_i = N$ when $pass_i$ executes, $round_{i+1}$ is assigned N and $given_i$ is assigned N. Because $round_i \leq N$, we have shown that all executions of $pass_i$ preserve I4.

There is also a very important property with respect to *pass*.

P5 if $pass_i$ is enabled, then $pass_i$ eventually fires.

Note that property *P5* does not imply that $pass_i$ fires for each enablement. Property P5 is proved as follows. If $pass_i$ is enabled, then $given_i < round_i$ and $round_{i+1} < N$. The only way to disable $pass_i$ is for $pass_{i-1}$ or $pass_{i+1}$ to execute. The execution of $pass_{i-1}$ cannot decrease $round_i$ (nor change $given_i$). Thus after $pass_{i-1}$ executes, $round_{i+1}$ is unchanged, $given_i < round_i$ is still true, and $pass_i$ is again enabled. The execution of $pass_{i+1}$ cannot change $given_i$ or $round_i$ or $round_{i+1}$. This means $round_{i+1} < N$ and $pass_i$ is still enabled after $pass_{i+1}$ executes. Because no interaction can execute more than N times, a state must be reached where $pass_i$ is enabled with neither of its conflicting neighbors enabled. By the weak fairness property of Raddle (i.e., if an interaction becomes enabled, it will become disabled), $pass_i$ must execute.

```
team Leader2(N)
   integer N ;

< || i : 0≤i≤N-1 ::
elector_i(id_i, im_leader)
   integer id_i,
      minid_i := id_i,
      round_i := 1,
      given_i := 0
   boolean im_leader;

   round_i < N
     & pass_(i-1)mod N [[ minid_i := min(minid_i, minid_(i-1)mod N),
                          round_i := min(round_(i-1)mod N + 1, N)
                       ]]
   []
   given_i < round_i
     & pass_i [[ given_i := round_i ]]
   []
   round_i = N and given_i ≥ N-1
     --> im_leader := (id_i = minid_i)
     --> return
>
end
```

Figure 6. Leader2 - second decomposition.

Now let us prove the correctness of *Leader*2. Correctness means the following:

Theorem. If all roles are invoked with a unique positive *id*, then all roles return with *im_leader* set true for the role with the minimum *id* and false for all other roles.

Proof. The partial correctness follows from invariant I1 because if a role returns, $round_i$ must be N and therefore $minid_i$ must be equal to the minimum of the id_i. *im_leader* is set true if and only if $id_i = minid_i$. Partial correctness is easy to show because the decomposition of the interactions preserves safety properties. Showing liveness properties is another matter.

Now termination is proved. We must show that

(1) eventually for all i, $round_i = N$ and $given_i \geq N-1$.

The proof is by contradiction. By assuming that (1) is not true, we show that there exists an enabled interaction, which by P5 must execute and thus take us a step closer to termination.[3] The negation of (1) says that it is always the case that there exists an i such that either

(a) $round_i = N$ and $given_i < N-1$

or

(b) $round_i < N$.

In case (a), by invariant I4

$$round_{i+1} - 1 \leq given_i$$

which combined with (a) yields

$$round_{i+1} - 1 \leq given_i < N-1$$

which yields

$$round_{i+1} < N$$

Therefore, $given_i < round_i$ and $round_{i+1} < N$, which means that $pass_i$ is enabled.

In case (b), then we show, for some j, $pass_j$ is enabled by showing $round_j > given_j$. By invariant I2, $given_{i-1} \leq round_{i-1}$. Thus either $pass_{i-1}$ is enabled (and we are done) or $given_{i-1} = round_{i-1}$. In the latter case by invariant I3, $round_{i-1} < round_i < N$. Because we are dealing with a ring, there must be a j such that $round_{j-1} > round_j$ and therefore $pass_{j-1}$ must be enabled. To summarize, we have proved that if (1) is not true, then an enabled interaction exists that eventually executes (by property P5), which brings the algorithm closer to termination because some $round_1$ increases as a result of this execution. ▯

3. More formally, the pairs $(round_i, given_i)$ together with the lexicographic ordering form a semilattice for each role. The Cartesian product of these semilattices is a semilattice, which provides a well-founded set for a termination proof.

4.2.3 Leader3 Now let us make a very simple observation: a role has something new to tell its left neighbor only if its current *minid* is greater than the previous value passed to the left. In the decomposition in Figure 7, the above observation is used to suppress interactions that are not required and arrive at an approximation of the algorithm of Chang and Roberts [21]. Note that an interaction is forced if $round_i$ becomes N and $given_i < round_i$.

```
team Leader3(N)
   integer N ;

< || i : 0≤i≤N-1 ::
elector_i(id_i, im_leader)
   integer id_i,
      minid_i := id_i,
      round_i := 1,
      given_i := 0,
      lastpass := 0
   boolean im_leader,

    round_i < N
      & pass_(i-1)mod N [[ minid_i := min(minid_i, minid_(i-1)mod N),
                           round_i := min(round_(i-1)mod N +1, N) ]]
   []
    given_i < round_i and (lastpass < minid_i or round_i = N)
      & pass_i [[ given_i := round_i, lastpass := minid_i ]]
   []
    round_i = N and given_i ≥ N-1
      → im_leader := (id_i = minid_i)
      → return
>
end
```

Figure 7. Leader3 - third decomposition.

4.2.4 Leader4 The final step in this exercise is to substitute a message passing team for the *pass* interaction. This is done with a team from the Raddle library that simulates message passing. Such a team is shown in Figure 8. Note that channel capacity N (equal to the number of lifts) is sufficient to ensure freedom from deadlock (and hence termination) because no role ever receives more than N messages.

5. Conclusions

We have revisited the Lift Problem to show a solution that is both cooperative and distributed. We have explored the advantages for the design of distributed systems of languages that have multiparty interactions. The major advantage is that the new abstraction (multiparty interaction) allows separation of concerns in a very natural way.

Next, we have pursued one concern (the decomposition of the *elect* interaction) to a natural end, a design for a unidirectional message passing ring. This requires a method of design that decomposes large synchronous interactions into groups of smaller interactions. Currently, these transformations are ad hoc; that is, each decomposition is proved correct independently; a tedious process, as Section 4 shows. A future important step in this research is to establish proof techniques to reduce the tedium. Others are working on this problem [22] for atomic actions, but not for multiparty interactions.

```
team Leader4(N)
      integer N
      team <,i : 0≤i≤N-1 ::
            channel_i := new Bounded_buffer(N)>;

< || i : 0≤i≤N-1 ::
elector_i(id_i,im_leader)
      integer id_i,
            minid_i := id_i,
            round_i := 1,
            given_i := 0,
            lastpass := 0
      list    msg
      boolean im_leader;

      round_i < N & channel_(i-1)mod N@receive(msg)
            ⟶ [[ minid := min(minid,nth(1,msg)),
                        round_i := min(nth(2,msg)+1,N) ]]
      []
      given_i < round_i and (lastpass < minid_i
                    or (round_i = N and given_i < N-1))
            & channel_i@send(list(minid,round_i))
              ⟶ [[ given_i := round_i, lastpass := minid ]]
      []
      round_i = N and given_i ≥ N-1
            ⟶ im_leader := (id_i = minid_i)
            ⟶ return
>
end
```

Figure 8. Leader4 - fourth decomposition.

Acknowledgements

I would like to thank Paul Attie, Glenn Bruns, Skip Ellis, Mike Evangelist, Noreen Garrison, Susan Gerhart, Mike Graf, Peter Marks, Colin Potts, Charlie Richter, and Vincent Shen for their comments on earlier versions of this report. Special thanks go to Paul Attie for improving the proof of Leader2 and his meticulous proofreading of this report. Thanks also go to Jay Misra for the many discussions from which the design of Raddle87 has greatly benefited. Finally, I would like to thank the referees their thoughtful comments.

References

1. C. A. R. Hoare, "Communicating Sequential Processes," *Comm. ACM* **21**(8) pp. 666-677 (August, 1978).

2. G. J. Milne, "CIRCAL and the Representation of Communication, Concurrency, and Time," *ACM Trans. on Programming Languages and Systems* **7**(2) pp. 270-298 (April, 1985).

3. G.-C. Roman and M. S. Day, "Multifaceted Distributed Systems Specification Using Processes and Event Synchronization," *Proc. 7th Int'l Conf. on Software Engineering*, Orlando, Florida, March 26-29, 1984, pp. 44-55

4. N. Francez and B. Hailpern, "Script: A Communication Abstraction Mechanism," *Proc. of the 2nd Int'l Symp. on Principles of Distributed Computing*, pp. 213-227 (1983).

5. A. Charlesworth, "The Multiway Rendezvous," *ACM Trans. on Programming Languages and Systems* **9**(3) pp. 350-366 (July, 1987).

6. R. J. R. Back and R. Kurki-Suonio, "Distributed Co-operation with Action Systems," *ACM Trans. on Programming Languages and Systems* **10**(4) pp. 513-554 (October, 1988).

7. S. Ramesh and S. L. Mehndiratta, "A Methodology for Developing Distributed Programs," *IEEE Trans. on Software Engineering* **SE-13**(8) pp. 967-976 (August, 1987).

8. IEEE Computer Society Press, *Proc. of the Fourth Int'l Workshop on Software Specification and Design*, Monterey, California, April 3-4, 1987.

9. I. R. Forman, "On the Design of Large Distributed Systems," STP-098-86 (Rev. 1.0), Microelectronics and Computer Technology Corp., Austin, Texas (January, 1987). (Preliminary version in *Proc. First Int'l Conf. on Computer Languages*, October 25-27, 1986, Miami, Florida.)

10. P. Attie, "A Guide to Raddle87 Semantics," STP-340-87, Microelectronics and Computer Technology Corp. (January 11, 1987).

11. I. R. Forman and M. Evangelist, "EFT: A Case Study in Design using Raddle," STP-121-87, Microelectronics and Computer Technology Corp., Austin, Texas (April, 1987).

12. I. R. Forman, "Raddle - An Informal Introduction," STP-182-85, Microelectronics and Computer Technology Corp., Austin, Texas (February, 1986).

13. I. R. Forman, "The Lift Problem Revisited," STP-269-87, Microelectronics and Computer Technology Corp. (September, 1987).

14. M. L. Graf, "A Visual Environment for the Design of Distributed Systems," *Proc. of the 1987 Int'l Workshop on Visual Languages*, Linkoping, Sweden, August, 1987.

15. M. L. Graf, "The Design of Distributed Systems Using A Visual Language," *Proc. of the 1987 IEEE Workshop on Lanugaes for Automation*, Vienna, Austria, August, 1987.

16. K. M. Chandy and J. Misra, *Parallel Programming Design: A Foundation,* Addison-Wesley (1988).

17. R. Back and R. Kurki-Suonio, *Co-operation in Distributed Systems Using Symmetric Multi-process Handshaking,* Swedish University of Abo (June, 1984).

18. E. Levy, "A Survey of Distributed Coordination Algorithms," STP-271-88, Microelectronics and Computer Technology Corp. (September, 1988).

19. N. Francez, *Fairness,* Springer-Verlag, New York (1986).

20. M. Chandrasekharan and C. McGowan, "Using Simulations to Resolve Practical Performance Issues of Specifications and Architectures," *Proceedings of the Fourth Int'l Workshop on Software Specification and Design,* Monterey, California, April 3-4, 1987, pp. 154-160

21. E. Chang and R. Roberts, "An Improved Algorithm for Decentralized Extrema-Finding in Circular Configurations of Processes," *Comm. ACM* **22**(5) pp. 281-283 (May, 1979).

22. J. L. Welch, L. Lamport, and N. Lynch, "A Lattice-Structured Proof Technique Applied to a Minimum Spanning Tree Algorithm," *Proc. of the Seventh ACM Symp. on Principles of Distributed Computing,* Toronto, Canada, August 15-17, 1988.

Appendix A.

The following is the original statment of the Lift Problem.

An N lift system is to be installed in a building with F floors. The lifts and the control mechanism are supplied by the manufacturer. The internal mechanisms of these are assumed (given). The problem concerns the logic to move lifts between floors according to the following constraints:

1 - Each lift has a set of buttons, one button for each floor. These illuminate when pressed and cause the lift to visit the corresponding floor. The illumination is cancelled when the corresponding floor is visited (i.e. stopped at) by the lift.

2 - Each floor has 2 buttons (except ground and top), one to request an up-lift and one to request a down-lift. These buttons illuminate when pressed. The buttons are cancelled when a lift visits the floor and is either travelling in the desired direction, or visiting the floor with no requests outstanding. In the latter case, if both floor request buttons are illuminated, only one should be cancelled. The algorithm used to decide which to service first should minimise the waiting time for both requests.

3 - When a lift has no requests to service, it should remain at its final destination with its doors closed and await further requests *(or model a 'holding' floor).*

4 - All requests for lifts from floors must be serviced eventually, with all floors given equal priority *(can this be proved or demonstrated?).*

5 - All requests for floors within lifts must be serviced eventually, with floors being serviced sequentially in the direction of travel *(can this be proved or demonstrated?).*

6 - Each lift has an emergency button which, when pressed causes a warning signal to be sent to the site manager. The lift is then deemed 'out of service'. Each lift has a mechanism to cancel its 'out of service' status.

Rooting UNITY

extended abstract

Rob Gerth*
Eindhoven University of Technology†

Amir Pnueli
Weizmann Institute of Science‡

February, 1989

Abstract

We take a theoretician's look at Chandy and Misra's UNITY and ask what it is that makes the UNITY methodology so easy to use and how it relates to alternative methodologies. Specifically, we show how UNITY might have been obtained as a specialization of Manna and Pnueli's temporal logic proof methodology together with Gerth's transition logic. This has the additional advantage of firmly rooting UNITY within a proof methodology that is sound and (relatively) complete, thus transferring these properties to UNITY itself.

1 Introduction

Despite the truism, the goal of program verification remains aiding the design of correct software. Because of this, Dijkstra's 1976 "A Discipline of Programming" [Dij76] still is a watershed publication: this monograph takes the earlier ideas on program verification of Floyd [Flo67] and Hoare [Hoa69] and builds a methodology with which a (sequential) program is developed through a number of successive steps, starting from some abstract specification from that program. This *stepwise development method* received a theoretical basis mainly through the work of Back [Bac80]. In modern terms, Back's formalism was the first example of a *mixed specification formalism* in which specifications and programs coexist on equal basis. The most important feature of Dijkstra's stepwise development method, however, is that it is easy to use *in*formally so that its use in the derivation of a program does not hinder the development of the underlying algorithm.

The obvious question is: what about parallel programs? For such programs the interest is in general temporal properties (as opposed to partial or total correctness). In a series of papers culminating in [MP83] Manna and Pnueli have generalized Floyd's inductive assertion method to proving such temporal properties. It can even be done compositionally, as Barringer, Kuiper and Pnueli have shown in [BKP84]. Mixed specification formalisms exist for *safety* properties; devised by Jonsson [Jon87], by Widdom [Wid87], and most extensively by Zwiers [Zwi89].

It is quite obvious that none of the latter three authors achieve comparable simplicity when set against Dijkstra's method for sequential programs. The main problem with these formalisms is the complexity of reasoning about computation histories.

Now, this may well be inherent to parallel programs — they are just so much more harder to design and to get correct. K. Chandy and J. Misra have claimed otherwise during the last three years and most forcefully in their recent textbook [CM88]. Summarized into one sentence, their thesis is that many if not all of the difficulties arise from the failure to separate the design

*The author is currently working in and partially supported by ESPRIT project P937: "Debugging and Specification of Ada Real-Time Embedded Systems (DESCARTES)".

†Department of Computing Science, Eindhoven University of Technology, P.O. Box 513, 5600 MB Eindhoven, The Netherlands. Email: wsdcrobg@heitue5.bitnet or mcvax!eutrc3!wsinrobg.uucp.

‡Department of Applied Mathematics and Computer Science, Weizmann Institute of Science, Rehovot, Israel.

of an (abstract) algorithm from the control flow that occurs in any of its realizations. Issues of sequential control flow — single (as in PASCAL) or multiple (as in CSP) —, uniprocessor versus distributed implementation, shared variable versus communication based interaction, synchronous versus asynchronous systems, etc. have no place in the initial design of an algorithm; they are later concerns, when the algorithm is specialized towards a specific architecture.

Instead, these authors propose a new programming language and design methodology — UNITY. Ignoring syntactic sugaring, a UNITY-program is a first-order transition system whose underlying graph has precisely one vertex and whose infinite execution sequences are constrained so that every transition occurs infinitely often on it.

Whatever one's initial reaction to this proposal or to the earlier claims might be, the sheer number and diversity of examples that Chandy and Misra tackle and their complexity comprise a convincing argument for the practical significance of this approach.

On a theoretical level this leaves two questions to be answered:

1. Exactly what is it that makes the proof theory of UNITY so much easier than those for other languages, and
2. How does the UNITY-methodology relate to its alternatives.

This paper attempts to address these questions. Specifically, we shall rewrite history and show how UNITY might have been embedded in Manna and Pnueli's temporal logic framework [MP83] together with Gerth's transition logic [Ger84], by asking how this framework can be simplified. If we succeed, this will give a sound and complete underpinning of the UNITY-approach, since it will then have been derived from a sound and complete system.

The remainder of this abstract sketches informally the derivation of UNITY and its proof system. We will concentrate mostly on the technical aspects of UNITY. The reader should consult [CM88] for methodological motivation.

2 Temporal and Transition Logic

We assume that the reader is familiar with linear temporal logic. Given some arbitrary class of first order transition systems[1] and some arbitrary set of justice and fairness constraints, [MP83] shows how to construct a proof system for proving program-properties expressed in linear temporal logic. Specifically, it is shown how proving such properties for a transition system, π, can be reduced to proving *transition properties* of the form $[p]\pi[q]$. Here, p and q are state-assertions and the intended meaning of $[p]\pi[q]$ is that "every transition in π that starts in a state satisfying p will terminate in a state satisfying q". The formulae in a transition property will have to refer to both the value of π's variables and to π's control-locations. The reduction in proof effort is that we started with a temporal logic assertion about π's computation sequences which is reduced to state assertions about the individual transitions of π.

Transition logic [Ger84] is motivated by Lamport's [Lam80] and is a logic for *compositional* reasoning about transition properties. Suppose that transition systems are generated using some set of syntactic combinators, $\mathcal{C}_i$ (and some set of primitive transition systems). Then, the most important proof rule in [Ger84] asserts (in first approximation) that for any combinator, $\mathcal{C}(\cdot, \ldots, \cdot)$ and any transition systems, π_i,

$$\frac{[p]\pi_0[q], \ldots, [p]\pi_n[q]}{[p]\mathcal{C}(\pi_0, \ldots, \pi_n)[q]}$$

is a valid inference.

This rule is a straightforward consequence of the fact that the transitions in $\mathcal{C}(\pi_0, \ldots, \pi_n)$ comprise precisely the transitions of its components, $\pi_0, \ldots, \pi_n$. Unfortunately, it does not achieve a reduction in the complexity of the state-formulae p and q in the initial specification. Here a problem arises because state-formulae depend on the control-locations of programs so that to simplify them we need to know the relations between control-locations in the different programs

[1] I.e., given a programming language whose operational semantics has been given by a transition system.

parts. Independently of how this is actually formalized — see [Ger84] for that — it is clear that if the rule is applied to, e.g., a sequential composition, $\pi_0 ; \pi_1$, we should be able to use, e.g., the axiom $in(\pi_0) \rightarrow \neg in(\pi_1)$ (where the proposition "$in(\pi)$" has its usual meaning and expresses that control resides somewhere within π or at its front), whereas if the rule is applied to a parallel composition, $\pi_0 \parallel \pi_1$, this axiom should not be used. In general, compositional proofs of such transition properties depend on a detailed analysis of the *syntactic* structure of programs; as is born out by the completeness proof in [Ger84]. This is what makes transition logic hard to use.

3 Redesigning the programming language

3.1 Normal forms of programs

If reasoning about arbitrary programs is too cumbersome, it might be possible to concentrate on restricted classes of programs. According to the previous section, the less syntactic structure a program has, the easier it becomes to reason about. On the other hand, we do want to maintain at least *universality*, so that every computable function is computable by a program from this restricted class.

For programs that compute over the integers, a classical result, [Wei87, section 1.4, theorem 5], says that the class of sequential while-programs is a universal class. Moreover, Mirkowska [Mir70,Har80] has shown that while-programs containing precisely one while-statement actually suffice.

If we use Dijkstra's guarded iteration construct [Dij76] instead of while-statements and admit *simultaneous*-assignments[2], we can go further yet:

3–1 THEOREM. *The class of programs of the form $S_0 ; \star[b_1 \rightarrow S_1 \,\square \cdots \square\, b_n \rightarrow S_n]$, where $b_1,\ldots,b_n$ are boolean tests and $S_0,\ldots,S_n$ are simultaneous assignments, is a universal class.*

The gist of the theorem's proof is conveyed by the following example: a program

$$\star[b_1 \rightarrow x := e\,; \textbf{if } b_2 \textbf{ then } y := f \textbf{ fi} \,\square\, b_3 \rightarrow z := g]$$

would be transformed into

$$\begin{aligned} t := 0\,; \star[b_1 \wedge t = 0 \rightarrow x, t := e, 1 \quad &\square \quad b_2 \wedge t = 1 \rightarrow y, t := f, 0 \\ &\square \quad \neg b_2 \wedge t = 1 \rightarrow t := 0 \quad \square \quad b_3 \wedge t = 0 \rightarrow z := g] \end{aligned}$$

The values of the fresh variable t identify the (syntactic) branching points in the original program. Observe that we can take $t := 0$ uniformly for every transformed program.

Since the goal is to remove all control-locations, we can one-up existing normal form theorems one more time, by allowing *conditional* assignments — e.g., $x, y := \begin{cases} x+1, 3 & \text{if } y > 0 \\ y, x & \text{if } y < 0 \end{cases}$, whence implicitly $x, y := x, y$ if $y = 0$. Also, we will replace the initial assignment by a specification of the initial state.

3–2 THEOREM. *The class* SLP *— single location programs — is a universal class. Here, an* SLP*-program has the form $I\colon \star[A_1 \,\square \cdots \square\, A_n]$; $A_1,\ldots,A_n$ are conditional assignments and I specifies the initial state.*

A computation-step of such a program is the execution of some assignment A_i. A computation is considered finished if none of the assignments can cause the state to change anymore; i.e., if and when the state *stabilizes.* To fix notation, assume that specifications of the initial state are given as simultaneous assignments in which "=" takes the place of ":=". Uninitialized variables have an arbitrary value.

[2] The variables on the left-hand-side of simultaneous assignments should not contain duplications.

As indication of proof of the theorem, a continuation of the previous example should suffice: the transformed program would be further transformed into

$$t=0{:}\star\left[x,t:=e,1 \text{ if } b_1\wedge t=0 \,\square\, y,t:=\begin{cases} f,0 & \text{if } b_2\wedge t=1\\ y,0 & \text{if } \neg b_2\wedge t=1\end{cases} \square\, z:=g \text{ if } b_3\wedge t=0\right]$$

The observant reader would notice that even SLP-programs are too baroque: clearly, we can do without general iteration and can assume that programs have the form $I\,;\star[A_1]$. The sequel will make it clear that this reduction is unnecessary. In fact, there are good reasons to *not* want it at all.

3.2 Parallelism

A reason to not simplify SLP any further, is that we intend to specify and develop parallel systems. For such, we want to control the extent to which the system's global state can change in one atomic step. Granting that SLP is used to describe parallel systems, then SLP's simultaneous assignment gives exactly this kind of control. Moreover, such control is obviously easier to achieve with general SLP-programs than with $I{:}\star[A]$-type programs.

In fact, Chandy and Misra maintain that SLP-programs should best be seen as system-descriptions before any implementation decisions have been taken. In their view, such architectural decisions are specific *interpretations* of the variables and the assignments in the SLP-programs. For example, by partitioning the variables, one can interpret each partition as a *synchronous* process that operates on the variables in the partition. The SLP-program then describes the lock-step execution of these processes. Alternatively, partition the assignments of the program and each partition corresponds to an *asynchronous* process, while the SLP-program describes the possible interleavings of the actions in these processes. Such architectural interpretations are a very effective tool in [CM88].

Such interpretations also induce notions of program-composition. For instance, we can define an asynchronous parallel composition as follows:

$$I{:}\star[A_1\,\square\cdots\square\, A_n]\parallel I{:}\star[B_1\,\square\cdots\square\, B_m] \quad \stackrel{\text{def}}{=} \quad I{:}\star[A_1\,\square\cdots\square\, A_n\,\square\, B_1\,\square\cdots\square\, B_m]$$

4 UNITY

The control-structure of a UNITY-program is exactly the same as in SLP. There is considerable syntactical sugaring which presumably stems from the wish to be able to suggest possible implementations within the syntax. This we shall ignore; as we shall ignore Chandy and Misra's insistence that assignments are deterministic.

There is one additional aspect to UNITY: *fairness*. On (infinite) execution-sequences, every assignment must occur infinitely often. In [MP83] this particular form of fairness is called *justice*.

We end this section with an informal definition of SLP-semantics and with a theorem relating UNITY and SLP.

4–1 DEFINITION (SLP semantics). *The semantics, $[\![S]\!]$, of an SLP-program, $S\equiv I{:}\star[A_1\square\cdots\square A_n]$, is a set of infinite sequences of states, such that every sequence is a suffix of a sequence satisfying*

1. *the first state is consistent with I,*
2. *for every pair of consecutive states, $\sigma\ \tau$, there is an assignment A_i such that $(\sigma,\tau)\in[\![A_i]\!]$*[3],
3. *for every assignment, A_i, there are infinitely many pairs of consecutive states, $\sigma\ \tau$, such that $(\sigma,\tau)\in[\![A_i]\!]$.*

[3] We assume that the semantics of an assignment, $[\![A]\!]$, has been given as a set of pairs of input and output states.

Note that this definition says that SLP-programs do *not* have finite execution sequences; which is consistent with Chandy and Misra's position. Termination of a program is replaced by reaching a *stable* state. We include all suffixes in the semantics in order to be consistent with [MP83].

Remark for the expert. The fairness-constraint is slightly weaker than the one used in [CM88], since we do not require that every assignment is taken infinitely often, but only that its effect is felt infinitely often.

4–2 THEOREM. *For any UNITY-program, U, there is an SLP-program, S, such that $[\![U]\!] = [\![S]\!]$.*

Because SLP-assignments can be nondeterministic, the converse of the theorem is not true.

5 Verifying SLP-programs

In this section we show how to tailor to SLP, (1) the transition logic proof system of Gerth [Ger84] and (2) the temporal logic proof system of Manna and Pnueli [MP83]. Since the latter proof system reduces verifying temporal properties to verifying transition properties, together they form a sound and relatively complete proof system for SLP.

Tailoring (2) is in fact quite straightforward. We can almost copy the proof rules in [MP83] while using the fact that for SLP-programs the so-called *justice set* is the set of all transitions.

Tailoring (1) is more complicated but also more interesting. It is here that the reduced syntax of SLP should pay off most, since it is here that we would have to do the reasoning about program-locations. In fact, we will see that for SLP-programs no location-predicate needs to appear at all in assertions.

For the rest of this section, fix some SLP-program, $I\colon S$, where $S \equiv \star[A_1 \,\square \cdots \square\, A_n]$.

5.1 Transition properties

If we were to prove $[p]S[q]$ using standard transition logic, we would use, amongst others, the following rule and location-axioms ($\bar{\vee}$ denotes exclusive or):

$$\frac{[p]A_i[q],\ i = 1 \ldots n}{[p]S[q]}$$

1. $at(S) \leftrightarrow \bar{\bigvee}_{i=1}^{n} at(A_i)$
2. $after(S) \leftrightarrow \bar{\bigvee}_{i=1}^{n} after(A_i)$
3. $after(S) \rightarrow at(S)$

Moreover, for an assignment, $A \equiv \bar{x} := \begin{cases} \bar{e}_1 & \text{if } b_1 \\ \ldots & \\ \bar{e}_k & \text{if } b_k \end{cases}$, where $\bar{x}$ is an m-tuple of variables and the $\bar{e}_i$ ($i = 1 \ldots k$) are m-tuples of expressions, we would use the transition logic assignment axiom

$$\frac{\begin{array}{c}\left(after(A) \wedge \bigvee_{i=1}^{k} \exists \bar{y}\ (p[\bar{y}/\bar{x}] \wedge b_i[\bar{y}/\bar{x}] \wedge \bar{x} = \bar{e}_i[\bar{y}/\bar{x}])\right) \rightarrow q, \\ \left(after(A) \wedge p \wedge \neg b_1 \wedge \cdots \wedge \neg b_k\right) \rightarrow q\end{array}}{[p]A[q]},$$

provided p does not contain any location-predicates.

Note that this is just Floyd's forward assignment axiom in disguise.

Now, what are the consequences of the restricted syntax for proofs in transition logic? We know that p and q can only contain the location-predicates, $at(S)$, $after(S)$, $at(A_i)$ and $after(A_i)$

$(i = 1 \ldots n)$[4]. If $p \equiv (at(S) \rightarrow p_0) \wedge \bigwedge_{i=1}^{n} (at(A_i) \rightarrow p_i)$, then axiom 1 implies that we can have $\models p_0 \rightarrow p_i$ for $i = 1 \ldots n$ by a judicious choice of p_0. This suggests that we can assume that p does not use any $at(A_i)$ (; just use p_0 wherever p_i was used). Likewise, we can assume that q does not use any $after(A_i)$. (Technically, we are postponing the use of the implication-rule to the end of the proof.)

Hence, we may assume that $p \equiv p_0 \wedge (at(S) \rightarrow p_1) \wedge (after(S) \rightarrow p_2)$, where p_0, p_1 and p_2 do not contain any location-predicates. Likewise for q. By axiom 3 we obtain that $\models q_2 \rightarrow q_1$, so that we may also assume that q does not use $at(S)$. That axiom also implies that $\models p_2 \rightarrow p_1$; and if we assume that $p_2 \equiv p_1$ (and we may) then we can assume that p does not use $after(S)$.

Next we use the fact that in transition logic it suffices to derive $[p \wedge at(S)]S[q]$ in order to prove $[p]S[q]$. This is in fact a special case of the strengthening-rule in [Ger84]. In its turn, this allows the conclusion that p need not contain location-predicates at all!

Thus p has the correct form for the assignment-axiom. Finally, the premiss of this rule assumes that $after(A)$ holds, from which we conclude that q, too, need not contain location-predicates.

We arrive at the following theorem:

5–1 THEOREM. *The following proof system is sound and complete for transition properties of* SLP*-programs (p and q do not contain location-predicates)*[5]*:*

$$C\colon \frac{[p]A_i[q]\ (i = 1 \ldots n)}{[p](I\colon \star[A_1 \,\Box \cdots \Box\, A_n])[q]}, \qquad I\colon \frac{p \rightarrow p', \quad [p']S[q'], \quad q' \rightarrow q}{[p]S[q]}$$

$$As\colon \frac{\exists \bar{y}\,(p[\bar{y}/\bar{x}] \wedge b_i[\bar{y}/\bar{x}] \wedge \bar{x} = \bar{e}_i[\bar{y}/\bar{x}]) \rightarrow q \quad i = 1 \ldots k \qquad p \wedge \neg b_1 \wedge \cdots \wedge \neg b_k \rightarrow q}{[p]A[q]}, \quad \text{where } A \equiv \bar{x} := \begin{cases} \bar{e}_1 & \text{if } b_1 \\ \ldots & \\ \bar{e}_k & \text{if } b_k \end{cases}$$

PROOF. The proof goes by showing how proofs in the SLP-proof system and proofs in the transition logic proof system can be intertranslated. It is in fact a formalization of the arguments leading up to the theorem. □

This three rule proof system is a marked simplification of the transition logic proof system with its 12 rules and infinite r.e. set of location predicate axioms.

5.1.1 Parallel composition

Because of the results of section 3.2, a parallel composition rule would be straightforward:

$$\frac{[p]A_i[q]\ (i = 1 \ldots n), \quad [p]B_j[q]\ (j = 1 \ldots m)}{[p](I\colon \star[A_1 \,\Box \cdots \Box\, A_n] \parallel I\colon \star[B_1 \,\Box \cdots \Box\, B_m])[q]}$$

5.2 Temporal properties

The temporal logic dialect used here is a classical 1st order logic extended with two temporal modalities: $\Diamond$ — eventually, and $\mathcal{U}$ — weak until. Traditionally, there is a third modality, $\bigcirc$ — next state. Since it is not used by Chandy and Misra, we shall ignore it too.

Instead of formally defining the meaning of temporal logic program specifications, S **sat** ϕ (S some SLP-program and ϕ some temporal logic formula), we just state that

- S **sat** $\Diamond\phi$ means that on every execution-sequence of S, ϕ will eventually become true, and
- S **sat** $\phi\, \mathcal{U}\, \psi$ means that on every execution-sequence of S, ϕ will continuously hold until ψ becomes true, if ever.

---

[4] $in(\cdot)$ is an abbreviation as it is always expressible in terms of the other predicates.

[5] An initialization-statement, '$x = e$ if b', has an obvious interpretation as an assertion: $b \rightarrow x = e$. We leave the general case to the reader.

Now, [MP83] offers three proof rules: one for proving properties of the form '$p \to q\,\mathcal{U}\,r$'; one for proving '$p \to \Diamond q$'-properties and one for combining these properties. Here, p and q are state-formulae that do not contain any modalities. Let $S \equiv I{:}\star[A_1 \,\Box \cdots \Box\, A_n]$.

$$U{:}\ \frac{\begin{array}{c}[\bar{q} \wedge \bar{p}]S[\bar{r} \vee \bar{q}],\ [\bar{p}]S[\bar{p}] \\ I \to \bar{p},\ p \wedge \bar{p} \to \bar{q} \vee \bar{r},\ \bar{q} \wedge \bar{p} \to q,\ \bar{r} \wedge \bar{p} \to r\end{array}}{I{:}\star[A_1 \,\Box \cdots \Box\, A_n]\ \mathbf{sat}\ p \to q\,\mathcal{U}\,r}, \qquad E{:}\ \frac{\begin{array}{c}[\bar{r}(\alpha)]S[r \vee \exists \beta \leq \alpha\, \bar{r}(\beta)],\ I \to \bar{q} \\ [\bar{q}]S[\bar{q}],\ q \wedge \bar{q} \wedge \neg r \to \exists \alpha\, \bar{r}(\alpha) \\ [\bar{r}(\alpha)]A_{f(\alpha)}[r \vee (\exists \beta < \alpha\, \bar{r}(\beta))]\end{array}}{I{:}\star[A_1 \,\Box \cdots \Box\, A_n]\ \mathbf{sat}\ q \to \Diamond r},$$

for any $f{:}\ \mathit{Ord} \mapsto \{1 \ldots n\}$.

$$A{:}\ \frac{S\ \mathbf{sat}\ \phi,\ S\ \mathbf{sat}\ \psi}{S\ \mathbf{sat}\ \phi \wedge \psi}$$

In rule E, f is a *choice function* that selects at every turn the helpful action that will cause q eventually to hold. In this rule we have already used the fact that every action gets executed infinitely often; i.e., that the justice-set comprises all the actions in S. The α and β are ordinals and Ord is the set of all ordinals.

In [MP83], Manna and Pnueli prove that these rules are relatively complete in the sense that any property of the form $p \to \Diamond q$ or $p \to q\,\mathcal{U}\,r$ can be proved using precisely one application of the respective rule (provided the 1st order logic is strong enough). Transition logic then supplies the means to reason about the transition properties in the premises of the rules. So, *these three rules together with the three rules of the previous subsection give a sound and relatively complete proof system for* SLP.

Now, what about Chandy and Misra's proof rules for UNITY? We claim that each of their rules is a derived rule in our system. An example has to suffice here.

Let us translate the property "q *ensures* r" ([CM88, section 3.4.4]) in our language as $q \to (q\,\mathcal{U}\, r \wedge \Diamond r)$. Their proof rule is ($S$ as above):

$$\frac{[q \wedge \neg r]S[q \vee r], \quad [q \wedge \neg r]A_i[r] \text{ for some } i = 1 \ldots n}{S\ \mathbf{sat}\ q\ \mathit{ensures}\ r}$$

Actually, this is how Chandy and Misra *define ensures*.

Now, the first premiss is used for the "$q \to q\mathcal{U} r$"-part; the second premiss for the "$q \to \Diamond r$"-part.

So, require in the U-rule that $p \equiv q$, $\bar{p} \equiv \mathit{true}$, $\bar{q} \equiv q \wedge \neg r$ and $\bar{r} \equiv r$. Then $[\bar{p}]S[\bar{p}]$ trivially holds; $(r \vee \bar{q}) \leftrightarrow (r \vee q)$; and the implications in the rule are true. Hence, the only premiss of the U-rule that needs to be proved is $[q \wedge \neg r]S[q \vee r]$; call it P.

Next, in the E-rule require the choice-functions, f, to be *constant* functions; take $\bar{q} \equiv \mathit{true}$; and $\bar{r} \equiv \alpha = 1 \wedge q \wedge \neg r$. Again, $[\bar{q}]S[\bar{q}]$ trivially holds and the implications in the rule are true. This leaves us with the transition properties: $[\alpha = 1 \wedge q \wedge \neg r]S[r \vee (\alpha = 1 \wedge q \wedge \neg r)]$ and $[\alpha = 1 \wedge q \wedge \neg r]A_f[r]$. We can derive within transition logic that it suffices to prove these properties with the "$\alpha = 1$"-parts removed — S does not depend on it. This renders the first property equal to P and the second property equal to $[q \wedge \neg r]A_f[r]$.

Combining the premises of the modified rules, we conclude that the *ensures*-rule, indeed, is a derived rule. Now, we have not been completely faithfull in our definition of *ensures*. Chandy and Misra define it in such a way that a *constant* choice function always suffices (as is clear from the proof rule). However, their proof rule, although less incomplete than it initially looked to be, still is incomplete: in general, one needs the $\bar{q}$ to characterize more fully the execution sequences of S; moreover, the fact that computations are initialized is not taken into account.

6 Conclusions

In this paper we have constructed a UNITY proof system by investigating the effects of program control on the standard temporal and transition logic proof systems and by aiming for the most simple proof system. Especially for transition property reasoning, the simplifications that can be achieved are considerable.

One might ask why the possibility of such simplifications has not been realized earlier by researchers in program verification, since the necessary theory is not particularly deep. Perhaps some did realize it. Only, it took a rare insight to see that the results would be more than a mildly interesting theoretical result, because many concurrent algorithms can be developed in such an impoverished language. Chandy and Misra had that insight.

The six proof rules in this paper form a sound and complete proof system for SLP (and hence for UNITY). Chandy and Misra's rules can be shown to be derived rules in our system. Their proof rules, however, do not comprise a complete proof system. In fact, that was not a goal for these authors. It does mean that the present paper supplies UNITY with a theoretical basis that has been missing until now.

A question with theoretical as well as practical significance is how far the SLP-syntax can be extended again while maintaining the simplicity of the proof system. One possibility is given by noticing that the particular form of the actions within the iteration of an SLP-program does not matter. It is the fact that these actions are executed *atomically* that counts. Accordingly, we can allow arbitrary programs instead of assignments as the atomic actions. The proof system would change only by the addition of rules to reason about these atomic programs; the existing rules would not change. Such an extension would make practical sense because sometimes it is easier to define the required state changes in a sequential manner.

Another possibility would be to add other composition operators. For instance, a synchronous parallel composition. This would be a first step in formalizing implementation decisions.

Acknowledgements

The first author thanks Willem P. de Roever for urging him to investigate the connection between transition logic and UNITY and Frank Stomp for his extensive comments.

References

[Bac80] R.J.R. BACK (1980), **Correctness preserving program refinements: proof theory and applications**, Mathematical Center Tracts, no. **131**, Center for Mathematics and Computer Science (CWI), Amsterdam.

[BKP84] H. BARRINGER, R. KUIPER, A. PNUELI (1984), "Now You May Compose Temporal Logic Specifications", *in* Proceedings 16th Annual Symposium on Theory of Computing (STOC), pp. 51–64, ACM.

[CM88] K.M. CHANDY, J. MISRA (1988), **Parallel Program Design**, Addison-Wesley.

[Dij76] E.W. DIJKSTRA (1976), **A Discipline of Programming**, Prentice-Hall.

[Flo67] R.W. FLOYD (1976), "Assigning Meaning to Programs", *in* Proceedings Symposium in Applied Mathematics, Vol. **19**, pp. 19–32, AMS.

[Ger84] R. GERTH (1984), "Transition Logic", *in* Proceedings 16th Annual Symposium on Theory of Computing (STOC), pp. 39–51, ACM.

[Har80] D. HAREL (1980), On Folk Theorems, *in* Communications of the ACM, Vol. **23**, No. **7**.

[Hoa69] C.A.R. HOARE (1969), An Axiomatic Basis for computer programming, Communications of the ACM, Vol. **12**, No. **10**, pp. 576–580.

[Jon87] B. JONSSON "Compositional Verification of Distributed Systems", Ph.D. dissertation, Uppsala University, Sweden.

[Lam80] L. LAMPORT (1980), The "Hoare logic" of concurrent programs, Acta Informatica, Vol. **14**, pp.21–37.

[Mir70] G. MIRKOWSKA (1970), "Algorithmic logic and its applications", Doctoral dissertation, University of Warsaw (in Polish).

[MP83] Z. MANNA, A. PNUELI (1983), "How to cook a temporal proof system for your pet language", *in* Proceedings 10th Annual Symposium on Principles of Programming Languages(POPL), ACM.

[Wei87] K. WEIHRAUCH (1987), **Computability**, EATCS Monographs on Theoretical Computer Science, Vol. **9**, Springer Verlag.

[Wid87] J. WIDDOM (1987), "Trace-Based Network Proof Systems: Expressiveness and Completeness", Ph.D. dissertation, Cornell University.

[Zwi89] J. ZWIERS (1988), **Compositionality, Concurrency and Partial Correctness: Proof theories for networks of processes and their connection**, Ph.D. dissertation, University of Eindhoven, The Netherlands. To appear in the LNCS-series , Springer Verlag.

Specifying Concurrent Systems with Δ-Grammars *

Simon M. Kaplan
Steven K. Goering
Roy H. Campbell
Department of Computer Science
University of Illinois at Urbana Champaign

Abstract

Specification of parallel and distributed systems is difficult because it involves describing a two dimensional relationship between the flow of control of many processes and the synchronized flow of data between those processes. Many researchers have turned to graphical representations for such specifications; perhaps one of the most well-known techniques involves Petri nets. However, parallel and distributed systems are often *dynamic*. The components' distribution and degree of parallelism vary with time. This is often difficult to express in existing graphical notations. The Actor approach has tried to capture such changing behavior (in a textual form) but can lead to system specifications that lack structure and are therefore prone to error.

In this paper, we introduce a new graph grammar based notation for specifying concurrent and distributed systems. The notation has a formal algebraic basis which both defines the meanings of graphs and forms the foundation for verifying transformations from specifications to code. Specifications show no implementation bias and are therefore independent of many low-level issues which clutter up conventional notations. The use of graphics greatly simplifies the tasks of writing and understanding specifications of concurrent systems.

The use of our approach is illustrated with two examples: The dynamic dining philosophers problem and the problem of establishing connections between clients in a multiple-server network with arbitrary topology in which the clients could be associated with any server.

1 Introduction

We introduce a formal approach to the specification of dynamic parallel and distributed systems that has a graphical visualization, imposes structure on dynamic systems, allows easy modification of specifications, has an algebraic basis, permits refinements of specifications to implementations, and permits deductions about dynamic systems. The specification technique is based on graph productions and uses theoretical results from the study of graph grammars. In this paper, we use the notation to specify two dynamic systems that have parallel activities and may be distributed geographically.

Specification of parallel and distributed systems is difficult. It involves describing a two dimensional relationship between the control flow of processes on the one hand and synchronized data flow on the other. Petri nets [13] are one popular approach to specifying such systems in a graphical manner. Such an approach allows a greater level of detail to be presented simultaneously to a specifier – the processing power of the eye may be used to search for patterns in the specification. Petri nets also have a formal basis that may be used to reason about the system.

However, the topology of Petri nets cannot change dynamically without augmentation of Petri net theory. Unfortunately, parallel and distributed systems are often dynamic. The components' distribution, and degree of parallelism vary with time. These systems are often difficult to express in existing graphical notations. This criticism is also true of

*Supported in part by the National Science Foundation under grants CCR-8809479 and CISE 1-5-30035 and by the AT&T Illinois Software Engineering Project. *Contact Author*: Simon M. Kaplan, 1304 W. Springfield Avenue, Urbana Illinois 61801. *phone*: 217 244 0392 *email*: kaplan@a.cs.uiuc.edu

another well-known formalism, CCS [10].

Dynamic behavior may be specified by Actor-based notations [1]. Actors may create new actors on receipt of messages or destroy themselves. Several dynamic systems involving parallelism have been specified this way. However, Actor specifications are behavioral and can lead to system specifications that lack structure. The lack of structure and the behavioral approach can impede reasoning about complex system specifications.

In previous work we developed GARP, a language for concurrent programming in which *graph grammars* are used to specify the topologies of concurrent systems [9] [8]. This work may be viewed as specifying permitted topologies for Actor systems. GARP may also be used as a design language [7]. In both of these projects, an extremely restrictive grammar formalism was used, in order to be guaranteed execution efficiency in the languages. A major contribution of this paper is the development of a declarative specification language based on graph grammars which does not suffer from these restrictions.

1.1 Goal of Research

The goal of our research has been to design a formal specification technique for parallel and distributed systems that both supports a graphical visualization that is easy to use in the specification process and describes the dynamic nature of systems using declarative techniques.

We believe *graphical representations* are an important design metaphor that both clarifies concepts and permits communication of those concepts. All structures have a natural graphical representation and there are many reasons *why* graphical representations of software systems have become popular. It has become standard practice to represent data structure, control, and data flow specifications graphically. It appears easier for a user to comprehend a two-dimensional diagram of a structure than a one-dimensional textual representation of that structure. Input to the user has a far greater bandwidth using graphical representation than using text. The human eye can aid the detection of complex patterns in graphical representations and this can take far less effort than the recognition of the equivalent patterns in textual form. For these reasons, a graphical representation of parallel systems would benefit system designers.

However, dynamic systems are more difficult to represent graphically than static ones. A behavioral specification of a complex dynamic system is difficult to analyze and is difficult to represent concisely in a graphical manner. A declarative specification is needed that represents the steps by which a system may change. Such a specification is provided by the use of graph productions.

1.2 Contents

In the remainder of the paper, we will explain the specification notation, describe its underlying formal properties, apply the notation to two examples, and summarize the contribution our work provides to the general understanding of specifications of parallel systems.

2 Overview of Graph Grammars

This section of the paper provides an overview of graph grammars. Although the review is self-contained, space does not permit a formal exposition; interested readers are referred to [12] [11] [3] for more details. We will informally review our grammar system, and then illustrate their use through several examples.

The particular graph grammar formalism we use is called Δ-grammars. This is based on Y-grammars [5]. A grammar consists of:

- An *initial graph*;
- A set of productions.

Each production is of the form shown in Figure 1. The production has a *context*, enclosed in a triangle (thus the name Δ-grammars). Each side of the triangle is identified as the *retraction*, *insertion* and *restriction* area as marked in the figure.

An example illustrates the use of our productions. Consider the graphs in Figures 2(a) and 2(b). To transform between them we must remove the vertex c (and its incident edges) from the graph, and insert a new vertex labeled d adjacent to vertex b. Although the graph does not show it, we can introduce a restriction: this transformation is not to take place if there is a vertex labeled e adjacent to vertex a. The production in Figure 2(c) expresses both this transformation and its restriction, as follows:

- The context – that relevant part of the graph that is not changed by the rewrite transformation – is in the triangle. In this case this is vertices a, b and the edge (a, b).
- The retraction – those vertices or edges that will be removed by the transformation – are on the upper left side of the triangle. In this case this is the vertex c and the edges (c, b) and (c, a).
- The insertion – those vertices and edges to be placed into the graph by the transformation – is the vertex d and edge (d, b).
- The restriction – the condition under which the transformation cannot be applied – is that there must not be a vertex e adjacent to the a in the context.

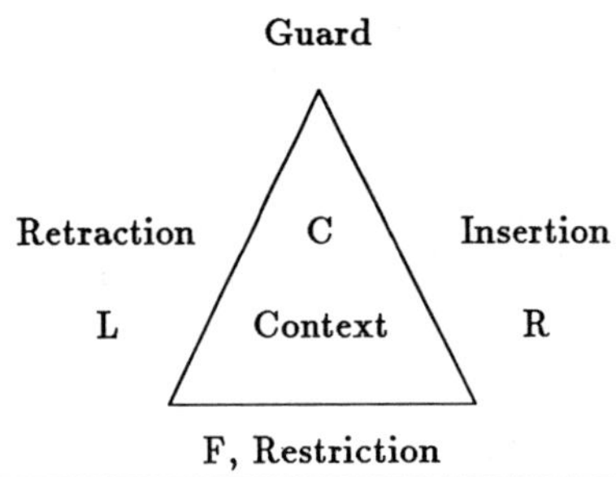

Figure 1: Form of Production

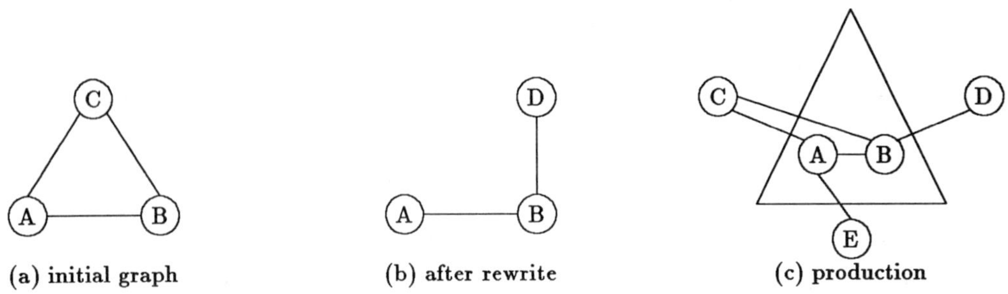

Figure 2: Introductory Example

- The guard – a further condition on the transformation – is usually some textually expressed restriction (such as a predicate on the labels of some subset of the vertices of the context, retraction and restriction) and written above the apex of the triangle. In our example there is no guard; their use is illustrated below.

Transforming a graph is known technically as a *rewrite*. We say that a production is applied to a graph. The graph to which the rewriting is applied is called the host graph. Applying a production p to a host graph H proceeds as follows:

1. The graph matching the graph of the context and the retraction is identified in the host graph (this is called the mother graph [6]). As this matching is done, the restriction is checked to ensure that a restricted graph is not being matched. The matching also involves unification of variables in the production with labels on the vertices in the host graph. If the mother graph cannot be identified then the production cannot be applied.

2. If the production has a guard, then that guard is evaluated. If it is not true, then the production cannot be applied.

3. The vertices (and all incident edges) and edges in the retraction are removed from the host graph (and by implication from the mother graph also).

4. A graph corresponding to the insertion is instantiated (this is called the daughter graph) and connected to the remainder of the mother graph as shown by the edges between the insertion and context in the production.

There are a few more details concerning graphs and productions:

- A vertex in a host graph may be attributed by a list of labels.

- Vertices in productions may be labeled either by literals or variable values. These are matched to actual label values by unification in the graph recognition phases of the rewriting algorithm given above. We will indicate literals in uppercase and variables in lowercase throughout this paper.

- Components of graphs in productions may also be marked with $*$ or $+$. These operators are used in the same way as in BNF grammars, *viz.* to indicate 0 or more, or 1 or more, occurrences of that part should be matched in the matching algorithm.

- It is possible to include several restrictions, so that the matching of any one precludes the application of the production.

- The algorithm for rewriting a graph in general is to pick repeatedly (nondeterministically) both a production and a vertex in the graph and attempt to apply that production there. Success means the graph will be transformed; failure means the graph is unchanged. In both cases another production and location will be selected and the process will continue.[1] To ensure fairness it is desirable that each node in the graph is given an equal opportunity to be rewritten.

- Rewritings are considered single-step operations in our model. Rewritings must be atomic within the area covered by the context and retraction of a production; other rewritings can take place elsewhere on the graph simultaneously. Thus, the model is inherently nondeterministic and concurrent.

- For specifications to be executable, we must achieve reasonable efficiency. Through static Δ-grammar analysis we can automatically find patterns to look for to improve execution efficiency.

- Where a large specification is made, Δ-productions may be hierarchically organized into groups. Such modularization is beyond the scope of this paper.

We use the following labeling conventions in our specifications. Objects (processes, actors, objects in object-oriented systems) are represented by circular vertices labeled by the type of the object and variables representing its state. Messages between objects are denoted by rectangular vertices, also labeled. The semantics of the system is specified by the grammar and initial host graph; the legal rewritings of the host graph provides an interpretation for the semantics. Thus, the specifications will inherently describe concurrent, nondeterministic systems.

We now consider a second, more interesting example. It will illustrate the extreme simplicity of our approach to specification, the lack of implementation bias, and the way in which extraneous details are avoided. The ease with which specifications can be extended will also become clear. The particular problem we consider here is the *dynamic* dining philosophers problem, based on the classic problem posed by Dijkstra [2].

Like the dining philosophers problem, there are several philosophers sitting around a table. There is a fork between each pair of philosophers. Philosophers alternate eating and thinking. When a philosopher wishes to eat, he must first pick up the forks to his left and right. He cannot take a fork currently being held by one of the other philosophers. When he is done he relinquishes the forks. Once we have described the actions of the philosophers we will describe the dynamic aspect of the problem.

The grammar for a solution to this system is shown in the first three productions of Figure 3. The *initial graph* shows the initial configuration of the system: two philosophers, two forks and each philosopher connected to each of the forks. Initially, both forks are available; we will indicate a fork being held by a philosopher by placing a vertex labeled H in the graph and connected to the fork being held and the philosopher holding it.

The diagram labeled *pick forks* shows the action of picking up the forks. The restriction indicates that the forks must not already be held. If this restriction is satisfied then the forks are picked up, and their in-use status is indicated by inserting H vertices and edges as shown between the philosopher and his forks. Note the cleanliness of this specification: details such as deadlock avoidance, sequencing or any other implementation details do not appear (of course, if the specifier *wanted* to constrain the possible implementations by providing any or all of the above he could do so).

The diagram labeled *put forks* describes the effect of relinquishing the forks.

Now, the dynamic dining philosophers problem is an extension of this problem in which the number of philosophers around the table can change dynamically, as philosophers arrive and leave. Each philosopher must bring one fork, and take it with him when he leaves. A philosopher cannot leave if he is holding a fork. When he arrives, he must end up between two forks in order to be able to eat; he must therefore insert himself between an existing philosopher and a fork adjacent to that philosopher, offering the fork he brought in as a replacement for the fork. It would be unconscionably rude of the newcomer to grab a fork already being used, so he cannot place himself between a philosopher who is already holding a fork and that fork. When a philosopher leaves he takes a fork with him, and the remaining philosophers and forks are reconnected to return the system to its correct configuration.

This extension to the problem is shown in the diagrams labeled *add philosopher* and *remove philosopher* in Figure 3. The most interesting thing to note is that this extension is orthogonal to the productions describing the original problem, *i.e.* no change is needed to the specifications for the non-dynamic case.

The diagram labeled *add philosopher* indicates that a new philosopher enters between a philosopher and a fork, connects the existing philosopher to the new fork and connects the new philosopher to the new and old forks. This cannot be done if the old fork is currently being held.

[1] Note that this is useful as a theoretical mechanism and a semantics for concurrent systems, but somewhat impractical due to the complexity of identifying the graphs in the general case. It is possible to transform a Δ-grammar specification to the more tractable – but both less readable and less clean – Garp [9] [4] model but this is beyond the scope of this paper.

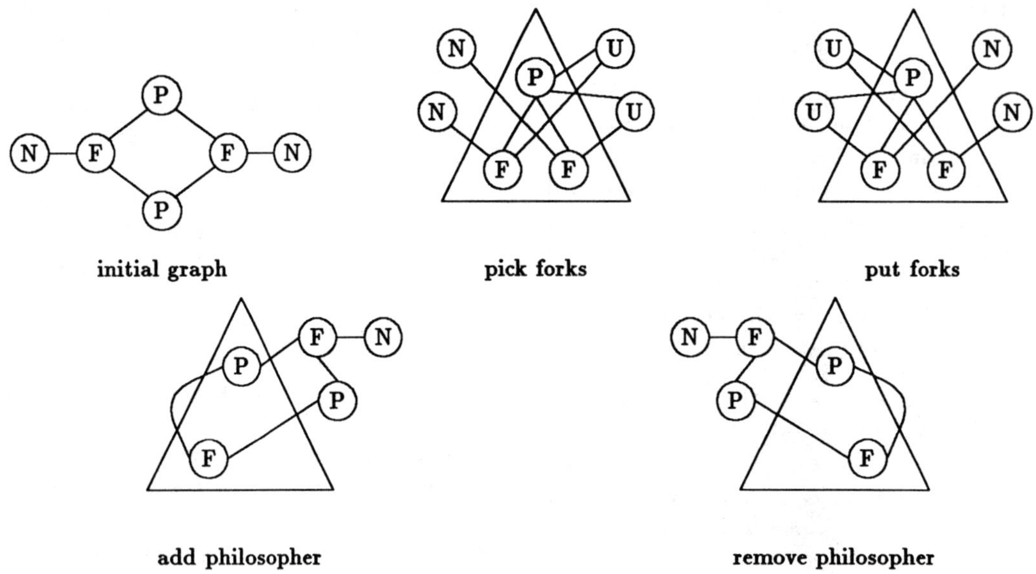

Figure 3: Dynamic Dining Philosophers Grammar

Similarly, the diagram labeled *remove philosopher* shows how to delete a philosopher. The philosopher takes one of his forks with him as he leaves. This fork cannot be held by another philosopher. The fork which the philosopher does not take is connected to the philosopher who loses a fork due to the removal of the philosopher.

Note this specification is deadlock free but not starvation free. A starvation-free solution could be specified by the introduction of an omnipotent additional agent into the system. This agent is usually called a *waiter*, and its behavior is to restrict the number of philosophers which eat at any time to be $n-1$, where n is the number of philosophers. Extensions to introduce a waiter and restrictions on the number of philosophers with the right to eat at any particular time are straightforward and therefore not shown here.

Again, we should stress that this is a specification, not a program. Being graphical, the specifications are easy to write given appropriate tools. There is no implementation bias in the specification. Production application (and therefore the behavior of the system) is entirely nondeterministic within the bounds specified by the productions. The rewriting mechanism captures the concurrent behavior of the system. Perhaps best of all, the notation is easy, simple to write and understand, and concise, making this a very usable specification language.

Once a specification is written, we can show it has certain properties. Since we have not introduced the grammar formalism formally in this paper, it would be difficult to try prove theorems here; instead we pose "conjectures" and "justifications", which would be theorems and proofs in a formal presentation. Here are some sample conjectures and justifications:

Conjecture 1 *When a new philosopher arrives, he never inserts himself between a philosopher and a fork which is in use by that philosopher.*

Justification: has already been argued above; is guaranteed by the restriction on the add-philosopher diagram.
□

Conjecture 2 *Every philosopher is always adjacent to two forks.*

Justification: proceeds by induction on the initial graph and considers addition and deletion of philosophers. This is true initially, and it is maintained by any addition or deletion of a philosopher (shown by considering the effects on the graph of the additions and deletions).
□

Conjecture 3 *The system can never deadlock.*

Justification: This follows immediately from the pick-fork and put-fork productions. Forks are picked up and put down *simultaneously* in pairs, by definition.
□

At some level of the implementation there may arise a deadlock problem in which case the implementor will have to ensure that his approach is faithful to the specification, *i.e.* deadlock free.

3 Another Example – Clients and Servers

This section of the paper considers a more complex example. Once again the specification will turn out to be natural, clean and concise.

Here is an informal specification of the problem:

> Consider a message based system with an arbitrary number of nameservers and clients. The number of nameservers and clients may change dynamically. Nameservers may be connected together in any arbitrary topology, but clients may only be attached to a single nameserver. A nameserver may take requests from any of its of clients and may make requests for services to one or more other nameservers. A client may make a request to a nameserver to be connected to another client in order to exchange date. The nameserver problem is to allow clients to connect to other clients in order to facilitate this exchange.

In more detail, an example system configuration is shown in figure 4(a). Client (C, a) (*i.e* the client with attribute a) requests connection to the client with attribute d. Such a client does exists in the system – (C, d), but neither (C, a) or its nameserver know this because (C, d) is attacked to a remote nameserver. The connection is requested by sending a message to client (C, a)'s nameserver (figure 4(b)), which then propagates the request through the system until it reaches (C, d) (figures 4(c) and (d)). When this client is identified, the connection is established (figure 4(e)).

The formal specification of the problem as a Δ-grammar is shown in figure 5.

The initial configuration is just a single server with no clients. Productions add clients to servers, add servers to servers, and send a connection request from a client to a server. These productions are all straightforward.

The production to propagate a message to all clients and servers connected to a particular client is labeled *propagate message*. Despite its seeming complexity, it is actually very simple:

- The client C with attribute a has sent a message indicating that it wants to connect to a client with attribute b. This message has reached server S.

- Server S has other servers and clients (with attributes c) in its neighborhood.

- The effect of the production is to propagate the message to all clients and servers which have not already received it (this is the restriction). This is an example of the specifier imposing a constraint on the implementation, and is necessary because an arbitrary topology of servers can include cycles.

- The guard $c <> a$ just prevents the message from being propagated back to the sender. (If such propagations were meaningful, then the guard could be removed, but we are assuming for the sake of the example that they are not. There is no loss of generality in this assumption).

The production to establish a connection and halt all further message forwarding once a matching client has been found is shown in the production labeled *connect.* The unification in the graph matching phase of the rewriting ensures that the b of the message and that of the client match. The message M is in the retraction; this indicates that the message vertex (and therefore all edges incident on it) are automatically removed as part of the connection establishment process. The actual connection is shown in the insertion part of the production.

The production to break a connection has the obvious semantics. There is presumably some reason why this production is applied; in a real-life example we would put a guard or restriction on the production to prevent it from being applied at the wrong time.

The final production is labeled *time-out* and implements the requirement that if, after n seconds, the match has not succeeded, the message is revoked (the connection request aborts). Note the restriction that the client cannot be connected when this happens; this is an example of a redundant restriction. We can show that the revocation cannot happen after the placement of the connection, simply by noting that that replacement removes the message, thereby making the match for the time-out production fail.

Note that many clients can be requesting connections at the same time (*i.e.* there is no restriction on the number of active messages in the system). It may be useful to restrict a client from requesting more than one connection at a time; we currently do not do this.

The diagrams of figure 4 illustrate a sample propagation in which a connection is to a remote client. Part (a) shows the configuration just before the message send, part (b) the send, parts (c) and (d) the propagation of the message and part (e) the connection. Note that parts (d) and (e) are immediately before and after the establishment of the connection respectively.

As before we can prove properties of the specification. One interesting property is that, assuming no timeout and no successful connection, the message is eventually propagated to every client and server in the system exactly once.

Conjecture 4 *Assuming the process is not interrupted by timeout or halted by finding a satisfactory connection, a connection request message will eventually propagate to all clients and servers in the system exactly once.*

Justification: By induction on the structure evolved by the grammar. This is true of a system with one server and

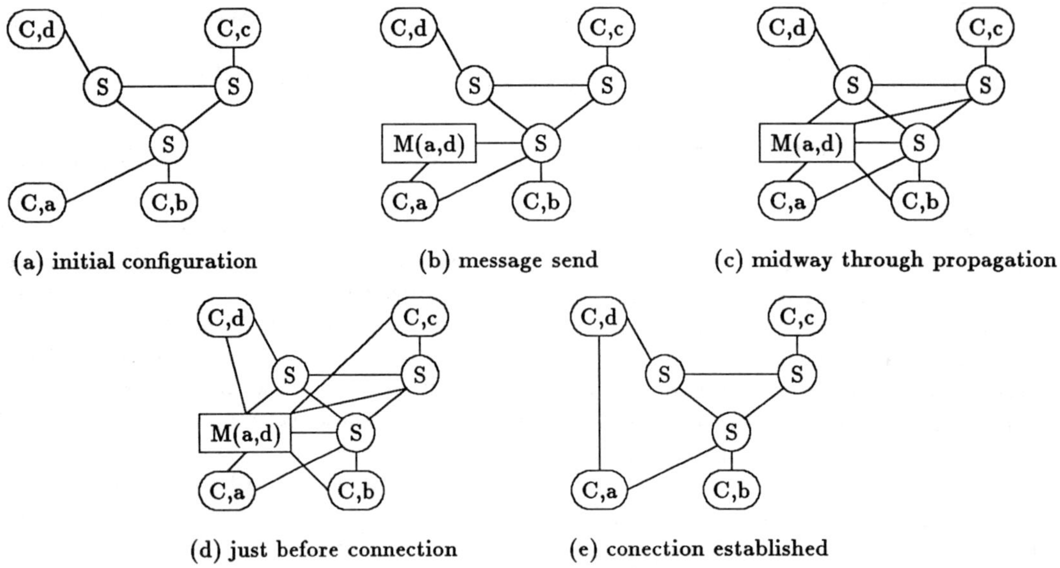

(a) initial configuration (b) message send (c) midway through propagation

(d) just before connection (e) conection established

Figure 4: Client-Server Example: Making the Connection

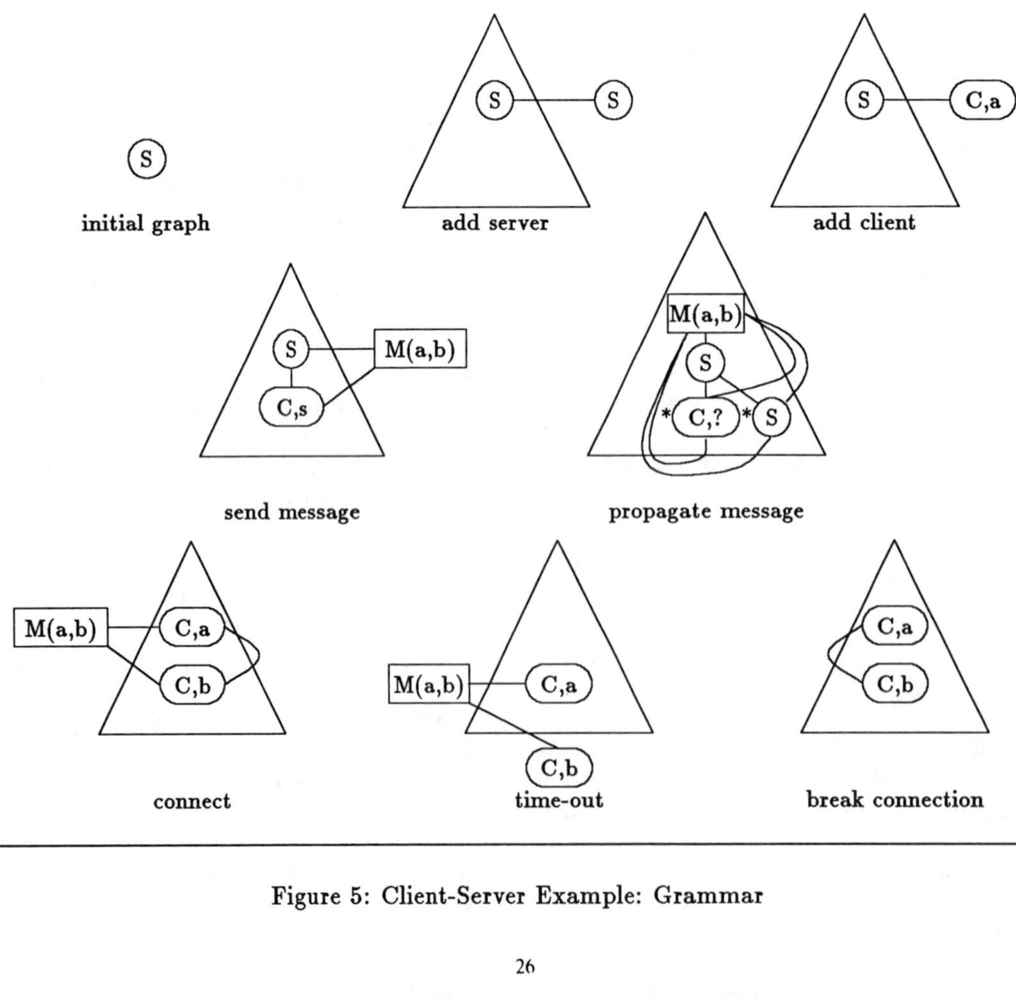

Figure 5: Client-Server Example: Grammar

client. Each client local to a server gets the message as soon as the server receives it, and similarly each server forward the message to its neighbors as it is received. However, the message is never forwarded to a server or client which has already received it. Thus, everyone will eventually get the message, and exactly once regardless of the topology of the system.

□

Conjecture 5 *When a client (server) is added to the system, any connection requests received by its server which have not yet been satisfied are propagated to this new client (server).*

Justification: This follows from the *propagate message* production. In this case just the new client (server) will match the context of the production and receive the message. The other clients (servers) will fail the restriction and therefore be ignored.

□

An obvious corollary is that, assuming no timeout, a connection will always be established if a suitable pair of clients exists.

4 Conclusions

We have introduced, and illustrated through examples, an approach to specifying concurrent systems via Δ-grammars. These specifications are:

- declarative;
- graphical, making them easier to read and understand than equivalent textual specifications;
- free of implementation bias;
- written in a formalism for which there is a formal algebraic basis.

Because of the absence of implementation bias, our approach allows the designer to concentrate on specifying the desired behavior of a system independent of low-level implementation and synchronization issues.

The two examples – dynamic dining philosophers and connecting clients in a distributed network of nameservers – illustrate the power, flexibility and readability of the formalism. Experience suggests that the specifications are easy to write, and developing Δ-grammar specifications aids in identifying parts of the problem which are not yet properly understood.

References

[1] Gul Agha. *ACTORS: A Model of Concurrent Computation in Distributed Systems.* M.I.T. Press, Cambridge, Mass., 1986.

[2] Edsger W. Dijkstra. Hierarchical ordering of sequential processes. *Acta Informatica*, (1):115–138, 1971.

[3] Hartmut Ehrig. Introduction to the algebraic theory of graph grammars. In Hartmut Ehrig Volker Claus and Grzegorz Rozenberg, editors, *Graph Grammars and their Application to Computer Science and Biology, LNCS 73*, pages 1–69, Springer-Verlag, Heidelberg, 1979.

[4] Steven K. Goering. *Message Passing Grammar Systems.* PhD thesis, University of Illinois, To appear, 1989.

[5] Herbert Gottler. Attributed graph grammars for graphics. In Hartmut Ehrig, Manfred Nagl, and Grzegorz Rozenberg, editors, *Graph Grammars and their Application to Computer Science, LNCS 153*, pages 130–142, Springer-Verlag, 1982.

[6] Dirk Janssens and Grzegorz Rozenberg. Graph grammars with node-label control and rewriting. In Hartmut Ehrig, Manfred Nagl, and Grzegorz Rozenberg, editors, *Graph Grammars and their Application to Computer Science, LNCS 153*, pages 186–205, Springer-Verlag, 1982.

[7] Simon M. Kaplan and Roy H. Campbell. Designing and prototyping in grads. In *Proceedings IEE/BCS Symposium on Software Engineering*, July 1988.

[8] Simon M. Kaplan and Steven K. Goering. Garp – a textual/graphical hybrid language for concurrent programming. In *Proceedings of the Workshop on Object-Based Concurrent Programming*, February 1989.

[9] Simon M. Kaplan and Gail E. Kaiser. Garp: graph abstractions for concurrent programming. In *ESOP '88*, Springer-Verlag, March 1988.

[10] R. Milner. A calculus of communicating systems. In *Lecture Notes in Computer Science, LNCS 92*, Springer-Verlag, Berlin, 1980.

[11] Manfred Nagl. Set theoretic approaches to graph grammars. In Hartmut Ehrig, Manfred Nagl, and Grzegorz Rozenberg, editors, *Graph Grammars and their Application to Computer Science, LNCS 291*, pages 41–54, Springer-Verlag, 1987.

[12] Francesco Parisi-Presicce, Hartmut Ehrig, and Ugo Montanari. Graph rewriting with unification and composition. In Hartmut Ehrig, Manfred Nagl, and Grzegorz Rozenberg, editors, *Graph Grammars and their Application to Computer Science, LNCS 291*, pages 496–514, Springer-Verlag, 1987.

[13] C. A. Petri. Concurrency. In *Net Theory and Applications, LNCS 84*, Springer-Verlag, Berlin, 1980.

Configuration Support for System Description, Construction and Evolution

"Doing it at the right level......"

J. KRAMER, J. MAGEE, M.SLOMAN

Department of Computing, Imperial College of Science and Technology,
180 Queen's Gate, London SW7 2BZ,
Great Britain.

ABSTRACT

Software systems can be conveniently described, constructed and managed in terms of their configuration, where configuration is the system structure defined as the set of constituent software components together with their interconnections. A specification of the system configuration can be used both to describe the required system structure and to generate the actual system itself. Evolution of the system is achieved by monitoring the status of the components and making extensions or changes to the system configuration by the addition of software components or the replacement of existing ones. The performance of these tasks at the configuration level is termed *configuration programming*, and is best supported by the use of a declarative configuration language and associated support tools. This paper discusses the main principles of this approach and illustrates its practice by describing the support which has been provided in the Conic environment for distributed systems.

1. INTRODUCTION

There is a need for a uniform approach and associated software tools to support system **specification**, **construction** and **evolution**. This is particularly necessary for large and complex systems which have a long lifetime. Ideally, specifications should provide clear and manageable descriptions of systems such that users can understand and manipulate them. Support tools are needed to validate the specification and to automatically construct the system from the specification. The system should then be constructed such that it corresponds to that specification, with support tools that facilitate system building, validatation and management. Finally, we desire the flexibility to make changes to the system in response to changes in requirements or technology. This may involve changes that were not predicted at the time the system was designed. Such evolution should be supported by the ability to make changes to the specification with the corresponding change reflected in the system itself, as shown in figure 1.

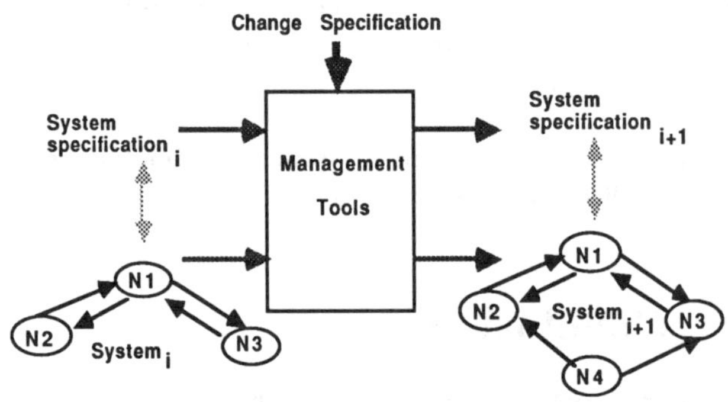

Figure 1 Correspondence Between System Specification and Actual System

Practical experience in software engineering has taught us that complex systems can be built and managed provided we adhere to some sound principles. Software modularity is essential, and permits the use of composition to form a system from reusable, context independent modules. The use of well-defined module interfaces permits validation of module interconnections. Hierarchies are a natural and convenient means for the support of submodule encapsulation and information hiding. These principles relate to structural concerns and can be combined by providing configuration level support. In particular, a declarative **configuration language** with associated tools provides the appropriate framework.

A configuration language can be used to provide a clear and manageable description of the structure of a system as the interconnection of instances of software modules. The structural nature of the configuration specification makes it natural to associate a graphical description with the textual form to facilitate comprehension and manipulation. Configuration tools can validate the description and use it to generate the corresponding system. Changes to the system and its specification are reflected as changes to the system structure, either by the addition of further modules, and/or the use of modified versions of selected modules. In addition, by supporting dynamic configuration, such change can be introduced into a system while the unaffected parts continue to operate. *"Configuration programming"* , the term we use to describe programming at the configuration level, thus provides a clear and flexible means for description, construction, modification and comprehension of complex systems. Configuration programming concentrates on the logical structure of a system, and abstracts from the algorithmic details of individual components. It is closely related to the ideas of *programming-in-the-large* [1] and the use of a module interconnection language outlined in [2,3].

There has been considerable research into distributed programming languages which emphasise modularity and reuse of components, such as Ada [4], SR[5], Emerald [6] and Argus[7]. Although these languages do have facilities for combining separately compiled components, they tend to treat the resultant system as a single large program. The system structure is thus embedded in the program itself rather than being explicitly and separately described. In addition, since the current structure is dependent on the state of the program, system modification and evolution is difficult to provide. A current configuration specification is needed to determine interactions and dependencies, particularly when managing change. For instance, although object-oriented programming lanaguages identify a type (class) hierarchy for objects, they do not provide explicit information on the object instance structure.

We recognise that the role of a structural view is accepted and used by some workers in the areas of software specification (such as PAISLEY[8]) and environments (such as STATEMATE[9]). However, our approach is novel in the emphasis on software structure and its direct use as a basis for system implementation and subsequent evolution.

Configuration programming is particularly appropriate for distributed processing where the software components may additionally reside on different machines. The Conic environment [10,11,12], developed by the Distributed Systems Group at Imperial College, provides support for configuration programming for distributed and concurrent programs. The environment provides support for two languages, one for programming individual task modules (processes) with well defined interfaces, and one for the configuration of programs from groups of task modules. In addition, the environment provides support for the reuse of modules in different contexts and support for dynamic configuration. This latter facility is achieved using on-line management tools which permit dynamic creation, control and modification of application programs. Recent work [13] has provided a sound basis for performing change in such systems while preserving consistency and without disrupting the unaffected components. The basic Conic environment has been in use for over 5 years, with dynamic configuration as a more recent facility. It has amply demonstrated the utility of configuration level programming and the need for the separate configuration perspective.

The rest of this paper outlines the configuration approach using the Conic environment to illustrate the concepts.

2. CONFIGURATION PROGRAMMING in CONIC

This section describes the configuration programming concepts embodied in the Conic distributed programming environment. These concepts are illustrated by using a simple example: a patient monitoring system (PMS)[14]. The intensive care ward in a hospital consists of a number of beds. Patients in each bed are continuously monitored for a number of factors, such as pulse, temperature and blood pressure. For each patient the current readings can be displayed both at the bedside and at the nurse unit. If any of the factor readings of a patient are outside of preset limits, then an alarm is sent to the central nurse station.

Module Types.

Module types must provide well defined interfaces for use and validation at the configuration level. This requires that a module must be context independent [10] in that it does not refer to any non-local entities, but can be integrated into any compatible context without redefining or recompiling it.

In Conic, the internal programming language is Pascal extended to support message passing for the distributed environment. The PMS system is constructed from the two module types defined both graphically and textually below in Figures 2 and 3. The interface to a module is defined by typed exit- and entryports. Messages are sent out of a module via exitports and received into modules from entryports. Messages can be of any Pascal datatype (except pointer types for obvious reasons). The type definitions are imported from definition units by the **use** clause.

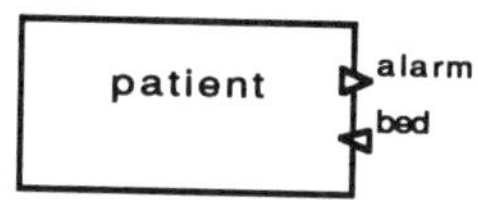


```
group module patient;
    use monmsg: bedtype, alarmstype;
    exitport alarm:alarmstype;
    entryport bed:signaltype reply bedtype;
    {
    - The module periodically reads sensors attached
    to a patient. Readings outside preset ranges cause alarm
    messages to be sent to the exitport alarm.
    A request message received on the entryport bed
    returns the current readings and ranges.
    }
end.
```

Figure 2 - The Patient Module

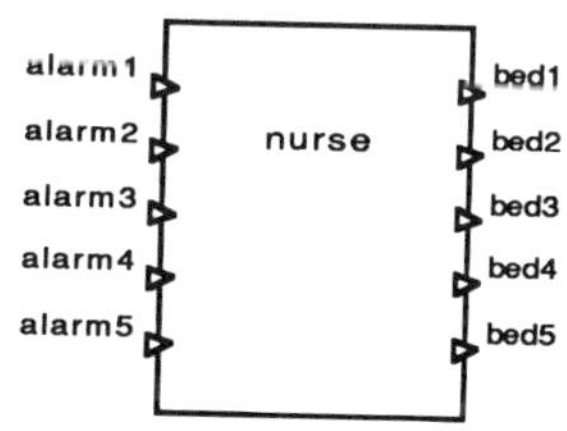


```
group module nurse (maxbed:integer=5);
    use monmsg: bedtype, alarmstype;
    entryport alarm[1..maxbed]:alarmstype;
    exitport bed[1..maxbed:signaltype reply bedtype;
    {
    - the module displays alarms received from alarm[]
    and can request the display for a particular patient from
    its exitports bed[].
    }
end.
```

Figure 3 - The Nurse Module

Module Hierarchies:

In the above, we have described the main module types to be used to construct the patient monitoring system. In fact, each of the two module types used are themselves configurations of modules. For example, the internal structure of the patient module is depicted in Figure 3. It is defined by instantiating an instance of each of a scanner and monitor module types and interconnecting their exit- and entryports. The links between exitports and entryports allow modules to communicate by message passing. The Conic environment permits only ports of the same type to be connected.

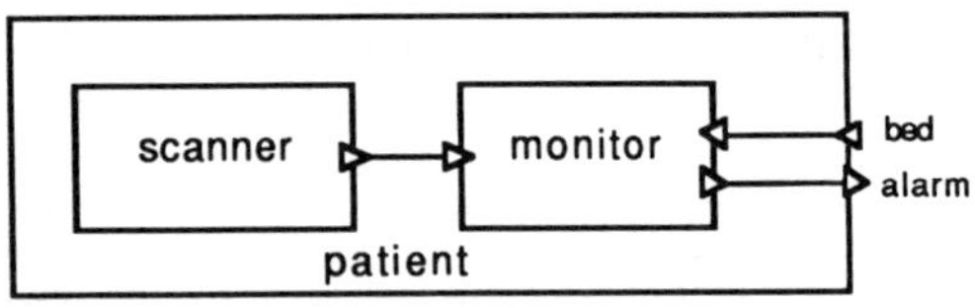


```
group module patient;
    use monmsg: bedtype, alarmstype;
    use scanner, monitor;
    exitport alarm:alarmstype;
    entryport bed:signaltype reply bedtype;
    create
        scanner;
        monitor;
    link
        scanner.reading to monitor.reading;
        bed to monitor.request
        monitor.alarm to alarm;
end.
```

Figure 4 - Internal structure of Patient Module

A system in Conic is thus an hierarchic structure of modules. The modules at the bottom of the hierarchy are **task** modules which are implemented in Pascal to which message passing constructs have been added. These task modules execute concurrently and are hierarchically structured using the configuration programming language into **logical nodes.** Logical nodes are simply group modules which include a run-time executive. Logical nodes are the unit of both distribution and change.

System Construction.

Given the hardware depicted in Figure 5, we can construct an initial patient monitoring system consisting of one nurse unit and one patient unit by instantiating one instance of each of the above module types and interconnecting their exit- and entryports. Again, the Conic environment permits only ports of the same type to be connected. The configuration program for this initial system is again shown both textually and graphically in Figure 5.

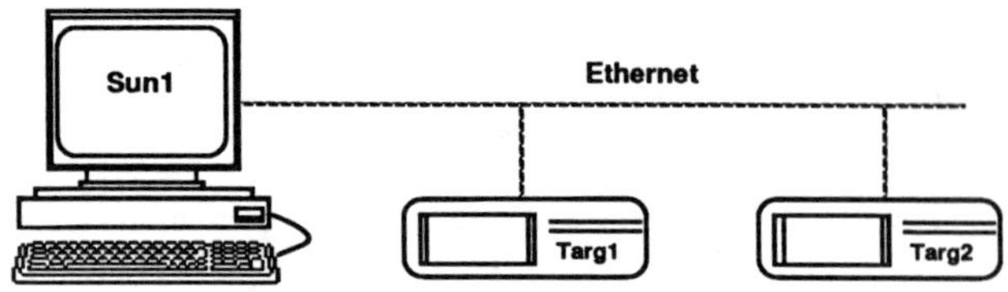

Figure 5 - Hardware Environment

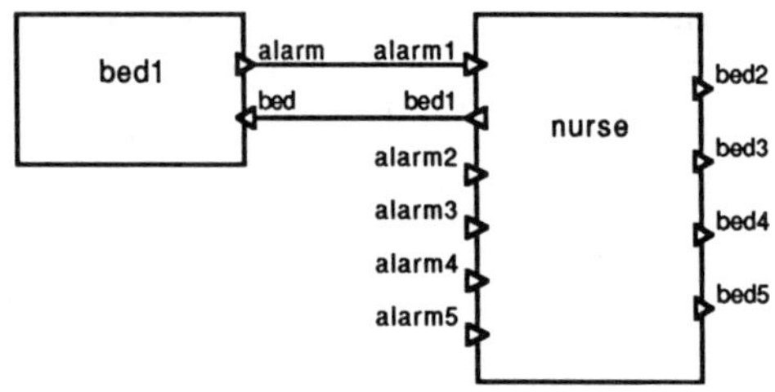


```
system ward;
    create
        bed1:patient at targ1;
        nurse: nurse at sun1;
    link
        bed1.alarm to nurse.alarm[1];
        nurse.bed[1] to bed1.bed;
end.
```

Figure 6 - Initial Patient Monitoring System

The system is created by submitting the configuration description to a configuration manager tool which downloads module code into target processors or instantiates processes under Unix as appropriate (figure 7). The configuration management tool and its supporting environment is described in [12]. The configuration description may be submitted directly as text to the configuration management tool or indirectly using a graphical editor described in more detail in [15]. Note that, in addition to instance creation and linking (interconnection), the configuration description includes module location (the **at** clause) and module parameters. For example the nurse module has a default parameter setting to the value 5 (Figure 3) however this could have been changed when the module instance was specified, eg. **create** nurse:nurse(3) **at** sun1.

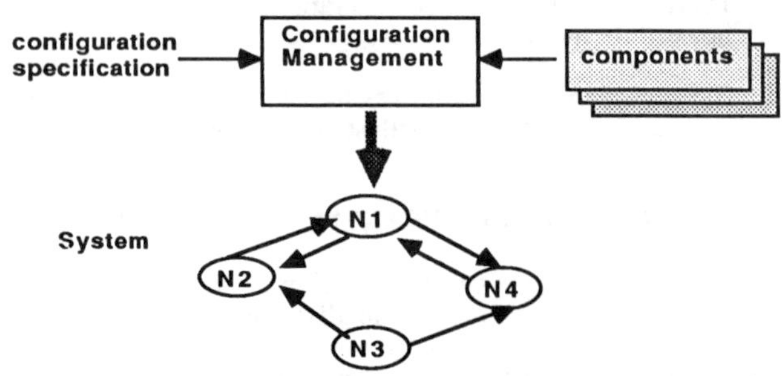

Figure 7 - System Configuration using Configuration Management

Note that the configuration language is declarative. This is more amenable to analysis and validation, and leaves the actual order in which configuration operations are performed to the underlying support system. It can then exploit the inherent parallelism of the underlying architecture where appropriate. If the configuration statements were embedded in a procedural language, the current state of the system configuration would depend on the state of the configuration program. This would complicate the user view of the system and the provision of support for system evolution and dynamic configuration.

System Evolution and Dynamic Configuration.

In addition to programming initial configurations, the Conic toolkit permits dynamic configuration: changes to running systems. For example, extending the above system to include an additional patient unit can be performed by submitting the following configuration change of the system 'ward' to a configuration manager:

```
change ward;
    create
        bed2:patient at targ2;
    link
        bed2.alarm to nurse.alarm[2];
        nurse.bed[2] to bed2.bed;
end
```

The resulting system is depicted grapically in Figure 8:

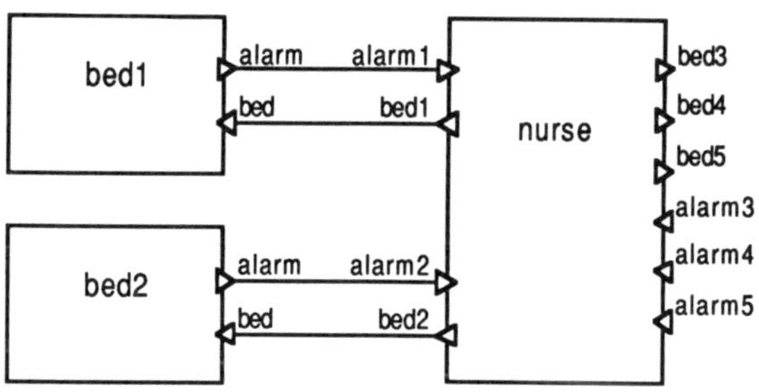

Figure 8 - Extended Patient Monitoring System

The change can be though of as an edit, in configuration terms, of the configuration specification *and* the system itself. As shown in figure 1 it results in both a new specification and a correspondingly changed system. Thus the system itself evolves rather than the traditional approach of regenerating the system *ab initio*.

Graphical Configuration Programming

In practice, we have found it convenient to create initial systems from the configuration specification. Once created, a graphics tool, ConicDraw, can be used to display and manage the system. As depicted in figure 9, ConicDraw maintains a graphic representation of executing Conic systems in terms of the module instances which exist in the system, their interconnections and their execution state. It gathers this information directly from the executing system by communicating with a configuration manager. Thus the graphics tool can be used in a monitoring mode to allow users an uptodate view of the system configuration. The diagram of Figure 6 was created by using the graphics tool to monitor a system created from the textual configuration specification shown.

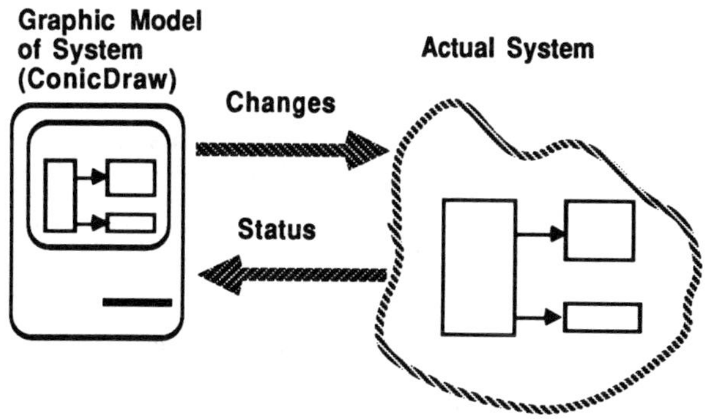

Figure 9 - Relationship between ConicDraw and System.

Changes to the system are reported to ConicDraw by configuration management to enable it to maintain an uptodate view of the system. ConicDraw can itself instigate changes to the system as a result of edits to the graphic representation. A change which has been performed graphically can be saved in its text form for later re-use. The system was extended by editing the diagram directly to create Figure 10. These edits caused the tool to send the extension configuration text to a configuration manager to change the actual system accordingly. Figure 10 shows a further bed, bed3, being linked into the existing system using the *link* tool in the tool palette. The link instruction generated by this graphic operation (link nurse.bed3 to bed3.bed) is shown at the bottom of the figure.

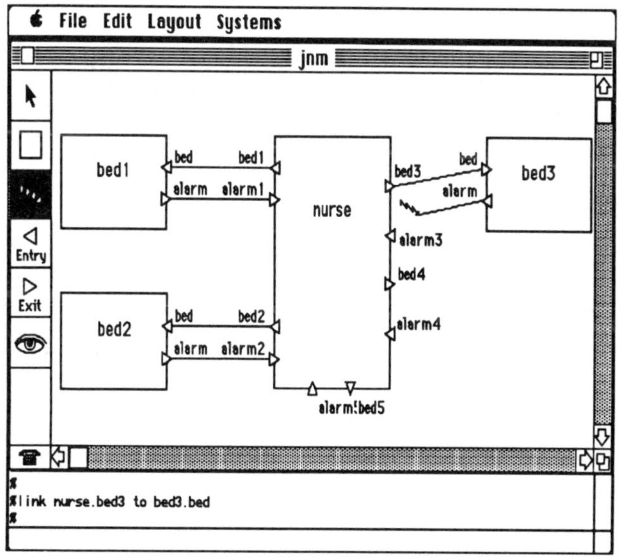

Figure 10 - System linking via ConicDraw.

Since ConicDraw always maintains a representation of the actual system, one or more workstations can be connected to the distributed system to allow a number of users to co-operatively manage and monitor the system. ConicDraw contains a comprehensive set of tools for creating and editing Conic configuration diagrams. As such, it can also be used as a standalone diagram editor. A full description of ConicDraw is given in [15].

Change Management

As mentioned, changes are specified declaratively at the configuration level in terms of structure. However, these changes must be applied to the system in such a way that the system consistency is preserved. In addition, we would like to minimise the disruption to the application during the change.

Recent work [13] has shown that it is possible to separate out the structural concerns from those at the application module level. Changes are specified purely structurally, in the declarative configuration language. Using a set of change rules, it is possible to derive a procedural change transaction which identifies those nodes in a system affected by the particular change, and includes the control operations and ordering decisions in order to apply the change transaction to the system itself. This change transaction puts the affected part of the system into a quiescent state in order to ensure that it does not contain the results of partial application transactions. It can be shown that this state is both reachable and sufficient for the application of the change. Terminating nodes are then given the opportunity to execute finalisation actions to leave the environment in a consistent state, and newly created nodes the opportunity to execute initialisation actions to make the node consistent with its environment. The system may then be permitted to actively participate with the rest of the system. The details of this approach are beyond the scope of this paper, but it has affirmed our belief in the separation of configuration concerns as an essential prerequisite for describing and supporting system evolution.

This section has briefly outlined how configuration programming is used and supported in the Conic environment. The interested reader can find a detailed description of the Conic Configuration and Task programming languages in [16] and [17], and the Conic environment in general in [12].

3. CONCLUSIONS

Configuration programming provides a clear and flexible means for system description, construction and evolution. Both initial system configurations and changes are specified in a declarative configuration language which clearly separates the issue of what structure is required from how that structure is constructed procedurally. Experience with the Conic system has demonstrated that, with adequate tool support, this structural specification can be used directly to construct and modify systems. The advantages of using a structural view has been recognised for both conventional software development, as in the use of interface specifications in the Inscape Environment [18], for reactive systems in STATEMATE [9], and in distributed systems such as Conic and, more recently, Durra [19]. Graphical support is particularly appropriate for the structural information used in configuration specifications.

Another set of approaches to the problem of system specification and construction advocates the use of formal specifications with transformation techniques to move to lower level specifications and finally to the system itself [20,21]. Although these approaches have produced some elegant techniques, they have still to be proven in practice on large systems. In addition, there has been little discussion of system evolution except for respecification and re-application of the transformations to a completely new system. If such approaches are to have any success in the long term, they must provide a practical *structure* or framework on which to compose their specifications and generate and evolve their systems. We believe that the configuration perspective provides such a framework, and that the transformation approach can benefit from adoption of such an environment. Similarly, we believe that our modules could benefit from a more formal specification of behaviour, with transformation techniques to decompose systems into constituent modules and composition rules to derive group module behaviour from constituent module behaviours. These techniques would be particularly useful in identifying respectively where changes should be effected and for predicting the affect of change.

Although this paper has only demonstrated the approach on a simple example, we have found it to be clear, useful and powerful in more complex cases. For instance, the configuration language can be used to describe complex interconnections. The following example forms part of a parallel implementation of the Fast Fourier Transform. It uses imported functions to control the internal connection pattern. Inputs are connected to the output which has a bit reversed value of their input index. The configuration language also permits the use of guards and recursion.

```
group module interleave(n:integer);
    use
        funcs:backwards,log2;
        compv:complex;
    entryport
        input[0..n-1]:complex;
    exitport
        output[0..n-1]:complex;

    link family k:[0..n -1]
        input[k] to output[backwards(k,log2(n))];
end.
```

The Conic environment has been applied to underground monitoring and communications in mines, plant automation, image processing, an object-oriented system manager, and multi-loop self-tuning adaptive controllers. Users of the Conic environment include a number of universities in the UK, Germany, Canada, France, Sweden and Japan, and a number of industrial research centres. Our experience has been very positive and leads us to believe that the configuration level is indeed the right level for system description, construction and evolution.

Acknowledgements

We would like to acknowledge the advice and expertise of Naranker Dulay and Kevin Twidle for their support in the implementation and interaction with the configuration managers, and Keng Ng for his work on ConicDraw.

REFERENCES

[1] F.DeRemer, H.H.Kron. "Programming-in-the-large Versus Programming-in-the-small, IEEE Trans. Software Engineering", Vol. SE-2, 2, June 1976.

[2] J.A.Goguen. "Reusing and Interconnecting Software Components", IEEE Computer, (Designing for Adaptibility), Vol. 19, 2, February 1986.

[3] T.J.LeBlanc and S.A.Friedberg. "HPC: A model of structure and change in distributed systems". IEEE Trans. on Computers, Vol. C-34, 12, December 1985.

[4] USA Department of Defense, "Reference manual for the Ada™ programming language", Proposed Standard Document, July 1980.

[5] G. Andrews, R. Olsson, "The evolution of the SR programming language", Distributed Computing, 1, July 1986, pp. 133-149.

[6] A. Black, N. Hutchison, E. Jul, H. Levy, L. Carter, 'Distribution and abstract types in Emerald', IEEE Trans. on Software Eng. SE-13(1), Jan. 1987, pp. 65-76.

[7] B.Liskov, R.Sheifler, 'Guardians and actions: linguistic support for robust distributed programs', ACM TOPLAS, 5 (3), July 1983, pp. 381-404.

[8] P.Zave, "An Operational Approach to Requirements Specification for Embedded Systems", IEEE Trans. on Software Engineering, SE-8 (3), 1982.

[9] D. Harel, H. Lachover, A. Naamad, A. Pnueli, M. Politi, R. Sherman, A. Shtul-Trauring, "STATEMATE: A Working Environment for the Development of Complex Reactive Systems", Proc. 10th. Int. Conf. on Software Eng., Singapore April 1988, pp. 396-406.

[10] J.Kramer, J.Magee, "Dynamic Configuration for Distributed Systems", IEEE Transactions on Software Engineering, SE-11 (4), April 1985, pp. 424-436.

[11] J. Kramer, J. Magee, M. Sloman. The CONIC toolkit for building distributed systems. IEE Proceedings, Vol. 134, Pt. D, No.2, March 1987.

[12] Magee, J., Kramer, J., and Sloman, M.S.,"Constructing Distributed Systems in Conic" Research Report DoC 87/4, (1987), 27 pages. To appear in IEEE Trans. on Software Eng., July 1989.

13] Kramer, J., and Magee, J., "A Model for Change Management", Proc.of IEEE Workshop on Trends of Distributed Computing Systems in the 1990s, Hong Kong, pp.286-295, Sept. 1988.

[14] W.P. Myers, G.F. Myers and L.C. Constantine. "Structured design", IBM Syst. J., vol. 13, no. 2, pp. 115-139, 1974.

[15] Kramer, J., Magee, J., and Ng, K,"Graphical Support for Configuration Programming", Proc. of 22nd HICSS, Vol.II (Software Track), Hawaii, pp. 860-870, January 1989.

[16] N.Dulay, J.Kramer, J.Magee, M.Sloman, K.Twidle, 'The Conic configuration language, version 1.3', Imperial College Research Report DoC 84/20, November 1984.

[17] J.Kramer, J.Magee, M.Sloman, K.Twidle, N.Dulay, 'The Conic programming language, version 2.4', Imperial College Research Report DoC 84/19, October 1984.

[18] D.E.Perry, "Software Interconnection Models", Proc. of 9th IEEE Int. Conf. on Software Engineering, Monterey, April 1987.

[19] M.R.Barbacci, C.B.Weinstock, and J.M.Wing, "Programming at the Processor - Memory - Switch Level", Proc. of 10th IEEE Int. Conf. on Software Engineering, Singapore, April 1988.

[20] M.M. Lehman, V. Stenning, W. M. Turski, "Another Look at Software Design Methodology", Software Engineering Notes, Vol. 9, No. 2, April 1984, pp. 38-53.

[21] R.M.Burstall, J. Darlington, 'A Transformation System for Developing Recursive Programs', JACN, 24, Jan.1977.

Action System Approach to the Specification and Design of Distributed Systems

R. Kurki-Suonio and H.-M. Järvinen

Tampere University of Technology
Software Systems Laboratory
Box 527, SF-33101 Tampere, Finland

Abstract

The notion of joint actions provides a paradigm that allows the specification and design of distributed systems to focus on cooperative events rather than on the behavior of individual processes. For concurrency this introduces an abstraction that is independent of process structuring and of communication mechanisms. For the designer this means replacing the conventional process-oriented view by an action-oriented one, which has a profound effect on thinking about a system and on the design process. The approach is especially suited for formal derivation of concurrent systems by a layered introduction of properties.

DisCo is an executable specification and design language based on joint actions. This paper introduces the basic principles of the joint action approach, together with the main capabilities of DisCo for supporting modularity and the derivation of distributed programs.

1. Introduction to Specification and Design by Joint Actions

The notion of *joint actions* [7] provides a novel approach to the specification and design of distributed systems. The key idea is that the traditional *process-oriented* viewpoint is replaced by an *action-oriented* one. Instead of describing the behavior of the individual processes the design focuses on the joint effects that the processes are to accomplish together. From an execution model point of view actions are *atomic events*. Different *interleavings* are possible by the *nondeterminism* that is inherent in the selection of actions for execution.

All cooperation is implicit in the actions and their enabling conditions, and no process communication primitives are therefore needed. This means that the level of abstraction is raised to independence of process structure and communication mechanisms. This makes joint actions a suitable basis for a specification language. Joint action specifications are *executable* (simulatable), and their simple execution model allows *proofs* either in *temporal logic* [24, 25] or in the logic developed for Unity [10].

External interactions are also modeled as joint actions, without committing to specific communication events between the system and its environment. This means that a joint action system is a *closed system* containing also a model of its environment. This has an effect on modularity, as will be seen below.

For the design process joint action systems provide a framework for *stepwise derivation*. The initial action system with which this process starts should be simple. Fortunately, the natural ways of structuring action systems support a layered introduction of properties. Bias towards machine architecture or communication primitives does not belong to the initial system, even if the eventual answers to such questions were known from the beginning. No harm is caused at this level by wasteful computations allowed by nondeterminism. Furthermore, the granularity of atomic actions can be coarser than would be feasible in a distributed implementation. Together with independence of communication mechanisms this helps in the avoidance of subtle timing errors.

The initial action system is the first baseline for the design process. Being amenable to both formal analysis and experimentation (by simulation and animation), it can be subjected to extensive verification and validation. From this stage the design proceeds by transformations that

- *refine* the *atomicity* of actions,
- *restrict* the *nondeterminism* by specific implementation strategies,
- *enrich* the system with additional properties,
- *refine data representations,* and
- *tailor* the system towards specific distributed architectures, communication mechanisms and decisions of distribution.

In principle, a joint action language can be used as a wide spectrum language from specification to implementation. Direct implementation as a programming language seems feasible only under restrictions that are too severe for a specification language. However, one of the goals in transforming an action system is to tailor it towards available implementation mechanisms. A compiler can be provided to produce the final program, once the required conditions for direct implementability have been achieved.

The role of the language and its environment is essential in supporting the correct use of transformations. Some of these can be performed by the computer, but their selection requires insight that is best provided by a human designer. Evidence from case studies [23] indicates a need for also non-standard transformations with specialized correctness proofs.

The notion of action systems was introduced in [3]. The associated design and proof methods were investigated further in [4, 21, 7, 2]. Its use as a basis for a practical design method was proposed in [5], and realistic case studies for its evaluation have been reported in [23, 22]. These reports also contain the first steps towards developing the ideas into a specification and design language.

Another action-oriented approach to the design of parallel systems is Unity, developed along with an associated proof system by K. M. Chandy and J. Misra [10]. The relationship between the two approaches is very close. In fact, under a specific fairness assumption called action justice in [6], any Unity program can be directly understood as an action system. Therefore, the methodologies of [10] can be used also with action systems. The problem of ensuring the validity of the fairness assumption in a distributed execution environment was addressed in [6].

This paper reports on an experimental specification and design language, DisCo (for *Dis*tributed *Co*operation), that is based on action systems. Emphasis is on its support for modularity and program derivation. An introduction to joint action systems is first given in Section 2. The basic entities of DisCo are then described in Section 3. The remaining sections are devoted to issues of modularity and transformations.

2. Action Systems as a Paradigm of Computation

Any execution model of computing involves a *state* (memory, registers, variables) and *actions* that modify this state (instructions, statements, transitions). Conventionally the state is partitioned into a *data part* (variables) and a *control part* (instruction counter). The von Neumann paradigm and structured programming are based on this partitioning and on sequential control. The same basic paradigm is preserved in the object-oriented approach, where control flow relations between objects are determined by messages instead of control transfer.

Concurrency and distributed systems have changed the situation by introducing more complexity into the control part, which has become the Cartesian product of the control parts of the component processes. In addition, deciding on process structure and distribution involves a tradeoff in implementing state components either in the data part or in the control part, and the von Neumann paradigm is clearly inadequate for dealing with such issues of design.

Action systems provide a model of computation with no such *a priori* partitioning of the state. State transitions are given as an *unordered* set of *actions* that have the form of *guarded commands.* Any of them can be executed whenever it is *enabled,* i.e., its guard is true. The commands themselves are assumed to be deterministic and to terminate in finite time. An execution of a system terminates if a state is reached where none of the actions is enabled; otherwise the execution is infinite.

In principle, an action system behaves like a single iteration statement in Dijkstra's guarded command language [12], or a production system like an OPS5 program [14]. There is a difference, however, in how this paradigm is used. In our case nondeterminism reflects an *interleaving* model of concurrency. Therefore, there is no need for conflict resolution, as in production systems, for determining which of the enabled commands to execute next.

With actions as atomic transitions, the execution model of [24] and temporal logic can be directly used for reasoning. With a specific fairness assumption the logic of Unity [10] can also be used. Atomicity of actions means that only one of them is thought to be in execution at a time. When it terminates, any of the actions that are then enabled can be chosen next. No concurrency of actions exists in this *sequential* execution model, which is a logical model for reasoning. Its relationship with realistic concurrent implementations is discussed below.

An implementation of an action system on a distributed architecture involves an allocation of state components to *processes.* In [3, 7] the state of an action system was given explicitly in terms of variables allocated to processes. Given such an allocation, the state components used in the command part of an action determine the processes that are needed to *participate* in it. An action can then be thought of as being executed jointly by these processes. Hence the name *joint actions.* For a singleton set of participating processes an action is called *private* by that process.

The guard of an action is called *local* if its evaluation involves the participating processes only; otherwise it is *global.* One of the simplifying properties to be achieved by transformations is that all guards are local (in the intended allocation), in which case the decision to execute an action can be based on communication between the participating processes only. A methodology for such transformations was the topic of [3].

Considered as a process communication mechanism joint actions are a generalization of the *synchronized rendezvous* of languages like CSP [18, 19] and Ada [1]. Notice that in our case the number of participating processes is not restricted to two, and guards can be arbitrary boolean expressions. There is also a more fundamental difference. In process-oriented languages a rendezvous is just another operation in which processes can get involved, while in our case joint actions are the active units of execution, and processes behave like passive resources. This distinguishes joint action systems from languages that are based on a multi-process handshake mechanism, like Raddle [15] and the shared action systems of [26].

During design, an action system is to be transformed into a form that reflects the properties of an implementation environment. For instance, if asynchronous messages are to be used for communication, the communication channels can be modeled as auxiliary state components that are used in a specific manner. Under certain conditions joint action systems are directly amenable for implementation. CSP implementation of two-process actions was studied in [3], and broadcasting network implementation of more general actions in [7].

A realistic execution model for an implementation of joint actions is a *concurrent model* where it is possible for several actions to be in progress simultaneously. Independent of how the guards are evaluated, synchronized *handshake* by the participating processes is required to start an action. After becoming committed to one by a handshake, a process cannot start another, until it has finished its part in the former.

Although no process can participate in more than one action at a time, several actions involving disjoint sets of them can proceed in parallel in the concurrent model. Depending on the length of time that different processes are needed in an action, they can be released at different times. When released, a process can immediately start participation in another action, if one is enabled and all other required processes are also free.

For details of the relationship between the two execution models, see [6, 7]. The sequential model is intended for reasoning, even if the implementation follows the more realistic concurrent model. The two models differ only in their *fairness* notions [2]. In practical design situations these differences do not seem very important, since mere fairness properties are insufficient, anyway, and more stringent real-time constraints are needed. For simplicity, fairness issues are ignored in this paper.

3. Basic Entities in DisCo

In DisCo the global state of an action system is partitioned into *objects* with *local states*. From an implementation point of view objects correspond to processes, data items, and physical resources. The allocation of objects to such implementation entities is not dealt with in the language.

An object can be characterized as a *data structure* (local state) together with the *capability to participate* in certain actions. In order to deal with collections of similar objects, the notion of object types or *classes* is adopted. This is significant also for the reusability of specifications. No explicit naming facility is provided for individual objects; their selection is always by class and properties of local state.

The behavior of a DisCo system is determined by a set of actions. These are, in fact, action schemes in the sense that the participating objects are specified only by their classes. Action guards can also be global; reference to other than the participating objects is by existential or universal quantification.

As an example, consider a situation with a number of Client and Server objects, such that each available Server is able to serve any Client that is requesting service. This can be expressed by an action Service of the form

> **action** Service **by** C: Client, S: Server **is**
> **when** C.requesting $\wedge$ S.free **do** ...

where the first line gives the participants, the guard is on the second line, and the body (or command part) of the action is omitted.

Comparing to [7, 10], unique identification of individual objects (by indexing, for instance) is avoided by binding formal names to actual participants. If all Servers, for instance, are interchangeable, they need no identification attribute. Notice that dynamic identification can easily be given when needed. For instance, if a longer-term association is required between a Client C and a Server S, this can be achieved by a data attribute S.c to which (a pointer to) C is assigned in Service. An action of the form

> **action** Continued_Service **by** C: Client, S: Server
> **is**
> **when** ... $\wedge$ S.c = C **do** ...

would then assume that such an association has been established.

Analogously to selecting the participating objects of an action, data values can also be selected by an action. Such *parameters* are *nondeterministically* chosen values that can be restricted by the guard. This provides an implicit mechanism for the participating objects to "negotiate" values as in LOTOS [8].

A DisCo program consists of two parts, called a *system* and a *creation*. The system part gives the class definitions and the actions, together with *invariants* that express safety properties. *Functions* and *relations* between objects can also be defined in this part to be able to express global properties in invariants and action guards. The *creation* part creates all objects and initializes them. The two parts are given separately in order to allow the execution of the same system part for different sets of objects.

Once all objects have been created, actions of the system part can start execution. These affect the global state of the system but cannot change its structure, i.e., destroy objects or create new ones. There is no need for this, either, since being destroyed can be understood as another state of an object, and new objects can always be taken in use if an infinite number of them have been created initially. Notice that infinite collections of similar objects cause no obstacle for the implementation of DisCo.

4. Structuring of Objects

Since action systems have no explicit control flow, the modularity of structured programming is not applicable. (For an illuminating discussion of the separation of modularity and control flow, see [10].) It should also be noticed that joint actions are only an execution model without any inherent structuring of the system. Attempts to use them in their bare form tend to lead to unstructured introduction of boolean flags and enumeration variables.

The purpose of classes and objects is to impose structuring on the global state of a DisCo system. The local state of an object is partitioned further into two parts, a *finite-state part* and a *data part*. The former is given as a hierarchical set of *states*, and it is an analogue of the nested control structure of a process. The latter consists of *variables* and *constants* that are associated with the states of the finite-state part.

There is no theoretical reason for including some components of the local state in the finite-state part. In principle, the finite-state part can always be omitted, in which case objects are just ordinary records. Notice that the structuring of an object is independent of its eventual implementation-oriented role. In particular, finite-state parts need not be mapped to the control part in a conventional implementation.

The finite-state part of an object provides an approximation of the local state that is representable as a *statechart*-like diagram [16]. Actions that change the finite-state part are given as *transitions* in the diagram. This leads to a structured way to look at an action system from the viewpoint of individual objects. The advantages of nested control structures and associated variable declarations are thereby achieved without committing to modules with executable code and specific entry and exit points.

As an example consider a class of Interface objects that connect environment objects to some system. The following diagram sketches the possible structure of such objects:

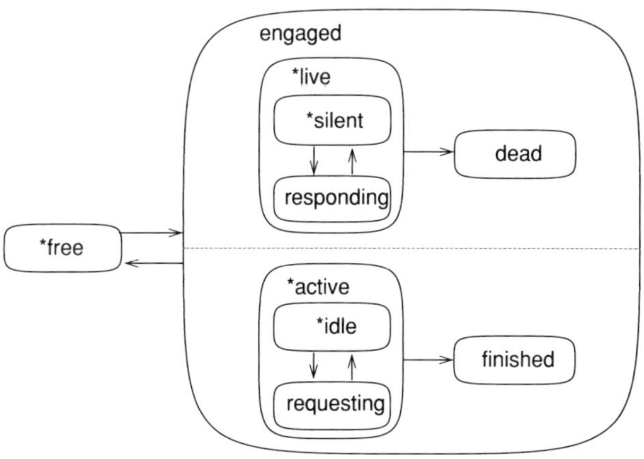

Each Interface is either free or engaged, depending of whether it is currently reserved to serve an environment object or not. The prefix (*) indicates an initial or default state. When engaged, an Interface has two faces, one towards the environment, the other towards the system. This is represented by the two parallel statechart components. Towards the environment an Interface is either live or dead, depending on whether it can still communicate with it or not. Similarly, it is either active or finished towards the system, depending on whether it can still affect it or not. When live, an Interface is responding when it has a response available for the user; otherwise it is silent. Similarly, when active, it is requesting when it needs to communicate with the system, and is idle otherwise.

As a class definition this hierarchical structure could be given as follows:

```
class Interface is
    state *free, engaged(u: User);
    extend engaged by
        state *live, dead;
        extend live by
            immediate_data: some_type;
            state *silent,
                responding(response: message);
        end live;
        state *active, finished;
        extend active by
            state *idle,
                requesting(request: message);
        end active;
    end engaged;
end Interface;
```

In addition to the finite-state part, the data part is also given here. Components that remain constant in a state are given in a parameter notation. Such are the User with which an Interface is associated when engaged, and the messages associated with the states responding and requesting. A variable, immediate_data, is associated with the state live. This is assumed to represent such information, to be collected by an Interface object, that can be used to respond to the User without consulting the system.

When comparing to statecharts [16] and their use in STATEMATE* [17], the following differences may be noted. Our statechart-like diagrams are associated with classes, not single objects, which enhances reusability. Our diagrams also apply to all classes, independently of their roles in the system. Furthermore, they are not given explicitly by the user, but are derived from class definitions and actions. Notice that an action, which is atomic in the execution model, may involve transitions in all participating objects. In STATEMATE, individual transitions are given separately, but they can trigger further transitions, thus forming larger atomic events that would correspond to our actions.

5. Superposition and Union

Superimposition, or superposition, is a design method that has proved useful especially in the development of distributed systems. In principle it is a layered approach where, starting from an initial solution satisfying some basic requirements, further properties are imposed without violating those that have already been established. An early use of the technique and the term was in [13]. Recently super-

*STATEMATE is a registered trademark of i-Logix, Inc.

position has been proposed as a control structure for concurrent and distributed programming languages [20, 9]. In [10] it was introduced as one of the main facilities for designing Unity programs in a modular fashion. In connection with action systems the technique has been successfully used in [3, 4, 21, 22].

In a conventional process-oriented description superposition easily involves modifications that are scattered all over the system. In an action-oriented description the corresponding modifications are local, which makes superposition an especially natural construction for this approach.

Although the key idea in superposition is that a new layer should not destroy properties that have already been established, there is no general agreement on its precise requirements. There are at least three possibilities: (i) a superposition construct should guarantee that all safety and liveness properties are preserved [3, 10]; (ii) preservation of safety properties should be guaranteed, but liveness properties may require separate proofs [9]; (iii) preservation of the specified safety and liveness properties needs a separate proof [20]. In view of our experience that safety properties are the more important ones in practice, and that nondeterminism often needs to be restricted during design, we have adopted alternative (ii). As there clearly exists a need for more liberal transformations also, option (iii) is separately available, but is not called superposition.

In DisCo superposition is allowed to extend the global state both by extending old objects (classes) with new components and by adding new objects (classes). For updating the new state components, old actions can be extended and new actions can be added. The guards of old actions can also be strengthened. What is essential is that projecting an execution of the resulting system to the original objects should always yield an execution of the original system. This can be guaranteed by the construction otherwise, but if guards are strengthened, separate proofs are needed to show that no computation is caused to terminate prematurely.

As an example, consider a sequence of Processor objects, each initialized with an integer x and with knowledge of the Processors to their left and right, if any:

```
class Processor(left, right: Processor) is
    x: integer;
end Processor;
```

The task of the Processors is to sort the integers x into a non-decreasing order from left to right.

An initial system, Basic_Solution, could contain the above class definition together with a simple Compare action:

```
action Compare by L, R : Processor is
when L.right = R do
    if L.x > R.x then
        L.x := R.x || R.x := L.x;
    end if;
end Compare;
```

This action is always enabled for any two neighboring Processors; its effect is to compare their numbers x and to exchange these if the order was not correct. (The parallel combinator || indicates that both right-hand sides are evaluated before the assignments.)

Obviously, Basic_Solution imposes no strategy on when to execute the comparisons, and it does not terminate. Suppose that we wish each Processor to communicate alternatingly with its left and right neighbor (except for the leftmost and rightmost ones, which have only one neighbor). This property can be superposed by *importing* the Basic_Solution and modifying its definitions as follows:

```
system First_Extension with Basic_Solution is
    extend Processor by
        state looking_left, looking_right;
    end Processor;
    extended action Compare is
    when ... L.looking_right ∧ R.looking_left do
        ...
        if L.left ≠ null then
            → L.looking_left;
        end if;
        if R.right ≠ null then
            → R.looking_right;
        end if;
    end Compare;
end First_Extension;
```

The Processor objects are extended here with states that indicate the directions of communication. The guard of Compare is strengthened with the aid of these states, and the body is extended to update the directions of communication. Ellipses stand for parts taken from the imported system, and arrows (→) express transitions in finite-state parts.

By importing two or more systems we get their *union*, i.e., a system that consists of all classes and actions of the component systems. The resulting system can then be transformed further by superposition. Union is especially useful when the component systems share some classes. This is the case when these systems have themselves imported such classes from a common source. Union is one of the modularity notions discussed in [10].

6. Inheritance

While superposition is suited for top-down design, *inheritance* is a closely related bottom-up technique for modular construction of reusable components. Language constructs for inheritance have been developed in connection with object-oriented programming [11].

Inheriting a previously defined class in DisCo means that, in addition to the specific attributes of the new class, all the attributes of the inherited class are also assumed, including the capability to participate in the actions defined for it. Inheritance of several classes, and multiple inheritance of the same class are also permitted.

Technically inheritance can be described as a form of superposition. Inheriting a class is, in fact, equivalent to superposition with predefined extensions that have been formulated in terms of a class.

In conventional, control flow-oriented modularity, a module and its interface are defined independently of those modules that can interact with it. In joint action systems the situation is different, as there are no interactions outside joint actions, and these cannot be defined without access to attributes of all interacting objects. This leads to a notion of modularity where using a module requires that this capability has been explicitly inherited from the module itself.

As an example consider the definition of a simple reliable Channel between a Sender and a Receiver, with capacity to transmit one message at a time:

```
system Simple_Channel is
    class Channel is
        state free, busy(m: message);
    end Channel;
    class Sender(to: Channel) is
        state preparing, giving(m: message):
    end Sender;
    class Receiver(from: Channel) is
        state ready, processing(m: message);
    end Receiver;
    action Send by s: Sender, c: Channel is
    when s.to = c ∧ s.giving ∧ c.free do
        → c.busy(s.m), s.preparing;
    end Send;
    action Receive by r: Receiver, c: Channel is
    when r.from = c ∧ r.ready ∧ c.busy do
        → r.processing(c.m), c.free;
    end Receive;
end Simple_Channel;
```

In addition to Channel objects, this module specifies the attributes that are required for their use. For instance, if objects of class Actual_Sender are to act as Senders to objects of class Actual_Receiver, the attributes of Sender and Receiver must be inherited by them as follows:

```
class Actual_Sender(to: Channel) is
    inherit Sender(to);
    -- other attributes of Actual_Sender
end Actual_Sender;
class Actual_Receiver(from: Channel) is
    inherit Receiver(from);
    -- other attributes of Actual_Receiver
end Actual_Receiver;
```

In this example inheritance creates parallel components to the outermost states of the new classes, which corresponds to the conventional idea of inheritance. The state structure of DisCo also allows inheritance to internal substates. An object of the inheriting class then belongs to the inherited class only when it is in the substate in question. This provides a flexible way to regulate the behavior of an object as an object of the inherited class.

7. Further Transformations

It is obvious that the above possibilities for modifying action systems and to use existing components for their construction are not sufficient in practice. In particular, there is a need to refine systems by splitting actions into smaller ones [2, 23]. General transformations can be found to accomplish this, but the possibility for specific transformations with individual proofs also remains. For such purposes the mechanism of importing and modifying a system can be used in DisCo also in a more liberal way where the restrictions of superposition are removed.

As a simple example, consider an action by two objects X and Y that has been massaged into a form reflecting an implementation where X first prepares a message to Y, and this message is subsequently processed by Y. Utilizing an asynchronous channel module, this action can be replaced by two separate actions, of which one is private for X, the other is private for Y, and actions Send and Receive of the channel module are executed between these.

8. Concluding Remarks

DisCo language and its environment are being developed in a project which is part of the FINSOFT programme of the Technology Development Centre of Finland. The first version of DisCo is purely experimental; more experience is needed to decide on a balanced set of properties for this kind of a language. For action bodies it seems that assignment statements (with conditions) are sufficient for the purposes we have in mind. The importance of conventional data structures is decreased by the possibility of treating their components as independent objects. On the other hand, there is an obvious need to support more abstract notions like sets, mappings and relations.

An interpreter and animation environment are being implemented on a workstation computer. The basic notions of action systems, i.e., objects and actions, provide a generic collection of entities to be visualized. With statechart-like structuring it seems that application-specific tailoring of animations can be kept to a minimum. When several layers of refinements exist, the user will be given the freedom to choose the level of abstraction in monitoring the system.

The approach presented in this paper seems also suitable for documenting a system in terms of the transformations that have been used in its derivation. It should be noticed, however, that there is not much experience in managing such derivations, and further work is required in this respect.

More understanding is also needed of the transformations to be used in the design process, and of the associated simulation mappings between consecutive design layers. Other areas for further research are computer-supported correctness proofs of action system transformations, and automatic compilation of (restricted) action systems.

References

[1] Ada Programming Language. ANSI/MIL-STD-1815A-1983.

[2] R.J.R. Back, Refining atomicity in parallel algorithms. Reports in Computer Science 57, Åbo Akademi 1988.

[3] R.J.R. Back and R. Kurki-Suonio, Decentralization of process nets with a centralized control. To appear in *Distributed*

Computing. An earlier version in *Proc. 2nd ACM SIGACT-SIGOPS Symposium on Principles of Distributed Computing*, Montreal, Canada, Aug. 1983, 131-142.

[4] R.J.R. Back and R. Kurki-Suonio, A case study in constructing distributed algorithms: distributed exchange sort. In *Proc. Winter School on Theoretical Computer Science*, Lammi, Finland, Jan. 1984, Finnish Society of Information Processing Science, 1-33.

[5] R.J.R. Back and R. Kurki-Suonio, A new paradigm for the design of concurrent systems. *Ada Letters VII*, 6 (Fall 1987), 110-112.

[6] R.J.R. Back and R. Kurki-Suonio, Serializability in distributed systems with handshaking. In *Proc. ICALP 88, Automata, Languages and Programming* (Ed. T. Lepistö and A. Salomaa), LNCS 317, Springer-Verlag 1988, 52-66.

[7] R.J.R. Back and R. Kurki-Suonio, Distributed cooperation with action systems. *ACM Trans. Programming Languages and Systems 10*, 4 (Oct. 1988), 513-554.

[8] T. Bolognesi and E. Brinksma, Introduction to the ISO specification language LOTOS. *Computer Networks and ISDN Systems 14*, (1987), 25-59.

[9] L. Bougé and N. Francez, A compositional approach to superimposition. In *Proc. 15th ACM Symposium on Principles of Programming Languages*, San Diego, California, Jan. 1988, 240-249.

[10] K.M. Chandy and J. Misra, *Parallel Program Design: A Foundation*. Addison-Wesley 1988.

[11] O.-J. Dahl, B. Myhrhaug and K. Nygaard, Simula 67 common base language. Report S-22, Norwegian Computer Center, Oslo, 1970.

[12] E.W. Dijkstra, *A Discipline of Programming*, Prentice-Hall 1976.

[13] E.W. Dijkstra and C.S. Scholten, Termination detection for diffusing computations. *Information Processing Letters 11*, 1 (Aug. 1980), 1-4.

[14] C. Forgy and M.C. Dermot, OPS, a domain independent production system language. In *Proc. Fifth International Joint Conference on Artificial Intelligence*, 1977, 933-939.

[15] I.R. Forman, On the design of large distributed systems. Microelectronics and Computer Technology Corporation, Report STP-098-86, Jan. 1987.

[16] D. Harel, Statecharts: a visual formalism for complex systems. *Science of Computer Programming 8*, 1987, 231-274.

[17] D. Harel et al., STATEMATE: A working environment for the development of complex reactive systems. In *Proc. 11th International Conference on Software Engineering*, Singapore, April 1988, 396-406.

[18] C.A.R. Hoare, Communicating sequential processes. *Commun. ACM 21*, 8 (Aug. 1978), 666-677.

[19] C.A.R. Hoare, *Communicating Sequential Processes*. Prentice-Hall 1985.

[20] S. Katz, A superimposition control construct for distributed systems. Microelectronics and Computer Technology Corporation, Report STP-268-87, Aug. 1987.

[21] R. Kurki-Suonio, Towards programming with knowledge expressions. In *Proc. 13th ACM Symposium on Principles of Programming Languages*, St. Petersburg Beach, Florida, Jan. 1986, 140-149.

[22] R. Kurki-Suonio, Specification of serializable databases by joint actions. Tampere University of Technology, Software Systems Laboratory, Report 2, 1988.

[23] R. Kurki-Suonio and T. Kankaanpää, On the design of reactive systems. *BIT 28*, 3 (1988), 581-604.

[24] Z. Manna and A. Pnueli, How to cook a temporal proof system for your pet language. In *Proc. 10th ACM Symposium on Principles of Programming Languages*, Austin, Texas, Jan. 1983, 141-154.

[25] A. Pnueli, Applications of temporal logic to the specification and verification of reactive systems: a survey of current trends. In *Current Trends in Concurrency* (Ed. J.W. de Bakker, W.-P. de Roever and G. Rozenberg), LNCS 224, Springer-Verlag 1986, 510-584.

[26] S. Ramesh and S.L. Mehndiratta, A methodology for developing distributed programs. *IEEE Transactions on Software Engineering, SE-13*, 8 (Aug. 1987), 967-976.

IMPLEMENTING A SHARED DATASPACE LANGUAGE ON A MESSAGE-BASED MULTIPROCESSOR

Gruia-Catalin Roman and Kenneth C. Cox

Department of Computer Science
WASHINGTON UNIVERSITY
Saint Louis, Missouri 63130-4899

ABSTRACT

The term *shared dataspace* refers to the general class of models and languages in which the principal means of communication is a content-addressable data structure called a dataspace. This paper reports on progress we have made toward the development of a prototype implementation of a shared dataspace language, *Swarm*, on a hypercube multiprocessor. The paper includes an informal overview of the Swarm language, describes the design organization of a transaction processing system which forms the kernel of a Swarm implementation, and explains the algorithms implementing a subset of Swarm embedded in the language C.

1. INTRODUCTION

Concurrent programming languages may be divided into four broad categories depending on the nature of the communication mechanisms they employ. *Shared variables* as used in Concurrent Pascal[5], for example, allow processes to communicate by reading and writing (directly or indirectly via monitors) the values of a fixed set of variables whose names are known to the communicating processes. *Message-based communication* requires all information sharing to take place by sending and receiving messages in accordance with some predefined protocol. CSP[8] and Actor languages[3] are representative of this category. *Remote operations,* such as the remote procedure call used in Ada[1], permit a process to invoke operations associated with some other process. The parameters and returned values represent the information shared by the processes involved in the exchange. The last category we choose to call *shared dataspace.* It is comprised of languages in which processes have access to a common, content-addressable data structure (typically a set of tuples) whose components may be examined, inserted, and deleted. Associons[10], Linda[4], SDL[11], Transaction Networks[9], Swarm[12], and some artificial intelligence languages such as OPS5[6] belong here.

During the past year our research group has embarked on a systematic study of the shared dataspace paradigm. The main vehicle for this investigation is the language *Swarm.* The design of Swarm takes a minimalist approach and provides a relatively small number of constructs which are believed to be at the core of a large class of shared dataspace languages and are helpful in the development and analysis of concurrent computations. In Swarm, a variety of computing styles have been brought together under a single unified model. Programming convenience has been achieved by the availability of powerful queries over the dataspace and by the ease with which unstructured and unbounded problems may be approached. The opportunities for temporal and spatial decoupling of computations characteristic of shared dataspace languages have been strengthened and enhanced. On-going work on a proof system for shared dataspace languages and on declarative visualization techniques promise to contribute to increased analyzability of shared dataspace programs.

This paper reports on progress we have made toward the development of a prototype implementation of Swarm on a hypercube multiprocessor. The implementation consists of a Swarm kernel designed to support dataspace transactions on a message-passing architecture and of a small subset of Swarm embedded in the language C, henceforth called Swarm/C. The Swarm kernel has additional capabilities beyond those required for Swarm/C; these additional capabilities will be used to extend the scope of our implementation.

The paper consists of four parts. Section 2 provides an informal overview of the Swarm language. Section 3 describes the Swarm kernel and its implementation on the NCUBE[2] hypercube multiprocessor. Section 4 defines the current Swarm/C language subset. Section 5 discusses the implementation of the Swarm/C subset using the kernel.

2. THE SWARM LANGUAGE

The purpose of this section is to give an introduction to the shared dataspace concept and some familiarity with the Swarm language and its computational model. In Swarm the state of a computation is represented by the contents of the *dataspace,* a set of content-addressable entities. The dataspace is partitioned into several subsets, including the *tuple space* (a finite set of data *tuples*) and the *transaction space* (a finite set of *transactions*). An element of the dataspace is a pairing of a *type* name with a sequence of *values.* In addition, a transaction has an associated behavior specification.

The execution of a transaction is modeled as a transition between dataspaces. An executing transaction examines the dataspace, then deletes itself from the transaction space and modifies the dataspace by deleting and inserting tuples and by inserting (but not deleting) other transactions. A Swarm program begins executing from a valid initial dataspace and continues until the transaction space is empty. On each execution step a transaction is chosen *nondeterministically* from the transaction space and executed. The transaction selection is *fair* in the sense that each transaction in the space will eventually be chosen.

Before explaining the syntax and semantics of programs, we need to introduce a few frequently used basic constructs. A constructor notation is used to form a set of entities and apply an operator to the elements of the set. It has the form:

[*operator variables* : *domain* : *operands*]

The *operator* field is a commutative and associative operator such as $\exists$, $\forall$, Σ, and Π. The *operands* field is a list of operands (separated by semicolons) compatible with the operator. The *variables* field is a (possibly null) list of bound variables whose scopes are delimited by the brackets. An instance of the constructor corresponds to a set of values for the bound variables such that the *domain* predicate is satisfied. (If the domain is blank, then the constant **true** is taken for the predicate.) The operator is applied to the set of operands corresponding to all instances of the constructor; if there are no instances, then the result of the constructor is the identity element of the operator.

Swarm predicates are first-order logical expressions which can examine the dataspace. For example, the predicate *has_intensity*(ρ,17), where ρ is a variable, examines the dataspace for an element of type *has_intensity* having two components, the first being an arbitrary value and the second the constant 17. If such an element exists, the predicate succeeds and the value of the first component of the matched element is bound to the variable ρ.

A special form of the constructor, called a *generator*, is used to form a set of entities, e.g., a set of tuples which form the initial tuple space. The operator fields of generators are blank; the domain predicates may not examine the dataspace.

A Swarm program consists of five sections: a program header, optional constant and macro definitions, tuple type declarations, transaction type declarations, and a dataspace initialization section. The syntax and semantics of these program sections are given below. Figure 1 shows a simple Swarm program to label each pixel in equal-intensity regions of a digital image with the smallest coordinate in the region.

Program header. The program header associates a name with the program and optionally defines a set of program parameters. An invocation of the program with specific argument values causes the substitution of the values for the parameter names throughout the program's body. The argument values must satisfy the constraint predicates given in the program header. The program in Figure 1 is named *RegionLabel1*; it has parameters *Rows, Cols, Lo, Hi,* and *Intensity* constrained as indicated. *Intensity* is an array of input values indexed by the pixel coordinates.

Definitions. The optional Swarm definitions section allows the programmer to introduce named constants and "macros" in a program. For example, *RegionLabel1* defines predicates *Pixel(P)*, *P* **neighbors** *Q*, and *P* **is_labeled** *L*. These predicates allow the other sections to be expressed in a more concise and readable fashion.

Tuple types. The tuple types section declares the types of tuples that can exist in the tuple space. Each tuple type declaration defines a set of tuple *instances* that can be examined, inserted, and deleted by the program. In Figure 1 tuple type *has_label* pairs a pixel with a label; *has_intensity* pairs a pixel with its intensity value.

Transaction types. The transaction types section declares the types of transactions that can exist in the transaction space. Each transaction type declaration defines a set of transaction *instances* that can be executed, inserted, or

```
program RegionLabel1 (Rows, Cols, Lo, Hi, Intensity :
        1 ≤ Rows, 1 ≤ Cols, Lo ≤ Hi,
        Intensity(ρ: Pixel(ρ)),
        [∀ ρ : Pixel(ρ) : Lo ≤ Intensity(ρ) ≤ Hi] )

definitions
    [ P, Q, L ::
    Pixel(P) ≡ [∃ x,y : P = (x,y) :
        1 ≤ x ≤ Cols, 1 ≤ y ≤ Rows ] ;

    P neighbors Q ≡ Pixel(P), Pixel(Q), P ≠ Q,
        [∃ x,y,a,b : P=(x,y), Q=(a,b) :
                a–1 ≤ x ≤ a+1, b–1 ≤ y ≤ b+1],
        [∃ ι :: has_intensity(P,ι), has_intensity(Q,ι)] ;

    P is_labeled L ≡ has_label(P,L)
    ]

tuple types
    [ P, L, I : Pixel(P), Pixel(L), Lo ≤ I ≤ Hi :
        has_label(P,L) ;
        has_intensity(P,I)
    ]

transaction types
    [ P : Pixel(P) :
    Label(P) ≡
            ρ,λ1,λ2 : P is_labeled λ1†, ρ is_labeled λ2,
                  ρ neighbors P, λ1 > λ2
                        → P is_labeled λ2
        ||  true        → Label(P)
    ]

initialization
    [ P : Pixel(P) :
        has_label(P,P), has_intensity(P,Intensity(P)),
        Label(P)
    ]

end
```

Figure 1: Nonterminating Region Labeling in Swarm

examined by a program. The program in Figure 1 declares a transaction type *Label(P)*.

The body of a transaction instance consists of a sequence of subtransactions connected by the || operator:

$$variable\_list_1 : query_1 \rightarrow action_1$$
$$\| \quad \ldots$$
$$\| \quad variable\_list_n : query_n \rightarrow action_n$$

Each subtransaction definition consists of three parts: the *variable_list*, a comma-separated list of variable names, the *query*, an existential predicate over the dataspace, and the *action* which defines changes to be made to the dataspace. If the variable list is null, then the colon that separates it from the query may be omitted.

A subtransaction's action specifies sets of tuples to insert and delete and transactions to insert. Syntactically, an action consists of dataspace insertion and deletion operations separated by commas. In the action of a subtransaction, the notation *name* (*values*) specifies that a tuple or transaction of the type *name* is to be inserted into the dataspace; a † appended to a tuple specifies that the tuple is to be deleted if it is present in the dataspace. Generators may be used to specify groups of insertions or deletions.

As a convenience, tuple deletion may be specified in the query by appending the symbol † to a dataspace predicate. *name(pattern)*† indicates that the matching tuple in the tuple space is to be deleted if the entire query succeeds. Any variables appearing in the *pattern* must be defined in the *variable_list* of the subtransaction (not in a constructor nested inside the query).

A subtransaction is executed in three phases: query evaluation, tuple deletions, and tuple and transaction insertions. Evaluation of the query seeks to find values for the subtransaction variables that make the query predicate true with respect to the dataspace. If the query evaluation succeeds, then the dataspace deletions and insertions specified by the subtransaction's action are performed using the values bound by the query. If the query fails, then the action is not executed. The subtransactions of a transaction are executed synchronously: queries are evaluated first, then the transaction itself is deleted and the indicated tuple deletions are performed, and finally the indicated tuple and transaction insertions are done.

Initialization. By default, both the tuple and transaction spaces are empty. The initialization section establishes the dataspace contents that exist at the beginning of a computation. The section consists of a sequence of generators separated by semicolons; each generator is like a subtransaction's action in syntax and semantics. Since the null computation is not very interesting, at least one transaction must be established at initialization.

3. SWARM KERNEL

The model underlying Swarm has properties that make it attractive for expressing large-scale concurrent computations and for investigating the visualization of concurrent computations. These capabilities, however, come at the expense of increased implementation difficulty imposed by the requirement for atomic execution of complex transactions. Although the problems which arise are not new and there is a large body of literature on implementing such database transactions, the low-level granularity of the dataspace and the large number of concurrent transactions demand different kinds of solutions and a much greater reliance on highly parallel machines.

Our investigation into realization strategies for Swarm is following two parallel paths: the design of a shared dataspace machine whose only primitive operation is pattern matching, and the development of a multiprocessor-based transaction system implementation. This section provides an overview of the design of the Swarm kernel which supports the transaction system. The first part gives an overview of the kernel design. The second part is a discussion of how this design is realized on the NCUBE, a hypercube-class message-passing multiprocessor developed by the NCUBE Corporation.

3.1. Kernel Overview

We want to be able to implement the kernel on a variety of message-based multiprocessors, including ones which do not support multiprogramming. In such a system, a processor cannot both support user application programs and service dataspace requests from other programs without greatly re-writing the user program. The transaction system therefore distinguishes between *user processes* and *dataspace processes.* The dataspace processes are responsible for storing tuples and handling dataspace requests from user processes. If the system permits, a single processor can run both user and dataspace processes; otherwise, the processors are partitioned into two groups, one used for user processes and one for dataspace processes. We use the term *site* to refer to a processor which is running a dataspace process.

At each site tuples are stored in a list. A position is assigned to each tuple when it is asserted; all positions are unique and increase by order of assertion time. The tuple position and site together form the tuple identifier, which is thus unique over the entire system.

The kernel acts primarily as a manager of *dialogs.* A dialog is the interaction between a single user process and a single site. A typical dialog consists of either two or three messages. The user program first issues a *request.* At some later time the site performs the request and returns a *reply.* The reply may complete the dialog, or the user process may be required to send a *confirmation.* These actions occur asynchronously, so the user process is free to continue with other processing after issuing a request.

A *dialog-id* is a type of object which identifies a dialog. Any object of type dialog-id is unique over the entire transaction system. When a user program issues a request, it receives a dialog-id. Dialogs may request operations on the dataspace, or may request bounds information from the site. The bounds information is simply a pair of integers containing the highest and lowest positions currently assigned to tuples at the site. This capability has been included for implementation of backtracking searches.

The supported dataspace operations are assert (add a tuple), query (examine a tuple), retract (remove a tuple), and modify (change a tuple). In the case of query, retract, and modify requests a *pattern* may be specified to be matched. The pattern includes constraints on the tuple data and the tuple identifier. When such a request is processed by a site the list of tuples at the site is searched in order until a match is found or there are no more tuples. A request can also specify a particular position at which the search is to start.

Matching requests may be issued in either *immediate* or *pending* operation-mode (several other modes are described below). In immediate mode, the site scans the tuples and replies; if no matching tuple is found, the reply contains a failure indication. In pending mode, the tuples are scanned; if no matching tuple is found, the site retains the dialog request until a matching tuple becomes available. When such a tuple becomes available, the request is performed and the reply is made. A pending request may be *released.* This action converts it to the immediate form, causing it to reply even if no matching tuple is available.

Any request may be *aborted.* If the site has already performed the request and sent a reply, the operation is not undone and the abort fails. If the abort is successful, the site returns a failure reply. Note in either case a reply is made and can be received by the user program. The *delete* operation behaves in the same manner but does not send a reply when the abort succeeds.

Tuples may be *locked* by requests. Each tuple has an associated *mark* which is modified by the request when it locks or unlocks the tuple. Several requests may hold locks on a tuple simultaneously. A request may be made in either *non-lock* or *lock* mode; lock mode specifies how the request modifies the lock. When a non-lock mode request matches a tuple, the request is immediately performed and the reply is sent; the dialog is then complete. When a lock mode request matches a tuple, the locking is performed and a reply is sent. The user process must complete the dialog by sending a confirmation. A confirmation may be either a *cancel* or a *commit*. Both confirmations unlock the tuple, but a commit performs the request operation while a cancel does not.

The effect of the tuple lock is to *block* certain searches. When a request matches a tuple against its pattern, it tests the mark to determine if the tuple is locked. If the tuple is locked, the search is suspended and the tuple mark is modified. When the tuple is unlocked (by a cancel or commit) or altered (by a modify or retract), any requests suspended at the tuple are permitted to continue. The requests resume scanning starting with that tuple; if the tuple was retracted, they proceed to the next.

Requests may be issued in *block*, *non-block*, or *ignore* mode. Block mode causes the request to halt as described above. Non-block mode causes the request to skip the locked tuple; it does *not* re-examine the tuple if it reaches the end of the tuple list. Both block and non-block modes have parameters describing what the request considers to be a lock; block mode has additional parameters which describe how the tuple mark is modified if the request blocks. Ignore mode causes the request to ignore the tuple locking and proceed with the operation and reply.

The functions provided to user processes by the kernel are summarized in Table 1. The functions may be divided into five broad categories: functions which *send requests* initiate a dialog and return a dialog-id; functions which *test for replies* allow examination of the replies which have arrived; functions which *receive replies* get the data from the replies; functions which *send confirmations* are used when the dialog requires a cancel or commit; and functions which *change transaction status* send abort, delete, and release requests. Space requirements prevent a complete explanation of these functions; a full discussion may be found in a recently released technical report[7].

Functions to send requests (S-class):

dialog-id **Sassert**(*site, tuple, lock-mode*)

dialog-id **Squery**(*site, position, pattern, operation-mode, lock-mode, block-mode*)

dialog-id **Smodify**(*site, position, pattern, operation-mode, lock-mode, block-mode, modification*)

dialog-id **Sretract**(*site, position, pattern, operation-mode, lock-mode, block-mode*)

dialog-id **Sbounds**(*site*)

Functions to test for replies (T-class):

boolean **Tavail**(*dialog-id*)

dialog-id **Tfirstreply**(*trans-type*)

dialog-id **Tnextreply**(*trans-type*)

Functions to receive replies (R-class):

boolean **Rassert**(*dialog-id, site, position, status*)

boolean **Rquery**(*dialog-id, site, position, tuple, status*)

boolean **Rmodify**(*dialog-id, site, position,* $tuple_1$, $tuple_2$, *status*)

boolean **Rretract**(*dialog-id, site, position, tuple, status*)

boolean **Rbounds**(*dialog-id*, p_1, p_2)

Functions to send confirmations:

boolean **Scancel**(*dialog-id*)

boolean **Scommit**(*dialog-id*)

Functions to change transaction status:

boolean **Sabort**(*dialog-id*)

boolean **Sdelete**(*dialog-id*)

boolean **Srelease**(*dialog-id*)

Table 1: Swarm Kernel Functions

3.2. Implementation of Kernel on NCUBE

The kernel is written in C under VERTEX, the NCUBE Corporation's proprietary operating system for the NCUBE node processors. This operating system supports message passing and message routing, but not multiprogramming. The nodes of an allocated NCUBE subcube are therefore partitioned into two sets, one set being available for user processes and one for dataspace processes. This partitioning is performed by a program running on the NCUBE host processor, which also loads the processes onto the dataspace nodes. This program is not part of the kernel so will not be discussed further.

The user processes are compiled with a library of functions which provide access to the Swarm kernel. The same library is used in the compilation of the dataspace process. This library provides many common structures to the two types of processes; for example, each process has a table which maps the logical sites to the physical NCUBE dataspace-node addresses. The two processes also have common protocols for formatting and transmitting messages using the VERTEX message-passing capabilities.

3.2.1. User package

When processing an S-class (send request) function, the user process first performs any necessary error-checking. It then generates a dialog-id and prepares a message containing an integer encoding the request type, the dialog-id, and the function arguments. The message is sent to the dataspace node corresponding to the site. The dialog-id and information about the dialog (including the request modes) are stored on the *outstanding list*. Finally, the dialog-id is returned.

Each user process has an internal counter for each of the dataspace nodes which it uses to generate the dialog-ids. System-wide uniqueness of dialog-ids is guaranteed by concatenating the counter with the address of the user process node and the site to create the dialog-id; the addresses and the counter can be recovered from the dialog-id.

When any of the package functions are called by the user program, the package first reads and queues any transaction-system messages (replies) which have arrived at the node. This transfers the messages from VERTEX operating system buffers into process buffers and reduces the possibility of a process blocking on a message send. The replies are then processed. Any replies that do not correspond to outstanding dialogs are discarded (it being assumed that these dialogs have been aborted or deleted). The remaining replies are added to the *available list* and the entry on the outstanding list is changed to show the reply is available.

The **Tfirstreply** and **Tnextreply** functions implement a list-traversal mechanism on the available list. The **Tavail** function simply examines the outstanding list to see if the reply has arrived.

When an **R**-class (receive reply) function is performed, the outstanding list is examined. If the reply is available, the reply contents are copied into the function arguments and the reply is removed from the available list. If the request was issued in non-lock mode, it is removed from the outstanding list; otherwise the outstanding list entry is modified to indicate the reply has been received.

When an **Scancel** or **Scommit** is issued, the outstanding list is checked to ensure that the dialog reply has been received. If it has, the confirmation is sent to the appropriate database process and the outstanding list entry is removed. Otherwise no action is taken.

When an **Sabort** is issued, the outstanding list is again checked. The function returns **false** if the dialog is not on the list. If it is on the list, the reply status is checked. If the reply has not yet arrived, an abort message is sent to the site and the outstanding list entry is modified to indicate it was aborted. If the reply has arrived, it and the dialog entry are discarded. The **Sdelete** function is similar but always removes the dialog's entry on the outstanding list.

When an **Srelease** is issued, the outstanding list is checked. The function returns **false** if the transaction is not on the list or is not pending. Otherwise the reply status is checked, and if the reply has not yet arrived a release message is sent to the site. Finally, the transaction mode is changed to immediate.

3.2.2. Dataspace processes

The dataspace process continually reads messages from user processes and performs the indicated action, perhaps sending a reply as a result. When the process receives a message, it first reads all transaction-system messages queued at the process site and places them in an internal queue.

Any abort, delete, release, cancel or commit messages are processed first. This is primarily for efficiency, since any of these may permit removal of dialogs from the site and reduce storage requirements. An abort or delete may also remove a message from the queue and save processing time. Request messages from a particular user process are performed strictly in increasing order of dialog-id. If a request arrives out of order, it is held until the intervening requests are obtained and processed. The process keeps the largest dialog-id (as determined by the counter portion) that it has received from each of the user processes.

All requests are stored on a master *outstanding list*; each entry contains all the information associated with the requests. A number of other lists of requests are described below. These are implemented as lists of pointers to entries of the outstanding list, so the data for a request only appears once. These lists have the property that a request appears on at most one such list. A part of the outstanding list entry indicates which other list, if any, the request is on.

The tuples are stored in a *tuple list*. In addition to the tuple data, each list element contains the *position*, a *mark* used for locking, and a *block list* of requests. The process maintains a counter which is used to generate positions. When an *assert* is performed, the tuple is appended to the tuple list with a new position, a zeroed (unlocked) mark, and an empty block list.

To support pending requests, the process maintains a *pending list* of unserviced requests. Any request issued in pending mode which does not produce results when first processed is appended to the list. After performing any action which asserts, alters, or unlocks a tuple, the pending list is scanned for a request which matches the tuple and considers the tuple unlocked. If such a request is found, the request is removed from the list and performed. If the request had no effect on the tuple, the scanning of the pending list continues from the selected request. If the tuple is altered (including locking information) a new tuple results and the scanning of the pending list starts from the beginning. If the tuple is retracted, scanning halts.

When a release request is processed, the largest dialog-id is examined. If the request to be released has not been processed yet, the release is held until the request is received, at which time it is changed to immediate mode. If the request is not on the outstanding list, the release is ignored. If the request is on the pending list, it is removed from the pending and outstanding lists and a reply containing a failure indication is sent. (The pending-list scan algorithm maintains the invariant 'a transaction is on pending list *if and only if* no unlocked matching tuple exists'; a final scan of the tuple list is therefore not necessary.) Finally, if the request is blocked at a tuple, its status is changed to immediate and, when it is unblocked, it is processed as such.

When a request pattern matches a tuple, the results depend on the blocking-mode in which the transaction was issued. If the request was issued in *ignore* mode, or the request was issued in *non-block* or *block* mode and the tuple is not locked, then the appropriate action is taken (either the operation is performed or a lock is applied) and a reply is sent. If the request was issued in *non-block* mode and the tuple is locked, the request proceeds to the next tuple. If the request was issued in *block* mode and the tuple is locked, the request becomes blocked. Requests which are blocked at a tuple are appended to the tuple's *block list*. When the tuple is modified the requests on the block list are re-examined and may continue searching. Processing of the blocked requests occurs before examination of the pending list.

Tuple locking and request blocking are carried out using the tuple *mark*. The mark consists of two elements, a bitfield *B* and integer *I*. The request may examine both elements to determine if the tuple is locked. The effect of a block or lock is to set some bits of the appropriate mark's bitfield and increment the mark's integer by some amount, while undoing a block or lock clears the same bits of the bitfield and decrements the integer by the same amount. The test for blocking examines the mark and blocks if particular bits are set or if the integer is greater than some value. In this manner multiple types of locks may be supported.

Issuing a request in either block or non-block mode requires the specification of a test to determine if the tuple is locked. This test consists of two values, a bitfield b_t and an integer i_t. Block mode also requires the specification of an alteration to be applied to the mark if the request is blocked. This alteration consists of a bitfield b_b and integer i_b.

Issuing a request in lock mode requires the specification of an alteration to be applied to the mark if the request succeeds in locking the tuple. This alteration consists of a bitfield b_l and integer i_l.

Let $\otimes$ be bitwise AND, $\oplus$ be bitwise OR, and $\overline{b}$ be bitwise NOT (of b). Then the lock/block actions are:

A request considers a tuple locked if

$$((B \otimes b_l) \neq 0) \vee (I > i_l)$$

When a request blocks on a tuple, it performs

$$B \leftarrow B \oplus b_b \qquad I \leftarrow I + i_b$$

When a request is unblocked, it performs

$$B \leftarrow B \otimes \overline{b_b} \qquad I \leftarrow I - i_b$$

When a request locks on a tuple, it performs

$$B \leftarrow B \oplus b_l \qquad I \leftarrow I + i_l$$

When a request unlocks a tuple, it performs

$$B \leftarrow B \otimes \overline{b_l} \qquad I \leftarrow I - i_l$$

When a request applies a lock to a tuple, the request is placed on a *confirmation list*. When a confirmation message (cancel or commit) is received, this list is searched for the request; if it is not found the confirmation is ignored. If the request is found, the confirmation is performed. If the confirmation is a commit, the request operation is applied to the tuple. For either a commit or a cancel, the tuple is unlocked and the request is removed from the confirmation and outstanding lists. The block list for the tuple and the pending list are then processed.

When an abort is received, the largest dialog-id is used to determine if the request has been processed. If it has not, the abort is held until the request is received, at which time the failure reply is made. If the request has been processed, the outstanding list is examined. If the request is found, the failure reply is made; otherwise no action is taken.

4. SWARM/C DEFINITION

Many of the Swarm kernel features described above are designed for later implementation of powerful transaction-processing capabilities. To test the kernal and provide a working transaction system, the kernel is being used to implement a subset of Swarm embedded in the language C, which we call Swarm/C.

Swarm/C provides a limited number of atomic transaction types implemented as function calls in the C language. Most of the complexities of the Swarm kernel are hidden from the user—for example, sites are completely hidden and all necessary site manipulations are performed by the Swarm/C runtime library. In addition, Swarm/C provides some capabilities not used for Swarm; for example, transactions may specify a timeout period and are aborted if they exceed this period. Obviously this is not needed for Swarm, which does not include information about time. In addition, there is a large suite of functions designed to make the creation and manipulation of tuples and patterns easier.

Swarm/C transactions are subject to the following restrictions:

(1) Each transaction consists of only one subtransaction—synchronous execution of multiple subtransactions is eliminated.

(2) Transactions can refer to only one tuple in the tuple space and may involve only simple comparisons among variables and constants (in the query part). The need for implementing backtracking is thus eliminated and transaction atomicity is easily ensured.

```
program RegionLabel2 (Rows, Cols, Lo, Hi, Intensity :
        1 ≤ Rows, 1 ≤ Cols, Lo ≤ Hi,
        Intensity(ρ: Pixel(ρ)),
        [∀ ρ : Pixel(ρ) : Lo ≤ Intensity(ρ) ≤ Hi] )

definitions
    [ P, Q, L ::
    Pixel(P) ≡ [∃ x,y : P = (x,y) :
        1 ≤ x ≤ Cols, 1 ≤ y ≤ Rows ] ;

    P is_next_to Q ≡ Pixel(P), Pixel(Q), P ≠ Q,
        [∃ x,y,a,b : P=(x,y), Q=(a,b) :
                a–1 ≤ x ≤ a+1, b–1 ≤ y ≤ b+1];

    (P,I) is_labeled L ≡ has_intensity_and_label(P,I,L)
    ]

tuple types
    [ P, L, I : Pixel(P), Pixel(L), Lo ≤ I ≤ Hi :
        has_intensity_and_label(P,I,L)
    ]

transaction types
    [ P,Q,L,I : Pixel(P), Pixel(Q), Pixel(L), Lo≤I≤Hi :
    Check(P,Q) ≡
            ι,λ : (Q,ι) is_labeled λ
                → skip
        ‖  [true  → Label(P,ι,λ), Check(P,Q) ;]
    Label(P,I,L) ≡
            λ : (P,I) is_labeled λ†, λ > L
                → (P,I) is_labeled L
    ]

initialization
    [ P,Q : Pixel(P), Pixel(Q), Q is_next_to P :
        has_intensity_and_label(P,Intensity(P),P),
        [Check(P,Q)]
    ]
end
```

Figure 2: Nonterminating Region Labeling in Swarm/C

(3) The single tuple referenced by the transaction may be examined, inserted, deleted, and modified. A modification involves a deletion followed by the insertion of a tuple of the same type in a single atomic operation.

(4) Transactions cannot refer in any way to the transaction space. The transaction space is essentially external to this implementation, because the transactions are issued from processes written in C.

Applying this set of restrictions to the region labeling program shown in Figure 1 leads to the version presented in Figure 2. The transaction type *Label(P)* had to be separated into two transactions each referring to a single tuple in the tuple space. Although the resulting solution is presented in Swarm, the reader is reminded that in Swarm/C one needs to create C programs which issue the transactions against the tuple space. To highlight this fact we placed a box around any actions which are actually performed in C without any support from the Swarm kernel.

5. IMPLEMENTATION OF SWARM/C

The four Swarm/C functions which user processes may invoke in a C program are *assert*, *query*, *retract*, and *modify*. An invocation of any of these functions is called a *transaction*. Assert inserts a tuple in the dataspace, returning its identification; query examines a tuple and returns the contents; retract deletes a tuple, returning the contents; and modify is equivalent to a retract and assert, returning both the previous and new tuple values.

The query, modify, and retract transactions specify a *pattern* which is used to determine which tuple is affected by the operation. A transaction can either succeed or fail. An assert transaction can only fail if the tuple cannot be added (due to lack of storage); the other types can fail if no appropriate tuple to access or alter can be found.

Each transaction acts on a single tuple, and any transaction may access any tuple. A transaction appears to the user as a single atomic action; that is, each transaction modifies the dataspace without interference from other transactions. In particular, the *modify* transaction is not identical to a *retract* followed by an *assert* because the modify is an atomic action while other transactions can be interleaved between the retract and the assert.

Implementation of Swarm/C on top of the kernel functions involves three major additions: automatic distribution of tuples to sites, a method of representing and controlling the multiple dialogs involved in a Swarm/C transaction, and protocols for the dialogs involved in each of the transactions.

5.1. Tuple Distribution Method

The tuple site is determined automatically when the tuple is asserted. For greater efficiency when a search of the dataspace is carried out, this assignment is done so the sites where a tuple may be found can be determined from a pattern matching the tuple. To do this, we require two functions; $F_t(tuple)$ produces the site at which a tuple is to be stored, and $F_p(pattern)$ produces a set of sites where a tuple matching the pattern may be stored. To be able to determine the possible sites from a pattern, we require $F_t(tuple) \in F_p(pattern)$ for *all* patterns which match the tuple.

Although this property of F_t and F_p appears difficult to realize, it is actually quite simple to develop appropriate functions. Assume that there are 2^n dataspace nodes (adaptations when there are not exactly 2^n dataspace nodes are simple). Each node is assigned a base-2 number consisting of n bits. Given a tuple to assert, an n-place vector of values is constructed from the tuple's structure and tuple data elements. A hashing function which produces 0 or 1 is then applied to each vector element, producing an n-digit binary number which is used as the node address.

A similar method is used for tuple matching. The pattern includes the structure of the tuple and some information about the values in the various fields. The same method as above is used to construct an n-digit number in which the structure and specified data element positions are 0 or 1 (as produced by the hashing function) and the unspecified positions are left empty. The set of possible tuple sites is generated by filling in the empty positions in all possible ways with 0 or 1.

The use of this method speeds up the process of searching for a tuple. However, it also requires that at all times $F_t(tuple)$ be the site where the tuple is stored. This means a tuple can only be modified if the new tuple has the same value of F_t as the old tuple, since tuples do not move once asserted.

The method used to guarantee this behavior uses the fact that tuples are vectors of data elements. A user program selects a number called the *cut*. Once a user process has asserted its first tuple, it cannot change the value of the cut. Any data elements whose position in the tuple is at or before the cut can be modified; data elements whose position is after the cut cannot be modified. The functions F_t and F_p use only information about positions after the cut.

5.2. Representation of Swarm/C Transactions

A Swarm/C transaction consists of a number of simultaneous dialogs with different sites. A transaction begins with the invocation of one of the Swarm/C functions and ends when the function returns; at this time all the dialogs have completed. No information needs to be kept from one transaction to the next.

With this information, design of the transaction representation is simple. Each transaction determines the sites with which it must interact, with *assert* using F_t to find the site where the tuple is to be stored and the others using F_p to find the sites that must be searched. Dialogs with each of these sites are initiated using the kernel functions.

The transaction then monitors the replies using the protocols described below. When the transaction selects a reply to be returned, it sends delete messages for any uncompleted dialogs and possibly a commit to complete the selected dialog. The transaction then returns. Any subsequent replies that arrive from the sites (due to transmission delays or two messages passing) are discarded by the user package as not belonging to active dialogs.

5.3. Protocols for Swarm/C Transactions

The assert transaction is the simplest, since a tuple is stored at exactly one site. The site for the tuple is selected using F_t and a request to assert the tuple is sent to that site. The assert request specifies no locking. The site either adds the tuple or fails (due to lack of storage) and replies accordingly. The site reply is passed on to the user.

The other transactions each permit pattern-searching. As such, they must interact with multiple sites. In the case of the query, the request is broadcast to all sites where tuples matching the pattern might be stored. The request specifies immediate mode, no locking, and block if a particular bit b of the mark bitfield is set. Each site eventually responds with a failure or with the contents of a matching tuple. If some site replies affirmatively, the transaction sends deletes to the sites with which it has active dialogs and returns the reply to the user. Otherwise, once all sites respond negatively the transaction returns a failure.

The retract and modify transactions are similar to one another. The request is broadcast to all sites where tuples matching the pattern might be stored. The request specifies immediate mode, lock by setting bit b, and block if the same bit b is set. Each site eventually responds. If some site responds affirmatively, the transaction sends deletes to all other sites to halt the dialog and unlock any other tuples it holds and sends a commit to the affirmative site to complete the operation and unlock the tuple. Otherwise, once all sites respond negatively the transaction returns a failure.

We now show that with the above scheme all transactions will complete. Clearly the possibility of deadlock exists. For example, assume transaction T_1 locks tuple τ_1 and transaction T_2 locks tuple τ_2. If T_1 blocks at τ_2 (i.e., waits for the results of a dialog which is blocked at τ_2) and T_2 blocks at τ_1, a deadlock condition results.

We use the following scheme to avoid this deadlock. The sites are ordered by their logical numbering. A transaction has only one dialog with a particular site, and hence holds at most one lock on a tuple stored at the site. Once a transaction has a lock on a particular tuple it renounces all interest in any sites following that of the tuple and terminates the dialogs with these sites using delete messages. In particular, it releases any locks it has at these sites and does not wait for the results of dialogs with these sites.

With these conventions, deadlock situations cannot develop. Consider the previous example with transaction T_1 locking τ_1 and T_2 locking τ_2. If τ_1 and τ_2 have the same site, T_1 cannot be blocked at τ_2 because it only has one dialog with the site, specifically the one which caused τ_1 to be locked. If τ_1 and τ_2 are at different sites, either (the site of) τ_2 follows τ_1 or τ_1 follows τ_2. In the first case transaction T_1 has no interest in τ_2 so cannot be blocked by transaction T_2; the other case is symmetric and T_2 is not blocked. This property also holds for larger systems of transactions, so we deduce that among the currently active transactions at any time there is always some transaction which is not blocked.

We can also show absence of individual starvation – that is, any particular transaction will eventually complete – given two assumptions. The first is that when a tuple is unlocked, the requests blocked at that tuple are permitted to proceed before any other request can lock the tuple. This guarantees a group of blocked requests will not be continually re-blocked at the same tuple by new requests. The second assumption is that blocked requests are processed strictly in the order in which they became blocked. This guarantees that each request blocked at a particular tuple will eventually progress. Accordingly, every dialog will eventually complete (or be deleted) and hence every transaction will complete.

Since the retract and modify protocols described above obey the protocol for absence of deadlock, and the Swarm kernel follows the two unlocking rules for absence of individual starvation, we can conclude that every Swarm/C function will eventually complete.

6. CONCLUSIONS

The shared dataspace paradigm is a novel approach to specifying, visualizing, and reasoning about concurrent computations. Despite its attractive features, the paradigm's full potential will be realized only if we are able to demonstrate that reasonably efficient implementations of shared dataspace languages are feasible. Multiple implementations of Linda already exist and a Linda machine is currently being built. Swarm, however, is significantly more complex than Linda. (SWARM/C already exceeds the feature set included in C-Linda.)

The implementation study presented in this paper is designed to probe the extent to which today's multiprocessors are capable of supporting the processing requirements of shared dataspace languages in general and Swarm in particular. The multi-phased implementation effort is also intended to be a vehicle for making available the shared dataspace paradigm to developers of multiprocessor-based applications and to researchers interested in program visualization techniques.

Acknowledgments: This work was supported by the Department of Computer Science, Washington University, St. Louis, Missouri. The authors express their gratitude to Jerome R. Cox, department chairman, for his support and encouragement. We also thank Conrad Cunningham for his input regarding this paper and his contribution to the development of the shared dataspace concept. The NCUBE is one of the computational resources maintained by the Computer and Communications Research Center of Washington University.

7. REFERENCES

1. "Reference Manual for the Ada Programming Language," ANSI/MIL-STD-1815A-1983, American National Standards Institute, Inc., Washington, D.C. (January 1983).
2. "NCUBE Users Handbook," Version P2.1, NCUBE Corporation, Beaverton, Oregon (October 1987).
3. Agha, G., *Actors: A Model of Concurrent Computation in Distributed Systems,* MIT Press, Cambridge, Massachusetts (1986).
4. Ahuja, S., Carriero, N., and Gelernter, D., "Linda and Friends," *Computer* **19**(8), pp. 26-34 (August 1986).
5. BrinchHansen, P., "The Programming Language Concurrent Pascal," *IEEE Transactions on Software Engineering* **1**(2), pp. 199-206 (1975).
6. Brownston, L., Farrell, R., Kant, E., and Martin, N., *Programming Expert Systems in OPS5: An Introduction to Rule-Based Programming,* Addison-Wesley, Reading, Massachusetts (1985).
7. Cox, K. C. and Roman, G.-C., "A Transaction System for the NCUBE," Technical Report WUCS-88-31, Washington University, Department of Computer Science, St. Louis, Missouri (October 1988).
8. Hoare, C. A. R., "Communicating Sequential Processes," *Communications of the ACM* **21**(8), pp. 666-677 (August 1978).
9. Kimura, T. D., "Visual Programming by Transaction Network," pp. 648-654 in *Proceedings of 21st Hawaii International Conference on System Sciences,* IEEE, Kona, Hawaii (January 1988).
10. Rem, M., "Associons: A Program Notation with Tuples Instead of Variables," *ACM Transactions on Programming Languages and Systems* **3**(3), pp. 251-262 (July 1981).
11. Roman, G.-C., "Language and Visualization Support for Large-Scale Concurrency," *Proceedings of the 10th International Conference on Software Engineering,* pp. 296-308. IEEE, April 1988.
12. Roman, G.-C. and Cunningham, H. C., "A Shared Dataspace Model of Concurrency — Language and Programming Implications," in *Proceedings of the 9th International Conference on Distributed Computing Systems,* IEEE (June 1989).

A Specification Language for Parallel Architectures and Algorithms

Thomas Bräunl

Universität Stuttgart, IFI
Azenbergstr. 12
D-7000 Stuttgart 1, FRG

University of Southern California
Computer Science Department
Los Angeles, CA 90089 (on leave)

E-mail: "unido!ifistg!braunl"@seismo.css.gov

Abstract

Most conventional programming languages rely implicitly on the von-Neumann model with its single processor unit. There is a need for a clear and safe programming environment to describe parallel execution explicitly for a modern computer architecture with many processing elements. The *Parallaxis* system enables the specification of the underlying hardware, consisting of processors and their interconnection network, as well as the declaration of the parallel algorithm to be performed on this particular hardware structure. Inter-processor communication is handled by a message-passing concept while an extended typing mechanism prevents errors by employing the concept of units. Thus, *Parallaxis* represents a tool for efficient concurrency exploitation with all benefits of a clear structured and safely restricted high-level language.

1. Introduction

Parallel Systems bear the solutions to future computational demands. Though the availability of highly parallel systems is increasing, there is still a lack of concurrent programming environments which account for both, high level language features, like structured design, clarity, legibility, etc., and the efficiency needed for a reasonable application.

This paper introduces a new concept for explicitly describing parallel resources and concurrent actions with any SIMD array-computer as target system. Essential is the syntactical splitting into two parts: first the hardware specification describing the interconnecting network structure and second the algorithm declaration for controlling the host and all parallel processing elements (PEs). This approach has benefits for all kinds of machines: Using a fixed wired SIMD computer it is desirable to adapt one´s algorithm, in order to achieve a better match to the available hardware with its structure reflected in the specification part itself. The better the match between software structure and hardware structure, the better the performance will be. Therefore, when using a reconfigurable SIMD computer (usually with reprogrammable network routers), it is straightforward to achieve an optimal match between the flexible hardware structure and the algorithm anticipated for solving a particular problem: all it needs is an appropriate hardware specification as a part of the *Parallaxis* program. Finally, considering a single-processor simulator of a parallel system, the hardware specification may be used for modeling, comparing, testing and debugging of algorithms for different network structures.

2. Historical Background

Several concurrent programming languages have been developed, however, none of them comprises the hardware structure that builds the basis for efficient parallel processing. Most conventional programming languages rely inherently on the von-Neumann single-processor model or consider only a few processors with common memory (*"coarse grained parallelism"*). This holds for Brinch-Hansen´s *"Concurrent Pascal"* [1] while Hoare´s *"CSP"* [2] and Inmos´*"Occam"* [3] are also appropriate for a larger number of PEs. All these languages allow the natural formulation of sequential and parallel subtasks, but they are short in specifying the underlying hardware structure they need to perform. Occam has only rudimentary specification constructs in the form of compiler directives. One of the latest challenges in parallel hardware is D. Hillis´ *"Connection Machine"* [4]. It is a true *"fine grained"* or *"data-parallel"* computer, for which conventional parallel programming languages do not fit. The *Parallaxis* model should be perfectly well suited for this class of architecture.

3. Specification of the Parallel Hardware

Specification of the hardware structure, of processors and network greatly increases the comprehensibility of a parallel algorithm, since the system structure is definitely crucial for understanding what is happening. Whether an algorithm is bound for a grid, ring, tree or even a hypercube topology should be stated crisply and clearly. After all, the

©1989 ACM 0-89791-305-1/89/0500/0049$00.75

topology greatly determines the algorithm applied! No matter, whether the actual hardware is reconfigured by this specification, interpreted by a simulator or just invariably stated: it certainly helps in reducing errors.

The *Parallaxis* system makes the assumption of a distributed system with many processing elements and only a single instruction stream, controlled by a central host. Processors do not have any common memory, but may exchange data by sending and receiving messages through bi-directional ports. All PEs are identical and therefore, have the same number of ports. This principally reflects a SIMD structure; any MIMD system may be programmed using *Parallaxis* as well, but it cannot take full advantage of its versatility. On the other hand, who wants to program, say, 1000 processors independently and take care of their synchronization? Many problems that can be solved in parallel exhibit some type of regular pattern, so it seems to be a good idea to take advantage of this regularity and use the simpler SIMD model that can be programmed much easier.

Parallaxis´ hardware specification takes two steps:

- First, the specification of the number of processors and their arrangement in dimensions through the CONFIGURATION specification.
- Second, the specification of the connections between the PEs, the network structure through the CONNECTION specification.

The configuration specification gives this processor pattern a name and defines a range (or just the number) of processors for each dimension enclosed in brackets. The connection specification defines a transformation function for each port of a processing element.

Since only regular patterns are of interest in a SIMD context, it is not necessary to define every single connection, but only one definition per port of the identical PEs. This greatly reduces the size of the specification: consider a system consisting of 1000 PEs with 5 ports each. Only 5 transfer functions in *Parallaxis* are sufficient to specify all 5000 connections.

The following example defines a two-dimensional grid of 1024 processing elements, arranged in 64 rows by 16 columns. Each PE is connected to its north, south, east and west neighbor. Border-PEs have connections to the inside of the grid only.

Example 1: *specification of a 2-dimensional grid (see fig. 1)*

```
CONFIGURATION grid [64] [16];
CONNECTION north: grid[i,j] → grid[i+1, j].south;
           south: grid[i,j] → grid[i-1, j].north;
           east : grid[i,j] → grid[i, j+1].west;
           west : grid[i,j] → grid[i, j-1].east;
```

Each transfer function specifies the neighbor to one port of every processing element. Therefore, the specification includes the port name, separated by a colon from its transfer function. The left hand side of the arrow describes a general PE as origin (here with coordinate variables i and j; one for each dimension) while the right hand side shows its destination or neighbor with coordinates computed from the original. After the period the corresponding entry-port of that neighbor is stated.

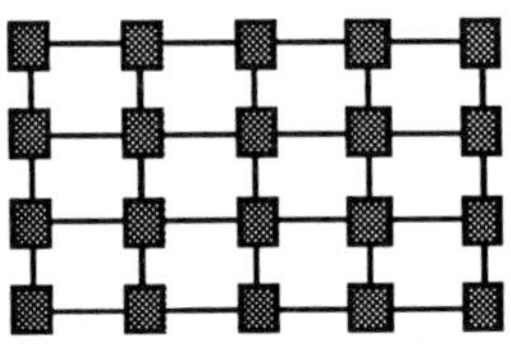

Figure 1: two-dim. grid

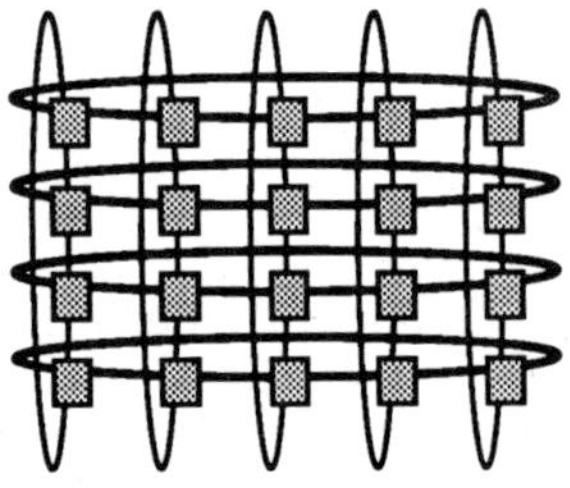

Figure 2: torus

If the coordinates of the neighbor PE are not in the appropriate range as stated in the configuration specification, then there will be no connection to this port of that particular PE. This happens in example 1 for all processing elements on the four borders. If one would like to have them connected to the border PEs on the opposite side (forming a *torus*), one could use the modulo-function with the row- or column-size in the destination coordinates´ expressions, as shown in example 2.

Example 2: *specification of a torus (see fig. 2)*

```
CONST rows = 64;  cols = 16;

CONFIGURATION  torus [rows] [cols];
CONNECTION
 north: torus[i,j] →torus[(i+1) mod rows, j].south;
 south: torus[i,j] →torus[(i-1) mod rows, j].north;
 east : torus[i,j] →torus[i, (j+1) mod cols].west;
 west : torus[i,j] →torus[i, (j-1) mod cols].east;
```

4. Message Passing

To exchange data between processing elements, a simple message passing protocol is being employed. The basic commands "send" and "receive" for passing messages consisting of single data objects are used to construct the more efficient command "propagate." It represents a *send* followed immediately by a *receive*, using the appropriate entry-port as denoted in the hardware specification. All communication is done synchronously and may only occur during parallel execution. That is, all active processors exchange data simultaneously, each to its appropriate neighbor as defined for that port. This statement for the grid from example 1 may look like the following:

```
propagate.north(send_expr, receive_var);
```

Here, "north" is the name of the exit-port while the entry-port is automatically determined to be "south." The expression contains the data to be transmitted while the variable takes the data received during the *propagate* operation. Remember that *propagate* in general operates with two different ports for each PE. In case there is an unconnected port, as in example 1, *propagate* will not send a message or will not receive one, depending on whether an exit-port or an entry-port is unconnected. In the latter case, the variable parameter simply receives the value of its own send-expression.

A similar problem arises when *propagate* occurs in an if-statement. While one PE is executing the "then"-branch, its neighbor might be inactive, waiting for the execution of the "else"-branch. This means, only one of them participates in the communication. The behavior is the same as above: no data exchange can be performed, because both partners have to participate in the communication process.

5. Parallel Execution

Algorithm declaration in *Parallaxis* is to some extend based on the *Modula-2* syntax [5]. There are some major extensions, however, to account for:

- the network structure of the abstract parallel machine,
- the mechanism for data exchange between the processing elements, and
- the explicit concurrent execution.

Concurrent execution in *Parallaxis* means that a specified subset of all available processors compute a certain statement block in parallel. That is, every processor executes the same instruction sequence broadcast by the host, but with its own local data. All action is synchronized by a global clock which also helps to speed up the message passing between processors. The keywords *"parallel"* and *"endparallel"* mark a statement block to be performed in parallel. *Parallel* takes a range or selection descriptor as argument for each dimension of the processor arrangement specified. Default value is the complete set of PEs. Each statement of this block is executed by every activated processor in parallel, while statements themselves are executed sequentially. Since the evaluation of expressions may depend on local data, the PEs may end up executing different code (e.g. if-statement).

Propagate-statements are restricted to the inside of a *parallel* block. Since every processing element executes the same code, there can never occur a programming error, like two neighbors both trying to send or both trying to receive simultaneously. The syntax of *Parallaxis* simply prevents this from being written down.

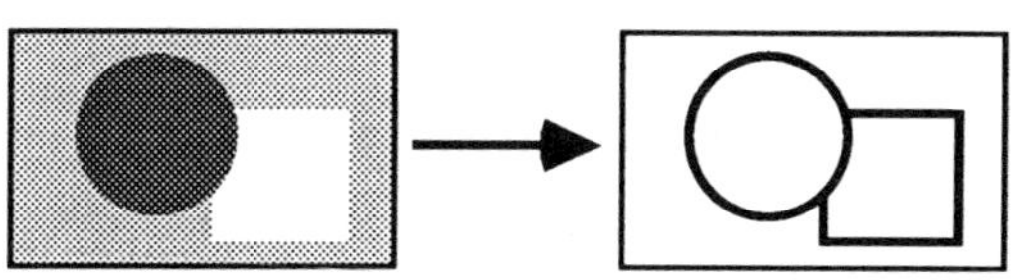

Figure 3: applying the edge detection program (ex. 3)

Example 3: *concurrent image operation on the grid of ex. 1*

```
PARALLEL
  propagate.north(brightness, b1);
  propagate.south(brightness, b2);
  propagate.east (brightness, b3);
  propagate.west (brightness, b4);
  brightness := brightness - (b1+b2+b3+b4) / 4
ENDPARALLEL
```

Ex. 3 shows a parallel implementation of the Laplace edge detection operator as it might be used for image analysis (see fig. 3), assuming the grid specification of ex. 1. For each PE, the local variable "brightness" is distributed to its four neighbors (by four consecutive *propagate* operations) and is then diminished by a fraction of these values. Points at a brightness discontinuity now get a high value, probably forming the outline of an object. The semantics of *propagate* guarantees proper algorithm execution even at the border of the grid (or any topology). For more elaborate *Parallaxis* applications, see [6].

6. Conclusion

The *Parallaxis* system provides a valuable tool for programming massively parallel SIMD machines, as well as performing simulations. Parallel computations employ the most difficult algorithms and are often hard to follow. So, tools that clarify algorithm and machine structure by providing parallel constructs help in preventing errors. Parallaxis achieves this by requiring a short and clear functional specification of the implied parallel hardware structure for every concurrent algorithm. *Parallaxis*-programs are not machine-dependent, for the requested parallel topology is included. This gives *Parallaxis* enormous flexibility that is still perfectly documented.

A compiler for *Parallaxis* is currently being developed for a Sun workstation while the corresponding concurrency simulator for a lowlevel parallel intermediate language is already working on Sun, Apollo, IBM-PC, and Macintosh.

Acknowledgements

Thanks to Prof. Arbab, Prof. Barth, and A. Zell for their support, discussions, and careful reading.

References

[1] P. Brinch-Hansen, *The Architecture of Concurrent Programs*, Prentice-Hall, 1977

[2] C. A. R. Hoare, *Communicating Sequential Processes*, Comm. of the ACM, vol. 21, no. 8, Aug. 1978, pp. 666 (12)

[3] Inmos Limited, *Occam Programming Manual*, Prentice Hall International, 1984

[4] W. D. Hillis, *The Connection Machine*, Ph.D. Thesis, MIT Press, 1985

[5] N. Wirth, *Programming in Modula-2*, Springer, 1982

[6] T. Bräunl, *Parallaxis: A Flexible Parallel Programming Environment for AI Applications*, Applications of Artificial Intelligence VII, Orlando Florida, March 1989

On the Algebraic Representation and Treatment of Processing Structures

Hermann von Issendorff

Forschungsgesellschaft für Angewandte Naturwissenschaften - FFM
D-5307 Wachtberg-Werthhoven
FRG

Abstract

The paper presents a novel style of programming, dealing with data dependencies only. It is based on a concise calculus which provides a language for the representation of partially ordered networks. It covers any style of programming no matter if it is sequential, concurrent, parallel, distributed, functional, or dataflow oriented. Programs are algebraic expressions which may be converted by simple and clear axioms and term replacement rules. The paper gives a short introduction to the theory and demonstrates partial order programming by a small example.

1. Introduction

The paper presents a novel approach of designing processing structures (e.g. programs) by means of the partial order of data dependencies only. A control structure, i.e. the order of execution is established in a separate step of design making use of a calculus. This calculus is the kernel of a general theory of organization [4,5]. It allows to arbitrarily map the processing structure to any control structure between the partial order of the data dependencies and the total sequential order. The calculus consists of an algebra and a set of term replacement rules. The algebra is based on par-tial order semantics. This means that periodic networks like parallel or concurrent programs are directly describable, in contrast to renowned theories like CCS [8], CSP[3], and TCSP[2], which are restricted to interleaving semantics.

The elements of the calculus, i.e. the elements performing the functions, are controlled multiple value single assignment statements, called actons. The operational control of an acton is achieved by a three-valued logic. This allows the joint representation of conditions and guards. Every processing structure, no matter if it is deterministic or nondeterministic, can thus be represented.

In this short paper we must confine ourselves to just a few aspects. These are aimed at giving an idea of the tremendous improvements which can be achieved with partial order programming. In fact, we cannot present the complete calculus consisting of an algebra with 24 axioms and 21 term replacement rules, the grammar coming along with the algebra, the treatment of nondeterminism, and correctness proofs, some of which can even be automated. These topics are presented in the paper mentioned above.

Partial order programming offers a number of important features:

First, it relieves the programmer from defining a control structure which especially with complex systems is very difficult and error prone.

Second, since such an acton structure is not superimposed by a specific control structure it represents a common base for all programs which are built up by the same functions. Depending on the size of a program there may easily be millions or billions of semantically equivalent programs. Hence, partial order programming unifies and considerably improves the readability of programs.

Third, partial order programming lends itself very well to evolutionary system development. Changing or extending a partial order program just means a local operation. The only functions which may be affected by a change are those immediately preceding or succeeding the point of change.

Fourth, the formal representation of programs by acton expressions facilitates the design of a programming support environment. For instance, tools for proving safety or liveness properties can be designed.

Fifth, acton structures can be graphically represented in very much the same way as Petri Nets [9,10]. The readability should even be better than with Petri Nets, because in general less elements are needed.

The methodology of partial order programming is not new, although it has not been used in data processing yet. Originally, the methodology had been developed for planning large industrial projects. It is generally called project planning and control by network analysis. Renowned methods are CPM [6] and PERT [11]. They follow the same line as partial order programming: A given project is stepwise dissected into subprojects until finally all activities and their mutual dependencies are clearly defined. The result is a network of activities. It allows a kind of real time control of the total project by estimating the execution time of each subproject and by calculating the critical path.

Here, we will be concerned with the functional design of a program and its algebraic treatment thereafter. We begin with a short but concrete introduction of the notion of acton followed by the definition of the connectives and the delimiters for loops and complete acton structures. We will then turn to the design of a small program in order to demonstrate the systematic way by which a program can be developed. Finally, we will indicate how an acton structure can be transformed to a sequential program or to a system of two communicating processes.

2. Actons and Acton Structures

An acton has a functional as well as an operational definition. Functionally an acton j is defined by the triple

$$(I_j, Alg_j, O_j),$$

where I_j and O_j are disjoint subsets of a finite set S of data, i.e. $I_j, O_j \subseteq S$, $I_j \cap O_j = \phi$, and where Alg_j is an algorithm, i.e. a recipe how to evaluate a function.. We further stipulate that the outputs of any two actons j and k are disjoint, i.e. $O_j \cap O_k = \phi$.

An acton needs to be generated and activated. It can only be activated once. This is done by a token, i.e. a storable and consumable signal.

Operationally, this gives rise to four different states, the state before activation, the state during activation, and two final states after activation, called termination and abortion. An acton entering the state of termination issues a token, while an acton entering the state of abortion will not react anymore to the outside world. An aborted acton appears as having ceased operating.

The operational states are controlled by logical expressions, making use of the three-valued logic as introduced by Kleene [7]. The values are true, false and undefined. They are associated with the meanings "proceed and terminate", "abort", and "wait". The "wait" state is an intermediate state. The logical expressions are represented by greek letters in square brackets. So, x[α] designates an acton x with a control expression α. In case α=true the control expression and the brackets may be omitted.

The results of the acton, i.e. the values of the output variables, become available to the outside world at first at termination, i.e. when the token has been issued. The behavior is like that of a latch in digital electronics.

Activation and termination are important predicates which will frequently be quoted in the sequel. Therefore we abbreviate activation by "A" and termination by "T".

As an example let us consider an acton for finding the minimum element mn of a list L of unordered natural numbers, described by ({L},min(L),{mn}). The algorithm is

```
          ⎧ begin                                  ⎫
          ⎪ i:=first; mn:=L[i];                    ⎪
min(L)=   ⎨ while i<final do begin i:=next;        ⎬
          ⎪ if mn>L[i] then mn:=L[i];              ⎪
          ⎩ end; end;                              ⎭
```

The acton performing just a (multiple value) single assignment is called neutral acton and designated by a $-symbol.

The four connectives between actons are defined by the predicates A and T. A first and fundamental one is designated by an arrow. It corresponds to the semicolon of programming languages. The definition is

$$x\text{->}y \overset{def}{<===>} T(x)=A(y).$$

It states that acton y will only be activated after acton x has terminated or, less precise, that acton x activates acton y.

There are two connectives for actons preceding another one. The first is designated by a delta and represents a kind of an AND-relation. The second one is designated by a nabla representing a kind of an OR-relation. Accordingly, they are called "and" and "or". Their definitions are:

$$(x\Delta y)\text{->}s \overset{def}{<===>} T(x)\wedge T(y)=A(s) \text{ and}$$
$$(x\nabla y)\text{->}s \overset{def}{<===>} T(x)\vee T(y)=A(s).$$

A last connective regards successor structures. As can be seen from the definition it establishes a relation between a predecessor acton and two succeeding actons similar to a logical AND.

$$p\text{->}(x\,|\,y) \overset{def}{<===>} T(p)=A(x)\wedge A(y)$$

In order to be able to build up networks we introduce three more constructs, i.e. the acton chain and two meshes. The acton chain is defined by

$$p\text{->}x\text{->}s \overset{def}{<===>} (T(p)=A(x))\wedge(T(x)=A(s)).$$

The chain is associative, i.e. (p->x)->s=p->(x->s).

A mesh representing a concurrent structure is defined by

$$p\text{->}(x\Delta y)\text{->}s \overset{def}{<===>} (T(p)=A(x)\wedge A(y)) \wedge(T(x)\wedge T(y)=A(s))$$

and likewise an alternative structure:

$$p\text{->}(x[\alpha]\nabla y[\beta])\text{->}s \overset{def}{<===>} (T(p)=A(x[\alpha])\wedge A(y[\beta])) \wedge(T(x[\alpha])\vee T(y[\beta])=A(s)).$$

In order to reduce the number of brackets we introduce a precedence Δ,∇,|,->, with Δ binding most.

Loops are defined and delimited by two special actons, called loop actons. Permanent loops are represented by

$$p\text{->}o\text{->}x\text{->}o'.$$

The loop is entered via a predecessor acton p and continues via the loop actons o' and o. Operationally, the loop actons regenerate the actons inside the loop and activate them again. Functionally, they transfer the results of cycle i to the input of cycle i+1, i.e. $I_{i+1}:=O_i$.

A conditional loop is represented in a similar way making use of the acton control.:

$$p\text{->}(o\text{->}(x[\alpha]\text{->}o')\,|\,y[\neg\alpha]\text{->}s).$$

Here, both actons x and y are activated once the loop is entered. Since they have complementary conditions one of them terminates and the other one aborts. Both are regenerated and reactivated as long as α=true. This acton structure corresponds to a conventional program of the form:

p; while α do x; y; s;

Complete acton structures are delimited in a similar way as loops. Here, special actons, called star actons, serve for this purpose. An initial star acton issues a token and a final acton absorbs it. By definition, an initial star acton has an empty output and a final one an empty input. A trivial example of a complete acton structure is

->aΔb->O->iΔk->'.

The introduction of the star actons provides us with three sorts of actons, i.e. head actons, body actons and tail actons, which are denoted by the letters h, b, t accordingly. In the trivial acton expression above, there are * and (*->x) of sort h, x of sort b, and *' and (x->*') of sort t. Furthermore, a predecessor p designates an element of sort h or sort b and a successor s designates an element of sort b or sort t. The notations are used for the representation of the transformation rules.

3. Partial Order Programming

As a small example of partial order programming, let us consider the well-kown set partition task. We use the same notation as Barringer [1]: There are two sets *L* and S of unordered elements, say of natural numbers. Both sets may be of different size. The intention is to write a program which orders the numbers so that all numbers of S are equal to or smaller than those of L, i.e. ∀x:L ∀y:S. x≥y.

The ultimate goal of this intention is to dissect the main task into a functional network of subtasks each of which is executable by a computer. The functional network is defined by the data dependencies between the actons. The dissection will be done by stepwise refinement. The specifications of the actons which are defined during the refinement are listed in the table below.

The most abstract representation of the task is the program

->SP->',

where SP designates the (yet undefined) acton of set partitioning. As can be seen SP has an empty input and an empty output. In a first step SP is split up in a read acton R , a set reordering acton O and a write acton W. R takes the sets *L* and S from the outside world and represents them as the arrays L and S. W returns the results.

Since reading or writing of each set is independent of the other we may refine R to a pair of read actons a,b and W to a pair of write actons i,k. The read and write actons are assumed to be executable. With that, the acton expression becomes

->aΔd->O->iΔk->'.

Next, we are going to refine O. There are several ways to solve the reordering problem. For instance, one could combine L and S in a single list, order this list completely and split it into L and S again. Another way is to repeatedly extract a maximum number mx∈S and a minimum number mn∈L and exchange them as long as mx>mn. Of course, the algebra does not provide criteria for the algorithm to be selected. Here, we will deal with the second one, because it allows for more parallelism.

One of the nice properties of the partial order approach is that the specification can be done in any order leaving it to a supporting system to put the actons in the right executional order.

Let us begin by defining an acton e taking mx and mn for input and terminating only if mx>mn. Since the acton does not perform any data processing it is a neutral acton with an empty output. Next, we need sources for mx and mn. These may be provided by two actons c and d, c realizing the function max(L) and d the function min(S). The functions max and min can be made available either by further dissection or by programming the functions by means of a conventional programming language. The latter has been done with the max function in the introductory example. Both actons c and d are independent of each other and immediate predecessors of e giving rise to a partial structure cΔd->e.

If acton e terminates, mx and mn have to be interchanged. This is done by an acton g taking care of L and an acton h taking care of S and results in two new sets L' and S '. The interchange function will not be further defined.

Next we are introducing repetition. This is done by two pairs of loop actons which apart from regenerating the loop structure serve for providing L' and S' as new sets for a next loop. Accordingly they assign L:=L' and S:=S'. The loop actons are providing the inputs for a next cycle and hence are placed in front of the actons c,d.

acton	input	partial function	output
SP	φ	set partitioning	φ
R	φ	{L,S}:=read(*L*,*S*)	L,S
a	φ	L:=read(*L*)	L
b	φ	S:=read(*S*)	S
O	L,S	{L,S}:=reord.(L,S)	L,S
c	L	mn:=min(L)	mn
d	S	mx:=max(S)	mx
e	mx,mn	skip[mx>mn]	φ
f	mx,mn	skip[¬(mx>mn)]	φ
g	mx,mn,L	L':=L\mn∪mx	L'
h	mx,mn,S	S':=S\mx∪mn	S'
o_1	L'	L:=L'	L
o_2	S'	S:=S'	S
W	L,S	write(L,S)	φ
i	L	write(L)	φ
k	S	write(S)	φ

Finally, we need a signal indicating that the job has been done. This is taken care of by creating another neutral acton f acting in parallel to acton e but with a complementary control, i.e. ¬(mx>mn). It aborts with every cycle as long as the condition has not become true.

We may now assemble the partial acton expressions to a complete one yielding

$$*\rightarrow(a\rightarrow o_1\rightarrow c)\Delta(b\rightarrow o_2\rightarrow d)\rightarrow(e[\alpha]\rightarrow(g\rightarrow o_1')|h\rightarrow o_2')|f[\neg\alpha]\rightarrow i\Delta k\rightarrow *',$$

where α=mx>mn.

As can be seen from the table each input is served by an output and there is no output which is not needed by an input.

The acton expression exhibits up to threefold parallelism, i.e. g,h,f may be executed in parallel. It will problably not be in a form suitable for execution. Thus we are now going to transform the acton expression, e.g. in a sequential form. This can easily be done by means of the following axioms and term replacement rules

$$p\Delta p=p \qquad (1)$$

$$t|t=t \qquad (2)$$

$$\frac{(p_1\rightarrow b_1)\Delta(p_2\rightarrow b_2)}{p_1\Delta p_2\rightarrow b_1\Delta b_2}\downarrow \qquad (3)$$

$$\frac{p_1\Delta b_2}{p_1\rightarrow b_2}\downarrow \qquad (4)$$

$$\frac{(b_1\rightarrow t)|(b_2\rightarrow s)}{b_1\Delta b_2\rightarrow t|s}\downarrow \qquad (5)$$

(1) and (2) are idempotency rules for a preceding acton p and a tail acton t. (3), (4), and (5) are term replacement rules. They state that if there is a partial expression of the form above the line, it can be replaced by the partial expression below the line.

Applying rule (3) twice and rule (5) once to the acton expression above gives the intermediate result

$$*\rightarrow a\Delta b\rightarrow o_1\Delta o_2\rightarrow c\Delta d\rightarrow(e[\alpha]\rightarrow g\Delta h\rightarrow o_1'|o_2')|f[\neg\alpha]\rightarrow i\Delta k\rightarrow *'.$$

Since the loop actons o_1, o_2 and o_1', o_2' are identical in function they may be reduced to a single acton each by rules (1) and (2). Finally, repeated application of rule (4) leads to the sequential expression

$$*\rightarrow a\rightarrow b\rightarrow o\rightarrow c\rightarrow d\rightarrow(e[\alpha]\rightarrow g\rightarrow h\rightarrow o')|f[\neg\alpha]\rightarrow i\rightarrow k\rightarrow *'.$$

It is one of 16 semantically equivalent sequential expressions. Of course, there are several other expressions exhibiting more or less parallelism. Figure 1 shows the structure of the original expression.

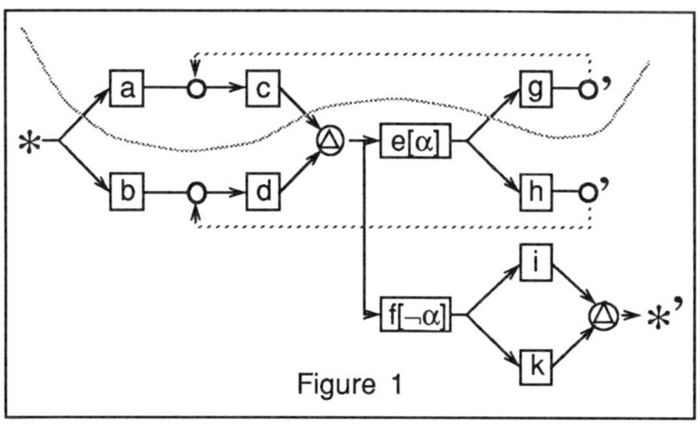

Figure 1

Aside from sequentializing the partial order program we can as well turn it into a system of communicating processes. This will be demonstrated by means of the graphical representation. The procedure is simple: First, a cut is made through the edges of the structure and then pairs of send/receive actons are attached to the open ends of inner edges, i.e. the edges which transfer data. Cuts of outer edges, i.e. of edges coming from a star acton or leading to a primed star acton, are supplied with separate star actons. In principle, any cut could be made. The cut being made here is indicated in figure 1 by a dotted line. Figure 2 shows the two communicating processes resulting from this operation. It is not a very good partition, because the upper process never terminates.

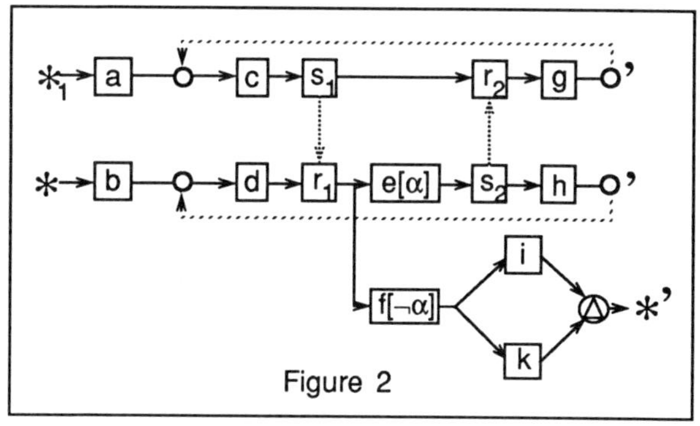

Figure 2

References

[1] H. Barringer, "A Survey of Verification Techniques for parallel programs," LNCS, vol. 191, Springer-Verlag, 1985

[2] S.D. Brookes et al., "A Theory of Communicating Processes," Journal ACM, vol.31, no. 3, p. 560, 1984

[3] C.A.R. Hoare, "Communicating Sequential Processes," Series in Computer Science, Prentice Hall Int., 1985

[4] H. von Issendorff, "The Theory of Organization - Approach to a Mathematical Treatment of Processing Structures," To appear in: Mitchell,R.J.(ed.) "Managing Complexity in Software Engineering", IEE Computing Series, Peter Peregrinus Limited, 1989

[5] H. von Issendorff, "The Theory of Organization," Submitted for publication in Acta Informatica

[6] J.E. Kelley, "Critical-path planning and scheduling: Mathematical basis," Operations Research, vol. 9, no. 3, p. 296, 1961

[7] S.C. Kleene, "Introduction to Metamathematics," p. 332, Princeton: Van Nostrand, 1952

[8] R. Milner, "A Calculus of Communicating Systems," LNCS, vol. 92, Springer- Verlag, 1980

[9] A. Petri, "Kommunikation mit Automaten," Schriften des Instituts für instrumentelle Mathematik, no. 2, Universität Bonn, 1962

[10] W. Reisig, "Petri Nets - An Introduction," EACS Monographs on Theor. Computer Science, vol. 4, 1985

[11] J. Roseboom et al., "Application of a Technique for Research and Development Program Evaluation," Operations Research, vol. 7, no. 5, 1959

Reflective Computation in Object-Oriented Concurrent Systems and Its Applications

Takuo Watanabe and **Akinori Yonezawa**
Department of Information Science, Tokyo Institute of Technology
2-12-1, Ookayama, Meguro-ku, Tokyo, Japan, 152
{*takuo,yonezawa*}*%is.titech.junet@relay.cs.net*

1 Introduction

1.1 What is Computational Reflection?

Reflection is the process of reasoning about and acting upon the system itself[2, 1]. In a conventional computational system, computation is performed on data that represent (or model) entities which are *external* to the system. In contrast, a reflective computational system must contain some data which represent (or model) the structural and computational aspects — the meta-level information — of itself. And such data, which is called *self-representation*, must be accessible and modifiable within the system itself, and more importantly, changes made to such data must be causally reflected/connected to the actual computations being performed. The motivation of computational reflection is to make the object-level computation perform effectively by *dynamically* modifying the internal organization of the system.

Recently, several programming languages which support computational reflection are proposed. Reflective facilities of such languages not only provide us with powerful expressiveness, but also encourage modular descriptions of computation — they introduce a new dimension (direction) of modularity, which is the separation of object-level descriptions and meta-level descriptions. 3-Lisp[2], 3-KRS[1], and ABCL/R[3] are examples of such languages. It is important that many of the special functionalities — often provided by *system calls* in conventional languages — can be described using reflective language constructs in a more natural and modular way. Notice, in such languages, that their language kernels are rather simple because of their powerful expressiveness. Many complex language features/constructs can be effectively defined using their reflective programming facilities. Thus, they are also useful to build prototypes of new language features.

1.2 Reflection in Concurrent Computing

In a sequential reflective system, when one wants to invoke a reflective operation, he must suspend the object-level computation which has been executed. *Reflective procedures* in 3-Lisp are typical examples — once invoked, the object-level computation is blocked until the reflective operation finishes. (This corresponds to the fact that man sometimes stops his work to look back upon his way or to make plans for future.)

In contrast, in a concurrent computational system, reflective operations and object-level computations may execute simultaneously. Each computational agent (process, object) in the system can observe or possibly modify the structure/behavior of other agents as well as itself. We present a monitor example later — modifying a running concurrent object and getting information about it. The technique of reflective computation used in the example can be extended to the gradual performance improvements of the entire concurrent system.

Reflective programming will become increasingly more important in concurrent computational systems such as: (distributed) operating systems, realtime systems, distributed simulation, distributed problem solving, planning/control of robots, and so on. We have designed and implemented a language ABCL/R which supports reflection in the framework of object-based concurrency. This language is a reflective dialect of ABCL/1[4].

Below we will briefly discuss our notion of reflection in object-oriented concurrent computing and then give an overview of the language ABCL/R.

2 Concurrent Computation Model

In our computation model, a system is a collection of *objects* — automonous information processing agents. Each object has an individual serial computation power, and may have local persistent memory called a *state memory*. Function and properties of a conceptual/physical entity in the problem domain are collectively modeled and represented by such an object. In order to use the functions and properties, a request *message* is sent to the object. When an object receives a message, if the message is acceptable to the object, it starts a sequence of actions which are requested by the message. In an object, the sequence of actions takes place one at a time. Thus, while an object is executing actions, messages arrive to the object is put in the *message queue*.

Actions performed by an object are combinations of inquiring/updating the object's local state memory, sending messages to other objects (including itself), creating new objects, and other symbolic/numerical operations. Basically, sequences of actions by objects in the system proceed asynchronously. This means that many objects perform their computation in parallel. In our model, the unit of concurrency is an object. Communication among objects and the synchronization of their computation are done only by message passing. Any two objects don't share any data other than the names (addresses, or pointers) of other objects. The state memory of each object cannot be accessed directly by other objects, and only indirect accesses through messages passing are permitted. The description of the behavior of an object is a collection of *scripts* (often called *methods* in other object-oriented languages), which consists of a message pattern and a sequence of actions. A script prescribes the sequence of the object's actions invoked when it received a message that matches the message pattern of the script.

3 Reflection in our Model

3.1 Meta-Object

To realize reflection, the *causally connected self representation* of the system must exist within the system. Formalisms to construct a causally connected self representation of a concurrent system is a primary concern of building a concurrent reflective

©1989 ACM 0-89791-305-1/89/0500/0056$00.75

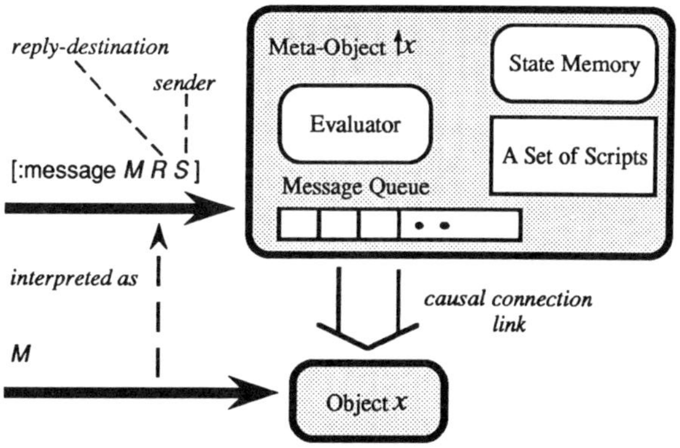

Figure 1: Meta-Object

system. There are two extreme approaches for object-oriented concurrent system: one end is to assume the existence of a datum which represent the *whole* system in a causally connected way, and the other end is to introduce the self representation of each object in the system individually. Our approach is the latter one. (Of course intermediate approaches are possible.)

The representation of an object contains the representations of the *message queue*, the *state memory*, the *set of scripts* and the *evaluator* of the object. Besides this structural aspect, the computational aspect of the object — *arrival*, *reception*, and *acceptance* of a message and the *execution* of a scripts — must be represented. Our approach is to represent each object as an object called a *meta-object*.

For each object x, there exists a meta-object $\Uparrow x$, which represents both the structural and computational aspects of x. $\Uparrow x$ contains the meta-level information about x. Meta-object $\Uparrow x$ represents the object x in a similar way that usual objects represent entities in the problem domain. The structure of x is represented as the data in the state memory of $\Uparrow x$, and the computational aspects of x is described as the scripts (methods) of $\Uparrow x$. An object x and the information about x in $\Uparrow x$ are causally connected. Thus the data stored in $\Uparrow x$ always represent the current status of x, and operations on the data cause the isomorphic effect on x. $\Uparrow x$ is an object. So $\Uparrow\Uparrow x$ also exists. This means that operations on $\Uparrow x$ are allowed. Thus, there is an infinite tower of meta-objects $\Uparrow x$, $\Uparrow\Uparrow x$, $\Uparrow\Uparrow\Uparrow x$, ...for each object x. In the actual implementation, meta-objects are created when their access takes place (by lazy creation). The correspondence between objects and their meta-objects is one to one.

To satisfy the requirement of the causal connection between an object x and its meta-object $\Uparrow x$, $\Uparrow x$ is used as the actual implementation of x. That is, the contents of the state variables of $\Uparrow x$ — a message queue, a set of scripts, a state object, and an evaluator object of x — are used for the actual computation of x. A message transmission to x is interpreted as the message transmission to $\Uparrow x$ (Figure 1). The evaluation of scripts is carried out by the evaluator object, which is also an ordinary object of ABCL/R. Thus every object of ABCL/R is implemented in a meta-circular way as its meta-object. A precise definition of a typical meta-object is found in [3].

The concept of meta-objects in our model is similar to that of meta-objects in 3-KRS[1]. In 3-KRS, structural/computational aspects of an object is also represented in its meta-object. But the way of modeling an object as its meta-object is different,

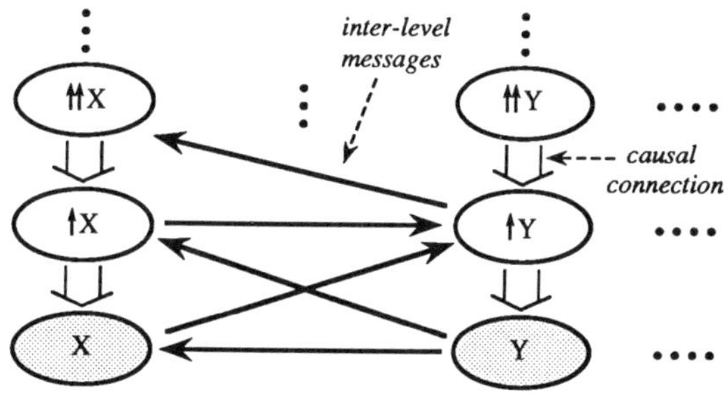

Figure 2: Reflection in Concurrent Objects

because an object is a unit of concurrency in our computation model.

3.2 Reflective Programming

Reflective computation in an object x is performed by x sending messages to its meta-object $\Uparrow x$. This enables x to inquire/modify itself through $\Uparrow x$, because the structural/computational aspects of x is represented in $\Uparrow x$ in a causally connected way. The causal connection link between x and $\Uparrow x$ is implicitly guaranteed by the language system. Note that appropriate scripts for operations on x must be prepared in $\Uparrow x$. Even if $\Uparrow x$ doesn't have such scripts, it is possible to modify $\Uparrow x$ using $\Uparrow\Uparrow x$ to acquire such scripts.

Of course, a meta-object $\Uparrow x$ can receive messages from other objects (other than x). In a system that consists of a collection of many objects, we can regard the meta-object of an object as the partial self-representation of the entire system. Thus the reflective computation in the system is realized by message transmissions among objects and their meta-objects. Note that such message transmissions may take place concurrently in our computation model (Figure 2).

By default, the definition of every meta-object is uniform: for each object x, the meta-object $\Uparrow x$ has the message queue, the state memory, the set of scripts and the evaluator for x as its state value, and actions in x — such as script search and execution — are uniformly defined as scripts in $\Uparrow x$. In ABCL/R, we can define an arbitrary *non-default* meta-object and can specify to use it when defining an object. For example, a meta-object which records the history of incoming messages, a meta-object which has an undo-operation, etc. can be defined.

4 Applications

4.1 Monitoring Running Object

To show the usefulness of reflective computation in a concurrent system, let us consider an example — monitoring the behavior of running objects. More technical details including programs are found in [3].

The internal structure of an object can be manipulated as data through its meta-object if the meta-object has scripts appropriate for such operations. For example, it is possible to add (delete) scripts to an object x by sending messages `[:add-script` S`]` (`[:delete-script` M`]`) to the meta-object $\Uparrow x$. Messages `:queue` and `:state` allows message senders to access the internals of an object. Note that these messages can be sent even when x is running. Since a meta-object $\Uparrow x$ is also an object, modification of the meta-object is also possible through its meta-object — namely, meta-meta-object $\Uparrow\Uparrow x$. We will present an example of such actions.

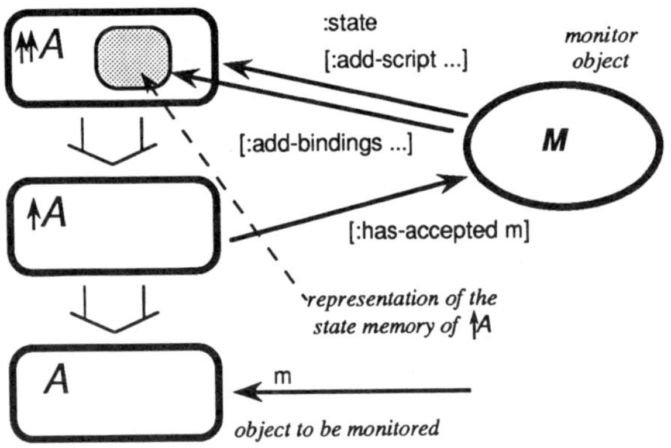

Figure 3: Monitoring Message Acceptance

Suppose one wants to monitor the behavior of a running object, say, A. Then the message passing involving A needs to take place in such a way that whenever A accepts a message m, a monitor object M receives a message `[:has-accepted` A m`]` from A. To realize this, we can directly modify every script of A by sending meta-level messages to $\uparrow A$. But it is somewhat cumbersome and not general. A more general solution is to modify a script of $\uparrow A$. As we have seen above, $\uparrow A$ represents the behavioral aspects of A — message reception, script search (method search), and script execution — by the scripts of $\uparrow A$. Actually, $\uparrow A$ has a script S for script search and execution[3]. This script is replaced with its *monitoring version* S', which sends a message `[:has-accepted` A m`]` to M when the script for a message m is found (Figure 3).

Since $\uparrow A$ does not know (the address of) M, before modifying the script, we have to modify the state memory of $\uparrow A$ to make M known by $\uparrow A$. To do so, we first get the state memory of $\uparrow A$, and send the state memory a message which introduces a new variable binding. Below is the message transmissions expressed in the ABCL/R notation. (The RHS and LHS of `<=`/`<==` are the message and its target respectively.)

```
[[↑↑A <== :state] <= [:add-binding 'Monitor M]]
```

The value of the expression `[↑↑A <== :state]` is an object representing the state memory of $\uparrow A$. Now the monitor object M can be accessible in $\uparrow A$ with name `Monitor`. After these message transmissions, the monitoring version S' (which contains the expression `[Monitor <= [:has-accepted` *message*`]]`) is added to $\uparrow A$ by the following message transmission.

```
[↑↑A <= [:add-script S']]
```

Actually, the newly added script S' is pushed and used prior to S for the same message. So S is not deleted. Thus, to stop monitoring, it is sufficient just to delete (pop) S'.

```
[↑↑A <= [:delete-script m_S']]
```

where $m_{S'}$ is a message which matches the message pattern of S'.

4.2 Other Applications

The reflective technique used in the previous section — dynamic modification (and acquisition) of scripts (methods) — can be extended to express fault-torelant computing, and dynamic repair and/or optimization of program components (including method search methods) in a uniform way.

Using the reflective language constructs of ABCL/R, a simple *Time-Warp* mechanism based on Jefferson's *Virtual Time* concept has been implemented[3]. This is a mechanism for managing temporal consistency in distributed discrete event simulation — object-based concurrency can offer a natural framework — using a *rollback* (a kind of undoing operations based on the timestamp of events) mechanism. Usually, the code fragments for the rollback are embedded in the code of simulation acts. In our implementation, the general rollback mechanism is defined in the meta-object of each simulation object, and such meta-objects are described using the meta-object specification facility of ABCL/R. Thus the code for the simulation acts and the rollback mechanism are clearly separated — this is an example of the program modularity reflective languages offer. This technique can be extended to other distributed algorithms and protocols — getting a snapshot of entire distributed system, deadlock detection and recovery, and so on. For further technical details, see [3].

As we noted earlier, one of the motivations of introducing reflective computation is that application programs (i.e., object-level programs) be able to influence the underlying computation environment dynamically. Since various resource management and control tasks can be modeled by meta-objects, powerful yet modular control over memory/processing power resource will be made available at application level. Also, scheduling in a real-time system can be handled at application level in a modular way. Furthermore, migration of objects among node processors in a multicomputer environment can be controlled by the objects themselves with reflective techniques.

5 Concluding Remarks

Research on object-based reflective concurrent computation has just started and most research issues have not been investigated. [5] mentions some of our potential research topics.

References

[1] P. Maes. "Concepts and Experiments in Computational Reflection". In *Proc. Object-Oriented Programming Systems, Languages, and Applications (OOPSLA)*, pages 147–155. ACM, 1987.

[2] B. C. Smith. "Reflection and Semantics in Lisp". In *Proc. Symposium on Principles of Programming Languages (POPL)*, pages 23–35. ACM, 1984.

[3] T. Watanabe and A. Yonezawa. "Reflection in an Object-Oriented Concurrent Language". In *Proc. Object-Oriented Programming Systems, Languages, and Applications (OOPSLA)*, pages 306–315. ACM, 1988. (revised version is in [4].)

[4] A. Yonezawa, editor. *ABCL: An Object-Oriented Concurrent System — Theory, Language, Programming, Implementation and Application.* The MIT Press, 1989. (in press.)

[5] A. Yonezawa and T.Watanabe. "An Introduction to Object-Based Reflective Concurrent Computation". *SIGPLAN Notices*, February 1989 (to appear.)

REAL-TIME, EMBEDDED AND REACTIVE SYSTEMS

A GENERAL WAY TO PUT TIME IN PETRI NETS

Carlo Ghezzi Dino Mandrioli Sandro Morasca Mauro Pezzè (*)

Dipartimento di Elettronica - Politecnico di Milano - Piazza L. da Vinci 32 - 20133 MILANO (ITALY)
(*) CEFRIEL - Politecnico di Milano - Via Emanueli 15 - 20100 MILANO (ITALY)

ABSTRACT

Petri nets have been widely used in the past to model various types of concurrent systems, including real-time systems. To do so, a variety of ad-hoc solutions have been proposed in order to allow time to be taken into account in specifications. In this paper, we initially survey these proposals and then we illustrate a new proposal (TB nets), that unifies and generalizes all previous ones. Next, we discuss how these and possibly other enrichments of the original model can be formally defined. This will be done in terms of a high-level net model, called ER nets. The ability of ER nets to express a variety of behaviors justifies our choice to use them as a kernel formalism of a specification support environment that we are currently developing. In this environment, it will be possible to define new graphical notations for formal specifications and give them formal semantics in terms of the underlying ER model. This allows the specifier to tune the notation used in formal specifications to the particular expressive needs arising while modelling an application and yet base the notation on firm and rigorous grounds.

1. INTRODUCTION

Several methods have been proposed to introduce time in Petri nets. Some authors (e.g. [12], [19]) propose stochastic models, while others (e.g., [1], [2], [11], [15], [17], [18]) propose non stochastic ones. While stochastic models are fairly well-suited to performance evaluation, they do not seem to be very useful for modelling real-time systems, i.e. systems whose correctness depends on timing bounds [20]. Since our main research interest is toward modelling and designing real-time systems, we will focus on non stochastic models.

Actually, the ways proposed so far for introducing time in Petri nets in a non stochastic fashion have been always presented as a support for solving particular classes of problems, like recoverability of communication protocols and performance evaluation, but none of them can be easily extended to provide a general model for representing time. They are ad-hoc notations that suffer from the lack of a formally defined semantics. Furthermore, their assumptions violate one of the fundamentals of Petri nets, that is the locality of the decision on the transition firing.

In this paper, we propose a new time model which includes the previous approaches and other features that may be useful in the modelling of timing issues. Unlike the previous time extensions, the model is fully consistent with the philosophy of Petri nets. This model, in turn, can be formally defined in terms of a still more basic net model: Environment/Relationship nets (ER nets). Actually, ER nets are proposed as a general and basic model that can be used as a kernel in a specification support environment where the specifier will be allowed to define new formalisms, enhance existing formalism, and so on, in order to tailor the specification language to the specific needs arising in an application. Formal semantics of these languages will be defined in terms of ER nets.

This paper is structured as follows. In Section 2 we start with a general introduction on representing time, where we briefly survey the main time extensions proposed so far and we stress the problems they raise (Section 2.1). A new notation (TB nets) is then proposed (Section 2.2) together with an intuitive definition of a possible time semantics. In Section 2.3 we assess the generality of the model by showing how previous models proposed in the literature and other useful features of time not yet modelled can be expressed in our notation. In Section 3 we formalize the proposal by introducing ER nets (Section 3.1) and then showing how these requirements can be satisfied within ER nets. In the conclusions (Section 4) we review the goals satisfied by the model proposed in this paper and we outline further goals of our current research.

2. REPRESENTING TIME

In this section we give a sketchy review of the main techniques so far used to represent (non stochastic) time within Petri nets and we analyze the major difficulties of time representation. After this discussion we introduce a new notation for describing time and we discuss informally two different types of semantics that can be given to it. The generality of the new model will be assessed by using it to express not only all of the previous proposals, but also other important time features that the previous proposals cannot formalize. The proposal will be justified in Section 3 where the formal semantics is given. We assume that the reader is familiar with Petri nets as defined in [16].

2.1 Survey

Two main techniques for representing time within Petri nets have been proposed in the literature: attaching time to transitions or, alternatively, to places. In this subsection, we will present in some detail some representative models; it is often the case that the time extensions provided by other authors are special cases of the ones we are now going to discuss, so that the review made here can be considered quite general.

In [11] each transition is associated with an interval $[t_{min}, t_{max}]$, where t_{min} and t_{max} represent the minimum and maximum time delay that must elapse between the enabling of the transition and its firing time, respectively. If $\bar{t}$ is the enabling time of the transition, i. e. the time of arrival in its input places of the last token of the enabling tuple, the transition fires in the time interval $[\bar{t}+t_{min}, \bar{t}+t_{max}]$. The firing is mandatory: the transition *must* fire at most t_{max} time units after its enabling (i.e. before or when time $\bar{t}+t_{max}$ has been reached by some implicit universal clock) provided that it is not disabled by some other transition firing occurring in the meanwhile.

[15] and [8] essentially propose to associate a firing duration Δ to each transition. A transition starts firing as soon as enabled and its firing takes exactly a time Δ, which means that (apart from conflicts) the behavior of the net would be deterministic.

In [2] and [18] Petri nets are augmented by attaching a waiting time to each place. Once a token has been produced in a place, it will not contribute to enabling any transition before the time associated to that place has elapsed. In addition, a transition must fire as soon as enabled.

All of these models are useful for the purpose they have, but they do not seem to be general enough for modelling all of the timing aspects that may arise in specifications, as we will see later. Thus, a number of criticisms, both theoretical and practical, can be made of such models. From a theoretical viewpoint, in all these approaches, there are particular timing conditions *forcing the firing* of a transition: in [11], for instance, a transition must fire before t_{max} time units have elapsed. Thus, a transition T cannot fire if elsewhere in the net there exists another transition whose timing constraints would force it to fire before transition T can fire. Therefore, the firing condition cannot be determined only by locally examining the transition, but it could require a view of the whole net, which is in contrast with the philosophy of the original formalism. Moreover, there must exist an underlying and hidden mechanism to record the arrival times of the tokens in the places. Last, these extensions are always introduced as ad hoc extensions of the original net model, with little attention to assessing their mutual relationships, let alone providing a formal definition of their semantics.

From a practical viewpoint, these models do not cover all the situations that can be useful to model with a timed net. Moreover, their definition is not suitable to embody such cases with further extensions, but it is likely that for each new situation that cannot be expressed in the model a new kind of extension must be introduced. For instance, if the firing time interval of a transition must depend on the arrival time of a token in only one of its input places, this situation could not be represented in any of the previous models. Therefore, this would ultimately result in a proliferation of ad-hoc models without clearly defined semantics and no clear description of their mutual relationships.

2.2 A New Notation

In this section, we propose a general notation to describe the time behavior of Petri nets in a simple and natural way. The resulting net model will be called **TB nets** (Time Basic nets). The main idea consists of attaching a timestamp to each token in order to represent the "local" time of the token, i.e. the firing time of the transition which created it. Thus, tokens are no longer anonymous (see also [3], [4], and [9]). Actually, we will see in Section 3 that in our underlying formal model we assume that tokens can carry as much information as needed, including time information. The dynamic time evolution is represented by attaching suitable actions to the transitions, which represent how the timestamp of the produced tokens depends on the timestamp of the enabling tokens.

Let us describe our notation and informally introduce its possible semantics through some examples. We associate a *time condition* to each transition. A time condition is a function from the timestamp of the tokens in the input places to a set of time values (e.g., reals, in the case of a dense time model). The transition is enabled to fire if there is at least one token in each of its input places (we assume weight 1 for each arc of the net) and at least one value of the set produced by application of the time condition to the tokens' timestamps is not less than the maximum of such timestamps. The corresponding tuple of tokens will be called an *enabling tuple*, and the maximum timestamp will be called the *enabling time* of the transition for that enabling tuple. In what follows, we will assume that no more than one enabling tuple will ever occur for each transition, as most time models proposed so far explicitly or implicitly do; the restriction will be dropped in Section 2.3.2. The values in the time set evaluated by the time condition that are not less than the enabling time are the time values at which the transition may fire. As a result of firing, the enabling tuple is removed from the input places and all of the tokens produced by the firing have the same timestamp, which is the *firing time* that produced them.

In the following, we use the notation *time(p)*, where p is a place, to denote the value of the timestamp associated with a token in place p. Also, in all of the examples we give we assume that the time set is a closed interval; we associate the notation [expr1, expr2] with transitions, where expr1 and expr2 are expressions whose values are time values, to denote the extremes of the interval. The case where expr1>expr2 obviously represents the empty set of time values.

An example is illustrated in Figure 1: place P_2 represents availability of a perishable item (say, a bag of apples) stored in a storehouse, place P_1 represents a customer request to buy the perishable item, and place P_3 represents availability of other resources (e.g. sugar, preservatives, etc.) needed for making jam with the perishable item. Transition T_1 models the selling of the item to the customer, transition T_2 models the trashing of the rotten item, and transition T_3 models making jam.

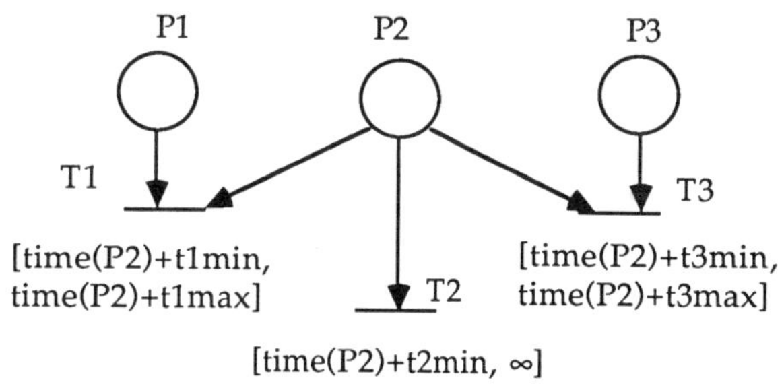

Figure 1

The firing of each transition depends not only on the presence of suitable tokens in their input places, but also on particular conditions on time. Namely, perishable items (e.g. apples) cannot be sold to a customer if they are still unripe or if they have gotten rotten. When the customer comes to the storehouse, he or she may or may not decide to buy the item: thus transition T_1 must not be forced to fire. It may fire (i.e. the item can be sold) if it is ripe but not rotten; this is represented by the time interval I_1=[time(P_2)+t_{1min}, time(P_2)+t_{1max}] associated to transition T_1. Also, notice that the customer may arrive at the store when the item is already unavailable for sale; this means that the token enters place P_1 at a time time(P_1) greater than time(P_2)+t_{1max}. Likewise, the item can be used for making jam from the time when it is rather ripe until it becomes not too rotten. This can also be represented by an interval I_3 = [time(P_2)+t_{3min}, time(P_2)+t_{3max}] attached to transition T_3 as in Figure 1. The two intervals, I_1 and I_3, can partially overlap ($t_{1min} < t_{3min} < t_{1max} < t_{3max}$). In fact, for a while the item could still be good to be sold, but also available for making jam. At last, the item can be removed from the inventory when it becomes completely rotten: a suitable interval (I_2 = [time(P_2)+$t2_{min}$, ∞]) attached to transition T_2 will represent this last timing constraint.

In the interpretation we implicitly gave to the system in Figure 1, a transition is not be forced to fire when its maximum firing time has been reached; what we express there is that, if it fires, it does so within the time set specified by the time condition. This interpretation of time will be called **Weak Time Semantics** (WTS): If a transition *ever fires*, its firing time must belong to its time set. However, the transition is *not forced* to fire.

WTS is adequate for modelling several real systems. For instance, a protocol for digitalized voice transmission is based on the principle that a voice packet is either received by a receiving station within a specified time or it is no more considered. This can be easily modelled by our model under WTS interpretation. A detailed description of a local area network protocol for voice transmission can be found in [7]. It is not reported here for the sake of brevity.

In other situations, the specifier might wish to represent a system where an action can be delayed *at most* for a specified time but, before that time expires, the action *must* take place. Such cases cannot be addressed correctly within the WTS framework. As an example, let us consider the Ada segment of Figure 2(a) describing a selective wait statement.

```
select
  accept E
or
  delay D
end
```

(a)

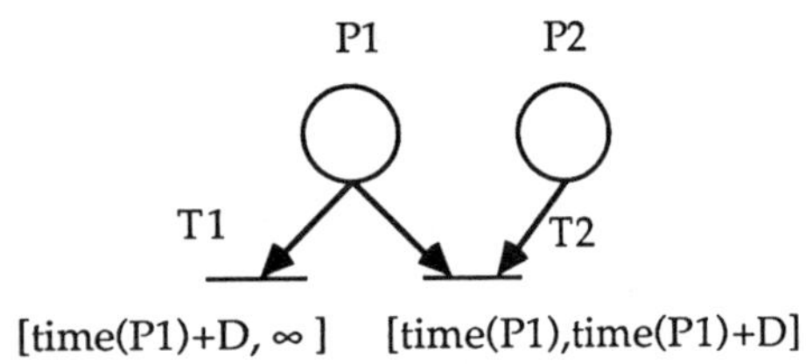

(b)

Figure 2

This construct can be modelled as in Figure 2(b), where place P1 represents an Ada task A executing the **select** statement, transition T2 represents the **accept** statement, and transition T1 represents the **delay** statement. After reaching the **select** statement, A can wait for another task B to call entry E up to D time units. The entry call issued by B is represented by a token in place P2. If the token gets into place P2 after this time has expired the transition cannot fire anymore with this tuple; in fact, the time condition associated to transition T2 is such that the enabling condition does not hold. However, within the framework of WTS, transition T2 cannot be forced to fire. Thus we cannot correctly represent the Ada requirement that indeed the rendezvous occurs if the entry call is issued before the maximum allowed waiting time is expired. In situations like this, a stronger requirement is therefore needed on the time intervals we attach to the transitions: a transition that is enabled to fire within a given interval, if not disabled before by some other firing, is forced to fire before the end of the interval. This will make the time model closer to the models we reviewed in the previous section.

This interpretation of time will be called **Strong Time Semantics** (STS): if a transition gets enabled by some tuple of tokens at some enabling time t, it must fire at some time t' ($t' \geq t$) of its associated time set.

Notice that a relevant particular case occurs when, for each transition, the set S of possible firing times is unbounded. In this case the two semantics coincide. In practice, such a particular case is useful when attention is focused only on the *minimum time* that is needed to perform any action. A model of this type can be used to answer questions of the type "Does there exist a system behavior that guarantees a given property?". Instead, questions of the type "Is a given property guaranteed by *any* system behavior?" cannot be addressed by considering only minimum firing times.

2.3 Assessing the Generality of the Model

In this section we assess the generality of the proposed model: first, previous proposals are shown to be particular cases of our definitions; then, we exemplify how the model can be naturally adapted to a variety of different needs that may arise during specification.

2.3.1 Previous Proposals Revisited

It is straightforward to use our notation to represent the time models proposed in the literature where time is attached to transitions, such as in [11]. Here we would like to point out how to use it to represent the case where time is attached to places. Let us consider a rather general situation, which extends the models so far proposed in the literature, where each place can be associated with a time interval $<\theta,\tau>$, where θ represents the minimum time that must elapse after a token arrives in the place before it becomes ready (i.e. it can contribute with others to enabling some transition), and τ is the maximum waiting time allowed for the token to contribute in any tuple. After τ time units elapse since the token reaches the place, it cannot participate anymore in any tuple for firing.

As an example, let us consider Figure 3, where the token in place P_1 represents a chemical compound that is created by the reaction modelled by transition T_1, the token in place P_2 represents a chemical compound created by the reaction represented by transition T_2, and both can match to produce a new chemical compound in the reaction represented by transition T_3. After the creation of each token a minimum constant time (respectively θ_1 and θ_2) must elapse; this models the fact that the compounds must become stable before they become ready for the next reaction. In addition, after a maximum time expires (respectively, τ_1 and τ_2 for the two compounds), the chemical compounds decompose and the reaction cannot take place anymore.

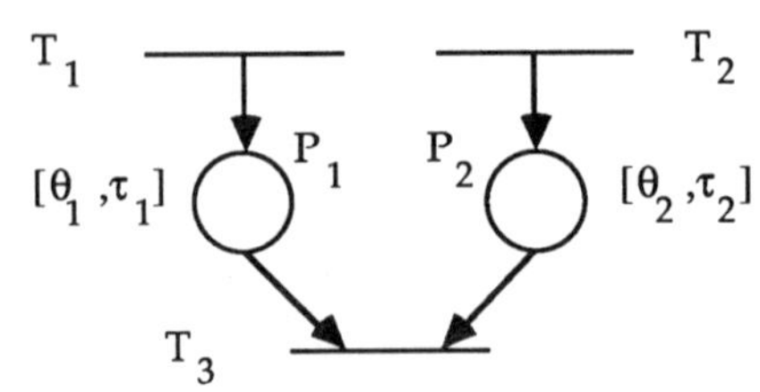

Figure 3

Such a representation can be straightforwardly translated into our model, where time constraints are attached to transitions and not to places. The time condition to be associated to transition T_3 is [θ, τ] where θ = max {θ_1+time(P1), θ_2+time(P2)}, τ=min{τ_1+time(P1), τ_2+time(P2)}. If for a given tuple $\theta>\tau$, the transition cannot fire.

In a practical environment supporting formal specification it would be nice to allow the user to tailor the specification language to the particular application area and perhaps even to his or her personal taste. This would make the notation easier to use and more expressive. For example, it would be nice to allow the specifier to use a notation like the one shown in Figure 3 instead of TB nets, if he or she wishes so. However, what is important to notice is that, although the external notation can be chosen to meet the specifier's taste, its meaning should always be specified rigorously and unambiguously in terms of a core model whose semantics is perfectly understood. Here we have done this in the case of TB nets. Actually, we believe that TB nets are not a sufficiently general and basic model to be assumed as the core formalism of an environment. Rather, they are one of the abstractions that may be built on top one such model. We will return to this important point later in Section 3 when we will introduce ER nets.

2.3.2 On the Re-firing of a Transition

We are now ready to remove the assumption that no more than one enabling tuple will ever occur for each transition. Consider the situation illustrated in Figure 4(a) in terms of the Merlin and Farber's notation, and suppose that a token enters place P at time 7 and, subsequently, another token enters at time 9. The semantics we give to this case, in terms of its equivalent TB net representation (Figure 4(b)), is that the possible firing time of T for the first token is in the interval [12, 19], whereas it is in [14, 21] for the second. For example, T can first fire at time 17 with the second token that entered P and then at time 18 for the first token; in WTS, it is possible that T only fires for the second token at time 20 and, consequently, that it will never fire with the first.

There is another interesting interpretation that one might wish to give to the net represented in Figure 4(a): T models a resource that exists in a single copy and that can be shared among several processes, each represented by a token in P. In this case, the interval [5, 12] would represent the minimum and maximum duration of the operation that processes perform on the resource. The behavior we would like to represent is the one in which if T fires (i.e. one process gets access to the resource) at time t, the next firing (i.e. access to the resource) can only occur between times t+5 and t+12. Note that this interpretation can be easily formalized within our model simply by adding a place to transition T, with a token whose timestamp records the last firing time of the transition, as in Figure 4(c). Each time the transition fires, the value of the timestamp of the token in place Q is updated to record the last firing time of the transition.

In practice, however, a specifier might find it more convenient to use Merlin and Farber's notation (Figure 4(a)) instead of that in Figure 4(c) to represent a behavior like the one we just discussed, and yet interpret the notation of Figure 4(a) *as if* it meant the behavior described by the TB net of Figure 4(c). As we discussed above in Section 2.3.1, an environment supporting formal specifications should support this attitude, and allow the specifier to give formal semantics to the newly defined notation in terms of a basic, predefined formal model.

2.3.3 Duration

As another example of a notation that the specifier might wish to adopt in formal specifications, consider the case illustrated in Figure 5(a), where the interval $[d_{min}, d_{max}]$ represents the possible duration of the operation modelled by transition T_1, as in the models proposed by [15] and [8]. In addition, as in [11], $[t_{min}, t_{max}]$ represents the (relative) firing time. In other terms, what the specification wants to say is that transition T_1 will start to fire $\bar{t}$ time units after it has been enabled and its firing will last $\bar{d}$ time units after the starting time, where $\bar{t}$ belongs

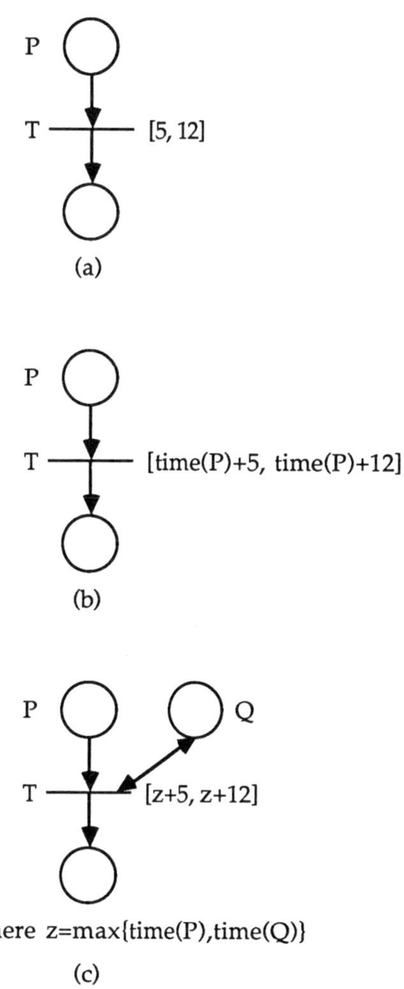

Figure 4

to $[t_{min1}, t_{max1}]$ and $\bar{d}$ belongs to $[d_{min1}, d_{max1}]$. During the firing of the transition, the tokens of the tuple that makes the transition fire should be no longer available for the firing of other transitions, although they remain in their places until the completion of the firing. The semantics of this behavior can be easily expressed in terms of TB nets, as shown in Figure 5 (b).

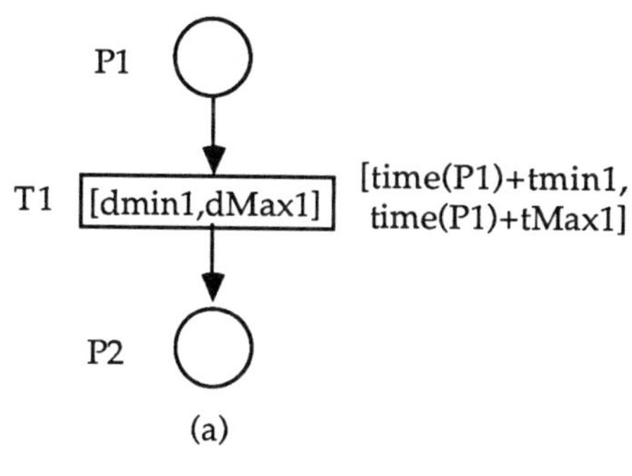

Figure 5

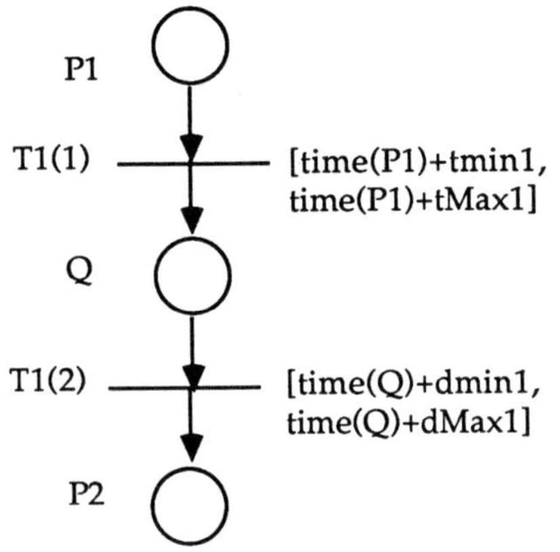

(b)

Figure 5

3. FORMAL SEMANTICS OF TIME

In order to give TB nets a formal semantics, we first introduce a general model, called **ER nets** (Environment/Relationship nets): a formal defintion of Environment/Relationship nets can be found in [13]. ER nets do not have any primitive concept of time; rather, they are high-level nets that can be used as a basis for building useful abstractions that may be needed in specifications [6]. In particular, here we show how to formally specify TB nets within the ER net formalism.

3.1 ER nets

ER nets are a high-level type of nets where tokens are environments, i.e. relationships between variables and values, and a predicate and an action are associated to each transition. Informally, token environments determine the firability of a transition by means of the associated predicate, which must evaluate to true, and are dynamically modified by actions, whose execution is part of the transition firing. ER nets are similar to Predicate/Transition nets [3], [4].

Definition

Let ID be a set of identifiers and V be a set of values (for simplicity, we ignore typing issues here: identifiers and values of the environments are assumed to be untyped); a ER net is a Petri net where:

- tokens consist of an *environment*, i.e. a subset of ID×V. Let ENV = $2^{ID\times V}$ be the set of all environments on ID and V. The tokens of a ER net will be called *environments*. Without losing generality it can be assumed that there are no repeated identifiers in the pairs of elements of each environment; i.e. environments are partial functions from ID to V.
- each transition T is bound to a predicate and an action. A *predicate* is a relation $p \subseteq ENV^k$ and an *action* is a relation $a \subseteq ENV^k \times ENV^h$ where k and h are the number of input and output places for transition T, respectively. As already mentioned, we consider only arcs with weight 1.
- a *marking* m is an assignment of a non-negative number of environments to all places. M denotes the set of all possible markings. m_0 denotes the initial marking.
- a transition T is *enabled* in a marking if and only if for each input place p_i, $1 \le i \le k$, in a given order, there is at least one environment env_i such that $<env_1, env_2, ..., env_k> \in p$. $<env_1, env_2, ..., env_k>$ is called a *k-tuple of enabling environments* for transition T (there can be more than one k-tuple of enabling environments for any given transition T and the same environment can participate in several enabling tuples).
- the *firing* of an enabled transition T consists of creating a new marking for the net, removing a k-tuple $<env_1, env_2, ..., env_k>$ of enabling environments from the input places, one for each input place in the given order, and inserting a h-tuple $<env'_1, env'_2, ..., env'_h>$ of environments in T's output places, in the given order, such that $<<env_1, env_2, ..., env_k>, <env'_1, env'_2, ..., env'_h>> \in a$.
- given an initial marking m_0, a *firing sequence* is a finite sequence

  $$<<T(1),m_1>, <T(2),m_2>, ..., <T(n),m_n>>$$

  where T(i) is a transition and m_i is a marking, such that for each i≥2, T(i) is enabled in the marking m_{i-1}, m_i is produced by the firing of transition T(i), and T(1) is enabled in the initial marking m_0. When markings are not important to consider, we simply write <T(1), T(2), ..., T(n)> to denote a firing sequence.

3.2 Requirements on Representing Time with ER nets

A natural way of modelling time is to represent it as an entry in each environment. The value associated to identifier *time* will represent the time of the transition firing that created the environment. If more than one environment is created by the same transition firing, the time of these environments is the same.

Dealing with time as if it were any other variable in the environment is not enough to guarantee that this variable actually models the intuitive notion of time: some properties of monotonicity must be satisfied. Here, we will discuss some of the most remarkable ones:

(R1) Local monotonicity: the time value of the environments produced by a transition firing cannot be less than the time value of any environment removed in the same transition firing; i. e., the firing time of a transition should not be less than the maximum time amongst the removed environments. This requirement expresses the fact that the execution of an action or the occurrence of an event (modelled by the transition firing) takes a non-negative time.

(R2) Monotonicity with respect to the firing time of each transition: the firing time of a transition cannot be less than the time of the previous firing of the same transition. This requirement expresses the fact that two consecutive executions of the same action must occur at non-decreasing time values.

(R3) Global monotonicity of time: the firing times of the transitions in a firing sequence <T(1), ..., T(i), ...> should be monotonically non-decreasing. This requirement expresses the fact that a sequence of firings that can occur in the model must represent a sequence of actions as they are observable in the modelled real world; such actions occur at non-decreasing time values.

Requirement R3 has been always implicitly assumed in the previous attempts to put time in Petri nets. However, sometimes it could overconstrain the system model.

3.3 Representing TB Nets with ER Nets

In this section we show how TB nets can be formally specified in terms of ER nets. Since timestamps are stored locally in the environments, they can be generated by the actions attached to transitions. Being actions expressed as relations in $ENV^k \times ENV^h$, they can model any kind of time set associated to a tuple of environments, not only time intervals. In the remainder of this section we will show how time requirements (R1, R2 and R3) introduced in Section 3.2 can be satisfied by means of conditions and actions.

In the ER net model, we use the notation *time(env)* to indicate the value associated to the time entry in the environment env. We extend *time* to any tuple of environments in the following way:

$$time(<env_1, env_2, \ldots, env_k>) = \max\{time(env_i) \mid 1 \le i \le k\}$$

This will be called the *characteristic time* of the tuple $<env_1, env_2, \ldots, env_k>$. The value of time in the environments of the tuple produced by the firing of a transition T will be referred to as the *firing time* of T.

Two firing sequences FS = <<T(1), m_1>, <T(2), m_2>, ..., <T(n), m_n>>, from the initial marking m_0 and FS' = <<T'(1), m'_1>, <T'(2), m'_2>, ..., <T'(n), m'_n>>, from the initial marking m'_0, are said to be *equivalent* if and only if $m_0 = m'_0$, $m_n = m'_n$, <T'(1), ..., T'(n)> is a permutation of <T(1), ..., T(n)> and for each i, $1 \le i \le n$, the effect of the firing of T(i) in FS is the same as that of the corresponding T'(j) in the permuted sequence, that is T(i) and T'(j) fire under the same enabling tuple and produce the same output tuple. To denote the time of the i-th firing (the firing that produced m_i from m_{i-1}) within a firing sequence FS we use the notation *f_time (FS, i)*. A firing sequence FS = (<T(1), m_1>, <T(2), m_2>, ..., <T(n), m_n>) is *time ordered* iff $\forall$ i, j | i < j $\Rightarrow$ f_time (FS, i) $\le$ f_time (FS, j).

Requirement R1, dealing with the local monotonicity, can be fulfilled by choosing suitable conditions and actions, such that the value of the time variable for the produced tuple is not less than the characteristic time of the removed tuple. Requirements R2 and R3 can be satisfied with different methods for Weak and Strong Time Semantics. Thus we will consider the solutions for the two kinds of semantics separately.

3.3.1 Weak Time Semantics

ER nets are defined in a way that is consistent with the underlying philosophy of Petri nets: Any transition may fire at any point provided that a *local* requirement based on the marking of input places is satisfied. Consequently, if we simply rely upon actions associated to transitions of ER nets to model time, nothing prevents the occurrence of a firing sequence like FS = <<T(1), m_1>, <T(2) ,m_2>, ..., <T(n), m_n>>, where f_time(FS, i) > f_time(FS, j) for some i, j, $1 \le i < j \le n$, which violates requirement R2 if T(i) = T(j) and, more generally, requirement R3. However, we show in this section that every feasible firing sequence is equivalent to a time ordered one. This implies that every observable behavior of the net represents (is equivalent to) a feasible behavior as far as time is concerned, provided that we assume WTS. Thus TB nets with WTS may be specified in terms of ER nets provided that actions satisfy requirement R1, without introducing any other extra mechanisms.

Theorem

Consider a ER net with a time entry in each environment and such that actions satisfy requirement R1. Then for each firing sequence FS = (<T(1), m_1>, <T(2), m_2>, ..., <T(n), m_n>) with initial marking m_0, there exists a firing sequence FS'=(<T'(1), m'_1>, <T'(2), m'_2>, ..., <T'(n), m'_n>) such that FS' is time ordered and FS' is equivalent to FS.

Sketch of the Proof

The theorem can be proved by induction on the length of the firing sequence.

Basis of the induction

A firing sequence composed of only one transition is trivially ordered.

Inductive step

For a given firing sequence FS_{h+1} = <<T(1), m_1>, <T(2), m_2>, ..., <T(h), m_h>, <T(h+1), m_{h+1}>> of length h+1, the subsequence of its first h transition firings can be assumed ordered from the inductive hypothesis. If f_time (FS_{h+1}, h+1) < f_time (FS_{h+1}, h), i.e. FS_{h+1} is not time ordered, we show that the firings of transitions T(h) and T(h+1) in the firing sequence FS_{h+1} can be swapped, thus obtaining a new, valid firing sequence FS'_{h+1} equivalent to FS_{h+1}.

Clearly, the firings of T(h) and T(h+1) can be swapped if the firing of T(h) does not produce any environment consumed by the firing of T(h+1). By contradiction, assume that at least one such environment env exists. Then time(env) = f_time(FS_{h+1}, h), since env is produced by the firing of T(h), and time(env) $\le$ f_time(FS_{h+1}, h+1), because of requirement R1. Thus f_time(FS_{h+1}, h) $\le$ f_time(FS_{h+1}, h+1): a contradiction.

After the swapping of the firings of T(h) and T(h+1) we obtain a firing sequence FS'_{h+1} = <<T'(1), m'_1>, <T'(2), m'_2>, ..., <T'(h), m'_h>, <T'(h+1), m'_{h+1}>> that is equivalent to FS_{h+1} and such that f_time(FS'_{h+1}, h+1) $\ge$ f_time(FS'_{h+1}, j), $\forall$ j with $1 \le j \le h$. Since, by induction, the theorem holds for the prefix of FS'_{h+1} of lengh h, it holds for FS'_{h+1}.

□

The theorem provides a partition of the firing sequences in a ER net: time ordered firing sequences can be considered as the natural representatives of each class. Also, each representative models a possible behavior according to WTS. Notice also that the result obtained is quite general as to the nature of the time sets and is not limited to time intervals only.

3.3. 2 Strong Time Semantics

According to the STS, a transition is forced to fire within its firing time set. Let us consider, for instance, the firing sequence FS = <T1, T3, T2> for the net of Figure 6, assuming an initial marking where there is one environment, with associated time 0, in each of P1, P2, and P4.

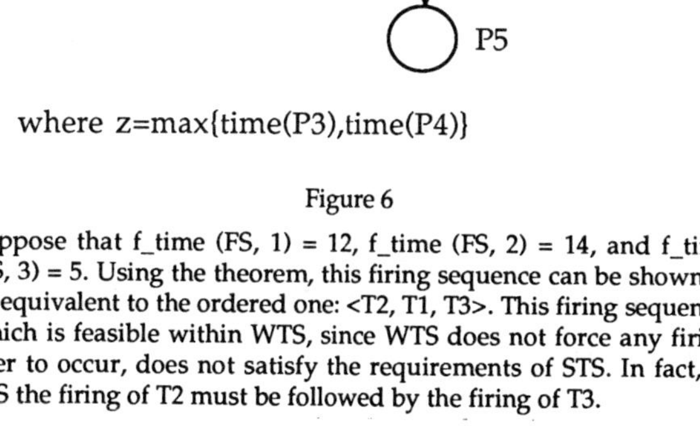

Figure 6

Suppose that f_time (FS, 1) = 12, f_time (FS, 2) = 14, and f_time (FS, 3) = 5. Using the theorem, this firing sequence can be shown to be equivalent to the ordered one: <T2, T1, T3>. This firing sequence, which is feasible within WTS, since WTS does not force any firing ever to occur, does not satisfy the requirements of STS. In fact, in STS the firing of T2 must be followed by the firing of T3.

The previous example shows that, in general, the application of the theorem to the firing sequences of ER nets does not guarantee that the generated firing sequences (which would satisfy requirements R2 and R3) are feasible according to STS. Thus extra mechanisms must be introduced to achieve this goal, as we show in this section.

Requirement R2 could be easily satisfied by adding to each transition a place which contains a environment acting as a "local timer" in much the same way as we did in Section 2.3.2. In fact, this guarantees that if the firing of a transition T occurs at time t, any subsequent firing occurs at time t', with $t' \geq t$. However, local timers cannot guarantee satisfaction of requirement R3, which requires a priority system among the enabled transitions according to their firing intervals, as shown in the example above. Our goal is to solve this problem without introducing in our net model any additional new concept. In a Petri net, the only way to (say) force a set of transitions to fire is to disable the other ones. Based on this observation, a solution for the system of Figure 6 is given by the model sketched in Figure 7.

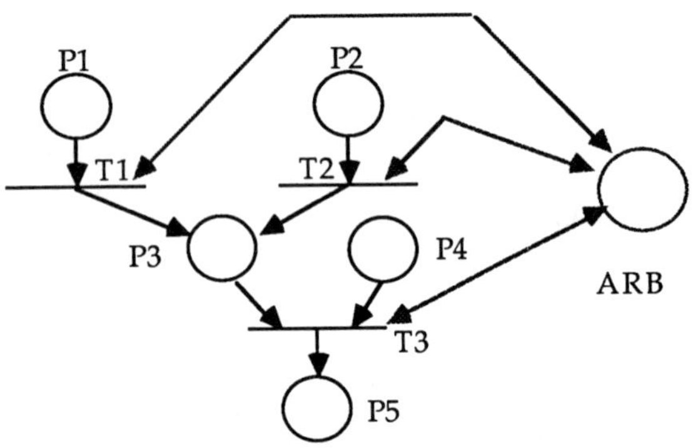

Figure 7

A place ARB ("arbiter") that is input and output place for every transition has been added to the net. In order to enforce STS, place ARB contains one environment, which will record the information needed to select the proper subset of transitions which can fire according to the time conditions, among those currently enabled. In addition, predicates and actions are attached to every transition. For instance, to enforce the firing of T1 after T3 fired, the values of the variables in the environment in place ARB would be such that the predicate attached to transition T1 is false while the predicate attached to transition T3 is true. This solution is somehow cumbersome. However, the problem intrinsically requires a great deal of global knowledge to correctly handle the general case.

4. CONCLUSIONS

In this paper we have discussed how to describe timing aspects in system models based on Petri nets. Initially, we have reviewed the models proposed in the literature and we have proposed a new model (TB nets) for dealing with time which is more general than the previous proposals. Also, we have motivated the need for two types of semantics of such model. Then we have addressed the problem of expressing all kinds of notations that may be useful for specifying real-time systems in terms of a basic, kernel formalism. In particular, we have presented a high-level net formalism (ER nets) and we have shown how time behaviors can be expressed in terms of ER nets. Another possible use of ER nets to model timing issues could address the case of a distributed systems with independent clocks. Following the same pattern we illustrated in the paper, one could also introduce time in a stochastic way as, e. g. in [19].

Apart from time, other useful abstractions that a specifier might wish to use in systems specifications can be expressed in terms of ER nets as well: for example, new kinds of places behaving like FIFO queues, which have proven to be useful for modeling the semantics of concurrent Ada programs [10], [5].

Since ER nets can be used as a kernel language to specify the semantics of new notations used for system specifications, we are currently in the process of designing an environment supporting formal specifications which uses ER nets as a kernel formalism. The goal of this environment is to allow the specifier to define new types of net based notations, or modify existing notations whenever the need arises to tailor the specification language to his or her expressive needs. Any new notation has its own external graphical syntax, but can be given precise semantics in terms of the kernel notation. According to this philosophy, the need to account for a variety of notations supporting specifications [5] will not produce, as a side effect, a proliferation of ad-hoc notations with little (if any) way to compare them and reason formally about them. Rather, every notation will be formally based on the grounds of a kernel formal model.

ACKNOWLEDGMENTS

This work has been partially supported by MPI 40% and by CNR - CSISEI. The research activity of Sandro Morasca is partially supported by Selenia S. p. A.

REFERENCES

[1] B. Berthomieu, M. Menasche, "An Enumerative Approach for Analyzing Petri Nets", *Information Processing 83*, R.E.A. Mason ed., Elsevier Science Pub. B.V. (North Holland).

[2] J. E. Coolahan, N. Roussopoulos, "Timing Requirements for Time Driven Systems Using Augmented Petri Nets", *IEEE Transactions on Software Engineering*, vol. SE9, September 1983.

[3] H.J Genrich, K. Lautenbach, "System Modelling with High-Level Petri Nets", *Theoretical Computer Science 13*, 109-136, 1981.

[4] H.J. Genrich, "Predicate/Transition Nets", in [14].

[5] C. Ghezzi, D. Mandrioli, "On Eclecticism in Specification: a Case Study Centered Around Petri Nets", *Proceedings 4th Workshop on Software Specification and Design*, Monterey, 1987.

[6] C. Ghezzi, D. Mandrioli, M.Pezzè, "Petri Nets as a Support to Symbolic Execution of Concurrent, Ada Programs", Dipartimento di Elettronica - Politecnico di Milano, Internal Report n. 87-007, 1987.

[7] C. Ghezzi, D. Mandrioli, S. Morasca, M. Pezzè, "A General Way to Put Time in Petri Nets", Dipartimento di Elettronica - Politecnico di Milano, Internal Report n. 88-011, 1988.

[8] M. A. Holliday, M. K. Vernon, "A Generalized Timed Petri Net Model for Performance Analysis", *IEEE Transactions on Software Engineering*, vol. SE13, December 1987.

[9] K. Jensen, "Coloured Petri Nets", in [14].

[10] D. Mandrioli, R. Zicari, C. Ghezzi, F. Tisato, "Modeling the Ada Task System by Petri Nets", *Computer Languages*, vol. 10, No. 1, 1985.

[11] P. M. Merlin, D. J. Farber, "Recoverability of Communication Protocols - Implications of a Theoretical Study", *IEEE Transactions on Communications*, vol. COM-24, September 1976.

[12] M. K. Molloy, "Discrete Time Stochastic Petri Nets", *IEEE Transactions on Software Engineering*, vol. SE11, April 1985.

[13] S. Morasca, M.Pezzè, "A Net-based Model for Time Dependent Systems", Dipartimento di Elettronica - Politecnico di Milano, Internal Report n. 89-05, 1989.

[14] "Petri Nets: Central Models and Their Properties", "Petri Nets: Applications and Relationships to Other Concurrency Models", *Advances in Petri Nets 1986, part I and II*, W. Brauer, W. Reisig, G. Rozenberg (eds.), Lecture Notes in Computer Science 254 - 255, Berlin, Heidelberg, New York; Springer Verlag 1987.

[15] C. V. Ramamoorthy, G. S. Ho, "Performance Evaluation of Asynchronous Concurrent Systems Using Petri Nets", *IEEE Transactions on Software Engineering*, vol. SE6, September 1980.

[16] W. Reisig, "Petri Nets: an Introduction", *EATCS Monographs on Theoretical Computer Science*, Berlin, Heidelberg, New York; Springer Verlag 1985.

[17] J. Sifakis, "Performance Evaluation of Systems Using Nets", *Proc. of the Advanced Course on General Net Theory*, W. Brauer ed., Lecture Notes in Computer Science 84, Berlin, Heidelberg, New York; Springer Verlag 1980.

[18] P. D. Stotts Jr., T. W. Pratt, "Hierarchical Modelling of Software Systems with Timed Petri Nets", in [19].

[19] 1st International Workshop on Timed Petri Nets, Torino, Italy, July 1985.

[20] N. Wirth, "Toward a Discipline of Real-Time Programming", *Communications of the ACM*, vol. 20, n. 8, August 77.

Toward Reliable Reactive Systems

Li-mei Gilham Allen Goldberg T. C. Wang

Kestrel Institute
1801 Page Mill Road
Palo Alto, CA 94304

1 Introduction

The goal of the work reported here is to construct a system that supports the acquisition and correct implementation of software specifications for reactive systems. The system utilizes a finite state machine formalism derived from the work of Harel [5], set-theoretic data structures as exemplified by [1, 8], and relies on both classic verification techniques and consistency-preserving transformational implementation of specifications. Formal reasoning and manipulation of programs is greatly simplified by *referential transparency*, which insures that the meaning of a program fragment is not dependent on context or state. The attractiveness of functional and logic programming derive from their maintenance of referential transparency. Although suppression of the notion of state makes manipulation of programs easier, it seriously detracts from their expressiveness. In particular, specification of a reactive system is extremely awkward without the notion of state. The challenge addressed in this work is to provide a notion of state and state change in a way that supports analysis and manipulation similar to that possible in functional and logic languages. The idea is to isolate state changes to those specified using a finite state machine formalism and to provide a functional language that specifies changes to abstract data structures when finite state machine transitions are executed. A system we are building to realize this goal is called REACTO.

REACTO uses graphically presented finite state machines (FSM) as the underlying framework to model reactive systems. A hierarchical notion of state is employed by REACTO to model the hierarchical, modularized structure of a complex reactive system, and to support stepwise refinement of the design. States are composed of substates in such a way that properties that are associated with a state apply to all of its substates. Thus a transition leaving a state is equivalent to a set of transitions each of which exits from a substate of that state.

The FSM formalism provides the top-level control structure allowing the specification of the state hierarchy of a reactive system. Associated with each state are variables, scoped with respect to the state hierarchy. Associated with transitions is a predicate over visible variables which guards the execution of the transition and and an action which consists of assignments of values to visible variables. The values assigned to variables are specified as an expression in a functional language.

Ease of specification is one design goal. Another is reliability. This is enhanced in two ways. First we are proving the correctness of the transformations implementing the compiler. Second the user may associate assertions with states. These assertions are redundant in the sense that the execution of the machine is not determined by the assertions. Their purpose is to specify invariants that the specifier believes must be true whenever the associated state is entered. We use traditional verification technology to discharge (verify) these assertions at compile time. Any remaining assertions are checked (by computation) upon entry to the associated state at run-time.

Specification acquisition is done via an interface consisting of a nested icon graphic display and hierarchy browser. The graphic display presents the finite state machine hierarchy of states and transitions.

©1989 ACM 0-89791-305-1/89/0500/0068$00.75

Text, such as variables associated with a state, and actions associated with a transitions are presented using the hierarchy browser. Within the browser there is mouse sensitivity to the syntax of program text.

This paper is organized as follows: The next section discusses related work. This is followed by a more detailed language overview. The semantics of REACTO is defined and then it is shown how to use the semantics to generate verification conditions. Next a section describes the functional language and our plans for its transformational implementation. Finally we describe the current implementation and state conclusions.

2 Related Work

The FSM mechanism used by the REACTO specification follows the statechart approach outlined in Harel [5, 4]. We have made some important modifications to it. The history mechanism has been restricted because the general history mechanism complicated the semantics.

One addition that we made to the formalism is the inclusion of substate calls. Substate calls of REACTO is quite similar to *subconversion invoking* in augmented transition networks (ATNs) [11]. ATNs allow a set of connected nodes to be named and "called" from another diagram. The use of substate calls and the restricted history mechanism have simple semantics and high expressiveness. We do not allow concurrent state machines. Our study in REACTO focuses on the formal semantics of the language, including the formal semantics of substate calls, the verification conditions related to the state hierarchy and assertion inheritance, and other techniques required for designing reliable software with REACTO.

3 Language Overview

REACTO is a two-tiered language. The top-level language constructs are used for specifying the finite state machine. Beneath this top-level, conditions and actions associated with transitions are specified with a high-level functional language. We describe the FSM facility.

3.1 States

A *state* is a named object with the following attributes: super-state, substates, initial-substate, local-variables, assertions.

The states are arranged in a tree, specified by the super-state and (redundantly) the substates attributes. A state with no substates is called a *primitive state.*

When the machine enters a non-primitive state it enters the unique designated initial substate of that state (except when the history mechanism is used). The rule is applied recursively if the initial state is not primitive.

Associated with a state is a set of typed variables. These variables are local to the state. Variables satisfy the usual visibility rules of a block-structured language, namely that a variable declared in a state S is accessible to S and all of its substates. Variables behave like Algol 60 *own* variables. They are lexically scoped and have dynamic extent. In particular, they are not allocated and deallocated upon entry and exit from a state. Rather they are allocated once and retain their value from one entry into the state to another.

There are two kinds of program variables, *interface variables* and *internal variables.* Internal variables are those that may only be written into by the program itself, whereas interface variables are those that may also be written into by an external agent. For example, if a user types a character on the terminal it is appended to an interface variable which is operating as a buffer. This distinction is useful for verification purposes since the value of internal variables can be assumed not to change unless done so explicitly by the program. A concurrent system may be specified by describing multiple machines communicating with shared interface variables.

The last attribute of a state is its assertions. *Assertions* are simply predicates over the state's visible variables which must be true each time the state is entered. These assertions are redundant to the specification itself; if no assertions are given a program will be able to execute. However these assertions serve a critical purpose of annotating the program with essential properties that give the user confidence that he/she has written what was intended. Verification of such assertions means proving prior to specification execution that the assertion holds upon entry to the state in any execution of the specification. Assertions not verified at compile time are checked at run time. The language in which assertions are written include (bounded) quantification, predicates, functions and sentential connectives, allowing concise expression of first-order formulas.

3.2 Transitions

A *transition* is a named object with the following attributes: originating-state, destination-state, predicate, action, history-flag, priority.

In a non-hierarchical finite state machine, transitions connect states with the intuitive meaning that if the machine is in the originating state and if the transition is taken the machine will enter the destination state. In a hierarchical finite state machine, the machine is never actually in a non-primitive state so the meaning of transitions from and to non-primitive states must be made clear. A transition from a non-primitive state is regarded as indicating a transition from every primitive substate, except a return state, to the destination state. A transition whose destination is non-primitive is regarded as a transition into the initial substate of the destination state. If that state is not primitive then the rule is re-applied so that the entrance is to the initial state's initial state, and so on.

The *action* associated with a transition is executed when the machine takes the transition. There are two kinds of transitions. One is called an *assignment transition*. Its action changes the values of variables visible within any superstate containing the originating and destination state. Specifically the action is specified as a multiple assignment, $x_1, \ldots, x_n := e_1, \ldots, e_n$, where each x_i for $1 \leq i \leq n$ is a program variable, each expression e_i, for $1 \leq i \leq n$, is an expression written in a typed functional sublanguage, $e_i \equiv f_i(y_1, \ldots y_m, x_1, \ldots, x_n)$. The idea here is to isolate state changes in the system precisely to variable updates on assignment transitions.

A transition whose action is to invoke via a *call* another portion of the finite state machine specification is called a ***substate call transition***. A substate call is specified by a `call-state` command followed by the name of a non-primitive state. The called state must be disconnected from the rest of the FSM. When a substate call action is taken, the machine will enter the initial primitive substate of the called substate. A substate call terminates when the execution of the call reaches a return state. A state is a *return state* if and only if it is a primitive state and it is not an originating state of any transition. The transitions contained in this substate may itself contain a substate call, however (mutually) recursive calls are disallowed. Thus the semantics of a substate call can be described textual substitution.

The predicate associated with a transition gives the condition required for the transition to be executed. There may be more than one transition leaving a state whose associated predicate are true and so it is ambiguous what transition the machine should take. Thus an integer is associated with each transition, called its *priority*, so that the transition with the highest priority is taken among those whose predicates are true.

Each transition contains a *history-flag*. If the value of this flag is false, then control passes to the initial substate of the destination state. If the value of this flag is true control passes to the most recently visited primitive state of the destination state. We require that when the history-flag of a transition is true, the originating state and the destination state of the transition must be identical, in other words the transition is a self-loop. This is useful since it allows a self-loop transition which is to be placed on each containing substate to be factored to the containing state. This history return mechanism is much simpler than the general history mechanism of Harel's statecharts. However in conjunction with the use of the substate call transition the control mechanism is sufficiently expressive.

3.3 The External Interface

This section describes how a FSM will interact with its external environment. Variables may be declared to be *interface variables*. These variables are shared so that they may be modified by an external process (e.g. another FSM).

An interface variable I of type T can be ***buffered*** or ***unbuffered***. A buffered variable is just an abbreviation for an unbuffered variable of type *seq(T)*, i.e. a sequence of elements of type T. The sequence acts as a queue — external writers append to the sequence, and the FSM reads from the head.

During execution an interface variable may be defined or undefined. An undefined interface variable has no unread data from its external source. Thus if it is buffered, the sequence representing it is empty. It is a run-time error to access undefined variables.

Interface variables can only be used as parameters to the following procedures.

- *Empty?(I)* if I undefined this function returns the value true.
- *Examine(I)* if I is unbuffered *Examine* returns the value of variable I. If I is buffered it returns the first element of I. If I is undefined this operation generates an error.
- *Read(I)* Returns the same value as *Examine(I)* and as a side-effect, performs the following action. If I is unbuffered set I to undefined. If I is buffered removes the head of I.

Reading an interface variable is a side-effecting action which can only occur within an action of a transition. *Examine* and *empty?* are predicates which may appear in any expression (including assertions).

3.4 Informal Semantics

The execution cycle of a REACTO finite state machine (FSM) is described as follows. Initially, the machine starts out in the initial substate of the top-level or root state of the FSM. At the start of the cycle interface variables are updated from any external source. Their values are then frozen until updated by a *Read* or the start of the next cycle. Any assertion on the state that has not been proved by the verifier to be an invariant is checked. If it evaluates to false the machine halts with an error. All the predicates on transitions from this state and its containing states are evaluated. Of those that evaluate to true the transition with the highest priority is executed. When a transition is taken the action associated with the transition is executed. If this transition is an assignment transition the current bindings of the variables are used to evaluate expressions appearing in the assignments and these values are used to simultaneously update the assigned variables. If the transition is a substate call, the semantics is the same as if the transition was replaced by an assignment transition which does not update any variables, but whose destination is the initial state of the called substate, and on all return states of the called substate there is a transition with predicate true and a null assignment pointing to the destination state of the original transition. Thus it functions as a call-by-name procedure call. This can all be done textually at compile time, since recursive calls are disallowed. The cycle then repeats. To deal with the possibility that all the predicates on all transitions evaluate to false, each state implicitly has a default transition whose predicate is true, whose priority is less than that of any other transition, its action is null, and its destination is the same state. Its effect is to keep the machine in an idle loop waiting for an external process to update an interface variable.

4 The Semantics of REACTO Specifications

In this section, we present a denotational semantics for the REACTO language. A reactive system typically does not terminate, thus the output value of such a system is undefined. Therefore the semantics formulates the input-output relation for each transition or a sequence of transitions. It also accounts for the computation process related to the interaction of the system with the outside world. Thus, our formal semantics is similar to a temporal logic formulation [7]. However, our approach is much simpler because it only uses first order logic.

The semantics of a REACTO program is defined with respect to an interpretation I of the data domain. For simplicity, we shall not present the detailed definition of this interpretation, but assume that I is the ***standard interpretation***. That is, I consists of a domain D and a mapping I_0, which assigns a standard meaning to operators of such standard types as Boolean and integer. Thus all logic and function symbols are interpreted naturally, such as $[true]_I = true$, $[false]_I = false$, $[\wedge]_I = \wedge$ (the logical "and"), $[+]_I = +$ (the plus operation in arithmetic), etc.

Let Σ be the set of all functions $\sigma : V \rightarrow D$, where V is the set of all program variables and D is the domain of the interpretation I. Each $\sigma \in \Sigma$ is called a *situation* of the interpretation I (usually, σ is called a *state* of the interpretation. Here we use the word "situation" to avoid confusion with the "state" of the FSM).

We formulate the semantics of a program by defining a transition function $exe_{(M,I)} : S \times \Sigma \rightarrow S \times \Sigma$. This function describes the next state and situation of the machine if currently in some given state s and situation σ. We have designed REACTO so that its semantics are easily described and the language remains expressive. The definition of *exe* must take into account substate calls, updating of interface variables, the history mechanism, and the state hierarchy. We leave the details to a longer version of this paper.

5 The Verifier

The REACTO verifier is designed to prove the consistency of the assertions associated to the state of a REACTO program with its operational behavior. It is based on an extension of Floyd's inductive assertions method [3]. Since the underlying structure of a REACTO program is a variant of a flowchart program, the use of Floyd's inductive assertion method is natural and convenient.

Although verification technology has been limited in its success their are two important advantages that our approach has that limits the burden placed on the theorem prover. First the problem is factored into small pieces, namely of verifying the correctness of each transition. Second verification is occurring at the specification level where operations are still suitably abstract and the theorem proving not overwhelmed by implementation detail.

Verification is done in two steps. The first step is to deduce the verification conditions. This is done mechanically by a *verification condition generator*. The second step is proving the truth of the verification conditions. This is done with a mechanical theorem prover.

Verification is done by proving by induction on the length of execution sequences that whenever a state is entered (actually after the interface variables are updated) its associated assertion is true. One can use as an induction hypothesis the claim that assertions associated with other states (in particular those with transitions into the state) are true. Verification of an assertion on a state S boils down to proving statement of the form, "if an assertion p holds and an action α is taken then an assertion q holds after α terminates." With the classical technique, this statement is proved by first deducing the weakest liberal condition $wlp(\alpha, q)$ from α and q, then proving that $p \rightarrow wlp(\alpha, q)$ holds. A condition, C, is called a *weakest liberal condition* of α and q if C holds if and only if α does not terminate or α terminates and q is true after α terminates. The formula $p \rightarrow wlp(\alpha, q)$, denoted by $vc(p, \alpha, q)$, is called the *verification condition* of α with respect to p and q. For a standard transition of a REACTO program, $wlp(\alpha, q)$ can be deduced mechanically. If α is a multiple-assignment statement,

$$\alpha : \quad x_1, ..., x_n := e_1, ..., e_n,$$

where no variables $x_1, ..., x_n$ are common, then it can be deduced from the formal semantics of the assignment statement that

$$wlp(\alpha, q) = q^{e_1,...,e_n}_{x_1,...,x_n},$$

where $q^{e_1,...,e_n}_{x_1,...,x_n}$ is obtained from q by a simultaneous substitution of x_i with e_i, for $1 \leq i \leq n$. Of course this is the most basic case. Substate calls, history returns, assertions inherited from containing states etc. must all be considered. The clean semantics makes this a manageable task. Each generated verification condition must be proved true by the theorem prover.

6 The Functional Language

The functional language is still under development, but major aspects of it has been determined. The language provides set-theoretic type constructors, such as finite sets, sequences, maps, tuples, and relations, which substantially relieve the programmer from having to choose data representations. A rich set of operations are defined on these types including, reduction, bounded quantification, set and sequence formation, lambda definitions, apply-to-all, etc. allowing concise algorithmic description.

A type system supporting polymorphism, type inference, user-defined types, and a restricted notion of subtyping is being defined. For greater reliability, types must be determined at compile time. We wish to provide the most powerful type system possible, but still maintain decidability of the type inference problem [2].

Although it does not make sense to insist that a reactive system terminate, it does make sense to insure that computational activities within the larger system do. In particular, we wish to guarantee the termination of the actions associated with (non substate call) transitions, i.e. the functional programs associated with an action. We do this by construction — it is impossible to write a program which does not terminate. Recursive calls are disallowed. An iteration construct has been designed which is flexible yet insures that all iterations are bounded. The language computes precisely the class of primitive recursive functions. The work of Martin-Löf [6] has demonstrated that the use of primitive recursive functions defined over a rich data domain provides a very-high level specification notation with attractive theoretical properties.

7 The Current Implementation

The current implementation includes a graphical interface for acquisition and editing of specifications, an execution simulator, and a verification system. The verification system consists of a verification generator as described in section 6, and a theorem prover which proves the generated conditions. The system, except for the theorem prover, which was developed by T. C. Wang [10, 9] is written in Refine [1]. The functional language described in the previous section is not fully implemented. The current prototype uses a functional subset of Refine. A fairly large example has been specified using the system. One component of the example system is a simple display-oriented editor. A screen dump taken from the system appears as figure 1. The system provides the capability to edit and view the specification either by manipulation of the graphical representation in the graphics window, by using a textual syntax representation in the LISP Listener, or by using the hierarchical presentation in the Outline Editor Window. Note that the icons in the Graphics Window are nested; you can zoom in and out of a portion of the diagram.

The major work to be done is the implementation of a provably correct transformation system that implements the language. We will start with the functional sublanguage. This language has simple control mechanisms, which are similar to those in the target language, Common LISP. Thus the major effort will be in proving the correctness of data type refinement transformations.

Figure 1: Screen Dump of REACTO

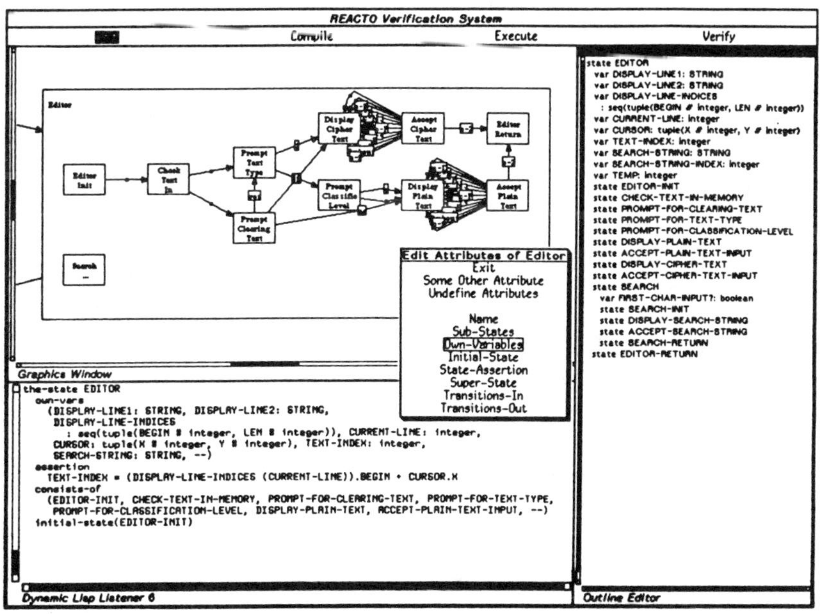

8 Conclusions

The system we are developing successfully integrates a number of useful concepts for the construction reliable software for reactive systems. These include

- A finite state machine formalism employing hierarchy and a "subroutine" call mechanism.
- A very convenient interface using a graphics presentation of the FSM and a hierarchical browser for the manipulation of program text.
- A verification system which checks the consistency of assertions associated with a specification and its operational behavior. The verification task is factored into manageable pieces, and the theorem prover operates on an abstract specification, not a detailed implementation.
- Specifications are executable, and so it provides a rapid prototyping capability.
- Termination of actions is guaranteed by construction of the program language.
- The system provides abstract type constructors which relieve the user of having to devise data representations.
- A rich notion of type is being incorporated into the language.
- A transformational compiler utilizing provably correct transformations is being developed.

References

[1] Leonor Abraído-Fandiño. An overview of $REFINE^{TM}$ 2.0. In *Proceedings of the Second International Symposium on Knowledge Engineering*, Madrid, Spain, April 8–10, 1987.

[2] L. Cardelli and P. Wegner. On understanding types, data abstraction, and polymorphism. *ACM Computing Surveys*, 17(4):471–522, December 1986.

[3] R. W. Floyd. Assigning meanings to programs. In *Proceedings of Symposia in Applied Mathematics XIX*, pages 19–32, American Mathematical Society, 1967.

[4] David Harel. On the formal semantics of statecharts. In *Proceedings of the Symposium on Logic in Computer Science*, pages 54–64, Ithaca, NY, June 22-25 1987.

[5] David Harel. Statecharts: a visual approach to complex systems. *Science of Computer Programming*, 8(3):231–274, June 1987.

[6] P. Martin-Löf. *Constructive Mathematics and Computer Programming.* 1979. Preprint, Department of Mathematics, University of Stockholm. Presented at *6th International Conference for Logic, Methodology and Philosophy of Science*.

[7] A. Pneuli. Applications of temporal logic to the specification and verification of reactive systems: a survey of current trends. In J. W. de Bakker et. al., editor, *Current Trends in Concurrency*, pages 510–584, Springer-Verlag, Berlin, 1986. Lecture Notes in Computer Science, Vol. 224.

[8] J. T. Schwartz, R. B. K. Dewar, E. Dubinsky, and E. Schonberg. *Programming with Sets: An Introduction to SETL.* Springer-Verlag, New York, 1986.

[9] T. C. Wang. Shd-prover at University of Texas at Austin. In J. H. Siekmann, editor, *Proceedings of 8th Conference on Automated Deduction*, pages 707–708, Springer-Verlag, Berlin, 1986. Lecture Notes in Computer Science, Vol. 230.

[10] T. C. Wang and W. W. Bledsoe. Hierarchical deduction. *Journal of Automated Reasoning*, 3(1):35–77, March 1987.

[11] A. I. Wasserman. Extending state transition diagrams for the specification of human-computer interaction. *IEEE Transactions on Software Engineering*, SE-11(8):699–713, August 1985.

An Operational Semantics of Real Time Design Language RT-CDL

Leo YuHsiang Liu and R. K. Shyamasundar

333 Whitmore Laboratory
Department of Computer Science
The Pennsylvania State University
University Park, PA 16802, U.S.A.

ABSTRACT

Any methodology for the design of a complex system needs a basis for specification and verification. This is particularly so for real-time systems since safety and reliability are extremely important for these systems. As a first step, we provide an operational semantics for the language RT-CDL (Real Time Common Design Language) employing Plotkin's labeled transition systems using the maximal parallelism model of Salwicki and Müldner. The language is based on the event-action model and is capable of (i) expressing various timing constraints, (ii) responding to various real-time exceptions, and (iii) specifying, reasoning, verifying about programs in a compositional manner. We show how to model the behavior of non-buffered broadcasts, durational events, priority, interrupts, and preemptive commands through the semantics. Our approach is compositional and thus provides a firm basis for compositional specification and verification of programs.

1. Motivation and Related Work

One of the primary objectives of Ada has been the programmability of real-time embedded systems. However, the definition of Ada [3] allows a high-priority task to wait for a low-priority task for an unpredictable delay. Furthermore, Ada lacks the power of harnessing the parallelism inherent in real-time systems. For instance, in Ada, we cannot even interleave some of the operations that are possible in the monitor-based languages—which is a disadvantage at many times. The rendezvous mechanism places a lot of restriction with reference to realizing multiform clocks and harnessing parallelism. Another notable point is that even though the traditional description tools of industrial process control systems are intrinsically parallel, it is paradoxical that the computerization of these systems results in the progressive replacement of these parallel tools by programming languages involving a great amount of sequentiality. There has been quite a substantial effort in looking for specification/programming languages for real-time distributed systems. However, if we look at requirements for real-time languages [4], we can come to the conclusion that most of these languages fall short of expectations. For example, many languages do not provide any explicit means of correctly specifying timing constraints, or are limited to either *delay* or *timeout* statement [10]. This limitation not only reduces the expressive power of languages (and hence cannot be used in certain applications such as switching and digital systems) but also makes it difficult to reason about the timing constraints of a given program text. RT-Euclid [8] is essentially a monitor-based language with features for expressing time-bounded loops; however, achieving data integrity through mutual-exclusion, again, is not desirable even in non-real-time languages [15].

Let us take a look at some of the major efforts towards a desirable specification/programming language for real-time systems. A first systematic study of considering the reasons for the lack of suitable specification/programming languages resulted in the language Esterel [2]. Esterel was designed for programming responsive systems assuming a *strong synchrony hypothesis* (i.e., control transfer and transmission of events are instantaneous) and thus overcame several of the deficiencies. In Esterel, there is no internal notion of time; the argument is that the local clock can be simulated through an external clock signal. Although such an assumption leads to efficient and nice structures, the assumption is questionable from a realistic point of view and may result in the causality problem (something like a short circuit cf. [1]). One important feature of reactive systems is that they are primarily event-based rather than transformational (state-based). With this view point, the efforts by Harel, Pnueli et al. started looking for pragmatic formalism (perhaps mixed specification and programming) that would aid in the design of reactive systems. Their study resulted in the formalisms referred to as *Statecharts* ([5, 6]). This formalism is based on state diagrams (thus providing graphic design aid) overcoming some of the drawbacks of state diagrams such as flatness, sequentiality, etc. Statecharts cater for hierarchical specification and multi-level concurrency via the broadcast communication mechanism. Although the language has great expressive power, the semantic of some features, e.g., micro-steps, is not very well understood [7]. Furthermore, Statecharts lack data abstraction in the current form. Also, even though the current technology looks for systems which are not necessarily text-based (perhaps one could consider graphic objects as primitive objects), we feel that a graphic based system may provide only an aid rather than a complete basis in the development of large systems.

The issues of safety and reliability are particularly important for real-time embedded systems because of the catastrophic consequences. This addresses the need of a sound methodology for the verification of *logical correctness* as well as *responsiveness* of real-time programs. Unfortunately, typical real-time embedded systems are large and complex; hence, it is difficult—if not impossible—for a programmer or a team to mentally comprehend. Thus, it is essential that we use a compositional methodology and realistic models. One important characteristic of real-time programs is to respond to external stimuli within a *controllable delay*. However, one cannot interpret this statement to mean *an arbitrary delay*. Thus, whenever we use *interleaving models*, we may not be able to satisfy the timing constraints as required.

RT-CDL (Real Time Common Design Language [11]), inspired by Esterel [2], has been proposed for the design of *real-time reactive* systems [17]. The primary goal of the RT-CDL project is to provide a tool to bridge the gap between specification and realization of programs. The language is based on the event-action model and is capable of (i) expressing various timing constraints in a natural way; (ii) responding to various real-time exceptions in a timely fashion; and (iii) specifying, reasoning, verifying about programs in a compositional manner. In this paper, as a first step, we discuss the primary real-time features of RT-CDL through an operational semantics. We employed *labeled transition systems* on the lines of Plotkin's work [16] to provide an operational semantics of RT-CDL using the *maximal parallelism* model of Salwicki and Müldner [20]. The maximal parallelism model is realistic in the sense that the number of actions which can be executed in parallel without violating synchronization constraints is maximized, and that no unnecessary waiting is modeled. Thus, it provides a realistic model—as opposed to the interleaving model—for real-time concurrency. We show how to model the behavior of non-buffered broadcasts, durational events, priority, interrupts, and preemptive commands through the semantics using discrete integer time domain. One nice feature of our approach is that it is compositional and thus provides a firm basis for compositional specification and verification of programs. From the semantics, we are able to show that the practical problems and the causality problems—due to the *strong synchrony* assumption—associated with Esterel are no longer there. It must be noted that one of the distinctive advantages of Esterel is the *compilability of the programs*; however, that the simplicity of Esterel would be lost if one has to specify timing constraints in a distributed program with reference to the local clock.

The remainder of this paper is organized as follows. Section 2 gives the language syntax and informal interpretation of RT-CDL. Section 3 overviews our notion of real-time and execution model. Section 4 provides the operational semantics of RT-CDL. Section 5 concludes with some remarks.

2. Language Syntax and Informal Interpretation of RT-CDL

In RT-CDL, a program is considered as a set of distributed processes: inter-process communication is achieved by broadcasting events (it is essentially the same as broadcasting a message over a bus in the case of ETHERNET). Note, however, that (i) our construct has the facility of broadcasting an event over a given period of time; (ii) there is no waiting associated with the broadcast command itself; and (iii) if the receiver is not ready to receive an event at the time of broadcast, then the event is simply lost (i.e., the event is not remanent).

Events may come from the process itself (local events) as well as from other processes (external events). We do not distinguish between the two. However, we partition events into *hard* and *soft* ones. An event is *hard* if an alternative action has to be taken as the current plan of action will not satisfy the intended goal. Examples of hard-events are exceptions, immediate time critical actions, and catastrophic events. An event is *soft* if it calls for some service through an external agent. Thus, in such a case, after servicing the external event, the agent may continue with its plan of action. Typical examples of soft events are *interrupts*. In RT-CDL, we abstract the underlying *bus* over which the message is broadcast as an event. It has the following structure:

EVENT E(v)

where E is the event name and v is the value of the message transmitted along with the event E.

In this paper, due to the lack of space, we only consider a subset of RT-CDL. For brevity, we will not go into the details of the declaration of events. Also, some features of the language such as internal parallel statements and during next statements are omitted since they do not play a role in highlighting the compositionality of the specification. In the following, we describe the relevant part of the abstract syntax as well as the context sensitive constraints of the language. For notational convenience, we adopt the following convention throughout this paper: We use P, Q, R for process names; C for set of joint input (E?) and output (E!!) events; x, y, z for variable names; e for expression; i, j, k, m, n for integer indices; E for event name; T for integer time expression; p for integer priority expression; and b for boolean expression. The abstract syntax of RT-CDL is given as follows:

- Network N ::= P | N_1 $//_C$ N_2 | [N $]_C$
- Process P ::= S
- Statement S ::= ε | x := e | **sleep** | **cast** E(e) **last** T |
  while b **do** S **end** | **during** Ev → A **do** S **end** |
  select $\mathbf{or}_{i=1}^{n}$ b_i; g_i → S_i **end** | S_1; S_2
- Action A ::= S
- Event Ev ::= **interrupt** E(x) **last** T | E(x) **last** T | T
- guard g ::= ε | **rec** E(x) **last** T **by** p | **delay** T

A program in RT-CDL must follow the above syntax as well as the context sensitive constraints described below:

- There are no shared variables between two processes.
- For each event, there is only one emitter but may have one or more receivers.

A brief informal interpretation of the above constructs is given as follows:

1. *Empty statement* (ε): This command does nothing and takes no time. This statement has been introduced purely for syntactical purposes of indicating that the program is complete (or terminated) if there is nothing to execute.

2. *Assignment* (x := e): Variable x gets the value of expression e.

3. *While statement* (**while** b **do** S **end**): Repeat (possibly zero times) the execution of body S until b is false.

4. *Sleep statement* (**sleep**): This statement does nothing but wait indefinitely; in fact, this statement is meaningful only in conjunction with a during statement (to be discussed in the sequel).

5. *Broadcast statement* (**cast** E(e) **last** T): Emit event E with value e for T time units. Durational events are captured by the *last* clause; we may omit the *last* clause when the duration is one time unit. Note that an event is simply lost if the receiver is not ready to listen to the event.

6. *During statement*: The receiver is ready to listen to an event while executing a during statement. An event can be a timeout, a hard event, and a soft event. Events prefixed by the word **interrupt** are soft events; otherwise, hard ones.

(a) *Timeouts* (**during** T → A **do** S **end**): The execution of the body S is continued until the expiration of period T, a timeout. If the timeout occurs before the end of the execution of S, then execute action A; the during statement terminates upon the completion of the execution of A. If the timeout does not occur before the completion of S, then the statement terminates.

(b) *Hard events* (**during** E(x) **last** T → A **do** S **end**): The interpretation of this construct is essentially the same as that of timeouts as given in (a) except that one looks for the event E rather than the timeout. Note that a durational event, E(x) **last** T, *occurs* only when event E has persisted for T contiguous time units, and that the value is exchanged when the event occurs.

(c) *Soft events* (**during interrupt** E(x) **last** T → A **do** S **end**): With the occurrence of the soft event E, the execution of S will be *suspended* after the completion of the current atomic command (essentially, assignment is atomic in our case). Then, the interrupt will be serviced by executing A. After completing A, the execution will resume from the point of suspension and continues until another interrupt E occurs or the the execution of S is complete. In the former case, the interrupt will be serviced, and then the execution will be resumed; in the latter case, the statement terminates.

Let us consider a during statement in conjunction with the sleep statement:

during E(x) **last** T → A **do sleep end**.

From the above interpretation, it should be clear that the statement can be interpreted as waiting indefinitely for the event E (it takes at least T time units for event E to occur). Note that if we add some non-empty statement S following the sleep statement, then the statement S has no effect at all as it will never be executed.

7. *Select statement* (**select** $\mathop{\mathbf{or}}\limits_{i=1}^{n}$ b_i; g_i → S_i **end**): A guard is *closed* if its boolean part evaluates to FALSE; otherwise, it is *open*. A guard can be a pure boolean guard, an input guard, or a delay guard. An input guard is of the form **rec** E(x) **last** T **by** p, where p specifies the priority for the receipt of event E. Since no waiting is associated with broadcast commands, we do not allow them to be guards. We say that an input guard is *enabled* when event E occurs. A delay guard is of the form **delay** T; it is said to be *enabled* with the expiration of the duration T. The select statement chooses an alternative according to the following procedure. If none of the guards are open, then the select statement aborts. Otherwise, check whether there are any open pure boolean guards (pure boolean guards are always enabled). If this is the case, choose one of them nondeterministically when there are choices, and execute the statement following the guard. In case there are open guards but no open pure boolean guards, then the execution proceeds as follows. Wait until some open input guards are *enabled*, and then execute the one with the highest priority; again, choose one nondeterministically if two or more enabled open input guards have the same highest priority. If none of the open input guards are enabled before an open delay guard is enabled, then execute the statement following the delay guard; again, choose one nondeterministically when there are choices. Let us demonstrate the semantics of the select statement using an example:

select true; rec E_1(x) **last** 1 **by** 1 → S_1
or **true; rec** E_2(x) **last** 2 **by** 2 → S_2
or **true; delay** 3 → S_3
end

Assume that the execution of the select statement is ready to choose an alternative at time 0. Then, consider the following three scenarios: (i) if only one event (say E_1) occurs before time 3, then execute the statement following that input guard (i.e., S_1); (ii) if both E_1 and E_2 occur at the same time before time 3, then execute S_2 since event E_2 has priority over E_1 (note that execution of S_2 may start only at or after time 2 since E_2 is a durational event of duration 2); (iii) if no events occur before time 3, then execute S_3 at time 3.

8. *Sequential composition* (S_1; S_2): Execute S_1, and then execute S_2 if and when S_1 terminates.

9. *Parallel composition* (N_1 $//_C$ N_2): Execute networks N_1 and N_2 in parallel. Actions of N_1 and N_2 can and will occur at the same time unless prohibited by the synchronization constraints imposed on the set of joint events, C. The composite construct terminates when both networks have terminated.

10. *Hiding* ($[N]_C$): Hiding operation has no effect on the execution of network N but changes the visibility of internal communication; i.e., communications via local events in C are internalized and cannot be observed any more.

3. The Real-Time Execution Model

Interleaving model has been used intensively as a vehicle for specifying, verifying, and reasoning about concurrent programs. In this model, there may be an arbitrary delay between the execution of two consecutive actions. On the other hand, Salwicki and Müldner [20] proposed the *maximal parallelism* model (referred to as the MAXPAR model) for the modeling of distributed systems. In the MAXPAR model, every process has its own processor, and hence the processor waits only when it cannot do anything else due to the synchronization constraints. In other words, communications will occur at the earliest possible time and no unnecessary waiting is modeled. Koymans et al. [9] reported that these two models are in fact two extremes of the general spectrum of models. They proposed the $MAX_\gamma(\delta, \varepsilon)$ model as the general spectrum of models, where γ is the transmission delay, δ and ε correspond to the minimum and maximum times for initiation and receipt of communication requests in a network. Recently, Pnueli and Harel [19] pointed out that analysis based on the interleaving model is *qualitative* rather than *quantitative.* The eventuality can be guaranteed only under some *fairness* assumption. Therefore, the interleaving model is *unrealistic* for real-time applications since the execution of a statement may take an arbitrary delay.

In this paper, for simplicity, we use the $MAX_0(0, 1)$ model, (i.e., the pure MAXPAR model) as our execution model. We consider the time domain to be the domain of natural numbers. We assume that every primitive instruction takes one unit of time, and that it takes no time to initiate or recognize a communication request. Real-time is modeled in the communication histories by relating the i-th element of a history with the i-th tick of a conceptual global clock. Note that the assumption does not imply the presence of a global clock, and thus it is appropriate for a distributed system. For purposes of reasoning, this can be achieved by assuming the the presence of a clock at a meta-level for reasoning about partial ordering of the events in the language. For every process, we assume that there is a local clock, and the clocks can be synchronized among processes through message passing. In other words, it would be a relativistic model. It must however be noted that by this assumption we do not imply anything about the presence of such a physical global clock or the tightness of synchronization of local clocks.

4. Operational Semantics of RT-CDL

We use Plotkin's transition systems to define the semantics of RT-CDL. The crucial points of the operation semantics are (i) to capture all possible transitions, and (ii) to eliminate all illegal transitions.

The state of a process is captured by a state configuration of the form $<S, \sigma>$ or **abort**, where S is the statement to be executed and σ is the state function. A final configuration is of the form $<\varepsilon, \sigma>$ or **abort**. In other words, once a transition reaches a final configuration, no further transitions can be made. The state function $\sigma = <\sigma_p, \sigma_e>$ consists of two parts: σ_p for program variables and σ_e for event (auxiliary) variables. In order to capture the behavior of durational events, we keep an event counter for each imported event to record the total number of contiguous existences of that event.

We use the labeled transition of the form $<S, \sigma> \underset{k}{\overset{h}{\rightarrow}} <S', \sigma'>$ to capture the possible transition from one state configuration to another. The above transition can be interpreted as follows: when a process is in state σ with statement S to be executed, it takes the process k time units in the communication environment described by h to enter state σ' with statement S′ still to be executed. The communication history h is a sequence of set of communication assumption records (CAR's) as described below: We use (E!!, v) to denote the broadcast of event E with value v; (E?, v) to denote the receipt of event E with value v; E? to denote the engaging with event E (in this case, event E must exist, but the value has not been exchanged); and E to denote the waiting of event E (in this case, event E must not exist). In other words, h is a sequence over 2^Σ, where $\Sigma = \{(E!!, v), (E?, v), E?, E \mid E$ appears in the program$\}$.

Notation

In this presentation, for simplicity, we assume that each primitive instruction takes one unit of time. We give transitions which take one unit of time. For notational convenience, we follow the convention below:

- For unit step transitions of the form, $<S, \sigma> \underset{1}{\overset{<A>}{\rightarrow}} <S', \sigma'>$, where A is a set of CAR's, we write $<S, \sigma> \overset{A}{\rightarrow} <S', \sigma'>$ instead. If the transition is a local one, i.e., $A = \emptyset$, we write $<S, \sigma> \overset{\square}{\rightarrow} <S', \sigma'>$ to indicate that it is a local computation.
- For some technical reason to be discussed in the sequel, we introduce the λ-transition, $<S, \sigma> \underset{0}{\overset{\lambda}{\rightarrow}} <S', \sigma'>$, to indicate a transition which takes no time (k = 0) and generates empty history ($h = \lambda = < >$).

We also need the following auxiliary constructs:

- To capture various cases of termination, we define the predicate *empty* as follows: empty(ε) holds; if empty(S) holds, then empty(**during** Ev **do** S **end**) holds; if both empty(S_1) and empty(S_2) hold, then both empty(S_1; S_2) and empty($S_1 //_C S_2$) hold.
- $\sigma(e)$ returns the value of expression e under state function σ.
- $\sigma[e_1/x_1, ..., e_n/x_n]$ replaces the value of variable x_i by the value of e_i under state σ for $1 \le i \le n$.
- $\sigma_1 \times \sigma_2$ returns the joint state of σ_1 and σ_2.
- Val(x) returns the set of possible values for variable x.

Operational Semantics

In the following, we define the operational semantics of RT-CDL using structural induction on the statement list. For brevity and simplicity, we ignore both the **abort** configurations arising out of expression evaluation and transitions involving the **abort** configurations.

1. *Empty statement* (ε): $$\frac{\mathrm{empty}(S)}{\langle S, \sigma\rangle \xrightarrow[0]{\lambda} \langle \varepsilon, \sigma\rangle}$$

It takes no time to pass an empty statement. This is reflected by the λ-transition.

2. *Assignment* (x := e): $\langle x := e, \sigma\rangle \xrightarrow{\square} \langle \varepsilon, \sigma[e/x]\rangle$

Assignments are local computations (reflected by the history □) and take one time unit (one is omitted).

3. *Sleep statement* (**sleep**): $\langle \mathbf{sleep}, \sigma\rangle \xrightarrow{\square} \langle \mathbf{sleep}, \sigma\rangle$

Note that the sleep statement should be used in conjunction with the during statement. More precisely, it should be the last statement of a during statement as mentioned already.

4. *Broadcast statement* (**cast** E(e) **last** T): Operationally, the values of e and T are evaluated only once at the very beginning of the broadcast statement; therefore, we introduce the auxiliary construct—**cast***—to reflect this fact (shown in the axiom below).

(a) $\langle \mathbf{cast}\ E(e)\ \mathbf{last}\ T, \sigma\rangle \xrightarrow[0]{\lambda} \langle \mathbf{cast^*}\ E(\sigma(e))\ \mathbf{last}\ \max(1, \sigma(T)), \sigma\rangle$

Since we have assumed that primitive instructions take one unit of time, the transition takes one unit of time even if T is less than one.

The following two transitions capture the property that there is no waiting associated with the broadcast.

(b) $\langle \mathbf{cast^*}\ E(v)\ \mathbf{last}\ 1, \sigma\rangle \xrightarrow{\{(E!!,\ v)\}} \langle \varepsilon, \sigma\rangle$

(c) $$\frac{T > 1}{\langle \mathbf{cast^*}\ E(v)\ \mathbf{last}\ T, \sigma\rangle \xrightarrow{\{(E!!,\ v)\}} \langle \mathbf{cast^*}\ E(v)\ \mathbf{last}\ T - 1, \sigma\rangle}$$

5. *While statement* (**while** b **do** S **end**):

(a) $$\frac{\sigma(b)}{\langle \mathbf{while}\ b\ \mathbf{do}\ S\ \mathbf{end}, \sigma\rangle \xrightarrow{\square} \langle S;\ \mathbf{while}\ b\ \mathbf{do}\ S\ \mathbf{end}, \sigma\rangle}$$

(b) $$\frac{\neg\sigma(b)}{\langle \mathbf{while}\ b\ \mathbf{do}\ S\ \mathbf{end}, \sigma\rangle \xrightarrow{\square} \langle \varepsilon, \sigma\rangle}$$

6. *During statement with the timeout event* (**during** T → A **do** S **end**): Similar to the case of the broadcast statement, we introduce the auxiliary construct—**during***—to reflect the fact that T is evaluated only once.

(a) $\langle \mathbf{during}\ T\ \mathbf{do}\ S\ \mathbf{end}, \sigma\rangle \xrightarrow[0]{\lambda} \langle \mathbf{during^*}\ \max(1, \sigma(T))\ \mathbf{do}\ S\ \mathbf{end}, \sigma\rangle$

(b) $$\frac{T = 1, \neg\mathrm{empty}(S'), \langle S, \sigma\rangle \xrightarrow{h} \langle S', \sigma'\rangle}{\langle \mathbf{during^*}\ T \rightarrow A\ \mathbf{do}\ S\ \mathbf{end}, \sigma\rangle \xrightarrow{h} \langle A, \sigma'\rangle}$$

The above rule corresponds to the case that the period has expired before the end of the body is encountered.

(c) $$\frac{T > 1, \langle S, \sigma\rangle \xrightarrow{h} \langle S', \sigma'\rangle}{\langle \mathbf{during^*}\ T \rightarrow A\ \mathbf{do}\ S\ \mathbf{end}, \sigma\rangle \xrightarrow{h} \langle \mathbf{during^*}\ T - 1 \rightarrow A\ \mathbf{do}\ S'\ \mathbf{end}, \sigma'\rangle}$$

The above rule corresponds to the case that the period has not yet expired.

7. *During statement with a hard or soft event* (**during [interrupt]** E(x) **last** T → A **do** S **end**): In addition to evaluating T only once like the case of the during statement with the timeout event, the event counter must be reset to zero. This is reflected in the following axiom:

(a) $\langle \mathbf{during}\ E(x)\ \mathbf{last}\ T \rightarrow A\ \mathbf{do}\ S\ \mathbf{end}, \sigma\rangle \xrightarrow[0]{\lambda}$

$\langle \mathbf{during^*}\ E(x)\ \mathbf{last}\ \max(1, \sigma(T)) \rightarrow A\ \mathbf{do}\ S\ \mathbf{end}, \sigma[0/E]\rangle$

Note that the clause *last T* specifies a contiguous existence of the event E for T time units, and that this axiom also applies to the case of soft events, i.e., events with **interrupt** option.

For purposes of easier understanding, we describe the transitions in terms of local and non-local events. To distinguish local events from non-local ones, we define local(E) to be **true** if E is emitted by the process itself. The following four rules are for local events:

(b) $$\frac{\mathrm{local}(E), \bigwedge_{v \in Val(x)} (E!!, v) \notin h, \langle S, \sigma\rangle \xrightarrow{h} \langle S', \sigma'\rangle}{\langle \mathbf{during^*}\ E(x)\ \mathbf{last}\ T \rightarrow A\ \mathbf{do}\ S\ \mathbf{end}, \sigma\rangle \xrightarrow{\{E\} \cup h} \langle \mathbf{during^*}\ E(x)\ \mathbf{last}\ T \rightarrow A\ \mathbf{do}\ S'\ \mathbf{end}, \sigma[0/E]\rangle}$$

If event E does not exist, then the event counter E is reset to zero. This rule is applicable irrespective of whether the event is hard or soft.

(c) $$\frac{\mathrm{local}(E), (E!!, v) \in h, \sigma(E) < T - 1, \langle S, \sigma\rangle \xrightarrow{h} \langle S', \sigma'\rangle}{\langle \mathbf{during^*}\ E(x)\ \mathbf{last}\ T \rightarrow A\ \mathbf{do}\ S\ \mathbf{end}, \sigma\rangle \xrightarrow{\{E?\} \cup h} \langle \mathbf{during^*}\ E(x)\ \mathbf{last}\ T \rightarrow A\ \mathbf{do}\ S'\ \mathbf{end}, \sigma[E+1/E]\rangle}$$

This rule corresponds to the case that the event does exist but has not yet persisted for the complete specified period. Thus, the event counter is incremented by 1. The rule is also applicable to soft events.

(d) $$\frac{\mathrm{local}(E), (E!!, v) \in h, \sigma(E) = T - 1, \langle S, \sigma\rangle \xrightarrow{h} \langle S', \sigma'\rangle}{\langle \mathbf{during^*}\ E(x)\ \mathbf{last}\ T \rightarrow A\ \mathbf{do}\ S\ \mathbf{end}, \sigma\rangle \xrightarrow{\{(E!!,\ v)\}} \langle A, \sigma[v/x]\rangle}$$

This rule corresponds to the case that the hard event has persisted for the specified period, and hence the internal communication succeeds. Note that there is no need to set the event counter E to zero as the statement terminates after executing A rather than returning to the unfinished part of the body of the during statement. The corresponding rule for the soft event is given below.

(e) $$\frac{\mathrm{local}(E), (E!!, v) \in h, \sigma(E) = T - 1, \langle S, \sigma\rangle \xrightarrow{h} \langle S', \sigma'\rangle}{\langle \mathbf{during^*\ interrupt}\ E(x)\ \mathbf{last}\ T \rightarrow A\ \mathbf{do}\ S\ \mathbf{end}, \sigma\rangle \xrightarrow{\{(E?,\ v)\} \cup h} \langle A;\ \mathbf{during\ interrupt}\ E(x)\ \mathbf{last}\ T \rightarrow A\ \mathbf{do}\ S'\ \mathbf{end}, \sigma'[v/x]\rangle}$$

This is the counterpart of (d) for soft events. It may be observed that even here there is no need for setting the event counter E to zero as the only way of listening to event E would be again by passing through the during statement; that is why there is no * in the during statement after the transition.

The following four rules consider the case of non-local events: they are essentially similar to the case of local events. The next two rules apply to both soft and hard events.

(f)
$$\frac{\neg\mathrm{local}(E),\ \langle S, \sigma\rangle \xrightarrow{h} \langle S', \sigma'\rangle}{\langle \textbf{during*}\ E(x)\ \textbf{last}\ T \rightarrow A\ \textbf{do}\ S\ \textbf{end}, \sigma\rangle \xrightarrow{\{E\} \cup h} \langle \textbf{during*}\ E(x)\ \textbf{last}\ T \rightarrow A\ \textbf{do}\ S'\ \textbf{end}, \sigma[0/E]\rangle}$$

(g)
$$\frac{\neg\mathrm{local}(E),\ \sigma(E) < T-1,\ \langle S, \sigma\rangle \xrightarrow{h} \langle S', \sigma'\rangle}{\langle \textbf{during*}\ E(x)\ \textbf{last}\ T \rightarrow A\ \textbf{do}\ S\ \textbf{end}, \sigma\rangle \xrightarrow{\{E?\} \cup h} \langle \textbf{during*}\ E(x)\ \textbf{last}\ T \rightarrow A\ \textbf{do}\ S'\ \textbf{end}, \sigma[E+1/E]\rangle}$$

(h)
$$\frac{\neg\mathrm{local}(E),\ \sigma(E) = T-1,\ \langle S, \sigma\rangle \xrightarrow{h} \langle S', \sigma'\rangle}{\bigwedge_{v \in \mathrm{Val}(x)} (\langle \textbf{during*}\ E(x)\ \textbf{last}\ T \rightarrow A\ \textbf{do}\ S\ \textbf{end}, \sigma\rangle \xrightarrow{\{(E?,\, v)\}} \langle A, \sigma[v/x]\rangle)}$$

For external events, we have to consider all possible values to be exchanged.

(i)
$$\frac{\neg\mathrm{local}(E),\ \sigma(E) = T-1,\ \langle S, \sigma\rangle \xrightarrow{h} \langle S', \sigma'\rangle}{\bigwedge_{v \in \mathrm{Val}(x)} (\langle \textbf{during*}\ \textbf{interrupt}\ E(x)\ \textbf{last}\ T \rightarrow A\ \textbf{do}\ S\ \textbf{end}, \sigma\rangle \xrightarrow{\{(E?,\, v)\} \cup h} \langle A;\ \textbf{during}\ \textbf{interrupt}\ E(x)\ \textbf{last}\ T \rightarrow A\ \textbf{do}\ S'\ \textbf{end}, \sigma'[v/x]\rangle)}$$

8. *Select statement* (**select** $\mathop{\textbf{or}}\limits_{i=1}^{n} b_i;\ g_i \rightarrow S_i$ **end**): Similar to the case of broadcast and during statements, we introduce the **select*** construct to reflect the fact that the evaluation of boolean expressions, durational expressions, and priority expressions of guards and resetting of event counters of input guards are done only once at the very beginning of the select statement.

(a)
$$\frac{\bigwedge_{i=1}^{n} \neg\sigma(b_i)}{\langle \textbf{select}\ \mathop{\textbf{or}}\limits_{i=1}^{n} b_i;\ g_i \rightarrow S_i\ \textbf{end}, \sigma\rangle \xrightarrow{\Box} \textbf{abort}}$$

If all the guards are closed, then the statement aborts.

(b)
$$\frac{\sigma(b_k),\ g_k \equiv \varepsilon}{\langle \textbf{select}\ \mathop{\textbf{or}}\limits_{i=1}^{n} b_i;\ g_i \rightarrow S_i\ \textbf{end}, \sigma\rangle \xrightarrow{\Box} \langle S_k, \sigma\rangle}$$

The rule corresponds to choosing nondeterministically an open pure boolean guard.

(c)
$$\frac{\bigvee_{i=1}^{n} \sigma(b_i)}{\langle \textbf{select}\ \mathop{\textbf{or}}\limits_{i=1}^{n} b_i;\ g_i \rightarrow S_i\ \textbf{end}, \sigma\rangle \xrightarrow{\Box} \langle \textbf{select*}\ \mathop{\textbf{or}}\limits_{\sigma(b_i)} \mathrm{eval}(g_i, \sigma) \rightarrow S_i\ \textbf{end}, \mathrm{reset}(\bigcup_{\sigma(b_i)} \{g_i\}, \sigma)\rangle}$$

where function *eval* evaluates the durations as well as the priority expressions, and function *reset* resets the event counters for the open input guards to zero. This rule corresponds to the case that there are some open guards but without any open pure boolean guards. Note that the **select*** construct consists of only open guards, and hence we omit the boolean guards in the **select*** construct.

The transitions for input and delay guards are skipped since they can be derived from the during statement as follows:

rec E(x) **last** T ≡ **during*** E(x) **last** T → ε **do sleep end**
delay E(x) T ≡ **during*** T → ε **do sleep end**

(d)
$$\frac{\bigwedge_{i=1}^{n} (\langle g_i, \sigma\rangle \xrightarrow{h_i} \langle g_i', \sigma_i\rangle \wedge \neg\mathrm{empty}(g_i'))}{\langle \textbf{select*}\ \mathop{\textbf{or}}\limits_{i=1}^{n} g_i \rightarrow S_i\ \textbf{end}, \sigma\rangle \xrightarrow{\bigcup_{i=1}^{n} h_i} \langle \textbf{select*}\ \mathop{\textbf{or}}\limits_{i=1}^{n} g_i' \rightarrow S_i\ \textbf{end}, \times_{i=1}^{n} \sigma_i\rangle}$$

The rule corresponds to the case that no guards will be enabled at the next time-point with respect to the particular set of transitions for guards, $\bigwedge_{i=1}^{n} \langle g_i, \sigma\rangle \xrightarrow{h_i} \langle g_i', \sigma_i\rangle$.

(e)
$$\frac{\mathrm{maxEnabled}(g_k),\ \bigwedge_{i=1}^{n} (\langle g_i, \sigma\rangle \xrightarrow{h_i} \langle g_i', \sigma_i\rangle)}{\langle \textbf{select*}\ \mathop{\textbf{or}}\limits_{i=1}^{n} g_i \rightarrow S_i\ \textbf{end}, \sigma\rangle \xrightarrow{h_k \cup \{E_i \mid g_i \equiv \textbf{rec}\ E_i\ \textbf{last}\ T_i\ \textbf{by}\ p,\ T_i = \sigma(E_i)-1,\ \mathrm{pri}(g_i) > \mathrm{pri}(g_k)\}} \langle S_k, \sigma_k\rangle}$$

where $\mathrm{maxEnabled}(g_k) \triangleq \mathrm{empty}(g_k') \wedge \bigwedge_{\mathrm{empty}(g_i')} \mathrm{pri}(g_k) \geq \mathrm{pri}(g_i)$,

pri(**rec** E **last** T **by** p) = p, and pri(**delay** T) = 0.

This rule corresponds to the case that there are guards which will be enabled at the next time-point with respect to the particular set of transitions for guards as in (d), and a guard with the highest priority is selected. Note that the semantics gives the execution of input guards priority over that of delay guards. Hence, an delay guard can be selected only if no input guards are enabled at the next time point. Here, we have to ensure that all input guards having priority over the selected guard indeed cannot be enabled at the next time point. Thus, the communication history should consist of at most a communication symbol (if the selected guard is an input guard) and perhaps some waiting symbols for input guards which have priority over the selected guard (reflected by $\mathrm{pri}(g_i) > \mathrm{pri}(g_k)$) and might be enabled in the next time point with respect to another set of transitions (reflected by $T_i = \sigma(E_i) - 1$).

9. *Sequential Composition* (S_1; S_2):

(a)
$$\frac{\langle S, \sigma\rangle \xrightarrow{h} \langle S', \sigma'\rangle}{\langle S; S_1, \sigma\rangle \xrightarrow{h} \langle S'; S_1, \sigma'\rangle}$$

(b)
$$\frac{\mathrm{empty}(S),\ \langle S_1, \sigma\rangle \xrightarrow{h} \langle S', \sigma'\rangle}{\langle S; S_1, \sigma\rangle \xrightarrow{h} \langle S', \sigma'\rangle}$$

10. *Parallel Composition* ($N_1 //_C N_2$): The idea of binding two networks is to check if the communication histories over the joint events are compatible at all the time points. The set of joint events C can be computed from the declaration (specification) of the networks. Let us consider the following two cases:

(1) If network N_1 imports event E while network N_2 exports event E, then both E!! and E? are in C. In such a case, at every time point, the following conditions must hold: (i) the value received and emitted over a joint event must be the same; (ii) if the receiver claims the receipt or engaging (i.e.,

the existence) of a joint event, then the emitter must have broadcasted that event; and (iii) if the receiver claims the waiting of a joint event (i.e., the event must not exist), then the emitter must not broadcast that event.

(2) If both networks import event E, then only E? is in C and E!! is not in C. In this case, similarly, at every time point, the following conditions must hold: (i) if both receivers claim the receipt of a value over a joint event, then the value must be the same; and (ii) if a receiver claims the existence of a joint event, then the other receiver must not claim the non-existence of the same event, and vice versa.

Since there are no shared variables between two processes, for simplicity, we assume that each process uses distinct program variable names. Now, we can formally define the predicate *compat* as follows.

compat(h_1, h_2, C) holds if the following conditions hold:

(i) $\forall$ E? $\in$ C, E!! $\in$ C, i $\in$ {1, 2}:

$$(1)\ (E?, v) \in h_i \rightarrow (E!!, v) \in h_{3-i} \wedge$$
$$(2)\ E? \in h_i \rightarrow \exists v\, [(E!!, v) \in h_{3-i}] \wedge$$
$$(3)\ E \in h_i \rightarrow \forall v[(E!!, v) \notin h_{3-i}]$$

(ii) $\forall$ E? $\in$ C, E!! $\notin$ C, i $\in$ {1, 2}:

$$(4)\ (E?, v_1) \in h_i,\ (E?, v_2) \in h_{3-i} \rightarrow v_1 = v_2 \wedge$$
$$(5)\ E \in h_i \rightarrow \bigcup_v \{E?, (E?, v)\} \cap h_{3-i} = \emptyset$$

Note that the durational events have been captured in the communication histories. Therefore, when we compose two networks, we can check the compatibility of histories over the joint events without considering the state function for event variables σ_e. The parallel operator, $//_C$, is commutative (i.e., $N_1 //_C N_2 \equiv N_2 //_C N_1$), and the parallel composition of networks is reflected in the following two rules:

(a)
$$\frac{\bigwedge_{i=1}^{2} \langle N_i, \sigma_i\rangle \xrightarrow{h_i} \langle N_i', \sigma_i'\rangle,\ compat(h_1, h_2, C)}{\langle N_1 //_C N_2, \sigma_{1_p}\times\sigma_{2_p}\rangle \xrightarrow{h_1\cup h_2} \langle N_1' //_C N_2', \sigma_{1_p}'\times\sigma_{2_p}'\rangle}$$

Here, σ_p denotes the state function for program variables. Note that auxiliary event counters are no longer required for the composed network.

(b)
$$\frac{\langle N, \sigma\rangle \xrightarrow{h} \langle N', \sigma'\rangle,\ empty(N_1),\ compat(h, \Box, C)}{\langle N //_C N_1, \sigma_p\rangle \xrightarrow{h} \langle N' //_C \varepsilon, \sigma_p'\rangle}$$

This rule provides the transition for the case that one component network has terminated. The composed network terminates when both the component networks have terminated. From this rule, it should be clear that the state configuration $\langle N //_C \varepsilon, \sigma\rangle$ is not equivalent to $\langle N, \sigma\rangle$.

11. *Hiding of Networks* ($[N]_A$):

$$\frac{\langle N, \sigma\rangle \xrightarrow{h} \langle N', \sigma'\rangle}{\langle [N]_C, \sigma\rangle \xrightarrow{h\uparrow C} \langle [N']_C, \sigma'\rangle},\ \text{where}$$

$$h\uparrow C \triangleq h - (\{E, E?, (E?,v) \mid E? \in C\} \cup \{(E!!,v) \mid E!! \in C\}).$$

The transition corresponds to internalizing the local events. In other words, the transition can be obtained by considering the transitions of the network and projecting them onto the external events.

5. Concluding Remarks

The operational semantics we presented in this paper is based on the pure maximal parallelism model. The extension to a general one can be obtained by associating different waitvalues—instead of unit waitvalue—with each primitive instruction and considering the overhead required for communication requests. The operational semantics of RT-CDL not only gives information regarding the implementation details but also provides a base for the denotational semantics and the proof-system. In fact, we can derive a denotational semantics and a trace-based proof-system for RT-CDL easily based on the given operational semantics.

Our main aim is to bridge the gap between specifications and realization of real-time programs. In another paper [12], we showed the specification of programs in RT-CDL and discussed the usefulness of RT-CDL. Our investigation so far indicates that RT-CDL is a language suitable for most real-time reactive systems such as elevator control systems, robotics control systems, telecommunication systems, device control systems, and digital systems. We also showed that the real-time features provided by RT-CDL can be adapted for various exception handling mechanisms.

As mentioned in [18], the main thrust of constructing reliable reactive systems is towards a methodology that starts with a specification of a reactive system and gradually approaches a correct implementation. We are currently investigating how to develop RT-CDL programs from the behavior specifications. Since real-time reactive systems tend to be large and complex, the verification of such systems cannot be done without the aid of automatic tools. In [13, 14], we proposed a systematic way of reasoning about the temporal behaviors for real-time distributed systems in CSP-R (a CSP-like language with the delay construct [9]). One nice feature of the above approach is that the static analysis can be done in a *compositional* manner. We are currently working on the extension of such an approach to Ada as well as to RT-CDL. Our initial investigation revealed that the notion of static proof systems, syntactic proof systems, and general proof systems defined in [21] becomes handy in developing a sound methodology for deriving timing properties of programs in RT-CDL. Our approach not only provides a framework for the compositional specification and verification of real-time programs, but also can be used to detect and handle various real-time exceptions. Thus, our work leads to the development of reliable real-time systems.

ACKNOWLEDGEMENT

We would like to thank an anonymous referee of Fifth International Workshop on Software Specification and Design for the valuable comments.

REFERENCES

1. Benveniste, A., A Model to Analyse the Causality in Synchronous Real Time Systems, *IRISA/INRIA, Campus de Beaulieu, F 35042 RENNES CEDEX* , FRANCE, Apr. 1985, 1-28.

2. Berry, G. and Cosserat, L., The ESTEREL Synchronous Programming Language and its Mathematical Semantics, *LNCS 197* (1984), 389-448.

3. DoD, Reference Manual for the Ada Programming Language (American National Standards Institute/MIL-STD-1815A), Jan. 1983.

4. Gligor, V. D. and Luckenbaugh, G. L., An Assessment of the Real-Time Requirements for Programming Environments and Languages, *IEEE Real-Time Systems Symp.*, 1983, 3-19.

5. Harel, D., Pnueli, A., Schmidt, J. P. and Sherman, R., On the Formal Semantics of Statecharts (Extended Abstract), *Proc. Symposium on Logic in Computer Science*, 1987, 54-64.

6. Harel, D., Statecharts: A Visual Formalism for Complex Systems, *Science of Computer Programming 8* (1987), 231-274.

7. Huizing, C., Gerth, R. and de Roever, W. P., Modelling Statecharts Behaviour in a Fully Abstract Way, *Technical Report, Eindhoven University of Technology*, 1988.

8. Kligerman, E. and Stoyenko, A., Real-Time Euclid: A Language for Reliable Real-Time Systems, *IEEE Trans. on Software Eng. SE-12*, 9 (Sept. 1986), 941-949.

9. Koymans, R., Shyamasundar, R. K., de Roever, W. P., Gerth, R. and Arun-Kumar, S., Compositional Semantics for Real-Time Distributed Computing, *Proc. Logics of Programs, LNCS 193 (Extended full version to appear in Information and Computation)*, 1985.

10. Lee, I. and Gehlot, V., Language Constructs for Distributed Real-Time Programming, *IEEE Real-Time Systems Symp.*, 1985, 57-66.

11. Liu, L. Y. and Shyamasundar, R. K., Specification of Real-Time Programs in RT-CDL, *IEEE Fourth Workshop on Real-Time Operating Systems*, Cambridge, MA., July 1987, 110-119.

12. Liu, L. Y. and Shyamasundar, R. K., *Programming for Real-Time Reliable Reactive Systems*, Technical Report, Penn. State University, University Park, PA 16802, 1988.

13. Liu, L. Y. and Shyamasundar, R. K., Static Analysis of Real-Time Distributed Systems, *The 1988 Symposium of Formal Techniques in Real-Time and Fault-Tolerant Systems, University of Warwick, U.K., LNCS 331*, Sept. 1988, 134-138.

14. Liu, L. Y. and Shyamasundar, R. K., *Static Detection for Deadlocks, Distributed Terminations, and Timing Errors of Real-Time Distributed Programs*, Technical Report, Penn. State University, University Park, PA 16802 , 1988.

15. Parnas, D. L., The Non-Problem of Nested Monitor Calls, *ACM Operating Systems Review 12, 1* (1978), 12-14.

16. Plotkin, G. D., An Operational Semantics for CSP, *Formal Description of Programming Concepts - II, North Holland, IFIP*, 1983, 199-225.

17. Pnueli, A., Applications of Temporal Logic to the Specification and Verification of Reactive Systems: A Survey of Current Trends, *LNCS 224*, 1986, 511-584.

18. Pnueli, A., Specification and Development of Reactive Systems, *Information Processing 86, H. J. Kugler (ed.)*, 1986, 845-858.

19. Pnueli, A. and Harel, E., Applications of Temporal Logic to the Specification of Real Time Systems, *The 1988 Symposium of Formal Techniques in Real-Time and Fault-Tolerant Systems, University of Warwick, U.K., LNCS 331*, Sept. 1988, 84-98.

20. Salwicki, A. and Müldner, T., On the Algorithmic Properties of Concurrent Programs, *LNCS 125*, 1981.

21. Shyamasundar, R. K., Hooman, J. and Gerth, R., Proof Systems for Real-Time Distributed Programming, *Penn. State University CS-87-19*, June, 1987.

TIMING EXTENSIONS TO STRUCTURED ANALYSIS FOR REAL TIME SYSTEMS

Lawrence Peters
Software Consultants International, Limited
P. O. Box 5712
Kent, Washington 98042
(206) 631-4212

Abstract

The Structured Analysis method has been modified and extended to incorporate techniques for accurately estimating the execution time for real time systems during the analysis and/or design phases. This estimating technique enables the software engineer to incorporate the effects of external hardware devices, concurrency of processing, synchronization, priorities, interrupts, and other factors traditionally excluded from consideration by the *Structured Methods*. The methods which have been incorporated into Structured Analysis in order to address real time systems include an object oriented view of the relationship of priority to data items, formal means of evaluating system partitioning, and a specialized form of notation. Best, worst, and nominal times, blockage probabilities, and the effects of various resource allocation strategies can be evaluated in a timely and cost effective manner using this revised form of these methods. These extensions support safety and hazard analyses by cataloguing all possible modes of operation of the system being modeled. The application of this methodology is supported by and demonstrated on a software tool. This extension of Structured Analysis is referred to as HRT/DM (Hard Real Time Development Method).

Background

Structured Analysis [1] and its subsequent variations are the result of an evolutionary process. This process began with the need to write larger and more complex software systems which resulted in the use of the concept of a module as a vehicle to help control complexity. With this new found tool came a new problem, modules could interact in ways that produced undesirable side effects. Clearly, some rules or guidelines were needed to assist the software designer in creating a blueprint for a successful software system. Structured Design filled this need so well that it is probably the singly most widely used software design method today. But Structured Design is a product of its times and it does not address the needs of an intervening decade of technical advancement in software systems. Specifically, the focus of attention in the early to mid-seventies when Structured Design was first published were the dual issues of correctness and maintainability. The definition or specification of the problem a design was to be developed to solve was an additional concern addressed by Structured Analysis. More recently, modifications of the Structured Analysis method have been created in an attempt to address the issues associated with real time systems [2,3,4]. These extensions focussed on the incorporation of control flows into dataflow diagrams to better visualize real time systems [2,3]. While such modifications to the notation aid development of some systems, the two primary issues presented by real time systems have, heretofore, remained unaddressed. These issues are:

1. Establishing that the system can meet timing requirements

2. Cataloguing in a disciplined, deterministic manner the population of states the system may exhibit

None of the extensions previously published address either of these issues as expanded herein. Clearly, dataflow diagrams, even with control flow information added, cannot directly provide timing insights. Also, the concept of state has been treated in a largely subjective manner by previous extensions to Structured Analysis. That is, given the same information, would two different software engineers, working independently, create identical lists of states and time estimates? If a disciplined approach were used, the answer would be yes. An approach has been developed which makes this possible.

The examination of the issue of execution time also involves better graphic methods and a more disciplined view of the concept of priorities and states. These concepts have been combined together with elements of an advanced form of Structured Analysis and Design [4] in a methodology referred to as HRT/DM (Hard Real Time Development Method). This paper describes the features of HRT/DM which adequately addresses the multiple and interacting problems of fixed time requirements under a wide range of operating conditions, multiple processors, periodic and aperiodic interrupts, task prioritization, and system adaptation/reconfiguration in order to accommodate special situations.

Extensions to Structured Analysis

The Structured Analysis method has proven itself to be an effective means of defining and partitioning systems [4]. This effectiveness on simpler classes of systems has lead to it being applied to more complex systems, including real time applications. In order to make it more effective on real time systems, the data flow diagram notation has been modified to include both data and control flows. It is now evident that this form or extension does not address the primary problems associated with the analysis of real time systems. The nature of the problem makes it clear that modifying the notation cannot meet our needs. The methodology itself must be modified.

Conceptual Basis for HRT/DM

HRT/DM employs all of the concepts associated with Advanced Structured Analysis and Design [4] and supplements them, as necessary. These may be summarized as extending the scope of inquiry of the structured methods to supplement the Process view (data flows, pseudocode, structure charts) with two other complementary and necessary views. All three views are described below:

- *Process View* - This view graphically and conceptually presents the system as a set of interacting, mutually supporting processes. The techniques utilized in this view are data flow diagrams, structure charts, pseudocode, and dictionary to document the contents of these.

- *Event View* - This view presents the system as being composed of several states or modes of operation. The system is described as being able to move from one mode to another due to the occurrence of events or interrupts. Graphical techniques used to accomplish this include the use of event diagrams, state reachability matrices, and dictionary to document the contents of these.

- *Information View* - This view describes the relationships which exist between/among groups of data objects (referred to as entities). Entity relationship diagrams and dictionary are usually used to document these. However, this view is probably the least important and applicable view of the three to the problem of hard real time systems.

These dimensions form a "Systems Space" [5] within which systems reside (Figure 1). The problem with this approach is that there has not been agreement on what the conceptual and notational elements are which constitute the Event dimension.

The addition of control flows in the form of flags and signalling arrangements on data flow diagrams [2] has not shown itself to be effective at increasing our ability to address the timing issue [6]. This graphical approach was not adopted in HRT/DM. Rather than modifying an information flow oriented graphic technique such as the dataflow diagram, a different graphic technique was employed whose basis was oriented toward the general problem of asynchronous and concurrent processing.

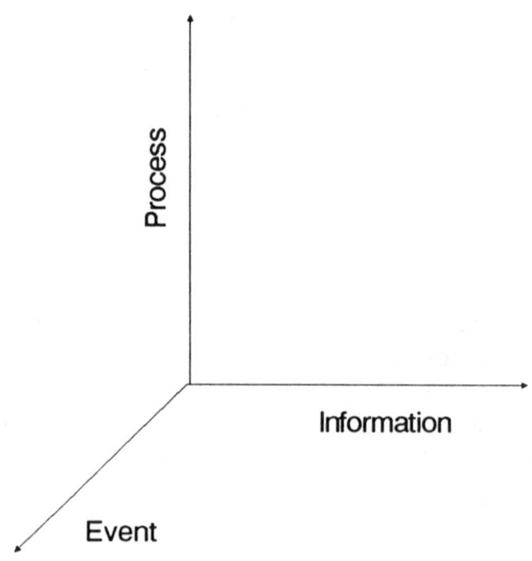

Figure 1: *The Assumed Systems Space*

To the previously listed set of methods and techniques, HRT/DM combines several supplementary and complementary concepts to address three areas of concern. These concerns are:

1. Validation and Refinement of the results of the analysis phase

2. Estimation of the timing of the (eventual) system

3. Safety and hazard analysis

To address the above concerns, the following concepts were tailored and introduced into Advanced Structured Analysis [4]:

- *Priority Attribution* - Priority has typically been thought of as being an inherent property of a module in the design and implementation phase and of a process in the analysis phase. HRT/DM views priority as being an inherent property of data NOT the process or module which produces that data. Another way to view this is that it is the output of a process which is vital, not the process itself. Hence, priority is a property which is inherent to data and this property can be imparted to the processes or modules which are involved in the production of a critical result. This may seem to be an unimportant distinction until one considers that priorities change as the operational state of the system changes. Hence, we need to be able to have a mechanism by which the priorities of processes and modules change as a natural outcome of state transitions taking place. This is easier to capture and refine using the data or object view than it is using the functional or modular view.

- *Input/Output Matrix Methods* - The role that Structured Analysis plays with respect to the design phase is much larger and important than previously recognized [4]. As a result, poor partitioning in the Structured Analysis work results in a poor starting point for the Structured Design activity. HRT/DM incorporates mathematical analyses in order to objectively evaluate the quality of the partitioning of the results of Structured Analysis activity.

- *Timing Estimation and Safety Analysis* - None of the currently available software system analysis and design methods address the estimation of execution time of the system being developed. One of the primary reasons for this is that the graphical methods employed by current methods were created to communicate among a large group of client and contractor personnel at technical as well as management levels. This notational need still exists and is not ignored by HRT/DM. However, HRT/DM does recognize the need for graphical representations which lend themselves to mathematical analysis and transformation into a form which is suitable for computation. HRT/DM has incorporated a modified form of the Petri net [7] which meets this need. With it, software engineers can identify potential timing problems early in the analysis phase and explore various options in order to resolve or improve problems.

- *Stimulus-Response Analysis* - The validation of data flow diagrams is a topic that has largely been treated from a subjective rather than an objective and deterministic standpoint. The idea of examining data flow diagrams from a stimulus-response standpoint has shown itself to be effective at detecting errors in systems which had been previously accepted as correct [8].

The remainder of this paper will focus on the use of the techniques related to timing estimation.

Notational Conventions

The notational components of HRT/DM are listed in Table 1. Most of the notational techniques shown in the figure have been described in considerable detail elsewhere [4,5,6]. However, the rules applied to the use of the Petri net within this context differ significantly from other applications [7]. These rules are presented in Table 2.

The graphical notation which leads to timing estimation is developed in conjunction with the DFD. The DFD is not used directly to obtain timing estimates but is used as a means of developing the Petri net from which these estimates can be obtained. Translation of the DFD into the Petri net appears to be simple. Each process in the DFD becomes a

Pseudocode
Data Flow Diagrams
Dictionary
Structure Charts
Event Diagrams
Input/Output Matrices
Stimulus-Response Tables
Petri nets
Entity-Relationship Diagrams

Table 1: *Notational Components*

- A transition can only "fire" if it is enabled
- A transition is enabled when all of its input places have a token in them
- A transition requires a finite time to complete
- A transition does not necessarily fire when it is enabled
- At any time, at least one transition will be firing
- A transition fires by removing tokens from its input and tokenizing its output places
- Places do not have duration (time)
- Places may contain multiple tokens
- A marking describes a condition or a set of conditions
- A state is a unique set of markings
- The reachability set is composed of all markings that are reachable from a predecessor state

Table 2: *Timing & Safety Analysis Conventions*

combination of Place (condition) and Transition (processor) in the Petri net. But there is semantic content in the DFD which must be retained in the Petri net. For example, in Figure 2, the DFD implies that any request is either of two types while the Petri net resulting from literal translation would behave differently. This Petri net would result in both the Perform_Proc_A and the Perform_Proc_B transitions being enabled. This is not consistent with the intent of the DFD from which this Petri net was derived. To address this, the "Guarded Conditional" construct has been introduced to aid in retaining the "sense" of the DFD in the resulting Petri net. The use of this construct is demonstrated in Figure 3.

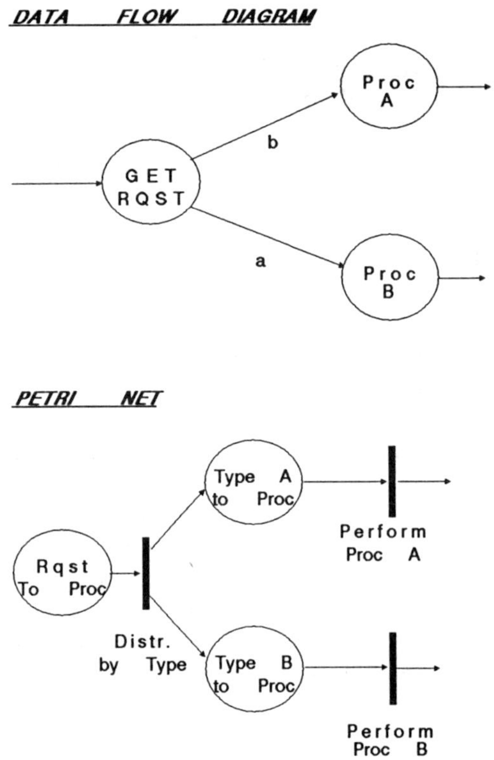

Figure 2: *Relationship Between DFD & Petri Net*

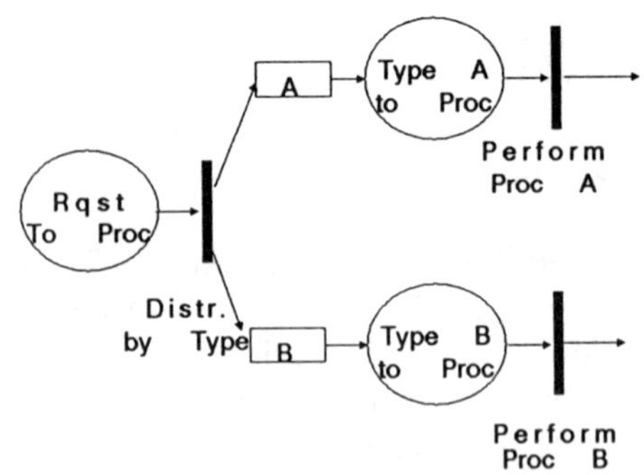

Figure 3: *Use of the Guarded Conditional*

The primary reason for initially incorporating Petri net concepts into Structured Analysis is the fact that Petri nets can quickly be represented mathematically. The timing equation for any given Petri net can be arrived at manually through appropriate linear combinations of the form:

$$t = SUM(i=1 \text{ to } n)\ N*D(T_i)$$

where

t = traversal time (i.e. the time required for the system to proceed from an initial to desired final state)
N = the number of transactions
D = stands for duration
T = stands for Transition or Process

Execution times for loops and other constructs can be developed in a similar manner. Due to the complexities involved, in this paper and other studies, we use a software tool to collect, store, document, validate, compute times and analyze safety factors for these networks. Although timing was the original goal, the use of safety and hazard analysis available from this technology is potentially as valuable.

In our timing analyses, it is assumed that the duration or delay associated with a transition may have a fixed value or be represented by a user defined function.

Since there may be variation in duration even for "fixed" times, it is recommended that three values for duration be employed. These are the minimum, maximum, and nominal. Some process durations are of this type. For example, in modeling the accessing of information from a fixed disk, we can quickly establish what the best or fastest access time will be (read head in best position), worst, and nominal access time. Nominal will correspond to the statistical average over a large number of cases.

The process for establishing a timing estimate using HRT/DM is relatively straightforward. However, it does require performance data that is both accurate and complete. Also, the rules regarding concurrency and synchronization of processes are not always as well defined in the analysis phase as they will be later. This results in an iterative process of "discovery." In addition, timing evaluation must be done on a computer. The steps leading up to a timing model of this type are listed below:

- Develop levelled and balanced data flow diagrams, dictionary, and pseudocode describing all processes.
- Detail and document via the dictionary each of the external systems and hardware devices interfaced with including but not limited to the microprocessor and communications link.
- Establish a conversion system from pseudocode to execution time for the target programming language(s) the system will be implemented in.
- Compute the maximum, minimum, and nominal execution times associated with each process (or module in the design phase) and record these in the dictionary data base.
- Develop a timed Petri net for the top level process treating other processes as externals for the time being.
- Create a set of data profiles for the top level process and compute the maximum, minimum, and nominal time values as predicted by the model.
- Calibrate the model by establishing the correlation between times predicted by the model and measured times on similar or analogous systems. If this is not possible, apply a "reasonableness" test on a temporary basis until such time as confirmation of these numbers is possible.
- Refine the model, necessary before proceeding to the incorporation of each of the systems and processors previously treated as externals. Recalibrate/cross check each one before incorporating the next.
- Create a data base of performance and interface values which will facilitate the exploration of "what if" scenarios with regard to the details of preliminary and detailed design issues. For example, these should include parameters which will enable the software engineer to study the effects of various prioritization schemes, mixes of processes running concurrently, processor performance characteristics, external device

performance characteristics, and other factors.

It is apparent that the full benefit of this methodology can only be realized through the extensive use of automation. Note that the graphics associated with the timing net are simple enough to be supported by a number of mechanisms ranging from specially developed to modification of existing packages. However, the interplay between an extensive and flexible data dictionary and pre-defined time equations which can be quickly and easily assembled to describe any data flow or structure chart situation is another matter.

Timing Estimation Example

For the purposes of this discussion, we will assume that the preliminary steps have all been completed successfully. Also, for this discussion we will assume that we are attempting to compute the average or nominal execution time for this system rather than the extremes. Hence, we will be using single valued times for the transitions. For this example, all transitions are assumed to have durations of 1 time unit. The dataflow diagram for the system being examined is presented Place-Transition-Interaction (PTI) format in Figure 4. It describes a previously published Petri net [9]. Execution time estimates, statistical analyses, and unique marking derivation were accomplished via a specialized software tool [10].

The results of this work take three forms. The first is the set of unique markings or states which can occur given the network and the timing characteristics of the transitions in it (Figure 5). The second is the timing analysis itself (Figure 6). For this example, the system was allowed to run to "exhaustion." That is, it ran until no more transition firings could occur. The third result is the transition statistics set (Figure 7). These detail how many times each transition fired, blockages that occurred and other factors. It should be noted that the concept of network reachability is not applicable in this method in the same way as it has been applied in other applications of Petri net technology. This is because of the role that transition times play. Changing transition times will change the unique marking set. For example, the combination of places 3 and 11 being marked is considered hazardous. These represent the crossing gate being up while the train is in the crossing. This can be eliminated in several ways. If we increase the duration of transitions associated with the train's approach (transitions t1 and t2) thus making the train travel slower in its approach to the crossing, we obtain a different unique marking set which does not contain the hazardous marking (Figure 8).

```
                        Transition #

Place # 01 02 03 04 05 06 07

     01        [I  -  -  -  -  -  -]
     02        [O  I  -  -  -  -  -]
     03        [-  O  I  -  -  -  -]
     04        [-  -  O  -  -  -  -]
     05        [O  -  -  I  -  -  -]
     06        [-  -  -  I  O  -  -]
     07        [-  -  -  O  I  -  -]
     08        [-  -  O  -  I  -  -]
     09        [-  -  -  O  -  -  I]
     10        [-  -  -  -  O  I  -]
     11        [-  -  -  -  -  O  I]
     12        [-  -  -  -  -  I  O]
```

Figure 4: *PTI Representation of Network*

```
                 Place #

 01 02 03 04 05 06 07 08 09 10 11 12

[1, 0, 0, 0, 0, 1, 0, 0, 0, 0, 1, 0]
[0, 0, 0, 0, 0, 1, 0, 0, 0, 0, 1, 0]
[0, 1, 0, 0, 1, 1, 0, 0, 0, 0, 1, 0]
[0, 0, 0, 0, 1, 1, 0, 0, 0, 0, 1, 0]
[0, 0, 0, 0, 0, 0, 0, 0, 0, 0, 1, 0]
[0, 0, 1, 0, 0, 0, 0, 0, 0, 0, 1, 0]
[0, 0, 1, 0, 0, 0, 1, 0, 1, 0, 1, 0]
[0, 0, 0, 0, 0, 0, 1, 0, 1, 0, 1, 0]
[0, 0, 0, 0, 0, 0, 1, 0, 0, 0, 0, 0]
[0, 0, 0, 1, 0, 0, 1, 1, 0, 0, 0, 0]
[0, 0, 0, 1, 0, 0, 1, 1, 0, 0, 0, 1]
[0, 0, 0, 1, 0, 0, 0, 0, 0, 0, 0, 1]
[0, 0, 0, 1, 0, 1, 0, 0, 0, 1, 0, 1]
[0, 0, 0, 1, 0, 1, 0, 0, 0, 0, 0, 0]
[0, 0, 0, 1, 0, 1, 0, 0, 0, 0, 0, 0]
```

Figure 5: *Unique Markings for Example*

```
Net run cycle at clock = 0
   [0,0,0,0,0,1,0,0,0,0,1,0] t1 initiated.

Net run cycle at clock = 1
   [0,1,0,0,1,1,0,0,0,0,1,0] t1 terminated.
   [0,0,0,0,1,1,0,0,0,0,1,0] t2 initiated.
   [0,0,0,0,0,0,0,0,0,0,1,0] t4 initiated.

Net run cycle at clock = 2
   [0,0,1,0,0,0,0,0,0,0,1,0] t2 terminated.
   [0,0,1,0,0,0,1,0,1,0,1,0] t4 terminated.
   [0,0,0,0,0,0,1,0,1,0,1,0] t3 initiated.
   [0,0,0,0,0,0,1,0,0,0,0,0] t7 initiated.

Net run cycle at clock = 3
   [0,0,0,1,0,0,1,1,0,0,0,0] t3 terminated.
   [0,0,0,1,0,0,1,1,0,0,0,1] t7 terminated.
   [0,0,0,1,0,0,0,0,0,0,0,1] t5 initiated.

Net run cycle at clock = 4
   [0,0,0,1,0,1,0,0,0,1,0,1] t5 terminated.
   [0,0,0,1,0,1,0,0,0,0,0,0] t6 initiated.

Net run cycle at clock = 5
   [0,0,0,1,0,1,0,0,0,0,1,0] t6 terminated.

End of net run at clock = 5
```

Figure 6: *Timing Results for Example*

ID	XC	IA	BT	FR	BP	DT
[t1,	1,	4,	0,	1,	0,	1]
[t2,	1,	4,	0,	1,	0,	1]
[t3,	1,	4,	0,	1,	0,	1]
[t4,	1,	4,	0,	1,	0,	1]
[t5,	1,	4,	0,	1,	0,	1]
[t6,	1,	4,	0,	1,	0,	1]
[t7,	1,	4,	0,	1,	0,	1]

```
Notes:
        ID = identifier of transition
        XC = execution count
        IA = # of cycles inactive
        BT = # of cycles blocked by transition
        FR = # of cycles firing
        BP = # of cycles blocked by place
        DT = duration time

Duration of Run: 5 time units
```

Figure 7: *Transition Statistics for Example*

ID	XC	IA	BT	FR	BP	DT
[t1,	1,	8,	0,	5,	0,	5]
[t2,	1,	8,	0,	5,	0,	5]
[t3,	1,	12,	0,	1,	0,	1]
[t4,	1,	12,	0,	1,	0,	1]
[t5,	1,	12,	0,	1,	0,	1]
[t6,	1,	12,	0,	1,	0,	1]
[t7,	1,	12,	0,	1,	0,	1]

```
Duration of Run: 13 time units
```

Figure 8: *Transition Statistics for Revised Network*

In this example we have concentrated on a simple, single level network. More complex models can be addressed. Due to the relationship between the DFD and the Petri net, the decomposition of various processes in the DFD would be paralleled in the Petri net. Since each process in the DFD results in at least one place and one transition, additional simplification techniques must be employed to reduce the complexities of the resulting graphs. One effective technique is to replace selected portions of a Petri net at a given level with a single transition. The timing associated with this transition would be derived from the lower level graph associated with it through this imposed process of decomposition. These techniques result in Petri net models which have transitions which decompose into subordinate networks or "subnets." These may contain transitions which also decompose into subnets. Timing and other analyses of these more complex models make manual evaluation impractical and require automated support [10].

Conclusions

A viable means of determining the timing characteristics of hard real time systems has been developed. It is an extension of an established software analysis methodology. The primary emphasis of this method is the effective use of the synergism which exists among data flow, logic flow, and concurrency oriented techniques. It is not suggested that the DFD be abandoned in favor of the Petri net as employed here nor is the reverse position being promoted. Rather, the specialized, mutually supportive role that both concepts play in an improved technology has been described and demonstrated.

References

1. "Structured Analysis and System Specification," T. De Marco, Yourdon Press, New York, N.Y., 1978.

2. "Structure Analysis of Real Time Systems," P. Ward and S. Mellor, Yourdon Press, New York, N.Y., 1981.

3. "Strategies for Real Time System Specification," D. Hatley and I. Pirbhai, Dover Press, New York, N.Y., 1987.

4. "Advanced Structured Analysis and Design," L. Peters, Prentice Hall, Englewood Cliffs, N.J., 1988.

5. "Structured Development of Real Time Systems," Seminar by Software Consultants International Limited, Kent, WA., 1988.

6. "Computer-Aided Systems and Software Engineering Products for Time-Critical Applications Development," Software Productivity Solutions, under NADC contract N6229-86-C-0415, April 1988.

7. "Petri Net Theory and the Modeling of Systems," J.L. Peterson, Prentice Hall, Englewood Cliffs, N.J., 1981.

8. Deutsch, M.S., "Focusing Real-Time Systems Analysis on User Operations," IEEE Software, Vol. 5, No. 5, (1988), pp. 39-49.

9. Leveson, N.G. and Stolzy, J.L., "Safety Analysis Using Petri Nets," IEEE Trans. on Software Engineering, Vol. SE-13, No. 3, (1987), pp. 386-397.

10. "ProTEM Systems Modeling Tool," Software Consultants Intl. Ltd.; Kent, WA, 1988, 1989.

REASONING OF REAL-TIME DISTRIBUTED PROGRAMMING LANGUAGES *

R.K. Shyamasundar
Pennsylvania State University and
Tata Institute of Fundamental Research

J. Hooman, R. Gerth
Eindhoven University of Technology

Abstract

Two important features of a real-time distributed programs are: establishing the logical correctness of the program using realistic models and establishing timing properties or deriving timing constraints. In this paper, we provide a hierarchy of proof techniques for deriving the timing properties of real-time distributed programs. First, we provide a static characterization of real-time distributed programs using the maximum-parallelism model and show that several interesting timing characteristics can be derived from such an analysis. The static analysis is based on complete trace structures and hence, we can specify various classes of safety (including deadlock), eventuality properties uch as eventual stability (persistance), recurrence, progress etc as well as parallel actions, and timing constraints. Based on prefix-closed trace structures (under the maximal parallelism model), we define two proof systems referred to as syntactic and general proof systems. The syntactic proof system uses assertions (postulates) attached to the I/O commands (essentially, reflecting the enablement or otherwise of the guards) rather than state information. Using such a system, we establish that we can refine several of the timing properties obtained by the static analysis. All the proof systems are compositional and they form a hierarchy. The hierarchy not only establishes the consistency of the systems but also provides the user a selection of proof systems depending on the requirements. Further, the algorithms based on the static analysis lead to algorithmic derivation of the timing properties of a wide variety of real-time programs.

1 Introduction

The major criterion in real-time programming is to write a program to respond to externally generated input stimuli within a controllable delay (cf. [Yo 83]). In spite of a proliferation of real-time embedded systems since a long time, there has been very little attention given to the development of a sound methodology for the development and reasoning of real-time programs. Wirth [Wir 77] was the first to highlight the importance of real-time programs and the difficulties of reasoning of real-time programs. There has not been a good progress towards a sound methodology even though there has been a considerable amount of work on real-time systems (cf. [Da85, JM 86]) with an emphasis on specifying/validating the timing constraints. One of the major reasons for such an approach is the following. In the case of real-time systems, one would typically be interested in verifying only certain parts of the timing constraints or the program properties rather than a complete verification of the program ([Ho 87]). For example, one could be interested in verifying timing properties or the constraints given the functional or the relational properties (which in turn might have been established by some other means (formal or otherwise)). In other words, there is a growing need [1] for the investigation of a spectrum of methods from which the programmer can choose the method according to his requirements. Further, if the systems of reasoning form a hierarchy, it it would be very attractive as the user can refine the timing constraints derived using the next system in the hierarchy. In this paper, we outline such an investigation.

We follow the general definition of a real-time distributed system to be a system in charge of controlling and monitoring a physical process that is governed by a set of internal laws given a priori [LL 83]. Such internal laws which define the *natural* behaviour of the physical process are functions of a parameter usually known as the ***physical time***. We consider languages which are capable of modeling such behaviour as real-time distributed programming languages. In [KSR 85], we have carried out an investigation to obtain a semantic characterization of real-time distributed programming language using realistic models. The investigation has led to a compositional semantics for CSP-R (extension of CSP with real-time features) using a spectrum of models ranging from interleaving to maximum-parallelism. One of the main features of the semantics described in [KSR 85] is that it is compositional and thus supplies a basis for compositional specification and verification technique. In this paper, we investigate techniques for deriving properties of real-time distributed programs in CSP-R based on the semantic foundations provided in [KSR 85]. The main results are summarized below:

1. First, we provide a static characterization of real-time distributed programs using the maximum-parallelism model and show that many interesting timing characteristics can be derived. The characterization is based on complete trace structures and thus enables one to specify various classes of eventuality properties such as eventual stability, recurrence, progress etc. The trace structure has very nice properties such as closed under parallel composition, hiding etc. Another interesting feature is that it is amenable for automation. Thus, it is very useful in practice for deriving timing properties for a wide class of real-time programs.

2. Next, we develop two classes of proof systems referred to as syntactic proof system and general proof system based on prefix-closed sets of traces. In the syntactic proof system, we use assertions (postulates) attached to the I/O commands (essentially, reflecting the enablement or otherwise of the I/O guards) instead of the state information. Using this proof system, we show how we can refine various timing properties of real-time programs that require some state information. The general proof system uses the complete state information and can be shown to be complete.

*The work is done as part of the Esprit Project 937: *Debugging and Specification of Ada Real-Time Embedded Systems(DESCARTES)*; The financial support is gratefully acknowledged.

[1] The view of Amir Pnueli (cf.[Pn 86]) that *reactive systems* are systems that cannot be adequately described by the relational or functional view reaffirms such a need.

3. Finally, we show the consistency of the proof systems with reference to the semantics and establish that the three systems actually form a hierarchy. This feature gives a choice of verification systems for verifying timing properties.

1.1 Language Syntax

In CSP-R, processes communicate via unidirectional channels and a channel connects exactly two processes.

D,W - stand for channel variables;
x,u - stand for program variables;
e - stands for expressions;
b - stands for boolean expressions.

Program: P ::= S | N
Statement: S ::= x:=e | skip | g | wait d | $S_1; S_2$ | A | *A | [N]
guard: g ::= b | D?x | W ! e | wait d | b;D?x | b;W!e | b;wait d
Alternative: A ::= [$[]_{i=1}^{n} g_i \rightarrow S_i$]
Network: N ::= $S_1 || S_2$

The informal semantics of the language follows on the lines of the semantics of CSP-R given in [KSR 85, GHR 86]. For the sake of completeness, we provide the interpretation of those commands that deviate from that of CSP [Hoa 78].

Interpretation of ***alternative command:*** first check if none of the guards is open. If this is the case, the execution aborts; otherwise, check whether there is at least one open pure boolean guard and select one of them nondeterministically. In case there is no open boolean guard but there is at least one other open guard the execution proceeds in the following way. The ***waitvalue*** is defined to be infinite if there are no open wait guards; otherwise, it is defined to be the maximum of 1 and the minimum of the values of the durations of the open wait guards. Let us the denote the waitvalue by d. As soon as there is a possible semantic match for the open I/O command, the communication action takes place (the selection of the semantically matching commands is nondeterministic). However, if no semantic match occurs within this d units, then one of the open wait guards with waitvalue equal to d is selected nondeterministically. It may be observed that we have assumed a priority for the boolean guards over the communication guards.

The interpretation of a ***repetitive command*** is the repeated execution of the alternative command contained in it. However, the execution terminates properly whenever none of the guards is open.

Hiding has no effect on the execution of S but changes what can be observed about such executions: communications along channels in N are internalized and cannot be observed any more.

1.2 Model of Real-Time and Execution

We assume that time proceeds in discrete time steps. Our time domain is the set of natural numbers. For the sake of simplicity, we further assume that all elementary actions (such as assignment and communication) take one unit of time. Parameterization with respect transmission time of the network, range of values for actions (cf.[KSR 85]) are ignored for the sake of simplicity. In other words, real-time is modeled by relating the ith element of a history with the ith tick of a conceptual global clock. However, it should be noted that we do not either imply the existence of a global clock or assume the tightness of synchronization of the processor clocks.

A real time execution model is only useful, if we can make some assumptions about the progress each process is due to make. In this paper, we use the ***maximum parallelism*** model (MAXPAR for short). In MAXPAR model, at any instant of time all actions that can be started without any conflict will be initiated. In other words, we assume the existence of a processor for every process. That is, a process is only allowed to idle only if all communication partners are unwilling to communicate and there are no local actions possible at that point.

2 Static Characterization of Real Time Processes

A general idea for the description of processes is to characterize the behavior of a process by the set of all possible execution sequences. In the absence of shared variables, communications are the reactions of the processes with the environment. In other words, the main events of the system are the communications of each process. In a real-time system where time response is critical, one reasonable assumption is to place a bound on the time from one event to another event. In other words, the bound on the time indicates the time required for the local computation or the time for which the process would wait for external stimuli. Now, we can capture the environmental behavior of each process if we can specify the relative timing constraints between events of each process. The main events could be classified as :

1. communication points,
2. readiness points (the point at which a process could be ready to communicate on various channels),
3. local actions

We statically characterize each process a priori through a regular expression over the alphabet of events. Such a characterization for CSP programs has been studied in [Apt 83]. However, note that Apt does not discuss either real-time or algorithms for the composite description of processes. bf Alphabet: Our basic alphabet is given by, $\Sigma = D \cup \{\Box\} \cup \{R(A)\}$, where D is a set of channel names, $\Box$ represents an internal action and R(A) represents the set of channels,A, over which the process is willing to send or receive. As we would like to represent concurrent actions, we extend the alphabet to the power set of Σ denoted by P(Σ) (i.e. 2^{Σ}).

Notational Interpretation:

1. (D) represents an input/output event over channel d. Note that in these events the actual value received or sent is of no concern to us.
2. R({D}) represents the readiness of the process to receive/send a message (value) over channel D.
3. Let A be a set of channel names. Then, R(A) represents represents the readiness of the process to do any of the actions in A. We follow the convention that when A = ϕ then R(A) is the same as $\Box$.
4. We assume for the sake of simplicity that each action takes one unit of time and hence $\Box_t$ corresponds to some internal action(s) that takes a total time of t units.
5. $[R(A)]_0^t = \cup_i [R(A)]^i \forall 0 \leq i \leq t$ and
$[R(A)]^* = \cup_i [R(A)]^i \forall 0 \leq i \leq \infty$.

Language: We define a ***language*** L(Σ) to be a subset of $\rho(\Sigma)^*$; note that ϵ denotes the empty string. In other words, the language denotes some subset of sequences over $\rho(\Sigma)$. Note that using $\rho(\Sigma)$ instead of just Σ enables us to consider possible parallel actions and thus, enables us to specify true parallelism.
As in regular languages, if L1 and L2 are two languages then L1 L2 stands for the ***product*** of languages and L^* stands for the Kleene closure of L(i.e. $L^* = \cup_i L^i$).

For the sake of easy reference, the languages will be referred to as *L-exprs*.

Abbreviations:

1. We represent singleton sets of the form {X} where X is some sequence over $\rho(\Sigma)$ by X itself.
   For example $\{\{\Box\}\{\Box, R(D)\}\{D\}\}$ is denoted by $\Box\{\Box, R(D)\}D$; and $\Box\Box\Box$ denotes $\{\{\Box\}\{\Box\}\{\Box\}\}$.

2. $\Box^0$ denotes $\{\epsilon\}$; $\Box^d$ denotes $\Box\Box...\Box$ (i.e. $\{\{\Box\}\{\Box\}...\{\Box\}\}$ – repeated d-times); $\Box^\infty$ denotes $\cup_{i=0}^{\infty}\Box^i$.
   We use the same notation for elements of the form R(D).

3. A set of more than one sequence is often denoted by means of the union, i.e. $\{seq_1, seq_2\} = \{seq_1\} \cup \{seq_2\}$. For example, $\Box\Box B \cup R(D)\{\Box, \Box\}$ denotes $\{\{\Box\}\{\Box\}\{B\}, \{R(D)\}\{\Box, D\}\}$.

In static evaluation, we need to know whether an expression (arithmetic or boolean) can be evaluated statically. For this purpose, we assume a function, *stat* from Exp $\rightarrow$ {true false} ; stat(e) = true corresponds to the interpretation that the expression is statically evaluatable and stat(e) = false corresponds to the fact that the expression cannot be evaluated statically.

3 A Priori Static Characterization

We associate a regular language to a process P_i using structural induction on the statement-list of each process as follows.
1. L(*skip*) = L(x:=e) = $\{\Box\}$
2. L(*wait d*) = $\{\Box^{d_v}\}$ where d_v = *if* stat(d) *then* value of d *else* *.
Note that "*" corresponds to considering all the possibilities since there is no bound on d statically.
3. L(D?x) = $\{[R(D)]^*(D)\}$
Here, R(D) denotes the readiness of the process to receive a message (value) over channel D and (D) reflects the actual communication; note that the actual value received is not of relevance. The implicit operator between the two terms is the usual ***concatenation*** operator.
4. L(W!e) = $\{[R(W)]^*(W)\}$
5. *Sequential Composition*: $L(s_1; s_2) = L(s_1)\ L(s_2)$
In other words, we associate the product of the languages of the component processes for the sequential composition.
6. *Alternative Command:* $[[]_i^m\ b_i; g_i \rightarrow S_i]$

As we are looking for a regular language that can be associated with a process ignoring the boolean guards, we have to consider all the possible waiting times ignoring the boolean guards. Essentially, we have to evaluate (i) waiting possibilities (bounded/unbounded) and (ii) the possible set of actions at a selection point statically.

Static Delay Information:

Assuming the wait values to be statically evaluatable (in a sense, this reflects the assumption that we know the time bound for each action and delay a priori), let $W = \{d_1, d_2, ..., d_r\}$ be the set of wait values. In case we do not have any a priori bound on d, we have to consider all possible values that can be taken by d. Without loss of generality, we assume that d_i is nonnegative for all i. Without evaluating the boolean guard, we can say that the delay would be bounded only if there exists a true boolean guard irrespective of the state of the process. In other words, we can say that the delay can be bounded if there is a wait guard (or a pure boolean guard) that can be syntactically transformed to TRUE. Let $W\prime \subseteq W$ be the set of wait values for which the corresponding boolean guard is always true irrespective of the state. Let d be the maximum waiting period at the alternative command. The value of d can be evaluated as follows:

if there exists a pure boolean guard which is always true
  then d = 0
  else
    if $W\prime \neq \phi$ then d = MIN($W\prime$)
      else d = ∞

In other words , if $W\prime = \phi$ and there is no pure boolean guard that is true always then d = ∞ (i.e. unbounded); otherwise d will be bounded a priori. Also note that a negative delay value is the same as zero delay.

Set of Ready Actions:

Let type(D?x) = type(D!e) = D. Note that whether a channel is an output channel or an input channel can be statically determined.

The maximum set of possible communication actions corresponding to this alternative command ignoring the boolean guards is given by, $A_{max} = \{type(g_i) | \forall i\}$.

The minimum (always guaranteed irrespective of the state) set of communication actions corresponding to this alternative command is given by $A_{min} = \{type(g_i) | \forall i,\ such\ that\ b_i \equiv TRUE\}$.

As the boolean guards are uninterpreted, all the possible set of actions ranging between these the sets A_{max} and A_{min} have to be considered (essentially possible world of actions). Assuming that there is no guard that can be syntactically transformed to FALSE, the behaviour expression is given below:

$L([[]_i^m b_i;\quad g_i \rightarrow S_i]) =$
(1).. $\quad L(S_i)\ if\ g_i \equiv\ skip\ i.e.\ it\ is\ a\ pure\ boolean\ guard;$
(2).. $\quad \cup_{A_{min} \subseteq A \subseteq A_{max}} [R(A)]^* (\cup_i L(b_i; g_i \rightarrow S_i))$
$\qquad \forall g_i\ of\ the\ form\ D?x\ or\ D!e\ in\ A\ if\ d = \infty$
(3).. $\quad \cup_{A_{min} \subseteq A \subseteq A_{max}} [R(A)]_0^{d-1} (\cup_i L(b_i; g_i \rightarrow s_i))$
$\qquad \forall g_i\ of\ the\ form\ D?x\ or\ D!e\ in\ A, d \neq \infty$
(4).. $\quad \cup_{A_{min} \subseteq A \subseteq A_{max}} \cup_i [R(A)]^{d_i} L(s_i)$
(5).. $\qquad \forall\ d_i \epsilon W\ if\ d = \infty$
(6).. $\qquad \forall\ d_i \epsilon W\ and\ d_i \leq d \neq \infty$
$\qquad for\ guards\ of\ the\ form\ b_i; wait\ d_i$

(1) corresponds to the case of pure boolean guards; associating an empty language with pure boolean test is reflected here; The relation (2) reflects the semantics of the alternative construct with delay guards and corresponds to the behavior corresponding to the case when there is no a priori bound on the delays. Note that, we consider all subsets of ready actions ranging from the minimum possible to the maximum possible. This is expressed by : $A_{min} \subseteq A \subseteq A_{max}$ as the boolean guards are ignored. Note that A = ϵ is ruled out as we are considering the corresponding action to be in A. Relation (3) corresponds to taking the action after the delay value of the concerned guard corresponding to the situation of a priori bounded delay. As we are ignoring the boolean guards, we have to consider all the wait values irrespective of whether it is the minimum or not. However, it cannot be more than the minimum wait-value,i.e. d; that is the reason for considering all the values from 0 to d-1; Relation(4) corresponds to the language associated with the delay guards. In the case of the delay guards, the statement-list can be executed after a time equal to the delay value; in case there is an a priori bound the values which are higher than the minimum wait-value can be ignored. The relation(5) corresponds to the case when there is no a priori bound on the minimum wait – in such a case all the possible wait values are to be considered. When there is an a priori bound, we have to consider only those that are less than the minimum (i.e. d) – this is reflected in (6). Also, note that R(A) when A = ϵ is the same as $\Box$.

7. Test : $L(b_i) = \{\epsilon\}$

As we are ignoring the time for evaluation of the boolean, we are associating ϵ (i.e. the empty string) with the boolean test; another possibility would be to associate a unit time cost; in the latter case the language associated would be $\{\Box\}$. Note that we cannot associate an empty set (ϵ) for obvious reasons.

8. *Iteration:* $L(*A) = L(A)^*$

Simple Example:
$P \equiv [D?x \rightarrow T_1\ []wait2 \rightarrow W?x]$
$L(P) = [R(\{(D)\})]_0^1 (D) \Box^{T_1} \cup [R(\{D\})]^2 (W)$
where T_1 represents the time for the local action.

3.1 Parallel Composition of Processes

In the following, we define some operations on the languages that will enable us to characterize parallel composition of processes given the characterization of individual processes under the MAXPAR model.

Notation:

1. If C is a set of communication channel names then $h|C$ denotes the sequence obtained from h by ignoring the elements not in C and deleting all the ready-records. Note that the empty set is denoted by □ and thus the projection preserves the length (or the time-points). We use the notation $h^C[k]$ to represent the kth element of $h|C$.

2. We define the projection of any element to its ready-set by, $h^r[k] = \cup_{R(A)\epsilon h[k]} A$. That is, $h^r[k]$ gives the ready-sets of the kth element of the sequence h.

Definition 1: Let h_1, h_2 be any traces in the behaviour expressions L(P_1) and L(P_2) of processes P_1 and P_2 respectively. Let *cset* be the common set of channels in P_1 and P_2 (note that cset could be a superset of the common set of channels). Then, h_1, h_2 are said to be *consistent* iff $\forall c \epsilon cset$, $\forall$ k, $h_1^c[k] = h_2^c[k] \wedge h_1^r[k] \cap h_2^r[k] = \epsilon$.
Informally, h_1, h_2 are consistent means that the sequences are communication compatible and satisfies the MAXPAR property i.e. there is no unnecessary waiting.

Definition 2: Given that h_1, h_2 are consistent, $h_1 \# h_2$ is defined as follows:
Let $h1\#h2$ = H[1]...H[m] where m = max(|$h1$|, |$h2$|) and H[i] is defined below: $H[k] = h1[k] \cup h2[k]$ *for* $1 \leq k \leq min(|h1|, |h2|)$, and for $min(|h1|, |h2|) < k \leq max(|h1|, |h2|)$, it is given by

$$H[k] = \begin{cases} h1[k]\ if & |h1| > |h2[k]| \\ h2[k]\ if & |h2| > |h1[k]| \end{cases}$$

Definition 3: The *merging* of two languages L(P1) and L(P2), denoted $L(P1)||L(P2)$ is defined as follows:
$L(P1)||L(P2) = \{h1\#h2 | h1 \epsilon L(P1), h2 \epsilon L(P2)\ are\ consistent\}$.

Definition 4: The parallel composition of two processes is given by $L(P1||P2) = L(P1)||L(P2)$.

Definition 5: $L([N]) = \{hide(h, jchan) | h \epsilon L(N)$, *jchan* is the set of internal channels of N$\}$, where *hide(h,jchan)* is the sequence obtained from h after mapping the communication records and ready records corresponding to the channel names in *jchan* to □ (thus preserving the time point).

Illustrative Example: We use the notation of enclosing a non-singleton element of a sequence within angle brackets. Singleton sets will not be enclosed within angle brackets. Consider the program given below.

```
Cons:: *[D?x → Compute(2 time units)
        [] W?y → Compute (3 time units) ]

P1:: *[ D!e → Compute (3 time units)]
P2:: *[W!e → Compute (4 time units) ]
```

L(Cons) = $\{([R(\{D,W\}]^*(D□□ \cup W□□□))\}^*$
L(P1) = $\{([R(\{D\})]^*(D□□□))\}^*$
L(P2) = $\{([R(\{W\})]^*(W□□□□))\}^*$

Using the merging definition we get,

$$L(Cons||P1) = (D□□ R(\{D,W\}) \cup(< W, R(\{D\}) > R(\{D\})R(\{D\})R(\{D\}) \cup D□□ W R(\{D\})R(\{D\})R(\{D\}))*$$

$$L(Cons||P1||P2) = \ < D, R(\{W\}) > [R(\{W\})R(\{W\})W R(\{D\})R(\{D\})R(\{D\})D]* \cup < W, R(\{D\}) > [R(\{D\})R(\{D\})R(\{D\})DR(\{W\})R(\{W\})W]*$$

From the merged expression, it can be observed that the the producers alternate as unnecessary waiting is disallowed (the first communication is nondeterministic). From the expression it is clear that the process CONS never waits for an input. That is, P1 and P2 succeed in sending the value in every 8 units.

In general, the timing behavior can be obtained by considering the maximum distance between consecutive communication elements of the alphabet. Also, the maximum delay for an action could be obtained by considering the maximum length of the consecutive *ready* elements.

The following closure properties lead to the development of algorithms for deriving timing properties.

Theorem 1: The behaviour expressions are closed under parallel composition and hiding.

Proof: The closure properties follow by transforming a behaviour expression into a finite state machine and then constructing [2]a finite state machine for the parallel composition of the machines.

Using the above closure properties, efficient algorithms have been developed for deriving safety, liveness and timing properties in [LS 87].

Nonterminating Systems: Many times, it is convenient to distinguish two states: never terminating and finite behaviors. The former is essential, when we want to treat reactive systems. The construct of the language that could lead to nonterminating behaviour is the iterative construct. In the case of nonterminating systems, the language associated with the iterative command can be obtained as follows:
Consider the nonterminating process,
$S \equiv *A$ where $A \equiv *[true \rightarrow D?x]$. The language for this process is given by,

L(S) = $L(A)^*$ if there is no pure boolean guard that is always true
= $L(A)^*@$ if there is one guard that is always true
where @ is some new symbol.

As a result of the above definition, the sequential composition is redefined as follows:

L(S1;S2) = L(S1) L(S2) if L(S1) is not of the form ending in @;
= L(S1) if L(S1) is of the form that ends in @.

The other analysis remains the same. The sentinel symbol, @, will enable us to consider *never-terminating* behaviors. This modified language will be used to distinguish the nonterminating and plausibly terminating states. The language synthesis can now be done using a Büchi automaton instead of the finite state automaton. The details of construction are given in [LY 88].

Consistency: Now, let us consider the consistency of the analysis with reference to the semantics of CSP-R. For convenience, we have provided the semantic equations in Appendix A. It should be clear from our analysis that the behaviour expressions are based on complete-trace structures as opposed to the prefix-closed sets for the semantics of CSP-R. In order to show the consistency, we need to remove from the semantics of CSP-R the state information as well as the incomplete trace structures. Once, it is done we would be in a position to compare the two analysis.

Let L(S) be the regular language description of S (as per the static analysis). Let $M[\![S]\!]\sigma$ be the denotational semantics of S (cf. Appendix A for the semantic equations of CSP-R).

[2]Note that the proof does not follow on the lines of the usual trace theory techniques as we are interested in maximum parallelism and timing restrictions.

Let $trim(M[\![S]\!]\sigma) \triangleq \{ h \uparrow$ channels $|h\epsilon M[\![S]\!]\sigma$ such that there is no $h\prime$ such that $h \leq h\prime \}$ where $h \uparrow$ channels is the history obtained after removing the values sent or received.

In other words, *trim* yields the set of histories such that all prefixes of terminated computations are removed as well as the state information (i.e. the values sent or received are also trimmed). Now, we have the following relation:

Theorem 2 : $L(S) \supseteq$trim$(M[\![S]\!]\sigma)$
Proof: proved in the complete paper.

4 Syntactic Proof System

As discussed already, if the external behaviour of the program depends on the state information, then the static analysis would lead to approximate timing properties. For example, consider the following simple program:

```
Cons::m:=0;n:=0;
      * [ m-n ≥ 2;D?x → Compute( 2 time units);n:=n+1;
      []m − n < 2;W?y → Compute (3 time units);m:=m+1;
      ]
P1::  *[ D!c → Compute (3 time units)]
P2::  *[W!c → Compute (4 time units) ]
```

For this program, the timing characteristic derived ignoring the boolean guards does not match with the timing characteristic derived considering the boolean guards. In other words, the static analysis provides an approximate timing behavior.

Now let us look at ways of refining our analysis without using complete state information. One natural way is to associate distinct labels with I/O commands and associate assertions with these labels. For example, let us assume that distinct labels are associated with I/O commands and these labels become part of the behavior expression, i.e. L(r:D?x) = (r:D) and L(k:D) = (k:D) as already highlighted. The alphabet of the composed process has the form (r:k:D) corresponding to the interpretation that the commands labeled r and k matched, i.e., two internal processes arrived at points r and k respectively and the handshake took place. If we associate assertions with labels r and k, we can derive information as to whether it was indeed possible or not; i.e., if the assertion associated with one of the labels was *false* then the handshake could not have been possible. Now, let us see the possible ways in which we can associate assertions with the labels:

A associate *yes* or *no* type of assertions; if we allow only these type of assertions, we would not be able to distinguish distinct control points corresponding to the same labeled I/O command (for example, consider an I/O command in a loop) and such an association would be completely static. For example, consider *[k:D?x → compute]. If we attach assertions of the form *yes* or *no* then it would amount to saying whether this point is reachable or not. Many times, we would like to attach assertions that becomes true only after some number of repetitions of the loop. This can be accomplished in the following type.

B assertions that map syntactic traces along with the labels to true or false, i.e. assertions are of the type $H \times L \rightarrow \{true, false\}$ where H corresponds to the set of syntactic traces and L the set of labels with which the assertions are associated. Again, these assertions would not be able to consider whether certain branches of a selection command are open or closed as the guards could be arbitrary boolean expressions using complete state information. Such types can be described as follows:

C assertions of the type $H \times L \times B \rightarrow$ {true,false} where B is the set of guards associated with the given label (in a sense enabling information of the respective guards).

In the following, we describe a syntactic proof system using assertions that refer to syntactic traces only (i.e. the values sent or received are ignored). As the guards in a selection or an iterative command can in general be composed of the whole state, our assertions have the form (B).

4.1 Correctness Formula

Correctness formula [3] is of the form

$$< (\iota_1.a_1,...,\iota_r.a_r)|I : \{p\}S\{q\} >$$

where I is a set of prefix-closed syntactic traces (L-exprs) of S referring to the channels of S only. It does not contain any program variable or labels of the I/O commands and does not refer to any value sent or received on any channel. The trace projections are referred through $\pi_c set$ where $cset$ is the set of channels over which the projection is considered; the projections preserve the length i.e. channels not in $cset$ are mapped to $\Box$.

A labeled *trace or history* is a sequence similar to the structure of behavior expressions discussed earlier except that the channel names are labeled (e.g. ι:D, ν:W). Normally, this will be referred through variable h. Note that the set of lables are finite.

The notation $\iota_i.a_i$ denotes the assertion associated with label ι_i. Note that assertion a_i maps from the domain of labeled syntactic histories and labels to {true,false}, with the restriction that one can refer to the trace projections of the channels between the two processes only. For example, in ι: D?x , the assertion associated with this label can use only the communication traces on channel D and the channels connecting the process under consideration with the process connected through channel D.

The assertions p, q are first-order assertions over syntactic traces (including the length of traces) and do not use state variables.

Let $[a_k]$ denote the interpretation of a_k in the environment of syntactic traces and the labels. Let $h^{(k)}$ represent the subsequence of h upto the kth labeled element of h (say $\iota_k : a_k$).

A syntactic labeled trace h is said to be ***valid*** denoted $\models$ h , iff $\forall \iota_k$ in h, $[a_k]$ $(h^{(k)}, \iota_k)$.
The notation $h|NL$ is used for the trace obtained from h ignoring the labels of the channels.
A correctness formula is said to be ***valid*** denoted
$\models < (\iota_1.a_1,...,\iota_r.a_r)|I : \{p\}S\{q\} >$
iff $\forall \overline{h}$, [p] $(\overline{h}) \rightarrow \forall h\epsilon M[\![S]\!]$, such that $\models \overline{h} \circ$ h, we have
$[[I](\overline{h}|NL \circ h|NL) \rightarrow [q](\overline{h}\circ$h) where $\circ$ denotes the concatenation operator.

In the following, we denote the set of labelled assertions by $\mathcal{D}$.

Remarks: Note that we consider only valid extensions of the traces. It may be observed that L-exprs capture all the finite behaviors. It is for this reason, we have not considered the condition that reflects whether the state is terminating one or not (as is normally used in partial correctness formulae). The extension to nonterminating behavior will be discussed later.

4.2 Proof System

For unlabeled statements, we ignore the declarations (assertions) part of the correctness formula.

1.**skip:** $\{I[\pi \circ \Box/\pi] \wedge p[h \circ \Box/h]\}skip\{p \wedge I\}$

[3]Note that the interpretation of the correctness formula I: {P} S {Q} has the interpretation (cf.[ZRB 85]) that if S is started in an initial state and trace for which P holds then the invariant I holds for the trace of S at any moment during the execution of S (including the moment of termination, if S terminates). Also whenever S terminates q will hold for the final state and trace of S.

2. Assignment:

$$\{I[\pi \circ \Box/\pi] \wedge p[h \circ \Box/h]\} x := e\{p \wedge I\}$$

As the states are ignored there is no distinction between a ***skip*** and an ***assignment*** (or any unlabeled action).

3. Wait Statement:

$$\{I[\pi \circ \Box^{d_v}/\pi] \wedge p[h \circ \Box^{d_v}/h]\} \text{ wait d } \{p \wedge I\}$$

where d_v = if stat(d) then *value of d* else "*". If we do not know the value of d (i.e. it cannot be statically computed), we have to consider all possible values for d.

4. Input

$$\frac{\{I \wedge p \wedge a_\iota(h) \rightarrow \forall t[I[\pi \circ [R(D)]^t \circ (D)/\pi] \wedge q[h \circ [R(D)]^t \circ (\iota : D)/h]]\}}{\{< \mathcal{D}|I : \{p\}\iota : D?x\{q\} >\}}$$

The universal quantifier for t essentially corresponds to the indefinite waiting for the communication labeled ι over channel D. As we are ignoring, the state information there is no need for considering the values that can be received.

5. Output Command: The rule is exactly the same as the input command as the values sent or received are ignored.

6. Alternative Command

Let A_{min}, A_{max} be defined as earlier; note that the two sets essentially define the minimum and the maximum set of ready actions respectively that could be offered when the control arrives at the alternative command. Let W be the set of wait values of the alternative command. Let d be the maximum waiting period for a communication at this point – this is as defined earlier.

$$\begin{array}{ll}
(1).. & < \mathcal{D}|I : \{p\}S_k\{q\} >, \forall b_k \rightarrow S_k \\
(2).. & I \wedge p \wedge a_{\iota_k}(h) \rightarrow \forall_{A_{min} \subseteq A \subseteq A_{max}}, \\
& \quad \forall_{t \leq d}, I[\pi \circ [R(A)]^t \circ (D)/\pi] \wedge p\prime, < \mathcal{D}|I : \{p\prime\}S_k\{q\} > \\
& \quad \textit{where } p\prime \equiv p[h \circ R(A)]^t \circ (\iota_k : D)/h] \\
& \quad \forall \textit{ guards of the form } b_k \; ; \; \iota_k : D?x \rightarrow S_k, \\
(3).. & I \wedge p \wedge a_{\iota_k}(h) \rightarrow \forall_{A_{min} \subseteq A \subseteq A_{max}}, \\
& \quad \forall_{t \leq d}, I[\pi \circ [R(A)]^t \circ (D)/\pi] \wedge p\prime, < \mathcal{D}|I : \{p\prime\}S_k\{q\} > \\
& \quad \textit{where } p\prime \equiv p[h \circ [R(A)]^t \circ (\iota_k : D)/h], \\
& \quad \forall \textit{ guards of the form } b_k; \iota_k : D!e \rightarrow S_k, \\
(4).. & I \wedge p \rightarrow \forall_{A_{min} \subseteq A \subseteq A_{max}}, \forall_{d_k \epsilon W} \wedge d_k \leq d, \\
& \quad I[\pi \circ [R(A)]^{d_k}/\pi] \wedge p\prime, < \mathcal{D}|I : \{p\prime\}S_k\{q\} > \\
& \quad \textit{where } p\prime \equiv p[h \circ [R(A)]^{d_k}/h], \\
& \quad \forall \textit{ guards of the form } b_k; \textit{wait } d_k \rightarrow S_k \textit{ for } d_k \leq d, \\
\hline
& < \mathcal{D}|I : \{p\}[[]_{i=1}^m b_i; g_i \rightarrow S_i]\{q\} >
\end{array}$$

The relation(1) corresponds to the establishment of the consistency for the pure boolean guards. Relations (2)-(3) correspond to the I/O guards. The important thing to be noted is that assuming the consistency of the labelled asssetions with respect to the trace, the consistency for the extension of the traces are to be established in the usual style. Realtion(4) corresponds to the wait guards; as there is no assertion attached with respect to the wait guards, the postulates are not used.

7. Iteration

$$\frac{< \mathcal{D}|I : \{p\}A\{p\} >}{< \mathcal{D}|I : \{p\} * A\{p\} >}$$

8. Sequential Composition

$$\frac{< \mathcal{D}_1|I : \{p\}S_1\{r\} >, < \mathcal{D}_2|I : \{r\}S_2\{q\} >}{< \mathcal{D}_1, \mathcal{D}_2|I : \{p\}S_1; S_2\{q\} >}$$

provided label $(\mathcal{D}_1, S_1) \cap label(\mathcal{D}_2, S_2) = \epsilon$. Note that r is the intermediate assertion.

9. Parallel Composition

$$\frac{\begin{array}{l} < \mathcal{D}_i|I_i : \{p_i\}S_i\{q_i\} > \;\; for \; i = 1,2 \\ I_1[\pi_1/\pi] \wedge I_2[\pi_2/\pi] \rightarrow I[\pi_1 \# \pi_2/\pi] \\ q_1[h_1/h] \wedge q_2[h_2/h] \wedge \; consistent \; (h_1, h_2) \rightarrow \\ \mathcal{D}_1, \mathcal{D}_2 \; Cooperate \; \wedge q[h_1 \# h_2/h] \end{array}}{< \mathcal{D}_1, \mathcal{D}_2 \mid I_1 | \mid I_2 : \{p_1 \wedge p_2\}S_1||S_2\{q\} >}$$

provided label$(\mathcal{D}_1, S_1) \cap label(\mathcal{D}_2, S_2) = \epsilon$, and chan$(I_i, p_i, q_i) \cap chan(S_j) \subseteq chan(S_i)$ for (i,j) = (1,2) and (2,1) where *consistent* and *cooperate* are defined below:

Consistent: $consistent(h_1, h_2)$ is true iff
$\forall c \epsilon chan(S_1) \wedge \text{chan}(S_2)$,$\forall j$, $h_1^c[j] = h_2^c[j] \wedge \forall$ i, $h_1^r[i] \cap h_2^r[i] = \epsilon$
That is, the histories are time compatible and communication compatible.

Cooperate: The cooperation of assumptions or postulates can be approached in two ways. The first is to consider all the static matching pairs which can be obtained by computing STAT(L(S_1),L(S_2)) [4] and show that for each (k,r) in this set the assertion at k and r are the same. The other way is show the cooperation relative to h_1 and h_2. The latter can be done as follows: Find the matching pair of synchronization labels in the histories and show that the assertions at these points are consistent with respect to the histories upto this point. Formally, the latter can be written as:
$\mathcal{D}_1$ and $\mathcal{D}_2$ cooperate relative to h_1 and h_2 iff: $\forall a_k, a_r$ in $\mathcal{D}_1, \mathcal{D}_2$, a_k $(h^{(j)}) \wedge a_r$ $(h^{(j)})$ where h_1^C[j] = k:C and h_2^C[j] = r:C for C in chan$(S_1) \cap chan(S_2)$ and $h^{(k)} = h_1 \# h_2$[k]
where $h^{(j)}$ stands for the first j-1 elements of h as defined earlier.
The notation is the same as that used in the definition of the validity of the correctness formula.

10. **Extension:** $(\pi \geq t) : \{\pi = t\}S_1||S_2\{\pi \geq t\}$
As the length of the sequence indicates the time this can also be considered as an extension axiom for time as well.

11. **Hiding**

$$\frac{< \mathcal{D}|I : \{p \wedge h|jchan(S_1, S_2) = <>\}S_1||S_2\{q\} >}{< \mathcal{D}\prime|I : \{p\}[S_1||S_2]\{q\} >}$$

provided Chan(I,p,q) $\subseteq$ chan$(S_1||S_2)$, and no assertion corresponding to an external channel should contain internal channels. The set of new declarations is given by $\mathcal{D}\prime$ obtained from $\mathcal{D}$ after removing the assertions attached to I/O commands between S_1 and S_2 only. In the above rule <> stands for the empty sequence.
Standard rules for consequence, invariance, conjunction, and ghost variable substitutions are given in the complete paper.

Illustrative Example: In the following, we provide a simple specification. The formal proof is given in the complete paper.

```
C1::b1:=true; b2:=false ;
    *[ b1; k:D?x → compute (2 time units); b1:=false; b2:=true
     [] b2; r:W!e → compute (4 time units); b2:=false; b1:=true]
C2::b3:=true; b4:=false;
    *[b3; m:D!x→ compute (3 time units); b3:=false; b4:=true
     [] b4; n:W?e→ compute (4 time units); b4:=false; b3:=true ]
```

Assertions:
a_k: # D = # W ; a_m is the same as a_k.
a_r: # D = # W+1;a_n is the same as a_r.
$I : 0 \leq \#D - \#W \leq 1$

Discussion and Refinements

Several times, use of some state information leads to the detection of errors, exceptions etc. In the case of syntactic system, we would like the state information to be just a postulate. For example consider the following program:

[4] The definition of statically matching pairs is given below:
$STAT(H1, H2) = \{(k : r)|h1 \epsilon H1, h2 \epsilon H2$ are consistent and $h1^c$[j] = k:D and $h2^c$[j] = r: D where D is the common channel in H1 and H2 and k and r are the labels of the synchronized I/O commands in the respective processes}. In other words, the set STAT(H1,H2) captures the compatible control points in the languages H1 and H2 respectively. Note that the set of ***semantically matching*** pairs (i.e. considering the boolean guards) is not computable [Apt 83].

```
C1:: *[ C?x → process x (time T1)
      [] D?y   → process y (time T2)
      [] wait T → ERROR]
P1 :: *[C!e1   → gen-item (time T3)
      [] wait T4→ e1-item-missed]
P2 :: *[D!e2   → gen-item (time T5)
      [] wait T6→ e2-item-missed]
```

For describing the post-condition for such a program, it would be nice to include postulates such as: if one of the communications has not happened then it is an *error* or some *exception* etc . For this purpose, we need to include some postulates about the state information. The composition of states would give an overall behavior of the program. However, note that they cannot be checked as we don't have the state information as the condition may very well depend on some values that have been exchanged between processes.

Let us consider the power of the label assertions in deriving properties. Consider the following program:

```
P1:: * [ true →b1:=true; b2:=true;
              [ b1; k1:D?x → compute; b2:=false;
              [] b2; r1:D?y → compute; b1:=false; ]
              [ b1; k2:W!e1 →compute
              [] b2; r2:W!e2 →compute]
       ]
P2:: * [ true →b3:=true; b4:=true;
              [ b3; k3:D!e3 → compute
              [] b4; r3:D!e4 →compute]
              [ b3; k4:W?e1   → compute
              [] b4; r4:W?e2   → compute]
       ]
```

Let us assume that we want to place the restriction that whichever receives in P1 must be enabled to send it (similarly in P2). That is label k2 is followed by k1 and similarly r1 is followed by r2. It is obvious that this can be captured through assertions on labels. In fact, this can be captured by the assertions at labels k2 and r2 and similarly at labels k4 and r4. For example consider the post-condition for P1 (by fixing T1 = 2 and T2 = 8), we get
h = ... R(D)* D $\Box\Box R(W) * W\Box\Box \ldots \vee \ldots R(D) * D\Box^8 R(W) * \Box^8 \ldots$
Note that the dots denote the behavior sub-expressions that are not relevant for the discussion. The behavior can be established by appropriately attaching the assertions to the labels as in our system *communication and time* are observable. However, if we want to include state information, we need labels in the pre- and post-conditions. For example, assume that the computation corresponding to labels k1 and k2 are the inverse of the computation in the other. Thus, to include these aspects in the post-condition, we need to use labels in the assertions; otherwise, the labels are not required in the assertions or the postulates.

The above proof rules can be modified for nonterminating systems very easily. We will not go into details here for lack of space. It may be noted that syntactic proof systems are a natural generalization of the use proof-outlines [5] (cf.[deR 85]). Thus, based on the annotations (or the specification language of assertions) one can obtain a varieties of proof systems that would enable one to derive various classes of timing properties.

5 Outline of a General Proof System

For lack of space, we just discuss the outline in an informal way. Let us first discuss the information that needs to be captured in assertions to prove general time-related properties of real-time programs and then outline the components of the general proof system.

[5] or annotated programs

A discussion of the matching of I/O commands with reference to time will enable us to understand the difficulties in providing global time assertions with reference to I/O commands. In the case of real-time distributed languages such as CSP-R, we are interested in time-points. Suppose a process P has arrived at a time point, say T, and it is willing to communicate with some other process. The pertinent question to ask is: how long it would have to wait to interact with some other process say Q. This would enable one to derive common time-points at which the I/O commands α, β can ***statically match***.

We say that I/O commands α and β in process P_1 and process P_2 respectively ***statically match at time point*** T iff the following conditions are satisfied:

1. There exists $t1 \leq T$ and $t2 \geq T$ such that there exists a proper terminating computation of P_1 via α and there exists a proper terminating computation of P_2 via β that statically match.
2. (t1 = T) or (t2 = T).

Now, if we are given the time points at which the I/O commands statically match, we can remove the nondeterminacy arising due to the assumptions that the handshake can take place at any time after t1 and t2. This is the essential property expressed in condition (b). Thus, it is not possible to decide about the earliest possible action ignoring the boolean guards. This is illustrated in the following example:
Example :

```
P1 ≡ *[ D?x → T1
       [] wait 2 → W ? x]
P2 ≡ *[b; D ! e → T1
       []¬b; wait1 → W ! e]
```

Though, from the timing behavior we can see that for every D? from P1 there is a corresponding D! from P2, we cannot ignore the actions W? and W! completely as communication over D will not be possible if the boolean guard **b** is false. To show that it is always the case that the communication takes place between P1 and P2 via channel D, we need stronger assumptions in the isolated proof of the processes and the consistency has to be verified while composing the processes. One of the ways of achieving this is to provide assertions at the I/O commands postulating the times at which the synchronization starts. One potential type of assertions would be of the type mapping from the trace (history), the next action and the current time to the common time at which the synchronization could start. In other words, if the assertion is defined through the relation, say *start(h,ι:D,t)* would yield the earliest time, say *t′*, at which the communication could start (obviously *t′* ≥ t).

The correctness formula and the complete proof rules are given in the full paper.

6 Relationship Among Various Proof Systems

In this section, we show that the systems described above form a hierarchy.

Let $M[\![S]\!]\sigma$ and $trim(M[\![S]\!]\sigma)$ be as defined earlier.

Let L(S) be the regular language obtained from S ignoring the state information (as in section 2).

Let $D|L(S)$ be the language obtained from S with a given set D of postulates, i.e. assertions associated with the labels before i/o commands.

$D^+|L(S)$ is the same as $D|L(S)$ except that we use the general labels in the postulates D^+.

The consistency of the analysis done so far with respect to the semantics is captured by the following theorem.

Theorem 3: The following hierarchy holds:

$L(S) \supseteq D|L(S) \supseteq D^{+}|L(S) \supseteq trim(M[\![S]\!]\sigma)$ for each σ satisfying the postulates in D and D^{+}.

*Proof:*see full paper.

7 Conclusions

In this paper, we have provided an outline of a hierarchical methodology for establishing the correctness of real-time distributed programs emphasizing on the timing and communication synchronization of distributed programs rather than the performance point of view. Our analysis is based on the maximum-parallelism [6] model and can be broadly categorized into:

1. a static characterization of real-time distributed programs enabling us to obtain a static timing characterization of programs.
2. a syntactic proof system that uses postulates attached to I/O commands.
3. a general proof system.

The first characterization is useful as it is amenable to automation. The static analysis leads to development of efficient algorithms for the composition operations. The latter in turn allows us to specify and verify timing properties as has been shown in [LS 88]. In fact, the underlying transition system (or the Buchi automaton) enables us to derive various intersting classes of properties such as eventual stability (persistance), recurrence, progress etc. This turns out to be extremely useful, as in practice one tries to derive the timing constraints after deriving the safety properties (thus, making the static analysis very useful). The second one enables us to provide stronger specifications and derive program properties (timing behaviour) without explicitly using the state information. As already discussed, the system generalizes the use of proof outlines at a syntactic level which has great advantages in the derivation of timing properties. Further investigation is in progress to arrive at results to show what classes of properties can be derived without using the state information. Finally, the general proof system enables us to obtain a priori characteristics of processes which is very useful. The latter can be shown to be complete and various eventuality properties that are often required for real-time distributed programs can be derived using complete state information. However, we feel the ths static and syntactic techniques will greatly help the programmer in deriving the timing properties. The extension of our analysis to Ada rendezvous mechanism, and asynchronous languages, (based on the semantics of the analysis in [SNP 87]), and strongly synchronous languages such as RT-CDL (cf.[LS 87]) is in progress.

References

[Apt 83] K.R. Apt(1983) *A Static Analysis of CSP Programs* LNCS, 164, pp 1- 17.

[Da 85] B. Dasarathy(1985) *Timing Constraints of Real-Time Systems: Constructs for Expressing them and Methods for Validating them* IEEE Tr. on Software Engg, SE-11, pp 80-86.

[deR 85] W.P.de Roever(1985) *The Quest for Compositionality– a survey of assertion-based proof systems for concurrent programs* Proc of IFIP Working Conference on the Role of Abstract Models in Computer Science, (E.J.Neuhold(Ed)), North-Holland Publishing Co., 1985.

[6]the analysis can be easily extended to $max_{\nu}(\delta,\epsilon)$[KSR 85].

[GHR 86] R.Gerth, C. Huising and W.P. de Roever(1986) *Full Abstraction of a Real-Time Denotational Semantics for an OCCAM-like language* TR, EUT, Aug 86

[Ho 87] J.Hooman(1987) *A Compositional Proof System for an OCCAM-like REal-Time Language* CSN 87/14, EUT, Eindhoven, November 1987.

[Hoa 78] C.A.R. Hoare(1978) *Communicating Sequential Processes* CACM, 1978.

[JM 86] F. Jahanian and A.K. Mok(1986) *A Graph-Theoretic Approach for Timing Analysis in Real-Time Logic* IEEE Real-Time Systems Symposium, 1986, pp 98-108.

[KSR 85] R. Koymans, R.K. Shyamasundar, W.P. de Roever,R.Gerth and S.Arun- Kumar(1985) *Compositional Semantics for Real-Time Distributed Computing* Proc. Logics of Programs, LNCS 193, (fullpaper in **Information and Computation**, 79, December 1988,pp 210-256).

[LL 83] G. Le Lann(1983) *On Real-Time Distributed Computing* Proc. IFIP-83 (Ed. by R.E.A. Mason), North-Holland Publishing Co.

[LS 87] L.Y.Liu and R.K. Shyamasundar(1987) *Specification of Real-Time Programs in RT-CDL* IEEE Fourth workshop on Real-Time Operating Systems, Cambridge, Ma. July 1987, pp 110-119.

[LS 88] L.Y.Liu and R.K.Shyamasundar(1988) *Static Analysis of Real-Time Distributed Programs* Symp. on Formal Aspects of Real-Time Programming and Fault Tolerant Computing, University of Warwick, UK, Sept. 1988.

[Pn 86] A.Pnueli(1986) *Specification and Development of Reactive Systems* IFIP 1986 (ed. H.J. Kugler), North-Holland Publishing Co.

[SNP 87] R.K.Shyamasundar,K.T.Narayana, and T.Pitassi(1987) *Semantics of Nondeterministic Networks* ICALP 87, Karlshruhe, West Germany.

[Wir 77] N. Wirth(1977) *Towards a Discipline of Real-Time Programming* CACM, 20, 577-583.

[Yo 83] S.J.Young(1983) *Real-Time Languages : Design and Development* Ellis Horwood Publishers.

[ZRB 85] J. Zwiers, W.P. de Roever and P. van emde Boas (1985) *Compositionality and Concurrent Networks: Soundness and Completeness of a Proof System* ICALP 85, LNCS 194.

Appendix A Denotational Semantics of CSP-R

In this section, we briefly describe the formal denotational semantics. For details, the reader is referred to [KSR 85, GHR 87].

The domain is, D = $P(\overline{S} \times H)$
where $\overline{S} = S \cup \{\perp\}$, S being the *set of proper states* (i.e. partial functions from Id (set of identifiers) to V (set of expression values), and
H = sequences of sets of communication records of the form:
1. **Communication records** of the form (D,v) where D is a channel name and v ϵ VAL (domain of values). If the ith element is of the form (D,v), it can be interpreted as sending the value v over channel D at the ith tick of the conceptual global clock.
2. **Ready records** of the form R(A) where A is a subset of channel names. If the ith element of a history is R(A), it can be interpreted as the willingness of the process to communicate over the channels in A at the ith tick of the conceptual global clock.
3. **internal moves** (denoted □). If the ith element is □ , it can be interpreted as a local action at the ith tick of the conceptual global clock.

In other words, the observable actions are : (a) communication actions, (b) the time of the observable actions and (c) the state of the time of termination.

Now, $\overline{S} \times H = \{ <\sigma, h> | \sigma \epsilon S, h \epsilon H \text{ and } |h| < \infty \}$.
The domain consists of all nonempty prefix-closed elements of D.
A set $X \epsilon (\textit{state} \times \textit{history})$ is *prefix-closed* iff $\forall <\sigma, h> \epsilon X$, if $h' \leq h$ then $<\perp, h'> \epsilon X$.

The *prefix-closure* of X, denoted PFC(X), is defined as

$$X \cup \{<\perp, \lambda>\} \cup \{<\perp, h'> | \exists \sigma \exists h\ (<\sigma, h> \epsilon X \wedge h' \leq h)\}.$$

Note that the domain forms a complete lattice with set-inclusion($\subseteq$) ; the lub is obtained by $\cup$ (set-union) and the least element is $\{<\perp, \lambda>\}$.

The meaning function is of the form, $M[\![\text{Statement}]\!] : \overline{S} \rightarrow D$ defining the meaning of statements from $\overline{S}$ to D. For defining the meaning of alternative command compositionally, we define an auxiliary function $G[\![g,A]\!]$ from $\overline{S}$ to D which gives the meaning of the guard g in the context of a set A of alternative guards. Denoting the set of alternative guards by A, we get:
$G[\![g]\!] : A \rightarrow \overline{S} \rightarrow D$.

Let ϕ be a function from S to D. Then ϕ' is the function from $\overline{S}$ to D defined by
$\phi'(\sigma) = \textbf{if } \sigma \epsilon S \text{ then } \phi(\sigma) \textbf{ else } \text{PFC}(\{<\sigma, \lambda>\})$.

Further, ϕ^* is the function from D to D defined by,
$\phi^*(X) = \{ <\sigma', h \circ h'> | <\sigma, h> \epsilon X \text{ and} <\sigma', h'> \epsilon \phi'(\sigma)\}$.

The function G is defined using the following two auxiliary functions.

$$\Gamma(\{b_1; \overline{g}_1, ..., b_n; \overline{g}_n\}, \sigma) = \{R(D) | \exists i\text{: } W[\![b_i]\!]\sigma = tt \wedge (\overline{g}_i = D!e \vee \overline{g}_i = D?x)\},$$

$$\begin{aligned} \text{waitvalue}(b\ ; \overline{g}, \sigma) &= 0 \text{ if } \overline{g} = \lambda \wedge W[\![b]\!]\sigma = tt \\ &= \max(n, 1) \text{ if } \overline{g} = \textit{wait } n \wedge W[\![b]\!]\sigma = tt \\ &= \infty \text{ otherwise} \end{aligned}$$

$M[\![S]\!] \perp = \{<\perp, \lambda>\}$ *for any S*; λ is the empty sequence.

$M[\![\textit{skip}]\!]\sigma = \text{PFC}(\{<\sigma, \{\square\}>\})$.

$M[\![x := e]\!]\ \sigma = PFC\{<\sigma[V[\![e]\!]\sigma/x], \{\square\}\}$
where V is the semantic function (assumed to be given) for evaluating the arithmetic expressions.

$M[\![g]\!]\sigma = G\ [\![g, \phi]\!]\ \sigma$ where g is a i/o command.

$M[\![S_1; S_2]\!]\sigma = M^*[\![S_2]\!]\ (M[\![S_1]\!]\ \sigma$

$G[\![b, A]\!]\sigma = \textbf{if } W\ [\![b]\!]\sigma \textbf{ then } \text{PFC}\ \{<\sigma, \lambda>\} \textbf{ else } \{<\perp, \lambda>\} \textbf{ fi}.$

where W is the semantic function (assumed to be given) for evaluating the boolean expressions.

$$\begin{aligned} G[\![\textit{ wait } d,\ A]\!]\sigma = \ & PFC(\{<\sigma, \Gamma(A, \sigma)^t> | \\ & max\{V[\![d]\!]\sigma, 1\} = minwait(A \cup \{\textit{ wait } d\}, \sigma) \underline{\Delta} t\}) \end{aligned}$$

where minwait(A,σ) gives the minimum of the waiting periods corresponding to elements of A.

$$\begin{aligned} G[\![D?x, A]\!]\sigma = PFC(\{&<\sigma[v/x], \Gamma(GRDS, \sigma)^t> \circ <D, v> | v \epsilon V, \\ & 0 \leq t < minwait(A, \sigma),\ GRDS = A \cup \{D?x\}\}). \end{aligned}$$

$$\begin{aligned} G[\![D!e, A]\!]\sigma = \quad PFC(\{&<\sigma, \Gamma(GRDS, \sigma)^t> \circ <D, V[\![e]\!]\sigma> | \\ & 0 \leq t < minwait(A, \sigma),\ GRDS = A \cup \{D!x\}\}). \end{aligned}$$

$G[\![b; g, A]\!]\sigma = G[\![g, A]\!]^*(G[\![b, A]\!]\sigma)$, *where* $g \equiv D?x$ *or* $D!e$ *or wait d*.

$$\begin{aligned} & G[\![[\square_{j=1}^n g_j \rightarrow S_j]]\!]\sigma = \\ & \quad \textbf{if} \vee_{j=1}^n W[\![g_j^b]\!]\sigma\ (\textit{where } g_j^b \textit{ is the boolean part of} g_j)\textbf{then} \\ & \quad\quad \cup_{j=1}^n M[\![S_j]\!]^*(G[\![g_j, \{g_k | 1 \leq k \leq n, k \neq j\}]\!]\sigma) \\ & \quad \textbf{else } PFC(\{<\perp, \lambda>\})\textbf{fi} \end{aligned}$$

$$\begin{aligned} G[\![*A]\!]\sigma = \mu\phi.\lambda\sigma.\textbf{if } \exists i : W[\![b_i]\!]\sigma) = tt \\ \textbf{then } \phi^*(M[\![A]\!]\sigma)\textbf{else } PFC(\{<\sigma, \epsilon>\})\textbf{fi} \end{aligned}$$

$$\begin{aligned} M[\![S_1 || S_2]\!]\sigma = \\ PFC\{<\sigma_1 \times \sigma_2, h_1\#h_2> | \forall i \epsilon \{1, 2\} :<\sigma_i, h_i> \epsilon M[\![S_i]\!]\sigma \\ \wedge \textit{consistent}(\sigma_1, h_1, \sigma_2, h_2)\}, \end{aligned}$$

$$\begin{aligned} \textit{where } \sigma_1 \times \sigma_2(x) &= \sigma_i(x) \textit{ if } \sigma_1, \sigma_2 \neq \perp \wedge x \epsilon var(\sigma_i) \\ &= \sigma(x) \textbf{if} \sigma_1, \sigma_2 \neq \perp \wedge \neg(x \epsilon var(\sigma_i)) \wedge x \epsilon var(\sigma) \\ &= \perp \textbf{otherwise} \end{aligned}$$

and $h_1\#h_2$ and *consistent* are as defined below. assuming *cset* to be the set of common channels in S_1 and S_2.

$$\begin{aligned} (h_1\#h_2)[j] = \{&<D, v> | \exists i, j : j \leq |h_i| \wedge <D, v> \epsilon h_i[j]\} \\ \cup \{&R(D) | \exists i, j : j \leq |h_i| \wedge <D, v> \epsilon h_i[j] \wedge D \textit{ not in cset}\}. \end{aligned}$$

$$\begin{aligned} & \textit{consistent}(\sigma_1, h_1, \sigma_2, h_2, cset) \underline{\Delta} (\sigma_i = \perp \rightarrow |h_3 - i| \leq |h_i| \\ & \quad \wedge \forall j, D, v : D \epsilon \textit{ cset} \rightarrow (<D, v> \epsilon h_1[j] \textit{ iff } <D, v> \epsilon h_2[j]) \\ & \quad \wedge \forall j, D : R(D) \textit{ not in } (h_1[j] \wedge h_2[j]) \end{aligned}$$

$$M[\![[S]]\!]\sigma = PFC\{<\sigma, h> | \exists h' :<\sigma, h'> \epsilon M[\![S]\!]\sigma \wedge h' \uparrow cset = h\}$$

where $h' \uparrow cset$ is the history obtained after removing all the communications and readies on channels *cset* from h′ (cset are the internal channels of S). Note that the empty set is represented by □ and hence the time points are preserved.

Analysis Capabilities for Requirements Specified in Statecharts [1]

Bonnie E. Melhart
Nancy G. Leveson
Dept. of Information and Computer Science
University of California, Irvine

Matthew S. Jaffe
Hughes Aircraft Company
Ground Systems Group
Fullerton, California

Abstract

This paper considers various types of analysis that are possible for formal requirements specifications in the Statecharts language. The application of recently developed criteria for completeness analysis of embedded systems requirements to specifications in Statecharts is discussed, in particular. Additions for the language that will enable such analysis are indicated.

Introduction

As today's computer systems are asked to perform more and more complex tasks, the individual components of the task or system and their interface become more complex, and the difficulty increases of assuring such properties as consistency, completeness, and unambiguity in the specifications. Embedded systems, in particular, have become increasingly complex as the software is tasked to interface with many machines and humans at once, often with stringent fault tolerance, safety, and reliability requirements. Evaluation for correctness and other properties is essential early on, i.e. at the requirements level, before commitment is made to a physical solution that may be costly or even impossible to change. Postponing such analysis is inadvisable: time and effort spent on verification of the design or the implementation to the requirements specification are wasted if the requirements are incorrect.

Work is ongoing at the University of California, Irvine to develop a formal model that can be used to determine and describe the features required for a real-time requirements specification language suitable for embedded systems and to develop completeness analysis methods based on this model. The focus has been on those aspects of the requirements specification that are often handled poorly or inadequately such as safety, robustness, timing, and the human-machine interface.

[1] This work has been partially supported by NSF Grant CCR-8718001, NSF VPW Grant 8800505-RII, NSF CER Grant DCR-8521398, and NASA Grant NAG-1-668.

The language used to specify software requirements is important not only for its ability to express and to communicate the requirements, but also for its ability to enable analyses of the requirements specification. It is therefore interesting and appropriate to consider such analysis capabilities in Statecharts [Har87], a state-of-the-art language for the specification of complex embedded systems.

In [MLJ88], the authors present a critical evaluation of Statecharts as a language that enables such analysis and suggest some additional features that are needed to completely specify real-time embedded systems. The application of the completeness analysis procedures that we have developed to an example specification in Statecharts is examined there as well. A brief description of a few of the results of this work is given here.

Statecharts

Statecharts is a language under development at Weizmann Institute in Israel by David Harel and his colleagues. It is intended for use in defining real-time reactive systems and is appropriate for the embedded applications on which this research is focused.

There are several characteristics of a language used for specifying software requirements that enable the application of various analyses of the resulting system description. In general, to preclude the need for some sort of natural language processor to manipulate the description, a formal, nonprose language is desired for requirements specification. On the other hand, formal languages can be hard to read and understand; tradeoffs are necessary when selecting a language that must be appropriate for use on many levels (i.e., design, validation, specification, analysis). As Statecharts employs a graph structure with multiple abstraction levels to represent an underlying formalism based on finite state machines, formal analysis can be focused on a certain level of detail in the specification or on parts of the representation that are relevant without looking at the entire specification.

Timing is an essential consideration for real-time embedded software. A means for representing minimum and/or maximum times for certain activities is present in the language. Syntax is provided to specify desired transition in the event of a time-out; that is, the passing of a given time since the last occurrence of a specified event. This capability is important to most analysis techniques. Another important feature for requirements analysis is the capability to include an environmental model as an orthogonal (independent, parallel) state to the software decription. Thus analyses of the requirements specification can include analysis of the software model interacting with its environment.

The next two sections describe two specific analyses for requirements level descriptions that have been considered for application to a Statecharts model.

Safety analysis

Leveson and Stolzy [LS87] have developed analysis techniques for timed Petri net specifications to analyze a model for safety and fault tolerance properties and to derive associated timing and functional requirements from a global system model. These techniques basically require a finite state machine formalism, the ability to derive at least a partial reachability graph, and the specification of maximum and minimum timing for state transitions. These capabilities are all a part of the Statecharts formalism, though not entirely backed by the current formal semantics. The procedures and algorithms can be transferred to Statechart specifications, with certain additions to the basic Statecharts model for modeling failures. There may even be advantages in the use of Statecharts for the specification since they allow the possibility of concentrating on detailed specification of hazardous states while performing less detailed analysis of non-critical functionality and performance.

Some additional features, however, may be necessary to completely specify and analyze timing requirements. In Statecharts, a state configuration of the software system is actually a tuple of substates of orthogonal components. If this "system state" then has a timing requirement, it should go into effect when the last orthogonal substate is entered. Sometimes it is desirable to give certain transitions priority over others for safety considerations; it is not clear how to give priority to a transition with timing on such a system state, since the substates may have starting times at quite a distance (time and space) from each other. Much work remains to be done in the area of time modeling.

There are five basic elements of a failure model considered in the Leveson and Stolzy work:

- a required event that does not occur,
- an undesired event,
- an incorrect sequence of required events,
- two incompatible events that occur simultaneously, and
- timing failures in event sequences.

These can be modeled in Statecharts by making use of the maximum and minimum timing features. Additional features are recommended to express, in particular, the case of incompatible simultaneous events. If the events are at the top level of the software description, a global transition is appropriate for the simultaneous occurrence. In fact, global transitions are quite useful for handling undesired events that require the same transition for all states. However, the general case demands a feature that transitions from perhaps widely separated internal states. To further facilitate analysis, there should also be some distinction between the normal, expected (desired) transitions and the error transition, which is usually, but not always, a time-out transition. The Leveson and Stolzy notion of a failure transition can be added to the Statecharts model in a straightforward way.

Completeness analysis

There is little consensus on what constitutes completeness in a requirements specification. Jaffe and Leveson [JL88] have attempted to provide a formal definition of completeness in real-time requirements specification and to identify criteria that can be used to detect and generate missing requirements for a particular specification. The analysis is applied to a black-box behavioral description that is composed of a set of assertions of the form: *trigger* $\Leftrightarrow$ *output*. The triggers and outputs are described using first-order predicate calculus and a simple state machine model. The general format of a requirements assertion in the model is:

$$\exists E_1, \ldots, E_i \ni P_E \Leftrightarrow \exists! O \ni P_O$$

where:

E_i: observables in environment (including passage of time), inputs and/or outputs,

P_E: predicate on trigger events, and

P_O: predicate on outputs (the trigger must existentially quantify any events used in the definition of P_O).

The E_i are the necessary state history or conditions for an output O.

Criteria have been developed to formally define completeness of both trigger conditions (i.e., robustness criteria) and output predicates using logical completeness to "close" the set of requirements. Closure with respect to trigger conditions ensures that undesired or unexpected events are considered and the behavior desired should they occur is specified, while closure with respect to outputs ensures that all relevant output behavior is specified. In addition, application-dependent rules and heuristics can be developed to close the output specification with respect to various criteria important in the controlled system. Criteria have been developed for safety, reachability, and path robustness (i.e., fault tolerance).

These criteria require a language for specification capable of expressing time and value for outputs, assumptions of timing and value ranges for environmental triggers and internal state information. Statecharts environmental model and state representation provide an appropriate format and necessary information to allow most analysis for the completeness of environmental assumptions and requirements that concern states. It may be desirable, however, to express time and value range assumptions elsewhere with reference to these specifications on the corresponding transitions so that arcs in the representation do not become cluttered. To specify exceptions to these assumptions of range and timing of input triggers, an additional state is generally required for each assumption. Addition to the Statecharts formalism of a specific mechanism for modeling exceptions would promote readibility and allow analysis.

It is important to have an appropriate syntax and semantics for expressing timing requirements, as certain analyses rely heavily on a formal semantic representation of timing and time-outs. Most critical states will require double timing specifications for minimum and maximum timing of certain activities that result in output. Notation for these should be made less confusing. In particular, expression of periodic functions is ambiguous in most representations as one description can allow or disallow phase shift depending on the interpretation. (This problem is described in detail in [JL88].) Constructs to make the desired timing explicit are necessary before these requirements can be completely specified.

Summary

No current real-time requirements specification language contains all the features we feel are necessary to completely specify a real-time, embedded system. Many features of Statecharts facilitate the analysis of the requirements. Orthogonality and hierarchy structuring, which augment the underlying finite state machine model, provide the modular breakdown needed for dealing with large, complex systems and allow specification of prerequisite inputs to assure their existence before use. The state representation allows evaluation for dynamic properties through reachability analysis. Some analysis is simplified as the specification of global requirements is possible with superstates in the hierarchy. The inclusion of the environmental model and means for expressing timing constraints are important for embedded systems; in particular, time-outs allow expression of some exceptions to timing assumptions for the environment.

Some additions have been suggested for the language that would enable analysis for safety and completeness of a Statecharts model. The Statecharts language is still under development, and it is hoped that the formal semantics will be completed in the near future. Semantics for maximum and minimum timing and time-out transitions are especially important. Features to describe value ranges and exceptions concisely and to indicate error and undesired event transitions are recommended. More details about how analysis might be done and suggestions for adding missing capabilities to the Statecharts language may be found in [MLJ88].

In general, there is a need for more scientific approaches to analyzing requirements specification documents for correctness. Informal techniques do not provide the reliability or confidence demanded for today's complex safety-critical systems. Techniques for analysis of the external completeness of the model and methods to analyze the specification of undesired event handling for completeness and consistency are a critical need for real-time embedded systems specification. Special modeling abstractions may be required to make complete specification of these models possible. While developing formal analysis methods is a complex endeavor, there are real benefits for doing so, as the alternative may mean incomplete and incorrect specifications that result in systems expensive to correct and that may even lead to disaster.

References

[Har87] David Harel. Statecharts: A Visual formalism for complex systems. *Science of Computer Programming*, 8:231–274, 1987.

[JL88] Matthew S. Jaffe and Nancy G. Leveson. Completeness, robustness, and safety in real-time software requirements specification. Technical report, Dept. of Information and Computer Science, University of California, Irvine, September 1988.

[LS87] Nancy G. Leveson and Janice L. Stolzy. Safety analysis using Petri nets. *IEEE Transactions on Software Engineering*, SE-13(3):386–397, March 1987.

[MLJ88] Bonnie E. Melhart, Nancy G. Leveson, and Matthew S. Jaffe. Analysis capabilities for requirements specified in Statecharts. Technical report, Dept. of Information and Computer Science, University of California, Irvine, September 1988.

ABSTRACTION AND STRUCTURE

Interface Specification with Temporal Logic

Martin Kooij*

PTT Research, Neher Laboratories
P.O. Box 421, 2260 AK Leidschendam, The Netherlands

Abstract

This paper describes developments and experience in the ESPRIT project 1283: "VDM for Interfaces of the PCTE". It shows the way temporal logic is used in combination with the relational VDM method in order to write interface specifications for large reactive systems. It is shown that in this way a specification can be written both usable for implementors and users of an interface. The ability to distinguish within the logic between an internal and an external action appears to be very important.

1 Introduction

This paper describes developments and experience resulting from ESPRIT project 1283: "VDM for Interfaces of the PCTE" (further on abbreviated as VIP). The goals of this project were to deliver a precise specification of the interfaces to PCTE[13] ("Portable Common Tool Environment") that would serve the following purposes:

- it should be usable for both users and implementors;
- it should identify weaknesses in the PCTE interfaces and suggest improvements;
- it should provide a basis for long term evolution of PCTE, not biased by any language binding.

The specification was to be based on VDM as it is a well developed method and relatively well known in industry. An interface specification in the style of VDM, using the 'British School' style of specification[5], was combined with a method for modularisation and parameterisation of specifications. Temporal logic was added to the method to be able to describe aspects of the system that are related to its reactive nature, and a method for separating special cases from normal ones was defined. The main focus of this paper will be the addition of temporal logic to the more conventional relational interface specifications. Then a short section will be devoted to a discussion about the features of the language used, and the way its semantics is defined. Three examples of use can be found in the appendix.

*Supported by the European Communities under ESPRIT project 1283: VIP. The VIP consortium consisted of Praxis Systems plc, Centre for Mathematics and Computer Science, PTT Research Neher Laboratories, Océ Nederland bv and the University of Leicester.

2 The Interfaces to PCTE

PCTE is a system that is designed to be a good basis for building tools for Software Engineering in an environment with workstations. The system is built around a distributed data base of objects, with variable user defined properties. Every process can install its own view on the database. The views can be installed such that the database looks like a UNIX filesystem, thus tools for UNIX can be reused easily. The PCTE system gives the possibility to lock objects in such a way that the database can be rolled back to a consistent state in the case of non successful termination.

The interfaces are given as a set of function calls to the PCTE. Currently there are two language bindings of this interface, one to C[13] and one to ADA[14].

3 Relational Interface Specifications

The interfaces are described as interfaces to a system that is abstractly modelled by a collection of variables, conventionally called "the state", written in VDM. An interface call is modelled as a VDM operation with input parameters and possibly output parameters (informally to be defined as return values to the program doing the interface call) and changing the state of the system. In the rest of this paper this model for interface calls will be taken for granted and instead of the interface call the paper will concentrate on the operations that form their model.

Assuming that an operation works in isolation, the operation can be written in VDM, relating the input parameters, initial state, output parameters, and final state. This relation is not necessarily a function from the starting state (with its parameters) to the final state (with its outputs), so several choices can be left open. Nor is the algorithm to arrive at the final state given.

An operation defined in VDM has the following syntax close to the one mentioned in Jones's book on VDM[5]:

$OP(x_1 : T_1, \ldots, x_n : T_n)\, r_1 : T_{n+1}, \ldots, r_m : T_{n+m}$

ext rd *readvars* wr *writevars*

pre *pre*

post *post*

This operation has as its the parameters $x_1, \ldots, x_n$ and as its the results $r_1, \ldots, r_m$ with the respective types $T_1, \ldots, T_{n+m}$. These types are assumed to be defined elsewhere in the specification. After the keyword rd a number of variables from the state are expected (with their types), called the read variables for this operation. After the keyword wr the write variables are named, all different from the read variables. The precondition *pre* is a logical expression containing the read and write variables and the parameters, defining the condition under which the operation should define the relation satisfying the postcondition *post*. This condition is a logical expression containing the parameters, the results, the read variables, and the write variables. The write variables can occur twice, once referring to the "old" value, and once referring to the "new" value. The read variables are assumed not to change. As the operation is meant to be implemented eventually every VDM operation is obliged to satisfy the "implementability proof obligation"[5]: for every precondition true there must be some assignment of all variables such that the postcondition is satisfied.

4 Problems with the Relational Approach

The relational approach of describing an interface call is based on the idea that the user of the interface is interested in the effect of its calls upon the state. This implies a kind of sequentiality of the interface calls. A user of an interface does one call, waits for the effect and does another. The observation of the state is through the sequential execution of interface calls. It is shown now that this view was inadequate for the purposes of the VIP project.

PCTE is based on a concurrent environment. The interface works on a central database controlled by a locking mechanism. This can cause some interface calls to wait for some time until a lock has been released. The relation between the starting state and end state gets very weak in these cases; think of how the state of the system can have changed while waiting half an hour for some lock! A simplified but typical example can be found in the second example in the appendix where the postcondition is indicating that the only thing we actually know about the counter is that it is greater or equal to the amount incremented. This is due to the fact that we have been waiting for a flag to go down. Apart from being quite uninformative it gives no clue for the implementation of this operation. It would seem that it is allowed to increment the counter with any value greater then n.

Moreover the user of PCTE cannot only observe the state through sequential calls but can also observe the state through an interface call parallel to other ones made by him. So the intermediate behaviour is of importance even to the user of an interface and not only to the implementor.

5 Temporal Logic

As the interface could also be observed in a concurrent way the relational view on an interface specification was not good enough. The approach we chose to solve the problem was to introduce the concept of intermediate states. So in addition to the relation between the start states and the end states allowed sequences from start states via intermediate states (if any) to the end states are described.

A useful formalism for describing sequences of states is Temporal Logic. We have chosen to use linear discrete time temporal logics[8] as a basis to describe the allowed sequences. To the conventional precondition and postcondition of VDM we added a, what we called, intercondition: a temporal formula describing properties of the state sequence. The syntax was extended to include the intercondition:

$OP(x_1 : T_1, \ldots, x_n : T_n)\, r_1 : T_{n+1}, \ldots, r_m : T_{n+m}$

ext rd *readvars* wr *writevars*

pre *pre*

post *post*

inter *inter*

Here *inter* is a linear discrete time temporal logic formula containing the parameters and the results as variables with a fixed value, and the read and write variables as temporal variables that can be different on every state in the sequence. The intercondition thus does not refer to any variable that is not mentioned as either a read or a write variable.

The intuition is that the intercondition restrict the possible paths leading from a state that satisfies the precondition to a state satisfying the postcondition. The relation between start and end states is the most important part, the intercondition can only be used to give an operational condition under which this relation is established and is as such more concrete. The form of postcondition *post* was also changed slightly; it now became an expression that could also contain both forms of a read variable, the "old" and the "new" ones. Previously only the write variables could have been changed between the start state and the end state.

The logic, however, did lack one property we needed that had to do with compositionality. This is discussed in the next section.

6 Internal and External steps

When combining interface specifications the actor that causes some property in the execution sequence can be very important. Temporal logic describes the properties of some sequence. By stating just the properties, however, it becomes for example impossible to specify that an operation must wait for a lock to become free and doesn't take some action itself such that the lock becomes free (same property established in two quite different ways).

For this we labelled the steps in an execution sequence of an operation to be either *internal* or *external*. To the logic two predicates were added indicate whether the next step is internal or external, respectively. Much more complicated suggestions were considered but this simple approach appeared to work. Intuitively the internal steps are atomic actions of the operations changing the state of the system in one indivisible step. The external steps are steps done by the system with the operation not changing anything in the system itself. In this way we are able to indicate the difference of waiting for a lock and establishing a lock yourself. Also it opens the way for building a system specification from its interface specifications (see for example [1] or in a CSP setting [9]). This is not tackled by the VIP project as it was not one of our primary tasks.

The two kinds of transitions allowed us to be more precise also about the meaning of the read variables and the write variables. As we had to drop the restriction that read variables could not change in the relation between the first and the last state, the read and write variables were used in exactly the same way. Intuitively there is a more fundamental idea behind the statement made in VDM that read variables are not changed in the relation: the read variable is not changed by the operation *itself*. This amounts to the same thing if one looks at operations in isolation, but just saying that read variables are not changed is not adequate for our purpose. The fact that the read variable is only changed by the environment can be made more precise by stating that a read variable may *not* be changed in an internal step. Furthermore we can now also state the role of the "other" variables that are not mentioned as either read or write: the operation itself may not change them: none of the "other" variables may be changed in an internal step. Thus all three kinds of variables have their own role:

- "Read" variables cannot be changed during an internal step, may change during external steps, and are relevant for the behaviour;
- "Write" variables can be changed during any step, and are relevant for the behaviour;
- "Other" variables cannot be changed during an internal step, may change during external steps, and are not relevant for the behaviour. This irrelevance to the behaviour can be seen from the way the conditions are defined; in none of the conditions defining an operation one of the "other" variables may be mentioned.

7 Semantics

In this section we present some of the elements that are used to model the the operations, here called valid full computations.

Notation: In the sequel, we will use the notation S_{rd} (S_{wr}, S_{other}) to refer to the set of all tuples of values that can be taken by the read-variables (write variables, other variables, respectively). These sets are projections of the global state space. The notation T_j, ($j = 1, 2, 3, \ldots$) will be used to refer to the types of the parameters and results. The notation $SL^{\dagger}$ will refer to the labelled state sequences as defined below. If the we want to refer to the set of finite state sequences we will write SL^{*}, and SL^{ω} for the set of infinite sequences. We take a partially interpreted version of the text of an operation and consider the pre-, post- and interconditions to be predicates of a certain type, and will not be concerned with how the translation from the text to the predicates is done.

Definition 1 *A* computation *of an operation is a sequence of zero or more transitions between states, i.e., instances of* $S_{\mathsf{rd}} \times S_{\mathsf{wr}} \times S_{\mathsf{other}}$, *where every transition (or "step") between consecutive states is labeled by either "I" or "E". The labels indicate whether the steps are taken internally or externally.*

$$\sigma \equiv \sigma^{(0)} \xrightarrow{\lambda_0} \sigma^{(1)} \xrightarrow{\lambda_1} \sigma^{(2)} \xrightarrow{\lambda_2} \cdots$$

in the infinite (non-terminating) case, or

$$\sigma \equiv \sigma^{(0)} \xrightarrow{\lambda_0} \sigma^{(1)} \xrightarrow{\lambda_1} \sigma^{(2)} \xrightarrow{\lambda_2} \cdots \xrightarrow{\lambda_{n-1}} \sigma^{(n)}$$

otherwise.

In the latter case, the length *of the computation,* $|\sigma|$, *is defined as* $|\sigma| = n + 1$.

Moreover, in every step with label "I" the sets S_{rd} *and* S_{other} *must be left unchanged, i.e., their variables are not affected. In every step at least one of the write or read variables has to change. This can only be a write variable in the case of an internal step and can be either a read or a write variable in the case of an external step. An exception is made for the tail of infinite sequence that may have an endless repetition.*

Notation: We will refer to a state projected to the read variables and the write variables as $\sigma^{(j)}_{\mathsf{rd,wr}}$ and refer to sequences where all states have been projected to the read and write variables as $\sigma_{\mathsf{rd,wr}}$.

The state sequence is built with the restriction that at least one variable changes from the viewpoint of the operation. This makes the next-time operator used in the logic more like the next-change operator as in [4]. This is done to be sure that an operation stays independent from any of the "other" variables as was already indicated to be desirable from an engineering point of view in the previous section. Being able to detect changes in these "other" variables would destroy this property and would give the writer of an operation the chance to write expressions that would be dependent on them.*

Definition 2 *A* full computation *of an operation is a computation together with the values of the parameters at the time of call and the result variables. This means that the full computation is an element from the set:*

$$T_1 \times \cdots \times T_n \times SL^{\omega} \\ \cup \\ T_1 \times \cdots \times T_n \times SL^{*} \times T_{n+1} \times \cdots \times T_{n+m}$$

Notation: We will write a full computation as $\bar{\sigma}$ and write

$$\bar{\sigma} \equiv (x_1, \ldots, x_n, \sigma, r_1, \ldots, r_m)$$

if the computation is finite,

$$\bar{\sigma} \equiv (x_1, \ldots, x_n, \sigma)$$

otherwise. Also we will use the shorthand $\bar{\sigma}_{\mathsf{rd,wr}}$ for full computations where the computations have been projected.

Definition 3 *A full computation $\bar{\sigma}$ of an operation is called* relationally valid *if*

- *the precondition doesn't hold on the first state*

$$\neg pre(\sigma^{(0)}_{\mathsf{rd,wr}}, x_1, \ldots, x_n)$$

or,

- *the computation is infinite and the precondition holds*

$$pre(\sigma^{(0)}_{\mathsf{rd,wr}}, x_1, \ldots, x_n) \wedge |\sigma| = \omega$$

or,

- *the computation is finite, say $|\sigma| = n$, the precondition holds on the first state and the postcondition holds on the last state*

$$pre(\sigma^{(0)}_{\mathsf{rd,wr}}, x_1, \ldots, x_n) \\ \wedge \\ post(\sigma^{(0)}_{\mathsf{rd,wr}}, x_1, \ldots, x_n, \sigma^{(n)}_{\mathsf{rd,wr}}, r_1, \ldots, r_m).$$

Every computation that starts in a state not satisfying the precondition is considered valid. This reflects the fact that nothing is guaranteed about the behaviour in such a case.

*Note that one external step from the viewpoint of an operation could thus actually be several steps in the system.

Definition 4 *A full computation $\bar{\sigma}$ of an operation is called* operationally valid *if*

- *the precondition doesn't hold on the first state*

$$\neg pre(\sigma^{(0)}_{\mathsf{rd,wr}}, x_1, \ldots, x_n)$$

or,

- *the precondition holds on the first state and the intercondition holds on the state sequence (with the point "now" as the first state in the sequence).*

$$pre(\sigma^{(0)}_{\mathsf{rd,wr}}, x_1, \ldots, x_n) \wedge inter(\bar{\sigma}_{\mathsf{rd,wr}}).$$

Definition 5 *A full computation $\bar{\sigma}$ of an operation is called* valid *if it is both relationally valid and operationally valid.*

In principle the semantics of an operation is formed by taking as a model all the possible sets of valid (full) computations. As the operations are meant to be implemented eventually, however, we allow only sets that fulfil the implementability proof obligation which is now interpreted as the existence in the set of some finite valid full computation from every state (with parameters) satisfying the precondition. We will call an operation for which such sets cannot be found unimplementable.

Furthermore we defined a methodological requirement on the operations that we call the maximal relationship requirement. Intuitively this means that we will let the relations contain the maximum amount of information that we can possibly give, or equivalently that will will not cut down on the reachable postcondition by the intercondition. First we define when an operation is relationally maximally defined:

Definition 6 *An operation is said to be* relationally maximally defined *if for all states, parameters, results $\sigma^{(0)}, \sigma^{(n)}, x_1, \ldots, x_n, r_1, \ldots, r_m$ such that the precondition and the postcondition are satisfied*

$$pre(\sigma^{(0)}_{\mathsf{rd,wr}}, x_1, \ldots, x_n) \\ \wedge \\ post(\sigma^{(0)}_{\mathsf{rd,wr}}, x_1, \ldots, x_n, \sigma^{(n)}_{\mathsf{rd,wr}}, r_1, \ldots, r_m)$$

it is the case that there is a valid computation $\bar{\sigma}$ relating the mentioned states:

$$\bar{\sigma} \equiv (\langle \sigma^{(0)}_{\mathsf{rd,wr}}, \ldots, \sigma^{(n)}_{\mathsf{rd,wr}} \rangle, x_1, \ldots, x_n, r_1, \ldots, r_n).$$

The maximum relationship method is that for every operation it is required that it is relationally maximally defined. Though it seemed to us a desirable goal we did not invest the full consequences and are not sure whether it will be feasible for all kinds of specifications.

Now we are able to define an atomic operation, one that corresponds most closely to a VDM operation. This was important to the VIP project as many operations had to be written as close as possible to normal VDM. For these operations the relation is defined to be a relation between two states where only the write variables may differ, as in conventional VDM. The operational behaviour of an atomic operation is assumed such that it relates two successive states via one —internal— step if something is changed and relates the state with itself if nothing is changed. Syntactically we indicated an atomic operation by the absence of an intercondition.

Definition 7 *An* atomic *operation is an operation where the relation in the postcondition is defined to be a relation between two states possibly differing in the write variables but in no other variable with the implicit intercondition stating that the operation can take either one internal step or non at all:*

inter $(\neg \bigcirc \text{true}) \vee (\text{is-}I \wedge \bigcirc \neg \bigcirc \text{true})$.

Here $\neg \bigcirc$ true is used to indicate that there is no next state, and is-I is a proposition added to conventional temporal logic that indicates the fact that the next state will be reached through an internal step.

Note that by defining the relation of the post condition in this way for the atomic operation, every atomic operation is relationally maximally defined.

8 The Specification Language

To meet the requirements of the VIP project a language VVSL[15] (VIP VDM Specification Language) was designed with the following properties:

- based on VDM;
- ability for structuring and reusing specification parts;
- ability to describe operational aspects in addition to the relation aspects;
- ability to separate "exceptional" from normal cases.

In order for the extensions to be well defined VVSL has been given a formal semantics; it was decided not to develop this from scratch but to use the formal design language COLD-K[3] (Kernel COLD) as a basis. This provided the mechanisms for structuring and parameterisation.

VVSL is mainly defined via syntactic transformations to COLD-K. The temporal part, however, is defined as a semantic extension to COLD-K. Furthermore, well thought out (syntactic) extensions appeared to be necessary in order to be able to manage specification of the size the VIP project had to cope with. Especially a facility for separation of "normal" and "exceptional" cases proved quite valuable.

9 Concluding remarks

The VIP project has been able to successfully describe the interfaces to a large system formally by combining relational interface description with temporal logic extended with the concept of external and internal steps. The temporal logic is only explicitly needed in the cases that the operational aspects are needed to describe some aspects of the system that cannot be expressed relationally. In this way we could be as abstract as possible. The possibility to synthesize systems from their interface specifications seems to be there, although this was not investigated within the project.

The conciseness of the language used appeared to be of crucial importance to specifications of this size and the language VVSL caters for that by giving the possibility to reuse specification parts, to modularise the specification and to separate the normal and exceptional cases in operations.

The transformational semantics given to VVSL by defining VVSL in terms of COLD-K appeared to be feasible. One of the drawbacks was that we lost the ability to use higher order functions. Often is said that for interface specifications these higher order functions are not needed. However aspects of user definable reactions on asynchronous signals could not be specified. Although in the particular interface these kind of constructs were of relatively low importance, systems that are based on these can easily be imagined.

Acknowledgements

I want to acknowledge the help of Kees Middelburg, who gave VVSL a formal semantics, and was always eager not to believe me when I said I needed some feature in describing the interfaces to PCTE. This kept VVSL clean. I want to thank Jeroen Bruijning for his constant effort of helping me to be clear, and all the other people in the VIP project for the numerous fruitful discussions about PCTE and VVSL.

References

[1] H. Barringer. The use of temporal logic in the compositional specification of concurrent systems. In *Temporal Logics and their Applications*, chapter 2, Academic Press Limited, London, 1987.

[2] J. Bruijning and M. Kooij. *Temporal Constructs and Error Conditions in VVSL.* Working Paper VIP.T.D.JB6, VIP, September 1988.

[3] L.M.G. Feijs, H.B.M. Jonkers, C.P.J. Koymans, and G.R. Renardel de Lavalette. *Formal Definition of the Design Language COLD-K.* Preliminary Edition METEOR/t7/PRLE/7, METEOR, 1987.

[4] M.D. Fisher. *Temporal Logic for Abstract Semantics.* PhD thesis, University of Manchester, Department of Computer Science, 1986.

[5] C.B. Jones. *Systematic Software Development Using VDM.* Prentice-Hall, 1986.

[6] M. Kooij. *An abbreviation for the PCTE specification.* Working Paper VIP.T.D.MK10, VIP, September 1988.

[7] M. Kooij. *LaTeX macros for VVSL.* Working Paper VIP.T.D.MK6, VIP, April 1988.

[8] F. Kröger. *Temporal Logic of Programs.* Springer Verlag, EATCS Monographs on Theoretical Computer Science, 1987.

[9] Z. Manna and P. Wolper. Synthesis of communicating processes from temporal logic specifications. *ACM Transactions on Programming Languages and Systems,* 6(1):68–93, January 1987.

[10] C.A. Middelburg. *Translation from VVSL to COLD-K.* Working Paper VIP.T.D.KM15, VIP, May 1988.

[11] C.A. Middelburg. VVSL: a language for structured VDM specifications. *Formal Aspects of Computing,* 1(1), 1989.

[12] C.A. Middelburg. *VVSL: Examples of Use.* Working Paper VIP.T.D.KM10, VIP, January 1988.

[13] *PCTE Functional Specifications.* ESPRIT, 4th edition, June 1986.

[14] *PCTE Functional Specifications (ADA interface).* ESPRIT, 1st edition, 1987.

[15] VIP Project Team. *VDM Extensions: Final Report.* Report VIP.T.E.4.3, VIP, December 1988.

[16] VIP Project Team. *Kernel Interfaces: Final Specification.* Report VIP.T.E.8.2, VIP, December 1988.

A Examples

Three examples are given. One atomic operation that changes the value of a variable in the state, and one that waits for a flag to go down before it changes the variable. With somewhat less detailed comments also a system is described with two interface calls: a producer and a consumer. The examples are focussed on the description of the temporal logic constructs available in VVSL. For a detailed example of the modularisation and parameterisation constructs see [11]. The abbreviation constructs for separating special cases are extensively used in [16].

A.1 Atomic

The following operation is atomic and increments the counter. It cannot be interrupted by other operations and will take only one internal step that increments a counter with the amount specified in its input parameter. Both to implementors and to users it is clear that after doing this call the counter is incremented with the amount specified.

module
  state
    counter : $\mathbf{N}$
    flag : $\mathbf{B}$
  operations
    $COUNT\_UP(n : \mathbf{N})$
    ext   wr *counter* : $\mathbf{N}$
    pre $n \geq 1$
    post $counter = \overleftarrow{counter} + n$
end

Comments on this example:

The state the state consists of two variables a boolean flag and a counter that is a natural number.

The externals there is one variable known to the operation: *counter*. It is a write variable.

The precondition the precondition is that n must be 1 or larger. The operation is only defined in that case.

The postcondition the postcondition defines a relation between two states where the new value of *counter* is n plus the old value (indicated by $\overleftarrow{counter}$).

The intercondition the intercondition is absent: the operation is atomic. The change of the *counter* variable is accomplished in one internal step. The value of the flag is implicitly not changed by this operation.

A.2 Interleaved

This operation waits for a flag to go down before it changes a variable. The operation does not influence the state (this is modelled by external steps) until a boolean flag becomes "false". Then in one internal step it increments the counter by the amount specified in its input parameter. The postcondition does not give the implementor enough information. It would seem from this postcondition that it would be possible to increment the counter with any number greater or equal than the input parameter indicates. An observer with the possibility of parallel composition of interface calls would conclude otherwise. The intercondition restricts the computations paths to the desired ones.

module
  state
    $counter : \mathbf{N}$
    $flag : \mathbf{B}$
  operations
    $COUNT\_UP(n : \mathbf{N})$
    ext wr $counter : \mathbf{N}$,
        rd $flag : \mathbf{B}$
    pre $n \geq 1$
    post $\neg flag \wedge counter \geq 1$
    inter (is-$E \wedge flag$) U
        ($\neg flag \wedge$ is-$I \wedge \bigcirc counter = counter + n \wedge$
        $\bigcirc \neg \bigcirc$ true)
end

Comments on this example:

The state the state consists of the same variables as the previous operation.

The externals Both variables in the state are visible to the operation: *counter* is a write variable and *flag* is a read variable.

The precondition The precondition is that n must be 1 or bigger. The operation is only defined in that case.

The postcondition The postcondition cannot say as much about the state as in the previous case. Other operation may change the state in the mean time. The only thing we know is that the counter will be greater than zero as we will increment it by at least one (and the other operations can not decrement it below zero) and we know that the flag is down. This is the maximally known relation between the first and the last state.

The intercondition The intercondition tells us that external steps are taken as long as the flag is up (is-$E \wedge$ *flag*) until the flag is down and then the counter is incremented by n in an internal step. The temporal operator U is used to indicate the weak until, also often called the *unless* operator. $\phi\ U\ \theta$ means that ϕ will be true up to a point in time where θ is true or ϕ will be true at all points in time.

A.3 Produce/Consume

This example describes a interface to a producer / consumer system. The producer is in this system unlimited and can produce always. The consumer waits until the buffer is not empty and assigns the first item to its result parameter.

module
  types
    Item free
  functions
    $empty(b : \text{seq of } Item)\ \mathbf{B}$
      $\triangleq b = \langle\rangle$
  state
    $buffer$: seq of $Item$
  operations
    $PRODUCE(i : Item)$
    ext wr $buffer$: seq of $Item$
    pre true
    post $buffer = \overleftarrow{buffer} \frown \langle i \rangle$

    $CONSUME()\ i : Item$
    ext wr $buffer$: seq of $Item$
    pre true
    post $\neg empty(\overleftarrow{buffer}) \Rightarrow \overleftarrow{buffer} = \langle i \rangle \frown buffer$
    inter (is-$E \wedge empty(buffer)$) U
        ($\neg empty(buffer) \wedge$ is-I
        $buffer = \langle i \rangle \frown \bigcirc buffer \wedge$
        $\bigcirc \neg \bigcirc$ true)
end

It can be seen that the producer can fill the buffer with its input parameter in one (atomic) step and thus is not hindered by interfering interface calls. The consumer can take only something out of the buffer in one atomic step if the buffer is not empty. The intercondition specifies that the consumer "idles", takes external steps, as long as the buffer is empty and takes an item out as soon as possible. Note that this system could be extended with more operations on buffers (such as a producer with that produces more than one item at a time) without changing that specification of the consumer.

Viewpoint Analysis: A Case Study

Julio Cesar S. P. Leite
Departamento de Informática
Pontifícia Universidade Católica do Rio de Janeiro
R. Marquês de S. Vicente 225 Rio de Janeiro 22453
Brasil

Abstract

Requirements modeling demands that the knowledge of what should be modeled be available. Acquiring this knowledge or eliciting the necessary requirements is recognized to be a very hard problem. Different suggestions have been made to alleviate this problem. We examine the application of one such approach, viewpoint resolution, towards the IWSSD library problem. This approach is based on the idea of very early validation. The case study presented helps justify the claim that early validation is a desirable characteristic of the software construction process. Four different views of the library problem are analyzed by an automated analyzer, which is capable of identifying problems of correctness and completeness in a pair of views. The results obtained, besides showing the benefits of early validation, show how viewpoint resolution can help very early validation.

1 Introduction

Viewpoint resolution was proposed by Leite [9] as a means for very early validation in the process of requirements elicitation.

Requirements elicitation is the process in requirements analysis responsible for understanding, finding and gathering information. As a part of requirements elicitation, the objective of *fact-validation* is to make sure that the facts gathered reflect the original intent, as well as to help unfold the knowledge not yet recorded as facts[1].

Viewpoint resolution is a different approach to very early validation. It takes place in the process of fact-validation, and it is based on the acknowledgement that software requirements can be elicited from different *viewpoints*.

Our objective is to show, using a "seemingly simple" problem description, how a early validation scheme, based on viewpoints, is capable of identifying and classifying problems related to correctness and completeness. Our results help to show that comparing different perceptions about a problem helps the understanding of the problem being addressed.

The study presented here is very similar to the study done by Wing [16] on the twelve articles addressing the library problem presented at the fourth IWWSD. Wing compares the different approaches and how they reveal problems in the description of the library example. Wing's comparison produced a list of problems of "ambiguities" and "incompletenesses" of the library description. She correctly pointed out that: "the interesting result of the specification exercise is not the specification itself by the insight gained about the specificand". From our viewpoint, Wing performed a viewpoint resolution over the 12 cases analyzed. In our study, we show how our viewpoint resolution framework is applied to the same problem analyzed by Wing.

In the next sections, we will present the overall understanding of viewpoint resolution, the cases analyzed, the results of the study, and conclusions based on these results.

2 Why Viewpoints?

In the task of modeling the users' expectations in the universe of discourse,[2] a systems analyst may encounter, and usually does, different opinions about the problem being addressed. Different systems analysts, when modeling the users' expectation in the **same** universe of discourse, produce different models. The same systems analyst when modeling the same universe of discourse may do so by using different perspectives (e.g.., a data model *versus* a process model).

All the above is common knowledge. The important point is that some software engineering methods use this fact with the objective of producing a model that "better" mirrors the users' expectations in the universe of discourse.

[1]A fact is a relationship between keywords of the application vocabulary

[2]Universe of discourse is the overall context in which the software will be developed. The universe of discourse includes all the sources of information and all the people related to the software. These people are referred to as the **actors** in this universe of discourse.

An example of such a method is CORE [10].

The principle that more sources of information provide a better understanding of a subject has been used for centuries in court investigation. Different witnesses may have conflicting or complementary recollections. By using this principle in the process of elicitation, the "chances" of detecting correctness and completeness problems will be greater. To effectively profit from this principle it is necessary to compare and analyze different views.

The analysis and comparison of viewpoints as proposed by Ross' SADT [13] and Mullery's CORE are informal tasks. They are similar to what we [9] call "Using Informal Checking." They rely heavily on the "good" systems analyst.

Although CORE and SADT advocate the use of viewpoints, neither one has a structured model to explicitly state how to profit from doing so. That is, besides the reliance on inspection procedures and some general guidelines, no model is presented for the use of viewpoints with the results derived from their inspection.

In order to properly profit from considering different viewpoints, there is a need for what we call viewpoint resolution. Next, we describe viewpoint resolution and define the terminology used in this framework.

3 Viewpoint Resolution

Viewpoint resolution is a means for very early validation in the process of requirements elicitation. It assumes a process oriented definition of requirements analysis as proposed in [2]. According to this definition, requirements analysis is seen as composed of two processes: requirements elicitation and modeling (see Figure 1).

- Requirements Analysis
  - **Modeling**
    - *Representation*
    - *Organization*
  - **Elicitation**
    - *Fact-finding*
    - *Communication*
    - *Fact-validation*

Figure 1: Parts of the Requirements Analysis Process

> Viewpoint resolution is the process which identifies discrepancies between two different viewpoints, classifies and evaluates those discrepancies and integrates the alternative solutions into a single representation (Figure 2).

By examining the model presented in Figure 2 and the definition of requirements analysis (Figure 1), it is easy to note that there are some viewpoint resolution tasks belonging to *fact-validation* and others belonging to *communication*. The tasks related to fact-validation are called **viewpoint analysis** and the tasks related to communication are called **viewpoint reconciliation**. Our work [9] does not deal, in detail, with viewpoint reconciliation. Our work has focused on the problems of identification of discrepancies and the classification of these discrepancies, thus providing an *agenda* upon which the evaluation and integration of viewpoints can be based.

In the next section we present the overall strategy for identification and classification of discrepancies in viewpoint resolution. The terms and their definitions used thereafter in the text are as follows. **Universe of discourse** – Universe of discourse is the overall context in which the software will be developed. The universe of discourse includes all the sources of information and all the

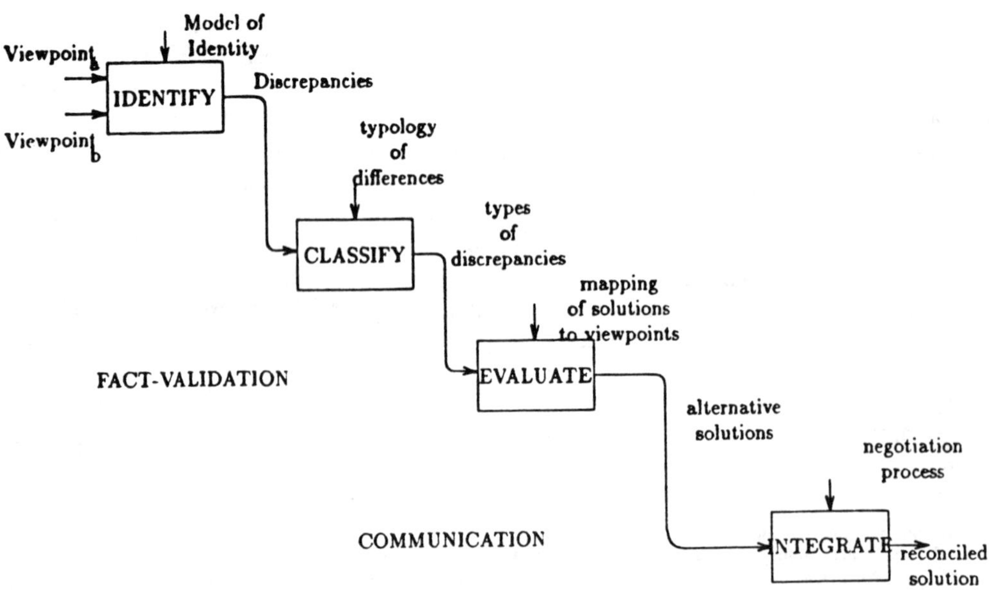

Figure 2: Viewpoint Resolution

people related to the software. These people are referred to as the **actors** in this universe of discourse. **Viewpoint** - A viewpoint is a standing or mental position used by an individual when examining or observing a universe of discourse. A viewpoint is identified by an individual (e.g., his name) and his role in the universe of discourse (e.g., a systems analyst, programmer, or manager). **Perspective** - A perspective is a set of facts observed and modeled according to a particular modeling aspect of reality and a viewpoint. An example of such a particular modeling aspect is what is known as data modeling. In our method we use three modeling aspects: the data perspective, the actor perspective, and the process perspective. **View** - A view is an integration of perspectives. This integration is achieved by a view-construction process. **Hierarchies** - The is-a hierarchy of concepts in the universe of discourse and the parts-of hierarchy of concepts in the universe of discourse.

4 Proposed Strategy for Viewpoint Analysis

The proposed strategy comprises procedures to formalize viewpoints (method), procedures to analyze the formalized viewpoints (static analyzer), and a special language, VWPl, to represent viewpoints. The language provides the representation which registers the formalism, and makes possible its analysis.

The language is derived from PRISM [5], a production system architecture. As such, our viewpoint analysis strategy is basically a process for finding discrepancies between two rule bases, each one representing a different view or perspective according to a viewpoint.

The process of validating facts is dependent on the process of finding facts. It is assumed that the facts (keywords) are available before the application of the viewpoint resolution strategy. Next we present the overall method behind producing a viewpoint, the description of the VWPl, and an overall description of the procedures that analyze different viewpoints.

4.1 Method

In Figure 3 there is an overall description of the strategy. John and Mary, both systems analysts, perform the task of modeling users' intentions. They both use the VWPl language to express their perception of the universe of discourse. They use different perspectives (process, data, and actor) and different hierarchies (is-a, and parts-of) to improve their own view. Once a series of critiques is provided, each analyst alone, solves the internal conflicts and integrates their final perception into a view. This "final" view is expressed in the process perspective together with the hierarchies. After that, both viewpoints are compared and analyzed.

Thus, in order to identify and classify discrepancies between different viewpoints, views are to be taken from the viewpoints. Views are produced by a process called view construction. The construction of a view is based on the following.

- A fact-finding method is defined,

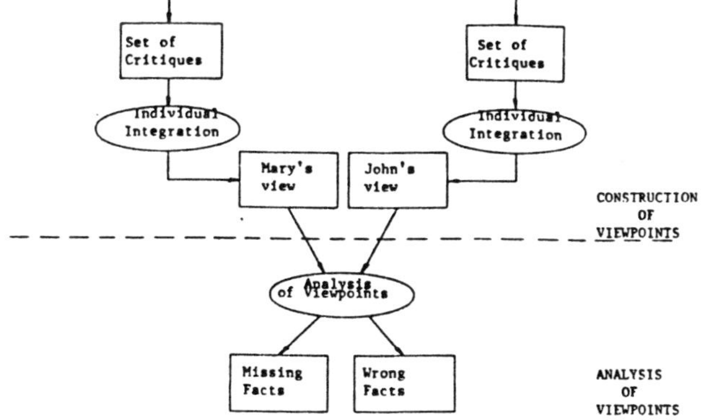

Figure 3: The Proposed Strategy

- a viewpoint holder with a specific role in the universe of discourse,[3] uses different perspectives and hierarchies in modeling his viewpoints,
- perspectives and hierarchies are analyzed by a static analyzer, and
- a view is a model integrating the different perspectives and hierarchies taken from the same viewpoint.

After two views are available it is possible to compare different viewpoints.

As noted above, it is common knowledge that systems analysts, when modeling the universe of discourse, may do so by using different perspectives. An example is the usual modeling of data and processes. This work, in addition to data and process modeling, uses actor modeling [7]. The idea behind actor modeling is to model using the perspective of those who are responsible for the processes, i.e., human agents or devices. The objective of using hierarchies is to try to attach some "semantics" to the information encoded on the viewpoint language. A specialization relationship between keywords is established as well as a decomposition relationship.

In order to construct a view a systems analyst describes the problem using the three perspectives and two hierarchies. The perspectives are: the actor perspective, the data perspective, and the process perspective. The hierarchies are the is-a hierarchy and the parts-of hierarchy. The perspectives and hierarchies are compared, and the "list of discrepancies" and "types of discrepancies" are produced. A view is the integration of perspectives and hierarchies,[4] achieved by the viewpoint holder, with the help of an "agenda", which is produced by the analysis of perspectives. When no more feedback is available from the analysis of perspectives, then an integration can occur.

The construction of a perspective is a process in which there is the assumption that the systems analyst uses the concept of "application vocabulary" [2], such that the keywords of the universe of discourse are carried into the viewpoint representation. The basic idea is that a systems analyst first analyzes a problem and writes down his findings using the VWPl actor perspective. Sometime later, without looking at the result of the actor perspective, the analyst does the same using the data perspective and the process perspective. The same approach is used in acquiring the hierarchies. It is assumed that the comparison of those perspectives and hierarchies held by the same systems analyst will provide him with clues to produce a "better" process perspective and hierarchies which are then considered to be the representation of his viewpoint about the problem.

The general guidelines for acquiring hierarchies and perspectives are as follows. Provide is-a and parts-of hierarchies for the concepts presented in the universe of discourse. For each perspective

- find the facts;
- express the facts using keywords of the application domain;
- classify the facts into: objects facts, actions facts, and agents facts; and
- define functionality of facts by coding them as productions.

Objects represent both the "objects" and the *states* of these objects (that is, objects are the facts that could not be classified under action or agent). There are no constraints on providing the hierarchies; an item is chosen to be in the hierarchy by the sole judgement of the viewpoint holder. The guidelines are purposely loose to make it simpler for the viewpoint holder to express his views.

In order to use the method as described above a representation in which this information will be cast is necessary. The description of such representation is given below.

4.2 The Viewpoint Language

A language was created for representing viewpoints, and its syntax and semantics were defined. This language is derived from PRISM [5], a production system architecture. As such our viewpoint resolution strategy is basically a process for finding discrepancies between two rule bases, each one representing a different perspective or viewpoint. This representation's main objective is to register early results of the fact-elicitation process in the requirements elicitation effort. It is not intended to be a requirements language. Its usefulness is restricted to the fact-validation process.

Our research has been exploring the use of a rule base language as a way of expressing functionality and constraints for the process of elicitation in requirements analysis. A claim made earlier [8] and the empirical evidence available from our work [8], together with references from the literature [4], allows us to hypothesize that expressing functionality and functionality-related constraints in production rules is simple and fairly easy to use.

The overall idea of VWPl is to have a predefined structure for the construction of rules. The imposition of a further constraint on the usual scheme of the left hand side being conditions and the right hand side being actions, makes it possible that some static semantic information is made available by the rule structure itself. The approach used in VWPl is similar to the one used in *case grammars*

[3] Our work used a fixed role of the viewpoint holder, that is the role of a systems analyst.

[4] It is important to note that in the construction of a view there is no need for the tasks related to the communication process (see Figure 2). Since the discrepancies in view construction are related to a single person, the systems analyst, the "mapping of solution to viewpoints" and the "negotiation" are not a problem, since they only depend on one single individual.

[11], where the structures produced by the grammar rules correspond to semantics relations rather than to strictly syntactic ones.

In the case of VWPl the semantics relations are achieved by using what we call *types* and *classes* constraints. Types are the differents sorts of facts used, that is, the object facts, the action facts, and the agent facts. Classes are the different roles each fact may have in a rule. In a rule a fact can:

- be deleted from working memory[5] (we call that the *input class*),
- be added to the working memory (we call that the *output class*), or
- remain in working memory (we call that the *invariant class*).

A *fact* is a relationship between keywords. The keywords used for expressing facts in VWPl are checked against a type list before being parsed. In other words, a set membership "semantic' check is performed on the keywords provided for describing the view.

The general structure of the rules are described by the VWPl grammar [9]. For each perspective there is a special combination of types and classes. In this article we only use the process perspective, for which the rule structure is as follows.

- LHS – **input** is an action and objects (optional), **invariant** can be an agent and/or an object.
- RHS – **output** is an object.

A fact is composed of a *fact-keyword* and *fact-attribute*. An example is "(book =book-id =author =title)." In this case we have the fact-keyword "book" and the attributes: "book-id", "author", and "title.". By using a nondeterministic control, it is possible to use the process perspective as an early, executable, expression of the requirements [8].

Hierarchies are encoded as lists. The lists are organized by the kind of hierarchy (is-a, or parts-of) and the type of the facts. For each kind and type the root in the hierarchy is the head of a list followed by the leaves of that hierarchy. Next, we describe the automated static analyzer implemented in Scheme [14].

4.3 The Static Analyzer

The analysis of different perspectives and different views is achieved by a set of procedures, which perform an analysis of two sets of perspectives or views. The perspectives and/or views are represented using VWPl. Because VWPl is a rule based representation, the static analysis is really performed between two rule sets (Figure 4).

Comparing two rule sets only makes sense when there is enough similarity between them. In our case there is a series of factors that leads to that similarity; below we list the most important ones.

- The fact that viewpoint holders are viewing the same universe of discourse.
- The use of a method which stress the importance of maintaining the concept of "application vocabulary" when modeling a view or a perspective.
- The use of a special language which constrains how the rules are expressed.

The static analyzer proposed and implemented has two major tasks: finding which rules are similar between each other, and, once rules are paired, identifying and classifying the discrepancies between them. Rules that are not paired are classified as missing information. The pairing of rules and their further analysis are basically syntactic oriented.

Being based on the syntactic representation of terms, the analyzer depends basically on pattern matchers and partial matchers. Those matching procedures, which are applied between facts of the two different rule sets, have different scoring algorithms depending on the "semantic" information available from the *types* and *classes* of each fact.

The classification of discrepancies, that is, determining which are the missing information discrepancies and which are the wrong information discrepancies, is done based on scores resulting from the matchers and on the information available in the hierarchies. In designing the static analyzer we borrowed several ideas from the work on analogy in Artificial Intelligence and used a descriptive framework described by Hall [3][6] (Figure 4). Simple "semantics" hints, such as: using hierarchies and case grammars, are used to enhance the performance of the analyzer. It is obvious that the static analyzer can not say anything about two rules that do not have discrepancies but which are not correct with respect to the universe of discourse.

5 Case Study

The case study undertaken by this article is based on four articles presented at the fourth IWSSD: ***A Larch Specification of the Library Problem*** [15], ***What Does it Mean to Say that a Specification is Complete*** [17], ***Toward a Requirements Apprentice*** [12], and ***SXL: An Executable Specification Language*** [6]. Each of these articles has a different approach; Wing's work uses a formal language, Yue's is based on the notions of causation and conditionals in logic, Rich's work is based on the notions of domain knowledge, and Lee's is based on an executable language. All

[5] Working memory is the global database of a production system, where the facts are kept and changed.

[6] There are four general heuristics used in the static analyzer: partial matching heuristics, scoring heuristics, evaluation heuristics, and classification of discrepancies heuristics [9].

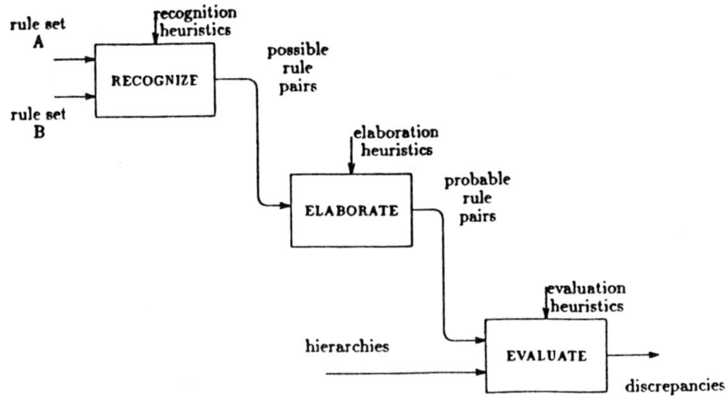

Figure 4: The Static Analyzer Heuristics

the papers deal with the library problem. Since we believe that the audience of this article is familiar with the library problem we do not describe it here.

In order to make it possible to present in a short paper the details of viewpoint analysis, we restricted ourselves to the action "check-out" and on the constraints of the library problem. In [9] longer cases are reported. Next we outline the main assumptions used in the study, as well as the heuristic used to transform each author description into a view.

5.1 Premises and General Heuristic

The ideal case study would be to have each of the authors describe the library problem using our viewpoint language, VWPl, and using the method we prescribed. Since this is not the case, we simulated their use of VWPl. This simulation is believed to be realistic because of the following assumptions. Each of the authors, independent of the approach used, performed a elicitation process. Each author produced a "model" of the problem using their preferred approach. The universe of discourse is the library statement, augmented by each author preconcived notion of a library. Most of the authors used the concept of "application vocabulary". The actions and the agents are easily identified. Each author has already "debuged" his understanding of the problem, such that we can consider their representations to be their final "view" of the problem.

The general heuristic used to construct each author viewpoint is as follows:

> Find where the author describes the action "check-out" and base the construction of the rule(s) in that description. Use the same keywords, used by the definition of operations or entities in the author method, for naming the facts. Use as attributes of the facts the parameters or the attributes of each operation or entity. In the approaches where there is separation between data and process, use the data portion to help constructing the hierarchies. Also, use the data portion to help the identification of the attributes. Distinguish agents from objects based on a "well behaved guess"; for the action there is no doubt, since that the process "check-out" is very well distinguished in all the four works.

Using the above set of heuristics it was relatively straightfoward to come up with VWPl rules for each of the approaches. The less easy tasks were: choosing the right attributes in order to give the "execution flavor" of VWPl (process perspective), and describing the notion of number of books checked out to a customer.

It should be clear that some of the papers do not intend to give explicit descriptions, let alone complete ones. Because of that, it is not fair to suppose that one approach is more complete or more correct than the others. On the other hand, since some of the approaches were less complete than others, we could demonstrate the capability of our automated viewpoint analysis. Next we present the "codified" view of each author.

5.2 VWPl Descriptions

The descriptions use the perspective rule described above. The fact *delete-from* the working memory (RHS) is the pre-condition **input** (LHS). A pre-condition **input** is discarded in order to maintain the working memory consistency. The fact *add-to* the working memory (RHS) is the post-condition **output**. The other facts in the LHS are the pre-conditions that did not change, that is, the **invariants**. In the hierarchies *is-a* and *parts-of*, the head of the list is the root of the hierarchy. We will provide a brief comment for the first rule of these descriptions, to help the understanding of the VWPl syntax.

```
YUE
(
 (21 ((check-out =borrower =copy)
  (book =author =title =copy)
  (library-copy =copy)
  (<not> (copy-borrower =borrower =copy)))
    -->
   (($delete-from wm (check-out =borrower =copy))
   ($add-to wm (copy-borrower =borrower =copy))))
; rule 21 CHECK-OUT is the input, BOOK,
;  LIBRARY-COPY and <NOT> COPY-BORROWER are
;  invariants and COPY-BORROWER is the output.
;  The attributes are: borrower, copy,
;  author, title and copy.
 (22 ((countofcopy =user =n)
  (greater =n =n-minus-one))
  (checkout-limit =user =n-minus-one)
    -->
  (($add-to wm (error checkout-limit))))
 )
```

```
(is-a (1 (user borrower library-staff)))
(parts-of (2 (book author title copy)))
;  In the is-a hierarchy the agent user is
;  the higher generalization of borrower
;  and library-staff.  In the parts-of
;  hierarchy; author, title and copy are
;  parts of the object book.

RICH
(
 (51 ((check-out =isbn) (library =isbn)
  (user =user-name) (staff =staff-name))
     -->
  (($delete-from wm (check-out =isbn)
   (library =isbn))))
 (52 ((check-out =isbn) (<not> (library =isbn)))
     -->
  (($add-to wm (error library))))
 )
 (is-a (2 (library repository)
        (library copies-of-books)))
 (parts-of (2 (repository itens place staff users)
             (copy-of-a-book title author isbn)))

WING
(
 (1 ((user =name =status =usr-books)
  (library =users =lib-books)
  (book =title =author =subject)
  (<not> (notavail =library =book))
  (<not> (overlimit  =user =size))
  (<not> (hascopy =user =book))
  (check-out =library =user =book))
     -->
  (($delete-from wm
    (check-out =library =user =book))
  ($add-to wm (checkedout =library =book))))
 (2 ((user =name =status =usr-books)
  (library =users =lib-books)
  (book =title =author =subject)
  (<not> (notavail =library =book))
  (<not> (overlimit  =user =size))
  (<not> (hascopy =user =book))
  (check-out =library =user =book))
     -->
  (($delete-from wm
    (check-out =library =user =book))
  ($add-to wm (responsible =book =user))))
 (3 ((limit =anumber) (overlimit =user =size))
     -->
   (($add-to wm (error limit))))
 (4 ((<not> (notavail =library =book))
     (checkedout =library =book))
    -->
    (($add-to wm (error notavail))))
 (5 ((notavail =library =book)
   (<not> (checkedout =library =book)))
    -->
   (($add-to wm (error checkedout))))
 )
 (is-a (1 (user regular staff)))
 (parts-of (1 (users name status books))
           (2 (book title author subject)
              (library users books)))

LEE
(
 (41
  ((check-out =user =title-of =author-of =borrower)
   (book =author-of =title-of)
   (book-available =author-of =title-of)
   (is-staff =user)
   (user =borrower))
     -->
   (($delete-from wm
    (check-out =user =title-of =author-of =borrower))
   ($add-to wm
   (checked-out-to =title-of =author-of =borrower))))
 (42
  ((check-out =user =title-of =author-of =borrower)
   (book =author-of =title-of)
   (book-available =author-of =title-of)
   (is-staff =user)
   (user =borrower))
     -->
   (($delete-from wm
    (check-out =user =title-of =author-of =borrower))
   ($add-to wm
    (last-borrower =title-of =author-of =borrower))))
 (43
  ((<not> (book-available =author-of =title-of))
   (<not>
    (checked-out-to =title-of =author-of =borrower)))
     -->
   (($add-to wm (error book-available))))
 (44 ((book-available =author-of =title-of)
   (checked-out-to =title-of =author-of =borrower))
     -->
   (($add-to wm (error checked-out-to))))
 (45 ((<not> (bounds =books =borrower)))
     -->
    (($add-to wm (error bounds))))
 (46 ((book =author-of =title-of)
   (<not>
   (card-catalogue =author-of =title-of =subject)))
     -->
   (($add-to wm (error card-catologue))))
 )
 (is-a (1 (user normal staff)))
 (parts-of (2 (book author-of title-of)
              (card-catalogue subject author-of title-of)))
```

5.3 Results

The static analyzer is not intended to be a perfect analyzer, neither it could be. Its performance is dependent not only on its heuristics as well as on the descriptions being analazed. A demonstration of this is that perspective analysis have, always, had a better performance than viewpoint analysis in the cases studied [9]. Performance here is understood as how well the messages compare with the possible messages produced by an inteligent agent performing the analysis. It also should be kept in mind that the messages produced by the analyzer are advices.

We should note that the analyzer besides producing **relevant** messages, also produces a series of redundant messages and messages that could have been dismissed by an intelligent agent. Unfortunately, this last side effect is not easy to overcome. In the next section, we list some of the messages produced by the analyzer that could be classified under the category of undesirable effects.

We performed three viewpoint analysis, each taking a pair of VWPl descriptions. We compare Rich's rules with

Yue's rules, Yue's rules with Wing's rules, and Wing's rules with Lee's rules. For each comparison; we list the probable rule pairs found by the recognition and elaboration parts of the analyzer (Figure 4), and list, in a prettyprinted format, the *relevant* messages produced, that is, we present a filtered result of the static analyzer. After each comparison there is a brief analysis of the messages produced.

Rich – Yue: The probable rule pairs are (51 21) and (52 21). Follows the *relevant* messages produced.

1. Rich's rules are missing a rule similar to Yue's rule 22.
2. Yue's rule 21 is missing the agents 'user and 'staff with respect to Rich's rule 51.
3. Comparing Rich's rule 51 and Yue's rule 21 the following objects are in contradiction: 'none and 'copy-borrower.
4. The attributes of Rich's 'library and Yue's 'library-copy and Rich's 'check-out and Yue's 'check-out do not correspond.
5. Comparing Rich's rule 52 and Yue's rule 21, the following objects are in contradiction: 'not-library and 'not-copy-borrower.

All these messages, being part of the "agenda" produced by the viewpoint analysis, will bring up discussions between the viewpoint holders about the following problems: constraint on the borrowing limit (1), error messages for not hold constraints (5), the role of the agents 'user and 'staff (2), the question of responsibility of a user (3), and the questions about attributes (4). These discussions are part of, what we have called, viewpoint reconciliation (Figure 2).

Yue – Wing: The probable rule pairs are (21 02), (21 01) and (22 03). The *relevant* messages are listed below.

1. Yue's rules are missing rules similar to Wing's rules 5 and 4.
2. Yue's rule 21 is missing the objects 'not-notavail and 'not-overlimit and the agent 'user with respect to Wing's rule 1.
3. Comparing Yue's rule 21 and Wing's rule 2, the following objects are in contradiction: 'copy-borrower and 'responsible.
4. Comparing Yue's rule 21 and Wing's rule 1, the following objects are in contradiction: 'copy-borrower and 'checkedout.
5. The attributes of Yue's 'checkout-limit and Wing's 'limit do not correspond.
6. The attributes of Yue's 'book and Wing's 'book and Yue's 'check-out and Wing's 'check-out do not correspond.

The messages produced by this comparison raises the questions about: the constraints (5 and 4), the role of the agent 'user (2), the notions of responsability and 'checked-out-to (3 and 4), and the different attributes used (5 and 6). These questions, by being part of the agenda for viewpoint reconciliation, should be resolved by the actors involved in the process of elicitation.

Wing – Lee The probable rule pairs are (1 41), (1 42) (2 41), (2 42), (3 43), (3 44), (4 43), (4 44), (5 43), and (5 44). Next we list the *relevant messages* produced by the analyzer.

1. Wing's rules are missing a rule similar to Lee's rule 46.
2. There is 54%[8] of chance that Wing's rule 2 is missing the object 'is-staff and Lee's rule 42 is missing the object 'not-overlimit.
3. There is 11% of chance that Lee's rule 42 is missing the object 'library and Wing's rule 2 is missing 'last-borrower.
4. Lee's rule 42 is missing the object 'not-hascopy.
5. The attributes of Wing's 'user and Lee's 'user do not correspond.
6. The attributes of Wing's check-out and Lee's check-out do not correspond.

The messages reported in this comparison bring up the following problems: the necessity of adding a 'card-catalogue constraint (1), the need to establish the role of 'library (3), the role of the object 'is-staff (2), the attributes of 'book, 'user and 'check-out (5 and 6), and the necessity of checking if a borrower has, already, a copy of a book (4). As with the other comparisons, this agenda will drive the processes of evaluation and integration of viewpoints.

6 Limitations of our Method and Future Work

The analyzer, as expected, generated some non relevant messages. For example: in the case of the Yue – Wing comparison, one message "mistakenly" compares Yue's 'countof-copy with Wing's 'overlimit and Yue's 'greater with Wing's 'limit, when the comparison should be the other way around; In the case of Wing –Lee comparison, the pairs (1 42), (2 41), (3 43), (3 44), (4 45) and (5 44) were considered to be "probable rule pairs", when in "reality" they should not; in the case of Rich – Yue the attribute diagnosis for the pair (51 21) was repeated for the (52 21) pair.

The heuristics of the analyzer could be improved mainly by using better pattern-matchers and by eliminating redundant messages.

By heavily relying on the "application vocabulary" concept [2], the strategy is very much syntax

[8]This percentage represents the message degree of belief, it is attributed according to the results of the set of scoring heuristic.

oriented. Although being syntax oriented the experiments done so far have demonstrated its usefullness. These experiments used, at a maximum, rule bases of 20 rules. Its use for larger rule bases was not investigated, but an incremental use of the strategy, for different levels of abstraction [9], could help in addressing this problem. Another aspect not dealt with, so far, is the construction of human-interfaces for the strategy.

Further experiments with viewpoint analysis, will not only evaluate its uselfulness in the process of elicitation, and thus on the process of knowledge acquisition, but will possibly suggest improvements that will make its application more productive.

7 Conclusions

The case study helped to show that it is higlhy desirable to have an early validation in the software construction process. By doing so, it also showed the role of a viewpoint analysis strategy in pointing out problems in the understanding of the situation which we are trying to model. Although the "agenda" produced by the viewpoint analysis distinguishes between completeness and consistencies problems between views, it raises a series of `problems` that may show "ambiguities" or "incompleteness" of the source of information in the universe of discourse. By examining different views of the same universe of discourse we are obtaining a meta insight about what Wing calls the specificand.

The evaluation and the integration of views has to deal with those problems, and has to perform the formation of the reconciled view (Figure 2). It should be noted that this process is not a simple technical problem, but it is, in reality, a problem which is related to social aspects of computing, since it deals with several different actors of the universe of discourse. It is interesting to observe that Wing [16] did a sort of viewpoint resolution in her analysis of the library problem, since she acknowledged the change of information between the several authors involved, but in that case she was the final judge of the analysis. Viewpoint reconciliation should try to be a participative process with all the actors involved in the process.

The distinction of completeness problems from consistency problems is one of the greatest advantages of using a domain based approach [12] [1]. In this approach, a requirements is validated against the domain. Our approach, although not providing the same performance as compared to a domain based validation, has the advantage of not needing the costly construction of a domain.

References

[1] Fickas, S. Automating the Analysis Process: An Example. *In 4th International Workshop on Software Specification and Design* (Monterey, CA, 1987), IEEE Computer Society Press, pp. 58-67

[2] Freeman P. and Leite J.C.S.P. Requirements Techniques and Languages: A Survey. *Dept. of Computer Science. Univesity of California Irvine*, submitted for publication (1988)

[3] Hall, R. Computational Approaches to Analogical Reasoning: A Comparative Analysis. *Artificial Intelligence 21*, 1 (Jan. 1988), 241-250.

[4] Kowalski, R. Software Engineering and Artificial Intelligence in New Generation Computing. 1984. from an Award Lecture on May 15, 1984 in London.

[5] S. Ohlsson and P. Langley; *PRISM Tutorial and Manual*. Tech. Rep. 86-02, University of California, Irvine - Dept. of Computer Science, Feb. 1986.

[6] Lee S. and Sluizer S. SXL: An Executable Language. *In 4th International Workshop on Software Specification and Design* (Monterey, CA, 1987), IEEE Computer Society Press, pp. 231-235

[7] Leite, J. *The Agent Viewpoint*. Tech. Rep. RTP 070, Dept. of Comp. Science, Univ. of Calif., Irvine, Mar. 1987.

[8] Leite, J. *A Proposal for Applied Research on Requirements Elicitation*. Tech. Rep. RTP 072, Dept. of Comp. Science, Univ of Calif., Irvine, Jul. 1987.

[9] Leite, J. *Viewpoint Resolution in Requirements Elicitation*. PHD thesis, Dept. of Comp. Science, Univ. of Calif., Irvine, 1988.

[10] Mullery, G. CORE - A Method for Controlled Requirement Specification. In *Proc. 4th Int. Conf. on Softw. Eng.* (1979), IEEE Computer Society Press, pp. 126-135.

[11] Rich E. *Artificial Intelligence*. Mc Graw-Hill, New York, 1983.

[12] Rich, C., Waters, R., and Reubenstein, H. Toward a Requirements Apprentice. *In 4th International Workshop on Software Specification and Design* (Monterey, CA, 1987), IEEE Computer Society Press, pp. 79-86.

[13] Ross, D. Structured Analysis (SA): A Language for Communicating Ideas. In *Tutorial on Design Techniques*, Freeman and Wasserman, Eds., IEEE Computer Society Press, Long Beach, CA 1980, pp. 107-125.

[14] Steele G., and Sussman, G. *The Revised Report on Scheme, a Dialect of LISP*. Tech. Rep. AI Memo No. 452, MIT, Jan. 1978.

[15] Wing J. A Larch Specification of the Library Problem. *In 4th International Workshop on Software Specification and Design* (Monterey, CA, 1987), IEEE Computer Society Press, pp. 34-41.

[16] Wing J. A Study of 12 Specifications of the Library Problem, *in IEEE Software 5,4* (Jul. 1988), 66-76.

[17] Yue K. What Does It Mean to Say that a Specification Is Complete? *In 4th International Workshop on Software Specification and Design* (Monterey, CA, 1987), IEEE Computer Society Press, pp. 34-41.

Specifying Reusable Components Using Z: Realistic Sets and Dictionaries

Ralph L. London
Kathleen R. Milsted*

Tektronix Laboratories

Abstract

We use the Z specification language to specify the designs of two reusable components and their interfaces. The components are based on sets and dictionaries from Smalltalk, each of which can provide surprises to users. We prove a significant property of desired behavior of the specifications under the precondition expected by the implementations. Specification and proof played an important role in our understanding of the components.

1 Introduction

Many people believe that reusable software components will increase software productivity and quality. To support that achievement, we believe that specifications have several contributions to make toward the realization of software components. First, specifications are needed so that potential users who are searching or browsing through a catalog of components will be able to learn what is available and what they may expect from each component. Second, specifications are needed so that suppliers of components may know what they must provide. Suppliers need to be free to change implementations subject only to still meeting the specifications. Providers may also supply more, or better capabilities, as long as doing so does not contradict the specification. Third, creating specifications can provide one more useful approach and discipline to understanding existing components as well as to providing guidance in formulating requirements, capabilities and implementations. The act of writing a specification usually raises questions, concerns and points of view that would otherwise be missed.

To study how components could best or reasonably be specified, we decided to use the specification language Z [2,5] to specify designs of reusable components. These designs are based on similar designs of several real and often reused components from Smalltalk [1]. We assume the reader is familiar with Z; only minimal knowledge of Smalltalk is needed. Our choice of components to specify, sets and then dictionaries, exposed us to very interesting examples not fully understood by us or our colleagues. It provided an opportunity to derive and prove a significant property of the specifications under the assumption expected by the implementors. Although the components are derived from Smalltalk, their use is more widespread. Separate implementations of the specification can be provided in other languages, such as C++. In summary, then, we define reusable software components and their interfaces, all in Z, and we provide verifications of the specified properties. We also report on using Z for this work.

We consider the Smalltalk set abstraction to be an industrial-strength example because it is a careful, efficient, practical and robust implementation that is very commonly used as part of a real system. However, users of Smalltalk sets often experience surprises because sets can appear to behave in unexpected, even counterintuitive ways. It would be helpful if set users could be given a specification that captured the set abstraction succinctly. The specification should explain sets, and in particular, the surprises, without revealing unnecessary features of

*Also Programming Research Group, Oxford University, England

the implementation. Our specification is detailed enough to explain surprises without having to replicate all of the language details of Smalltalk. The other Smalltalk class of interest here is the dictionary abstraction, a subclass of sets. It can be specified largely in terms of sets even though the implementation partly uses more primitive operations. Such uses need not be revealed in a specification of dictionary.

In the following sections we first briefly describe abstract sets and note relevant equality operations. Next we discuss the main technique used in the Smalltalk implementation of sets and discuss the implementation precondition. It is helpful to give examples of what can happen without this precondition. We then give the Z specification of a design for sets with commentary; the specification is a model of the actual code. In all cases we motivate, state and verify what the specification yields under the implementation assumption. In fact, it yields abstract sets, fortunately. We then specify dictionaries largely in terms of the set interface. We close with observations and conclusions. Throughout this paper, our mention of Smalltalk should be interpreted generally as "Smalltalk-like" or "Smalltalk-inspired."

2 Abstract Sets and Smalltalk Sets

Abstract sets correspond to a requirements-level specification of our reusable set component. Based on classical sets, they may be empty, or may contain elements of different kinds. One may ask whether a particular element is a member of a set. One may add an element to a set or remove an element. Finally, one may apply a function to each element of a set and form a new set of the results. The main difference from classical sets is that the equality relation among elements of an abstract set is not assumed to be pure identity; we only insist that it be an equivalence relation.

The design-level specification, which is our main concern, is modelled after the Smalltalk set implementation. Here, an empty set is obtained with the message new. The other operations are implemented by the message names includes:, add:, remove: and collect:. The equality relation that holds among elements of a Smalltalk set need not be identity since redefinition of the symbol = is allowed in different classes. A point on our notation: use of the symbol = to represent the equality relation among elements would introduce a conflict with our later Z specification where = is predefined and always means identity. For this reason, we shall use the symbol E for element equality. Surprises may result from not having the expected equality, especially if it arises through inheritance.

Let us now describe briefly in words the Smalltalk implementation, called linear probing [3]. Elements of a set are stored in an array. An element is put at the index of the element's hash value, or at the first available unoccupied index following the index of the hash value. An element is not stored again if an already existing equal element is found. Searching for an element starts at the element's hash value and continues until an equal element is found or an unoccupied index permits the search to end. Removing an element may require some adjusting of existing elements (called "fixing collisions") to permit later accurate searching. The searches for an unoccupied index and for an element may wrap around to the first index of the array. The object nil is used to indicate an unoccupied index and thus serves as a terminator of a search for an element. Adding the element nil to a set is ignored. This design for a set is good because searches are shortened, removes are relatively easy, there are no restrictions on the elements, and there are no assumptions on element density.

We can motivate the data structure of sets in three steps. Start with a table that does pure linear search with no hashing. Introduce hashing and provide each slot in that table with its own linear search table to allow for hash collisions. The hash collision tables are disjoint from each other and from the main table. Finally, place all the hash collision tables back into the main table where they will now generally overlap but will still be linearly searched.

The relations E and *hash* are not independent of each other. The Smalltalk book [1, p. 96] states, "Any two objects that are equal must return the same value for hash." It also advises (using = for our E), "Any time = is redefined, hash may also have to be redefined in order to preserve the property that any two objects that are equal return equal values for hash." This property that equal elements hash equally, i.e. if x E y then *hash* x = *hash* y,[1] we

[1] One might argue that the = here should be E for comparing two integer responses to Smalltalk hash. We prefer saying we are comparing two results of a Z function *hash*.

shall call the equal-hash property. Maintaining it is another way to avoid surprises as we shall show that sets behave as expected when it holds. The equal-hash property is certainly not part of abstract sets. One might consider it to be a property of the sets' elements. It is definitely a precondition or constraint on the use of this implementation if one expects abstract set behavior. In any case, it is not possible to abstract it away.

It helps to understand the specification below of Smalltalk-like sets if one considers an example where the equal-hash property does not hold. Suppose we have a set of rational fractions with E being equality of values. Thus 1/2 E 2/4. Let *hash* (n/d) be n, i.e. the numerator. We used this E and this hash on an example Smalltalk set of rational fractions and confirmed the behavior we now show.[2] Now *hash* (1/2) $= 1 \neq 2 =$ *hash* (2/4), so equal elements need not hash to equal values. One mild surprise is that s ← Set new. s add: (1/2). s includes: (2/4) will give false. A way to eliminate the surprise is to modify the hash function to reduce its argument to lowest terms before computing the hash.

This example can also produce another group of surprises. For instance, s ← Set new. s add: (1/2). s add: (3/6). s includes: (2/4) gives false. If we continue with s, then s add: (2/3). s includes: (2/4) now gives true. Continuing again, s remove: (2/3). s includes: (2/4) gives false. In this case, the presence or absence of 2/3 changes the result of s includes: (2/4)! Or consider s ← Set new. s add: (1/2). s add: (1/3). s add: (2/4) which constructs a set waiting to surprise. Now s add: (1/2). s includes: (1/2) gives true, as expected. However, continuing, s remove: (1/2). s includes: (1/2) still gives true, but not as expected! To a carefully rigged set we've added an element, immediately removed that same element, but it appears to remain. These surprises each occur because of the absence of search properties that the equal-hash property would provide. In essence equal-hash means that searches for equal elements start at the same index, and furthermore, that searches are not extended or shortened based on the accident of an occupied or unoccupied index.

There is a final irony and surprise to mention. With all the emphasis on equality of elements, there has been no mention of equality of sets! In Smalltalk, equality of sets becomes == (identity) through inheritance from Object, meaning that two sets with equal elements might not be equal. For abstract sets we think two sets should be equal when they contain equal elements. It is easy to obtain this and to restore the equal-hash property.

3 Specification of Sets

This section will provide a design-level specification of sets, a Z model of the Smalltalk implementation. There is a fundamental difference between the two because Smalltalk is object-oriented, doing much of its computation by side-effect, while Z is inherently functional (but see Conclusions). In the interest of simplicity and clarity of specification, we chose to specify the implementation as if it were functional. This captures the essence of the implementation. The operations in the Z model return copies of the inputs rather than returning changed inputs.[3]

Some simplifying assumptions were made for the model. E and *hash* are defined as global functions instead of reflecting the situation in Smalltalk where their definitions depend on the class to which an object belongs. E is also assumed to be an equivalence relation. We believe this to be a reasonable requirement of an equality relation, but in Smalltalk this may not be the case.

No explicit mention will be made of a set's maximum size. For completeness we should introduce it because we are dealing with finite sets. However, we felt this added unnecessary formal clutter, and we will assume it exists implicitly. This means that the values produced by the Z hash function are assumed to be less than the maximum set size. (In fact, the Smalltalk code achieves this by taking the hash value modulo the size of the hash table.) The Smalltalk implementation also involves "growing" of the table: an array of fixed size is initially allocated and as the array gets fuller through addition of elements, the elements may be transferred to a larger array (up to the maximum object size). Our model of the table in Z as a number-to-object function abstracts away the need for such a process; growing is neither required nor precluded. It also allows us to model the Smalltalk object nil as the absence of a number in the domain of the function representing the hashtable.

[2] Do not confuse this with the Smalltalk class Fraction which does not exhibit this strange behavior.

[3] Certain Smalltalk set operations return the element rather than the set. We chose to return the set.

3.1 The Data Model

Let $[OBJECT]$ denote the intended members of our sets. The equality relation E and hash function *hash* on objects are defined globally, and if two objects belong to the same equivalence class under E, we shall say they are *surrogates* of each other.

$$
\begin{array}{|l}
\_\mathrm{E}\_ : OBJECT \leftrightarrow OBJECT \\
hash : OBJECT \rightarrow \mathbb{N} \\
\hline
x \mathrel{\mathrm{E}} x \\
x \mathrel{\mathrm{E}} y \Rightarrow y \mathrel{\mathrm{E}} x \\
x \mathrel{\mathrm{E}} y \wedge y \mathrel{\mathrm{E}} z \Rightarrow x \mathrel{\mathrm{E}} z
\end{array}
$$

The hashtable[4] of a set, in which an element occurs only once, is modelled in Z by a finite injective function between numbers and objects.

$$
\begin{array}{|l}
\_SET\_\_\_\_ \\
hashtable : \mathbb{N} \rightarrowtail\!\!\!\!\!\!\!\!\!\;\;\;\;\rightarrow OBJECT
\end{array}
$$

SET will be extended by two subsidiary components which will facilitate later definitions and reasoning: a contiguous *subtable* starting from a given index and a *bucket* of objects at a given index (which are just the objects in the contiguous subtable starting from that index).

$$
\begin{array}{|l}
\_SET\_\_\_\_ \\
SET \\
subtable : \mathbb{N} \rightarrow (\mathbb{N} \rightarrowtail OBJECT) \\
bucket : \mathbb{N} \rightarrow \mathbb{F}\, OBJECT \\
\hline
(m, x) \in subtable\ n \Leftrightarrow (m, x) \in hashtable \wedge \\
\qquad [n..m) \subseteq \mathrm{dom}\ hashtable \\
bucket\ n = \mathrm{ran}\ (subtable\ n)
\end{array}
$$

The notation $[n..m)$ is meant to denote the set of numbers from n to, but not including, m; this may involve wrapping around in the table (m may be less than n). The maximum set size would be involved in its definition, so we chose not to define it formally. We trust however that its meaning is clear.

We shall say a set has well-formed buckets if it satisfies two conditions. First, any object in the hashtable must be in the bucket associated with its hash value, i.e. x must be in the bucket at *hash* x. Second, no individual bucket may contain multiple surrogates.

[4]To improve formatting of Z specifications in this paper, we shall sometimes use *ht* as a synonym for *hashtable*.

$$
\begin{array}{|l}
\_WFBUCKETS\_\_\_\_ \\
r : SET \\
\hline
\forall x : \mathrm{ran}\ r.hashtable \bullet x \in r.bucket\ (hash\ x) \\
\forall x, y, n \mid x, y : r.bucket\ n \bullet x \mathrel{\mathrm{E}} y \Rightarrow x = y
\end{array}
$$

It will be shown that *WFBUCKETS* is a data type invariant of sets, i.e. it holds after the initial operation and is preserved by set operations. Defining it separately here emphasizes the fact that the set operations do have a well-defined behavior even if the property does not hold.

3.1.1 The Equal-Hash Property

The equal-hash property, *EQUAL_HASH*, is the precondition for reasonable behavior of sets. It states simply that two surrogate objects have the same hash value.

$$
\begin{array}{|l}
\_EQUAL\_HASH\_\_\_\_ \\
\forall x, y \bullet x \mathrel{\mathrm{E}} y \Rightarrow hash\ x = hash\ y
\end{array}
$$

Its importance, and that of well-formed buckets, is demonstrated by the following theorem: under equal-hash, a set with well-formed buckets will not have more than one surrogate in its entire hashtable.

$$EQUAL\_HASH;\ WFBUCKETS(r) \vdash$$
$$\forall x, y : \mathrm{ran}\ r.hashtable \bullet x \mathrel{\mathrm{E}} y \Rightarrow x = y$$

Assume $x, y : \mathrm{ran}\ r.hashtable$ and $x \mathrel{\mathrm{E}} y$.

By $WFBUCKETS(r)$, $x \in r.bucket\ (hash\ x)$ and $y \in r.bucket\ (hash\ y)$.

But by *EQUAL_HASH*, $hash\ x = hash\ y$.

So, $x \in r.bucket\ n$ and $y \in r.bucket\ n$ and $n = hash\ x = hash\ y$.

Therefore, by $WFBUCKETS(r)$, $x = y$.

3.2 Set Operations

3.2.1 New

The operation *new* is obviously modelled as a set with an empty hashtable; trivially, it has well-formed buckets since all its buckets are empty.

$$
\begin{array}{|l}
new : SET \\
\hline
new.hashtable = \{\}
\end{array}
$$

3.2.2 Includes

The set operation *includes* is a test of set membership: a set r includes an object x if and only if a surrogate of x exists in the bucket at $hash\ x$.

$$
\begin{array}{|l}
\_includes\_ : SET \leftrightarrow OBJECT \\
\hline
r\ includes\ x \Leftrightarrow \\
\quad \exists\, y \bullet y \in r.bucket\ (hash\ x) \wedge y \ \mathrm{E}\ x
\end{array}
$$

This definition says that the search for an object's surrogate is restricted to a specific portion of the hashtable. With well-formed buckets and under equal-hash, the following theorem and proof justifies this; under these conditions *includes* will therefore behave as expected.

$$EQUAL\_HASH;\ WFBUCKETS(r) \vdash \\ \quad r\ includes\ x \Leftrightarrow \exists\, y : \mathrm{ran}\ r.hashtable \bullet y \ \mathrm{E}\ x$$

$$
\begin{array}{l}
r\ includes\ x \\
\Leftrightarrow \exists\, y \bullet y \in r.bucket\ (hash\ x) \wedge y \ \mathrm{E}\ x \\
\qquad\qquad \text{by definition of } includes \\
\Leftrightarrow \exists\, y \bullet y \in r.bucket\ (hash\ y) \wedge y \ \mathrm{E}\ x \\
\qquad\qquad EQUAL\_HASH \\
\Leftrightarrow \exists\, y \bullet y \in \mathrm{ran}\ r.hashtable \wedge y \ \mathrm{E}\ x \\
\qquad\qquad WFBUCKETS(r)
\end{array}
$$

3.2.3 Add

If an object to be added to a set is already included, nothing further occurs. Otherwise, if there is space for it, the object is added to the hashtable at the "next free hole," i.e. the first unoccupied index, at or beyond (possibly involving wraparound) the object's hash value index.

$$
\begin{array}{|l}
nexthole : SET \times \mathbb{N} \twoheadrightarrow \mathbb{N} \\
\hline
nexthole\ (r, n) \cong m \ \Leftrightarrow\ m \notin \mathrm{dom}\ r.ht \ \wedge \\
\quad [n..m) \subseteq \mathrm{dom}\ r.hashtable
\end{array}
$$

$$
\begin{array}{|l}
\_add\_ : SET \times OBJECT \twoheadrightarrow SET \\
\hline
r\ includes\ x \Rightarrow r\ add\ x = r \\
\neg\,(r\ includes\ x)\ \wedge\ \exists\, m \bullet m = \\
\quad nexthole\ (r, hash\ x) \Rightarrow (r\ add\ x).ht = \\
\quad r.ht \cup \{nexthole\ (r, hash\ x) \mapsto x\}
\end{array}
$$

The interesting feature of *add* is that addition of an element may cause buckets to merge. This, in fact, is the reason for some of the surprises in the examples of section 2. However, it can be shown that *add* preserves well-formed buckets if equal-hash holds.[5] Using this fact, we will now prove that *add* produces results consistent with expected behavior if equal-hash holds and the original set has well-formed buckets.

$$EQUAL\_HASH;\ WFBUCKETS(r);\ r\ includes\ x \\ \vee\ \exists\, m \bullet m = nexthole\ (r, hash\ x) \ \vdash \\ \quad (r\ add\ x)\ includes\ y \Leftrightarrow r\ includes\ y \vee y \ \mathrm{E}\ x$$

$$
\begin{array}{l}
(r\ add\ x)\ includes\ y \\
\Leftrightarrow \exists\, z \bullet z \in (r\ add\ x).bucket\ (hash\ y) \wedge z \ \mathrm{E}\ y \\
\qquad\qquad \text{definition of } includes \\
\Leftrightarrow \exists\, z \bullet z \in (r\ add\ x).bucket\ (hash\ z) \wedge z \ \mathrm{E}\ y \\
\qquad\qquad EQUAL\_HASH \\
\Leftrightarrow \exists\, z \bullet z \in \mathrm{ran}\ (r\ add\ x).hashtable \wedge z \ \mathrm{E}\ y \\
\qquad\qquad add \text{ preserves } WFBUCKETS \\
\Leftrightarrow \exists\, z \bullet (z \in \mathrm{ran}\ r.hashtable \vee z = x) \wedge z \ \mathrm{E}\ y \\
\qquad\qquad \text{definition of } add \\
\Leftrightarrow (\exists\, z \bullet z \in \mathrm{ran}\ r.hashtable \wedge z \ \mathrm{E}\ y) \vee x \ \mathrm{E}\ y \\
\Leftrightarrow (\exists\, z \bullet z \in r.bucket(hash\ z) \wedge z \ \mathrm{E}\ y) \vee y \ \mathrm{E}\ x \\
\qquad\qquad WFBUCKETS(r) \\
\Leftrightarrow (\exists\, z \bullet z \in r.bucket(hash\ y) \wedge z \ \mathrm{E}\ y) \vee y \ \mathrm{E}\ x \\
\qquad\qquad EQUAL\_HASH \\
\Leftrightarrow r\ includes\ y \vee y \ \mathrm{E}\ x \\
\qquad\qquad \text{definition of } includes
\end{array}
$$

3.2.4 Remove

If an object to be removed from a set is not included, nothing further occurs. Otherwise, the index in the hashtable where the object's surrogate occurs is found. All elements in that bucket at the index and beyond (possibly with wraparound) are then removed from the hashtable; those which were exclusively beyond the index are then added back one by one. This is the process of "fixing collisions" noted earlier.

$$
\begin{array}{|l}
fixCollisions : SET \rightarrow \mathbb{N} \rightarrow SET \\
\hline
fixCollisions\ r\ index = \mathrm{reduce}\ add \\
\quad (\mu\, r' \mid r'.ht = r.ht - r.subtable\ index) \\
\quad (r.subtable\ (nextindex\ index))
\end{array}
$$

[5] This and other omitted proofs may be found in [4].

$$
\begin{array}{|l}
\_remove\_ : SET \times OBJECT \rightarrow SET \\
\hline
r\ includes\ x \Rightarrow r\ remove\ x = \\
\qquad \mu\, y \mid y \in r.bucket\ (hash\ x) \wedge y\ \mathrm{E}\ x \bullet \\
\qquad fixCollisions\ r\ (r.hashtable^{-1}\ y) \\
\neg\ (r\ includes\ x) \Rightarrow r\ remove\ x = r
\end{array}
$$

As with *add*, we can prove that *remove* preserves well-formed buckets if equal-hash holds. Under these conditions, *remove* will then behave as expected, and a proof outline is given.

$$
\begin{array}{l}
EQUAL\_HASH;\ WFBUCKETS(r)\ \vdash \\
\qquad (r\ remove\ x)\ includes\ y \Leftrightarrow \\
\qquad\qquad r\ includes\ y \wedge \neg\ (y\ \mathrm{E}\ x)
\end{array}
$$

For $\Rightarrow$, define the property $P(s)$ of any set s as: $\forall y \bullet s\ includes\ y \Rightarrow (r\ includes\ y \wedge \neg\ (y\ \mathrm{E}\ x))$. From *fixCollisions*, P holds of $\mu\, r' \mid r'.hashtable = r.hashtable - r.subtable\ index$. P also holds after every iteration through *reduce*, if it held before. Hence, P holds after all the iterations, i.e. $P(r\ remove\ x)$. For $\Leftarrow$, the proof is straightforward.

3.2.5 Collect

The set operation *collect* is modelled as taking an object-transforming function as an argument. This function is then applied to the objects in the set's hashtable, the results of which are then added one by one to a new set.

$$
\begin{array}{|l}
\_collect\_ : SET \times (OBJECT \rightarrow OBJECT) \\
\qquad \rightarrow SET \\
\hline
r\ collect\ b = \mathrm{reduce}\ add\ new\ (b \circ r.ht)
\end{array}
$$

A set produced by *collect* has well-formed buckets if equal-hash holds, but interestingly, the original set is not required to have well-formed buckets. Under equal-hash, *collect* behaves as expected.

$$
\begin{array}{l}
EQUAL\_HASH\ \ \vdash\ (r\ collect\ b)\ includes\ x \Leftrightarrow \\
\qquad \exists\, y : \mathrm{ran}\ (b \circ r.hashtable) \bullet y\ \mathrm{E}\ x
\end{array}
$$

This is proved similarly to the analogous theorem for *remove* but with the property P taken as: $\forall x \bullet s\ includes\ x \Rightarrow \exists\, y : \mathrm{ran}\ (b \circ r.hashtable) \bullet y\ \mathrm{E}\ x$. Trivially, P holds of *new*, and is preserved by every iteration of *reduce*.

4 Specification of Dictionaries

In Smalltalk, dictionary is a subclass of set. A dictionary is defined and usually viewed as a set of associations where an association is a key-value pair. Dictionaries may also be viewed as "a collection whose elements are unordered but have explicitly assigned keys or names. From this perspective, the elements of a dictionary are arbitrary objects (values) with external keys." [1, p. 148] One might consider this view to be a finite partial function. All the dictionary operations can be defined in terms of sets of associations. Then dictionaries can be consistently viewed as sets of associations, as collections or as a mixture. Our Z specification of dictionaries will be as an extension to sets, whose elements are associations.

Equality of associations is defined as just equality of keys, and thus the value part is ignored in membership tests. Similarly, the hash of an association is the hash of its key. The *EQUAL_HASH* property plays a similar role for dictionaries as for sets. With or without it, the dictionary operations do have a defined behavior, but with it dictionaries behave as expected with no surprises.

Comparing the dictionary specification with the Smalltalk code led us to an inconsistency between the Smalltalk dictionary operations keyAtValue: and includes:, both of which use equality of values in their search. The code for keyAtValue: uses Smalltalk ==, i.e. = of Z, while includes: uses Smalltalk =, i.e. E. This we claim is a bug in the code and have not replicated it in the specification.

4.1 The Data Model

The Z types *KEY*, *VALUE* and *ASSOC*, which represent the types of keys, values and associations, are defined as being equivalent to objects. The constructor *association* and selectors *key* and *value* then map between these types as expected.

$$
\begin{array}{l}
KEY \mathrel{\widehat{=}} OBJECT \\
VALUE \mathrel{\widehat{=}} OBJECT \\
ASSOC \mathrel{\widehat{=}} OBJECT
\end{array}
$$

$$
\begin{array}{|l}
association : KEY \times VALUE \rightarrowtail ASSOC \\
key : ASSOC \twoheadrightarrow KEY \\
value : ASSOC \twoheadrightarrow VALUE \\
\hline
\text{dom } key = \text{dom } value = \text{ran } association \\
key\ (association(k, v)) = k \\
value\ (association(k, v)) = v
\end{array}
$$

Equality and hashing of associations are based respectively on equality and hashing of keys thus:

$$
\begin{array}{|l}
\forall a, b : \text{ran } association \bullet \\
\quad hash\ a = hash\ (key\ a) \ \wedge \\
\quad a \mathrel{\mathrm{E}} b \Leftrightarrow (key\ a) \mathrel{\mathrm{E}} (key\ b)
\end{array}
$$

A dictionary is then modelled as a set containing only associations in its hashtable.

$$
\begin{array}{l}
DICTIONARY \ \widehat{=}\ SET \mid \\
\quad \forall x : \text{ran } hashtable \bullet x \in \text{ran } association
\end{array}
$$

4.2 Dictionary Operations

The Smalltalk message category for accessing dictionaries provides three operations: *associationAt* returns the association at a key, *at* returns the value associated with the key and *keyAtValue* returns a key associated with a particular value. These operations are all partial since the input key/value might not occur in the dictionary. Note too that since the same value may be associated with many keys, *keyAtValue* may return any of these keys; our specification allows this non-determinism, by simply accepting each possibility, even though the actual code always returns a particular one.[6] Testing a dictionary for inclusion of an association, key or value is performed by the three operations *includesAssoc*, *includesKey* and *includes*.

An association may be added directly to a dictionary using *addAssoc* (named just add: in Smalltalk) or by giving its key and value components as arguments to the operation *at_put*.

$$
\begin{array}{|l}
\_addAssoc\_ : DICTIONARY \times ASSOC \twoheadrightarrow \\
\qquad\qquad DICTIONARY \\
\_at\_put\_ : DICTIONARY \times KEY \times \\
\qquad\qquad VALUE \twoheadrightarrow DICTIONARY \\
\hline
d\ addAssoc\ a \cong (d\ remove\ a)\ add\ a \\
d\ at\ k\ put\ v = \\
\qquad d\ addAssoc\ (association(k, v))
\end{array}
$$

[6]Space allows showing only the Z specifications for adding associations to dictionaries; the others are in [4].

Adding an element to a dictionary is different in one respect from adding an element to a set: if the element occurs already, a dictionary overwrites the old occurrence with the new[7] whereas the set does not. This accounts for the rather strange definition of *addAssoc*, which is not necessarily an identity operation since all the equality tests involved are based solely on the keys.

Removing an entry from a dictionary is specified either by the association to be removed (use *removeAssoc*) or simply by its key (use *removeKey*). The enumerating operations, *associations*, *keys* and *values*, return groupings of the entries in a dictionary: The associations are returned as a number-indexed set of associations (modelling a Smalltalk OrderedCollection), the keys are returned as a finite set while the values are returned as a bag.

5 Conclusions

We have written a Z design specification that models essentially all the details of an industrial-strength implementation of sets. The complexity results from our desire to explain the actual implementation, complete with various surprises if an assumed but unchecked property of the implementation does not hold. Because we wished to prove properties of specifications, we then proved that the equal-hash property and well-formed buckets are sufficient to ensure that this reusable component really behaves as abstract sets. It is just that result which would encourage a potential user of this component to use it. The result also warns the user to make certain the equal-hash property holds.

The Z specification meets the needs of users, implementors and those seeking understanding and guidance. Users can read the specification to see what the implementation provides with or without the equal-hash property. Implementors can learn what must be provided, why the implementation works, and perhaps what they may safely alter. Both groups must expect to read the specification carefully for it is a formal, technical document rather than a tutorial. Those seeking understanding can gain much from reading the specification and its commentary. The specification process itself also provides understanding and guidance to the specifiers. Specifically, our understandings of individual

[7]Note that only the value is overwritten in Smalltalk.

components have been improved by the discipline that writing specifications provides.

Z is suitable for specifying the major implementation inspired by Smalltalk sets. However, because Z is functional and property-oriented rather than operational and object-oriented, a specification of the actual workings of the set implementation would also have to include a specification of certain operational aspects of Smalltalk, such as method lookup. Z is certainly capable of providing this, but adding so much detail could easily lose the essence of the set implementation. The other difference between Z and Smalltalk is that Z is generally nonexecutable which means that a proposed answer, however obtained, can be judged to be acceptable or not. The answer, by intent, can often not be computed from the specification alone.

In writing a specification one must invent a model, in Z, for what is being specified. In the sets example, the introduction of *subtable* and *buckets* seems, in retrospect, natural and obvious because together they do represent the implementation. That they were far from obvious as we began is what one should expect. Convincing ourselves that the implementation of dictionaries could be modelled as sets of associations took a bit of time. Getting exactly the right model with appropriate properties is no more algorithmic than other design tasks. We sometimes think we are "programming in Z," and sometimes that view may help the specification. Like data abstractions and invariant assertions, specification abstractions exist and need to be found.

No special proof techniques are expected for, or excluded from Z specifications. For sets standard data type induction was used to show that well-formed buckets is a data type invariant. Ordinary loop invariants were used to prove the implicit loops in *remove* and *collect*. Usual kinds of proofs were sufficient for the rest. We are pleased that the proofs could be written to exhibit interesting structure at the same time capturing our intuitions. Z has its own style of specifications and corresponding styles of proof and approaches, all of which we are still learning.

It is important to realize some special circumstances of this effort. First, we started from the actual implementation rather than from the abstraction. Second, the implementation is very real, as noted. Third, we came to understand Smalltalk sets only after much iteration among the code, specification attempts, conjectured properties and proof attempts; these, and the iteration itself, were valuable, mutually reinforcing, and perhaps crucial. Our understanding is in three parts: the Z specification, the proved properties and the explanation which we feel is essential for others to be able to use the specification.

Like many other Z specifications in the literature, what we present here represents much reworking. As an alternative, for example, our companion technical report [4] contains a more detailed presentation of the specifications. There we formally define abstract sets separately from the specification of the implementation. An explicit abstraction function is used to perform standard data refinement, and therefore more proofs (with a few more steps) are included.

Acknowledgements

Thanks to our Tek colleagues Norman Delisle, Robert Duisberg, David Garlan and Mayer Schwartz for helpful discussions, especially in the beginning.

References

[1] Adele Goldberg and David Robson, *Smalltalk-80: The Language and its Implementation*, Addison-Wesley, 1983.

[2] Ian Hayes (editor), *Specification Case Studies*, Prentice-Hall International, 1987.

[3] Donald E. Knuth, *The Art of Computer Programming*, Vol. 3, Addison-Wesley, 1973.

[4] Ralph L. London and Kathleen R. Milsted, Specifying and Verifying Reusable Components Using Z: Sets and Dictionaries, Technical Report No. CR-88-10, Tektronix Laboratories, October 1988.

[5] J. Michael Spivey, *The Z Notation: A Reference Manual*, Prentice-Hall International, 1989.

Authors' present addresses: Ralph L. London, Tektronix Laboratories, P. O. Box 500, MS 50-662, Beaverton, OR 97077 USA. Kathleen R. Milsted, Programming Research Group, 11 Keble Road, Oxford OX1 3QD ENGLAND.

A Look Through PRISMA: Towards Pluralistic Knowledge-based Environments for Software Specification Acquisition

Celso Niskier [1] Tom Maibaum [1] Daniel Schwabe [2]

[1] Department of Computing
Imperial College of Science and Technology
180 Queen's Gate
London SW7 2BZ

[2] Departamento de Informática
Pontifícia Universidade Católica do Rio de Janeiro
Rua Marquês de São Vicente, 225
22.453 Rio de Janeiro

ABSTRACT

A pluralistic attitude to software specification acquisition is proposed, where multiple viewpoints/formalisms are simultaneously used to describe more comprehensively the required system. Syntactic, semantic and pragmatic (heuristic) aspects of Entity Relationship Models, Data Flow Diagrams and Petri Nets are captured using Prolog as a metalanguage. More general heuristics indicating complementarity consistency between methods are also formalised. The construction of PRISMA - a pluralistic knowledge-based system - is described, and the approach is ilustrated via examples. Theoretical and practical issues related to specification processes and environments supporting a pluralistic paradigm are also discussed.

1. Introduction

Requirements analysis has been recognized as one of the most critical and difficult tasks in the construction of software systems. As one moves from an informal description of an application to a formal (or at least "formatted") representation of it, errors are often introduced due to incorrect or ill formed understanding of the desired properties of the system [11,15].

Recently attention has been given to the idea of combining specification styles according to problem characteristics. This focus of research originates from the observation that one formalism alone cannot hope to support very well, if at all, the need to say different kinds of things about the intended software system.

In practice, specifications themselves do not live over a single formalism. For example, it has been pointed out that a requirements specification of a real-time system may involve a temporal component for reasoning about timing constraints, a different temporal system for reasoning about the sequencing of various actions, a deontic element for reasoning about "rights" and "obligations" of various users or components, and finally some non-monotonic component for reasoning about states of some database.

However, although past experience in diverse areas such as programming language semantics [7] and database systems [27] suggests that the integration of different styles/aspects/perspectives would seem to be a sound methodological compromise, there is the problem that we do not as yet have any sound theory underpinning it. More specifically, there are several questions that need to be answered, particularly with relation to the notions of views, formalisms and processes to support a pluralistic approach to software specification in general.

One the other hand, many recent efforts have been reported on the possibility of relating Software Engineering to Artificial Intelligence [1,13]. Some of them refer, in particular, to the current need for a better formalisation of the software development process to allow for a more extensive automation of software production. AI can be associated to this problem in two ways. In one hand, it can provide new formalisation tools (e.g. logic programming) to the expression of software engineering concepts. On the other hand, it is possible to draw an analogy between studies on the classification of the heuristics for problem solving in AI and the classification of the heuristics that exists when one is involved with the more general question of solving a problem through a software system.

In our approach, specifications written in different formalisms (logics) are seen as different theory presentations expressing particular *views* of reality, each one comprised of limited aspects or perspectives (properties) of the system to be constructed [18]. In this framework, the process of software specification acquisition is modeled as a dynamic integration of different sources of knowledge about the intended application [19,9].

In adopting such an approach, our research methodology has been the following:

• To capture syntactic, semantic and pragmatic (heuristic) aspects of well-known methods by interpreting them into a common logical notation;

• To construct a suitable knowledge-based tool supporting the coherent construction and integration of different views;

• To acquire higher-level guidelines and heuristics for the combination of methods according to classes of problems through experimentation within the exploratory environment.

This paper reports on the work going on, both at Imperial College and PUC/RJ, based on the experience started with the construction of PRISMA (Portuguese for prism), a prototype version of a pluralistic knowledge-based environment centred around well-known methods such as Data Flow Diagrams, Entity Relationship Models and Petri Nets.

In the following section we present an introductory discussion on requirements of a formal framework to support a pluralistic approach to software specification. Some important points are made, and few challenging problems are outlined. In section 3 the experience gained with the construction of PRISMA as a partial answer to some of the outlined problems is discussed. We emphasize particularly the interpretation of formalisms into (a Horn Clause restriction of) first-order logic, the formalisation of heuristics for structuring, validation and achievement of complementarity between views and the construction of a knowledge-based tool supporting the whole process of specification using multiple views. Finally, we conclude by discussing the main contributions of our work, new developments that are being made and some points for further research.

2. The Multiple View Specification Process

Many different analogies can be made to describe the process of software specification acquisition. An interesting one relates specification building to scientific theory construction [15]. In Science, a theory is put forward to describe the system under consideration, the theory is analysed to see if it matches expectation (validation), and the theory is used to make predictions which can then be put to the test by experimentation (to see if the predicted property matches reality). The analogy is important because, like a scientific theory, a specification (especially the original design or formal requirement specification) can never be proved correct. It can only provide more and more confidence as it passes more and more tests until if fails some test or makes an unacceptable prediction. The specification must then be tinkered with until it is improved. In extreme cases, a completely new theory must be proposed.

Specification building differs from the scientific paradigm in a very important sense. There is generally no part of the world being modelled. The specification describes an imagined artifact whose realisation will become part of the world. This compounds the difficulty of scientific hypothesising in at least two ways. Firstly, the 'knowledge' of the imagined artifact is much less precisely delineated - no 'world' to act as a check.

Further, the very act of realising the artifact may profoundly change the world. Secondly, it is our firm belief that what we can say through a software specification is heavily dependent on the choice of specification language (or logic) used to express it. Moreover, we believe that, during early steps in the process of software specification acquisition the choice of any specific formalism could severely restrict or bias our ability to prescribe the nature of the intended system.

Therefore, in the following discussion we attempt to generalize current specification theories based on the step-wise sequential development process to a pluralistic multiple view specification process, where several complementary views, expressed in different formalisms, can be constructed and implemented in parallel.

We will denote a *logic* **L** by a pair

$$\langle \mathcal{L}_L, \vdash_L \rangle$$

with $\mathcal{L}_L$ defining the legal expressions in the logic (generally in terms of basic symbols and formation rules) and $\vdash_L$ defining a derivability relation (generally in terms of logical axioms and rules of inference). Examples of logics used in specification are MAL [16] for real-time systems, Temporal Logic for concurrent systems [2] and database systems specification [3], and Many-Sorted First Order Logic (MPC) for abstract data type specification [14].

Program development as a sequential formal activity may be seen simplistically in terms of the following diagram:

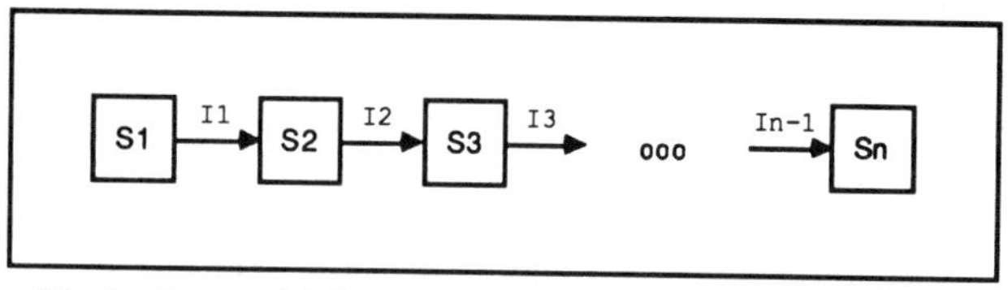

Fig.1 - Sequential Step-wise Program Development Process

Here S_1 is some specification with which we start the development process, S_n is supposed to be the running system and $S_2, \ldots, S_{n-1}$ are intermediate representations of the original specification used to derive S_n. The I's are meant to name the property-preserving transformations mapping one representation into another. Note that we are not assuming a priori a uniform logic for all representations. For example, the first level of a real-time system specification may be expressed in temporal logic, and reasoning about the final program can be done using an assertion language in a Hoare logic style.

Now, generalizing upon this picture we can formulate a new diagram of what we call a *multiple view specification process*:

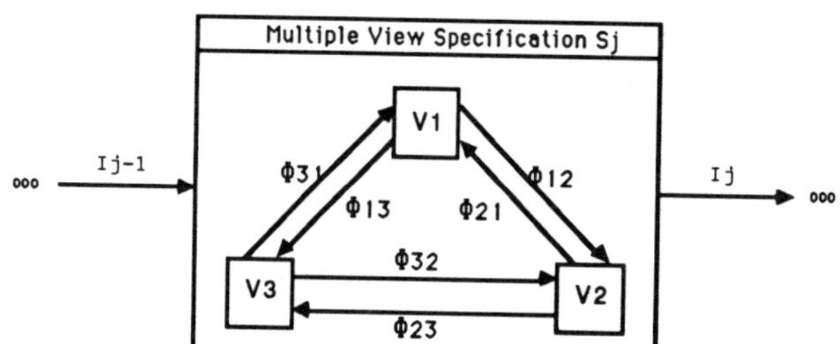

Fig.2 - Multiple View Specification Process

In this framework, at each specification level several different views are constructed in parallel. A *multiple view specification* is then composed of a collection of views, together with a collection of mappings (Φ's) between them. The above picture shows a three-view specification, together with their internal mappings. Note that there is no pre-specified order in which different views are constructed.

We represent a *view* by a theory presentation in some logic **L**. We will denote such a theory presentation by a pair

$$<L,\Delta>$$

where L is the choice of extralogical symbols used to define the current system representation and Δ is the set of axioms used to define the properties of the representation as captured by the view. If the logic within which we are presenting the theory is not obvious from the context, we write $<L,\Delta>_{\mathbf{L}}$.

Note that we again are not assuming a priori an uniform logic for all views. However, having assumed an uniform description of the concept of a specification view, we would also like to assume that the Φ's are instances of the same relationship between them. The intuition behind these mappings is that properties "observable" in one view should be mapped to corresponding properties "observable" in another view. The differences in views arise through the simple, direct expression of some property in one view and its possibly complicated, tortuous coding in another. In this way, we would be assured that we are actually describing the same object from multiple points of view. Two theoretical problems have to be solved in order to achieve such framework.

Firstly, the notion of translation between views written in different formalisms is not yet clear enough, so the existence of an unifying treatment for all Φ's (regardless the logics being translated) is still an open problem. Secondly, we cannot guarantee that for each pair of views V_i and V_j, expressed in logics $\mathbf{L}_i$ and $\mathbf{L}_j$, there exists a total mapping between them that preserves all properties from one into another. Some properties are usually lost (or gained) in the form of extralogical language, axioms and/or logic restriction (extension).

Our approach to the first problem has been its reduction to that of finding mappings between different views expressed over the same logic, with the construction of suitable interpretations of each formalism into the setting of first-order logic. In this context, (total) property-preserving translations are well-known as *interpretations between theories* ([8], [26]), and can then be treated uniformly.

An interpretation between views (as theories in MPC)

$$\Phi_{ij}: <L_i,\Delta_i> \longrightarrow <L_j,\Delta_j>$$

is generally defined in terms of an underlying interpretation between languages such that sorts, constants, variables, function and relation symbols of L_i are mapped to (tuples of) sorts, constants, variables, function and relation symbols of L_j, and, given such correspondence between languages, the following condition holds:

$$\textbf{If } \Delta_i \vdash A \textbf{ then } \Delta_j \vdash \Phi_{ij}(A)$$

This meta-property (property about views) is called the *property-preserving* condition, and ensures that the properties attributable to symbols of L_i are *simulated* for the corresponding symbols of L_j. Here simulation is applied to properties and derivations thereof, not behaviour, as commonly understood. The idea is simply: once a property of a system has been derived in a view, it has to be always there, suitably translated, in other views. This property holds for total interpretations.

However, the existence of the second practical problem has suggested the use of heuristics. Heuristics are normally regarded as rules of thumb, guiding the search for a solution in a space of problem representations [12,21]. In our context, we regard heuristics as rules helping us search for a proof of partial translation correctness between different views. Intuitively, they act as guidelines in constructing such proof, indicating ways of verifying that some properties in one view are correctly represented in other views. They represent therefore *incomplete proof procedures*. Their incompleteness results from the fact that their use cannot guarantee that a proof is going to be found. Moreover, the partiality problem indicates the need to "localize" adequately the application of heuristics. In other words, the environment should provide efficient advice on *when* and *where* the use of heuristics is more effective.

The application of heuristics in proving partial translation can be driven by dialogical activities, for example by interacting with the specifier giving suggestions on properties that should be checked for complementarity. This characteristic is being investigated in detail in [20], and was adopted as an underlying mechanism in the construction of PRISMA, as we shall see next.

3. The PRISMA Experience

The choice of Data Flow Diagrams [6], Entity Relationship Models [4] and Petri Nets [22,23] as test-case methods was based on a few assumptions about their nature. Firstly, each one of them focuses on different aspects of software description, respectively *functional*, *informational* and *operational* aspects [17,28]. Secondly, they represent well-known and widely used methods, so the fact that they have been heavily tested in practice adds both to the quantity and quality of the methodological knowledge available. And, finally, all three methods make use of graphical formalisms to express the knowledge about the system. This uniform characteristic, apart from rendering the approach much more intuitive and appealing - adding the effective possibility of *visualizing* in different ways the system behaviour and structure - favoured the use of a common conceptual basis and an unifying metalanguage in the form of Horn clauses [10,5].

3.1. Logical Interpretation of Specification Formalisms

3.1.1.Primitive Sorts

For each graphical formalism we have identified primitive sorts, i.e., conceptual units used to describe real world phenomena. We consider two types of primitive sorts: *object* sorts and *relation* sorts. Thus, for example, in a Data Flow Diagram primitive object sorts corresponding to each graphical symbol are: *process*, *dataflow*, *file* and *external_entity*. Primitive relations are of two kinds: *input* and *output*. Similarly, for an Entity Relationship Model we were able to identify objects of three kinds: *entity*, *relationship* and *attribute*. Interestingly, the non-primitive notion of a relationship between two entities could be partitioned into two primitive relations: *one* and *many*. Moreover, there is also the primitive relation *has_attribute*. Finally, in a Petri Net two types of primitive objects were pointed out: *event* and *condition*. Their relations are easily identified: *precondition*, *postcondition* and *has_token*, the latter expressing the idea that an event can be marked. Fig. 3 ilustrates the process of decomposition of an instance of a multiple view specification into its primitive sorts, and their interpretation into Horn clauses.

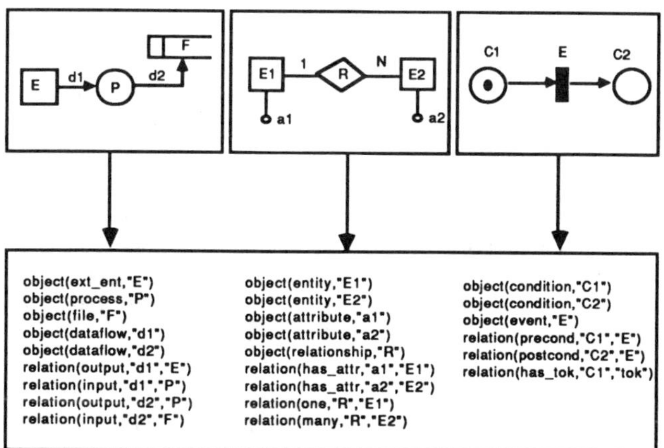

Fig.3 - Decomposition of a Multiple View Specification into its Primitive Sorts

Two observations can be made:

• The 'semantical net' treatment given to formalisms, with their consequent formalisation in logic, appears to be generic enough to suggest an uniform treatment for a wide class of graphical formalisms;

• Once primitive sorts are identified, we observe that if it is possible to decompose any instance of a view into its primitive sorts, then it seems reasonable to suppose that we can use different combinations of them to describe syntactic and semantic properties of the view.

3.1.2. Syntactic Properties

These properties are related to diagram well-formedness. They are represented by syntactic correctness rules. For instance, each situation below

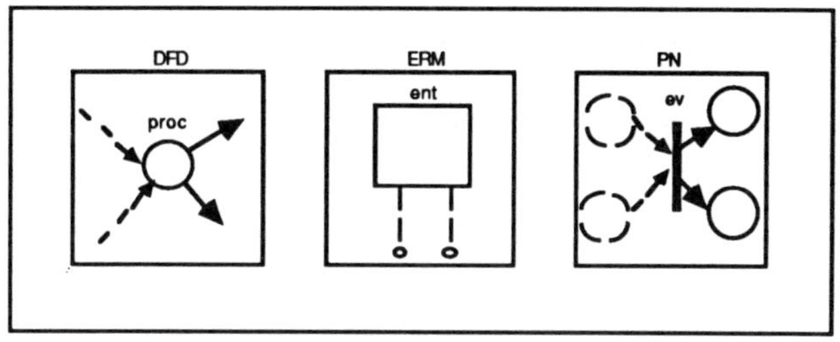

Fig. 4 - Syntactically Incorrect Situations

can be captured in Prolog-like notation as rules:

```
has_no_inputs(Proc) :-
        object(process,Proc),
        findall(Y,relation(input,Y,Proc),Inputs),
        empty(Inputs).

has_no_attributes(Entity) :-
        object(entity,Entity),
        findall(Y,relation(has_attr,Y,Entity),Attrs),
        empty(Attrs).

has_no_preconditions(Event) :-
        object(event,Event),
        findall(Y,relation(precond,Y,Event),Preconds),
        empty(Preconds).
```

In this notation variables are represented by upper-case arguments, and constants by lower-case arguments.The *findall* clause can be interpreted as a set constructor. As will become clear later on, these properties, together with advice-giving heuristics, are used to produce an agenda-driven process of view construction.

3.1.3. Semantic Properties

These are properties that capture expected behaviours of the specified system. In most graphical formalisms, much of the semantic information is attached to the meaning of primitive sorts, and is given through generic definitions and practical examples. The following rules capture particular behaviours that may be observed in DFDs and PNs. They are later used to generate natural language paraphrases for the validation of each view:

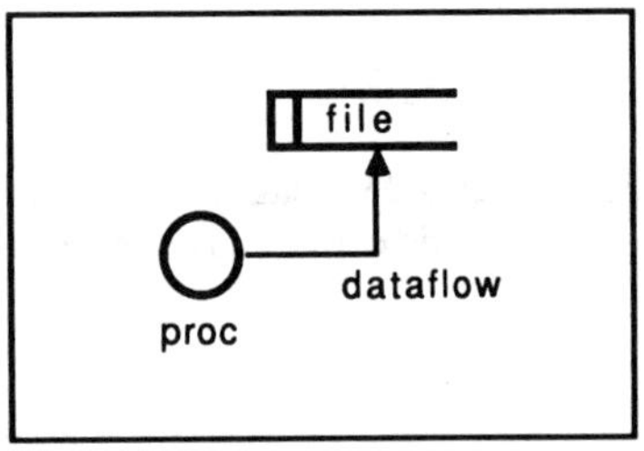

Fig. 5(a) - Process updating a file in a DFD

"If a dataflow is an output of a process and an input to a file,then the process isupdating the file".

```
update(Proc, File) :-
        object(process,Proc),
        object(file,File),
        object(dataflow,Dataflow)
        relation(output,Dataflow,Proc),
        relation(input,Dataflow,File).
```

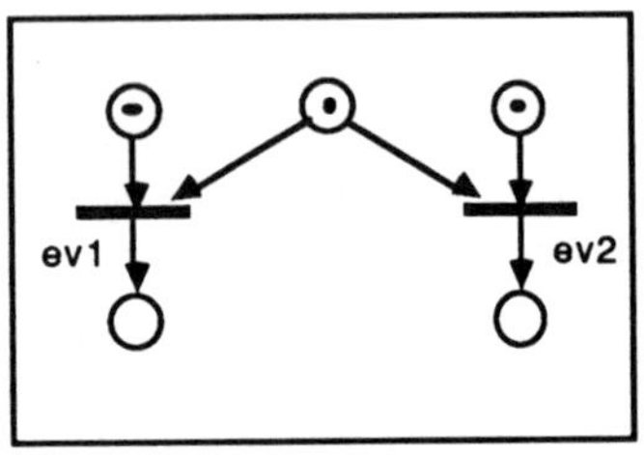

Fig. 5(b) - Events in conflict in a Petri Net

"If two events have common preconditions, and they aremarked, then they arein conflict"

```
conflict(Ev1,Ev2)  :-
        object(event,Ev1),
        object(event,Ev2),
        not(equal(Ev1,Ev2)),
        findall(Y,relation(precond,Y,Ev1),Preconds1),
        findall(Y,relation(precond,Y,Ev2),Preconds2),
        marked(Preconds1),
        marked(Preconds2),
        intersection(Preconds1,Preconds2,Comm_conds),
        not(empty(Comm_conds).
```

3.2. Formalisation of Heuristics

Heuristics in PRISMA are represented as pairs <*situation,action*>, where *situations* are characterized by a conjunction of satisfiable queries to an instance of a view. *Actions* are then specification tasks that need to be performed according to the situation. Examples of specification tasks are the definition of new concepts, verification of properties or validation of a current view against the specifier's original intention. According to previous discussion (section 2), situations and actions characterize *when* and *where* heuristics should be effectively applied. In the following we classify specification heuristics by task and formalism, starting with structuring heuristics.

3.2.1. Structuring Heuristics

These are advice-giving heuristics, capturing past experience in the application of the methodology to specific problems. They make use of syntactic properties to characterize unsatisfactory situations in a view - usually caused by minor inconsistencies or incorrectnesses - and provide advice on how to overcome these problems.

Thus, an example of a structuring heuristic for a DFD is shown below:

"If there is a process with only output dataflows then define its input dataflows looking for the sort of information needed to produce the outputs"

```
context(rule(20),structure_rep,dfd)  :-
        /* if_situation */
        has_outputs(Proc,Outputs),
        has_no_inputs(Proc),
        /* then_action */
        show_task('Define inputs of process',Proc),
        show_advice('Look for information needed to
                produce',Ouputs).
```

The interpreter applies the set of structuring rules to a current view. Every time the premisses of a rule are satisfied - meaning that the particular situation is identified for that view - two types of action are produced. The first one, expressed by the predicate *show_task,* produces a new entry in the view agenda, indicating that the required action needs to be done. The second one produces an advice on how to accomplish that task, thus incorporating useful information based on past experience in the application of the methodology. Here follows another example of structuring heuristics, now for a PN view:

"If there is an event with only preconditions, then define its postconditions looking for the conditions identifying the state of the system after the event occurs"

```
context(rule(34),structure_rep,pn)  :-
        /* if_situation */
        has_preconditions(Event,Preconds),
        has_no_postconditions(Event),
        /* then_action */
        show_task('Define preconditions of
                event',Event),
        show_advice('Look for  conditions identifying
                the state of the system
                after',Event,'occurs').
```

3.2.2. Validation Heuristics

There are many different ways in which specifications can be validated. For example by:

(a) *Proving* properties capturing expected behaviour of the specified system. This activity justifies and underlines the use of formal specification methods as a way of formally deriving properties (e.g. by theorem-proving) from the original specification;

(b) Direct proof of well-known scenarios - tantamont to *symbolic execution* (or evaluation) of the system, given inputs corresponding to situations for which the behaviour of the specified system is known. Petri Net specifications, given their operational nature, are particularly suitable to this kind of activity.

(c) *Paraphrasing* in natural language - by producing a stylised natural language description of the system, it is expected that the specifier will be able to recognize mismatches between his (her) *intentions* and what was actually specified. An example of this approach has been used in GIST [1].

In the PRISMA context, a particular example of validation heuristics consists of rules capturing "interesting" properties of specifications in the form of *natural language paraphrases*. A specification may be syntactically correct, but may not have some desired property, or may have some non-desired property, thus indicating a possible semantic mismatch. Examples of these properties used to generate paraphrases are:

" In a file, all information being recovered is derived from some input"

```
context(rule(53),validate_rep,dfd) :-
        /* if_situation */
        has_inputs(File,Inputs),
        has_outputs(File,Outputs),
        /* then_action */
        show_paraphrase(Outputs,'are derived from some
                input to',File).
```

"If an entity has a one to many relationship with another entity, then an instance of it interacts with many instances of the other; but an instance of the other interacts with only one instance of it"

```
context(rule(64),validate_rep,erm) :-
        /* if_situation */
        one_to_many(Ent1,Rel,Ent2),
        /* then_action */
        show_paraphrase('An instance of',Ent1,'interacts
                via relationship',Rel,'with many instances
                of',Ent2),
        show_paraphrase('An instance of',Ent2,'interacts
                via relationship',Rel,'with one instance
                of',Ent1).
```

3.2.3. Complementarity Heuristics

These are the most crucial heuristics in the context of a multiple view specification, as they act as guidelines in assuring the partial consistency of different descriptions. In PRISMA, a partial translation between views is a mapping relating sorts and properties of one view to corresponding (tuples of) sorts and properties of another view, as outlined in section 2. In this context, complementarity heuristics indicate when and where the property-preservation condition should be enforced.
Thus, for example, we can associate to each entity in an ERM a corresponding file in a DFD, as expressed by the following rule:

```
context(rule(75),change_view(dfd),erm) :-
        /* if_situation */
        object(entity,Entity),
        /* then_action */
        show_comp_check('Check that the
                entity',Entity,'is possibly associated with
                a file').
```

Similarly, we can identify complementarity heuristics when going from a DFD to a PN. For instance, to each process representing a data transformation there is an associated event representing the occurrence of that transformation:

```
context(rule(87),change_view(pn),dfd) :-
        /* if_situation */
        object(process,Proc),
        /* then_action */
        show_comp_check('Check that the
                process',Proc,'is possibly associated with
                an event').
```

It is imporant to note that these and other identified complementarity heuristics are partial as they only apply to limited properties of views. They are also incomplete, once, although they suggest complementarity checks, they do not constitute complete translation proofs.

3.3. The Environment

The paradigm for the utilization of PRISMA as a knowledge-based tool for software specification is based on the idea of an user-specifier, sitting in front of his/her workstation, trying to build up a structured description of the desired system from informal concepts (e.g. annotations, tables, natural language statements) previously obtained in a preliminary brainstorming session with the client. For that purpose, different views suggest complementary ways to look at these concepts. Heuristics were organized in a set of tools aiming to provide efficient advice for the main activities arising in his/her work.

The basic "desktop" indicates major activities along the top of the screen. In PRISMA, the user enters an activity as a subsidiary screen. The options *file* and *edit* are the usual "bookkeeping" ones, the first dealing with file manipulation functions such as save, load, etc. while the second calls a specific diagram editor for each formalism (still being implemented).

Besides these common facilities, the PRISMA environment provides the user with three sets of tools associated with each view: the *agenda*, the *paraphraser* and the *complementarity checker* (view change mechanism).In the following sections we present an overall idea of these features with a simplified example extracted from the traditional *academic information system* specification problem.

3.3.1. Agenda

The agenda mechanism implements the set of advice-giving heuristics, driven by syntactic rules. At any step, during a view construction, the user-specifier can query, through a *tasks window*, a list of the remaining and most promising tasks to be done, with advice suggesting how to do each task.

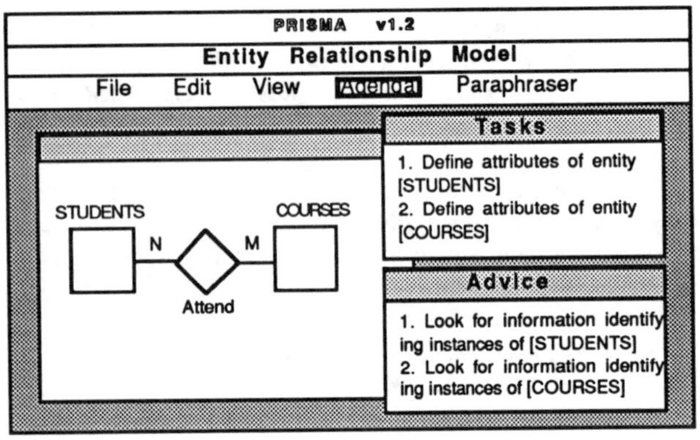

Fig. 6 - ERM Agenda

3.3.2. Paraphraser

The paraphraser makes use of the set of validation heuristics to generate sentences in natural language. Similarly, a *paraphrases window* is produced whenever the user wants to scrutinize the current state of a view in order to see if its properties satisfy his original intention.

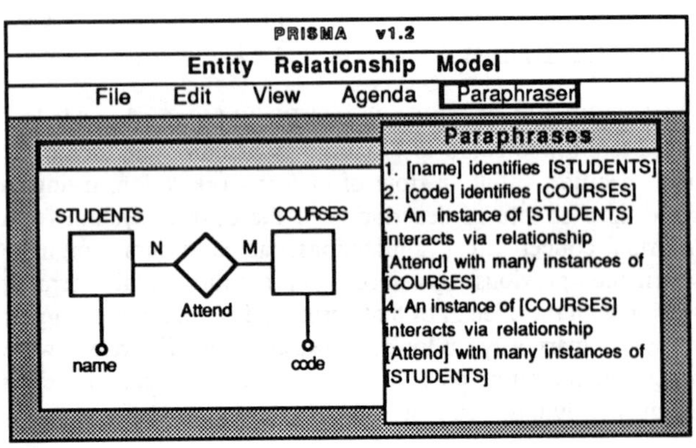

Fig. 7 - ERM Paraphraser

3.3.3. Complementarity Checker

Finally, once he is happy with the possibilities of one view, he/she is allowed to shift to another one. When selecting a new view, the control mechanism automatically switches to the complementarity checker, which promptly presents a set of "hints" through a special *comp_checks window* indicating associations that must be observed between properties of the current view and properties in the new view. This tool can be used in a dual sense: as an aid in constructing a new view from the previous one or as support for checking partial consistency of two complementary views already obtained.

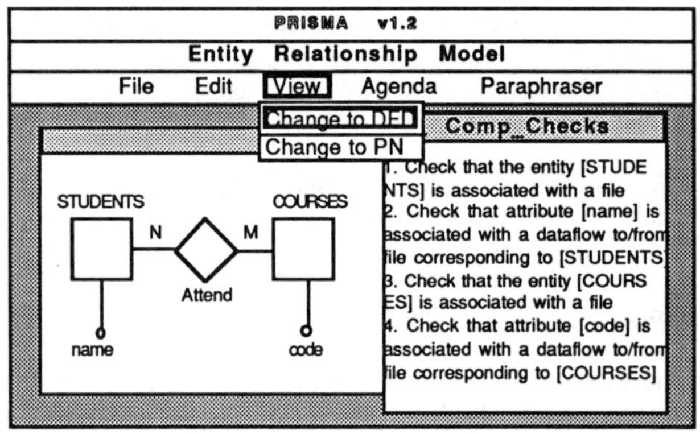

Fig. 8 - Changing views from ERM to DFD

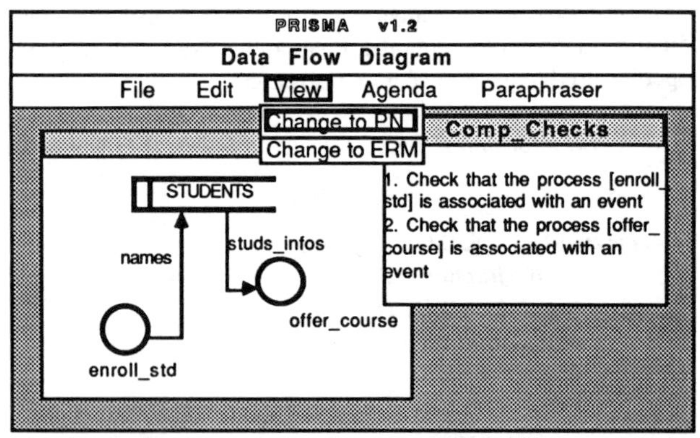

Fig. 9 - Changing views from DFD to PN

The fact that some properties that are easily observed in one view are implicit or non-existent in other views is a powerful motivation for the use of an integrated multiple view environment for software specification. Although we have followed a specific direction when shifting views, according to our own intuition, there is no pre-specified way to move across them, as partial translations (remember the mappings in section 2) connect every pair of views. It is left to the specifier to choose the best approach to his/her problem, possibly according to its own characteristics. At the end, the result of this process is a multiple view specification that captures more comprehensively the knowledge about the intended application. Moreover, each view presents information in a way which makes a certain class of properties easier to and more directly comprehendable.

4. Conclusions and Research Perspectives

We have shown how software specification methods and their heuristics can be classified and formalised according to a pluralistic paradigm of software specification acquisition. As a by-product, we have constructed a knowledge-based tool supporting software specification from multiple viewpoints. PRISMA has been intensively tested with many toy-problems of medium complexity. The results have been satisfactory, giving us confidence that the combination of multiple viewpoints with effective heuristics provides a good paradigm for software specification acquisition. In fact, we believe that the model can be easily extended to encompass other methods and areas of expertise.

At a more foundational level, we aim at identifying classes of logics/formalisms more suitable to combination. We are particularly interested in investigating the relationship between the concept of modularity internal to a specification - a technical requirement for the formalism - and the concept of modularity of a multiple view specification - a requirement on the common metalogic. We are also investigating formal dialogue models for view translation [9,20]..

On the practical side, we are looking at extensions to the basic primitives to provide for *refinement* and *abstraction* in a given formalism. For example, we might wish to allow a node in a Petri Net to be replaced by another Petri Net, which refines its specification, or the converse operation of abstracting a (sub) net into a node. These extensions allow the specifier to be working with several diagrams, in the same formalism, at the same time, and to keep track of the relationships between them. To support these operations, an additional set of rules is being added, capturing the syntactic restrictions for each formalism (in which refinement and abstraction is defined).In addition, a new set of heuristics is being incorporated into the system, to guide the specifier in applying these operations;

Also, an improved natural language paraphrase generator is being designed. Besides linguistic "clarity" and "good style" requirements imposed on the paraphrases it produces, it is also required that they be complete in the following sense: if a person "ignorant" of the system being specified, but fluent in the formalism, is given the paraphrase of a specification, this person should be able to produce another specification which is essentially equivalent to the original one. This equivalence can be reduced to the fact that the two descriptions are syntactic variations of each other. A strong requirement can be made when two people can go through the same input procedure to PRISMA. In this case, (s)he should produce the same semantic information as it was originally produced.

At the moment, the formalism being investigated is DFD. To be able to produce meaningful output, the user is required to provide, during input, semantic information which is in addition and complementary to the specificaton itself. This semantic information is, in essence, a description of the *functions* computed by each process to produce each of its output flows. In each case, the specifier is prompted to give a verb and a semantic category (from a previosly defined universe of categories) that describes the function under consideration. The user is also requested to describe, if desired, the kinds of operations it does to its input and output flows. An interesting development of this work is the fact that this semantic information gives rise to a series of heuristics that produces "better" DFD's. This topic is also being investigated [24].

Finally, the agenda mechanism can be worked in two modes - active and passive. In the passive mode, the user is allowed to build incorrect and/or inconsistent specifications, and the agenda will contain "suggestions" to eliminate these problems. This is how it actually works in the current version of PRISMA. In the active mode, however, the system functions as a driver, guaranteeing that only well-formed specifications are produced. This is a generalisation of the structured editor concept. This new mode is also being implemented in new versions of PRISMA.

Acknowledgements

Prof. Carlos Lucena has been an inspiring source of many of our ideas back at PUC/RJ. Among our colleagues at Imperial College Hugo Fuks, Anthony Finkelstein and Martin Sadler have significantly contributed with many useful comments to this work. Celso Niskier is supported by the Brazilian National Research Council CNPq, grant no. 20.2518/86-CC. Daniel Schwabe was partially supported by Projeto ESTRA, SID Informática, São Paulo.

References

[1] Balzer, R. (1985); A 15 Year Perspective on Automatic Programming, IEEE Trans. on Software Engineering, Vol. SE-11.

[2] Barringer, H. (1987); Using Temporal Logic in the Compositional Specification of Concurrent Systems, in Galton, A.P. (ed.), Temporal Logics and their Application,Academic Press, London.

[3] Castilho, J.M.V., Casanova, M.A., Furtado, A.L.(1982); A Temporal Framework for Database Specification, Proc. 8th International Conference on Very Large Databases.

[4] Chen,P.(1976); The Entity-Relationship Model - Toward a Unified View of Data, ACM-TOD, vol.1, no.1.

[5] Clocksin,W.F., Mellish,C.S. (1981); Programming in Prolog, Springer-Verlag, Berlin.

[6] DeMarco, T. *Structured Analysis and System Specification*, Prentice-Hall, 1979

[7] Donahue, J.E.(1976); Complementary Definitions of Programming Language Semantics, LNCS 42.

[8] Enderton, H.B. (1972); A Mathematical Introduction to Logic, Academic Press, New York.

[9] Finkelstein, A., Fuks, H., Niskier, C., Sadler, M. (1987); Constructing a Dialogic Framework for Software Development, Proc. Fourth International Software Process Workshop, Devon, U.K.

[10] Kowalski, R. (1979); Logic for Problem Solving, North-Holland, Amsterdam.

[11] Lehman, M.M., Stenning, V. & Turski,W.M. (1983); Another Look at Software Design Methodology, Imperial College of Science and Technology, Research Report DoC 83/13.

[12] Lenat, D.B. (1982); The Nature of Heuristics, Artificial Intelligence 21(1).

[13] Lucena, C.J.P. (1987); Inteligência Artificial e Engenharia de Software, Publicações Acadêmico-Científicas PUC/RJ - IBM Brasil, Jorge Zahar Editores.

[14] Maibaum, T.S.E., Veloso, P.A.S., Sadler, M. (1985); A Theory of Abstract Data Types for Program Development: Bridging the Gap ?, Mathematical Foundations of Software Development, Vol. 2, LNCS 186, Springer-Verlag.

[15] Maibaum, T.S.E. (1986); The Role of Abstraction in Program Development, IFIP 86, North-Holland

[16] Maibaum, T.S.E. (1987); A Logic for the Formal Requirements Specification of Real-Time Embedded Systems, FOREST Project Report.

[17] Mastro, V.A. (1985); Three Dimensional System Development, SEN 10 (5).

[18] Niskier, C. (1986); PRISMA: Utilização de Paradigmas Complementares para a Aquisição da Especificação de Software, M.Sc. Dissertation, Depto. de Informática, PUC/RJ.

[19] Niskier, C.(1987); Using Multiple Views for Software Specification, presented at the Fifth International Workshop on Specification of Abstract Data Types,Gullane, Scotland.

[20] Niskier, C., Fuks, H., Sadler, M. (1988); Changing Views in Software Specification: Interpretation Between Theories using Dialogue, in preparation.

[21] Pearl,J. (1984);Heuristics, Addison-Wesley.

[22] Peterson,J.L.(1981); Petri Net Theory and the Modeling of Systems, Prentice-Hall, Englewood Cliffs.

[23] Reisig,W.(1985); Petri Nets, Springer-Verlag, Berlin.

[24] Scott, D. & Souza, C.S. (1989); Conciliatory Planning for Extended Descriptive Texts, submitted to IJCAI '89

[25] Turski,W.,Maibaum,T.S.E.(1987); The Specification of Computer Programs, Addison-Wesley.

[26] Veloso, P.A.S., Pequeno, T.H.C. (1978); Interpretations Between Many-sorted Theories, 2nd Brasilian Colloquium on Logic, Campinas.

[27] Veloso, P.A.S., Casanova, M.A., Furtado, A.L. (1984); Formal Data Base Specification - An Eclectic Perspective, Research Report 1/84, Depto. de Informática, PUC/RJ.

[28] Yourdon,E.(1986); What Ever Happened to Structured Analysis ?, Datamation, June 1986.

A NET METHOD FOR SPECIFICATION OF REUSABLE SOFTWARE

H. S. Dhama

MITRE Corp.
Burlington Road
Bedford, MA 01730

V. Shtern

Metropolitan College
Boston University
Boston, MA 02215

ABSTRACT

A method, called the Net Method, has been developed for specifying software components based on Petri nets. Using two types of nodes and three types of connectors, five primitives of the specification method have been constructed. Only these five primitives are then used as building blocks to specify software. Although the Net Method was originally designed for software components, it has been found to be particularly suited for specifying systems that have a number of parallel processes and require the synchronization of a number of activities.

A graphics editor for the Net Method has been implemented and a Net simulation package is under development.

1. The High Cost of Software and Reusability

Reduction in the cost of software production through software reusability has been an aim of software producers for quite some time.

Reusability efforts have come a long way with many different paradigms being used for the production of reusable software components [1, 6, 8, 10]. However, the concept of "mass produced software components" remains a long way off since, among other problems, the problem of functional specification of software components still looms large.

2. Projected View of Reusable Software

This paper tackles only the problem of functional specification of functionality of reusable software components, irrespective of the model that was used for their development. However, for the sake of clarity and for ease of giving examples we would like to keep the paradigm of Ada packages and call the software components Logical Software Units (LSUs). This paper assumes that LSUs will come off-the-shelf in a standardized certified form and will have customization capability within a given functionality.

3. Development of a Specification Method for Reusable Software

Specification methods can be categorized under two broad headings:

(a) Those that have a mathematical formalism as their base and use some type of algebraic notation.
(b) Those that have a graphical notation whether they have a mathematical foundation or not.

We would like to develop a specification method belonging to the second category because we wish to follow the paradigm of the Sears' catalog in providing the user with hierarchically arranged information on the large number of LSUs that, we hope, will be available on the market at some future date. The LSU catalog will have a pictorial functional description of the LSU at a high level of abstraction (like pictures of tires in a Sears' catalog) followed by one or more levels of description in increasing detail just as tire specifications, other than price and size, are given removed from the picture of the tire.

Existing methods of graphical specification [4, 5, 9, 11] suffer from one or more of the following drawbacks:

(a) They are geared either towards representation at the architectural level of detail or towards representing details at the coding level without the ability to specify interactions at all levels of abstraction.
(b) They do not make a distinction between an active choice and a passive choice and thereby mask the identity of the activity participant that makes the decision. An "active choice" is a decision made by a participant of an activity; a "passive choice" is made by default for other participants of the activity as a result of the active choice.
(c) They do not distinguish between sequential activities and those activities that are independent and can be carried out in parallel, but are often carried out sequentially because of limitations of resources.

The Net Method of specification that we have developed addresses these issues and is due largely to the work of Holt and Commoner [2, 3] which in turn is based on the work of Petri [7].

3.1 Elements of the Specification Method

The elements of the specification diagrams are: entities, activities and connectors (fig. 1). Entities participate in system activities and the relationships between these two elements are shown by directed connectors. These form directed graphs in three dimensions which are system space, time and choice.

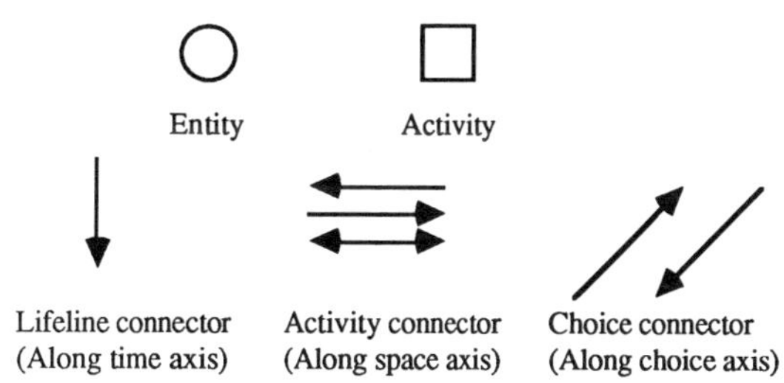

Fig. 1 - Elements of the Specification Method

3.2 The Five Primitives of the Specification Method

Using the elements of the specification method, five primitives of the specification method have been developed. Only these five basic representations combined in various ways, are needed to express the functional specifications of LSUs. Although we do not offer a proof of this sufficiency, we make this statement on the basis of our considerable experience with the Net Method.

1. Sequential Activities are joined by vertical connectors (Fig. 2). The figure shows an entity A which is transformed by activities 1, 2 and 3 and then leaves the system.

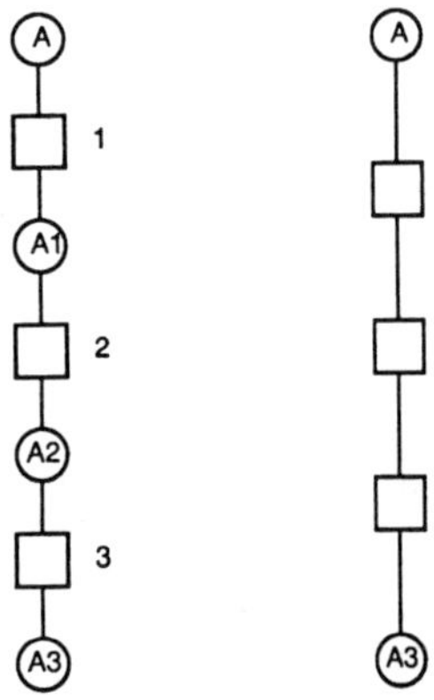

Fig. 2a Fig. 2b

Fig. 2 - Entity A Engages in Sequential Activities 1, 2, and 3

Since only one entity can cascade down a life-line connector, it is not necessary to show an entity node after each sequential activity. For this reason figure 2a has been abbreviated to fig. 2b where the entity nodes are understood to exist between activities.

2. Potentially Parallel Activities (fig. 3) are represented by cloning the entity that takes part in independent actions. In figure 3, entity B is a sorting program that is called upon to sort two unrelated files A and C. B is cloned into entities E and F thereby enabling the indepenedent activities 1 and 2. After the need to show independent actions is over, the clones G and H are merged.

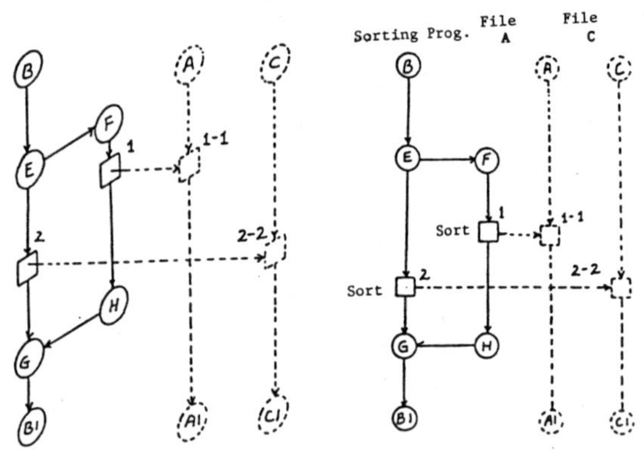

Isometric view of fig. 3b. Normal view

fig. 3a fig. 3b

Fig. 3 - Potentially Parallel Activities

From the graphical construct alone, two activities can be known to be independent if one cannot be reached from the other following connectors and using only nodes as crossover points.

Activities 1 and 1-1, and 2 and 2-2 are coincidental activities that must take place at the same moment. They are connected by horizontal connectors along the space axis. These connectors reflect multiple views of the same activity from the perspective of different entities.

3. and 4. Active Choice and Passive Choice (fig. 4) reflect the "master-slave" relationship between activities.

The Active Choice is made by entity A in activity 1 and is shown as a fork. Unlike A, entity B has no control over the two activities, 2 or 3, in which to participate and is said to make a Passive Choice.

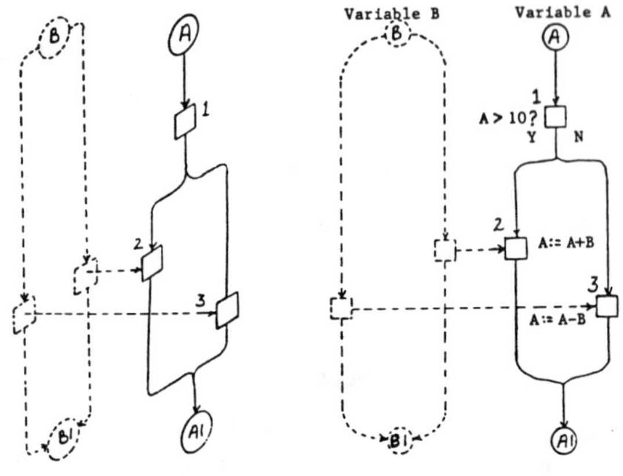

Isometric view of fig 4b Normal view

fig. 4a fig. 4b

Fig. 4 - Active and Passive Choice made by Entities A and B Respectively

5. Dispersion of Co-present Entities (fig. 5) - makes a temporary distinction between members of a group of entities, e.g. making a distinction between one field of a record and the rest of the record.

   This is shown by entities D and E taking part in independent activities 1 and 2. After the need for distinction is over, the record is treated as a single entity.

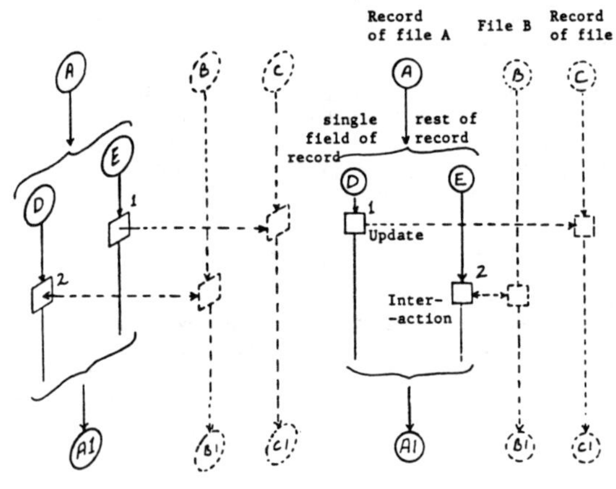

Isometric view of fig. 5b Normal view

fig. 5a fig. 5b

Fig. 5 - Two Co-present Entities Engage in Independent Action.

4. Example of use of the Specification Method

Through this example we would like to illustrate the ability of the Net Method to draw attention to errors of representation of a reusable software component.

A Logical Software Unit, L, has been designed to accumulate key input from a keyboard, K. Each character is stored in the buffer and the LSU gets ready to accept the next character from the keyboard. When a <CR> character is entered from the keyboard, the contents of the buffer are transferred to main memory. Fig. 6 shows these activities at the highest level of hierarchy.

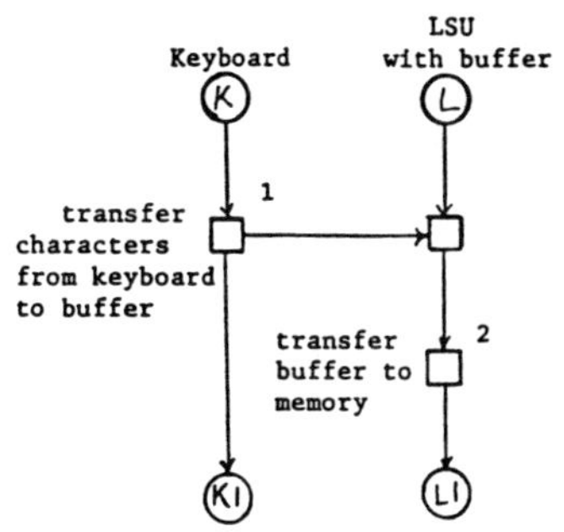

Fig. 6 - Input Characters from Keyboard Transferred to Main Memory

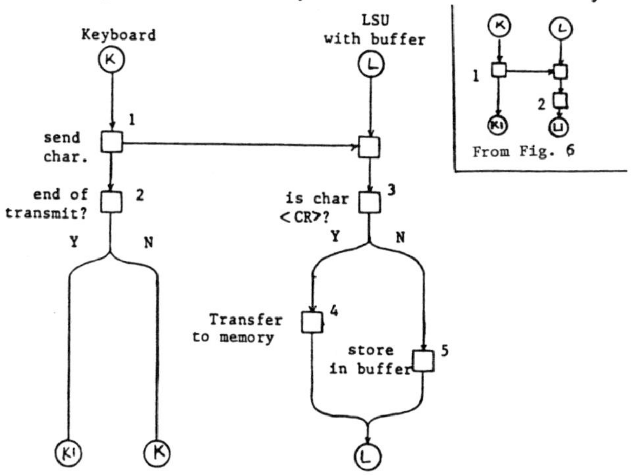

Fig. 6A - Transfer of Characters from Keyboard to Buffer

Fig. 6 has been expanded in fig. 6A which shows the details of character by character transmission from keyboard to buffer. The end of transmission is determined by the keyboard (activity 2). If it is not the end of transmission K gets ready to transmit the next character otherwise the entity K leaves the system. The diagram clearly shows us the error in the design: when K makes a decision to end transmission without sending <CR> as the last character, L is not informed of it, and the contents of the buffer will be left forever. This problem has been rectified in figure 6B.

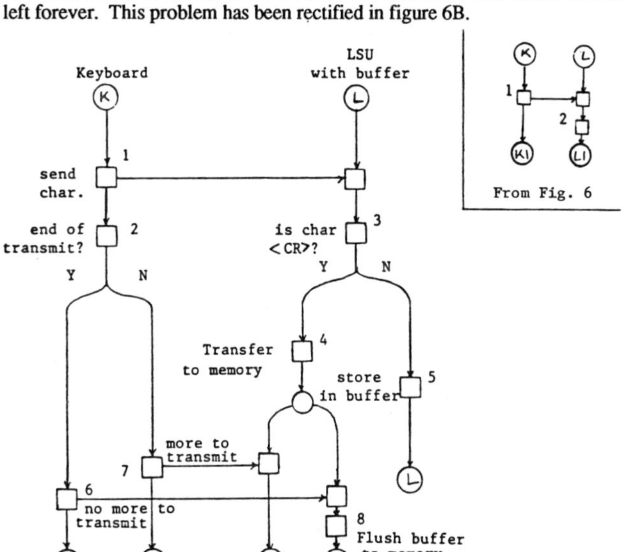

Fig. 6B - Transfer of Characters from Keyboard to Buffer
Last Character must be a <CR>

In fig. 6B, activities 1 through 5 are the same as in fig. 6A. In activity 6, when entity K has decided to end transmission, a signal to this effect is sent to L. On the receipt of this signal, entity L transfers its contents to main memory and goes out of the system with entity K doing the same. If it is not the end of transmission a signal to this effect is sent to L (activity 7) and both K and L get ready for another cycle of transmission and receipt of characters. Note that entity K makes the active choice to end transmission and entity L makes the passive choice of accepting this decision.

5. Advantages of the Net Method and Future Work

The advantages of the Net Method over existing graphical specification method are:

1. The high level representation is convenient for the creation of catalogs of LSUs. The same representation technique is used for specifying top level and low level details of LSU functionality.
2. Both flow of data and flow of control can be represented by the vertical and horizontal connectors used in the Net Method constructs.
3. Distinctions are made between active and passive choices and between sequential, coincidental (synchronized in time) and independent (potentially parallel) activities.
4. The technique is particularly suited for specifying software components that have a number of parallel processes and require synchronization of activities.

A graphics package for the Net Method has been designed and implemented, on the IBM PC. A Net simulation method is in the advanced stages of implementation, also on the PC. The simulation will enable us to see problems of synchronization, deadlocks and bottlenecks at all levels of system design.

References

1] Biggerstaff, T. J., Perlis, A. J., "Forward," IEEE Trans. on Software Engineering, Vol. SE-10, No. 5, Sept. 1984, pp. 474-476.

[2] Holt, A. W., "Final Report for Contract N00014-76-C-0781 titled 'Research on Information Systems Specification'," Massachusetts Computer Associates, Inc., Wakefield, MA, 1977.

[3] Holt, A. W., Commoner, F., "Events and Conditions Part I, Part II, Part III," Information Systems Theory Project, Applied Data Research, Inc., New York, NY, Dec. 1969.

[4] IBM Corp., "HIPO - A Design Aid and Documentation Technique," publication number GC 20-1851-1, Technical Publications/Systems, Dept. 824, IBM, White Plains, NY, 1975.

[5] Jackson, M., "System Development," Prentice/Hall International, Englewood Cliffs, NJ, 1983.

[6] Lanergan, R. G., Grasso, C. A., "Software Engineering with Reusable Design and Code, "IEEE Transactions on Software Engineering, Vol. SE-10, No. 5, Sept. 1984. pp. 498-501.

[7] Petri, C. A., "Communication with Automata, "Translated by Greene, C. F., Jr., Applied Data Research, Inc., Princeton, NJ, 1965.

[8] Prieto-Diaz, R., Freeman, P., "Classifying Software for Reusability," IEEE Software, Jan. 1987, pp. 6-16.

[9] Ross, D. T., "Structured Analysis: A Language for Communicating Ideas," IEEE Transactions in Software Engineering, Jan. 1977.

[10] Webster, D. E., "Mapping the Design Information Representation Terrain," Computer, Vol. 21, No. 12, Dec. 1988, pp. 8-23.

[11] Yourdon, E., Constantine, L. L., "Structured Design: Fundamentals of a Discipline of Computer Program and System Design," Prentice/Hall, Inc., Englewood Cliffs, NJ, 1979.

Software Development Using Models

Richard S. D'Ippolito Charles P. Plinta

Software Engineering Institute
Carnegie-Mellon University
Pittsburgh, PA 15213-3890

Abstract

We have been observing the design methods of software practitioners and engineers in other disciplines and have noticed differences. The most notable difference is the lack of models available to the software practitioner. We have reached several conclusions as a result of our observations and work:

- what is currently being called software engineering is not really engineering in the traditional sense
- there are important lessons about the design process to be learned from traditional engineering disciplines
- the application of one of the key concepts in engineering, the process of *modeling*, has the potential for high payoff

This report describes our experience and successes with modeling.

Traditional engineering practices

Before we discuss our experiences in the creation and use of models for software development, we will present a brief tutorial describing what models are and how they are applied in traditional engineering practices to solve everyday problems.

All engineering has a common basis.

Engineering is an applied science. All engineering disciplines have a defined body of scientific knowledge and the techniques to apply it. The key elements of the knowledge bases are codified as formal models. Each discipline also has a set of specialized techniques for applying its models to the solution of everyday problems. These techniques consist of formal methods of analyzing the problem in order to express its requirements in terms of existing model solutions. The parts of the problem that do not map on to existing model solutions must have the models created.

Automotive engineers have models of cars, civil engineers have models of bridges, mechanical engineers have models of rolling mills, electrical engineers have models of motors, and architects have models of Gothic cathedrals. The Gothic cathedral model is particularly instructive, as it is easy to separate into the component parts. The style of a design is inherited from the style of its model elements. Thus, a stylistically good design will be composed of model elements in compatible styles. Extracting the model elements of a Gothic cathedral yields spires with conical tops of constrained proportions; archways, false and real, composed of nested joined curves, also of constrained proportions, and supported by columns; windows outlined by the same arch curves, etc. Each of these model elements can be considered a model itself, as it is a replicable, validated design component. We know that these design components have been validated because they have survived repeated use while demonstrating their utility.

By now you should conclude that we classify engineering designs by the inherited characteristics of the component models, the ***domain*** and the ***style***. Furthermore, we respect the separation of domains. We never expect a good civil engineer to design a church. Neither should we expect an architect specializing in Gothic cathedrals to design good Jewish temples, for the styles are entirely different, although the domains are the same. Finally, we judge the quality of designs within the various domains and styles; we don't make abstract value comparisons between pens and pencils, or cathedrals and school buildings.

Capturing the design.

Finally, we need to be able to assemble models so that two goals are achieved: Models must express the design in a way that the requirements being met by the model are evident. The models must also contain the implicit translation rules. The ability to look back from the model to the requirements we shall call *saleability*, and the ability to look forward from the model to the implementation we shall call the *scaleability*.

Architects sell their designs from the scale models. The customer can see from the model how the space and activity requirements will be met. This is the way that the architect (designer) conveys the design to the user in terms of common understanding. Continuous use of these types of models have nearly eliminated all possibility of misunderstanding as to what the model actually conveys. For example, customers never challenge the absence of light switches, glazing, and plumbing fixtures; nor do they poke their fingers through the balsa wood floors while exclaiming, "This will never hold my grand piano!"

Furthermore, the more complex the design problems, the more likely there will be the need for several models. The wind-tunnel model for an automobile has different requirements than does the interior mock-up. The equivalents in software engineering would be models used to test certain performance characteristics *vs.* models used to present the user's view of the system.

Once the selling job is complete, the designer's models are turned over to detailers. The product of the detailers is really the translation of the models to the complete design. To do this, the detailers use specific and rigorous procedures to add the missing details and translate each model component into a set of plans and specifications that can be used for implementation. In order to be effective detailers, they must possess both the knowledge of the functions implied by the model and the knowledge of the construction techniques applicable to the domain. The plans and specifications are drawn in a familiar and common way, so that any builder skilled only in construction techniques can build or buy the components and implement the design.

Let's look at a success story from chemical engineering.

A real-world engineering example, with lessons.

> Successful start-up of Honam Oil Refinery Co. Ltd.'s 120,000[1] metric-ton-per-year polypropylene plant at Yocheon marked the first outside licensee with a world-scale application of the Union Carbide/Shell Oil (USA) Unipol PP process. "Compared with a conventional slurry process, the Unipol process has proven to be stable and simple when it comes to resin property control," according to C.N. Son, plant manager. "Start-up of the plant was smoother and quicker than expected," he says. His proof: The polymerization reaction began 20 minutes after catalyst injection and production hit design values in two hours.
>
> Just two reactors can produce an entire range of polymer products.
>
> Chemical Business, September, 1988.

This project is a stellar example of the application of modeling in engineering, and represents the kind of engineering process we should apply to software development. When we presented this example to a colleague in the software industry, the response was:

> If we knew all of the facts about the quoted chemical plant we would probably discover that all of the work leading up to the "start-up" took longer than most software products, probably more than ten years.
>
> Anonymous Critic

In fact, depending on how you measure it, the work took only either 18 or 7 months. This plant is based on a process that was developed in 1982, and is only the second such plant. The first plant, with a capacity of 80,000 metric-tons per year, was in Texas. Eighteen months before the Honam plant was started, the scaled-up design was issued. Construction began in July 1987, only seven months before startup, and was completed in November. The remaining two months were devoted to clean-up, safety inspections, instrument testing, and leak testing with nitrogen gas. *There were no pilot batches run.*

What lessons should we learn from this example? The first lesson is that at no time during the construction and commissioning of the plant were any tests of the design made. All the tests were to verify that the plant was an accurate implementation of the design. This is possible only when the design is composed of validated component models, validated interface models, and validated control models.

The second lesson is that the way chemical engineers are trained has changed recently and is worth emulating. Chemical engineers are not taught how to design polypropylene plants; they are taught the unit operations and the objects that provide them, such as distillation columns, heat exchangers, reactors, and pumps. The students are then told to go design various plants with the unit operators. Note again that this means that the focus of software engineering should be on identifying and characterizing the unit operators and their interfaces. By the way, we are not far behind because this paradigm shift in chemical engineering occurred in the fifties. This means that we can improve on their record because we are at an earlier stage of professional maturity than the chemical engineers were when their shift was made.

Modest beginnings -- contributions from us.

Nowhere in our software development travels through various application domains have we seen a similar application of models. In fact, we saw no models to speak of. We will describe three projects where we have made successful attempts to use engineering models in the software development process.

Example 1: Where, oh where, have my engines gone?

We were involved as technical consultants for the Ada Simulator Validation Program (ASVP). This was a research and development effort by two aerospace contractors to redesign and re-implement in Ada subsets of two existing flight simulators. The Software Engineering Institute's (SEI) project team supported the Air Force System Program Office by attending reviews and acting as technical consultants. As part of our involvement we developed a software architecture (model style) for flight simulator systems.[2] The software architecture has received wide acceptance in the flight simulator domain and is the ancestor of a model in use on full-scale developments by contractors in the domain.

[1]The original article misstated the capacity as 77,000.

[2]This work is described in more detail in SEI-TR-30 "An OOD Paradigm for Flight Simulators."

What did we do? Well, at first we didn't know what we were doing and after we had finished, we weren't quite sure what we had done. Now that we have had time to reflect on the effort, we can extract the lessons from it. Actually, we took on the project with the specific intent to explore design methods. We now realize that the original FORTRAN designs did use a form of modeling, but that the model used was inappropriate to meet the system enhancement requirements. The simulator was based on mathematical models and tables constructed from engine test-stand and flight-test data. The simulator program was simply used to solve the simultaneous equations and to do the table lookups.

However, the problem with this model was that it made fault injection (the important use of a simulator is emergency, and not normal, flight training), modification, and enhancement difficult. This is because the flight equations hid and combined the effects of the aircraft objects, e.g., there was no software "engine," let alone "engine rotor shaft bearing" to simulate the wear of. Our contribution here was to develop a model (report reference above) for enclosing objects and updating object states in a consistent manner. The same model was used for the electrical and engine systems, and had universal applicability within the simulator.

We derived these models using the components and interfaces from the real engineering models, the ones used to create the aircraft systems, and added the updating components. For domains that deal with real-world entities, it seems eminently sensible to capture the modeling work already completed and tested at the appropriate level of detail.

Example 2: Did you get my message, General?

The Granite Sentry Program is a phased hardware and software replacement of the systems in the Cheyenne Mountain Complex of NORAD. Our team supports the Program Office by attending reviews and acting as technical consultants. In addition, the team participates in design discussions and working group meetings with the lead system designers. As part of our involvement we developed a model and the software to perform message translation and validation. This model solution is now being incorporated into Phase II of the Granite Sentry System.

The message translation and validation model solution is well-defined and has known properties. Based on a message description, a detail designer using it can calculate timing estimates, sizing estimates, and will know the effects of the model on the software architecture. In order to guarantee identical instantiations of the solution model and enhance the probability of reuse, we have provided templates for the detail designer. Using these templates, it now takes only one to two hours to produce and test the software for translating and validating a new message type.

There are other recurring problems within this system where we can effectively apply a model solution. In order to develop a consistent set of models for use within a domain, we have to develop a domain-specific modeling style. The component models for the Gothic cathedral domain, for example, are all done in the same style. This insures the unity and harmony of the whole when the various models are assembled into a complete design.

We are now working with the Granite Sentry Phase II design team to codify the style to be used for developing the remaining models for the Phase II System, with the intent that they will be used in the remaining phases of the Granite Sentry Program. We will also transition these models and style to the Command, Control, Communications, and Intelligence (C^3I) system community to provide them with an initial experience base. Designers in the domain can be trained to understand the models and use them in future system developments.

Example 3: Pin the missile on the tank.

We have just begun working with the design team for the Advanced Millimeter-Wave Seeker (AMMWS) anti-tank missile project. This is a redesign of the Maverick missile, where the heat-sensing head has been replaced with millimeter-wave radar. The command and signal processing functions are being redesigned in Ada from the original JOVIAL and will reside on an embedded 80286/87 microcomputer.

The contractor has chosen to do an object-oriented design. After examining some design sketches for the top-level objects, we suggested the use of the OOD Paradigm architecture that we developed for the ASVP Project, as both executive structures were similar. We are currently applying the OOD Paradigm as a mechanism for updating objects that belong to a closed-loop control system.

Conclusions and future directions.

We have tried to show with our examples how extracting the lessons from traditional engineering and applying the modeling approach to software design has rewarded us with success. We now have validated models for two domains, and have begun to test the transfer of a model from one domain to another, leaving the basic features intact. Our current focus, when we begin involvement on a new project, is to seek out the recurring problems and use the best designers to develop a model solution applicable to each occurrence of the problem. In this way, we solve the problem only once, and the detail designers are able to build upon the work of the experts.

Larger Scale Systems Require Higher-Level Abstractions

Mary Shaw

Computer Science Department and
Software Engineering Institute
Carnegie Mellon University
Pittsburgh, Pennsylvania 15213, U. S. A.

Abstract

Over the past thirty years, abstraction techniques such as high level programming languages and abstract data types have improved our ability to specify and develop software. However, the increasing size and complexity of software systems have introduced new problems that are not solved by the current techniques. These new problems involve the system-level design of software, in which the important decisions are concerned with the kinds of modules and subsystems to use and the way these modules and subsystems are organized. This level of organization, the *software architecture* level, requires new kinds of abstractions that capture essential properties of major subsystems and the ways they interact.

1. Introduction

The development of abstraction techniques has been a major source of improvement in programming practice. It has provided programming language constructs, specification techniques, program structures such as algorithms and data types, strategies for modular decomposition, and more [8].

The essence of abstraction is recognizing a pattern, naming and defining it, analyzing it, finding ways to specify it, and providing some way to invoke the pattern by its name without error-prone manual intervention. This process suppresses the details of the pattern's implementation, reduces the opportunity for clerical error, and simplifies understanding of the result.

There are, of course, many kinds of detail associated with software. It is possible to identify abstractions of many kinds, specifying different sorts of detail—about functionality, implementation, performance, physical properties, and so on. At any given time, some of these details are significant and others irrelevant. Consequently, different abstractions are appropriate at different points in the software design and development process. In other words, good abstraction is ignoring the right detail at the right times.

The development of individual abstractions often follows a common pattern. First, problems are solved *ad hoc*. As experience accumulates, some solutions turn out to work better than others, and a sort of folklore is passed informally from person to person. Eventually the useful solutions are understood more systematically, and they are codified and analyzed. This enables the development of models that support automatic implementation and theories that allow the extension or generalization of the solution. This in turn enables a more sophisticated level of practice and allows us to tackle harder problems—which we often approach *ad hoc*, starting the cycle over again. As time passes, the abstractions capture larger and larger amounts of detail with more and more precision. This allows increasingly complex programs to be described with a given amount of effort. This pattern can be seen, for example, in the development of higher-level programming languages and abstract data types.

2. The Software Architecture Level of Design

Just as higher-level languages and abstract data types emerged because good programmers recognized useful structures, good programmers now recognize useful system organizations. Some of the popular system organizations are

- *Pipes and Filters:* Each module accepts a stream of inputs and emits a stream of outputs; usually the output stream involves local transformation of the input stream, making the module a *filter*. As indicated in Figure 2-1, modules are strung together by connecting the output stream of one module to serve as the input stream of its successor (a *pipe*).

Figure 2.1: Pipes and Filters

This work was supported by Carnegie Mellon University and the Mobay Corporation.

- *Data abstraction:* Abstract data types provide a useful way to organize a software system. With the addition of inheritance of definitions, it is known as *object-oriented programming* [5]. Figure 2-2 suggests a typical system organization, in which a number of independent objects (*obj*) invoke each others' operations (*op*).

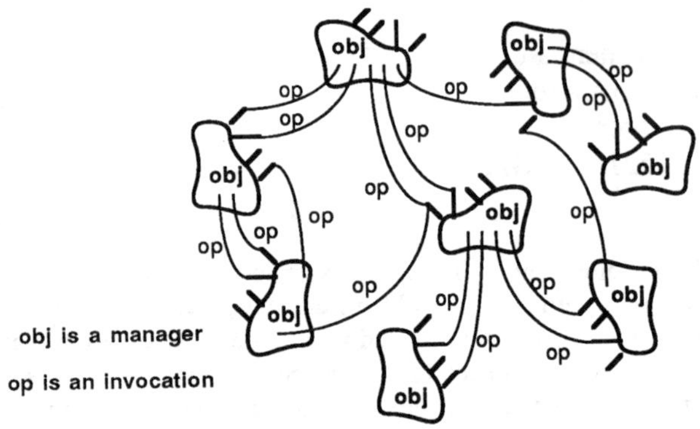

Figure 2.2: Data Abstraction

- *Layered Systems:* The system is organized hierarchically, with each layer providing service to the layer above it. Inner layers are usually hidden from outer layers, except for certain functions carefully selected for export [6]. Figure 2-3 gives an example of such an architecture.

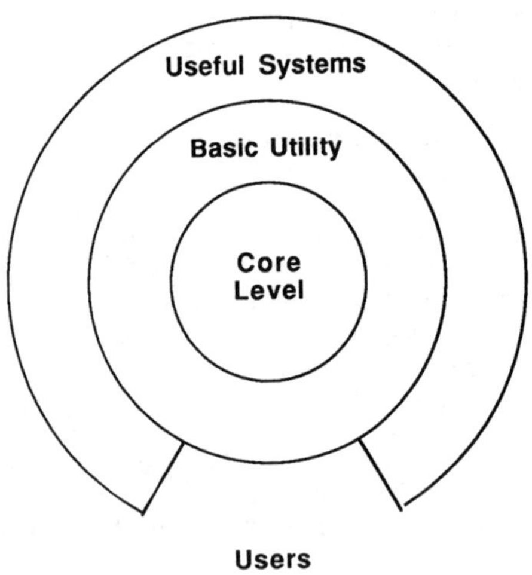

Figure 2.3: Layered System

- *Rule-Based Systems:* The computation is organized as an unordered collection of rules, each of which gives a condition under which the rule applies and an action to take when it does apply [3]. Figure 2-4 shows a typical system organization in which an inference engine interprets the rules that define the knowledge base for a particular application.
- *Blackboard Systems:* A central data structure represents the current state of the computation; a collection of independent processes, each responsible for a certain kind of knowledge, check the current state and update it if they can. As indicated in Figure 2-5, processes, or knowledge

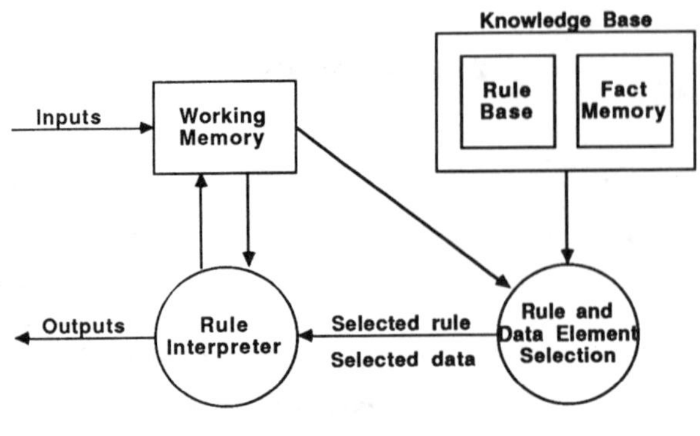

Figure 2.4: Rule-Based System

sources (*ksi*), are invoked when they are able to improve the current state; the progress made by each knowledge source should enable some other process to operate. This organization is useful for applications in which diverse kinds of knowledge must be brought to bear on interpretation of raw data; the current state represents the current state of the interpretation and the various processes augment that interpretation using whatever expertise each one implements [1].

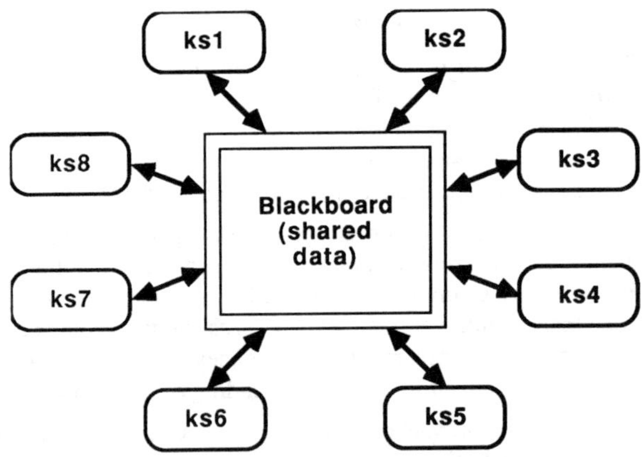

Figure 2-5: Blackboard System

This level of system organization and design is the *software architecture* level. Software organizations like these are used informally, but they are not systematically understood. Nor are they taught systematically, with guidance about reasons for choosing one rather than another for a given application. Nevertheless, software designers sometimes describe the architectures of particular systems. Most commonly, such a description includes a block diagram of the major subsystems and labels the elements in terms that refer to their specific function in the system.

In particular problem domains or user communities, a single pattern may predominate. This pattern may be used because it is familiar, or it may be used because other alternatives are not considered, even when some other organization might be better. Consider, for example, the Unix community, in which pipes and filters are clearly the preferred system structure. In any case, the resulting uniformity of program structure may permit the development of utilities to support the structure [2] or partial automation of program construction.

In order to design effectively at this level, we need to be able to describe and analyze architectures of software systems in uniform, comparable terms. The remainder of this paper sets forth the tasks required to do so.

3. Composition of Systems from Subsystems

System organizations such as those described above are constructed by combining subsystems. Sometimes, as for most of the examples cited above, the subsystems are independently compilable modules, linked by shared data or procedure calls. At other times the subsystems are sets of design decisions (for example, the choice of a synchronization strategy,) and the code that implements them is woven together with the code for other subsystems.

Each subsystem performs some clear function within the system. In current architectural descriptions of systems, this function is often specific to the system being implemented; but it may also be a more common function such as communication or storage. For example, compilers include lexical analyzers, which are actually instances of *filters* (that is, functions that perform local processing on a stream of input tokens to yield a stream of output tokens). Identifying and classifying the system functions that are common to many applications is a significant first step to the development of software architecture.

Subsystems have internal structure. It is often useful to design that substructure at an architectural level before implementing it. The internal structure of a subsystem is often not the same as the structure in which the subsystem is embedded. For example, many of the filters provided with Unix are not organized internally as filters. At some point, of course, it is necessary to drop from the architectural design level to the programming level. At this point, the programmer can choose from a variety of programming paradigms, such as imperative code, rule-based systems, functional systems, and table-driven interpreters.

Subsystems allow a variety of implementations of the functions they provide. The choice of implementation strategy depends on characteristics of the application. For example, the strategies for implementing the storage function include files, data bases, symbol tables, and arrays. These have different access patterns, different data models, slight variations in the detail of the function they provide. They also have different abilities to accommodate heterogeneous or variable-sized data, different response times, latencies, and overheads.

Subsystems are combined into systems in a number of ways. The most common are the usual mechanisms for combining units of code: invocation (e.g., of procedures), instantiation (e.g., of generic definitions), and replication (e.g, of program text). In these cases, implementations of subsystems may be constrained to a single programming language, hence a single paradigm. Other mechanisms for combining subsystems, such as communication links and pipes, are not sensitive to the implementation paradigm of individual units, though they often require that the individual units observe certain protocols with respect to the communication. In cases where subsystems are not independent compilation units, systems are composed by mingling code for one subsystem with code for another.

4. Codification and Specification

Engineering disciplines rely on shared understanding of design and implementation strategies and standards. This shared understanding is based on extensive experience; in engineering disciplines other than software it is codified and disseminated through handbooks. Some of these handbooks cover entire fields; Perry's Chemical Engineers' Handbook [7] and Kent's Mechanical Engineers' Handbook [4] are examples. Other handbooks concentrate on specialized areas such as waste management or pesticides. These handbooks serve not only as repositories of information, but also as carriers of the conceptual structure of the field. The information they contain ranges from narative design options to mathematical models and experimental data.

For software architectures, it is not sufficient to identify system structures, subsystem types, and techniques for composing subsystems into systems. These elements are sufficiently complex that they can't be reconstructed from memory, and their analysis requires detailed information about alternatives, tradeoffs, and interactions. Knowledge about them must be codified in a uniform way, and implementation should be automated whenever feasible. Informal analysis and the organization of data from experience must precede formal specification. The basis for developing formal specifications includes

- *Informal description:* purpose of element, general domain of utility
- *Abstract model:* basis for specification, either formal or informal
- *Syntax:* notation, signatures of operations
- *Semantics:* meanings of primitive elements and for the rules for composition
- *Evaluation criteria:* correctness, generality, performance, adaptability, domain-specific power, etc.
- *Implementation:* template for structure, system support
- *Design dimensions:* implications of design decisions
- *Engineering considerations:* interactions, good practice
- *Selection criteria:* indicators and contraindicators
- *History:* primary users, major upgrades

This task has been started for lower-level abstractions such as algorithms and data structures, but architecture-level design is not yet mature enough to support it.

5. Summary

Large-scale systems involve design at a level above the traditional module. At this design level the objects of interest are subsystems and their interactions, rather than data structures and algorithms. Support for design at this level requires systematic identification and analysis of useful system organizations and the components from which they are constructed.

Many system descriptions already provide evidence of informal abstraction at the architectural level. These factors suggest that the step to software architecture is now possible. *Identification, codification,* and *dissemination* are the three major problem areas to attack.

References

1. Erman, L. D., Hayes-Roth, F., Lesser, V. R., and Reddy, D. Raj. "The Hearsay-II Speech-Understanding System: Integrating Knowledge to Resolve Uncertainty". *Computing Surveys 12*, 2 (June 1980), 213-253.

2. Gammage, Neil, and Casey, Liam. "XMS: A Rendezvous-Based Distributed System Software Architecture". *IEEE Software 2*, 3 (May 1985), 9-19.

3. Hayes-Roth, Frederick. "Rule-Based Systems". *Communications of the ACM 28*, 9 (September 1985), 921-932.

4. Kent, William. *Kent's Mechanical Engineers' Handbook.* John Wiley & Sons, New York, NY, 1950.

5. Liskov, Barbara. Data Abstraction and Hierarchy. OOPSLA '87 Addendum to the Proceedings, New York, NY, October, 1987, pp. 17-34.

6. Oberndorf, Patricia A. "The Common Ada Programming Support Environment (APSE) Interface Set (CAIS)". *IEEE Transactions on software Engineering 14*, 6 (June 1988), 742-748.

7. Perry, Robert H., et.al.. *Perry's Chemical Engineers' Handbook.* McGraw Hill, New York, NY, 1984.

8. Shaw, Mary. "Abstraction Techniques in Modern Programming Languages". *IEEE Software 1*, 4 (October 1984), 10-26.

Discovering, Visualizing, and Controlling Software Structure

R. W. Schwanke, R. Z. Altucher, and M. A. Platoff

Siemens Corporate Research, Inc.
755 College Rd. East
Princeton, NJ 08540

1. Introduction

Although many good principles, methods, and notations for large system design have been developed in the last two decades, they have seen little application to software system maintenance. The reasons seem to be the large cost and the diminishing value of writing specifications after the code already exists. This paper describes research that is attempting to bridge the gap between software design and software maintenance. The MAINTAINER'S ASSISTANT project at Siemens Research is researching ways to make the software maintainer more productive, in part by helping him contend with the enormous amounts of information in the project database. A sub-project, ARCH[1], is developing a new approach to controlling the structure of a large software system during maintenance. The approach assumes that a large body of code may already exist before the structure is formally specified. The ARCH methodology includes

- a practical notation for specifying software structure,
- a graph editor to help the architect visualize and construct the specification,
- a tool that extracts the actual structure of a system and compares it to the specification, and
- an automatic classification tool that helps an architect analyze existing code to discover an appropriate structure specification.

This paper describes the specification method used in ARCH, the *condensation* method that aids visualization, and the classification tool, which uses *conceptual clustering* to help the architect discover the structure of the system. The clustering is based on detailed cross-reference information, which we hypothesize provides useful "light semantic" profiles of the parts of a system. The paper includes preliminary results from some experiments in analyzing a real system, and describes the full-scale experiment we plan to carry out next.

[1]The name is drawn from "architecture" and from bridging the gap between design and maintenance.

2. How ARCH Will Be Used

The focal point of ARCH is an architecture specification that documents the intended structural design of a large program, and controls its evolution. We use the term "architecture" to refer to structural aspects of the program, and not its function.[2] The structure of a program is the set of connections between software units. The architecture is a set of *allowed* connections. ARCH controls the structure by checking the actual connections to see if they are allowed. This checking is incorporated in the system building process, so that errors are reported to the programmer as early as possible.

Typically, the structure of a system contains far too many connections for the architecture to list each of them individually. Instead, the architecture specifies a subsystem tree that places software units in groups, and those groups in larger groups, and so on. Then, the set of allowed connections can include connections between groups, as well as individual units.

Keeping the specification separate from the code distinguishes "what is allowed" from "what is". The architecture permits a large set of possible structures that are equally acceptable from the point of view of the overall design. The import/export clauses in the code of, say, an Ada program, describe only the current structure of the actual code.

This distinction is very useful for coordinating teams of programmers. An individual programmer is expected to take advantage of as much existing code as possible, by importing it into his modules and invoking its procedures, types, and so on. Therefore, he is authorized to modify his import/export clauses to fit the needs of his code.

[2]Reasonable persons might disagree with our choice of terms. Nonetheless, the need to control structure is apparent.

©1989 ACM 0-89791-305-1/89/0500/0147$00.75

The system architects, on the other hand, are responsible for making all the pieces fit together. They can't possibly review every change to an import or export clause to analyze its impact on the overall structure. By specifying the architecture, they can constrain the set of allowable imports and exports without embedding too many design details in the specification. Then, the programmers are free to modify portions of the structure independently, without constantly consulting the architects. Like every other aspect of software, architecture specifications will change. However, we expect that they will change much more slowly than the actual structure of the system.

3. ARCH Specifications

An ARCH specification consists of *subsystem trees* and *constraint graphs*. A subsystem tree divides the system into subsystems, and the subsystems into sub-subsystems, to an arbitrary depth. The leaves of the tree represent the smallest software units that the project wishes to consider separately when analyzing and enforcing structure. The tree need not be balanced. A specification may have several subsystem trees, representing different views of the system. One tree may reflect a managerial viewpoint; another may reflect a resource viewpoint; another may reflect division into cooperating processes.

A constraint graph is a multi-colored, directed graph over the nodes of the subsystem trees. Each color denotes a type of connection. Each edge from, say, node X to node Y, permits connections from leaves of the subtree rooted at X to leaves of the subtree rooted at Y. A software system satisfies its architecture if every connection between its software units is permitted by some edge of its architecture.

4. Visualizing System Structure

One way that we understand either the architecture or the structure of a system is to draw it. So, ARCH provides a graph editor that can automatically lay out large graphs. The prototype implementation uses Edge [1], which topologically sorts the nodes so that most edges in the graph will point down(right), and only a few will point up (left). It then applies the Sugiyama layout heuristic to minimize edge crossings.

However, just having good layout heuristics cannot make up for graphs that are too large. For example, we used Edge to display the *includes* graph for a 56,000 line C program. The graph had 100 nodes and 630 edges. The displayed graph was 25 screens wide, and had 48,000 edge crossings. Many regions of the graph were blackened by criss-crossing edges. Plainly, the graph was too detailed to draw in any meaningful way. Therefore, ARCH (through Edge) provides facilities for summarizing graphs semi-automatically.

The summary technique is *condensation*. A condensation is a many-to-one mapping from a large graph *onto* a smaller graph. Each node in the smaller graph corresponds to one or more nodes in the larger graph. Each edge in the smaller graph corresponds to one or more edges in the larger graph, with corresponding vertices. A condensation is useful because it does not discard any of the edges in the original graph. Although the condensed graph does not tell us which particular members of one group are connected to members of another group, we can be sure that there are *no* edges between members of two groups unless the summary shows an edge between the groups.

When a good subsystem tree is available for the nodes of a graph, the analyst can use it to select a condensation. Each node in the tree represents the leaf nodes in the subtree below it. The analyst can indicate details to ignore by selectively pruning nodes from the subsystem tree. The pruned nodes are then condensed onto their parents to produce a summarized graph.

5. Automatic Classification

Effective condensation depends on selecting a good mapping, based on the subsystem tree. Often, however, a large graph or large system does not have a good subsystem tree to use for condensation. Many old systems have only informal structure above the file level. Other systems have an obsolete subsystem structure that combines managerial, political, and historical factors with technical decisions. During years of maintenance, many interdependencies may have appeared that were not intended in the original design.

For these reasons, ARCH is developing automatic classification methods to help the architect create a subsystem tree where none existed, or revise a tree that has become obsolete. The classification methods can be applied to actual code, or to architecture specifications that have become too detailed to adequately understand.

The next three sections discuss the information we use to classify software, describes the classification method that we are using, and presents the results of some preliminary experiments.

5.1. Characteristics of Software

We have chosen to classify software on a "light semantics" basis. We feel that deep semantic analysis, which discovers the "meaning" of a procedure or module by determining what the code does, is beyond current technology. Instead, we use a model taken from the information retrieval domain, in which the "meaning" of a document is nothing more nor less than the set of nontrivial words it uses. This model is commonly used to classify documents in retrieval systems (e.g. [2]).

The names used in a procedure frequently give the reader hints about the subject matter of the procedure. For example, if you noticed that a certain module called the procedures `FileOpen`, `FileRead`, and `StringCompare`, you might guess that it was doing some kind of lexical analysis on the contents of files.

There are several reasons why names may be good indicators of the subject of a software unit:

- Names are frequently chosen for their mnemonic value. Even though the computer may not know the mnemonic relationship, the name still represents a concept.
- In a well-designed program, there are many procedures whose purpose is to read and/or write a certain data structure or data type. The name of this structure or type partially characterizes what the procedure does.
- There are no synonyms in programs, except for aliases, which are hopefully becoming rare. Therefore, two procedures that access different data structures are "talking about" different subjects.
- In a well-designed program, the scope of most names should be relatively small [3, 4]. Therefore, two procedures that use several of the same names often should be placed in the same module, or at least the same subsystem.

Most of the rationale given above can be reworded to support the hypothesis that a procedure can also be characterized by where it is used. For example, if most of the procedures in a given system that invoke the macro `XtWindow` also invoke `XtDisplay`, you might guess (correctly) that the two macros are related.

Therefore, as a working conjecture, ARCH characterizes a software unit by the names that it uses, which we call its *names-used*, and the names of the places where it is used, which we call its *user-names*. This information is extracted from programs by a typed, scoped, cross-reference tool, currently based on `cxref`.

5.2. Overview of the Method

Our classification method builds a tree of categories and subcategories, placing similar software units together in the same category. The tree is a variable-arity tree, where the arity is chosen heuristically to achieve "natural" categories, rather than rigidly following a plan of predefined branching factors and category sizes. As a by-product, the method produces, for each category and subcategory, a statistical summary of the characteristics of the members of the category.

The classification method is a *conceptual clustering* method [5], and the tree it creates is a concept tree, in which each category represents a concept. The concept is described in two ways: by a list of examples (the members of the category), and by the statistical summary, identifying the common features of members. Unlike some conceptual classification methods, the concepts are defined *probabilistically*. A deterministic concept would list a set of features shared by all examples of the concept; these features would define the concept. In ARCH, not every member of the category shares every feature; the statistical summary records how many members of the category have each feature.

Since there are exponentially many different classification trees possible for a given set of objects, we must define criteria for a good tree. There are actually two related *evaluation functions* needed: a similarity function, which measures the similarity between two objects and between two groups of objects, and a function which measures the "goodness" of the tree overall.

ARCH currently provides two classification algorithms, an incremental algorithm and a batch algorithm. The incremental algorithm, based on the Cobweb system [5], builds the tree by classifying one object at a time, locally reshaping the tree each time to hill-climb towards a good set of categories. The batch algorithm classifies all of the objects at once, by repeatedly combining objects into groups, and groups into larger groups, using the tree evaluation function to select the best group sizes.

We now feel that a batch algorithm is more suited to our problem domain, because the objects to be classified are all available at the time the computation takes place, and the number of new objects added later will be relatively small compared to the number of objects already classified. However, batch algorithms are generally in higher time-complexity classes than comparable incremental algorithms, so we will be experimenting to see the sizes of systems that we can afford to analyze with the batch method.

5.3. Experiment: Understanding a Call Graph

To test whether *names-used* and *user-names* are useful features for clustering software, and also to test whether our clustering methods were valid, we used automatic clustering to help summarize the structure of a large call graph.

The code we studied was the TML subsystem of DOSE. (DOSE is a structure editor prototyping environment; TML is a language and interpreter for incremental semantic actions.) TML contains 82 procedures. The internal call graph contains 155 edges. A legible plot of the call graph would require three pages of this proceedings, arranged vertically, to present. It is complicated enough that its "overall structure" is not obvious, although a knowledgeable maintainer could trace individual paths through it without trouble.

The clustering algorithm was presented with 392 features (2 per edge, plus a self-reference for each node so that a node would have itself as a neighbor). It created a subsystem tree consisting of 29 clusters, including the root cluster comprising the entire system, yielding an average branching factor of 3.8. The run time was 323 seconds on a 12 Mbyte diskless Sun 3.

To test whether the clusters were meaningful, we attempted to write a short descriptive name for each cluster, based on the shared features of its members and our knowledge of the code. We were able to do so for 26 of the 29 clusters. One of the three unnamed clusters was made up of two procedures that had nothing in common, which were apparently "left over" after everything else had been classified. The other two unnamed clusters were bottom-level clusters where the algorithm had paired two members of a meaningful cluster because the cluster was a little too large.

To demonstrate that the clustering was useful for understanding the graph, we edited the cluster tree to move the "left over" cluster up to the root level, then fed the cluster data and the original call graph to Edge for display. We then generated summaries of the graph at many different levels of detail, forming a tutorial sequence for absorbing details of the graph in small, manageable increments.

We conclude from this experiment that clustering objects in a software interconnection graph according to their *names-used* and *user-names* is useful for understanding the overall structure of the graph.

6. Our Next Experiment

To apply conceptual clustering to a more practical problem, we will be analyzing data from the Siemens BS2000 operating system. This system comprises 1 million lines of code, has been maintained for 15 years, and currently employs 300 programmers. The architects have recently gone through the painstaking process of formally specifying its structural architecture, using a "virtual machine layer" methodology. They have classified the edges in the actual cross-reference graph into 7 different kinds of dependencies, some of which imply a dependency in the same direction as the cross reference, and others which imply a dependency in the reverse direction. The project has included a graph editor for displaying the specification, and will include a validation tool for detecting architecture violations in the code.

Our experiments will try to reproduce, through semi-automatic means, the architecture they have extracted manually. This will necessarily include statistical methods for initializing the weights of different identifiers for use in the similarity measures, and will probably include "relevance feedback", in which the classifier compares some of its results to the human's work, and improves its performance by adjusting weights.

7. Future Work

Although our current algorithms generate concept trees that do not share subtrees, we expect to find algorithms that will let us discover useful internal design concepts that cross subsystem boundaries. This would correspond to a concept graph that formed a general DAG, such as found in a thesaurus. Our Maintainer's Assistant project will include such a thesaurus to use for similarity-based search, and also to relate code to documentation and other project artifacts.

The production-quality clustering tool we would eventually like to see built is a structure browser/editor which would provide incremental, interactive clustering services to help the maintainer study and modify a large system. For example, he may have the task to restructure a subsystem, and ask the tool for suggestions on which procedures to move. He would like to try small changes first, to preserve as much of the "known world" as possible. Therefore, the services should be arranged to "hill climb" from the existing structure to a better one. He would also like to do similarity-based search, either to help him find existing code to edit and reuse, or to help him find code similar to the code he has just modified, in case it needs the same kinds of changes.

8. Conclusions

The ARCH project has shown that automatic clustering of large graphs, combined with manual labelling, effectively supports graph summarization. ARCH will use this technique to discover, visualize and control the structure of large software systems.

9. Acknowledgements

Gail Kaiser encouraged us to pursue this project before we were sure we should. Francie Newbery kindly supplied us with the source code for Edge, and lots of cooperation as we stress-tested it with large graphs. George Drastal introduced us to conceptual clustering and told us about Cobweb.

1. Frances J. Newbery, "An Interface Description Language For Graph Editors", *IEEE 1988 Workshop on Visual Languages*, October 1988.

2. C. J. Van Rijesbergen, *Information Retrieval,* Butterworths, London, 1979, 2nd edition

3. William A. Wulf and Mary Shaw, "Global Variable Considered Harmful", Tech. report, Computer Science Department, Carnegie-Mellon University, 1972.

4. David L. Parnas, "On the Criteria To Be Used In Decomposing Systems Into Modules", Tech. report, Computer Science Department, Carnegie-Mellon University, August 1971.

5. Douglas Fisher, "Knowledge Acquisition Via Incremental Conceptual Clustering", *Machine Learning*, Vol. 2, No. 2, 1987, pp. 139-179.

REQUIREMENTS ELICITATION, ANALYSIS AND FORMALIZATION

DOMAIN ANALYSIS
- From Art Form To Engineering Discipline -

Guillermo Arango

Advanced Software Engineering Project
Department of Information and Computer Science
University of California, Irvine, CA 92717

Abstract

A precondition for reusability in software development is the existence of reusable resources. There is a lack of systematic methods for producting reusable information. Within the "reuse community", there is belief that *domain analysis* will facilitate the identification and capture of reusable abstractions for restricted classes of applications. This belief is grounded on successful experiences conducted by some very capable individuals. However, for domain analysis to become a practical technology we need: 1) to understand the conceptual foundations of the process; 2) to produce an unambiguous definition in the form of specifica techniques; and, 3) to provide adequate support tools.

In this paper we advance a conceptual framework. We do not offer a detailed, cannonical scheme of how *every* type of domain analysis is or ought to be done. We have identified a set of principles providing coherence to a diverse set of findings about domain analysis. Within this framework we have explored techniques for *practical* domain analysis. The framework is useful for comparing between different approaches to domain analysis, and can be used as guidance in developing other instances of methods and representations.

Keywords: reusability, reuse methodology, domain analysis, conceptual modelling.

> *"Software is often expected to provide a formal description of the very same properties for which mankind has yet failed to evolve and accept a satisfactory linguistic system ... We, the software makers, are contributing to the development of application domain theories by exposing, albeit in a painful and costly way, highly concentrated consequences of the inadequacies of available domain descriptions."* W. Turski [43].

> *A domain analyst is a machine for turning coffee into reusable abstractions.* *

1. Purpose and viewpoint

We need a theory of the process of domain analysis to help us synthesize domain analysis methods and compare between different methods. The purpose of this paper is to outline one such framework and *not* to present a particular method for domain analysis. The framework is at a meta-level with respect to actual analysis techniques- [2] discusses specific methods.

We adopt the viewpoint of researchers in*reusable software engineering* [15]. An engineering approach---controlled approximation to satisficing solutions---is at the core of our framework. Our software engineering bias is reflected in the structure of a development cycle for reuse infrastructures modelled after the established software development cycle. We believe in the need for domain-specific approaches to reusability. We conjecture that there exists no universal characterization of the information that could be of value to a reuse algorithm.

The domain engineering (DE) framework [2] resulted from many years of research on software reusability. A view of reusers as learning systems captures the essence of a variety of reuse situations in conventional software and expert-systems development. The DE framework has helped us: 1) to analyze and compare existing approaches to domain analysis, 2) to establish an operational definition for practical domain analysis, and 3) to design practical domain analysis techniques and representations.

Outline. Section 2 sketches the emergence of the notion of domain the study of domain analysis and Section 3, the basics of the DE framework. Section 4 examines the established view on ``problem domain" and ``domain analysis". We argue that these shared, intuitive notions are non-operational and that do not allow for a meaningful comparison between analysis techniques. Section 5 proposes an operational definition for the task of domain analysis. Section 6 outlines a model of reusers as learning systems and proposes a general strategy for the design of domain analysis techniques appropriate to particular reuse situations. Section 7 discusses how this view could be applied to assessing progress and defining stopping conditions in the process domain analysis. Finally, Section 8 discusses the conditions under which different methods to domain analysis can be compared.

2. A bit of history

The concept of software reusability can be traced back to the beginning of computer programming and it saw the light as a software engineering topic at the 1969 NATO Conference. Little progress was made until the mid- to late-1970, when some organizations put to a test the promise of productivity through reusability. In the early 1980's software reusability regained stature as a topic of software engineering research [14]. The Workshop on Reusability in Programming sponsored by ITT in 1983 was a milestone in that process. Early research on reusability focused on methods and mechanisms to perform reuse, on the representation of reusable components and on the organization of repositories of components. Comprehensive surveys are available from [6], [16] and [42].

Jim Neighbors introduced the expression *domain analysis* to refer to the activity of surveying a class of problems with the purpose of developing the problem-oriented specification languages and formal transformations employed by the Draco system [29]. The expression was adopted by a limited number of specialized research groups which shared the goal of automating some aspect of software development.

* Paraphrasing Paul Erdös' "A mathematician is a machine for turning coffee into theorems."

This research was supported in part by the University of California and Aluminum Company of America under the MICRO program, and by the National Science Foundation under grant DCR-85-21398. At the time of the writing, the author is visiting at Departement Applications de l'Intelligence Artificielle, Division Structures et Logiciel pour la Conmutation, Centre National d'Etudes des Telecommunications, France Telecom, Lannion, France.

For example, domain-specific automatic programming [5], specification analysis [11], verification [17][19], application-generator generators [30], software portage [1]. They also shared a prevailing view in the expert-systems area, that mechanical reusers perform well on restricted classes of problems when they have access to problem-specific knowledge. These experiences uncovered the dominant role of domain-specific information in the definition and organization of reusable resources.

The importance (and difficulty) of identifying ``appropriate" reusable information soon became clear as a larger segment of the software engineering community attempted to realize the promise of reusability. One of the recommendations from the 10th. Minnowbrook Workshop on Software Reuse in July 1987, suggests ``concentrating on specific applications and domains (as opposed to developing a general reusability environment)" [26]. The Rocky Mountain Workshop on Software Reuse acknowledged the lack of a theoretical or methodological framework for domain analysis [37] . More recently, the need for a unifying framework to compare different approaches to domain analysis became apparent at the first Domain Analysis Workshop organized in the context or OOPSLA'88.

3. The domain engineering perspective

There exists a wide gap between the kinds and form of knowledge available about problem domains and the content and form of the items of information that can be reused in software construction. For instance, knowledge about a problem domain is often implicit and nonformal, while reusable information must be usually represented explicitly and formally. We use the term *reuse infrastructure* to refer to the information that must be made available to the software developer, together with the auxiliary information needed to locate and manipulate it. An example of a reuse infrastructure is a collection of catalogued and documented software components. Bridging the problems-infrastructure gap is a difficult and expensive process. The bridging process must be decomposed into a system of well-defined activities and intermediate work products---a *domain engineering process* ---supporting three fundamental concerns:

1. *Domain analysis:* the identification, acquisition and evolution of reusable information on a problem domain to be reused in software specification and construction. There are two aspects to domain analysis:

   Conceptual analysis: the identification and acquisition of information required to *specify* systems in the domain.

   Constructive analysis: the identification and acquisition of information required to *implement* those specifications.

Relevant information is captured in a *model of the domain.* The information in the model allows the reuser to achieve specific levels of performance (Section 6) in the software construction task.

2. *Infrastructure specification:*: the selection and organization of reusable information in the model to fit the patterns of reuse in the environment of the reuser. As a result, an architecture for reusable information is specified. For example, a library of programs, an object base, a library of transforms, a data base schema.

3. *Infrastructure implementation*: the design and encoding of the pieces resulting from the specification process using particular representations required by the technology of the reusers; for example, encoding the specified programs using Ada or Lisp, indexing them using a particular classification scheme, etc. (This is a task closely related to conventional software engineering).

This decomposition is a ``convenient fiction" analogous to the waterfall view of program development---requirements analysis, specification, design and coding. It helps to distinguish between the pursuit of different goals. The motivation for distinguishing between models of domains and reuse infrastructures is analogous to the reasons for distinguishing between representations for systems specification and programming languages for systems implementations.

As an illustration of the kinds of research questions that need to be answered, let us consider the following: Given a class of similar problems, how to identify reusable problem-specific information. How to modularize the information and to package it into reusable components. If a component is changed, what is the impact on a reuser's ability to specify and construct systems in a domain? If the class of problems evolve, how can the changes be propagated to the collection of components to maintain the level of performance of the reuser? How to organize a collection of reusable component to improve the efficiency of the actual reuse process?

Similar questions are routinely asked in the context of conventional software development with regard to the relation between requirements and executable programs. Software engineering has emerged as a pragmatic response to the need to bridge that gap in a controlled, systematic manner. A similar approach, *domain engineering,* is needed in the field of domain-specific reuse.

Our research is based on the following hypotheses: 1) problem domains exist; 2) problem domains evolve gradually; 3) there are communities that need to develop large numbers of similar software systems within those domains; 4) there is expertise in building systems in those domains; 5) reusers follow systematic approaches to reuse. Our focus is on domain analysis and infrastructure specification, the upstream activities in the infrastructure development cycle.

4. ``Pure" vs. ``practical" domain analysis

The shared view

A *problem domain* is defined by consensus, and its essence is the shared understanding of some community. There seems to be general agreement among reusability researchers, that a shared paradigm [23] is a precondition for domain analysis. As a result of such consensus a language with shared semantics may emerge. The goal of domain analysis is to make that language and its semantics explicit. We could summarize the intuitive notion of problem domain following [38, p.525]:

> In a given community, items of real-world information come to be associated as bodies of information or problem domains having the following characteristics:
>
> 1. deep or comprehensive relationships among the items of information are suspected or postulated with respect to some class of problems,
>
> 2. the problems are perceived as significant by the members of the community, and
>
> 3. there exists the knowledge to produce solutions to the problems.

We impose no a priori restrictions on the number, complexity or kinds of problems, nor on the amount, kinds or level of detail of the real-world information involved.

The commonly held view of *domain analysis* was formulated by Neighbors:

> ``A domain analysis is an attempt to identify the objects, qperations and relationships between what domain experts perceive to be important about the domain"

Other definitions have been proposed but they are essentially variants of this one. As a whole, they capture the shared intuition of what domain analysis is about, but they are insufficient from the point of view of the practice of domain analysis:

1. they are not ``true" definitions, since there is no precise definition of terms such as ``important" or ``domain".
2. they are not operational definitions, there is no clear statement of goals, nor completion predicates that could answer questions such as: ``Are we done with the analysis of this domain?"
3. Finally, they do not suggest how to assess progress in the process of domain analysis.

The essential difficulty of ``pure" domain analysis

Domain analysis is an *essentially* difficult problem. Quoting (out of context!) from [43]:

> ``... an application domain, is often natural, or has a major natural component, or while man-made, has no discernible prior design. Thus,its properties are difficult to describe and the resulting descriptions are quite complex. It is because of these complexities that some software is intrinsically complex."

> ``...Thus, software is inherently as difficult ... as science where it is concerned with the description of properties of nonformal domains."[p. 1078]

We argue against the possibility of practical procedures for capturing the ``true" ontology and semantics of arbitrary problem domains. If they existed we would have succeeded in formalizing the scientific method. The history and philosophy of science show how elusive is this goal [8] [20] [33] [34] [36] [40]. Instead, we strive for techniques for *practical* domain analysis, based on the *systematic and incremental approximation* to a definition of an ontology and semantics for a problem domain.

5. Towards ``practical" domain analysis

``Pure" domain analysis is an instance of the theory formation problem routinely confronted by scientists or systems analysts. We propose a new formulation for the problem of ``practical" domain analysis. The new formulation, distinct from ``Which are the appropriate, reusable abstractions in a problem domain?" [9] [29], is

> *How is a model of a domain incrementally constructed/evolved to achieve a specified level of performance with a given target reuser?*

This, in contrast to the old question, is a thoroughly practical problem. By adopting this new viewpoint we move towards operational definitions for practical domain analysis, and away from the view of domain analysis as an art, i.e., ``a domain analyst is a machine for turning coffee into reusable abstractions."

Given:
1. a partial, nonformal description of a problem domain
2. a model of a reuser as a learning system

Find: a systematic method to
1. *identify* information in the problem domain which, if available to the reuser in appropriate form, would allow it to attain a specified level of performance.
2. *capture* the information identified as relevant, and
3. *evolve* the acquired information to enhance or maintain the performance of a reuser.

Practical domain analysis methods must be based on a view of reusers as learning systems. On such a foundation, a method for practical domain analysis is a method for the systematic evolution of a reuser's model of the domain, to attain and maintain a desired level of performance.

* A goal is operational for an agent in a particular environment if that agent, by performing some computation using the available information, can determine whether the goal is achieved [7].

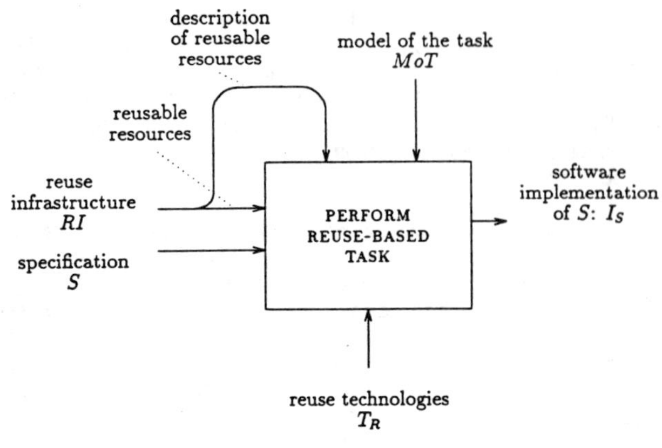

Figure 1. The reuse system P = [MoT, T, RI, S, I]

This perspective agrees with the shared view on the assumption that problem domains exist, and on the overall goal of identifying appropriate, reusable abstractions in problem domains. It differs from the shared view in that it incorporates a notion of performance of the reuser, which makes possible an operational characterization of the domain analysis task.

To make this perspective precise, we must define what do we mean by learning system, level of performance, systematic evolution and model of a domain. We begin by outlining the structure of reusers as learning systems.

6. Reusers as learning systems

A reuse system **P** is described by a set of primary traits abstracted by state variables:

- o a model of the reuse task, **MoT**
- o a pool of technologies to support reuse, **T**
- o a reuse infrastructure, **RI**
- o a class of specifications, **S**
- o a class of implementations, **I**

Figure 1 represents **P** as a directed system. Output variables are those whose value is determined from within the system, **I = MoT (S, RI)**.

A **Model of the reuse Task** is a rigorous characterization of what kinds of reuse are performed and how, (i.e., kinds of reusable information, operators for manipulating it, their applicability conditions, and the control strategy for achieving the goal of implementing a specification through reuse). Ideally, the value of the **MoT** variable would be an algorithm; for example, Draco [29]. In practice, people are often involved in the reuse process, and the **MoT** becomes a combination of algorithms and informal guidelines. (For brevity, we will refer to a variable **X**, meaning ``the value of the system variable **X**").The model of the task is realized by a set of support technologies, **T**. These may include people, languages, tools.

* The boxes and arrows diagrams follow the SADT [27] convention. Boxes represent activities; the subject matter is inside the box. The four sides of the boxes are called: Input (left), Control (top), Output (right) and Mechanism (bottom). Arrow connections make the interface between the subjects.

Example---The GTE Assets Library System. The environment of the GTE Assets Library System [35] is GTE Data Services, in which a management structure, the Assets Management Program, has been set up to create, maintain and make available a collection of reusable assets; in particular, software components. The task to be supported is reuse-based software construction. A ``Help Support Group" in charge of training provides guidelines for reuse. The Model of the Task is typical of the reuse of libraries of components:

1 Encode specification as a library query using a keyword, faceted scheme .
2 Submit query to the library system.
3 Select a ``best candidate" from the set of candidate components with the help of thesauri and heuristic metrics describing conceptual distances between terms in each facet.
4 Adapt---a programmer ``copy-and-edit"s---the best candidate to fit the structure of the system under construction.
5 Integrate the adjusted component into a system.

The second and third steps are well-defined. The remaining steps are performed by people under programming guidelines or reuse guidelines and on the basis of their own judgements. These steps are not formal, and little direct support for reuse can be provided. The reuse infrastructure, **RI**, could be further decomposed into a Catalogue part and a Shelf part corresponding to the two aspects of the Assets Library. The Shelf part corresponds to a collection of (mostly) Cobol programs of various size and complexity. The supporting technologies, **T**, include software engineers, programmers programming languages, and software development tools. The part of **T** that supports the management of this collection is a relational data base management system on a personal computer.

A reuse infrastructure, **RI,** must be in place for a software developer to practice reuse. The reusable information must be such that, 1) it is of the type required by the **MoT**, and 2) it is encoded in a form that allows for manipulation by the technology, **T**, of the reuser. For example, if the target reuser is a system like Draco [30], then the reusable infrastructure is encapsulated as formal grammars and libraries of tree-to-tree transformations. If the target reuser is a programmer using the Ada technology, a reusable infrastructure may include collections of Ada generics built according to DoD-STD-2167A, set in a storage and retrieval system such as [28], [35], or [41]. For each value of **MoT**, **RI** could take different values depending on the values of **T**. For example, for software construction based on a compositional model, the reuse infrastructure could be realized by Ada generics or, Lisp functions or, Smalltalk objects, indexed in some way.

We propose a *characterization* of a problem domain for the task of implementing specifications as a set of *exemplar specifications*, **S**, and the corresponding exemplar implementations **I.**

Reusers are embedded in a *reuse environment*. For the purpose of this discussion, a reuse environment is an organizational context in which information is systematically acquired and reused in software construction under the control of some management guidelines and costing models. Many other reuse tasks of interest in software development, for example, the reuse of problem domain theories in the analysis of specifications [12], the reuse of theorems in verification [17] [19], the reuse of implementation plans in mechanical debugging [21], etc., are outside the scope of this paper.

The *state* of a reuse system is characterized by the value of each of the state variables at a given time. Instances of reuse systems are compared by comparing the values of their state variables. Time is used to distinguish between different observations of the same attribute of a reuse system.

Goals of a reuse system

We have defined an initial vocabulary for the description of reuse systems. For the purpose of this discussion we will assume that the goals of a reuse system **P= [MoT,RI,T,{ S,I }]** are:

1. to construct satisficing implementations, **I,** for all specifications in **S** by reusing information from a reuse infrastructure **RI** under the control of **MoT**, and
2. to produce those implementations as efficiently as possible.

Other goals could be specified, for instance, to produce implementations that uses storage or CPU efficiently, or, to produce implementations that are safe. We do not exclude these or other properties of the implementation process or of the implementations themselves, as long as they are measurable properties of the state of the reuse system. Measurable properties of the state of **P** are Boolean or real-valued, time-dependent function, such as:

o *Coverage.* If the system **P**, in state *S*, can produce implementations for a set of specifications **S** we say that **P** *covers* **S**,

$$\mathbf{S} \subseteq \mathbf{C}(S)$$

o *Size of the reuse infrastructure.* Measured as the number of distinct items in **RI**, e.g., the number of generics in a library, number of transforms. A reuse infrastructure is said to be *parsimonious*, if every item in the infrastructure is necessary for the implementation of at least one specification in **C(** *S* **).**

o *Implementation cost.*
Quantitative measures associate a value to the resources expended in the implementation process. The definition of the cost functions, is a management issue and depends on the technologies of the reuse system, and on the economic/productivity goals defined for the system. In a mechanical transformational system, cost could be measured as the length of derivations, number of designer interventions, or CPU time expended. In a reuse system implemented by programmers and a data base of reusable components, cost could be computed as a function of hours of programmer time expended and number of data base transactions.

The learning component in a reuse system

To describe the process of convergence to a goal we propose an enhanced view of reuse systems (Figure 2). The purpose of the learning component **L** is the (goal-directed) generation of new values for the goal-related variables of **P** with the intention of increasing the performance of the reuse system. Given the goals defined above, the learning component is defined by the following traits:

- o a model of the problem domain, **MoD,**
- o a method for increasing the coverage of the reuser, **Lc,**
- o a method for improving the efficiency of the reuser, **Le,**
- o the expertise available in the environment of the reuse system, *Exp,* and
- o a historical record of feedback received from the actual reuser, *ReuseLog*
- o a set of technologies **TL** to realize the learning component, that is, to support the representation and evolution of the **MoD.**

Other traits may be defined to represent for methods for improving the performance of **P** along other dimensions, besides coverage or cost.
The **MoD** structure is a data structure for representing information about the domain that is relevant to the problem solving task facing the reuser. For example, if the task to be supported is the implementation of software specifications using components, the **MoD** structure may support the representation of the semantics of entities and activities used to specify systems in the domain, their interconnections [32] and other perhaps supporting information regarding, for example, design decisions, implementation plans, etc. If the task was fault diagnosis using an evidential model, then the **MoD** structure would need to support a different ontology, possibly including causes, symptoms, causal relations, tests to discriminate among causes, and so on.

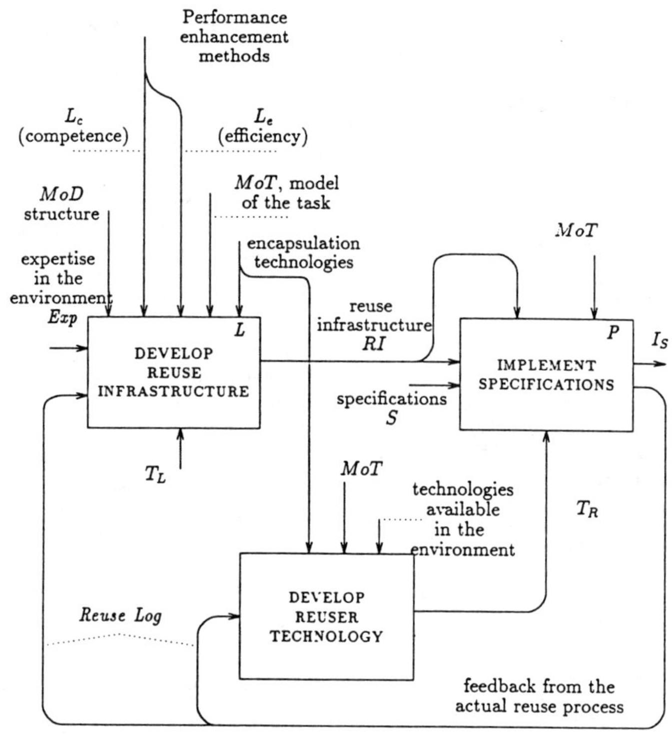

Figure 2. The reuse system as a learning system

The variable **Exp** abstracts problem domain expertise available in the environment of the reuse system. It may exist in many forms: as the knowledge of human experts, explicit in the technical literature, or compiled in implemented systems.

The outputs of the **L** component are values for the reuse infrastructure, that is, inputs to the performance component in the reuse system, **P**. The values of **RI**, the reuse infrastructure, are derived from the state of **MoD.** Figure 3 ``explodes" the **L** component and uncovers the stages of the infrastructure development lifecycle outlined in Section 3.

The *ReuseLog* variable is used to abstract the feedback from the performance component of the reuse system. This feedback may take different forms depending on the reuse system. In general, it includes a record of the specifications submitted to the system, measures of properties of the reuse process and measures of properties the resulting implementation (including failures to implement a specification).

Domain analysis as learning

Domain analysis techniques can be thought of as the controls on the learning component of the reuse system. The values for the state variables **Lc** and **Le** are learning methods. ``Learning denotes changes in the system that are adaptive in the sense that they enable the system to do the same tasks or tasks drawn from the same population more efficiently and more effectively the next time" [39].

In our research we have chosen to assume that the values of state variables **MoT** and **T** remain fixed. The motivation for this assumption is that differences in performance can be attributed *exclusively* to the evolution of values of the **MoD**, thus, of the **RI**. Changes in our understanding of the problem domain are reflected as changes in the values of *Exp*, (for example, as additions or deletions to **{ S , I }**) or *ReuseLog*. The application of the learning methods results in a corresponding evolution of the values of **MoD** and **RI**, that puts the reuse system in a new stable state where the performance goals are met again.

The mechanisms which realize **Lc** evolve the information in the **MoD** through the acquisition of new expertise, *Exp*, or through the analysis of the state of the **MoD.** The choice of knowledge acquisition techniques depends on thesources of information; on the **MoT** (role-limiting methods [24][25]); and on the information already captured (knowledge-based knowledge acquisition). For example, [2] uses as inputs pairs of specifications-implementations of existing systems and an expert's advice, and applies a technique for *design recovery* reusing the information already available in the **MoD.**

The analysis of the state of the **MoD** is focused by the performance measures selected to guide the learning process. For example, if the purpose is to develop a library of software components, and coverage is the measure selected, then typical techniques include clustering and induction over the abstractions captured in the **MoD** [2]. In the case of fault diagnosis if accuracy is the measure selected, then techniques such as, path differentiation, symptom distinction, test conditionalization, etc. [18] are appropriate. The application of these techniques is constrained by the representations chosen for the **MoD.**

The mechanisms which realize **Le**, focus on tuning the structure of the reuse infrstructure to *patterns of reuse* in the environment of the system. Patterns of reuse can be defined in many ways: as statistics of frequency of reuse of components or derivation fragments (in transformational systems), distributions of parameters in specifications submitted to the reuser, etc. Very little research has been done in the formalization of patterns of reuse. We have experimented with a conceptual clustering scheme proposed by [13] to identify candidate

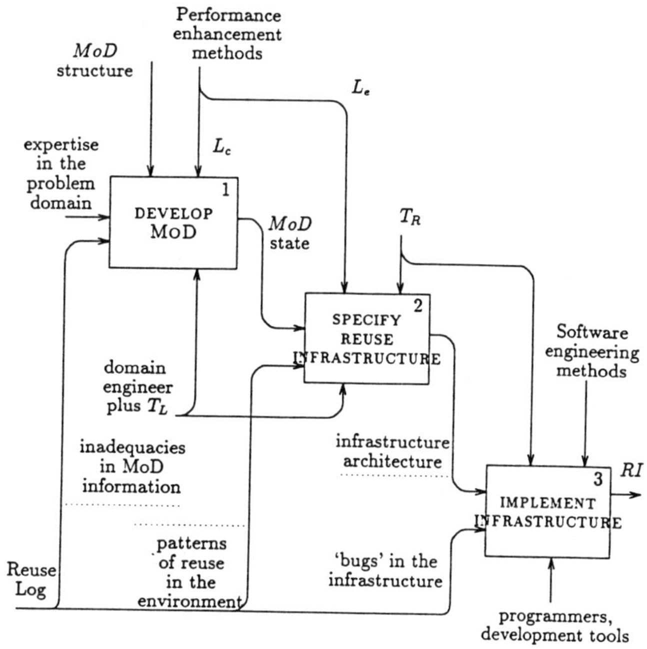

Figure 3. Phases in the infrastructure development cycle

generics for a software library [4]. In that case, patterns of reuse are formally represented as probabilistic classification trees of specification descriptors.

Strategy for the design of domain analysis methods

Now that we have established a basic vocabulary we can outline a generic strategy for designing (or assembling) a collection of domain analysis methods.

Given: a reuse situation characterized by a description of a reuser and its environment.

Produce: the methods to drive the learning component of the reuse system.

Strategy:

1. produce a precise definition of the reuser and its environment. Characterize:
   - o the model of the reuse task, **MoT,**
   - o a set of measures of reuser performance,
   - o the problem domain (e.g., **{ S, I }**),
   - o the set of technologies that implement the reuser, **T**, and those that could be used to support the operation of the learning component being designed, **TL**,
   - o the patterns of reuse in the environment, *ReuseLog,*
   - o a cost-benefit model to determine under which conditions it is economical to invest in the development of a reuse infrastructure.
2. Identify the information needs of a reuser operating under **MoT**.
3. Design a **MoD** structure:
   - o to capture the kinds of information required by the **MoT**,
   - o using the representation technologies available from **TL**,
   - o to support and enhance the application of evolution procedures **Lc** and **Le**.
4. Design methods **Lc**, based on the structure of the **MoT**, to evolve the information represented in the **MoD** with the goal of enhancing the performance of the reuser.
5. Design methods **Le**, based on the structure of the **MoT**, to select and organize the information in the **MoD** according to the patterns of reuse in the environment.
6. Lay out a scheduling policy for the evolution of reuse infrastructures according to cost-benefits analysis in the environment [4].

In [2] we demonstrate the application of this strategy to the design of domain analysis methods to support the reuse of software components. By instantiating the parameters in this guideline to the characteristics of different reuse environments, different domain analysis methods result. Our reliance on **MoT** as a source of constraints on methods parallel s a similar approach in knowledge acquisition for expert systems based on what McDermott calls *role-limiting methods* [19][24].

7. Assessing progress and stopping conditions

To assess the performance of a reuse system **P**, we must introduce a notion of *goal state, **G***. A goal state is a particular configuration of values of the state variables of **P**. A notion of distance, ***d***, over values of measurable properties of the states of **P** is needed to compare the current state of reuse system with respect to a goal state. To illustrate this point we will use two forms of distance: one, call *competence*, is based on the coverage measure defined above; the second one, called *efficiency*, is based on a measure of implementation cost.

Given two states of a reuse system, ***S*** and ***S'***, the distance in competence is defined to be the cardinality of the difference between their covered sets:

$$dc\,(S, S') = |\,C\,(S) - C(S')\,|$$

Intuitively, ***dc***, is the number of specifications that can be implemented by one and only one of the systems. (To make this distance computable in practice, we introduce the notion of *benchmark* **B**, a selected set of specifications)

Given a cost function **f** that depends on the technology of a reuse system, the difference in efficiency between two states ***S, S'*** is defined using a benchmark **B(S)**, as

$$de(S, S') = f(S) - f(S')$$

The performance of a reuse system is a measure of the degree to which it satisfies a goal. Separate goal states can be defined to establish standards of competence or efficiency. We measure the performance of a reuse system **P** in state *S*, relative to a goal state *G*, using a selected distance between *S* and *G*.

For example, **P** satisfies a competence goal (formalized as a goal state *G*) if

$$C(G) \subseteq C(S)$$

The degree to which **P** may satisfy a competence goal, i.e., a relative measure of competence, can be obtained as

$$1 - dc(S,G)/C(G)$$

P satisfies an efficiency goal (formalized as a goal state *G*) if the cost of implementing s selected benchmark is less than cost of using *G*, for the cost function, *f*. To improve the performance of a reuse system we must modify the appropriate system variables to reduce their distance along the desired dimension. A performance function **w**, defined over pairs of states:

$$w : \text{state} \times \text{state} \longrightarrow [0..1]$$

can used to represent the *degree* to which a state approximates a specified goal state relative to other known states. Given a set of known states *Y*, with *G* in *Y*, and a distance *d* (e.g. competence, efficiency, or other), the performance function can be defined by [22]:

$$w(S,G) = 1 - d(S,G) / dm(S,S')$$

where,

$$dm(S, Y) = \max d(S,S') \quad \text{for } S' \text{ in } Y$$

Intuitively, if a state *S* satisfies the performance goal, the difference ***d(S, G)*** is null, and ***w(S, G)*** is 100 percent. If ***dm(S,S') = d(S, G)***, the performance of *S* is null.

Given a goal state *G* and performance function *w*, and two states of a system *S* and *S'*, *S* is said to be *goal-oriented* [22] with respect to *S'* if and only if ***w(S,G) > w(S',G)*** that is, if the reuse system in state *S* performs better with respect to *G*. The value of

$$dw(S,S' | G) = w(S, G) - w(S', G)$$

is called the *degree of goal-orientation* of *S* with respect to *S'*.

Goal orientation provides direction for the application of learning techniques that *incrementally* and systematically evolve the state of a reuse system towards a goal state. Theoretical stopping conditions are defined by achieving a goal state. In practice, it is often cost-effective to get the reuse system to a state that is "close enough" to the goal state. Cost-benefit models in the environment of the reuser provide such stopping conditions. "Close enough" becomes a synonym for "the estimated cost of evolving the model of the domain to cover case **X** is higher than the perceived benefit of reuse-based construction of systems of type **X**".

To conclude, we must observe that the number of specifications covered by a reuser is potentially infinite. In practice, performance properties are measured over a selected set of sample specifications, a *benchmark* set. Benchmarks are designed to reflect patterns of reuse in the environment of the reuse system, based on such properties as recency of reuse, frequency of reuse over some period of time or some measure deemed relevant to the purpose of the study. Benchmarking is a standard approach to assessing the performance of software or hardware systems.

8. Comparing between domain analysis methods

A practical motivation for comparing between methods is to discover which one ``does better". However, approaches to domain analysis may or may not be comparable. When comparing between two domain analysis methods we must assume:

- o a single target reuse system,
- o a single set of reference measures (e.g., coverage, cost, size of the infrastructure, ...)
- o a common set of problems to act as a benchmark for the resulting infrastructures.

From the DE perspective, domain analysis methods are the controls of the learning component in the reuse system. Two domain analysis methods are comparable if the values of theremaining state variables in the reuse system---***MoT, RI, T, S, I**, Exp, ReuseLog*---remain fixed. **TL** is an exception, since it may be expected that different approaches will be supported by different technologies. Variations in **TL** impact the results of the comparison if the measures selected refer to properties of the domain analysis process itself, for instance, time to completion.

Domain analysis methods that have been designed to realize learning in different reuse situations cannot be compared directly. For instance, comparing the approach followed by Fickas [11] [12] to build his domain theory of Library Systems for specification analysis, and the approach followed by Gary Kahn [18] to build a knowledge-base of diagnosis rules for the MUD expert system cannot be compared. Still both are examples of practical domain analysis approaches tuned to particular reuse situations. Similarly, comparisons made without establishing explicitly the measures to be used are useless. These observations are common sense rules (do not compare "apples and oranges"), still, they are routinely ignored in discussions on the nature and merits of domain analysis approaches.

9. Conclusions

Our interest in the process of domain analysis originated in our work on the reuse of domain-specific information in the context of Draco [3]. We have argued hat the established view of domain analysis is not operational and that it does not allow to compare between domain analysis methods. In this paper we have outlined some aspects of the Domain Engineering framework that address those problems. By analogy with software engineering, the aim of domain engineering is to provide methods and representations to help in 1) the construction and analysis of models of problem domains to support software specification and construction; and, 2) the transformation of those models to enhance the performance of reuse systems.

Modelling reusers as learning systems indicated the need for representations and methods to record and enhance that learning process. In particular, it prompted us to make explicit the purpose, the content and the form of the information used at each step in the reuse process and its effects on the performance of the reuser.

Some of the central ideas of the DE perspective are:

- o We must support a formal development cycle for reuse infrastructures. Domain analysis, infrastructure specification and infrastructure implementation are activities with separate concerns.

- o "Pure" domain analysis strives for the synthesis of (anticipatory!) theories about domains of reality. This task has eluded systematization for centuries and nothing suggests that effective procedures will be developed in the near future.

- Experience shows that problem domains are relatively stable. "Practical" (i.e., systematic, incremental) domain anlaysis methods can be based on information acquisition for experts and the analysis of historic information.

- Models of domains and reuse infrastructures should be treated as separate entities, conceptually and practically. Models of domains capture the results of the learning process in domain analysis and support the application of learning techniques. Reuse infrastructures are specified to support the efficient reuse of the information from the model in particular environments.

- Modeling reusers as learning systems leads to operational definitions of domain analysis.

- Under the domain engineering framework, the scope of application of a domain analysis method is explicitly defined by the class of reuse systems that are instances of the model of the task used to constrain the design of methods.

- Explicit measures of performance for a reuser and costing models reflecting the economics of its environment are the basis for assessing progress in domain analysis and for defining completion predicates.

- Potentially, there is a need for a large number of *practical* domain analysis methods, at least as many as there are types of reuse system and measures of performance for those systems.

A research program in domain analysis must include the analysis of approaches to reusability to identify useful **MoTs** and the knowledge they employ. On such basis, practical knowledge representations and evolution methods for **MODs** can be developed.

References

[1] Arango, G., Baxter, I., Freeman, P., and Pidgeon, C., "TMM: Software Maintenance by Transformation," *IEEE Software 3*,3 (May 1986), 17-39.

[2] Arango, G., "Domain Engineering for Software Reuse," *ICS-RTP-88-27*, Dept. of Information and Computer Science, U. of California, Irvine, 1988.

[3] Arango, G., "Evaluation of a Reuse-based Software Construction Technology," *Proc. Second IEE/BCS Conference on Software Engineering 88*, The British Computer Society, (July 1988), pp. .

[4] Arango, G., "The Reuse Working Set Model of Library Evolution," Submitted to Conference on Software Maintenance, Pensacola, FL, (September 1989).

[5] Barstow, D., "Domain-specific Automatic Programming", *IEEE Transactions on Software Engineering SE-11*, 11 (November 1985), 1321-1336.

[6] Biggerstaff, T., "Reusable Software", Addison Wesley, Reading, MA, 1989.

[7] Dietterich, T., and Bennet, J., "Improving Machine Learnikng Terminology: Operationality," Dept. of Computer Science, Oregon State University, Corvallis, OR, and Tecknowledge Inc., Palo Alto, CA, 1987.

[8] Dilworth, D., "Scientific Progresss," D. Reidel Publishing Co., Boston, 1981.

[9] Department of Defense, "Reusability Guidebook," (draft), in *STARS-4th. Applications Workshop*, San Diego, CA, (September 1986).

[10] Fickas, S., "A Knowledge-based Approach to Specification Acquisition and Construction," Tech. Rep. *CIS-TR-85-13*, U. of Oregon, 1985.

[11] Fickas, S., "Automating the Specification Process," Tech. Rep. *CIS-TR-87-05*, U. of Oregon, December 1987.

[12] Fickas, S., "Problem Acquisition in Software Analysis: A preliminary study," Tech Rep. *CIS-TR-87-04*, U. of Oregon, August 1987.

[13] Fisher, D., "Knowledge Acquisition Via Incremental Conceptual Clustering," *Machine Learning 2*, (1987), 139-172.

[14] Freeman, P., "Reusable Software Engineering: A statement of long-range research objectives," *ICS.TR-159*, Dept. of Information and Computer Science, U. of California, Irvine, November 1980.

[15] Freeman, P., "Reusable Software Engineering: Concepts and Research Directions," in *ITT Proceedings of the Workshop on Reusability in Programming*, (Stratford, CT, 1983), pp. 129-137.

[16] Freeman P., "Software Reusability," IEEE Computer Society Press, March 1987.

[17] Gerhart, S., "Reusability Lessons from Verification Technology," in *ITT Proceedings of the Workshop on Reusability in Programming*, (Stratford, CT, 1983), pp. 110-121.

[18] Kahn G., Nowlan S., and McDermott, J., "Strategies for knowledge acquisition," *IEEE Transactions on Pattern Analysis and Machine Intelligence PAMI-7*, (September 1985), 511-522.

[19] Good, D. "Reusable Problem Domain Theories," Tech. Rep. 31, Institute for Computing Science, UT Austin, September 1982.

[20] Hadamard, J. "The Psychology of Invention in the Mathematical Field," Dover Publications, New York, 1945.

[21] Johnson, W., and Soloway, E., "PROUST: Knowledge-based Program Understanding", *IEEE Trans. on Software Engineering SE-11*, 3 (March 1985), 267-275.

[22] Klir, G., Architecture of Systems Problem Solving, Plenum Press, New York, 1985.

[23] Kuhn, T., The structure of scientific revolutions, The University of Chicago Press, 1970.

[24] Marcus, S., Automating Knowledge Acquisition for Expert Systems, Kluwer Academic Publishers, Boston, 1988.

[25] McDermott, J., "Preliminary Stpes Towards a Taxonomy of Problem Solving Methods", in Automating Knowledge Acquisition for Expert Systems, (Ed.) S. Marcus, Kluwer Academic Publishers, Boston, 1988.

[26] McGarry, F., "Software Reuse--Repoort 10th. Minnowbrook Wrokshop," *DACS Newsletter VI*, 3 (September 1987), 1.

[27] Marca, D. and McGowan, C., SADT: Structured Analysis and Design Technique, McGraw-Hill, New York, 1988.

[28] Mittermeir, R. and Oppitz, M., "Softare Bases for the Flexible Composition of Application Systems," *IEEE Trans. on Software Engineering SE-13*, 4 (April 1987), 440-460.

[29] Neighbors, J., "Software Construction Using Components," PhD. Thesis, Dept. of Information and Computer Science, U. of California, Irvine, 1981.

[30] Neighbors, J., "The Draco Approach to Constructing Software from Reusable Components," *IEEE Trans. on Software Engineering SE-10*, (September 1984), 564-573.

[31] Neighbors, J. "Why do Domain Analysis?", in *Proc. Reuse Workshop*, (October 1988), Rocky Mountain Institute of Software Engineering.

[32] Perry, D., "Software Interconnection Models," in *Proc. 9th. IEEE Int. Conference on Software Engineering*, (March 1987) IEEE Computer Society Press, pp. 61-69.

[33] Poincare, H., La Science et L'Hypotese. E. Flammarion, Paris, 1968.

[34] Polya. G., Mathematical Discovery-On understanding, learning and teaching problem solving, John Wiley and Sons, New York, 1981.

[35] Prieto-Diaz, R., Breathing New Life into Old Software, *GTE Journal 1*, 1 (1987), 23-31.

[36] Blake R. and Ducasse E., Theories of the Scientific Method, University of Washington Press, Seattle, 1960.

[37] Workshop on Software Reuse - Participant Proceedings (Boulder, Colorado), October 1987, Rocky Mountain Institute of Software Engineering.

[38] Shapere, D., "Scientific Theories and Their Domains," In The Structure of Scientific Theories, (Ed.) F. Suppe, U. of Illinois Press, 1977, pp. 519-565.

[39] Simon, H. "Why should machines learn?" In Machine Learning, Tioga, Palo Alto, CA, 1983, pp. 25-38.

[40] Suppe, F., The Structure of Scientific Theories, U. of Illinois Press, 1977.

[41] Sommerville, I. and Wood, M. "A Knowledge-based Software Components Catalogue," Tech. Rep. CS/ST/5/86, U. of Strathclyde, Glasgow, Scotland, 1986.

[42] Tracz, W., Software Reuse: Emerging Technology, IEEE Computer Society Press, New York, 1988.

[43] Turski, W., "And no philosopher's stone either," in Information Processing 86 (September 1986), North Holland, pp. 1077-1080.

A LOGIC OF ACTION FOR SUPPORTING GOAL-ORIENTED ELABORATIONS OF REQUIREMENTS

Eric Dubois

Philips Research Laboratory,
2, Avenue van Becelaere, B-1170 Brussels (Belgium)

Abstract

Constructing requirements specifications for a complex system is a quite difficult *process*. In this paper, we have focussed on the *elaboration* part of this process where new requirements are progressively identified and incorporated in the requirements document. We propose a requirements specification language which, beyond the mere expression of requirements, also supports the elaboration step. This language is a Gist's dialect where the concepts of *goals* and the one of *agent* characterized by some *responsibility* are identified. A formalization of this requirements language is proposed in terms of a non standard modal logic of actions.

1 Introduction

Expressive power and formality

To support requirements analysis, the current state of practice provides us with a number of languages with a semi-formal 'syntax' and an informal semantics. Most popular examples include SADT [14], SREM [1] or PSL [19]. New languages are now emerging, examples include RML [11], GIST [8], MAL [10], ERAE [7] or OBLOG [16]. Besides a formal syntax, these languages exhibit two essential features, i.e. *expressive power* and *formality*.

Expressive power and formality of a language are two complementary features. The former supports the 'modelling' (encoding) of requirements while the latter provides guidance in the 'control' of this modelling. In other terms, expressive power is needed at the level of the *product* (the requirements document) while formality is advocated to support the *process*, i.e. the progressive and systematic construction of the final product. Let us consider two examples:

- the operational semantics associated with GIST supports the use of symbolic evaluators which can be used to execute the specification and thereby, to check its conformity with the customers' intuitions [3];
- in ERAE, the use of deductive power associated with temporal logic supports the derivation of new statements from the available ones and to propose them for validation to the customers [5].

The scope of this paper

In this paper, we investigate the use of a specific formal framework that could be associated with a suitable requirements language that permits to address some non-usual issues like:

- at the **product** level, the use of a language including the following concepts: static and temporal constraints, description of agents belonging to the system or specification of the admissible actions that an agent can perform;
- at the **process** level, the formality associated with the language at the product level supports an incremental *elaboration* of the requirements document where a distinction is made between (a) general objectives and constraints (requirements' goals) that are first identified and (b) finer requirements specifications that are assigned to different agents and that should meet goals.

This paper elaborates on ideas preliminary introduced in [6]. It should be mentioned that Feather's work within the framework of the Gist language has strongly influenced our work [8] [9].

In Section 2, we present informally the *process* according to which the requirements document is incrementally elaborated. In this Section, for expressing the product, we use a requirements language that can be considered as a Gist's dialect.

Section 3 presents with the formal framework associated with the Gist's dialect introduced in the previous Section. This framework is based on a specific non-standard modal logic originally introduced by von-Wright [21]. This logic is powerful enough for capturing the language's concepts in a natural way. Furthermore, we will suggest how the deductive power associated with this logic supports the validation of the elaboration steps followed at the process level.

Finally, Section 4 ends with a brief comparison of other existing approaches and indicates some of our current research directions.

All along this paper, we will illustrate our ideas on a fragment of a library case study inspired by [17]. Here is a excerpt of a slightly revised description:

> *We consider a library with the following transactions:*
>
> 1. *Check out a book / Return a book;*
> 2. *Add a book to / Remove a book from the library.*
>
> *We will consider two types of users: the librarian and borrowers. Transaction 1 is restricted to the borrowers while transaction 2 is restricted to the librarian. The library management system must satisfy the following constraints:*
>
> - *The library can never become empty, i.e. at least, one book should be available on the shelves of the library.*
> - *No book may be available in the library for an unlimited time.*

2 The process of elaborating requirements

2.1 The world-oriented paradigm

We call Requirements Analysis (RA) the activity of the software development where initial specifications are produced. We call *analysts* those who are in charge of RA.

Analysts should investigate *customers'* requirements on the future application to be developed. As many other authors, (see, e.g. the concept of *closed-system* in [8]), we advocate that analysts are in charge to produce *world-oriented* descriptions, i.e. descriptions which pay attention to the desired behavior of:

- the *system* to be developed later on. This system does not only include requirements on a computerized part to be implemented but also requirements on manual procedures to be installed or on specific hardware to be developed;
- the *environment* in which the system will operate. The description will include assumptions about the application domain in presence of the system. Describing the environment helps to perceive the impact of the introduction of a system in its environment.

As in [8] [10], we call *agents* those who contribute to the behavior exhibited by the various components of the system and its environment.

- The behavior of agents belonging to the system should be defined by the analyst. Their description will form the *contractual* part of the requirements document. It will result from a negotiation with customers and *designers*: (a) customers will have to agree that the proposed solution meets the objectives and constraints that they assign to the future application; (b) designers will have to guarantee the feasibility of the system that should be implemented.[1]
- The behavior of agents belonging to the environment is not under the responsibility of the analyst. Its description can be considered by the analyst as given. It should be guaranteed by customers.

Let us now turn our attention to the library case-study. One can isolate two specific agents, respectively, the **librarian** in charge of managing the library and the **borrowers** who want to checkout/return book. For a matter of convenience, we will consider that the librarian cannot be a borrower himself.

- the librarian is considered as an agent of the system. It is the person whose the behavior will have to guarantee the effective management of the library. Therefore, the analyst will have to analyze and to design his future behavior.
- borrowers are clearly responsible of their own behaviors. They choose the book they want to checkout or to return. Therefore, borrowers are considered as agents belonging to the environment.

In the figure below, we show this starting point in a specific requirements language. The syntax of the latter is largely inspired of notations used by Feather [9] within the framework of the Gist language. However, for the purpose of this paper, we will use some additional specific notations. In the next Section, we will discuss the formal framework associated with the proposed language. In the following, keywords are underlined throughout while italics are used to comment the specification.

[1] Let us notice that we call designers not only those who are in charge of developing software but also those who elaborate hardware pieces or even those who can be in charge of implementing new manual procedures in an organization

```
book | type BOOK ||
 {IN-LIBRARY | relation (book) }
```

We declare a value type associated with a book variable. For a matter of convenience, we consider any copy of book as distinguishable. IN-LIBRARY is a subsidiary declaration of an unary relation on BOOK. IN-LIBRARY(book) stands for the presence of a specific book in the library.

```
,
librarian | agent ||
 {ADD | procedure(book) || insert book:IN-LIBRARY
  ,
  REMOVE | procedure (book) || delete book:IN-LIBRARY
 }
```

Librarian is declared an agent in the system. ADD and REMOVE are subsidiary declarations of procedures associated with primitive changes causing a "transition" to a new library's state. Both changes are under the control of the librarian. ADD takes one argument of type book and inserts (in the state) a IN-LIBRARY relation on this argument. REMOVE takes one argument of type book and deletes an existing IN-LIBRARY relation on this argument.

```
,
borrower | external agent ||
 {CHECKOUT | procedure (book) ||
                          delete book:IN-LIBRARY
  ,
  RETURN | procedure (book) || insert book:IN-LIBRARY
 }
```

Borrower is declared an agent in the environment. To make the distinction with agents of the system, we use an additional external agent notation not available in the Gist language. CHECKOUT and RETURN are subsidiary declarations associated with procedures under the control of borrowers. CHECKOUT takes one argument of type book and deletes an existing IN-LIBRARY relation on this argument. RETURN takes one argument of type book and inserts a IN-LIBRARY relation on this argument.

2.2 The identification of goals

Constructing a requirements specification is an incremental *process*. The *elaboration* part of this process is concerned with the activities where analysts are in charge of progressively acquiring and incorporating new requirements in the current state of the *product*. Those requirements express properties about the agents' behaviors in the future system and its new environment.

Still, the analyst should be assisted in his elaboration process. A part of this assistance may be provided by the identification of *goals*. The latter are basic objectives and constraints that customers want to be met by the behavior resulting from the combination of the system and its environment both together. They correspond to what is called "requirements goals" in [12].

In the library case-study, two specific constraints are given. Those are goals that we will describe by again introducing a new specific notation.

```
library-objectives | goal ||
 {NEVER-EMPTY | relation ||
     exists book || book:IN-LIBRARY
  ,
  NEVER-EVER | relation ||
     forall book || if book:IN-LIBRARY
                 then not ever more book:LIBRARY
 }
```

The library's constraints are declared a goal. Goal is a new predefined type that we consider as an extension to the Gist language. NEVER-EMPTY is a subsidiary 0-ary predicate which means that there exists at least one book in every state of the library. NEVER-EVER is another subsidiary predicate which means that a book cannot stay for ever in the library. It should be noted the use of the ever more temporal reference which means 'always in the future'.

2.3 Refining goals

In the next step of the requirements elaboration process, the analyst is in charge of refining the initial goals in terms of finer requirements that can be assigned to system's agents. In no case, they can be assigned to environment's agents since their behavior cannot be controlled.

In the library case-study, there is a unique system's agent called the librarian. The original 'library-objectives' should therefore be refined in terms of finer requirements that will be under the librarian's responsibility.

A new concept should be introduced in the requirements language considered so far. This concept deals with the *responsibility* associated with a system's agent with respect to requirements to be guaranteed. Up to now, in the specification, we introduced the concept of "procedure" denoting a possible state's change. Responsibility is concerned with the control of these changes. We will describe the concept of responsibility in terms of *activity*. The latter are denoted with the Gist's notation used by Feather [9].

In the case of the library, we introduce a specific activity associated with the librarian. At any moment, he can modify the library's content by adding or removing a book or he can let unchanged the library's content.

```
librarian | agent ||
 {IN-LIBRARY | relation (book)
 ,
  LIBRARY-MANAGEMENT | activity (book) ||
      choose      { ADD(book), REMOVE(book), null }
 }
```

LIBRARY-MANAGEMENT is a subsidiary declaration of an activity parameterized by type book. An activity is a statement that gets invoked in every state for each possible instantiation of its parameter. In every state, the status of a book (being or not in the library) can be changed (ADD,REMOVE) or stay unchanged (null).

The librarian's activity is not only concerned with the responsibility that he can exercise with respect to his possible changes brought to the library's content. We can also imagine that he can exercise his responsibility with respect to changes that other agents want to bring to the library's content. In our case, this responsibility can be concerned with the possible changes (CHECKOUT and/or RETURN) that can be applied by borrowers.

In the requirements language, we introduce two specific additional constructions to express the responsibility that a system's agent may exercise on possible changes brought by agents of the external environment. "allows" means that a change is permitted to another agent. "prevents" means that a change is forbidden to another agent.

```
librarian | agent ||
 {LIBRARY-MANAGEMENT | activity (book) ||
      choose      { ADD(book), REMOVE(book),
                    allows CHECKOUT(book),
                    allows RETURN(book),
                    prevents CHECKOUT(book), null }
 }
,
borrower | external agent ||
 {CHECKOUT | procedure (book) || delete book:IN-LIBRARY
 ,
  RETURN | procedure (book) || insert book:IN-LIBRARY
 }
```

The definition of LIBRARY-MANAGEMENT given in the previous specification is now extended with three new cases. The librarian may allows or prevents the CHECKOUT of a book. He may allows the RETURN of a book

In the specification presented above, for each book, at each time, the librarian has the choice between 6 different actions ('null' being considered itself as an action). However, this choice can be restricted because preconditions associated with procedures. For example, REMOVE(book) can only be performed if the intended book is in the library. This precondition is enclosed in the delete clause.

Besides choice's restrictions due to preconditions, there are additional restrictions that can be expressed about under what circumstances an agent is permitted or forced to perform an action. These restrictions are expressed as a collection of safety and liveness requirements (like in MAL [10] or in OBLOG [16]).

Behavioral conditions are expressed using a specific such that construct. Here is an example of its use in the library case study.

```
book | type BOOK ||
 {IN-LIBRARY | relation (book)
 ,
  UNIQUE | relation (book) ||
      not exists book.1 ||
                 not (book = book.1) and
                 (book.1:IN-LIBRARY)
 }
```

UNIQUE is an additional subsidiary declaration of a unary relation on BOOK that we will need later on. UNIQUE(book) means that this specific book is the only one currently available in the library.

```
librarian | agent ||
 {LIBRARY-MANAGEMENT | activity (book) ||
      choose      { ADD(book), REMOVE(book),
                    allows CHECKOUT(book),
                    allows RETURN(book),
                    prevents CHECKOUT(book), null }
      such that { if prevents CHECKOUT(book)
                     then book:UNIQUE
                  and
                  if book:UNIQUE then
                         not (allows CHECKOUT(book)
                              or REMOVE(book))
                  and
                  some more REMOVE(book) }
 ,
  ADD | procedure(book) || insert book:IN-LIBRARY
 ,
  REMOVE | procedure (book) || delete book:IN-LIBRARY
 }
```

The first condition means that the action of *prevents CHECKOUT can only be applied when there is only one book available in the library. The second condition means that two actions (respectively* *allows CHECKOUT and REMOVE)* cannot be applied on a book which is the last one available in the library. Finally, the last condition means that, for any book in the library, a REMOVE book action will be applied soon or later on this book. It should be noted the use of the some more temporal reference which means 'sometimes in the future'

During this step of the process, the analyst assigns changes' responsibilities and conditions to agents of the system but he has also to ensure the the agents' activities are compatible with the overall goals that have been previously identified. These goals should follow from the agents' activities.

In the library case-study, two goals were identified, respectively the existence of at least one book in the library and the limited time of presence of a book in the library. These two goals seem to be met by the admissible behavior of the librarian. Still, it should be helpful to show a formal *proof* of this compatibility. That will be made in the next Section where we propose an appropriated formal framework associated with the Gist's dialect used in this Section.

3 A formal logic of actions and agents

In the introduction, we advocated that a suitable formal framework should encompass two essential features: formal semantics and deductive power. In other terms, we argued in favour of the use of a *logical* framework. Still, in this case, the degree of expressiveness and of deductions is heavily depending on the kind of logic chosen. Many new languages are based on typed first order predicate calculus (see, e.g. RML [11]). Semantics and deduction rules associated with this logic are well-known. However, for some kinds of descriptions, the formalism is not powerful enough for expressing them in a natural way and making possible useful deductions.

Let us illustrate this with a little example concerning the treatment of the *time* dimension in two specific formal frameworks. A first one could be the classical first order logic where each predicate is equipped with an extra explicit time argument, and the second one could be the temporal logic with its specific operators (e.g. always and possibly). The temporal framework is more appealing because there exists a specific deductive power associated with the time component. In the classical logic, this deductive power is reduced to first order derivation rules.

In this Section, we introduce a specific non-standard variety of modal logic. providing a formal interpretation to specifications written in the Gist's dialect. In the first sub-Section, we show how the specifications of temporalities and agents' activities are built in this logic. In the second sub-Section, we suggest how its associated deductive power supports the validation of the goal-oriented process followed in Section 2.

3.1 Expressiveness

We will present the formal framework in successive stages. For each of them, we will illustrate the expressive power associated with.

3.1.1 A logic of admissible states.

Standard first order predicate calculus is the base of our formal framework. The following conventions will be used throughout. Predicates and constants will be in upper case character, and variables will be in lower case. Usual truth connectives and quantifiers will be used in their standard interpretation: $\neg, \wedge, \vee, \Rightarrow, \Leftrightarrow$ for negation, conjunction, disjunction, (material) implication, and (material) equivalence respectively; quantifiers all ($\forall$), exists ($\exists$) and unique existence ($\exists!$). Any variables that appear with no quantifier are assumed to be universal variables. Finally, the Greek alphabet will be used for denoting metavariables for formulas.

Typically, typed first order logic deals with the description of admissible *states*. Let us illustrate this on a fragment of the specification introduced in the previous Section. The following declaration is possible; it consists of four basic relation schemes expressed in terms of predicates:

IN-LIBRARY: BOOK
NEVER-EMPTY:
NEVER-EVER:
UNIQUE: BOOK

Static integrity constraints are statements characterizing possible configurations of admissible states.

In the specification of the library, the following constraints were identified:

```
{NEVER-EMPTY | relation ||
     exists book || book:IN-LIBRARY
...
  UNIQUE | relation (book) ||
     not exists book.1 || not (book = book.1)
              and (book.1:IN-LIBRARY)
```

Their interpretation in typed first order logic is:

book, book1 :BOOK

NEVER-EMPTY $\Leftrightarrow \exists$ book: IN-LIBRARY(book)

$\forall$ book: (UNIQUE(book)
$\Leftrightarrow \neg\exists$ book1: $\neg$ (book = book1) $\wedge$ IN-LIBRARY(book1))

The deductive power of the language is associated with the existence in first order logic of a set of axioms schemas and of rules of inferences [15]. Examples of typical axioms schemas are those based on De Morgan's laws (ϕ and ψ being two well formed formulas)

$$\phi \vee \psi \Leftrightarrow \neg(\neg\phi \wedge \neg\psi)$$

Typical inference rule is the so-called *modus ponens*:

$$\phi, \phi \Rightarrow \psi \vdash \psi$$

3.1.2 A logic of admissible histories.

In the previous sub-Section, we introduced a formal framework supporting the description of admissible *states*. A first extension deals with the description of admissible *histories*, i.e. admissible sequences of those states. This extension is required to support the expression of dynamic constraints referring several states at different moments in time.

Temporal logics are a classical mean to express dynamic constraints. There are several different temporal logics (see, e.g. [13] for a survey). For our current purpose, we choose a specific temporal logic known in the literature as the System T (of Feys). The *vocabulary* of this logic is the vocabulary of first order logic enriched by the following connectives:

$\Box$ (in all future states),
$\Diamond$ (in some future state)

Considering ϕ as a first-order well-formed formula, *expressions* of the temporal logic are:

$\Box\phi$ means that ϕ is true in all future states (or now)
$\Diamond\phi$ means that ϕ is true in some future state (or now)

Using the temporal logic framework, we can associate a formal interpretation with the following dynamic integrity constraint considered in the previous Section:

NEVER-EVER | relation ||
forall book || if book:IN-LIBRARY
then not ever more book:LIBRARY

This constraint can be expressed straightforwardly by:

NEVER-EVER $\Leftrightarrow$
(IN-LIBRARY(book) $\Rightarrow \neg\Box$ IN-LIBRARY(book))

It should be noted that the ever more notation is associated with the $\Box$ symbol. Similarly, the counterpart of the some more notation is the $\Diamond$ symbol.

Temporal logic is characterized with a set of axioms schemas and rules of inferences. Axioms schemas are,

$$\Box(\phi \Rightarrow \psi) \Rightarrow (\Box\phi \Rightarrow \Box\psi)$$
$$\Box\phi \Rightarrow \phi$$
$$\Box\phi \Leftrightarrow \neg\Diamond\neg\phi$$

while a typical rule of deduction is,

if $\vdash \phi$ then $\vdash \Box\phi$

3.1.3 A logic of admissible transitions.

Again, we consider a new extension to the logical framework, this extension is required for capturing the semantics associated with the concept of procedure.

The notion of procedure deals with primitive changes causing a "transition" to a new state. In terms of temporal sequences of states, that means that we need to be able to denote two successive states. Again, different variants of temporal logics propose new connectives for denoting the *next moment in time*. We will consider a specific "And Next" logic discussed in [20]. The *vocabulary* of this logic extends the vocabulary considered so far with the following T connective which is read "and next". Considering ϕ and ψ as two well-formed formulas, a valid *expression* is:[2]

$\phi T \psi$ means that ϕ now and ψ in the next state (moment)

We propose five axioms schemas characterizing the T connective:

$$\Box(\phi T \psi) \Rightarrow (\Box\phi T \Box\psi)$$
$$(\phi \vee \psi) T (\rho \vee \sigma) \Leftrightarrow (\phi T \rho) \vee (\phi T \sigma) \vee (\psi T \rho) \vee (\psi T \sigma)$$
$$(\phi T \psi) \wedge (\phi T \rho) \Rightarrow (\phi T (\psi \wedge \rho))$$
$$\phi \Leftrightarrow (\phi T (\psi \vee \neg\psi))$$
$$\neg(\phi T (\psi \wedge \neg\psi))$$

In the library's specification, a typical statement was:

procedure(book) || delete book:IN-LIBRARY

The formal interpretation associated with this statement is:

IN-LIBRARY(book) $T\neg$ IN-LIBRARY(book)

It should be noted that the implicit precondition associated with a delete procedure is now made explicit.

A similar formal interpretation can be associated with the statement on the insert procedure of a book:

[2]It should be noted that the notation introduced by von Wright can be compared with a notation based on the monadic $\bigcirc$ (next) connective introduced by Scott. The formulation $\phi \wedge \bigcirc\psi$ has been proved equivalent by Prior [13], p. 184.

$\neg$ IN-LIBRARY(book) $\mathcal{T}$ IN-LIBRARY(book)

We have still to associate a formal interpretation with the specific *null* procedure. It is convenient to use the word "change" so that it includes also non-changes, i.e. immediate progressions in time with the same initial and end-state. Thereby, the two following axioms are added:

IN-LIBRARY(book) $\mathcal{T}$ IN-LIBRARY(book)
$\neg$ IN-LIBRARY(book) $\mathcal{T}\neg$ IN-LIBRARY(book)

In this way, we have formally described the four possible changes that can affect the library's content. Still, using static and temporal connectives introduced above, we cannot express specific conditions under which these changes can happen. These conditions will be described later on after having introduced a last ingredient in the formal theory.

3.1.4 A logic of admissible actions.

Finally, we have to consider a last extension to our formal logic framework to cope with the concept of activity under the control of *system's agents*. This control is concerned with the responsibility that system's agents may exercise on changes brought to the current state. We will first define formally this concept of *responsibility*; then, the concept of activity will be defined.

The concept of action and responsibility

We first extend our formal framework considered so far with the new concept of *action* in order to make explicit the concept of responsibility related with. It should be noticed that two types of actions should be distinguished. On the one hand, there are actions performed by the system's agents when they want to bring changes in the current state of affairs and, on the other hand, there are actions that the system's agents may perform to allow or prevent changes brought by the environment's agents.

In the previous Section, we noticed that the librarian (the system's agent) may perform actions to bring his own changes (i.e. ADD and REMOVE) but that he may also perform actions to allow or prevent changes (i.e CHECK-OUT and RETURN) brought by a borrower (external agent)

Up to now, the two types of actions could not be distinguished in our logical framework. Assuming the following statement,

IN-LIBRARY(book) $\mathcal{T}\neg$ IN-LIBRARY(book)

nothing can be concluded about the role of the librarian; he could REMOVE the book or to allow the CHECKOUT of the book by a borrower.

In order to distinguish these two cases, an additional connective $\mathcal{I}$ is introduced to express the type of interference the librarian had on the state. This $\mathcal{I}$ dyadic connective was introduced by von Wright [21] to express the correlation existing between (i) the state in which the world is when an action has been completed and (ii) the state in which the world would be, had the agent not interfered with it but remained passive. Let us consider two examples:
IN-LIBRARY(book) $\mathcal{T}$
($\neg$ IN-LIBRARY(book) $\mathcal{I}$ IN-LIBRARY(book))
asserts that had the librarian remained passive, the change would not have taken place. Then, we can conclude that the librarian *brought about* the change, i.e. that he was directly responsible of the REMOVE of the book

IN-LIBRARY(book) $\mathcal{T}$
($\neg$ IN-LIBRARY(book) $\mathcal{I}\neg$ IN-LIBRARY(book))
asserts that, independently of the librarian, the change would nevertheless have occurred. Thereby, we can conclude that the librarian *let* the change happen, i.e. he allowed the borrower to check out the book.

It results that the general form which a description of action may become extracted is "-$\mathcal{T}$ (- $\mathcal{I}$ -)". The expression says that the world initially is in a certain state *and* *next* is in a certain total state *instead of* being in a certain third total state. $\mathcal{T}$ coordinates the world which *is* now and the world which *will be* next; $\mathcal{I}$ co-ordinates the world *as it is* with a system's agent in and the world *as it would be* if the system's agent remained passive. Thereby, the rules of inference governing the connective $\mathcal{I}$ present some similarities with those characterizing the connective $\mathcal{T}$:

$$(\phi \vee \psi)\mathcal{I}(\rho \vee \sigma) \Leftrightarrow (\phi\mathcal{I}\rho) \vee (\phi\mathcal{I}\sigma) \vee (\psi\mathcal{I}\rho) \vee (\psi\mathcal{I}\sigma)$$
$$(\phi\mathcal{I}\psi) \wedge (\phi\mathcal{I}\rho) \Rightarrow (\phi\mathcal{I}(\psi \wedge \rho))$$
$$\phi \Leftrightarrow (\phi\mathcal{I}(\psi \vee \neg\psi))$$
$$\neg(\phi\mathcal{I}(\psi \wedge \neg\psi))$$

The overall logical framework including static, temporal, $\mathcal{T}$ and $\mathcal{I}$ connectives was proved decidable and complete [21].

Considering the IN-LIBRARY (book) predicate, there are 8 (2^3) different possible actions.

The concept of activity

Having introduced a formal logic of *actions*, we are now able to describe the concept of activity in formal terms.

In the previous paragraph, we declare eight possible actions. There can be restrictions on the performance of these actions, these restrictions are linked to the description of activities associated with.

First of all, there can exist situations where an action can never be performed. In the library's specification, we had the following statement:

librarian | agent ||
{LIBRARY-MANAGEMENT | activity (book) ||

choose { ADD(book), REMOVE(book),
allows CHECKOUT(book),
allows RETURN(book),
prevents CHECKOUT(book), null }

It results that the action prevents RETURN(book) can never be performed. In more formal terms, this forbidding is expressed using the $\Diamond$ temporal connective:

$$\neg \Diamond [\ \neg\text{IN-LIBRARY(book)}\mathcal{T}\ (\neg\text{IN-LIBRARY(book)}\mathcal{I}\ \text{IN-LIBRARY(book)})\ ]$$

Other restrictions on the performance of actions are due to safety and liveness restrictions associated with activities. In the library's case, we found the following restrictions:

such that { if prevents CHECKOUT(book) then book:UNIQUE
and
if book:UNIQUE then
not (allows CHECKOUT(book)
or REMOVE(book))
and
some more REMOVE(book) }

The following axioms can be associated with these three constraints:

$$(\text{IN-LIBRARY(book)}\mathcal{T}\ (\text{IN-LIBRARY(book)}\mathcal{I}\neg\ \text{IN-LIBRARY(book)}))\ \Rightarrow \text{UNIQUE(book)}$$

$$\text{UNIQUE(book)} \Rightarrow \neg\ (\ [\text{IN-LIBRARY(book)}\mathcal{T}\ (\neg\text{IN-LIBRARY(book)}\mathcal{I}\neg\text{IN-LIBRARY(book)})]\ \vee\ [\text{IN-LIBRARY(book)}\mathcal{T}\ (\neg\text{IN-LIBRARY(book)}\mathcal{I}\ \text{IN-LIBRARY(book)})]\ )$$

$$\text{IN-LIBRARY(book)} \Rightarrow \Diamond[\text{IN-LIBRARY(book)}\mathcal{T}\ (\neg\text{IN-LIBRARY(book)}\mathcal{I}\ \text{IN-LIBRARY(book)})]$$

3.2 Formal deduction

In the Introduction, we suggested how the deductive power associated with a formal requirements language could provide support to various activities performed during the *process*.

In this Section, we would like to detail how the deductive power associated with the logic considered so far supports the specific *elaboration* activity described in Section 2. In this activity, *goals* (objectives and constraints) are first identified before to be refined in terms of finer behaviours exhibited by *agents* in the final system. Still, to support a *formal* elaboration, it would be convenient to *prove* how goals are met by the finer requirements.

Let us consider the NEVER-EVER goal identified in the library case-study.

$$\text{IN-LIBRARY(book)} \Rightarrow \neg\ \Box\ \text{IN-LIBRARY(book)}$$

We can show how this goal is proved by the axiom characterizing the REMOVE of a book, i.e.

$$\text{IN-LIBRARY(book)} \Rightarrow \Diamond[\text{IN-LIBRARY(book)}\mathcal{T}\ (\neg\text{IN-LIBRARY(book)}\mathcal{I}\ \text{IN-LIBRARY(book)})]$$

In the proof below, we establish this derivability.

1. $\text{IN-LIBRARY(book)} \Rightarrow \Diamond[\text{IN-LIBRARY(book)}\mathcal{T}\ (\neg\text{IN-LIBRARY(book)}\mathcal{I}\ \text{IN-LIBRARY(book)})]$
   - assumption
2. $\text{IN-LIBRARY(book)} \Rightarrow \Diamond[\text{IN-LIBRARY(book)}\mathcal{T}\ \neg\text{IN-LIBRARY(book)}]$
   - $\mathcal{I}$ elimination
3. $\text{IN-LIBRARY(book)} \Rightarrow \Diamond[\text{IN-LIBRARY(book)} \wedge \circ\neg\text{IN-LIBRARY(book)}]$
   - $\mathcal{T}$ definition (see p. 6)
4. $\text{IN-LIBRARY(book)} \Rightarrow \Diamond\neg\text{IN-LIBRARY(book)}$
   - $\wedge$ elimination
5. $\text{IN-LIBRARY(book)} \Rightarrow \neg\ \Box\neg\text{IN-LIBRARY(book)}$
   - $\Box$ definition

It would also have been possible to give a formal proof of the second goal (i.e. NEVER-EMPTY). However, because of lack of place, we only informally suggest how this proof could be established. The library will never become empty because of restrictions that are imposed on activities performed by agents when only one book is available in the library (UNIQUE(book)). In this case, allows CHECKOUT and REMOVE are two forbidden activities. Thereby, it ensures that at least one book is always present in the library.

4 Conclusion

Constructing requirements specifications for a complex system is a quite difficult *process*. In this paper, we have focussed on the *elaboration* part of this process where new requirements are progressively identified and incorporated.

Feather's work within the framework of the Gist language [8] [9] has strongly influenced our work. So, we proposed a requirements language where the concepts of *goals* and the one of *agent* characterized by some *responsibility* were identified.

Establishing *goals* is a classical way used for decomposing systems in terms of more finer systems (for example, in SADT [14], activities are decomposed in terms of a graph of more finer activities). Still, in most cases, there is no precise characterization of the decomposition. Let us mention two relevant contributions where the decomposition criterion is analogous to the one we consider. The first one is done by [2] where a clear distinction is made between goals requirements and solution-oriented requirements. In the second one [18], the distinction is made between the behaviour of a "business system" and the behaviour resulting from the combination of various actions performed by agents of the system.

The concept of responsibility is informally introduced in some requirements specification languages. For example, it is denoted by the *processor mechanism* in SADT. More complete characterizations of responsibility with respect to activities performed by agents can be found in the Forest project [10] or in OBLOG [16]. In the former, responsibility is expressed through the concept of action performed by an agent to guarantee a certain behaviour of the system. In the latter, knowledge is described about acts performed by agents as well as the interaction between them.

Still, another major contribution should be done at the level of the *elaboration* part of the process. Heuristics should be proposed based on properties associated with the various concepts introduced at the level of the requirements language. Up to now, we have identified some of these heuristics informally. In the future, we intend to formalize these heuristics, this formalization being a first step in the formalization of the *process*.

Acknowledgment: This work was partially supported by the European Community under Project 2537 (ICARUS) of the European Strategic Program for Research and Development Technology (ESPRIT). We are indebted to A. Rifaut for helpful comments and suggestions.

References

[1] M.W. Alford, "A Requirements Engineering Methodology for Real-time Processing Requirements," *IEEE Trans. Soft. Eng.*, SE-3(1), pp. 60-69, 1977.

[2] J.A. Bubenko, "On Concepts and Strategies for Requirements and Information Analysis, " in *Information Modeling*, J.A. Bubenko (ed.), Chartwell-Bratt, pp. 125-169, 1983.

[3] D. Cohen, "Symbolic Execution of the Gist specification language," in *Proceedings of the Eighth IJCAI*, pp. 17-20, 1983.

[4] E. Dubois, J. Hagelstein, E. Lahou, F. Ponsaert, A. Rifaut and F. Williams, "The ERAE Model: a Case Study," in *Information Systems Design Methodologies: Improving the Practice*, T.W. Olle, H.G. Sol and A.A. Verrijn-Stuart (eds), North-Holland, pp. 87-105, 1986.

[5] E. Dubois, J. Hagelstein. "Reasoning on Formal Requirements: A Lift Control System," in *Proc. Fourth International Workshop on Software Specification and Design*, pp. 161-168, 1987.

[6] E. Dubois, "Logical Support for Reasoning about the Specification and the Elaboration of Requirements," in *The Role of Artificial Intelligence in Databases and Information Systems*, WG2.6/WG8.1 Conference, Guangzhou, China, pp. 29-48, July 1988.

[7] E. Dubois, J. Hagelstein and A. Rifaut, "Formal Requirements Engineering with ERAE," to appear in the *Philips Journal of Research*, 43, nos. 3/4, 1988.

[8] M.S. Feather. "Language Support for the Specification and Development of Composite Systems," in *ACM TOPLAS*, vol. 9, 2, pp. 198-234, April 87.

[9] M.S. Feather. "Constructing Specifications by Combining Parallel Elaborations," to appear in *IEEE Trans. Soft. Eng.*.

[10] A. Finkelstein, C. Potts. "Building Formal Specifications Using 'Structured Common Sense'," in *Proc. Fourth International Workshop on Software Specification and Design*, pp. 108-113, 1987.

[11] S.J. Greenspan, A. Borgida and J. Mylopoulos, "A Requirements Modeling Language and its Logic," *Information Systems*, vol 11(1), pp. 9-23, 1986.

[12] W. L. Johnson, "Deriving Specifications from Requirements," in *Proc. 10th Int. Conf. on Software Engineering*, Singapore, pp. 428-438, 1988.

[13] A. Prior, "Past, Present and Future," Oxford University Press, 1967.

[14] D.T. Ross and K.G. Schoman, "Structured Analysis for Requirements Definition," *IEEE Trans. Soft. Eng.*, SE 3(1), pp. 1-65, 1977.

[15] J.R. Schonfield, "Mathematical Logic," Addison-Wesley, 1967.

[16] A. Sernadas, C. Sernadas and H.-D. Ehrich, "Abstract Object Types: a Temporal Perspective," *Colloquium on Temporal Logic and Specification*, Barringer, H. (ed), (to be published).

[17] "Library (R.A. Kemmerer, Testing formal specifications to detect design errors," *ACM SIGSOFT Software Engineering Notes*, vol. 11,2, pp.

[18] R. Stamper, K. Althans and J. Backhouse, "MEASUR: Method for Eliciting, Analyzing and Specifying User Requirements," in *Computerized Assistance during the Information Systems Life Cycle*, T.W. Olle, A.A. Verrijn-Stuart and L. Bhabuta (eds), North Holland, pp. 67-115, 1988

[19] D. Teichroew and E.A. Hershey, "A Computer Aided Technique for Structured Documentation and Analysis of Information Processing Systems," *IEEE Trans. Soft. Eng.*, SE-3(1), pp. 41-48, 1977.

[20] G.H. von Wright, "And Next," *Acta Philosophica Fennica*, Fasc. 18, pp. 293-304, 1965.

[21] G.H. von Wright, "An Essay in Deontic Logic and the General Theory of Action," *Acta Philosophica Fennica*, Fasc. XXI, North-Holland, 1968.

Detecting Interference when Merging Specification Evolutions

Martin S. Feather

USC / Information Sciences Institute
4676 Admiralty Way, Marina del Rey CA 90292

ABSTRACT

We have been studying a model of software specification design which begins with a trivially simple specification, incrementally elaborates it in a number of parallel "lines" of design, and merges the specifications that result from each of those divergent lines to achieve the fully detailed specification. We employ "evolutionary" transformations - that is, transformations whose very purpose is to change meaning - to perform the elaborations in the design lines, and thereafter achieve merging by replaying the transformations in a serial order. Merging does not always proceed smoothly: on occasions the different lines of design interfere with one another in some manner, inhibiting the serial replay of their evolutionary transformations. We show that by comparing how the transformations change specification properties (herein we consider the properties of terminology and usage), certain kinds of interference can be detected, and in some cases means to deal with it suggested.

1. Specification evolution via transformation

While traditionally the software design process has started with a specification and worked towards an implementation, we have come to believe that the construction of the starting specification is also an important and complex design process. We have studied a process in which specification construction is incremental - the specification is gradually evolved from a trivially simple starting point by means of a series of evolutionary steps. We have built mechanisms for performing these via "evolutionary transformations", akin to the transformations of conventional program transformation work, except they deliberately *change* the meaning of the specifications to which they are applied. In contrast, conventional transformations generally keep the meaning of the specification constant (so called "correctness-preserving") while improving efficiency (sometimes they "shrink" the meaning, i.e., when the initial specification admits to alternative implementations, the transformations may be allowed to select from among those, but in any event they never introduce new possibilities).

Similar research has been done in the area of modifications to type lattices and database schemas: in [2] a classification of possible changes to a type lattice is given, and used to suggest means for adapting existing data and operations on that data accordingly. Similar changes are considered in [10], where the focus is on constructing methods to handle clashes between objects and programs created under different versions of the type lattice. Recently in [6] it is argued that several machine learning techniques can help in the task of making these same kinds of modifications to databases.

1.1 Parallel lines of design

We found that different evolution steps are often independent, or nearly so. This prompted us to apply those steps in parallel, giving rise to several different lines of design. The specifications that result from each line of design must thereafter be merged. Since the different specifications have been obtained by applying series of evolutionary transformations, we obtain the merge of those specifications by applying the same transformations in series. A more complete description of the overall approach may be found in [4]. The aspect that is of interest here is the desire to pursue separate lines of design independently, and thereafter merge their results. The ability to do this would have several beneficial characteristics:

- separation of concerns: the details introduced by one evolution can be ignored while conducting another evolution,
- distributed development: several people may independently evolve the same initial specification in different ways, and thereafter have their versions merged, and
- explicit combination: when the different lines of design are not completely independent, this will be recognized and dealt with explicitly at the time of merging.

1.2 Other work on merging

Previous work toward merging has addressed the merging of programs expressed in simplified languages, and concentrated upon those cases where the versions are non-interfering. The merging of extensions (as distinct from arbitrary modifications) to applicative programs is considered in [3]; the merging of versions of programs in a simplified assignment-based language, relying upon some coordination during creation of those versions to ensure consistency among use of names, is considered in [5]. Both of these efforts rely upon knowing only the initial program and its versions to be merged, and do not make use of knowledge of how those versions were obtained from the initial program. In contrast, we are assuming that the versions are derived from the initial specification by application of evolutionary transformations drawn from a pre-existing set. This provides the extra information that serves as the basis for increasing the robustness of the merging process in the face of interference (but relies upon the designer to perform all modifications by transformation). Also, we have concentrated on specifications rather than programs; we expect the latter to have a more "intertwined" nature, as a consequence of their goal of being efficient. We suspect that specifications, being more concerned with clarity than efficiency, may be more suited to our model of design.

AI planning research addresses the problem of efficiently discovering a linear plan to achieve multiple goals, where goals are represented as predicate logic formulas. Included in this are the activities of detecting and resolving interference between plan steps (e.g., [9], [1]). In order to make use of these results we would have to formulate specification evolution in terms of goals and operators, for which we need a far better understanding of the evolutionary process. Our current work is more modest, and focuses on accumulating a repertoire of conflict resolution techniques expressed directly in terms of the evolutionary transformations, rather than in terms of the goals of such transformations.

1.3 Merging by replaying evolutionary transformations

Our approach to merging is to replay the evolutionary transformations of the separate lines of design in a serial order. This proceeds smoothly if the parallel evolutions are completely independent, and leads to the same result regardless of the serial order followed. The simplest case of this, where there are just two lines of design and each line comprises a single evolution, is shown pictorially in the left hand side of figure 1: s0 is the initial specification, e1 and e2 the evolutions, giving rise to evolved specifications s1 and s2 respectively. To produce the specification that combines these elaborations, we replay them in serial order, that is, apple e2 to the result of applying e1 to s0, or apply e1 to the result of applying e2 to s0. This is shown in the right hand side of figure 1, where the two paths from s0 down to s3 represent the two serial replays. The result should be the same regardless of which serialization is followed, i.e. the diagram commutes.

For example, if one evolution removes an existing function F, and another evolution adds a new function G that does not refer to F, then clearly these can be replayed in either order and result in the same final specification. More problematic are those cases where the evolutions interfere with one another in some way. For example, interference may occur if one evolution renames function F to G, while another

```
                 parallel evolution

        specification s0 *
                        / \
          evolution e1 /   \ evolution e2
                      /     \
 specification s1 *           * specification s2

                  serializations

                      s0 *
                        / \
                   e1 /   \ e2
                     /     \
                 s1 *       * s2
                     \     /
                   e2 \   / e1
                       \ /
                    s3 *
```

Figure 1 - Serial replays of parallel evolution

evolution extends function F with an extra formal parameter; a serialization in which the renaming follows the extension will proceed without problem, whereas the alternative ordering in which the extension follows the renaming will fail (because the extension evolution refers to F, while the specification now contains G). Worse yet, evolutions developed in parallel may be contradictory. For example, when one evolution generalizes the input type of a function from integers to sets of integers, while another evolution generalizes the input type of that same function to sequences of integers. We would like our approach to be robust in the case of simple interference (e.g., continue to work in the event of simple renaming) and helpful in more complex cases (e.g., by identifying the occurrence and nature of interference, and, where appropriate, suggesting means of resolving it).

Typically, we apply evolutionary transformation to change some of the properties of the specification while leaving others invariant. For example, some modify the terminology (e.g., add a new formal parameter to an existing function), while others adjust which constructs are used (e.g., replace a call to one function with a call to another function). This suggests that we decompose the detection of interference into two stages:

- Determine the effects that each of the evolutionary transformations induces on each specification property, then

- make pairwise comparisons of changes within each property, and of changes between each property.

For example, if two evolutions each add a new named definition, in the first stage we determine that they each induce a change on the terminology. Then in the second stage we compare these changes to see if the names are the same, in which case there is interference - if the two definitions are the same, then only one of the evolutions should be replayed (to avoid duplicating the definition), otherwise one of the evolutions must be changed to give a different name to the definition it introduces. Evolutionary transformations may make several changes to a property or properties, in which case we would have to do the pairwise comparison of every possible cross-pairing of those changes. In some cases, transformations that make multiple changes may need to be decomposed into a series of simpler transformations so that their effects can be merged.

This is the approach we present in the rest of the paper. It has the virtue of permitting the easy extension of the set of evolutionary transformations - given a new transformation, we analyze it to determine what changes to specification properties are induced by an invocation of that transformation. Thereafter, we can use that transformation in our specification design process, and make the necessary comparisons of changes to specification properties. Thus the amount of work needed to add a new evolutionary transformation is not dependent upon the number of transformations already in the set.

Robinson has also studied the merging problem in this same context of evolutionary transformations [7, 8]. His approach is to build a collection of rules, used both for merging and to help in conducting evolutionary transformation. These rules reason simultaneously about data and control flow properties and development goals. In contrast, we have attempted to factor the problem based upon specification properties.

In the next section we present a small example, informally illustrating the kind of reasoning we wish to perform. Then in section 3 the formal details are introduced, and in section 4 we return to our example to see the formalisms at work.

2. An informal example of detecting interference

We draw our illustrative example from the specification of the "Patient Monitoring System", briefly, a software system that monitors the status of hospital patients and alerts nurses of unsafe conditions. This problem is taken from [11]. Design of the complete specification following our style of parallel evolution followed by merging is presented in [4]; for our present purposes we consider only portions of two of the lines of this design, those that:

- evolve the monitoring system from having direct access to patients' medical status values, to instead having indirect access via an intermediary device (e.g., thermometer), and

- evolve the model of each patient's medical status from a single value to a record structure of values, one for each medical "factor" (temperature, bloodpressure, pulse, etc.).

Examining the first evolution, we find that it induces the following changes:

- Terminology changes: new named objects are added to the specification, namely the type modelling devices, and the data structures modelling device values and recording which devices are linked to which patients.

- Usage changes: the monitoring system's uses of patient values are replaced with uses of device values, and the (new) devices introduce (new) use of patient values. patient values.

The second evolution induces the following changes:

- Terminology changes: new named objects are added to the specification, namely the types modelling factors and modelling record structures of values; the type of the patient's medical status is changed from a single value to a record structure of values.

- Usage changes: patients and the monitor now make use of the new data types modelling record structures of values.

We now compare the changes in the above categories to detect interference. The more interesting comparisons are discussed below. As we will see in section 4, our formal comparison process requires many comparisons to be made, most of which indicate no interference.

- Comparing terminology changes, we detect interference if any of the named constructs introduced in the separate evolutions happen to be given the same name. Since they are all intended to be distinct constructs, all their names should also be distinct. If this were not the case, we would systematically rename the offending new construct in one of the lines of design.

- Comparing usage changes, we find no interference, since the uses added by the second evolution are of the new structures it introduced (hence there can be no overlap with the changes to usage made by the first evolution).

- Comparing usage changes and terminology changes, we find that the first evolution adds uses of a data structure that the second evolution changes (namely, device uses patient's medical status, the type of which has changed from a single value to a record structure). This indicates interference: the change also must be applied to the new use (i.e., the new devices should read and forward record structures, rather than single values).

3. Formalizing the detection of interference

In this section we present the formal method that we use to detect interference between evolutions. We consider the changes induced by evolutionary transformations on the properties of:

- *terminology* (the set of signatures of the specification's constructs) - section 3.1, and

- *usage* (the uses that constructs make of one another) - section 3.2.

In the future we intend to do the same sort of analysis for properties of *dataflow* and *behavior* (the set of behaviors denoted by the specification).

We then consider comparisons between changes:

- terminology / terminology comparisons - section 3.3
- usage / usage comparisons - section 3.4
- terminology / usage comparisons - section 3.5

3.1 Changes induced on terminology By terminology we mean the set of the specification's constructs' signatures, i.e., their names, arities and formal parameter types. We assume that each construct has a name, and an associated set of parameters each of which is a pair comprising a name and a type (e.g., a definition of the form "`procedure PRINTINT[n of type integer] definition ...`" associates with the name "`PRINTINT`" the single parameter named "`n`" of type "`integer`"). We will assume that no two constructs can have the same name, and that no two parameters of the same construct can have the same name.

The possible changes to terminology are as follows (in each case the way that change is indicated in the columns of the comparison tables is shown between quotes; "...."):

- Add a construct named `c` with definition `d`; "`add construct c`".
- Remove the construct named `c` with definition `d`; "`remove construct c`".
- Add a parameter named `p` of type `t` to a construct named `c`; "`add parameter p/c/t`".
- Remove the parameter named `p` from the construct named `c`; "`remove parameter p/c`".
- Rename the construct named `c` to `c'`; "`rename construct c->c'`".
- Rename the parameter named `p` of construct `c` to `p'`; :`rename parameter p/c->p'`".
- Change the type of the parameter named `p` of construct named `c` to `t`; "`change parameter p/c->t`".

In this initial study we deliberately chose a rather coarse set of terminology changes. We could have further distinguished between several classes of type-changes, e.g., type refinement, in which a type is decomposed into several subtypes (human → male / female), vs. type extension, in which a more general type is substituted (surgeon → medical-professional). Finer distinctions such as these would give correspondingly finer distinctions between classes of interference, but would require larger comparison tables and more effort to analyze the changes induced by each transformation.

3.2 Changes induced on usage We take the "usage" property to encompass notions of reference (e.g., reference to a data structure) and invocation (e.g., invocation of a procedure or function).

The possible changes to usage that we consider are as follows:

- Add to construct c a use of construct d.
- Remove from construct c a use of construct d.
- Remove *all* construct c's uses of construct d.
- Replace one of construct c's uses of d with uses of constructs s (a set of constructs).
- Replace *all* of construct c's uses of d with uses of constructs s (a set of constructs).

3.3 Comparing terminology changes to detect interference

Table 1 displays the pairwise comparison of terminology changes.

The simplest entries have only a single keyword (e.g., "`ok`", indicating no interference). The other entries have associated conditions which have to be evaluated to determine which keyword applies. For convenience, "`if <condition> then <keyword> else ok`" is abbreviated as "`<condition> <keyword>`" (e.g., in the entry that compares `change parametertype r1/c1->t1` with `remove construct c2` there is the condition `c1=c2` and keyword `RM`, indicating that if `c1=c2` then we have an instance of the `RM` interference, otherwise it is `ok`).

The possible kinds of interference between terminology changes are as follows, presented in increasing order of conflict (the keywords used in the table are shown to the left):

`ok` - no interference: The transformations are completely independent with respect to terminology, and may be serialized in either order, resulting in the same specification. For example, if one transformation adds a new construct while another transformation removes an existing construct, they can both be performed (note that since we are interested in only the terminology, we do *not* consider here whether the definition of the added construct accesses the removed construct - this would be detected by the inter-property comparison in section 3.5.

`DUP` - duplication: The two transformations make the same terminology changes, hence in serializing, the terminology changes of only one of them (it doesn't matter which one) need be performed. This might necessitate decomposing a transformation that makes multiple changes into a series of smaller transformations, so that its duplicated terminology change is separated from the other changes, and can be omitted.

`RI` - renaming interference: One transformation renames something that the other transformation refers to. For example, if one transformation changes the type of some parameter of construct `c`, while the other transformation renames `c`. To resolve this, either the transformations are serialized so that the renaming transformation is applied second, or alternatively apply the renaming transformation first, then the other transformation modified by having had the renaming applied to it (i.e., transform the transformation).*

`DUPR` - duplication with renaming: The transformations make the same terminology changes modulo renaming. For example, if one transformation renames construct `c` to `c1'`, and the other transformation renames that same construct `c` to `c2'` (where `c1'`≠`c2'`). To resolve this, we apply the terminology change of only one of the transformations (whichever introduces the name we deem to be preferable).

`NNC` - new name clash: The transformations introduce the same name for different purposes. For example, if each adds a

*In general, whenever a renaming transformation is serialized before another transformation, the renaming should be applied to that other transformation.

Table 1 - Comparison of terminology changes

```
          |add      |remove   |add      |remove   |rename   |rename    |change
          |construct|construct|parameter|parameter|construct|parameter |parameter
          |c2       |c2       |p2/c2/t2 |p2/c2    |c2->c2'  |p2/c2->p2'|p2/c2->t2
----------+---------+---------+---------+---------+---------+----------+---------
change    |         | c1=c2   |         |c1=c2 &  | c1=c2   |c1=c2 &   |c1=c2 &
parameter |   ok    | R&M     |   ok    |p1=p2    | RI      |p1=p2     |p1=p2
p1/c1->t1 |         |         |         |R&M      |         |RI        | if t1=t2
----------+---------+---------+---------+---------+---------+----------+ then DUP
rename    |         | c1=c2   |c1=c2 &  |c1=c2 &  | c1=c2   |c1=c2 &   | else #
parameter |   ok    | R&M     |p1'=p2   |p1=p2    | RI      |p1=p2      \--------
p1/c1->p1'|         |         |NNC      |R&M      |         | if p1'=p2'|
----------+---------+---------+---------+---------+---------+ then DUP  |
rename    | c1'=c2  | c1=c2   | c1=c2   |c1=c2    |c1=c2     \ else DUPR |
construct | NNC     | R&M     | RI      |RI       | if c1'=c2'|----------+
c1->c1'   |         |         |         |         | then DUP  |
----------+---------+---------+---------+---------+ else DUPR |
remove    |         | c1=c2   |         |c1=c2 &  |\----------+
parameter |   ok    | R&M     |   ok    |p1=p2    |
p1/c1     |         |         |         |DUP      |
----------+---------+---------+---------+---------+
add       |         | c1=c2   |c1=c2
parameter |   ok    | R&M     | this case is further
p1/c1/t1  |         |         | divided into four
----------+---------+---------+ subcases, as follows:     |p1=p2 |p1≠p2
remove    |         | c1=c2   |                      ------+------+------
construct |   ok    | DUP     |                      t1=t2 |DUP or|DUPR or
c1        |         |         |                            |NNC   |ok
----------+---------+---------+                      ------+------+------
add       | if c1=c2 \-----\                         t1≠t2 | NNC  | ok
construct | then DUP or NNC |
c1        | else DUPR or ok |
```

Key

```
c1 c2 c1' c2' - construct names             #    - contradiction
p1 p2 p1' p2' - parameter names             DUP  - duplication of same change
t1 t2         - types (of parameters)       DUPR - duplication of same change modulo
p1/c1/t1      - parameter p1 of c1          NNC  - new name clash               renaming
                (parameter's type is t1)    ok   - no interference
                                            RI   - renaming interference
                                            R&M  - remove & modify ordering dependency
```

new construct with the same name, but the constructs are different. To resolve this, we systematically replace the new name being introduced in one of the transformations with a different name (new with respect to the original specification *and* the other transformation), then serially apply the transformations in either order.

DUP or NNC - duplication or new name clash: This choice arises when the two transformations each add some new construct, or each add some new parameter, and introduce the same name. In either case, the choice hinges on whether or not the additions are intended to be the same; the designer must make this determination. If they are to be the same, we have an instance of DUP, otherwise an instance of NNC.

DUPR or ok - duplication modulo renaming or no interference: This choice arises when the two transformations each add some new construct, or each add some new parameter, and introduce different names. In either case, the choice hinges on whether or not the additions are intended to be the same; the designer must make this determination. If they are to be the same, we have an instance of DUPR, otherwise an instance of ok.

RM - remove & modify: One transformation removes a construct that the other transformation modifies (e.g., adds a new parameter to). To resolve this, the modification transformation is applied *before* the removal transformation (if the modification transformation makes no other changes, it would be permissible to omit it entirely, and just do the removal).

- contradiction: At this level of description the transformations cannot both be performed. For example, if one transformation changes the type of a construct's parameter to some type `t1`, while the other transformation changes the type of that same parameter to type `t2`, where `t1≠t2`. Note that in some circumstances it may be possible to combine apparently contradictory type changes, e.g., if one modified type `x` into `set of x`, while the other modified type `x` into `sequence of x`, then it might make sense to combine these by modifying type `x` into `set of sequence of x`, or alternatively into `sequence of set of x`. This is a finer level of reasoning than our model of terminology deals with, hence the method as presented can only indicate a contradiction. For commonly occurring special cases of contradictions we intend to build mechanisms that take a more detailed view and hence might be able to resolve them.

3.4 Comparing usage changes to detect interference

Table 2 displays the pairwise comparison of usage changes. The possible kinds of interference are as follows (in increasing order of conflict):

ok - no interference: The transformations are completely independent with respect to usage, and may be serialized in either order, resulting in the same specification.

DUP - duplication: The transformations duplicate the same usage change, hence in serializing, the usage change of only one of them (it doesn't matter which one) need be applied.

DUP? - potential duplication: If both transformations are affecting the same instance of use, they are duplicating one another. For example, each transformation removes a use of d from c; with respect to our definition of use, the changes they make are identical, however in the specification they may or may not be removing the same *instance* of a use of d.

DUPall - duplication of a single change by the "all" transformation: Only the transformation that makes changes to all uses need be replayed.

A&M - add & modify ordering dependency: One transformation adds a use of the kind that the other transformation modifies. By choosing an ordering in which the addition precedes the modification, the modification will be applied to the added use; conversely, by choosing the opposite ordering, the modification will not be applied to the added use.

RorM - remove or modify choice: One transformation removes a use of the kind that the other transformation modifies. By choosing an ordering in which the removal precedes the modification, the use will be removed; conversely, by choosing the opposite ordering, the modification will be performed on that use and thereafter it will not be removed.

RorM? - potential remove or modify choice: If both transformations are affecting the same instance of use, they offer a remove or modify choice.

- contradiction: At this level of description the transformations cannot both be performed.

#? - potential contradiction: If both transformations are affecting the same instance of use, they are contradictory.

3.5 Comparing terminology changes with usage changes to detect interference

Lastly we compare changes to terminology with changes to dataflow - table 3.

ok - no interference. Columns in the table that would be completely filled with ok have been omitted (those corresponding to adding a new construct, to renaming a construct, and to renaming a parameter).

MNU - modify new use: One transformation introduces a new use of some construct that the other transformation is modifying, hence that new use may need to be modified

Table 2 - Comparison of usage changes

	replace all c2's uses of d2 with uses of s2	replace a use of d2 by c2 with uses of s2	remove all c2's uses of d2	remove from c2 a use of d2	add to c2 a use of d2
add to c1 a use of d1	c1=c2 & d1=d2 A&M	ok	c1=c2 & d1=d2 A&M	ok	c1=c2 & d1=d2 DUP?
remove from c1 a use of d1	c1=c2 & d1=d2 RorM	c1=c2 & d1=d2 RorM?	DUPall	c1=c2 & d1=d2 DUP?	
remove all c1's uses of d1	c1=c2 & d1=d2 RorM	c1=c2 & d1=d2 RorM	c1=c2 & d1=d2 DUP		
replace a use of d1 by c1 with uses of s1	c1=c2 & d1=d2 if s1=s2 then DUPall else #	c1=c2 & d1=d2 if s1=s2 then DUP? else #?			
replace all c1's uses of d1 with uses of s1	c1=c2 & d1=d2 if s1=s2 then DUP else #				

Key

c1 c2 d1 d2	- construct names
s1 s2	- sets of construct names
# (#?)	- (potential) contradiction
A&M	- add & modify ordering dependency
DUP (DUP?)	- (potential) duplication of the same change
DUPall	- duplication of a single change by the "all" transformation
ok	- no interference
RorM (RorM?)	- (potential) remove or modify choice

Table 3 - Comparison of usage changes with terminology changes

	remove construct c2	add/remove/change parameter p2/c2
add to c1 a use of d1	c1=c2 R&M; d1=c2 #	d1=c2 MNU
remove from c1 a use / all uses of d1	c1=c2 R&M	ok
replace a use / all uses by c1 of d1 with uses of s1	c1=c2 or d1=c2 R&M; c2∈s1 #	c2∈s1 MNU

Key

c1 c2 d1 - construct names
p2/c2 - named p2 of construct c2
s1 - sets of construct names

\# - contradiction
MNU - modify new use
ok - no interference
R&M - remove & modify ordering dependency

too. Note that the interaction between introducing new uses and renaming will have been handled by having pre-applied the renaming transformation to the use transformation, as mentioned in section 3.3.

R&M - remove & modify ordering dependency: One transformation removes a construct that the other transformation modifies. To resolve this, the modification transformation is applied before the removal transformation (see R&M in section 3.3).

4. Application to an example of merging

We now demonstrate the use of the comparison tables on the example of merging presented informally in section 2.

The first evolution (introduction of devices as intermediaries between the monitoring system and patients) induces the following changes:

Terminology changes:
1a) add construct named `device` with definition <u>type</u> `device`
1b) add construct named `device-readings` with definition <u>relation</u> `device-readings(device,value)` ...
1c) add parameter named `device` of type `device` to `device-readings`
1d) add parameter named `value` of type `value` to `device-readings`

Usage changes:
1e) replace all `monitor`'s uses of `patient-medical-status` with uses of {`device-of`, `device-readings`}
1f) add to `device` a use of `patient-medical-status`

The second evolution (elaboration of a patient's value from a single value to a record structure of values, one for each factor) induces the following changes:

Terminology changes:
2a) add construct named `factors` with definition <u>type</u> `factors = { temperature ... }`
2b) add construct named `record-of-values` with definition <u>type</u> `record-of-values = ...`
2c) change the type of the `pvalue` parameter of `patient-medical-status` from `value` to `record-of-values`

Usage changes:
2d) add to `patient` a use of `factors`
2e) add to `patient` a use of `record-of-values`
2f) add to `monitor` a use of `factors`
2g) add to `monitor` a use of `record-of-values`

Using table 1 we make pairwise comparisons of the terminology changes of the two evolutions.

- The add construct / add construct comparisons (e.g., 1a/2a) lead to the table entry `if c1=c2 then DUP or NNC else DUPR or ok`, where `c1` and `c2` are the names of the new constructs. Since in each comparison the names are distinct, the result is `DUPR or ok`, and since the constructs are indeed intended to be distinct, we conclude that the result is `ok`, i.e., no interference.

- All the other comparisons yield `ok`, i.e., no interference (e.g., 1c/2a is an add parameter/add construct comparison, whose table entry is `ok`).

Using table 2 we make pairwise comparisons of the usage changes of the two evolutions.

- The add use / add use comparisons (e.g., 1f/2d) yield the table entry** `if c1=c2 & d1=d2 then DUP? else ok` where `c1`(`c2`) is the construct to which a use of `d1`(`d2`) is being added. In each case the test `c1=c2` evaluates to false (e.g., for comparison 1f/2d, `c1=device` and `c2=patient`), so the result is `ok`, i.e., no interference.

- Similarly the replace all uses / add use comparisons (e.g., 1e/2d) evaluate to no interference.

Using table 3 we make pairwise comparisons of the terminology changes with the usage changes.

- The replace all uses / add construct comparisons (e.g., 1e/2a) and the use/add construct comparisons (e.g., 1f/2a) yield `ok`, i.e., no interference.

**Recall that in the tables `<condition> <keyword>` is an abbreviation for `if <condition> then <keyword> else ok`

- The replace all uses/change parameter comparison (1e/2c) yields the table entry `if c2∈s1 then MNU else ok`, where `c2` = `patient-medical-status` and `s1` = { `device-of`, `device-readings` }, so the result is no interference.

- The add use/change parameter comparison (1f/2c) yields the table entry `if d1=c2 then MNU else ok`, where `d1` = `patient-medical-status` and `c2` = `patient-medical-status`; thus `d1=c2` is true, so the result is the `MNU` kind of interference, indicating that the new use of `patient-medical-status` by `device` may need to be modified too.

- Finally, the add use/add parameter comparisons (e.g., 2d/1c) all yield the table entry `if d1=c2 then MNU else ok`. In each case the test `d1=c2` evaluates to false, so the result is no interference.

This concludes the comparisons. We see that the formal method has identified the same interference as did our informal reasoning of section 2, albeit requiring a large number of trivial comparisons. Since our goal is to automate this comparison process, the abundance of such trivial operations is not an impediment, what matters is that the method is able to recognize all the cases of interference.

5. Conclusions

Our concern has been to support the incremental and parallel design of software specifications. We suggested a design approach in which "evolutionary" (meaning changing) transformations are applied to make the increments, and thereafter are replayed serially to merge the specifications that result from the several diverging design lines.

Our focus has been on an important class of problems that can arise when replaying evolutions in a serial order - namely, interference stemming from the fact that the separate design lines may not necessarily be completely independent. We have exhibited a formalism capable of detecting, and some times resolving, this interference. Our formalism is based upon comparing the changes that the evolutionary transformations induce on several specification properties. As illustrated in the simple example, the comparison of changes is a repetitious but simple activity, and hence should be simple to mechanize (to date we have implemented a number of evolutionary transformations, but have *not* yet implemented the change comparison). The formalism has the desirable property that addition of a new evolutionary transformation requires only the analysis of how that transformation induces changes to the specification properties.

Acknowledgments

This research has been supported in part by Rome Air Development Center contract No. F30602-85-C-0221 and in part by National Science Foundation contract No. MCS-7918792. Views and conclusions contained in this document are those of the author and should not be interpreted as representing the official opinion or policy of RADC, NSF, the U.S. Government, or any other person or agency connected with them. The research has been conducted in the framework our software specification group, headed by Bob Balzer and including Neil Campbell,Don Cohen, Neil Goldman, Ed Ipser, Lewis Johnson, Dan Kogan, Yingsha Liao, Jay Myers, Steve Smoliar, Bill Swartout, Dave Wile, and Kai Yue. The author has also benefited from discussions with Steve Fickas and Bill Robinson.

References

1. Allen, J.F. & Koomen, J.A., "Planning using a temporal world model," in *Proceedings, 8th International Joint Conference on Artificial Intelligence, Karlsruhe, West Germany*, pp. 741-747, August 1983.

2. Balzer, R., "Automated enhancement of Knowledge Representations," in Joshi, A. (ed.), *Proceedings, 9th International Joint Conference on Artificial Intelligence, Los Angeles*, pp. 203-207, August 1985.

3. Berzins, V., "On Merging Software Extensions," *Acta Informatica* 23, 1986, 607-619.

4. Feather, M.S., "Constructing Specifications by Combining Parallel Elaborations," *IEEE Transactions on Software Engineering* 15, (2), February 1989, 198-208. Available as research report # RS-88-216 from ISI, 4676 Admiralty Way, Marina del Rey, CA 90292

5. Horowitz, S., Prins, J. & Reps, T., "Integrating non-interfering versions of programs," in *Conference Record of the Fifteenth ACM Symposium on Principles of Programming Languages*, January 1988.

6. Li, Q. & McLeod, D., "Object Flavor Evolution through Learning in an Object-Oriented Database System," in *Proceedings, 2nd International Conference on Expert Database Systems*, pp. 241-256, April 1988.

7. Robinson, W.N., Towards formalization of specification design, Master's thesis, University of Oregon, 1977.

8. Robinson, W.N., *Integrating Divergent Specifications: An Initial effort Using Flow Analysis*, University of Oregon, Technical Report, 1988.

9. Sacerdoti, E.D., "The nonlinear nature of plans," in *Advance papers of the 4th International Joint Conference on Artificial Inteligence, Tbilisi, Georgia, USSR*, pp. 206-214, 1975.

10. Skarra, A.H. & Zdonik, S.B., "The management of changing types in an object-oriented database," in *OOPSLA '86 Proceedings*, pp. 483-495, ACM, September 1986.

11. Stevens, W.P., Myers, G.J. & Constantine, L.L., "Structured design," *IBM Systems Journal* 13, (2), 1974, 115-139.

A Proposed Perspective Shift: Viewing Specification Design as a Planning Problem

John S. Anderson and **Stephen Fickas**

Department of Computer and Information Science
University of Oregon
Eugene, OR 97403

Abstract

Our interest is in formal models of the specification process. In this paper we argue that with the right perspective and set of assumptions, work in AI planning may be brought to bear on three aspects of designing a software specification: proposing a specification (generation); analyzing a proposed specification for problems (critiquing); and modifying a specification to mitigate problems (elaboration). We describe a program called ASAP which automates portions of the specification process.

1. Introduction

We view a specification designer's task as a kind of planning problem: from a given set of operators, select a subset that can be used to achieve a set of goals. One of our primary assumptions is that a designed artifact is intended to achieve one or more goals of the potential user(s) of the artifact. In particular, tools are designed to allow the user to carry out certain plans which will achieve his/her goals. The designer must understand what plans the user is likely to employ and design the artifact to accomodate those plans.

In our view, the expert knowledge that the designer uses can be encoded in the form of operators, together with the objects and relations manipulated by those operators. The designer finds a set of operators that can be used to achieve the client's goals, and ensures that the preconditions of those operators can be established and maintained.

While there are many similarities between specification and other planning problems, there are also many differences. One difference is that, rather than trying to solve a problem just once, a designer is concerned with providing an artifact which can be used many times, perhaps by many users, in a variety of situations. Thus, there is no single initial state from which a plan is to be executed. The designer tries to ensure that the user goals can be achieved regardless of what conditions are true at the time.

Another difference between specification and one-shot planning is that the designer is not only concerned with achieving a goal, but also with preventing certain *prohibited conditions*. Users not only want to achieve their goals, they also want to avoid a variety of unacceptable circumstances. The designer must anticipate user actions that, accidentally or intentionally, might result in an unacceptable state. To the extent possible, opportunities for those actions must be eliminated.

In this paper we describe ASAP (Automated Specifier And Planner), a program being developed to explore the automation of specification design using planning techniques. Within its domain of expertise, ASAP is able to assist a designer by 1) storing and retrieving operators and plans in an abstraction hierarchy, 2) suggesting methods for achieving user goals, 3) discovering plans that could result in undesirable outcomes, and 4) suggesting methods for preventing undesirable events.

ASAP's task is to find a set of operators which can be used to achieve the goals of the artifact users, but cannot be used to achieve a prohibited condition. It first generates a trial operator set by finding plans to achieve the user goals and collecting the operators from those plans. It then checks for faults in the proposed set by looking for plans which achieve the prohibited conditions. Finally, ASAP assists the human designer in modifying the operator set if faults exist. The test and modify steps are repeated as necessary.

The test domain for our system is that of physical resource management systems, such as libraries. Objects in this domain are things like BOOKS, VIDEO TAPES, PATRONS, CUSTOMERS, STAFF. Relations are things like ITEM-BORROWED, PASSWORD-OF. Typical operators are CHECK-OUT, CHECK-IN, QUERY-FOR-WHO-HAS-WHAT-ITEM. The domain knowledge we use is taken from 1) texts and articles on analyzing problems in the domain, and 2) protocols of human analysts, familiar with the domain, constructing and critiquing specifications [6].

The remainder of this section contains an example

problem. Section 2 discusses the specification problem representation, the input to the specification system, and the criteria used to identify a satisfactory specification. The next section describes the three phases of specification design: generation, critique, and modification. Section 4 discusses the use of abstraction and analogy in specification design. Finally, we discuss related work and the limitations of our system.

Example problem

An example will illustrate the types of problems we hope to address. Suppose we are trying to come up with a specification of a library record-keeping system. Our first version of the specification contains a variety of operations to be provided by the system, such as checking out and returning books, querying for various types of information, etc. Our next step is to critique the specification in order to discover any potential problems.

Suppose one of the prohibited conditions is allowing one user to know what another user has borrowed. In order to prevent users from violating other users' privacy, the query action has a precondition that users can only query on their own borrowing record.

The critic finds a plan which achieves the prohibited condition anyway. Given an initial state of two borrowers A and B, and a resource R to be borrowed, the plan for circumventing the system to reach this prohibited condition is as follows:

- borrower A checks out resource R;
- borrower B gains access to A's identity;
- B queries the system, as A, to find what resources A has checked out;
- B learns that A has checked out R.

The plan described above can be generated from the operator set by means-ends analysis. [The plan step not accounted for by the specification, gain-access-to-another's-ID, is assumed to be available to plans in this domain unless specifically prohibited by the user. Thus, the critic's domain model includes components in the environment as well as components in the system to be built.]

We have an undesirable situation: a prohibited condition is shown to be achievable with a particular plan. Can we modify the plan to avoid the bad outcome from being reached? One library analyst we interviewed suggested we focus on disabling the B-queries-as-A action by monitoring the query action with a staff person [6]. Most computer-based systems today take the other route, and attempt to make it difficult to carry out the gain-access-to-another's-ID action by including various password schemes.

Of course, one might question all of this intricate modification to the plan when we can simply remove the query operator from the specification, thus squashing the plan once and for all. This in fact would be feasible if the query operator was not playing a key role in any plan needed to satisfy a user goal. In other words, does removing the query operator from the operator set cause a user goal to become non-satisfiable?

We can see how this might happen by looking at another case, one that satisfies the goal of accounting for human forgetfulness. The plan is as follows:

- borrower A checks out resource R;
- A forgets the identity of R;
- A queries the system to find what resources A has checked out;
- A is reminded that A has checked out R;
- A checks resource R back in (eventually).

If the goal of accounting for human forgetfulness is considered important, then this plan or another like it must be made available. [The forgetting action is again part of the domain model of the critic, and is assumed to be available for any case that needs it in matching its plan.] If we remove the query operator, then one of three outcomes is possible:

1. Another operator from the specification's operator set can be found to complete this plan.
2. No other operator can be found to complete this plan, but yet another plan is found that satisfies the goal (i.e., this plan is redundant).
3. No plan can be found to satisfy the goal.

It is the third case that will lead us to consider the more subtle types of plan modifications to be discussed.

Finally, we note that these two examples can be reversed. We may start out with no query operator, note that a user goal is not being satisfied, add the query operator to remedy the situation, and then note that a prohibited condition can now be achieved.

2. Problem Description

In a traditional AI planning problem, the problem statement includes a goal, an initial state, and a set of operators. The planner returns a sequence of operators that transform the initial state into a state in which the goal conditions are satisfied. Our definition of a specification problem is a modified version of the general planning problem. The requirements of a specification problem are stated as policies rather than goals; operators are divided into distinct types; and 'initial conditions' can have several interpretations. The output is a set of operators plus a set of *start-up* conditions.

Figure 1 presents ASAP with its inputs and outputs and the interface between the specifier and planner modules. For this discussion, the planning module can be considered to be a generic AI planner similar to NOAH [10] or SIPE [12].

Policies

As mentioned earlier, a designed artifact is typically meant to be used many times by many users. Therefore, goals are generally stated in some aggregate form, rather than as a particular set of conditions to be achieved. We refer to these aggregate goals as *policies* (cf. [8]). Based on discussions with domain experts and

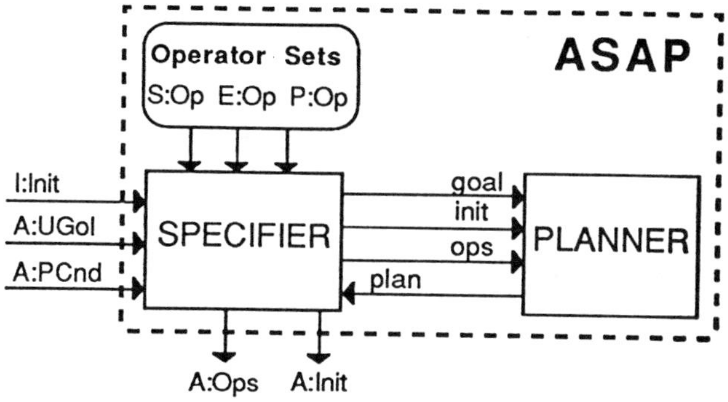

Figure 1. Overview of ASAP

a study of the domain literature, seven typical policies were defined for resource borrowing systems:

1. Allow users to have a large selection to choose from.
2. Allow users to gain access to a useful working set and keep it as long as necessary.
3. Maintain the privacy of users.
4. Recognize the human dynamics of group (patron, staff, administration) membership.
5. Account for human foibles, e.g., forgetting, losing items, stealing.
6. Account for development resource limitations, e.g., money, staff, and time available to develop the system.
7. Account for production environment limitations, e.g., money, staff, and time available to run and maintain the delivered system.

Each of these seven can be further refined. For example, policy 3 includes the sub-policies of maintaining the privacy of users' borrowing records, maintaining the privacy of users' queries, etc.

Note that policies frequently interfere with each other. Allowing one patron to keep a book for a long period (policy 2) reduces the selection available for the next patron (policy 1). One way to resolve this conflict is to have enough copies of the book for everyone, but this is very expensive, violating policies 6 and 7. In fact, most borrowing systems can be viewed almost solely as compromises between conflicting concerns. One key process in specification design, then, is coming to grips with conflicting policies through various forms of trade-off and compromise.

It is not possible for ASAP to plan in terms of policies directly. Instead, the policies must be translated into specific conditions to be achieved or avoided. For example, the policy of giving users a useful working set can be translated into the user goal of HAVE (PATRON, BOOK). The policy of maintaining privacy of users' borrowing record can be represented as a prohibited condition, BORROWING-RECORD-OF (RECORD, PATRON1) $\wedge$ HAS-ACCESS-TO (PATRON2, RECORD) $\wedge$ PATRON2 $\neq$ PATRON1. In ASAP, translating policies into goals and prohibited conditions is not automated but must be done manually.

Operators

ASAP uses traditional STRIPS-style operators, consisting of add, delete, and precondition lists. Operators that can be invoked by artifact users to achieve their goals are called *user-accessible* operators. User-accessible operators are divided into two categories: *environment* and *artifact* operators.

Operators that would be available whether or not the artifact existed are called *environment operators*. This set includes the normal things that people do every day such as move from place to place, pick objects up and put them down. These operators allow a specification designer to reason about the interactions between the artifact and the environment in which it is used.

Artifact operators are provided as part of the artifact being specified. They are selected from a catalog of potential operators. Typical examples in software systems are operators which store information, retrieve it, and modify it. Non-software examples include the "make toast" action provided by toasters and the "clean clothes" action performed by washing machines.

Most plans involve both environment and artifact operators. For example, a patron's plan to take a book out of a library includes environmental operators such as picking up the book and carrying it to the check-out counter, plus an artifact operator for actually checking out the book. It is important for the system to be able to reason about the environment in which the artifact is to be used, and not be restricted to a description of the artifact itself [4].

Environment operators are not under the control of the specification designer, and cannot be altered or removed from the set of user-accessible operators. The only way to prevent their use is to disable their preconditions. In contrast, artifact operators can simply be removed from the set of user-accessible operators by the specification designer.

A third class of operators is that of *start-up* operators. These operators are used to create an artifact but are not considered to be available to the typical user. Start-up operators are assumed to be relatively expensive, such as erecting a building or purchasing a central computer system. It is the expense of these operators that separates them from the user-accessible operators.

We characterize design as the need to apply an expensive plan once in order to establish a set of conditions which, once true, will enable the repeated achievement of one or more recurrent goals. Thus, establishing a library is a difficult and expensive process, but once done, makes it possible for large numbers of users to gain access to resources at a very low "per use" cost. Similarly, it is difficult for the average user to build a toaster, but simple to make toast hundreds of times once the toaster is available.

Initial Conditions

There are three ways to view the initial conditions of a specification. We refer to these three perspectives as the *user view*, the *artifact view*, and the *design view*, respectively.

In the user view, the initial conditions are those conditions that exist when a user wants to achieve a goal. These are the conditions that the planner needs to know about when generating a plan to achieve the user goal. Unfortunately, it is not possible to know exactly what conditions will hold when a user decides to execute a plan.

The only conditions that must be true when a user's plan is executed are those conditions that do not change over the lifetime of an artifact. We refer to these conditions as the *constant conditions* of the artifact. For example, the structure of the library building and the record-keeping system are assumed to be constant relative to patrons' activities. These conditions cannot be altered by any user-accessible operators.

The initial conditions for a user's plan will consist of the constant conditions plus any combination of conditions that can be achieved by any sequence of user-accessible operators. By specifying the constant conditions, the designer can enable or disable certain patron plans. For example, by specifying pens which are chained to the check-out counter, the designer enables filling out check-out slips while disabling taking the pens away.

From the artifact perspective, the initial conditions are the conditions that exist when the artifact is first put into use. We refer to these conditions as the *start-up conditions*. The specification may include a partial list of the start-up conditions of the artifact. In particular, all of the constant conditions must be included in the start-up conditions.

In the third view, the design view, the initial conditions exist before the artifact is built. We refer to these conditions as the *prior conditions*. The start-up operators are used to establish the start-up conditions from the prior conditions. The cost and availability of start-up operators restrict the changes that a designer can make in moving from the prior conditions to the start-up conditions.

Problem Definition

We now formalize our definition of a specification problem. All of the information relevant to the specification can be represented in terms of a set of objects **Obj**, a set of relations **Rel**, and a set of operators **Op** that add and delete members of **Obj** and **Rel**.

A functional specification of an artifact **A** consists of the *start-up conditions* **A:Init** and a set of *artifact operators* **A:Op**. The start-up conditions are a set of relations which describe the artifact when it is first put into use. We also define a set of *environmental operators* **E:Op**. The union of **A:Op** and **E:Op** is the set of *user-accessible operators* **U:Op**.

The *constant conditions* of **A** are those relations in **A:Init** which do not appear on the delete lists of any operators in **U:Op**. The *accessible states* of **A** are all states which can be reached from the start-up conditions by some sequence of operators in **U:Op**. A state is a conjunction of relations.

The input to ASAP includes a proposed set of start-up conditions, **P:Init**. In addition, ASAP starts with a database of three sets of operators: a set of *start-up operators*, **S:Op**; the set of environmental operators, **E:Op**; and a set of *potential operators*, **P:Op**, from which the artifact operators are selected.

The policies (i.e., requirements) of **A** are represented by a set of *user goals* **A:UGol** and a set of *prohibited conditions* **A:PCnd**. Each user goal or prohibited condition is a state.

A functional specification is said to be *non-satisfying* when a policy can be violated. *Incompleteness* is a type of non-satisfaction that occurs when a goal in **A:UGol** cannot be achieved from an accessible state using operators in **U:Op**. *Unsafeness* occurs when a prohibited condition **PCnd** can be achieved from an accessible state using operators in **U:Op**. *Superfluousness* occurs when an operator in **A:Op** does not participate in any plan needed to achieve a goal in **A:UGol**.

We now have a definition of a specification problem and criteria for a satisfying solution. Given that one is willing to live under these assumptions and definitions, we argue that construction of a functional specification can be viewed at least partly as a planning process. The specification designer's task is to provide the means for satisfying the user goals and avoiding the prohibited conditions. This requires finding a set of operators such that there exists a sequence of operators from that set (i.e., a plan) that satisfies each user goal but no plans that achieve any of the prohibited conditions.

3. The Specification Process

The designer must specify an operator set **A:Op** and a set of start-up conditions **A:Init**, given a set of user goals **A:UGol** and a set of prohibited conditions **A:PCnd**. One can view this as a three step process: 1) Generate a trial set of operators **T:Op** and start-up conditions **T:Init**. 2) Analyze whether specification **T** is satisfying, i.e., satisfies the policy requirements for artifact **A**. 3) If **T** is non-satisfying, modify **T:Op** and/or **T:Init** to overcome specification problems (e.g., unsafeness, incompleteness). We next describe each of these steps in more detail.

Phase 1: Propose a Specification

In the first phase, ASAP generates a trial set of operators, **T:Op**, as a first cut at producing **A:Op**. To obtain the operators, ASAP calls the planner once for each goal **UGol** in **A:UGol**. Each time, **init** is set to **I:Init** and **ops** is set to **E:Op** ∪ **P:Op**. Any operator from **P:Op** that appears in any plan returned by the planner goes into **T:Op**. Thus, **T:Op** is a subset of **P:Op** that achieves the goals in **A:UGol**.

As an example, suppose we want to set up a simple library system. Our goal is to allow people to use certain books and to keep track of who has what books. **A:UGol** consists of a single conjunctive goal, HAVE (PATRON, BOOK) ∧ CHECKED-OUT (BOOK, PATRON). **I:Init** contains the relations IN-LIBRARY (BOOK) and UNRESTRICTED-EXIT (PATRON, BOOK). The system operator CHECK-OUT (PATRON, BOOK) achieves the goal, so our initial **T:Op** consists of that operator. The contents of **I:Init** become the trial start-up conditions, **T:Init**.

Phase 2: Detect Policy Violations

In the second phase, ASAP looks for faults in the initial specification. Faults to be detected include incompleteness, unsafeness, and superfluous operators. ASAP detects unsafeness by using the planner as a devil's advocate, searching for a plan which achieves a prohibited condition. To do this, ASAP calls the planner with each prohibited condition in **A:PCnd** as a goal. Each time, **init** is set to **T:Init** and **ops** is set to **E:Op** ∪ **T:Op**. If the planner succeeds in finding a plan, it means that the proposed specification would allow a policy violation.

In the example above, we noted that we want to keep a record whenever a book is borrowed. Thus, one policy is that no book should be taken out without being recorded. We represent this as a prohibited condition, HAVE (PATRON, BOOK) ∧ ¬CHECKED-OUT (BOOK, PATRON). The planner finds that, indeed, there is an environmental operator that achieves the prohibited condition, namely, STEAL (PATRON, BOOK). Therefore, the initial specification is non-satisfying, and ASAP goes on to phase three, modification of the specification.

Phase 3: Modify the Specification

The next step is to modify the specification if it is non-satisfying, that is, if user goals cannot be achieved and/or prohibited conditions can. One possibility is to go back to phase one and generate a brand new specification. The problem with this approach is that it does not take advantage of the work that has already been done. We would prefer to modify the specification we have, based on the faults discovered in phase two. There are two ways to modify the specification: by altering **T:Init** or altering **T:Op**.

To modify a specification found to be incomplete, we must add operators or alter the constant conditions so additional operators are enabled. To modify a specification found to be unsafe, we must delete operators or alter the constant conditions so certain operators are disabled. To modify a specification containing superfluous operators, we must remove the extra operator(s) from the operator set. Altering the constant conditions can change the outcome of a plan by enabling or disabling preconditions. This approach has been used as a means of preventing undesirable conditions by McDermott [8] and Carbonell [3].

In our example, the prohibited condition is achieved by an environmental operator. No adjustment to **E:Op** is allowed, so our only option is to alter **T:Init**. We need to ensure that at least one of the preconditions of the offending operator is not true. Suppose the preconditions of STEAL (PATRON, BOOK) are IN-LIBRARY (BOOK) and UNRESTRICTED-EXIT (PATRON, BOOK). Then, to prevent someone from stealing a book from the library, we could either 1) keep no books in the library, or 2) restrict exiting in some way, such as with a magnetic detection device. These changes must involve constant conditions if the operator is to be permanently disabled.

Either one of these modifications will disable the STEAL operator, but each one also disables the goal. Legitimate borrowers as well as thieves will be prevented from taking a book out of the library. Therefore, we will need to modify the specification again.

For our example, no operator exists for obtaining a book unless it is in the library. Thus, modification number one simply fails. However, we do have another check-out operator that deals with modification two. We replace our original check-out with one that includes de-magnetizing the book after the transaction is recorded, call it CHECK-OUT2. In this way, theft is prevented while legitimate patrons are able to check out books.

It is not enough to be able to achieve user goals from the start-up conditions: the goals should be achievable from any accessible state of **A**. Fortunately, it is not necessary to check every accessible state to ensure that the user goals can be achieved. It is only necessary to ensure that, if any precondition of an operator can be deleted, that precondition can also be re-established. Alternatively, it may be possible to provide multiple paths to the same goal, starting from different states.

In our example, we have no way for a second user to obtain the book once it has been checked out. Since one of the preconditions of CHECK-OUT2 is that the book is in the library, and CHECK-OUT2 deletes that condition, ASAP reports that an operator to re-establish the condition is required. Thus, we need to add a RETURN (PATRON, BOOK) operator.

With the suggested modifications, no policies of our example specification are violated, so the specification is satisfying. ASAP returns a specification consisting of the operators CHECK-OUT2 and RETURN in **A:Op** and the condition IN-LIBRARY (BOOK) in **A:Init**.

If no specification can be found which allows achievement of all user goals and avoidance of all prohibited conditions, the policies must be altered. Our current system does not help in the modification of goals or policies, although this seems like a possibility for the future.

4. Research Issues

Viewing specification design as a planning problem brings certain research issues to the foreground. The central issues we are investigating involve the use of abstraction and analogy in specification design. We are looking at three areas in which abstraction and analogy appear useful. First, adaptive planning may be used to suggest modifications to the specification. Second, generalization allows extracting common features of a set of plans. Third, operators can be generated for a new domain by analogy with other domains. In addition, we are looking at ways to restrict the possible specification modifications to be considered.

The Planner

The generation system is built around a hierarchical planner that generates and uses abstract plans [2]. The planner is being used to explore issues in planning by analogy, planning given incomplete knowledge, and dealing with potential plan failures. We are using the design of formal specifications as one application of our planner.

The key features of our planning system are:

- A mechanism that builds up an abstraction hierarchy of operators, given a set of primitive (executable) operators as input. For example, checking out a library book shares certain aspects with checking out a basketball from the PE department. An abstract "check-out" operator is created and made the parent of the two primitive operators.
- A mechanism that builds up an object hierarchy, based on the roles of objects in similar operators. For example, "PE-dept-basketball" and "library-book" play corresponding roles in the two primitive "check-out" operators above. Thus, they both belong to the class of "check-out-able" objects. An abstract object is created to represent this class and to fill the appropriate role in the abstract "check-out" operator.
- A general-purpose, hierarchical planner. Our planner inherits many features from NOAH [10] and SIPE [12].
- A mechanism that generates abstract plans from executable plans by replacing the primitive operators with abstract operators. In this way, the system builds up a library of abstract plans which can be retrieved and specialized when needed.

Adaptive planning

We have implemented a mechanism that builds up an abstraction hierarchy of operators, given a set of primitive (executable) operators as input [2]. For instance, the two check-out operators in the example would be descendents of a single abstract check-out operator in the hierarchy.

The abstraction hierarchy should prove useful in the third phase of specification, modifying the operator set. If an operator is used to achieve a user goal, but also achieves a prohibited condition, it may be possible to find a closely related operator in the abstraction hierarchy which still achieves the goal but does not achieve the prohibited condition. The basic idea for this approach has been described as *adaptive planning* [1].

For instance, an analyst was asked to comment on a functional specification that included an operator that kept a history, for each book, of who had checked the book out in the past. She first commented on the negative aspects of such a query, i.e., that it may allow user confidential information to be given out illegally. This is a case that is also caught by our critic using a case similar to the one discussed previously of one user gaining access to another's ID.

However, she went further by suggesting a modification:

> "Library statisticians are interested in what category of borrower checks out what books. So they can look up and see that faculty checked it out or graduate students, or public borrowers, or even by department. I mean, it can be used for management information. However, you don't really need to know the individual who had it before."

The analyst's proposed modification is from recording the borrower's identity to one of recording the borrower's classification within the university. The effect of the modified query is to give status information about a borrower without identifying the individual.

In our system, as in Alterman's, operators are arranged in a generalization hierarchy. In that hierarchy, the modified query can be viewed as a sibling of the original query, one which satisfies the goal of the original query without allowing the invasion of privacy. The method for finding the sibling operator is discussed in detail in [1].

General plans

Most traditional AI planners stop when they have found a single plan that achieves a goal state. In detecting faults in a specification, however, we would like to know about all plans that lead to a prohibited condition. If possible, we would like to know if there is one change that will disable all of the prohibited plans at the same time. Thus, it would be useful to know the common elements of all of the prohibited plans. If one precondition could be disabled or one operator could be removed to disable many or all of the prohibited plans, many cycles of generate and test could be avoided.

A feature of our planner described in [2] is a mechanism that generates abstract plans from executable plans by replacing the primitive operators with abstract operators. This mechanism should prove useful in finding the most general plans which lead to prohibited conditions. By dropping the details that are unique to one plan, and preserving those aspects common to several plans, we can identify key changes which will disable a large number of similar plans.

Generate new operators

In the first part of the paper, we assumed that the operator database was complete and that every possible operator that could go into a specification was included. While this might be reasonable for certain well-defined domains, it is too limiting if we want to explore novel designs or uncharted domains. One source of new operators is to simply have the user define a new operator whenever it is needed.

Another source of new operators is analogy: using the operators of one domain as templates for the operators in a new domain. Using analogy, ASAP can generate an operator set for a domain it knows nothing about. ASAP "knows about" a domain if its database includes operators and plans for achieving goals in that domain. ASAP can generate an operator set for **A** if it knows about one or more domains which are analogous to **A**. For example, if ASAP has operators and plans about libraries but none about video rental stores, it will still be useful in designing a specification for a video rental system.

The key to this method is the use of an object hierarchy that parallels the operator hierarchy. For example, each check-out operator in Figure 2 has a corresponding "check-out-able" object in the object hierarchy. Given a new object defined in terms of its functional properties, ASAP automatically generates a set of proposed operators based on the operators defined for other objects with the same properties. For example, if ASAP is told that a video-tape is a "check-out-able" object, it will assume that there is a "check-out-video-tape" operator that is a child of the general "check-out" operator.

The user can save some effort by simply telling ASAP that video-tapes are like library-books. ASAP will assume that all operators that apply to library-books (e.g., browse, check-out, copy) have counterparts that apply to video-tapes. However, this method is likely to generate spurious operators (e.g., rip out a page of a video).

The result of this process is a set of new operators that are analogous to operators that have been found

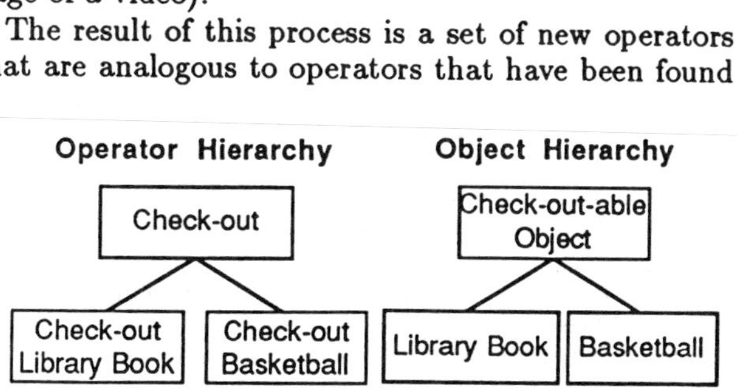

Figure 2. Portions of the operator and object hierarchies

useful in other domains. Stated briefly, we are using mappings provided by the user that tie the new domain into others that we have previously analyzed. Our planner stores its information in such a way that these mappings can be used to generate potential operators for the new domain.

The advantage of using an abstract planning mechanism is that we can find commonalities between the new domain and domains we know more about. These commonalities provide hints about the types of operators that will be needed to achieve our goals in the new domain.

Restricting modifications

It seems clear we must bring some discipline to modifications made to the operator set: a potentially infinite number are possible. We believe that this discipline can at least partially be achieved by representing the resource constraints of the system, and the cost a modification has in terms of resources used.

As an example, what would be the cost of having a staff person oversee (or actually carry out) all queries to the borrowing record, a modification suggested by one analyst to avoid user privacy being violated?

A related issue is trade-offs in the achievement of policies. While in the ideal case we would like to enforce all of the client's policies, the cost of enforcing a policy can often be greater than the cost of allowing the policy to be violated. Again, explicit representation of the cost of the operators and plans used in satisfying a policy is needed in order to evaluate the cost of enforcing that policy. This provides additional restriction on the set of feasible modifications.

Of course, there are other resources than the standard money and time. For instance, in an earlier specification we were working on in the domain of sporting events, the question came up of how to modify the specification to avoid tie games. Here the resource is human endurance. In some games, extra innings are allowed up until some maximum. In boxing, this does not work. Instead, judges are not allowed to produce ties, i.e., we do not allow a tie score after regulation time. In any case, paying attention to overall resources available and representing operator costs provides some restriction on the set of possible modifications.

5. Related research

We have pointed out that policies are often incompatible and therefore require some sort of compromise. Fortunately, conflicts arising in a specification of a well charted domain are typically not novel. Further, solutions to well known conflicts are often themselves well known to experts in the domain. For instance, librarians are well aware of the conflict between allowing long borrowing periods and having resources available to other patrons. How can we make use of known compromises when a conflict is encountered during the critique stage?

Sycara has explored the approach of cataloging compromise solutions in the domain of labor-management bargaining [11]. A member of our group, Bill Robinson, is attempting to incorporate a similar mechanism into a specification designer [9], a tool that we believe may play an important role in the operator selection and modification process.

Feather has begun to classify domain-independent specification changes in terms of the ramifications such changes will have on the existing structure [5]. The goal of this work is to 1) identify what type of specification modification steps lead to conflict, and 2) catalog strategies for dealing with it. In essence, Feather is analyzing the process involved in designing a specification rather than the product that ensues.

6. Limitations and problems

Along with its benefits, our approach has several shortcomings. Phase three, modification of the specification, involves a large number of choices. If a plan which achieves a prohibited condition is discovered, which operator(s) in that plan should be replaced? What operator(s) should be used instead to achieve the desired conditions without achieving the prohibited conditions? If these choices are not guided by heuristic selection rules, the size of the search space makes the problem intractable.

There is still much that is manual about our approach. First, the user must translate policies into user goals and prohibited conditions. These must match relations that are stored in the database of the system. Second, the user must propose a tentative set of start-up conditions. In addition, modification of a non-satisfying specification is currently more manual than automated. Finally, the generation of new operators requires a great deal of user intervention.

Finally, there are many policies that are considered common sense to humans and therefore are frequently not stated explicitly. The policies of avoiding health hazards and operating within the law are normally taken for granted. An automated specification development system should know about these unstated policies in order to recognize specifications in which they are violated.

7. Summary

We have argued that it may be useful to view certain types of specification problems from a planning perspective. In particular, if a specification can be viewed as a set of objects, relations, and operators, and the requirements as user goals and prohibited conditions, then results in AI planning may be brought to bear.

To support our arguments, we have presented a specification design system which uses planning techniques for specification generation, critiquing and modification. The planner is implemented and has been used in developing simple specifications (more complex than the example in this paper). The specifier has been designed and is now being implemented.

We are hoping to find a productive division of labor between the system and the user, according to the abilities of each:

- The system stores and indexes operators for its domain(s) of expertise.
- The user determines the combination of goals and prohibited conditions that is most appropriate for the given application.
- The system examines large numbers of operator sequences and combinations.
- The user provides additional domain-specific expert knowledge.

We expect our system to prove valuable in exploring additional issues in applying planning techniques to specification design.

Acknowledgments

We acknowledge the National Science Foundation for support of this work under grant CCR-8804085. We also thank Marek Lees for his initial insight into the planning view, and Martin Feather for comments on an earlier version of this paper.

References

[1] Alterman, R. 1988. Adaptive planning. *Cognitive Science* **12**, 393-421.

[2] Anderson, J. S. and A. M. Farley. 1988. Plan abstraction based on operator generalization. In *Proceedings of AAAI-88*, St. Paul, 100-104.

[3] Carbonell, J. 1981. Counterplanning: a strategy-based model of adversary planning in real-world situations. *Artificial Intelligence* **16**, 295-329.

[4] Feather, M. 1987. Language support for the specification and development of composite systems. *ACM Transactions on Programming Languages and Systems* **9**.

[5] Feather, M. 1989. Constructing specifications by combining parallel elaborations. *IEEE Transactions on Software Engineering* **15**.

[6] Fickas, S., S. Collins, and S. Olivier. 1987. Problem acquisition in software analysis: a preliminary study. Technical Report 87-04, University of Oregon.

[7] Fickas, S. and P. Nagarajan. 1988. Being suspicious: critiquing problem descriptions. In *Proceedings of AAAI-88*, St. Paul, 19-24.

[8] McDermott, D. 1978. Planning and acting. *Cognitive Science* **2**, 71-109.

[9] Robinson, W. 1989. Integrating multiple specifications using domain goals. To appear in *Proceedings of IWSSD-89*, Pittsburgh.

[10] Sacerdoti, E. 1977. *A Structure for Plans and Behavior.* New York: American Elsevier.

[11] Sycara, K. 1987. Resolving adversarial conflicts: an approach integrating case-based and analytic methods. Georgia Institute of Technology.

[12] Wilkins, D. 1988. *Practical Planning: Extending the Classical AI Paradigm.* Morgan Kaufmann.

Multi-party Specification

Anthony Finkelstein & Hugo Fuks

Imperial College of Science, Technology & Medicine (University of London), Dept. of Computing, 180 Queens Gate, London SW7. acwf@uk.ac.ic.doc

0 Abstract

This paper examines a formal model of how specifications can be constructed from multiple viewpoints and presents some tools to support this approach. The development of specifications is presented as a dialogue in which the viewpoints negotiate, establish responsibilities and cooperatively construct a specification. The model is illustrated by means of some small examples.

Keywords: formal specification, distributed artificial intelligence, dialogue, logic, tool support

1 Introduction

"Specification-in-the-large", that is the development of requirements specifications for systems of substantial complexity and scale, mirrors "programming-in-the-large" in raising a variety of difficulties that lie beyond the clerical problems of handling large amounts of information (Cunningham, Finkelstein et al 1985, Finkelstein & Potts 1987). One such difficulty is that of specification from multiple viewpoints (Niskier 1987). Specification-in-the-large is an activity in which there are many participants - clients, systems analysts, engineers, domain experts and so on. Each has differing perspectives on, and knowledge about, the object system, as well as a variety of skills, roles and so on. In some cases the perspectives may be based on underlying contradictions. To construct a specification the participants must cooperate; that is, contribute to the achievement of a joint understanding.

This contrasts with the approach taken by existing specification schemes, methods and tools which are generally based on specification from a single viewpoint and refined using examples that consolidate this weakness.

Our research objective is to develop a formal understanding of specification from multiple viewpoints so that we can both support the construction of formal specifications and reason about the process of specification itself. We aim to encapsulate cooperative specification development strategies, "replay" these strategies (Wile 1983) and develop appropriate support and coordination tools. To do so we have taken what might be broadly termed an AI approach - we have sought to model the mechanisms which underlie the way people carry out the complex task of specification.

2 Dialogue

Our model of specification from multiple viewpoints treats the development of a specification as a dialogue in which the viewpoints negotiate, establish responsibilities and cooperatively construct an overall specification. The term dialogue, as generally used, refers to a conversation or spoken interaction between two or more partners. This definition is suitable as a starting point. Our approach is related to the more restricted (and informal) metaphor of the contract model of specification, exploited in the ISTAR environment (Lehman 1985), in which tasks are shared through the negotiation and award of "contracts" among developers.

Before introducing our model in detail it may be useful to examine the intuitions that suggested this approach.

The most straightforward of these is that it directly mirrors the conventional setting of requirements specification in which clients and systems analysts sit around a table - the clients explaining the requirements, waving documents in the air and occasionally arguing among themselves while the developers ask guiding questions, seek clarification, point out inconsistencies and raise unanticipated consequences.

Examining the way in which complex specifications are built and documented - in natural language - is a well understood way of developing specification techniques with higher expressiveness (Balzer, Goldman & Wile 1978). The approach is exemplified by Gist (Balzer 1985) and Pure Tell (Horai, Saeki & Enomoto 1987). It is not such a great leap of the imagination to extrapolate from this to using the structure of dialogue as an overall setting.

Less directly we regard formal software development as making interpretations between theories (Maibaum, Veloso & Sadler 1985). This process of interpretation is, we suggest, dialogic in form. A formal account of interpretation based on dialogue is developed in Niskier, Fuks & Sadler (1988).

Finally it is hoped that by having a model which is based on dialogue we might have a convenient framework to understand empirical studies of specification, generally in the form of protocols, which are notoriously difficult to analyse (Soloway 1986).

3 Model

The model we present has two parts: an underlying *viewpoint architecture* and a *dialogue scheme* animated by that architecture. Our model also comes in two basic flavours. Two party dialogues (or multi-party dialogues consisting of many two party dialogues) and true N party (N>2) dialogues. Currently we have a detailed understanding of two party dialogues, which we will illustrate in this paper, and have established the formal underpinning for N party dialogue which will be briefly reviewed.

The underlying vehicle for defining our model is a formal account of dialogue. Such accounts have their roots in a number of different traditions:

the *game theoretic semantics tradition* in which dialogue "games" are used to define the meanings of components of a formal language, for example Lorenz (1982);

the *foundations of logic tradition* in which an understanding of the communicative context of argument is examined to understand the development of different logical traditions, notably Hamblin (1987);

the *computer human interaction tradition* in which representations of dialogues are developed for design and evaluation of user interfaces, for example Schneiderman (1982) and Green (1983);

the *rhetorical or argumentative tradition* in which a model of dialogue provides the normative base for deciding what constitutes rhetorical "competence", for example Allwood (1986);

the *natural language processing tradition* in which computationally tractable models are sought to provide a basis for automatically interpreting and generating dialogues, for example Carbonell (1982);

the *distributed artificial intelligence tradition* in which computational models of multi-agent "negotiation" are constructed to integrate diverse knowledge sources, notably Erman & Lesser (1975), Smith (1980), Smith & Davis (1981), Kornfeld & Hewitt (1981) and Lenat (1975).

We have sought to combine the formal apparatus - dialogue logics - of the foundations of logic tradition with the approach - cooperation and negotiation - of the distributed artificial intelligence tradition. We have explicitly rejected the competitive approach typical of the game theoretic semantics tradition and are not directly concerned with the discourse level issues that dominate both the natural language processing and the rhetorical tradition. The descriptive tools provided by the computer human interaction tradition lack the required expressiveness for the less highly constrained dialogues on which we have focussed.

3.1 Viewpoint Architecture

Figure 1 shows a block diagram of the viewpoint architecture. We have shown two main participants (Viewpoints A & B) in the diagram. Each additional participant in a dialogue (such as Viewpoint N) has a similar structure.

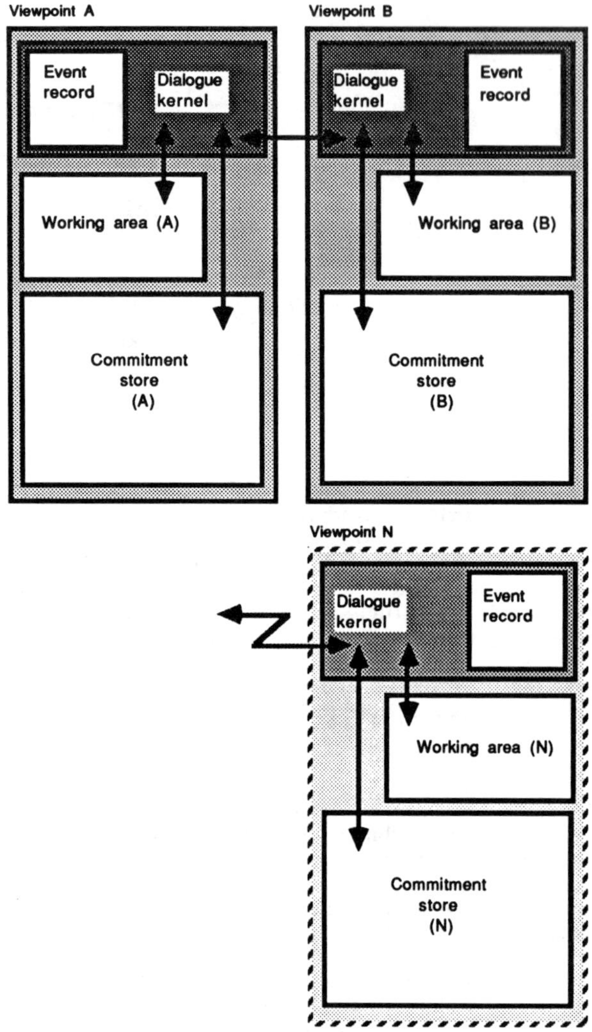

Figure 1 Block diagram of viewpoint architecture

The main building blocks of the viewpoint architecture are as follows:

Viewpoint

A viewpoint is a "logical" participant in the dialogue. We can loosely define a viewpoint as an agent responsible for maintaining a particular perspective. A physical participant in a dialogue may "act the part of" or "present" many logical viewpoints. For example, a librarian might be responsible for both acquisitions policy and disposals. Our model does not as yet include structured groups of viewpoints.

Commitment store

Each viewpoint has a commitment store which holds it's commitments within the dialogue. A commitment is the public engagement to a statement that restricts freedom of action. A commitment to a statement is, in effect, holding yourself out as liable for the consequences of that statement (just as clients in "real-life" software specification "commit" themselves by signing off a requirements statement). As a concept commitment needs to be carefully distinguished from epistemic notions such as belief, which are essentially private and which we exclude from our model both on philosophical and technical grounds. The general status and role of commitments is discussed by Winograd & Flores (1986). In the context of design Thimbleby (1988) suggests that "... abstraction and commitment are inverse processes - an abstraction is an outcome of relaxing commitments and a representation is the outcome of making commitments".

The contents of the commitment store of each participant changes as the dialogue progresses. A viewpoint can read from any store. The only way it can alter the commitments of any viewpoint, including it's own, is through participation in the dialogue. A specification is the pool of commitments that result from such a dialogue, an approach closely akin to that of the requirements analysis method CORE (Mullery (1985).

Working area

The private "sketch-pad" or database of the viewpoint. It contains the internal or working statements which do not have the full status of public engagement. No other viewpoint can directly access the working area nor is there any obligation for the viewpoint to maintain it's consistency. The working area is an essential element of the architecture but is not treated explicitly in the dialogue scheme outlined below.

Event store

The event store keeps a record of the "dialogue events". It is used by the dialogue kernel to maintain the legality of the dialogue. Dialogues are flexible and dynamic, participants make moves to realise their aims based on the revealed "record of play".

Dialogue kernel

The dialogue kernel is the independent controller of a viewpoint. The role of the dialogue kernel is to implement the common dialogue scheme for each (loosely coupled) viewpoint.

In the two party version of the model responsibility for issues such as control of the domain of discourse, initiation and completion of dialogues are implicitly assigned to the individual viewpoints. An alternative approach is to provide each dialogue with an "agenda" which explicitly handles these issues by establishing a larger set of commitments at the level of the dialogue itself (this can be thought of as analogous to the organising role played by a specification method). We are investigating this approach further in the context of N-party dialogues.

3.2 Dialogue Scheme

Formal schemes that fit with the architecture outlined above and with our overall approach to modelling dialogue have been proposed by Hamblin (1971) and more fully worked by Mackenzie (1981, 1985). We have adopted Mackenzie's dialogue system - DC - and, with some changes and substantial reinterpretation, are using it as the basis for validating our intuitions. Below we present a brief overview of the main elements of DC, using our own notation.

The scheme is presented in terms of three important constructs:

(i) Acts

Equivalent to "locutions", "utterances" or "speech acts". Consist of a statement and a modifier, represented **modifier**(Statement). Statements are constructed in a propositional language which includes negation, conditional and conjunction of statements.

Act modifiers are as follows:

Assertions, to be read as "It is the case that Statement", notationally **asserts**(Statement).

Denials, to be read as "I deny that it is the case that Statement", notationally **denies**(Statement).

Questions, to be read as "Is it the case that Statement?", notationally **questions**(Statement).

Withdrawals, to be read as "No commitment to Statement", notationally **withdraws**(Statement).

Challenges, to be read as "Why is it to be supposed that Statement", notationally **why**(Statement).

Resolution demands, to be read as "Resolve your commitments", notationally **resolve**(CS(Viewpoint)).

(ii) Events

Represented by a triple of the form <Stage, Viewpoint, Act>. Stage marks the progress of the dialogue, stage, stage+1 and so on. Viewpoint indicates the current speaker. A dialogue is a sequence of such events.

(iii) Commitments

Represented **committed**(Stage,Viewpoint).

These constructs are used in the rules of the scheme which are divided into three subsets:

(i) Dialogue rules

Establish the "etiquette" or rules governing the legitimate shape of the interaction, they provide a way of maintaining a "legal" dialogue.

For example:

<u>Dialogue rule Quest (Questions):</u>

After the questioning of a statement (**questions**(Statement)), the next event must be either the assertion (confirmation) of that statement, it's withdrawal or it's denial (**asserts**(Statement), **withdraws**(Statement) or **denies**(Statement)).

No legal dialogue of length stage+1 contains an event <stage-1,hearer,**questions**(Statement)> unless it also contains an event <stage,speaker,**asserts**(Statement)> v <stage,speaker,**withdraws**(Statement)> v <stage,speaker,**denies**(Statement)>.

(ii) Commitment rules

Set out how acts affect the commitment store of each viewpoint (we see these changes to the commitments as more or less equivalent to the "high level edits" described by Feather (1987)).

For example:

Commitment rule W:

After a withdrawal the statement is removed from the speaker's commitment store, the hearer's store remains unchanged.

After <stage,speaker,**withdraws**(Statement)>
committed(stage+1,speaker)=
    committed(stage,speaker) - {Statement}
committed(stage+1,hearer)=
    committed(stage,hearer)

(iii) Argument forms

Define, syntactically, the form of reasoning permissible within the dialogue and common to it's participants. Our presentation of DC primarily involves "modus ponens", though addition of other schemas to fit various logical tastes is a relatively simple matter. The argument form mechanism for modus ponens is embedded in the rule below:

Commitment rule G:

After an assertion (AnotherStatement) which occurs as a reply to a challenge (**why**(Statement)) both views are committed to the reply (AnotherStatement) and to the conditional (AnotherStatement -> Statement).

After <stage,speaker,**asserts**(AnotherStatement)>
where the preceding dialogue event was
<stage-1,speaker,**why**(Statement)>
committed(stage+1,speaker)=**committed**(stage,speaker) ∪
    {AnotherStatement, AnotherStatement -> Statement}
committed(stage+1,hearer)= **committed**(stage,hearer) ∪
    {AnotherStatement, AnotherStatement -> Statement}

As can be seen, not only was {AnotherStatement} added to both stores, as would be expected, but also {AnotherStatement -> Statement}. If we take {AnotherStatement, AnotherStatement -> Statement} and apply the modus ponens rule to it, we deduce {Statement} - exactly what was originally challenged.

4 Examples

Our overall approach may be clarified by looking at some examples. We shall use a small case study concerning description of an automated travel ticketing system. In this case study various statements about travel and travel discounts are distributed between the working area of two viewpoints.

Figures 2, 3 & 4 below, differ slightly from Figure 1 for ease and economy of presentation. The figures show two viewpoints called respectively A and B each represented by a shaded box. Each viewpoint has a working area with different contents (WA (A) and WA (B)). Commitments are represented in separate stores (CS (A') and CS (B')). The current dialogue event is given in a box at the top of the diagram alongside an arrow that points from the originator of the event (speaker) to the recipient (hearer). The commitments stores resulting from that dialogue event (CS (A) and CS (B)) are shown at the bottom of the diagram. Other figures just show the commitment stores with the original commitments in a box above a bar showing the dialogue event and the resulting commitments below. These commitments may in turn be altered by a subsequent event.

Figure 2 illustrates the addition of information to a description (Example A). Let us follow what happens in the process of making this addition.

Initially the commitment store is empty. The speaker (B) asserts the statement, in this case *ticket* ["can obtain a ticket"] (an immediate consequence of the content of its working area (*discount_fare, discount_fare -> ticket*) ["paid a discount fare" and "paying a discount fare implies that you can obtain a ticket]), and so by:

Commitment rule S:

If a statement has been made which is not the reply to a challenge then the speaker and the hearer are obliged to place it in their commitment store.

After <stage,speaker,**asserts**(Statement)>where the preceding dialogue event was not
<stage-1, hearer,**why**(AnotherStatement)>
committed(stage+1,speaker)=
    committed(stage,speaker) ∪ {Statement}
committed(stage+1,hearer)=
    committed(stage,hearer) ∪ {Statement}

The rule S defines an important feature of this dialogue scheme. A viewpoint is committed to anything stated by another viewpoint. This commitment can only be removed by a subsequent withdrawal or challenge.

The resulting commitment stores are CS (A) and CS (B). Both A and B are committed to *ticket* and must answer for any consequences of this commitment and other commitments added in a similar manner. This process of straightforwardly adding commitments, which we can clearly continue, can be termed "simple elaboration". An enhanced description or specification is built up in the commitment stores and shared between the participating viewpoints.

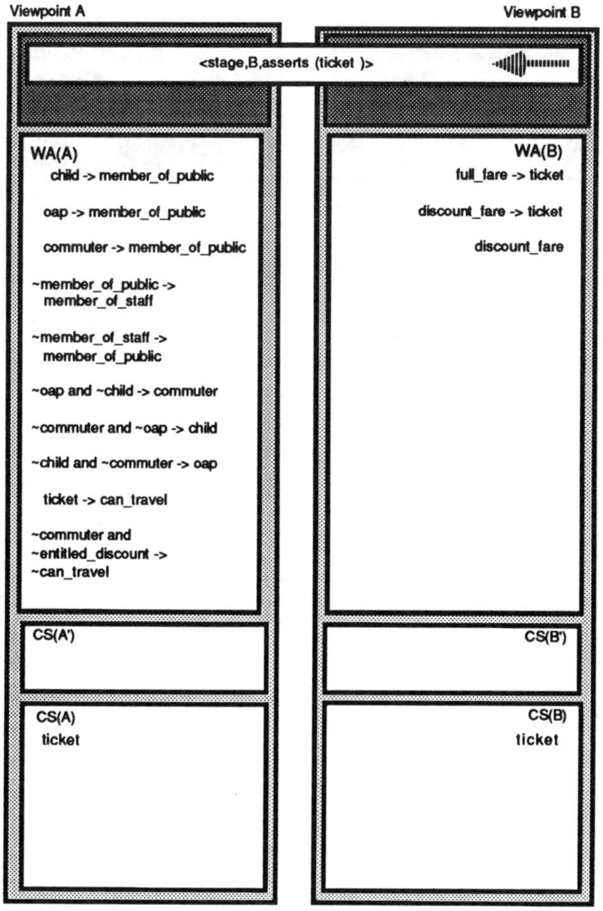

Figure 2 Example A (1 of 1)

Let us now consider a slightly more complicated example (Example B) illustrating refinement of a description. We start at a point some way into a set of dialogues (Figure 3) with CS (A') containing a commitment to *child -> ticket* ["a child can obtain a ticket"]. Viewpoint A, the speaker and initiator of this part of the dialogue, asks something along the lines of "why is it to be supposed that a child can obtain a ticket?".

It should be noted that in this setting asking why is a demand for evidence, not for an explanation. So by:

Commitment rule Y:

After a challenge the hearer adds the challenged statement to it's own commitment store and the speaker removes the statement from it's commitment store, replacing it by the challenge itself. This is necessary to avoid the problem of circularity ("Why is the book on loan?","Because it is out of the library!","Why is it out of the library?","Because it is on loan!!" and so on).

After <stage,speaker,**why**(Statement)>
committed(stage+1,speaker)=
  committed(stage,speaker) -
    {Statement} ∪ {**why**(Statement)}
committed(stage+1,hearer)=
  committed(stage,hearer) ∪ {Statement}

Observe that the placing of {Statement} in the hearer's commitment store forces a reaction - either a challenge to "give a good reason" for the statement or a withdrawal in order not to be committed to it. As a last resort the hearer may demand a resolution over the speaker's commitment store, we will illustrate this in a subsequent example.

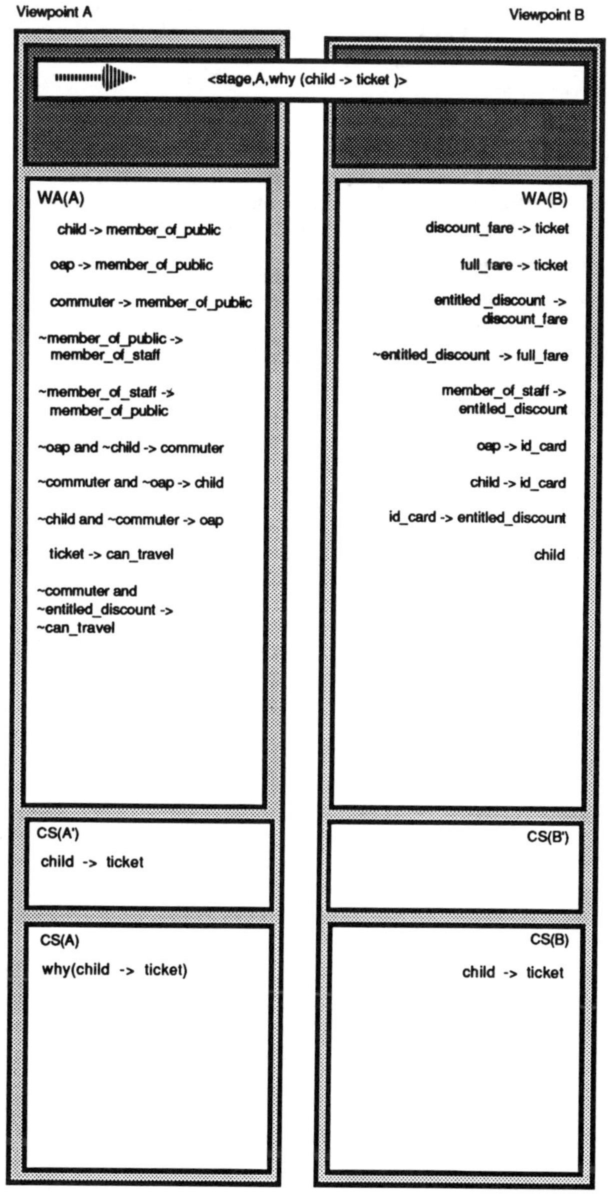

Figure 3 Example B (1 of 5)

CS (A) and CS (B) now form the commitments for the next stage of the dialogue and reappear as the new CS (A') and CS (B') shown in Figure 4. Viewpoint B replies to maintain dialogue legality as indicated by:

Dialogue rule Form:

Each viewpoint contributes an act at a time, in turn each act must be well formed that is a statement, question etc.

No legal dialogue contains an event <stage,given_viewpoint,Act> if it also contains an event <stage-1,given_viewpoint,AnotherAct> or if Act is not properly constructed.

The act that follows is the assertion of *discount_fare* which is taken from the statement contained in the working area that *discount_fare -> ticket*. The resulting commitment stores CS (A) and CS (B) are derived according to the rule below:

<u>Commitment rule G (for the challenge of an implication):</u>

After an assertion (AnotherStatement) which occurs as a reply to a challenge (**why**(Statement1 -> Statement2)) both views are committed to the reply (AnotherStatement) and to the conditional (AnotherStatement -> Statement2).

After <stage,speaker,**asserts**(AnotherStatement)>
where the preceding dialogue event was
<stage-1,speaker,**why**(Statement1 -> Statement2)>

committed(stage+1,speaker)=**committed**(stage,speaker) ∪
{AnotherStatement, AnotherStatement -> Statement2}

committed(stage+1,hearer)= **committed**(stage,hearer) ∪
{AnotherStatement, AnotherStatement -> Statement2}

Figures 5, 6 & 7 show the continuation of this dialogue in which the refinement (all the steps required to show why a child can obtain a ticket) is completed in a constructive manner by a process of "dialogue led" backward chaining.

Note that in Figure 5 Viewpoint A can challenge either *discount_fare -> ticket* or *discount_fare*. It chooses to challenge *discount_fare* because this was the actual reply of B, while *discount_fare -> ticket* is a construct of the commitment rule G.

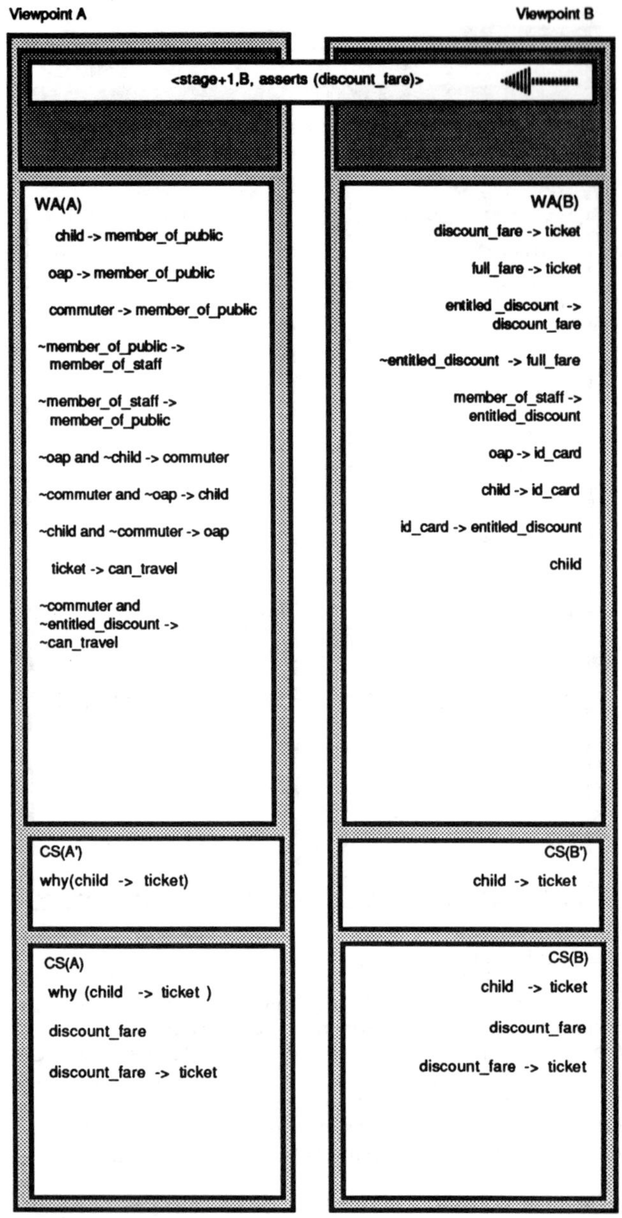

Figure 4 Example B (2 of 5)

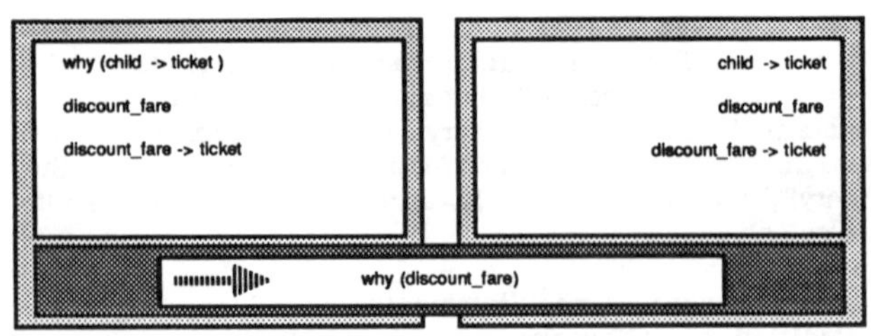

Figure 5 Example B (3 of 5)

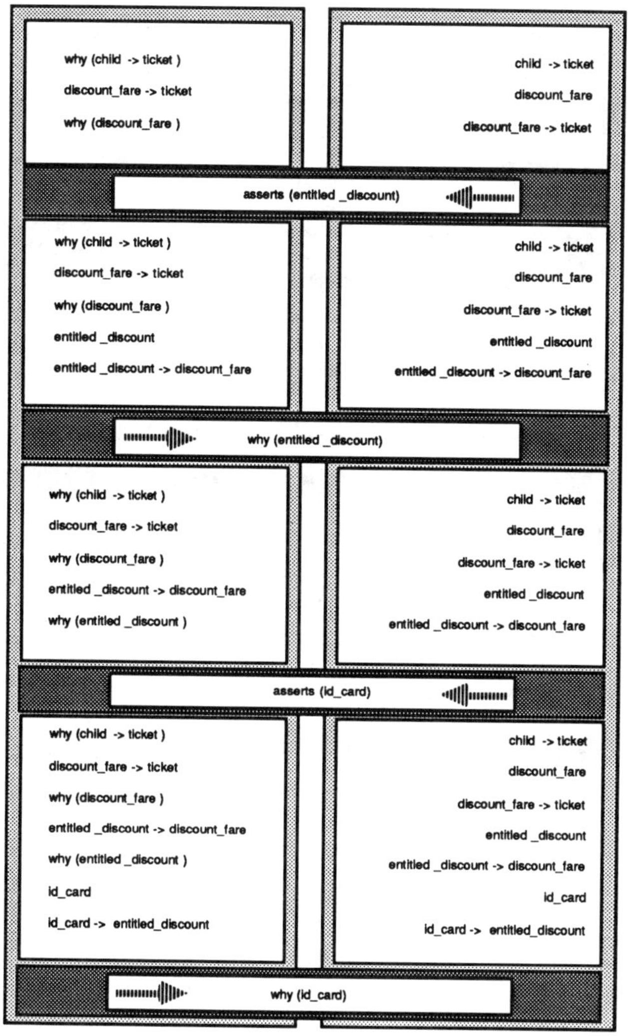

Figure 6 Example B (4 of 5)

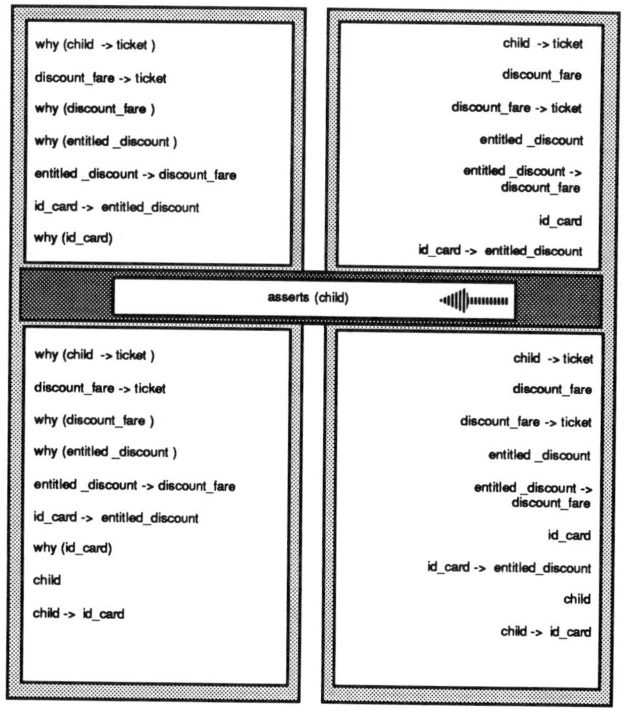

Figure 7 Example B (5 of 5)

The final example (Example C) we will consider is again more complex, illustrating a number of features including progressive verification of one viewpoint with respect to another. By looking at WA(A) in Figure 8 it should be easy to spot the inconsistency which has been introduced (*~id_card*) [" it is not the case that there is an id_card "], as a result of which notice the inconsistency that may possibly arise between Viewpoint B (which is working on the basis of *oap -> entitled_discount* ["oap's are entitled to a discount"] and Viewpoint A.

In Figure 8 Viewpoint B challenges *oap -> entitled_discount*. The resulting commitment stores, CS (A) and CS (B) are derived similarly to the previous examples.

B replies (Figure 9) by asserting *id_card* obtained by matching with the implication *id_card -> entitled_discount* and the commitments are established according to Commitment rule G (for the challenge of an implication) which we have also seen before. B now challenges *id_card* and A withdraws it being unable to deny it due to Dialogue rule Chall which, substantially abbreviated, states:

<u>Dialogue rule Chall (Challenges):</u>

The reply to a challenged statement must be the withdrawal of the statement <u>or</u> it must be the resolution demand of an immediate consequence conditional of the statement whose consequent is the statement and whose antecedant is a conjunction of statements to which the challenger is committed <u>or</u> it must be a statement to which the challenger is not committed.

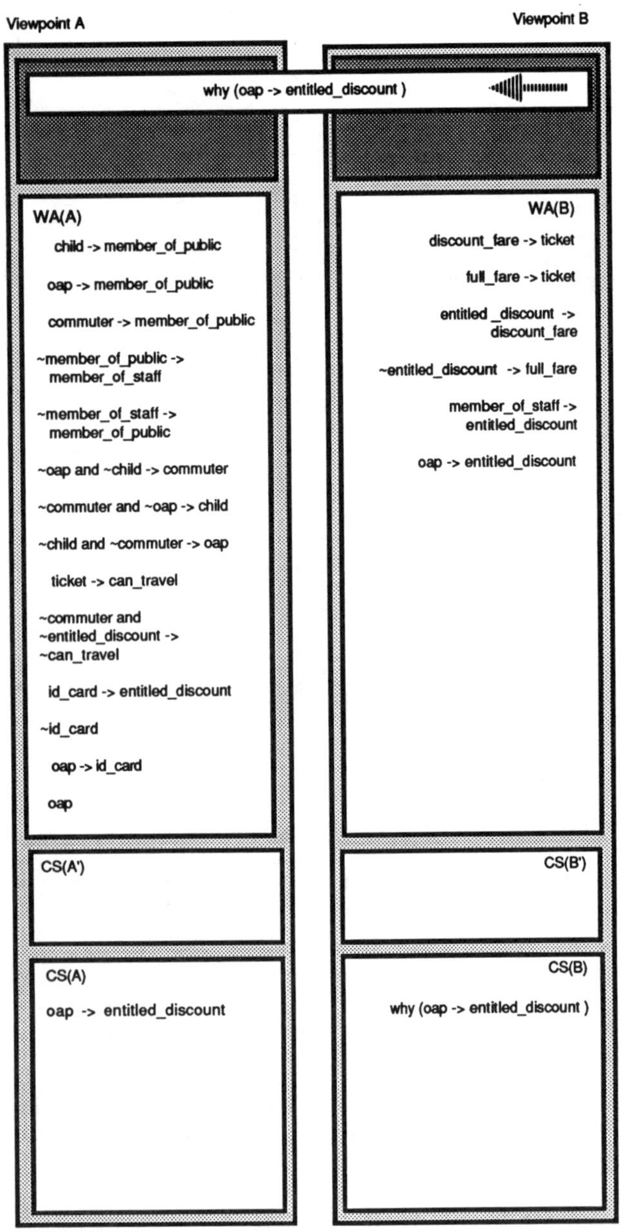

Figure 8 Example C (1 of 5)

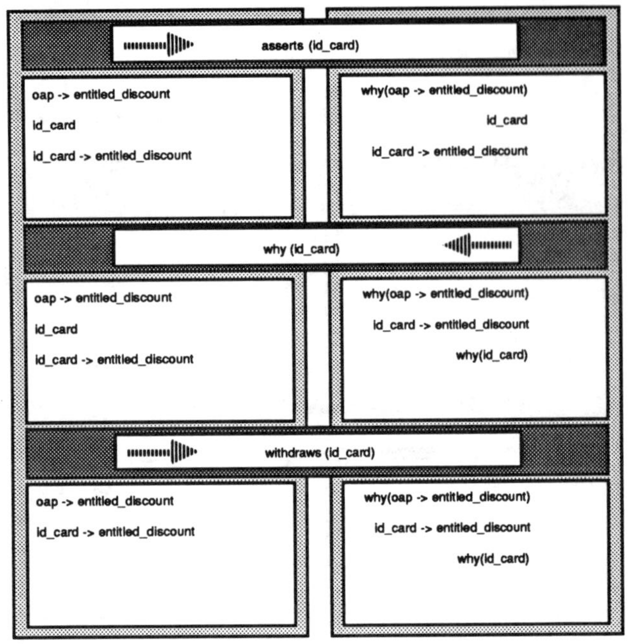

Figure 9 Example C (2 of 5)

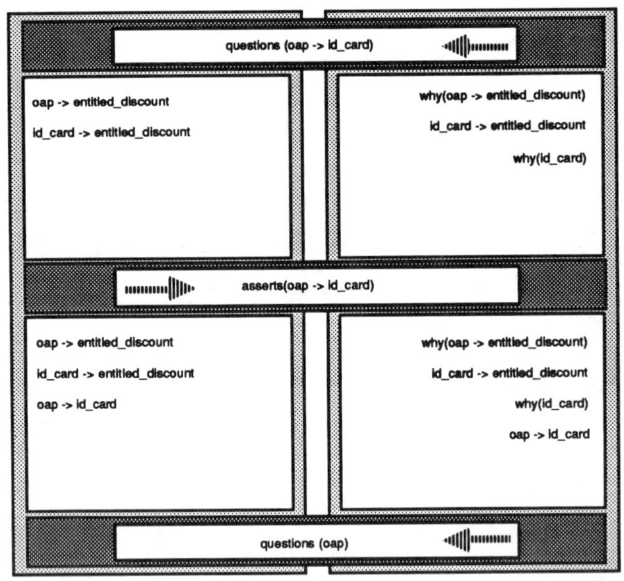

Figure 10 Example (3 of 5)

Some straightforward question and answer follows with the results determined by Commitment rule S above and:

Commitment rule Q:
Questions do not affect commitment stores.

After <stage,speaker,**questions**(Statement)>
committed(stage+1,speaker)=**committed**(stage,speaker)
committed(stage+1,hearer)= **committed**(stage,hearer)

By Figure 11 Viewpoint B questions *id_card*, which it is free to question because it is not on A's commitment store, and A, as a result of an inconsistency deep in it's working area, denies it with the resulting commitments derived by Commitment rule D:

Commitment rule D:

If a denial of a statement has been made then the speaker and the hearer are obliged to place the negation of the statement in their commitment store.

After <stage,speaker,**denies**(Statement)>
committed(stage+1,speaker)=

committed(stage,speaker) ∪ {~Statement}
committed(stage+1,hearer)=

committed(stage,hearer) ∪ {~Statement}

B immediately demands that A, having denied an immediate consequence of it's commitments resolve it's commitment store, which is now inconsistent (using modus ponens we have *{oap,oap ->id_card} —> id_card* which is of course inconsistent with *~id_card*):

Commitment rule R:

Resolution demands do not affect commitment.

After <stage,speaker,**resolve**(CS(hearer))>
committed(stage+1,speaker)=**committed**(stage,speaker)
committed(stage+1,hearer)=**committed**(stage,hearer)

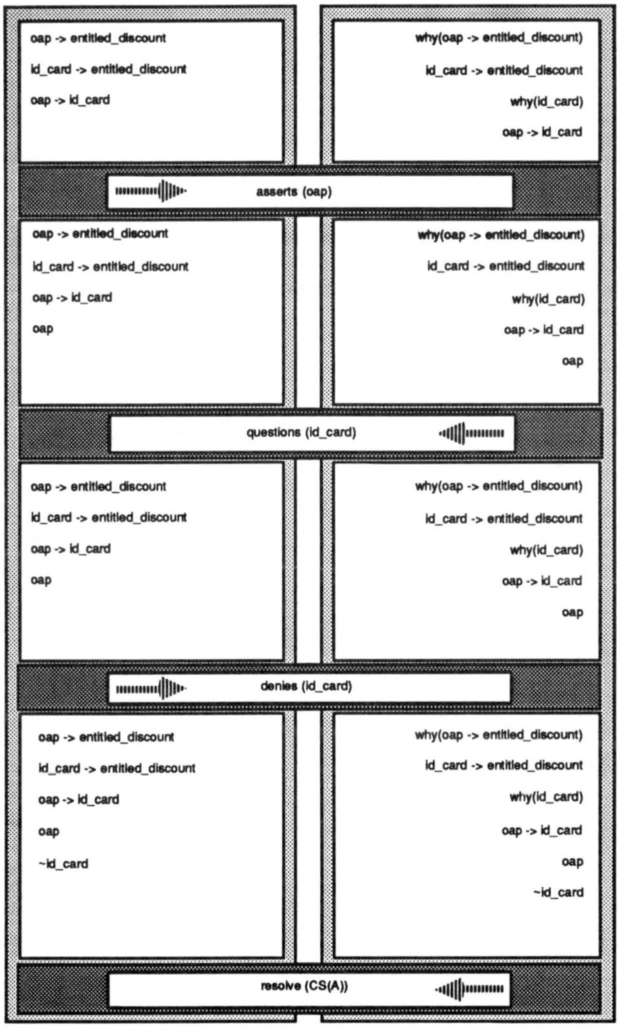

Figure 11 Example C (4 of 5)

In Figure 12 Viewpoint A withdraws it's previous denial (it is constrained to do so by the dialogue rules) restoring consistency by adjusting the commitments according to Commitment rule W given in our overview of the dialogue scheme.

B follows suit by also withdrawing the inconsistency, which if not removed would now leave it liable to a resolution demand from A, and so the dialogue concludes with a shared description and discovery of the "misunderstanding" hidden in A's working area.

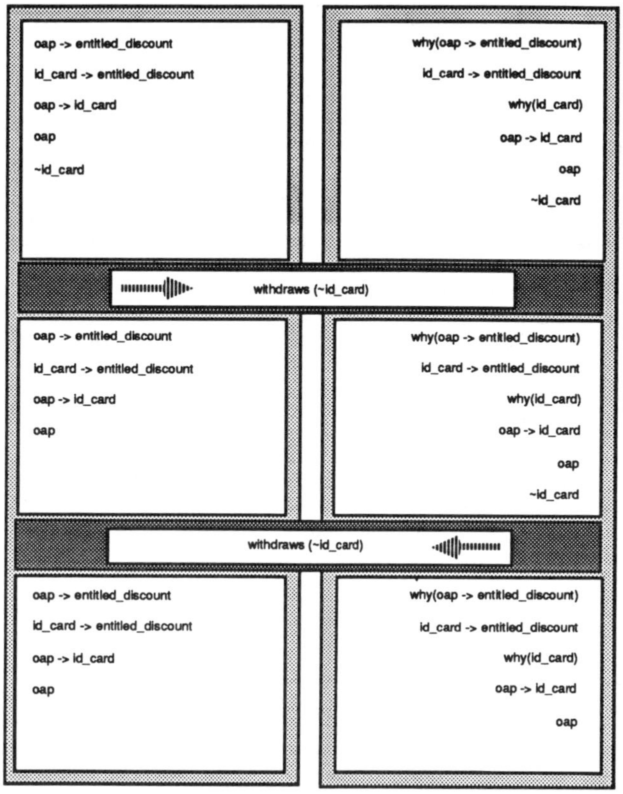

Figure 12 Example C (5 of 5)

5 N-party

An outline of the features necessary to extend the DC dialogue scheme to N-party (N>2) has been developed. The primary element of this extension is the addition of a typed interface to viewpoints that filters commitents. This addition introduces the idea of an audience and substantially changes the way in which the progress of the dialogue is marked, a change which in turn necessitates changes in the basic constructs of our scheme. Dialogue acts are grouped into those which are directed, that is intended to elicit a response from a specified viewpoint, and those which are general, to which any viewpoint can respond. Changes in the form of the two party DC rules are required to accommodate the enhancements notably additional commitment rules to prevent circularity in argument. A number of small examples have been developed and investigated using the outline scheme however there still remain difficulties that relate to the coordination of viewpoints and conventional distributed processing problems such as fairness. The agenda, briefly discussed earlier, provides a structure within which these issues might be resolved, this is the subject of further work.

6 Automated support

Our approach to specification development clearly requires automated support. Such support serves two purposes: to act as a workbench while developing an improved understanding of the model and enhancing dialogue schemes (without support even relatively simple examples are awkward to handle); to be used as the core of a specification support environment based on the principles we have outlined. In such an environment replaying a "development history" would be equivalent to running through a record of dialogue events (this can be compared to the approach of Conklin 1989). In principle it would also be possible to record and replay generalised dialogue "strategies" (an elaboration strategy, verification strategy and so on).

We have developed two dialogue support systems (IC~DC One & IC~DC Two) which animate, albeit in a simple minded way, the dialogue scheme. These tools allow the user to develop simple dialogues like the examples above and then replay them in whole or in part. IC~DC One is written in Prolog and has been used to help us to understand and enhance the dialogue rules. IC~DC Two is written in Smalltalk-80 and has been used to investigate an appropriate architecture for a specification support environment and N-party extensions to the model.

In both tools the dialogues are monitored for legality and illegal dialogues can be explained and rolled back to a legal state. Users may view the commitment stores of the participating views and may change the course of the dialogue by editing the commitment stores directly.

7 Conclusions

We have presented dialogue as a basis for constructing specifications from multiple viewpoints. This approach combines an intuitively appealing model with a non-classical formal framework. We have developed a detailed understanding of, and automated support for, cooperation and negotiation of two viewpoints and laid the ground work for N-party cooperation. The model has been validated by experience on a large number of small examples. Our approach links work on specification with advances in the foundations of logic, linguistic philosophy, distributed artificial intelligence (in which area we believe our model makes some contribution) and the use of social metaphors in computing.

Having made a radical departure from existing models it should stressed that there remains a substantial amount of foundational work to be done to make extended dialogue models which are both computationally tractable and formally sound. To this end we are currently engaged in the construction of a dialogic framework for theorem proving (Fuks, Pequeno & Sadler 1988). In this work we are developing an idea posed by Hintikka (1973), that the act of proving a theorem can be seen as a dialogue between "nature" and the logician.

It is important to emphasise that our model is very sparse. By basing our work on a formal model of argumentation there are practical limitations in both the underlying language and the dialogic strategies we can capture. Observational studies of specification construction (Fickas, Collins & Olivier 1987) show clearly the sophisticated strategies, such as example generation, which are employed during this activity. We aim, within our overall framework, to be able to capture such strategies but in doing so we must of necessity make the delicate balance between this concern and the formal properties of our model. Our argument is not that the strategies we have succeeded in capturing are sufficient in themselves for understanding specification but rather that our approach provides a foundation on which such an understanding may be built.

Our immediate aim is to continue work revising and extending the dialogue schemes, including generalising dialogue strategies, with the long term objective of developing a full specification support environment based on the approach we have outlined. Our vision of the future sees dialogue as providing the logical equivalent of Unix-style pipes and filters to support the communication of complex formal objects between distributed and cooperating communities of tools and users.

Acknowledgements

The authors would like to thank their colleagues and students most notably Wayne Butcher who has been responsible for implementing IC~DC Two, also Martin Sadler and Celso Niskier for the lively critical discussion which has contributed significantly to the work this paper reports. Hugo Fuks is supported by the Brazilian National Research Council CNPq, grant 202471/86-cc.

References

Allwood, J. (1986); Logic and Spoken Interaction; In: Myers,Brown & McGonigle (Eds), Reasoning and Discourse Processes, Academic Press Cognitive Science Series, pp 67-94.

Balzer, R. (1985); A 15 Year Perspective on Automatic Programming; IEEE Trans. Software Engineering; SE-11,11,pp 1257-1267.

Balzer, R. Goldman, N. & Wile, D. (1978); Informality in Program Specifications; IEEE Trans. Software Engineering; SE-4,2, pp 94-103.

Carbonell, J.G. (1982); Meta-Language Utterances in Purposive Discourse; Carnegie-Mellon University Tech. Report, CMU-CS-82-125.

Conklin, J. (1989); Design Rationale and Maintainability; Proc. 22nd Hawaii International Conference on Systems Sciences, V2, pp 533-539, IEEE CS Press.

Cunningham, J. Finkelstein, A. Goldsack, S. Maibaum, T. & Potts, C. (1985); Formal Requirements Specification - The Forest Project; Proc. 3rd IWSSD; pp 186-191, IEEE CS Press.

Erman, L. & Lesser, V. (1975); A Multi-Level Organization for Problem Solving Using Many, Diverse, Cooperating Sources of Knowledge; Proc. IJCAI-75, pp 483-489.

Feather, M. (1987); Constructing Specifications by Combining Parallel Elaborations; To appear IEEE Trans. Software Engineering.

Fickas, S. Collins, S. & Olivier, S. (1987); Problem Acquisition in Software Analysis: a preliminary study; University of Oregon Tech. Report, CIS-TR-87-15.

Finkelstein, A. & Potts, C. (1987); Building Formal Specifications Using "Structured Common Sense"; Proc. 4th IWSSD; IEEE CS Press.

Fuks, H. Pequeno, M. & Sadler, M.(1988); A Dialogic Framework for Theorem Proving, Imperial College, Department of Computing Tech. Report, DoC 88/4.

Green, M. (1983); Report on Dialogue Specification tools; In: Pfaff (Ed) Proc. Wrkshp. User Interface Management Systems 1983; Springer-Verlag.

Hamblin, C. (1971); Mathematical Models of Dialogue; Theoria, V2, pp130-155.

Hamblin, C (1987); Imperatives; Basil Blackwell, Oxford.

Hintikka, J (1973); Logic, Language-Games and Information; Clarendon Press, Oxford.

Horai,H. Saeki, M. & Enomoto, H. (1987); Specification Based Software Development System Pure Tell, IIAS Research Report No. 73.

Kornfeld, W. & Hewitt, C. (1981); The Scientific Community Metaphor; IEEE Trans Systems, Man & Cybernetics, SMC-11,1, pp 24-32.

Lehman, M. (1985); Approach to a Disciplined Development Process - The ISTAR Integrated Project Support Environment; Imperial College Dept. of Computing Tech Report 85/19.

Lenat, D. (1975); Beings: Knowledge as Interacting experts; Proc. IJCAI-75, pp126-133.

Lorenz, K. (1982); On the Criteria for the choice of Rules of Dialogic Logic; In Barth & Martens (Eds), Argumentation: approaches to theory formation, SLCS V8, John Benjamins, Amsterdam.

Mackenzie, J. (1981); The Dialectics of Logic; Logique et Analyse, V24, pp 159-177.

Mackenzie, J. (1985); No Logic before Friday; Synthese, V63, pp 329-341.

Maibaum,T., Veloso, P. & Sadler, M. (1985); A Theory of Abstract Data Types for Formal Development: bridging the gap?; Proc. Colloq. Software Engineering Berlin 1985; LNCS 186, Springer Verlag.

Mullery, G. (1985); Acquisition — Environment; In Paul, M. & Siegert, H. (Eds), Distributed Systems: methods and tools for specification, LNCS 190, Springer Verlag.

Niskier, C. (1987); Using Multiple Views in Software Specification; Proc. 5th Workshop on Formal Specification of Abstract Data Types, Gullane, Scotland.

Niskier, C., Fuks, H. & Sadler, M. (1988); Changing Views in Software Specification: interpretation between theories using dialogue; (In preparation).

Schneiderman, B. (1982); Multiparty Grammars and Related Features for Defining Interactive Systems; IEEE Trans Systems, Man & Cybernetics, SMC-12,1, pp 148-154.

Smith, R. (1980); The Contract Net Protocol: High-Level Communication and Control in a Distributed Problem Solver; IEEE Trans. Computers, C-29,12, pp1104-1113.

Smith, R. & Davis, R. (1981); Frameworks for Cooperation in Distributed Problem Solving; IEEE Trans Systems, Man & Cybernetics, SMC-11,1, pp 61-69.

Soloway, E. (1986); Meeting the Challenge of Programming-in-the-Large, 1st Workshop on Empirical Studies of Programmers 1986, pp 263-268; Ablex Publishing Corp.

Thimbleby, H. (1988); Delaying Commitment; IEEE Software; V5 N3, pp 78-86.

Wile D. (1983); Program Developments: Formal Explanations of Implementations; CACM 26(11), pp 902-911.

Winograd, T. & Flores, F. (1986); Understanding Computers and Cognition: A New Foundation For Design; Ablex Publishing Corp.

The Use of Lexical Affinities in Requirements Extraction

Yoëlle S. Maarek* and Daniel M. Berry§

Computer Science Department, Technion, Haifa 32000, Israel

Abstract

The use of lexical affinities to help a human requirements analyst find abstractions in problem descriptions is explored. It is hoped that a lexical affinities finding tool can be used as part of an environment to help organize the sentences and phrases of a natural language problem description to aid the requirements analyst in the extraction of requirements. An experiment to confirm its effectiveness is described.

1. INTRODUCTION

The first steps in the development of any computational system should be the writing of requirements with the client's help. It may be necessary to build a prototype first, but ultimately before building a production-quality version, it is necessary to agree upon what is to be in the system. Winchester and Estrin [34] list a number of requirements for the requirements themselves. The main of these from the programmer-client perspective are that the requirements must be understandable to both the customers and the designers and builders; the parts of the requirements must be consistent with each other; and the requirements must be complete so that the designers and builders do not have to make unintended value judgements during their work.

This paper deals ultimately with, describes, and determines the effectiveness of one tool designed to assist in one part of the process of writing requirements. It is essential that the reader understand the context in which this tool is expected to operate. Hence, Sections 2 through 5 are devoted to briefly describing this context.

2. THE PROBLEM

Many system design or programming methods, e.g, those of Jackson [19], Parnas [26], Booch [10], Myers [23], Orr [24,25], etc., start from a clear statement of the requirements and show how to arrive at a design of a program or even at a program meeting these requirements. However, none of these methods really explain how these requirements are obtained in the first place. It seems clear to us (at least) that the writing of the requirements is a *major* part of the problem, and that once these are available, the arrival at an implementation, by comparison, is relatively straightforward.

Large E type [20] software, for which it is difficult or even impossible to obtain clear requirements, is usually developed for a client organization in which there are many people who have some view or say as to what the desired system should do. These views range from being totally unrelated to each other to being totally inconsistent with each other. It is no wonder that the distillation of these views into a consistent, complete, and unambiguous statement of the requirements, albeit in natural language, is a *major* part of the problem of developing software which meets the client's needs. Therefore, it is essential to have methods and tools that help in distilling these many views into coherent requirements.

3. PAST WORK

There are already a variety of systems, tools, and methods for dealing with requirements. These include SADT [28,27], IORL [31], PSL/PSA [32], RDL [34], RSL [5,6,7], RML [11] and Burstin's prototype [12] tool. The first two are graphically oriented, and the second of these is automated. The remainder work from highly constrained subsets of English consisting of sentences, each of which states one requirement to which the final implementation must adhere. These sentences can be considered as relations in a database. Those which are automated have tools for working with the sentences and abstractions of the requirements document once these sentences and abstractions have been recognized and stated. Due to space limitations, only those having a direct impact on this work are described in detail herein. A more complete discussion can be found in [3]

Burstin's prototytpe tool allows tuples of a relation, i.e., sentences, each with a verb and objects, to be organized into a hierarchy of abstractions. Each abstraction contains those sentences sharing a common collection of objects, with the verbs representing procedures of the abstraction. There are tools for introducing and moving sentences to and from abstractions and for placing and moving abstractions in the hierarchy. There is also a rudimentary application-oriented expert system that helps recognize when two or more phrases of sentences may be talking about the same thing, e.g., "plane" and "airplane" or "passenger" and "flier."

All of the mentioned systems are useful for working with sentences and abstractions of a requirements document, once they are recognized and formed. Organizations implementing and using two of these, PSL/PSA and SREM, report much user satisfaction [32,7,30].

It is interesting that all of the above requirements analysis systems deal with relations and that all but the first two, which are not picture-oriented, have gone to the use of a relational database for storing the relations. All can be used to support an abstraction-based requirement development which leads naturally to an abstraction-based software development [9].

However, none of the methods and tools give much help in actually obtaining the sentences in the first place and in recognizing the relevant abstractions, especially in the context of a large client organization. The descriptions of all of the methods either fail to mention how to get the sentences or say something to the effect of "get them and write them down" as if there were nothing to it.

Teichroew and Hershey [32] offer that "since most of the data must be obtained through personal contact, interviews will still be required." PSA does help this gathering process in that its "intermediate outputs ... also provide convenient checklists for deciding what additional information is needed and for recording it for input."

Alford [5] says that the "SREM steps address the sequence of activities and usage of RSL and REVS to generate and validate the requirements. It

Address correspondence to the second author.

§ This work was supported in parts by the University of California MICRO program, Unisys Corporation, and NCR Corporation.

* Current Affiliation: IBM T.J. Watson Research Center, P.O.B. 704, Yorktown Heights, NY 10598

assumes [italics are not in the original] that system function and performances have been allocated to the data processor, and have been collected into a Data Processing Subsystem Performance Requirement or DPSPR."

Even eight years later, Scheffer, Stone, and Rzepka [30], from a completely different company which had been using SREM, state only that the "initial input to SREM is a system specification that is translated into RSL and interpreted to determine the interfaces with the outside world, the messages across these interfaces, and the required processing relationships and flows."

The first step of the TAGS method [31] is the conceptualization step, "User concepts and requirements are used to develop a conceptual model that is the basis for subsequent engineering." This conceptual model is the top level SBD. In the cited article, there is advice on the issues that should be dealt with in arriving at it. However, no tools are provided, since the TAGS method deals with activities that follow the production of this first SBD.

Therefore, we feel that the gap between the initial fuzzy natural language statements from the individuals in the client organization to the sentences, i.e., relations, with which these tools work is still too large. Methods and tools are needed to close this gap.

4. ENVISIONED REQUIREMENTS GATHERING ENVIRONMENT

We ultimately envision an integrated environment, REGEE, for gathering, sifting, and writing requirements. This environment may very well be part of a larger environment used for software development, deployment, and maintenance [1,2]. REGEE is in the very rudimentary prototyping stage, as we do not understand the process it is supposed to assist. For now, REGEE is described as helping the human requirements analyst (RA) massage transcripts of interviews with members of a client organization into a consistent, complete, unambiguous, coherent, and concise statement of what the organization wants. We do not care what language is being used either for the interview transcripts or for the final requirements. REGEE should support any possibility. Usually the input, transcript language will be some natural language, possibly with pictures [17]. However, the output language, in which the requirements are written, can be anything from natural language, possibly with pictures, to predicate calculus; in particular, it should be possible to use any of the requirements expression languages mentioned in Section 3.

We do not know enough about effective requirements writing in order to be able to codify the process. Thus at least for now, a completely automated expert-system approach is out of the question. We therefore envision an environment consisting of clerical tools that help with the tedious, error-prone steps of what one particular human RA, the second author, does.

We view a requirements document both in the process of being written and in final form as a network, very often a hierarchy, of nodes each denoting an abstraction and containing a description of all that is known and required about the abstraction. The arcs between the nodes can be used to describe the "uses" relation or any other basis for organizing the set of abstractions.

REGEE needs two basic kinds of tools,

1. to help identify the abstractions that will make the nodes from the transcripts of the interviews, and
2. to help organize the abstractions into a network of abstraction-nodes, each to contain a consistent, complete, unambiguous, coherent, and concise description of that abstraction.

This paper deals with a proposed tool of the first kind, a lexical affinities finder, to be described below. To understand the rationale behind the lexical affinities finder, it is useful to understand the envisioned tool of the second kind. We are building a significant enhancement of the Burstin tool mentioned in Section 3. This tool provides a medium in which nodes, implemented as windows on a work station screen, can be organized into a network, as suggested by Figure 1. Each window can be made to hold arbitrary text, including text that causes displaying of a picture. Any arbitrary element of the text of any window can be given links connecting the element to any window or to any element, possibly in another window. Figure 2 shows two windows from a description of an airline reservation system.

The links connect an element to windows giving more details about the element or to other elements talking about the same or related concepts, as

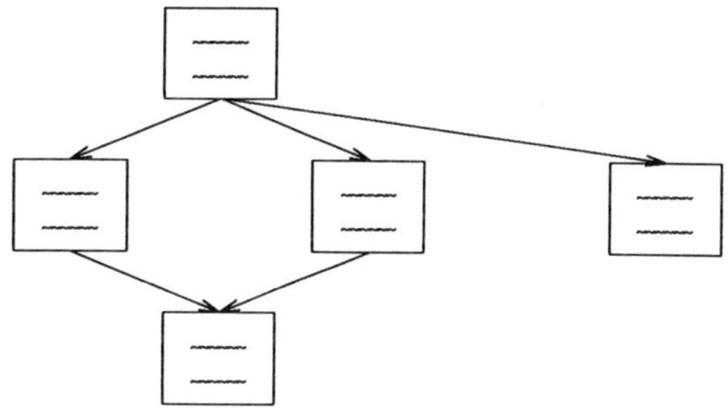

Figure 1: Network of Nodes

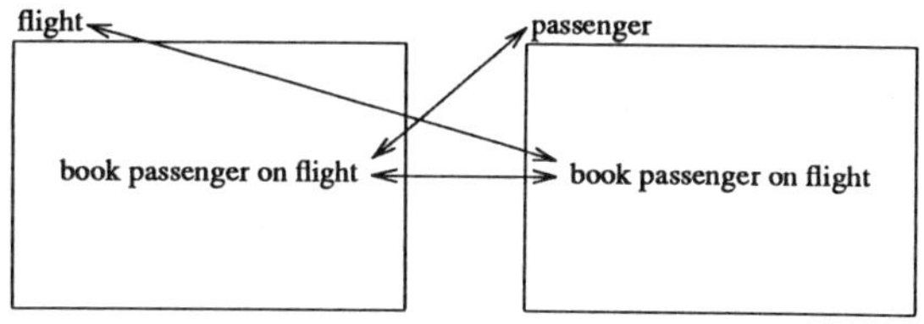

Figure 2: Links

the human RA desires. The RA can use these links to navigate through the windows as he or she is tracking down the information that allows the contents of each window to be refined into a consistent, complete, unambiguous, coherent, and concise description of the window's abstraction.

This description of the tool of the second kind suggests building it on top of some existing hypertext system [35,13,15]. Indeed, Garg and Scacchi have suggested maintaining all life-cycle documents as hypertext [16].

5. ABSTRACTION IDENTIFICATION

The way identification of abstractions is done now is that the human RA scans the transcripts trying to note important subjects and objects of sentences, i.e., nouns. The problem is that humans get tired, get bored, fall asleep, and overlook relevant ideas. So we want a tool that does the clerical part of the search without getting tired, getting bored, falling asleep, and overlooking anything. The human RA still does all the *thinking* with the output of this tool, confident that no occurrence of any noun has been overlooked.

Our first idea, reported in [8], was to use a parser to find the nouns. However, we tried it and found that the few errors it made were so distracting that it was more comfortable to do it by hand. Moreover, we realized that even a better, but still imperfect, parser would still be distracting. Thus, the program did not inspire confidence that it found everything. Maybe there was an important noun that was overlooked because it appeared to the parser as a verb. Even a better, but still ultimately imperfect, parser does not solve this confidence problem. We want something with guaranteed coverage, even if it is less intelligent. The lack of intelligence in the tool is no problem because a human is applying his or her intelligence to the output of the tool.

6. REPEATED PHRASE FINDER

A second idea, reported in [4,3], (Most of this introductory material is borrowed from this paper.) is to use findphrases, a repeated phrase finder. The idea is based on the observation that the frequency of occurrence of a term within a text carries much information on the importance of this term in the text. Indeed, it has been empirically verified that a writer repeats words of importance in a text as she explains or varies her argument [21]. Just counting repeated words within a document is not sufficient for identifying its major abstractions. In counting isolated single words, a lot of information is lost. In particular, information on the relationships in which words are involved is lost. Therefore, it is necessary to consider the phrases in which the words appear.

In its simplest application, the user provides findphrases with the text to be analyzed and a file containing punctuation and keywords. The punctuation and keywords are used by findphrases to break the text into sentences. findphrases processes the phrases of the sentences and produces a series of reports. The basic output contains: (1) the input file as is with lines numbered and the punctuation and keywords overstruck, (2) a frequency ranked table of repeated phrases, and (3) an alphabetically ordered table of repeated phrases. Each entry in these tables gives the numbers of the lines in which the phrase occurs, so that each phrase may be examined in its original context to decide which abstraction is really represented by the phrase. A number of options are provided that the user may use to control the parsing of the input text into tokens and phrases, to control the printing of the phrases in the tables of the output, and to indicate which additional tables are to be printed.

Observe that there is a learning process involved in using findphrases effectively. First, it appears that there are different characteristic punctuation-keyword, multi-token and initial ignored-phrases files for each language. These can be catalogued for general use. In addition for each class of applications, there appears also to be a characteristic set of additional ignored phrases. Finally, as one is doing a particular application, one finds it useful to extend the ignored phrases file with common words that are actually important abstractions, but whose presence skews the list and populates it with too much noise for finding the other abstractions.

The works [4, 3] describe tests of effectiveness of findphrases in helping the human RA identify abstractions.

The tests involved four examples of program development, each of which had multiple versions of the same program ranging from natural language descriptions, through designs, decompositions, etc., to code. Three of these had been published in the literature and one had not.

It was desired to determine if findphrases is effective in helping the human RA to find, in the natural language transcripts of interviews about a system under development, *all* of the abstractions that serve as the basis for the requirements, design, and implementation. It was deemed effective if we, as humans, do indeed recognize the same set of abstractions in the outputs of findphrases run (with the appropriate parameter files in each case) on all versions of the same problem. Finding the same set of abstractions in all versions says that the abstractions found in the first version, the natural language description, are sufficient to cover all abstractions that will be needed for all subsequent versions, including the code and that no other abstractions will need to be invented.

The first experiment is Abbott's example of programming with the help of natural language. This example is the focus of a paper [8] that points to the need of this phrase finding tool. For this experiment, three versions of the program solution are compared. The first version was written in standard English, the second in an Ada™[2]-based program design language, and the third in Ada. The second experiment is the problem of writing the phrase finder itself. In writing the phrase finder, the manual page served as the requirements document. findphrases was run with its own manual page to see if the same abstractions that formed the basis for the modular decomposition used in writing the code are identified from the information provided by findphrases. The third experiment takes Mitchell's text book [22] example of writing a sorting program starting from the English statement of the requirements and ending with a Pascal program developed with a structured programming method. Four versions of the program solution are compared, the initial English description, two program design language descriptions, and the final Pascal program.

The fourth experiment takes Wiener and Sincovec's text book [33] example of writing a spelling checker program. They start with a statement of the requirements, develop a modular decomposition for the solution, and produce an Ada program.

In these experiments, findphrases was found to be effective in aiding the human RA to identify abstractions. However, one particular weakness was noticed. A repeated phrase finder fails to count as a repetition of `book a flight` the phrase `book the flight`. Were each of these phrases to appear only once, the concept of *booking a flight* would not show up at all in the list of repeated phrases. In many cases, concepts do not appear as adjacent words but rather a set of words separated by not more than a few words. Most of these concepts appear as closely separated pairs of words standing for an agent-object relation. Moreover, this relational information often allows distinguishing between semantically distinct uses of the same word by showing the context from which the word comes.

7. LEXICAL AFFINITIES

We propose to take *lexical affinities* (LAs) as the atomic unit for identifying major abstractions within a text. An LA stands for the correlation of the common appearance of two items in sentences of the language [14]. For our purposes, we restrict this definition, by observing LAs within a finite document rather than on the whole language. For instance, in this paper, *requirement* and *analysis* are bound by a lexical affinity. For our purpose, we consider only LAs involving *open-class words* as meaning bearing. Open classes gather nouns, verbs, adjectives and adverbs whereas *closed-class words* are represented by pronouns, prepositions, conjunctions and interjections [18]. The LA finder's output is a list of lexical affinities with their associated frequency of appearance within the considered text. For instance, the analysis of the *rm* manual page in the UNIX™[3] environment, returns as the most frequent LAs, the list `(delete file)`, `(file file)`, `(file permission)`, etc. which all appear three times within the one-page document. Were the manual page taken as a statement of the requirements of rm, we believe that this list of LAs would be of great help for assisting the human RA in his or her process of extracting requirements. As we see in the above example, among the three LAs cited, two represent major abstractions. This can be much improved by accounting for the general context or universe to which the document belongs. This would allow filtering out such LAs as `(file file)` cited above.

In order to account for the general context or universe, LAs need to be scaled according to their specific contribution in the given document. As a measure of their contribution, we propose evaluating the *resolving power* of every LA. We define the resolving power ρ of an LA is a function of its quantity of information and its frequency of appearance within the considered text. The quantity of information represented by a word w in a given textual universe is defined as [29]

$$\textsc{Info}(w) = -\log_2 P\{w\}.$$

Thus, if a word `asterisk` occurs once in every 20 000 words, its quantity of information is estimated to be

$$\textsc{Info}(\texttt{asterisk}) = -\log_2 5\times10^{-5} = 14.29.$$

In contrast, the word `the` that occurs once in every 15 words, has its information contents estimated to be

$$\textsc{Info}(\texttt{the}) = 3.9.$$

Drawing on this definition of the quantity of information for single words, we define the resolving power of an LA within a document d as follows.

Let (w_1, w_2, f) be a tuple retrieved while analyzing a document d, where (w_1, w_2) is an LA appearing f times in d. The resolving power of this LA in d is defined as:

$$\rho((w_1, w_2, f)) = f \times \textsc{Info}(w_1)\textsc{Info}(w_2)$$

The higher the resolving power of an LA is, the more characteristic it is of the considered document. The best LAs, in terms of resolving power, within a document, represent key concepts of the considered document. These LAs may therefore provide valuable assistance to the human RA in the process of extracting requirements.

In order to conduct a first test of the effectiveness of LAs in helping the human RA to find abstractions, we have tried to use LAs to find the abstractions in one of the examples used to test findphrases, namely the findphrases manual page.

8. THE findphrases MANUAL PAGE

One of the original experiments for the repeated phrase finder considered the problem of developing a program for findphrases. That is, findphrases was tested using its own manual page, which is found in the appendix. The data abstractions identified by findphrases from this

[2]Ada was a trademark of the U.S. Dept. of Defense (AJPO).

[3]UNIX is a registered trademark of AT&T Bell Laboratories.

application were compared with the abstractions used in the decomposition for the final program. Space limitations prevent showing the actual output of the running of findphrases on the manual page. However, it can be found in [3].

The decomposition used to write the findphrases program includes fifteen different modules, as illustrated in Figure 3. (See Chapter 3, Section 3 of [4] for a description of the modules.) The modules with dashed outlines are built into the implementing programming language. Nine of the non-built-in modules, i.e., those with the thicker outlines, are data abstraction packages. Table 1 below shows the correspondence between these packages and some of the repeated phrases identified by findphrases from the manual page description:

The Data Abstraction Packages	The Repeated Phrases
string_type_file	`strings, character strings`
argument_line	`argument, option`
output_file	`output,` `tables of the output`
chunk_file	`file(s), free-format`

punct_keyword_table	`punctuation, keyword(s),`
	`punctuation/keyword(s),`
	`punctuation-keyword-file`

multi_tokens_table	`multi-tokens,` `multi-tokens-file`
text_file	`text, input,` `arbitrary text`

phrases	`phrase(s),`
	`ignored phrases,`
	`repeated phrases`

sentences	`sentence(s)`

Table 1:Packages and Phrases

The name of each abstraction, except for chunk_file, directly corresponds to at least one repeated phrase appearing in the manual page. Although the phrase `chunk` does not appear in the description, the chunk_file abstraction is implied by the phrases indicated above. During the program's development, chunk_file was recognized as the abstraction to be used by the procedures that read the various free-format files. Thus, this abstraction is indirectly identified by repeated phrases appearing in the tables. Note that it does not bother us that we had to do some thinking to make these connections. We believe that this kind of thinking is precisely what an RA is doing when presented with such a list of concepts.

In this experiment, the repeated phrases tables produced by findphrases include phrases that identify the abstractions that were used in the program decomposition. The tables act as guides to the user when looking for the abstractions. The user's attention is first focused on the phrases with the highest frequency and then on possibly related phrases. The line numbers printed in the tables enable the user to locate the phrases in the text. By analyzing the context of the sentences containing the phrase, the importance of the phrase as a potential abstraction can be determined.

In addition to finding the list of abstractions, as the user analyzes the context of each phrase usage, a list of statements related to that phrase can be extracted. For example, consider the phrases `multi-token`, `multi-tokens` and `multi-tokens-file`. By examining the context of the lines that contain these phrases, one finds the following information:

1. the optional *multi-tokens-file* contains in free format the list of character strings to be taken as multi-tokens;
2. a multi-token is a string consisting of more than one symbolcharacter (non-word character);
3. if the `-m` option is present, the input text is parsed using the information provided by the *multi-tokens-file*;
4. a token may be a multi-token;
5. if the `-v` and the `-m` options are present, the list of multi-tokens is printed.

These statements represent requirements for the data abstraction multi-token. Located by the manual method, these same statements were used when the initial decomposition and implementation were developed. The final program uses a procedure to read the *multi-tokens-file* and a package to handle a multi-tokens table. These statements also guided the development of the text parsing routines.

Thus, in this experiment, the human RA finds in the repeated phrases generated from the manual page the very abstractions used in the modular decomposition and implementation.

9. THE LAs for THE findphrases MANUAL PAGE

We have extracted the LAs from the findphrases manual page and ranked them according to their resolving power. The whole UNIX manual has been used as the textual universe, in order to determine the quantity of information of each word. The 30 LAs with the highest resolving power are given in Table 2.

Lexical Affinity	ρ
ignore-phrase	699.123546
phrase-repeat	696.600983
multi-token	483.353302
file-phrase	418.820829
contain-**phrase**	299.996707
file-keyword	281.335816
keyword-punctuate	271.657352
file-token	268.032537
file-punctuate	263.292488
format-free	232.582511
option-present	228.395449
begin-**phrase**	208.569285
phrase-table	207.914468
repeat-table	186.066941
file-ignore	163.864523
file-multi	160.532580
phrase-token	138.637142
entry-table	132.656315
contain-file	131.339831
list-token	128.602978
phrase-tally	124.433003
contain-ignore	122.670819
number-supply	119.521321
list-phrase	116.148446
occurrent-phrase	112.433009
contain-list	112.236757
phrase-sentence	111.806985
phrase-provide	106.772850
length-**phrase**	105.449181
free-token	102.949931

Table 2: Most significant LAs

As a first step, the human RA quickly selects, among the top LAs, the main abstractions which are marked in boldface in Table 2. In our example, these abstractions are `ignore-phrase`, `phrase-repeat`, `multi-token`, `keyword-punctuate` and `phrase-sentence`. Single words can also be selected when they are involved in many of the most significant LAs, for instance, in our example, the word `phrase` appears to be a major abstraction. Some other abstractions can also be found after a finer analysis[4], such as chunk, represented by `free-format`, argument-line represented by `option-present` or text_file by noticing all the occurences of `file-phrase` and `text`.

In a second step, the human RA obtains more information on the main abstractions by performing a keyword-based search on the whole list of the LAs. The correspondence between the abstractions, selected at the first step, and the LAs selected during this search is given in Table 3. The most significant LAs leading identification of abstractions are in italics. These might form an initial list of operations, attributes, or methods of the abstractions.

[4]Please note that at this stage, the human RA is required to *understand* the transcript.

ABSTRACTIONS	LEXICAL AFFINITIES
ignored phrase	*ignore-phrase*
	file-ignore
repetition	*phrase-repeat*
	repeat-table
	find-repeat
multi_tokens	*multi-token*
	file-token
	phrase-token
	list-token
punctuation_keyword	*keyword-punctuate*
	file-punctuate
	file-keyword
	keyword-phrase
sentence	*phrase-sentence*
	occurring-sentence
	consecutive-sentence
	sentence-token
	present-sentence
	entry-sentence
phrase	ignore *phrase*
	phrase-repeat
	file-*phrase*
	contain-*phrase*
	begin-*phrase*
	phrase-table
chunk	*format-free*
argument_line	*option-present*
	multi-option
	argument-present
	argument-option
text_file	*file-phrase*
	arbitrary-text
	phrase-text
	repeat-text

Table 3: Packages and LAs

10. CONCLUSIONS

The initial attempt to use LAs to assist a human RA in finding abstractions looks promising. The LAs help the RA identify the same abstractions that were used to build the implementation. In addition, the LAs were helpful in organizing the information in the descriptions and allowed the user to focus on the important phrases. It will now be necessary to try out the LAs on other problems.

It is not clear at this time which is better, LAs or repeated phrases. The use of LAs finds repeated phrases whose key elements are not necessarily adjacent and are not necessarily appearing in the exact same form each time. However, at present the LA finder does not find LAs consisting of more than two words. It finds only verb-noun, adjective-noun, and other common grammatical structure pairs. LAs of more than two words must be inferred as joins of binary relations. Of course, the repeated phrase finder has no problems finding phrases of more than two words. Perhaps both should be used, and tools for dealing with both should be available to the users of REGEE. Perhaps a combined tool should be built in which non-adjacency, synonyms, and varying parts of speech are tolerated in finding repeated phrases.

REFERENCES

1. "Requirements for the Ada Programming Support Environment: STONEMAN," Technical Report, U.S. Department of Defense (1981).
2. *IEEE Software* **5**(2) (March, 1988).
3. C. Aguilera and D.M. Berry, "The Use of a Repeated Phrase Finder in Requirements Extraction," *Journal of Systems and Software*(9) (1990 (To appear)).
4. C.S. Aguilera, "Finding Abstractions in Problem Descriptions using findphrases," M.S. Thesis, Computer Science Department, UCLA, Los Angeles, CA (October, 1987).
5. M.W. Alford, "A Requirements Engineering Methodology for Realtime Processing Requirements," *IEEE Transactions of Software Engineering* **SE-3**(1), pp. 60-69 (1977).
6. M.W. Alford, "Software Requirements Engineering Methodology (SREM) at the Age of Two," in *COMPSAC 78 Proceedings* (November, 1978).
7. M.W. Alford, "SREM at the Age of Eight; The Distributed Computing Design System," *Computer* **18**(4), pp. 36-46 (April, 1985).
8. D.M. Berry, N.M. Yavne, and M. Yavne, "Application of Program Design Language Tools to Abbott's Method of Program Design by Informal Natural Language Descriptions," *Journal of Software and Systems*(7), pp. 221-247 (1987).
9. V. Berzins, M. Gray, and D. Naumann, "Abstraction-Based Software Development," *Communications of the ACM* **29**(5), pp. 402-415 (May, 1986).
10. G. Booch, *Software Engineering with Ada*, Benjamin-Cummins, San Francisco, CA (1986). Second Edition.
11. A. Borgida, S. Greenspan, and J. Mylopolous, "Knowledge Representation as the Basis for Requirements Specifications," *Computer* **18**(4), pp. 82-91 (April, 1985).
12. M.D. Burstin, "Requirements Analysis of Large Software Systems," Ph.D. Dissertation, Department of Management, Tel Aviv University, Tel Aviv, Israel (1984).
13. J. Conklin, "A Survey of Hypertext," MCC Technical Report No. STP-356-86, Rev. 1, MCC, Austin, TX (February 9, 1987).
14. D.A. Cruse, *Lexical Semantics*, Cambridge University Press, Cambridge (1986).
15. N.M. Delisle and M.D. Schwartz, "Contexts — A Partitioning Concept for Hypertext," *ACM Transactions on Office Information Systems* **5**(2), pp. 168-186 (April, 1987).
16. P.K. Garg and W. Scacchi, "Maintaining Software Life Cycle Documents as Hypertext: Issues, Analysis, and Directions," Technical Report, University of Southern California, Los Angeles, California (1987).
17. D. Harel, "On Visual Formalisms," *Communications of the ACM* **30**(6) (June, 1987).
18. R. Huddleston, *Introduction to the Grammar of English*, Cambridge University Press, Cambridge (1984).
19. M.A. Jackson, *Principles of Program Design*, Academic Press, London (1975).
20. M.M. Lehman, "Programs, Life Cycles, and Laws of Software Evolution," *Proceedings of the IEEE* **68**(9), pp. 1060-1076 (September, 1980).
21. M. Luhn, "The Automatic Creation of Literature Abstracts," *IBM Journal of Research and Development* **2**(2), pp. 159-165 (April, 1958).
22. W. Mitchell, *A Prelude to Programming: Problem Solving and Algorithms*, Reston Publishing, Reston, VA (1984).
23. G.J. Myers, *Composite/Structured Design*, van Nostrand Reinhold, New York, NY (1979).
24. K.T. Orr, *Structured Systems Development*, Yourdon, New York (1977).
25. K.T. Orr, *Structured Requirements Engineering*, Ken Orr & Associates, Topeka, KS (1981).
26. D.L. Parnas, "On the Criteria to be Used in Decomposing Systems into Modules," *Communications of the ACM* **15**(2), pp. 1053-1058 (December, 1972).
27. D.T. Ross, "Structured Analysis (SA): A Language for Communicating Ideas," *IEEE Transactions on Software Engineering* **SE-3**(1), pp. 16-33 (January, 1977).
28. D.T. Ross and K.E. Schoman, Jr., "Structured Analysis for Requirements Definition," *IEEE Transactions on Software Engineering* **SE-3**(1), pp. 6-15 (January, 1977).
29. G. Salton and M.J. McGill, *Introduction to Modern Information Retrieval*, McGraw-Hill, New York (1983).
30. P.A. Scheffer, A.H. III Stone, and W.E. Rzepka, "A Case Study of SREM," *Computer* **18**(4), pp. 47-54 (April, 1985).
31. G.E. Sievert and T.A. Mizell, "Specification-Based Software Engineering with TAGS," *Computer* **18**(4), pp. 56-66 (April, 1985).
32. D. Teichroew and E.A. Hershey, III, "PSL/PSA: A Computer-Aided Technique for Structure Documentation and Analysis of Information Processing Systems," *IEEE Transactions of Software Engineering* **SE-3**(1), pp. 41-48 (January, 1977).
33. R. Wiener and R. Sincovec, *Software Engineering with Modula-2 and Ada*, John Wiley & Sons, New York (1984).
34. J. Winchester and G. Estrin, "Requirements Definition and Its Interface to the SARA Design Methodology for Computer-Based Systems," *AFIPS Conference Proceedings* **51**, pp. 369-379 (June, 1982).
35. N. Yankelovich, N. Meyerowitz, and A. van Dam, "Reading and Writing the Electronic Book," *Computer* **10**(18), pp. 15-30 (October, 1985).

Figure 3: findphrases DECOMPOSITION

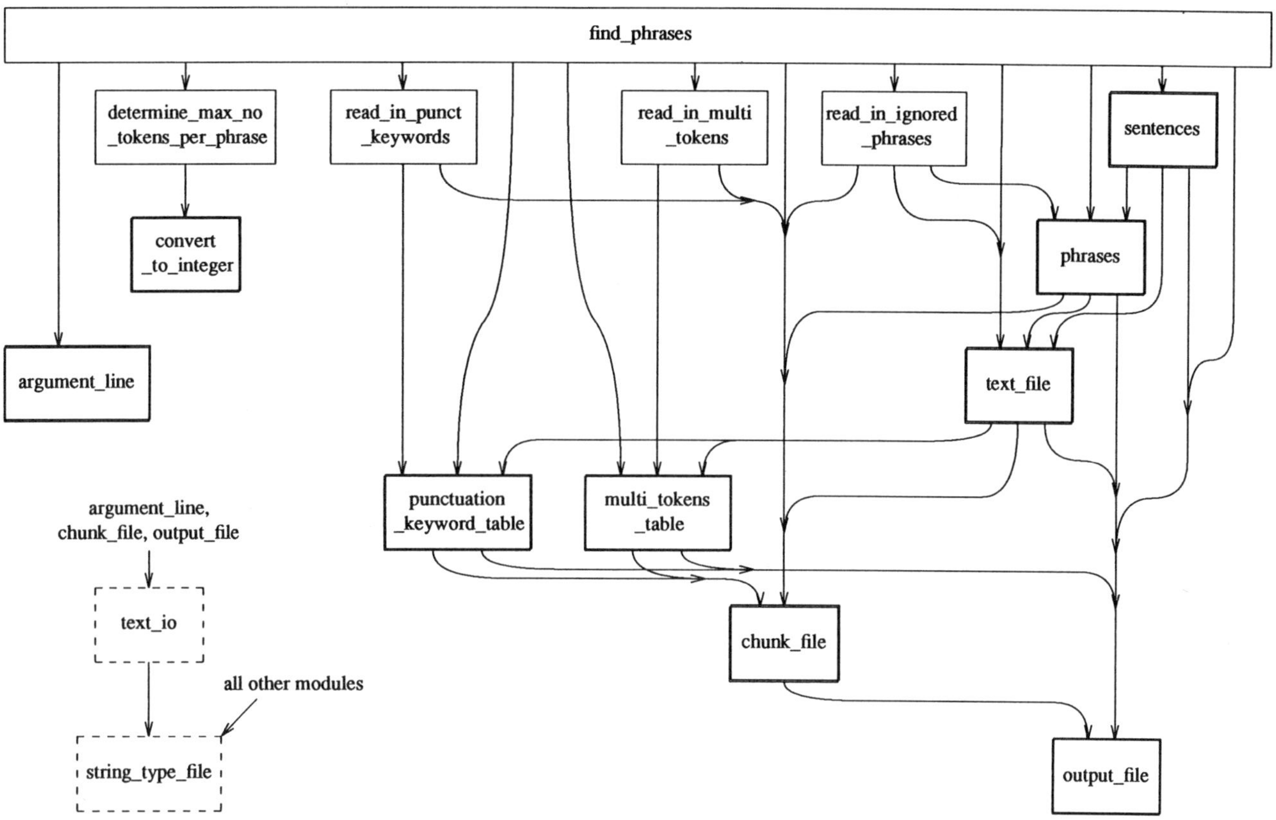

APPENDIX findphrases MANUAL PAGE

NAME

findphrases – find repeated phrases in an arbitrary text

SYNOPSIS

findphrases [**–n***number*] **–p***punctuation-keyword-file* [**–x***ignored-phrases-file*] [**–m***multi-tokens-file*] [**–u**] [**–b**] [**–s**] [**–t**] [**–v**] [**–c**]

DESCRIPTION

All files mentioned in the synopsis provide their data in what is referred to as free format subject to particular restrictions to be described for each case. In free format, the items of the file may be entered zero or several per line with a mixture of blanks and tabs before, in between, and after the items. Consequently, no item can include a blank, a tab, or a newline.

The **–n** argument is optional and if present provides a number *number* serving as the maximum length phrase (to be described later) to be tallied. If this argument is not present, if it does not supply a number, or if the supplied number is outside the reasonable range of greater than zero and less than or equal to 50, then *number* is taken as 10.

The *punctuation-keyword-file* contains in free format a list of those character strings to be taken as punctuation/keywords (see below). The optional *ignored-phrases-file* contains one-per-line a list of phrases to be ignored in the tallying (see below). In each line, the tokens (see below) are in free format. The optional *multi-tokens-file* contains in free format a list of those character strings consisting of more than one symbolcharacter (see below) which are to be taken as multi-tokens (see below).

No assumptions are made about the standard input, thus it may be an arbitrary text. The program parses the text into words and symbolcharacters. These in turn are formed and classified into tokens and punctuation/keywords based on the information provided by the *punctuation-keyword-file* and, when the **–m** option is present, the *multi-tokens-file*.

First some definitions are necessary:

Whitespace: blank, tab, newline, beginning-of-file, end-of-file

Wordcharacter: letter, digit, _

Symbolcharacter: any printable character which is neither a wordcharacter nor a blank

Word: any sequence of wordcharacters delimited on each side by whitespace or a symbolcharacter

Punctuation/Keyword: whatever is in the *punctuation-keyword-file*; the symbolcharacter strings are called punctuation and the wordcharacter strings are called keywords

Multi-token: whatever is in the *multi-tokens-file*

Token: any word, symbolcharacter, or multi-token which is not listed in the *punctuation-keyword-file*

Sentence: list of tokens delimited on each side by punctuation/keyword

Phrase: one or more consecutive tokens occurring within one sentence

The main job of this program is to tally the occurrence of all phrases in all sentences. The maximum length phrase that has to be considered is that of *number* tokens. If the *ignored-phrases-file* is provided, then the phrases given in the file are to be ignored in the tallying. If the **–b** option is used along with the *ignored-phrases-file*, then phrases which begin with an ignored phrase are also ignored in the tallying.

The standard output consists of:

a copy of the input as is, with the lines numbered and the punctuation/keywords overstruck two times (i.e., printed three times in place) so that they can be spotted easily,

a frequency ranked table of the repeated phrases. i.e., those appearing more than once among the sentences; that is the entries of the table are given in order of decreasing frequency, and

an alphabetically ordered table of the repeated phrases.

In the two tables, the entry for a repeated phrase consists of:

a sequence of asterisks indicating the phrase's frequency as a percentage of the maximum frequency; in this one asterisk represents 10%,

the actual number of occurrences of the repeated phrase,

the repeated phrase itself, and

a list of the numbers of all lines containing the beginning of the repeated phrase.

In printing the repeated phrase itself in a table entry, the underscores, i.e., ‘‘_’’, are printed as blanks. This means that an underscore can be used immediately preceeding or following a word that looks like a keyword to prevent it from being considered a keyword.

Note that the definition of ‘‘phrase’’ is independent of the number of times it occurs in the sentences. An *ignored phrase* is simply one to be ignored in the tallying but not in searching for phrases. A phrase which contains an ignored phrase which itself is not ignored is to be tallied. When the **–b** option is present, a phrase which begins with an ignored phrase is not to be tallied. A *repeated phrase* is one whose final tally is greater than one. Only the repeated phrases show up in the tables of the output.

Typically, the *ignored-phrases-file* will contain so-called noise phrases such as ‘‘a’’, ‘‘an’’, ‘‘the’’, ‘‘of’’, ‘‘of the’’, etc. plus any useless phrases found in previous runs of the program.

One particular configuration of the files is as follows:

Punctuation-keyword-file: **; [ ] abort accept access all and array at begin body case constant declare delta digits do else elsif end entry exception exit for function generic goto if in is limited loop mod new not null of or others out package pragma private procedure raise range record rem renames return reverse select separate subtype task terminate then type use when while with xor**

Multi-tokens-file: ** := <= >= /= .. <> << >>

This configuration is suited for finding repeated phrases in Ada™ (Ada is a trademark of the U. S. Department of Defense.) or in an Ada-based program design language.

If the **–u** option is present, then only the unique phrases that are not wholly and everywhere contained in another phrase are listed in the tables of the output. In addition to the already specified output, if the **–s** option is present, then all the sentences are listed; if the **–t** option is present, then all the tokens are listed; if the **–v** option is present, then the output is verbose with the punctuation/keywords listed, and when the **–m**, and respectively the **–x**, option is present, the multi-tokens, and respectively the ignored phrases, are listed. If the **–c** option is present, then upper and lower case distinctions are to be applied in determining whether a phrase is in a sentence. The default is to ignore case distinction in the comparisons.

DIAGNOSTICS

They are good, of course.

BUGS

There are none, of course.

As an example, when running findphrases against its own manual page, the following findphrases options were used:

i. The *punctuation-keyword-file* consisted of a standard set of punctuation: period, comma, colon, semi-colon, question mark, and exclamation point.

ii. The *ignored-phrases-file* consisted of a list of sixty-seven phrases to be ignored: apostrophe, opening and closing double quotes, opening and closing parentheses, opening and closing brackets, dash, colon, underscore, `10`, `a`, `ada`, `all`, `an`, `and`, `any`, `are`, `as`, `based`, `be`, `begin`, `beginning`, `below`, `by`, `called`, `can`, `configuration`, `course`, `described`, `e`, `each`, `end`, `entry`, `file`, `for`, `i`, `if`, `in`, `into`, `is`, `it`, `items`, `may`, `not`, `number is`, `of`, `on`, `or`, `respectively`, `see`, `so`, `synopsis`, `taken`, `than`, `that`, `the`, `then`, `this`, `those`, `thus`, `times`, `to`, `tokens`, `(see below)`, `when`, `which`, and `with`. These phrases were found in prior runs.

iii. The *multi-tokens-file* consisted of the following symbols: `''` `` `` `` `**` := <= >= /= `..` <> << >>

iv. The –u and –b options were used to print the Tables of Repeated Phrases. The –b option was used to ignore in the tallying of repeated phrases those phrases which began with an ignored phrase. The number used with the –n option was `11`.

ANALOGICAL APPROACH TO SPECIFICATION DERIVATION

Kanth Miriyala and Mehdi T. Harandi
Dept. of Computer Science,
University of Illinois, Urbana–Champaign

ABSTRACT

Software tools are essential for writing specifications. This paper describes how analogical reasoning can play an important role in such a tool. A knowledge base of specifications – informal and formal – of a representative class of problems and a set of heuristic rules analogical specification derivation are used to transform a given informal specification into a formal one. Analogies are detected between components of the given (target) informal specification and components of one or more (base) informal specifications from the knowledge base. Ordering of the analogies and subsequent selection is performed by invoking heuristics germane to the situation. Due to the nature of the analogy process, the derived specification may be incorrect. A heuristic has been developed to correct some such errors.

1. Introduction

Though the importance of formal software specification has been explicated for quite sometime [Parnas72 , Liskov75], writing formal specifications remains an expert's task. The difficulty stems from the fact that software specifications should be rigorous – precise, unambiguous, complete, consistent and irredundant. This makes the writing of formal specifications a tedious and error–prone task.

This work explores the merits of applying analogical reasoning techniques to derivation of formal specifications from informal ones (thus continuing the import of ideas from AI to software, successfully started by [Balzar73, Green76, Greenspan84] and others). Analogical reasoning has been studied by many researchers in relation to psychology and AI [Carbonell83, Gentner83, Greiner88, Winston80]. More recently [Dershowitz83] and [Bhansali88] have used analogy in the automatic synthesis of programs. We describe the application of analogical reasoning to the task of specification derivation, as part of a general specification derivation system. This system includes, in addition to the knowledge about analogical reasoning, domain models, specification schemata, knowledge for schema instantiation, knowledge of primitive data types, general purpose problem–solving rules (embodying strategies like divide and conquer, rules for synthesizing parts of the specification, rules for composing parts to get an integrated whole, etc), and appropriate mechanism for manipulation of such sources of knowledge.

When a new (target) problem is to be specified, its informal specification is given. Strictly speaking, we should call this semi–formal specification as it is a systematic representation of information about the *domain* – objects, their attributes and relations between objects – and *problem description*, that is, what are given and what is to be determined. This is illustrated in Fig. 1(a) which represents the informal specification for the traveling salesman problem (TSP). The informal specifications are analysed to detect analogies. These analogies are then utilized to derive formal specifications for the target problem. The formal specification is given in terms of *preconditions* and *postconditions*[Gries81]. The formal specification for the TSP is shown in Fig. 1(b). The predicates and functions used in the precondition and the postcondition are defined in the *required definitions* part.

The knowledge base of the specification derivation system contains records of previously derived formal specifications, together with the corresponding informal input specification. When a problem is stored in the knowledge base, a structure tree is also maintained. The structure tree (Fig. 1(c)), as the name suggests, stores the conceptual structure of the informal specification and is used for choosing applicable analogies. The known concepts are assumed to be organized in the form of a forest (in general, however, this can be a graph) in the knowledge base. In any tree, concepts at the root are most general and those at leaves are most specialized. The process of analogical specification is aided by a set of heuristics. In this paper we demonstrate these heuristics through some examples.

©1989 ACM 0-89791-305-1/89/0500/0203$00.75

2. Algorithms for analogy detection and analogy application

We are interested in analogies between the informal specification of the target problem and the informal specification of the base problem. In the analogy detection process:

1) Any two atomic objects are (abstractly) considered analogous.

```
Domain Model

(object :name city)

(attribute :of trip
           :is cost
           :which-is integer)
(relation :name trip
          :tuple-size  2
          :tuple-description <city city>
          :condition  true)
(relation :name  tour
          :tuple-description <(collection trip)>
          :condition (forms cycle (collection trip))  &
                     (includes cycle (all city))

Problem Description

(find  :what tour
       :condition (minimize (total cost tour))

(given (forall :city c1 :city c2
         (exists :relation trip
                 :from c1
                 :to c2)))
```

Fig. 1(a). Informal specification of the traveling salesman problem (TSP).

2) Attributes of the same type are analogous. For example, weight of an edge of a graph and cost of an edge in TSP are both of the type integer, and hence analogous.

3) Relations whose tuple descriptions are analogous are analogous.

4) Two concepts are analogous if

(a) they are the same or have a common ancestor, i.e., belong to the same tree of the forest (for example, the various kinds of collections like lists, sets, general collections, etc., are all analogous); and

(b) the number of arguments are the same. For example, if *(minimize (total tour cost))* of TSP has a match, the target should have concept matches for *minimize* and *total*, followed by match of number of arguments for total. The actual arguments can, of course, be different.

After the concept analogy has been obtained, the formal specification part that corresponds to the base concept should be transformed to suit the target concept. This is called *analogy application*. In the general case of concept analogy, the base and target concepts have a common ancestor. In such a situation, the formal base specification is successively abstracted till the common ancestor is reached and then specialized down to the target concept. Associated with every concept is the information necessary to perform this *abstraction* or *specialization*. For example, in Fig. 2, minimize is first abstracted to optimize and then specialized to (the target concept) maximize. If we take the traveling salesman problem as the base problem and 0–1 knapsack problem as the target[1] and apply the concept tree of Fig. 2 , we obtain the abstraction and specialization shown in Fig. 3. Usually the first analogies considered are concept analogies (this is formalized in the H_{STRUCTURE} heuristic discussed below). The predicates or functions used in the already defined part of specification are defined next. Normally predicates and functions are re-

```
precondition:
(∀ c1: city ∃ c2: city: edge(c1, c2))
postcondition:
(find t: tour(t) ∧ ∀ t': tour(t') → t-cost(t) ≤ t-cost(t'))
required definitions:
(tour(t)  = cycle(t))
(cycle(t)  =  ∀  c1: city: path(c1, c1, t)        ∧
              ∀  c1: city: degree(c1) = 2
(path (c1, c2, t) =  edge(c1, c2) ∨
              ∃ c3: city: edge(c1, c3) ∧  path(c3, c2, t)

(function :name t-cost
          :from (collection edge)
          :to  c
          :defined-by c = Σ_{e∈t} cost(e))
```

Fig. 1(b). Formal specification of TSP

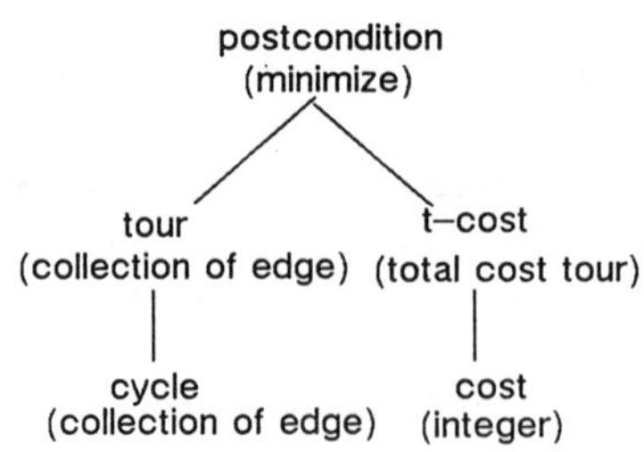

Fig. 1(c). Structure of the formal specification of the TSP. Associated informal concepts appear within parentheses.

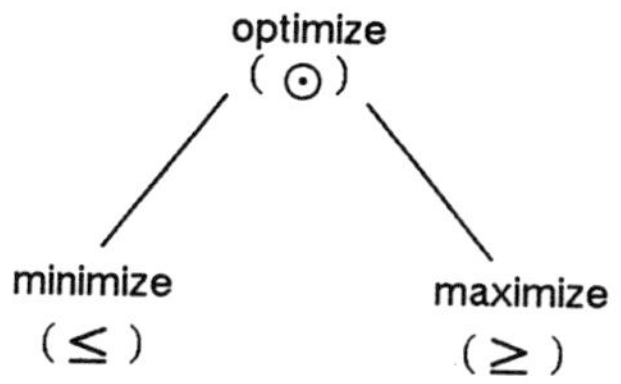

Fig. 2. A part of a concept tree with associated abstraction/specialization information.

---

minimize:
(the base problem is the traveling salesman problem)
(find t: tour(t) $\wedge$ $\forall$ t': tour(t')
$\rightarrow$ t-cost(t) $\leq$ t-cost(t'))

↓ abstraction

optimize:
(find t: P(t) $\wedge$ $\forall$ t': P(t') $\rightarrow$ Q(t) $\odot$ Q(t'))

↓ specialization

maximize:
(the target problem is the 0–1 knapsack problem)
(find t: filling(t) $\wedge$ $\forall$t': filling(t')
$\rightarrow$t-profit(t) $\geq$ t-profit(t'))

Fig. 3. Illustration of abstraction/specialization process of analogy application.

---

lated to relations and attributes, respectively, of the informal description. Therefore, when predicates or functions have to be specified, one looks for relation and attribute analogies. This process results in a *top–down* derivation of the formal specification. As the process percolates downwards, the analogical map is between more specific features.

The algorithms for analogy detection and application are shown in Fig. 4(a) and 4(b) respectively.

3. Heuristics

Our system employs a variety of analogical reasoning methods each aided by a specific heurisitc. In this section we will derive heuristics for the following methods of using analogy to derive specifications:
- direct analogy
- divide and conquer analogy,
- difference based analogy, and
- multiple analogies

An example will be used to derive the heuristic in each case.

[1]In the 0–1 knapsack problem we have a knapsack for which the volume of "filling" is limited. "Filling" is a collection of objects. Associated with each object is a volume and a profit. The idea is to obtain a filling with maximum profit.

```
ANALOGY(a1, a2)
{ takes two structures a1 and a2 and returns true
 if they are analogous; false otherwise}

analogous := true;
if object(a1) & object(a2)
then return(analogous)
else
if  attibute(a1) & attribute(a2)
then if   analogy(type(a1), type(a2))
        then  return(analogous);
else
if  relation(a1) & relation(a2)
then for all  e1 ∊ tuple-description(a1) & corresponding
                e2 ∊ tuple-description(a2)
                analogous := analogous ∧  analogy(e1, e2)
        return(analogous)
else  if  concept(a1) & concept(a2)
        then  if  a1 & a2 have a common ancestor
                then  return(analogous)
                else  return(false)
        else  return(false)
```

Fig. 4(a). Analogy Detection Algorithm

{takes the concept tree, c, the base concept node, b, the target concept node, t and the common ancestor, a, and applies the analogy.}

Successively abstract the base specification upwards from b till a is reached. At each level, abstraction is performed using the abstraction information associated with the node. This gives an abstract schema.

Successively specialize the abstract schema downwards instantiatling with specialization information obtained at each node. Stop on reaching t.

Fig. 4(b). Analogy application algorithm.

In the ensuing discussion it is assumed that the three specifications shown in Figs. 1, 5 and 6, for the traveling salesman problem(TSP), searching a 1–D array, and sorting a 1–D array, are in the knowledge base of the system.

3.1. Direct analogy

The minimum spanning tree (MST) problem will be used to illustrate this. The MST problem can be stated as follows:

Domain Model

```
(object :name A
        :isa array
             :from o
             :to n-1
             :of integer)

(object :name x
        :isa integer)
```

Problem Description

```
(given (occurs :element x
               :in A))

(find :what i
      :condition (equal x A[i]))
```

Fig. 5(a). Informal specification of 1–D search.

---

precondition:

$(x \in A)$

postcondition:

(find i : $0 \leq i \leq n-1 \;\wedge\; x = A[i]$)

Fig. 5(b). Formal specification of 1–D search.

Domain Model

```
(object :name A
        :isa array
             :from o
             :to n-1
             :of integer)
```

Problem Description

```
(find :what A'
      :condition (forall i
                   A'[i] ≤ A'[i+1]) &
                   permutation(A, A'))
```

Fig. 6(a). Informal specification of 1–D sorting

---

precondition:

$(A[0{:}n-1] = (a_0 \ldots a_{n-1})$

postcondition:

$(\forall i :\ 0 \leq i < n-1 : A[i] \leq A[i+1] \;\wedge$

$A = \text{permutation}(\, a_0 \ldots a_{n-1}))$

required definitions:

(permutation(s): set–of (s) = set–of(permutation(s)))

Fig. 6(b). Formal specification of 1–D sorting

Domain Model

```
(object  :name node)
(attribute :of edge
           :is cost
           :which-is integer)

(relation :name edge
          :tuple-size   2
          :tuple-description <node node>
          :condition   true)

(relation :name  spanning-tree
     :tuple-description <(collection edge)>
     :condition (forms tree (collection edge)) &
                (includes tree (all nodes))
```

Problem Description

```
(find  :what spanning-tree
   :condition (minimize (total cost spanning-tree)))

(given (connected (input (collection edge))))
```

Fig. 7(a). Informal specification of the minimal spanning tree problem.

---

precondition:

(connected (input (collection edge)))

postcondition:

(find t: spanning–tree(t) $\wedge$
$\forall$ t': spanning–tree(t') $\rightarrow$ t–cost(t) $\leq$ t–cost(t'))

required definitions:

(spanning–tree(t) $\rightarrow$ tree(t) $\wedge$ size(t) = n–1)

(tree(t) $\rightarrow$ connected (t) $\wedge$ $\forall$ t' $\subseteq$ t: $\neg$ cycle(t'))

(cycle(t) = $\forall$ c1: node: path(c1, c1, t) $\wedge$
$\forall$ c1: city: degree(c1) = 2

(path (c1, c2, t) = edge(c1, c2) $\vee$
$\exists$ c3: city: edge(c1, c3) $\wedge$ path(c3, c2, t)

```
(function :name t-cost
          :from (collection edge)
          :to  c
          :defined-by c = Σ cost(e) )
                          e∈t
```

Fig. 7(b). Formal specification of the minimal spanning tree problem.

Given a connected undirected graph, G = <V, E>, and a "cost" value associated with each edge, find a spanning tree (a spanning tree is one that connects all the vertices of G) of minimum cost. The informal specification for this problem appears in Fig. 7(a).

The analogy detection algorithm gives a set of analogies, which includes the *direct* analogy between the concepts *minimize* of MST and *minimize* of TSP. The match is confirmed by the existence of *spanning–tree* and *cost* in MST corresponding to *tour* and *cost* in TSP. Note that analogy is also detected between *city* and *node*, *edge* and *edge*, *cost* and *cost*, *total* and *total*, etc. We are interested in the analogy that occurs highest in the structure tree of the base problem. We see from the structure tree of the TSP (Fig. 1(c)) problem that *minimize* is such an analogy.

Application of the *minimize* analogy results in the postcondition:

(find t: spanning–tree(t) $\wedge$ $\forall$t': spanning–tree(t') –> t–cost(t) $\leq$ t–cost(t'))

Next t–cost gets defined by analogy. However, to define *spanning–tree*, the domain model will be used to get:

(spanning–tree(t) –> tree(t) $\wedge$ size(t) = n–1),

where *tree* is a predefined concept . Let us suppose that it is defined in terms of *cycle*. Then *cycle* can be defined by analogy again (but need not be as it is also a known concept, if we assume that the knowledge base had some graph theoretic knowledge). The complete formal specification for the MST is given in Fig. 7(b). Here the precondition has been left informal for simplicity (it is not relevant to the discussion; in practice however, the knowledge base has the definitions for these graph–theoretic terms and hence will supply one immediately). Of course, in a general case, preccondition (i.e., the *givens* of the program description) may be more complicated and hence require use of analogy to be formally specified.

Direct analogies are <base component, target component> pairs returned by the analogy detection algorithm. Using the notation of [Greiner88] we get the first heuristic to be:

$H_{STRUCTURE}$: From the set of analogies, choose that which is at the highest level in the structure tree of the base problem.

3.2. Divide and conquer analogy

Suppose we wish to specify the saddleback search problem [Gries81, p. 215] which can be stated as follows:

Domain Model

```
(object :name A
        :isa array
            :from 0, 0
            :to n-1, m-1
            :of integer)

(object :name x
        :isa integer)
```

Problem Description

```
(given (sorted row A) &
       (sorted column A))
(given (belongs-to x A))
(find :what <i, j>
      :condition  x = A[i, j]))
```

Fig. 8. Informal specification of saddleback search.

It is known that a fixed integer x occurs in a fixed 2–dimensional array, A[0:n–1, 0:m–1]. Further it is known that each row and each column is ordered by ($\leq$) . Find i, j such that x = A[i, j].

When a conjunctive form (such as the one given in Fig. 8) is checked for analogy and none is found, it is automatically split into individual conjuncts and analogy detection is carried out separately for each conjunct. In this case individual conjuncts of *given* part match with *find* part of the sort problem. Applying this analogy to both the subproblems that result from the split we get:

(x $\in$ A $\wedge$
$\forall$i: 0 $\leq$ i $\leq$ n–1: $\forall$j: 0 $\leq$ j < m–1: A[i, j] $\leq$ A[i, j+1] $\wedge$
$\forall$j: 0 $\leq$ j $\leq$ m–1: $\forall$i: 0 $\leq$ i < n–1: A[i, j] $\leq$ A[i+1, j])

Here, that part of the specification which says A is a permutation of the original array is omitted, as it is relevant only in the postcondition of sort (this is general specification knowledge available in the knowledge base). The postcondition is found by analogy with the stored 1–dimensional search problem to be:

(find i, j: 0 $\leq$ i $\leq$ n–1 $\wedge$ 0 $\leq$ j $\leq$ m–1: x = A[i, j]).

The complete formal specifications that are derived, are omitted for this and following examples in order to save space. Summarizing what was done to derive the formal specification for saddleback search: split the *given* which is a conjunctive form, found both the parts resulting from the split to be analogous to the same concept in the *find* part of the sort problem, and found the postcondition to be analogous to the postcondition of the search problem. This gives us the second heuristic:

$H_{SIMULTANEOUS}$: If more than one target subproblem is analogous to the part(s) at the same level of the structure tree of the base problem, apply both analogies simultaneously.

The fact that a *find* part of a base problem can be analogous to a *given* part of a target problem and vice versa is already taken care of by the analogy detection algorithm (because it treats all of them as concepts). Another point which we have not included in the above heuristic is the fact that different parts of a target problem can match with parts of different base problems (in this case the base problems used for analogy were – 1–dimensional search and 1–dimensional sorting). This will be incorporated in the $H_{STRUCTURE}$ of next section where we see a more general manifestation of this case wherein successive subproblems generated can be matched with different base problems.

3.3. Multiple analogies

It is possible that application of a concept analogy results in more subproblems. These subproblems are again (recursively) solvable by analogy. However, the important thing is that successive subproblems need not necessarily be analogous to successive subproblems of the same base problem. Instead they can match with different base problems. This will be illustrated using plateau problem [Gries81] as an example.

> *The Plateau Problem:* Given an array A[0:n–1] sorted in ascending order, find the longest plateau in A. A plateau is a sequence of equal values.

The informal specification is given in Fig. 9. The concept *longest* is related to *maximize*, as shown in Fig. 10(a). Prior to analogy match longest is transformed to (maximize (length plateau)). This results in a match. Application of this analogy defines the longest plateau postcondition as:

(find t: plateau(t) $\wedge$ $\forall$t': plateau(t') -> length(t) $\geq$ length(t'))

Next *plateau* has to be defined. From the informal specification in Fig. 9 we see that it is *a sequence of equal values*. This is related to a sequence of ascending values (Fig. 10(b)), which in turn is related to sort (not shown in the figure). Application of this analogy gives:

(plateau: $\exists$ j, k: $0 \leq j \leq k \leq n{-}1$: $\forall$i: $j \leq i < k$: A[i] = A[i+1])

Note that the facts that the sequence can be of any length and that A is an array from 0 to n–1, have been used to derive the existential bounds on i.

Domain Model

```
(object :name A
        :isa array
             :from o
             :to n-1
             :of integer)
(relation :name plateau
          :tuple-size n
          :tuple-description <(sequence A)>
          :condition (ordered (sequence A)
                        :by =)
```

Problem Description

```
(find :what plateau
      :condition (longest plateau))

          |  gets transformed to
          v

(find :what plateau
      :condition (maximize (length plateau))
```

Fig. 9. Informal specification of the plateau problem.

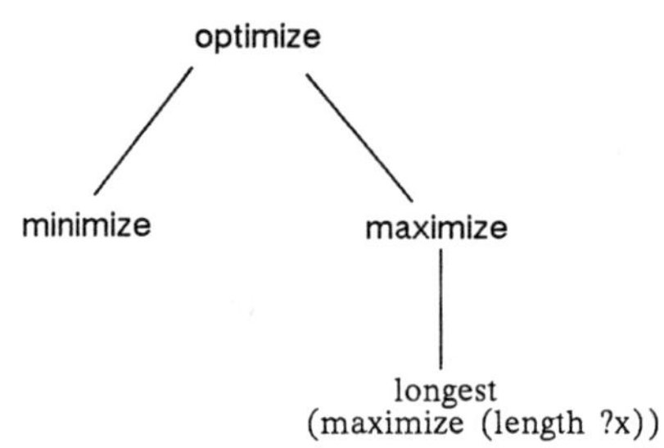

Fig. 10. (a) Part of concept tree showing *longest* concept

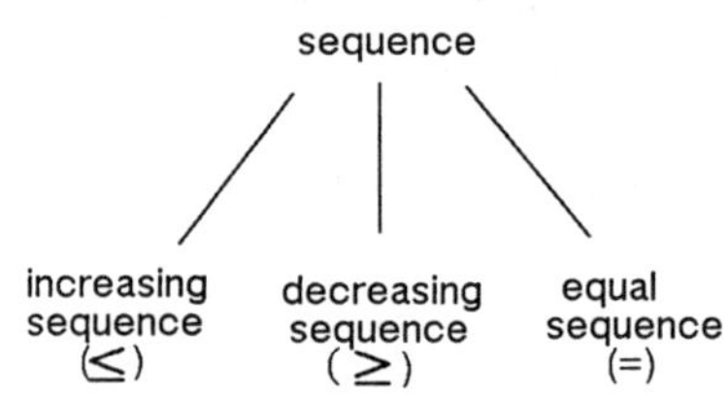

Fig. 10. (b) Part of concept tree showing *sequence* concept

In the example of section 3.3 we saw that various parts of the informal specification could have analogical matches with different base problems. Here we noticed that successive subproblems need not necessarily match with the same base problem. Hence we get the following heuristic:

$H_{MULTIPLE}$: If different parts of the target problem match different base problems, apply all those analogies in any order.

Consider the heuristic, $H_{SIMULTANEOUS}$, of section 3.3. It refers to the case wherein several parts of the target problem match the same (or parts of the same level of structure tree) part of the base problem. The reverse situation could occur, i.e., the same part of the target problem could be analogous to parts of several base problem(s). For instance, suppose that the 0–1 knapsack specification is also present in the knowledge base. Then the match would occur between *longest* and *maximize.* If all possible analogies were tried, *longest* would have been analogous to *minimize* as well. However we chose the closest match. A closest match is one for which $d_b + d_t$ is minimum, where d_b is the distance between the common ancestor and the base concept in the concept tree and d_t is the distance between the common ancestor and the target concept. This gives the next heuristic:

H_{CHOICE} : If the same part of the target problem is analogous to more than one part of the base problem(s), choose the most direct analogy, i.e., the analogy with the least $d_b + d_t$

3.4. Difference based analogy

Difference in two otherwise analogous problems [Falkenhainer88] could help in correcting erroneous specifications. Let the base problem specification be $\{Q_b\}\ S_b \{R_b\}$ and the target problem specification be: $\{Q_t\}\ S_t \{R_t\}$ where the 'Q's are the preconditions, 'S's are the programs and 'R's are the postconditions. Assume that the preconditions are collections of conjuncts. Then we treat Q_b and Q_t as sets. The possible relations between the two are: $Q_b \subseteq Q_t$, $Q_b \supseteq Q_t$, $Q_b = Q_t$, neither Q_b belongs to Q_t nor vice versa. When they are equal there is no problem. When $Q_b \subseteq Q_t$, we may have to prune R_b to get R_t. When $Q_b \supseteq Q_t$, R_b must be expanded by disjunction to get R_t. When neither belongs to the other, the differences are considered and both pruning and expansion might be needed to derive R_t.

However, not every difference is important, i.e., not every difference leads to pruning or expansion. An example is shown in Fig. 11. Let this be the base problem and the specification in Fig. 12 be the target. Comparing the preconditions we notice that the facts that x belongs to A and that A is sorted are missing in the target. The former difference is important and results in expanding the target postcondition. However, the latter difference is unimportant as the sorting or otherwise of A does not affect the presence or absence of x (The fact that A is sorted is important to the program development as it results in a much more efficient search. However, it does not concern the

precondition:

$(x \in A\ \wedge\ \forall i:\ 0 \leq i < n-1 : A[i] \leq A[i+1])$

postcondition:

$(\text{find } i : 0 \leq i \leq n-1\ \wedge\ x = A[i])$

Fig. 11. Formal specification illustrating the presence of an unimportant difference.

precondition:

true

postcondition:

$(\text{find } i : 0 \leq i \leq n-1\ \wedge\ x = A[i])$

Fig. 12. Erroneous (incomplete) formal specification derived by analogy.

specification postcondition). So there are three tasks involved in difference based analogy: (a) determining the differences; (b) classifying the differences as important or unimportant; (c) reasoning about the important differences and modifying the specification. Of these, task (a) can be done. Task (b) requires more work, but it appears that reasoning knowledge to determine the dependence of postcondition on the difference is required. In this case, we can say that there are two important parameters – x and A, and differences relating the two are important. If the difference affects the truth of postcondition and it is missing from the target, its negation should be added as a disjunct to the postcondition of the base. Similarly, if such a difference is missing in the base, its negation is pruned from the postcondition. For the specification in Fig. 12, the postcondition is expanded to:

$(\text{find } i:\ 0 \leq i \leq n-1 \wedge x = A[i]) \vee x \notin A$

Thus we have the heuristic:

$H_{DIFFERENCE}$: If postconditions match, determine differences in the preconditions and classify the differences as important or unimportant. If the difference is important then [if difference belongs to base precondtiion then [expand base precondition by adding the negation of the difference as a disjunct] else [if the difference belongs to the target precondition then prune the base precondition by removing the disjunct which is the negation of the difference]].

3.5. Applying the heuristics

In practice, the heuristics described above, are applied in the order:

H_{CHOICE}, $H_{MULTIPLE}$, $H_{STRUCTURE}$, $H_{SIMULTANEOUS}$, and $H_{DIFFERENCE}$.

That is, first the most direct analogy is determined for each part of the target problem. If there are multiple analogies, all of them are applied. If there are several analogical maps to parts of the same structure tree, the hightest level analogy is applied first. But if there is more than one analogical map to the highest level, apply all of them simultaneously (i.e., the order is unimportant). Finally, check the derived formal specification. If it has a postcondition which matches with a postcondition from the knowledge base, determine the differences in preconditions, if any, and reason from these differences and remove any errors in the derived specification detected thereof.

4. Conclusion

In this paper we have described a novel approach that uses analogy to automate specification derivation. Formal problem specifications from past experience are stored in the knowledge base along with the associated informal specifications. When a new (target) problem is to be specified, its informal specification is provided. This is used to obtain analogies from the knowledge base, which are then applied to the target problem to derive the formal specification. The informal specification is compared with those in the knowledge base, to determine all possible analogies. A set of heuristics have been designed to assist in pruning this set of analogies, in ordering them and in selecting one or more of them at every step of the specification derivation process. The selected analogies are applied and the formal specification is constructed piece by piece in a top-down manner. The formal specification at this stage may be erroneous. A heuristic has been developed to correct some such errors.

REFERENCES

[Balzar73] R. M. Balzar, A Global View of Automatic Programming, In *IJCAI*, 494–498, 1973.

[Bhansali88] S. Bhansali, Derivation of Unix Programs Using Analogy, Masters Thesis, University of Illinois at Urbana–Champaign, 1988.

[Carbonell83] J. G. Carbonell, Derivational Analogy and its Role in Problem Solving, *AAAI*, 64–69, 1983.

[Dershowitz83] N. Dershowitz, *The Evolution of Programs*, Birkhauser, Boston, 1983.

[Dershowitz85] N. Dershowitz, Program Abstraction and Instantiation, *ACM Trans. on Prog. Lang. and Systems*, 446–477, **7**(3), 1985.

[Falkenhainer88] B. Falkenhainer, The Utility of Difference–Based Reasoning, *AAAI*, 530–535, 1988.

[Gentner83] D. Gentner, Structure Mapping: A Theoretical Framework for Analogy, *Cognitive Science*, 155–170, **7**(2), 1983.

[Green76] C. Green, The Design of the PSI Program Synthesis System, In *Proc. Second International Conf. on Software Eng.*, 14–18, 1976.

[Greenspan84] S. Greenspan, Requirements Modeling: A Knowledge Representation Approach to Software Requirements Definition, Ph. D. Thesis, University of Toronto, 1984.

[Greiner88] R. Greiner, Learning by Understanding Analogies, *Artificial Intelligence*, 81–125, **35**, 1988.

[Gries81] D. Gries, *The Science of Programming*, Springer–Verlag New York Inc., 1981.

[Liskov75] B. H. Liskov and S. Zilles, Specification Techniques for Data Abstractions, *IEEE Trans. Software Eng.*, 7–19, **1**(1), 1975.

[Parnas72] D. L. Parnas, A Technique for Software Specification with Modules, *Comm. ACM*, 330–336, **15**(5), 1972.

[Winston80] P. H. Winston, Learning and Reasoning by Analogy, *Comm. ACM*, 689–703, **23**, 1980.

The Requirements Apprentice: An Initial Scenario

Howard B. Reubenstein & Richard C. Waters

MIT Artificial Intelligence Laboratory
545 Technology Square; Cambridge MA 02139

Abstract

The implementation of the Requirements Apprentice has reached the point where it is possible to exhibit a concrete scenario showing the intended basic capabilities of the system. The Requirements Apprentice accepts ambiguous, incomplete, and inconsistent input from a requirements analyst and assists the analyst in creating and validating a coherent requirements description. This processing is supported by a general-purpose reasoning system and a library of requirements clichés that contains reusable descriptions of standard concepts used in requirements.

1 The Requirements Apprentice

The philosophy underlying the Requirements Apprentice (RA) is laid out in detail in [14]. In the interest of brevity, this discussion will not be repeated here. However, it is important to keep in mind the position occupied by the RA in the requirements acquisition process. As illustrated by Figure 1, the RA is intended to assist a requirements analyst.

The analyst begins the requirements acquisition process by means of a "skull session" that illicits an informal idea of what is wanted. A good example of the result of such a skull session is the library database requirement sketch [1] that was used as a benchmark by previous Workshops on Software Specification and Design.

Starting from such an informal requirements sketch, the RA assists an analyst (and through the analyst, the end user) to arrive at a more complete and more formal requirement. In this, the RA continues in the tradition of the SAFE project[2] and differs from most current work on software requirements tools (e.g., [4, 7, 11]) that focuses instead on the validation of a requirement that is already stated in a formal way.

Viewed from an artificial intelligence perspective, the problem faced by the RA is essentially one of *knowledge acquisition*. Related systems in this area include KLAUS[10] and ROGET[5], which provide automated assistance for acquiring new rules for expert systems. These tools support the acquisition of vocabulary and new concepts and provide well-formedness and consistency checking.

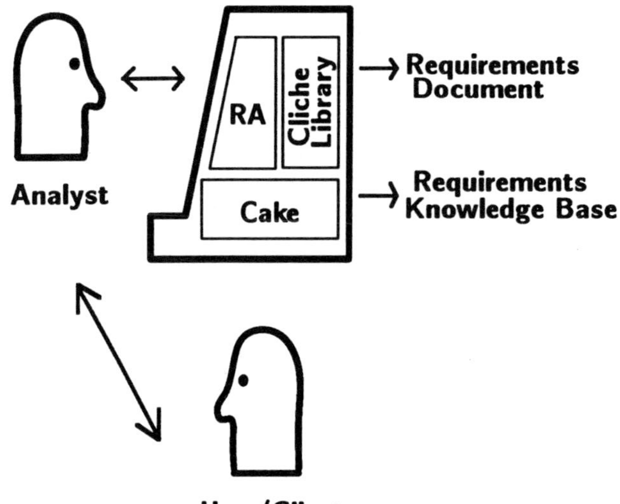

Figure 1: The Requirements Apprentice.

The current research with goals most similar to the RA is the KATE [8] system. Fickas has proposed an interactive system that will provide assistance over the entire requirements acquisition process emphasizing specification design. The system will critique an evolving specification [9] and will eventually be capable of generating examples to support its observations. To make this feasible, knowledge of a particular domain (resource management) will be provided to the system.

The RA produces three kinds of output. Interactive output notifies the analyst of conclusions drawn and inconsistencies detected while requirements information is being entered. A machine-manipulable *requirements knowledge-base* represents everything the RA knows about an evolving requirement. This knowledge-base will eventually be used by tools working on other parts of the software process. Finally, the RA will be able to create various kinds of written documents based on the requirements knowledge-base. Such documents can be used both by the end user (for validation) and by a system designer.

Figure 1 shows the internal architecture of the RA. The RA's basic reasoning abilities are supported by the Cake [13] system. Cake provides basic facilities for reasoning about equalities, propositional deduction (including the detection of contradictions), maintenance of dependencies between de-

©1989 ACM 0-89791-305-1/89/0500/0211$00.75

duced facts, and incremental retraction of previously asserted facts.

The RA proper handles interaction with the analyst and provides high-level control of the reasoning performed by Cake. The analyst communicates with the RA by issuing commands. Each command provides fragmentary information about an aspect of the requirement being specified. The basic implications of a command are processed by Cake, added to the requirements knowledge-base, and checked for consistency. If the analyst makes a change in the description (to correct an inconsistency or simply due to a change of mind) the RA incrementally incorporates this modification into the requirements knowledge-base, retracting invalidated information and replacing it with the new data. All of this processing is carried out in such a way that the net result is independent of the order of the commands.

The third box in Figure 1 is the cliché library. The cliché library is a declarative repository of information relevant to requirements in general and to domains of particular interest. Clichés define the key terms (e.g., "information system", "report", "transaction") used in stating the requirement. These definitions are the essential components from which a requirement is built. Most of the RA's knowledge of requirements in general and all of its knowledge of particular domains is encoded in clichés. As a result, the RA can be extended to cover new domains by defining new clichés.

Working Toward The RA

Research on the RA is aimed toward three mutually reinforcing goals:

- Developing a theory of coherent requirements descriptions.
- Identifying and codifying reusable components of software requirements.
- Demonstrating the feasibility of automated assistance for software requirements acquisition and analysis.

The initial RA proposal [14] outlines approaches toward each of these goals. In particular, using the library database problem as a point of departure, the proposal contains some document fragments showing what a requirement produced by the RA might look like, a discussion of what some of the clichés in the cliché library should be, and a proposed scenario illustrating how the RA might be able to assist a requirements analyst.

Initial work on the RA focused directly on supporting the proposed scenario. However, it gradually became apparent that it was not possible to support the scenario, nor even have a clear idea of the exact content of the scenario interaction, without having a clear idea of what the end product of the requirements analysis should express. In cognizance of this, the focus of research was temporarily switched to a detailed investigation of the contents of the requirement.

This second stage of research culminated in early 1988 with a concrete proposal for the requirements document to be produced by the RA for the library database problem. More importantly, it culminated in a general theory for how the requirement should be structured. The requirement has three main sections: *environment*, *needs*, and *system*. The environment section describes the context of the requirement: those aspects of the requirement that are not under the control of the end users and are therefore not up for discussion (e.g., the fact that a library of books exists). The needs section gives a high-level description of the desires of the end users (e.g., the need to keep track of which books are currently in the library). The system section contains an initial specification of a particular system that meets the needs (e.g., an information system that keeps track of particular pieces of data and furnishes particular kinds of reports).

Armed with a concrete requirement as the goal, the focus of research returned to implementation of the RA. The scenario in the next section shows the status of the RA in the fall of 1988. A basic suite of clichés has been developed. Further, the basic mechanisms underlying the interaction between the RA and an analyst have been implemented. However, the interface to the system is still primitive and, although the requirements knowledge-base contains the correct information, the RA is not yet capable of creating a requirements document.

The Proposed RA Interface

To put the scenario below in perspective, it is important to keep the intended RA interface in mind. As shown in Figure 2, this interface is expected to display at least four kinds of information. A dialog window is used for typing commands to the RA and for displaying the responses of the RA.

A window on the side displays a list of pending issues that need to be resolved. These issues can be viewed as requests from the RA for particular pieces of information. Merely listing these issues, allows the analyst to control the pace of

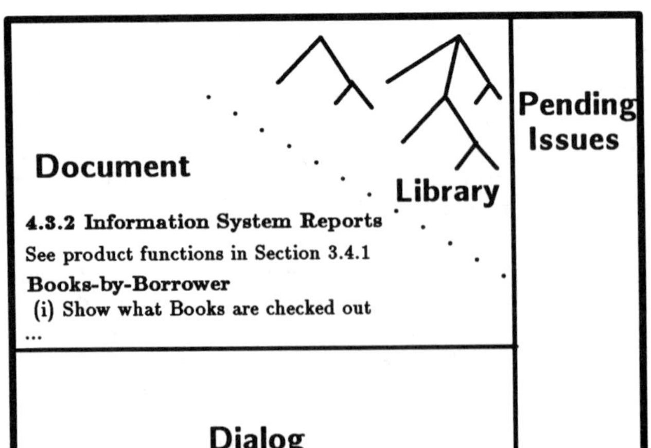

Figure 2: The proposed Requirements Apprentice interface.

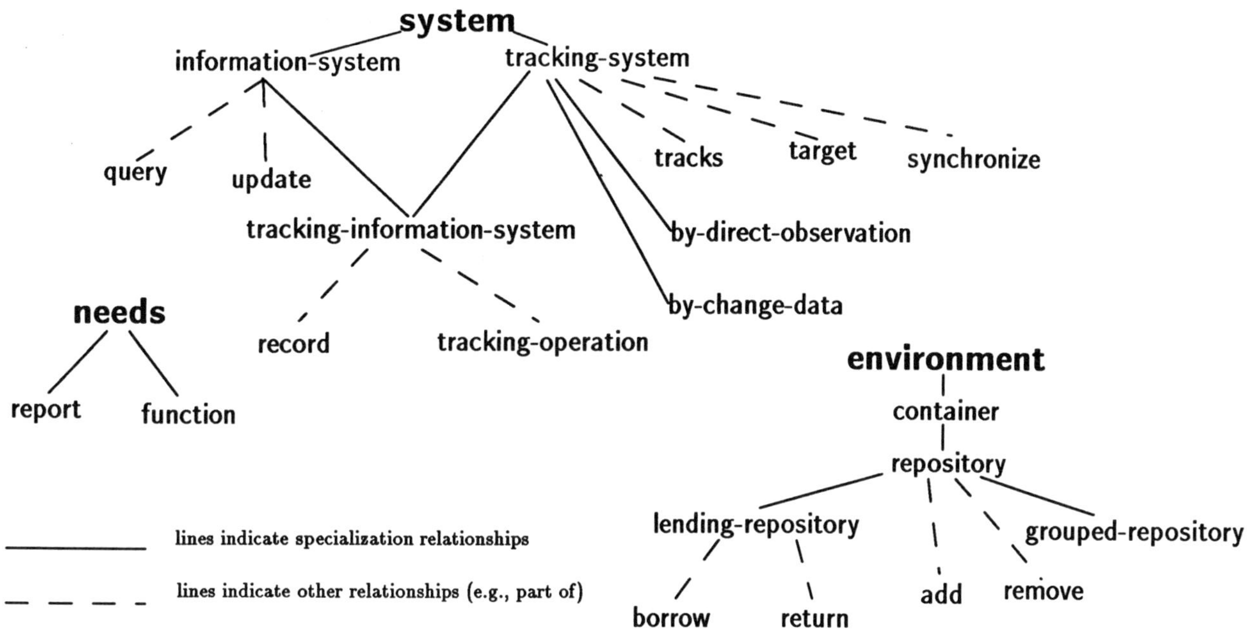

Figure 3: The structure of a fragment of the requirements cliché library.

the interaction. However, the requirement cannot be viewed as complete until all pending issues have been dealt with.

The main part of the screen can be used either to view portions of the requirements document being created or to browse through the requirements cliché library. At any moment the analyst can request the RA to generate a textual document corresponding to the current state of the requirements knowledge-base. In addition, the analyst can inspect the contents of the cliché library to gain a better idea of what the RA knows and what words are appropriate to use.

The Requirements Cliché Library

In the scenario below, the information unique to the particular problem comes from the analyst. However, the bulk of the information comes from the cliché library. The term *cliché* is used here to refer to a commonly occurring concept that underlies an area of expertise. Knowledge of the relevant clichés is the foundation for the competence of a person working in any given area. Recognition of the importance of codifying domain knowledge is a theme that the RA shares with systems such as Φ-NIX[3] and DRACO[12].

Figure 3 shows a schematic outline of part of the contents of the cliché library. The library contains clichés relevant to the three principal aspects of a requirement discussed above. Within each aspect, the clichés are arrange hierarchically. Clichés are represented as frame-like structures linked by constraints. Related ideas on how to apply knowledge representation techniques to software requirements can be seen in the RML language of Greenspan [6].

The specific clichés in Figure 3 are described in some detail in [14]. It suffices to say here, that in the realm of systems, an *information system* maintains a data base of information that can be updated and printed in reports and a *tracking system* follows the state of something in the environment. In the realm of environments, a *repository* stores objects for later retrieval.

The analyst is likely to initially provide high-level information, e.g., regarding which objects are information-systems or repositories, in describing the requirement. As more and more information about a requirement is collected, the RA "intersects" the information underlying these terms to determine the specializations of the terms that are relevant to the requirement. Each time a specialization is identified, significant amounts of additional information can be incorporated into the requirement by instantiating the more specialized clichés involved.

2 A Session with the RA

The following is an annotated trace showing an interaction with the currently running version of the RA. When looking at the trace, it is important to focus on its content, not its form. The content illustrates the fundamental capabilities of the RA. However, the form is at best a weak shadow of what the dialog portion of the interface should be like.

The RA is implemented in Common Lisp. Each command to the RA is a Lisp expression whose car specifies the type of command. As a prompt for a new command, the RA prints out an identifying number for the command. The output generated by the RA in response to a command is shown on the following lines. The particular commands shown were chosen based on the library data base problem [1]. They closely follow the proposed scenario in [14]. In command 1 (see below), the analyst directs the RA's attention to a requirement to be called 'library-system'. If there had already been a requirement of that name, the RA would have returned to a consideration of this requirement. In this case, there is no preexisting requirement. A new requirements knowledge-base is created and it is asserted that library-system is a requirement.

```
1: (Find-Requirement Library-System)
Beginning-A-New-Requirement-Called-The Library-System.
Library-System Is-An-Instance-Of Requirement.
```

The RA decides what to say in response to a command by monitoring changes in the requirements knowledge-base. Finding things to say is not so much the problem as deciding what *not* to say. The underlying reasoning system typically deduces an avalanche of facts, only a few of which are worth reporting. The RA collects a list of all the new and changed facts matching particular syntactic forms. It then filters these facts further to avoid redundancy. For example, if an object is deduced to belong to several different types, all but the most specific type assertions are pruned away. The RA then displays the remaining facts in an order based on the objects they refer to. (For a further discussion of the problems involved in choosing an appropriate level of explanatory detail see [15].)

A significant portion of the output generated by the RA essentially echoes the analyst's commands in a paraphrased form. This echoing allows the analyst to judge whether or not the RA has interpreted the command correctly. The rest of the output reports conclusions drawn by the RA. In the interest of brevity, the remainder of the trace suppresses the paraphrastic output and focuses on the deductive output.

In command 2, the analyst gives a name to the system being specified in the requirement. In a define command, the first argument is the word being defined. The word is often followed by one or more keywords specifying the type of the word. (As discussed above, the requirements library is organized as a hierarchy of types.) The remainder of the arguments to the define command are pairs of keywords and values, which specify particular features of the definition. In command 2, a short synonym (ULDB) is specified, which can be used on input and output when referring to the university library database.

```
2: (Define University-Library-Database :System
          :Synonym Uldb)
...
```

Command 3 specifies that the environment of the requirement is a library. In the output produced by the RA, the word library appears in quotes. This signifies that although the RA has recorded that the UL is a library, it does not know what a library is. Words are surrounded by quotes unless they are defined by requirements clichés or have been explicitly defined by the analyst in define commands. This is done to indicate that this term must eventually be defined.

```
3: (Define University-Library :Environment :Library
          :Synonym Ul)
Ul Is-An-Instance-Of "Library".
...
```

In this scenario, it is assumed that the RA has extensive knowledge of information systems, tracking systems, and repositories but no knowledge about libraries or library information systems. To operate in the intended manner, the RA must have a considerable amount of background knowledge relevant to the requirement at hand. However, it is unrealistic to assume that this knowledge will ever be complete.

Command 4 specifies the prime need in the requirement being constructed. The form `(!Logic ...)` specifies that its body is a logical formula. An interesting aspect of this command is the use of the word "tracks". The way the RA attaches a meaning to this word in this context is a simple example of what goes on in the RA when it tries to interpret the analyst's statements. Tracks has several specializations in the cliché library and thus the use of the word tracks is ambiguous. There is nothing directly connected to either ULDB or UL that can be matched up with the use of tracks as a relation between them. However, it turns out that the specializations of tracks that are consistent with what is known about ULDB and UL are all associated with various specializations of a particular kind of system called a tracking-system. As a result, the RA assumes that ULDB must be a tracking system. This is reported to the analyst, who could choose to override the assumption.

```
4: (Need (!Logic (Tracks Uldb Ul)))
Uldb Is-An-Instance-Of Tracking-System.
...
```

After processing command 4, the RA has not succeeded in totally disambiguating what tracks means. It has located an intermediate specialization of the term, which reflects its intermediate level of understanding. The cliché library is designed to be a multiple hierarchy with large numbers of intermediate terms that can be used in this way.

An important goal of the RA is to leave the analyst in control of the interaction. The RA is designed to be non-invasive in that it primarily just processes what the analyst says without much comment, even if it is not able to understand these statements completely. However, the RA maintains a list of issues that need to be resolved. This information should be displayed to the analyst in an unobtrusive way as a list of pending issues (see Figure 2). After command 4, four issues are pending. The word library needs to be defined. The word tracks needs to be further disambiguated. The fact that ULDB tracks UL means that there must be some state inside UL that is being tracked. The composition of this state and the parts tracked by the ULDB need to be specified.

This list of pending issues indicates one of the ways that the RA can assist in ensuring that a requirement will be complete. Terms mentioned by the analyst pull in clichés, which contain various places where additional information has to be filled in. Filling in this information makes the requirement more complete but may pull in additional clichés. This process continues until a point of closure is reached where filling in the remaining information does not lead to the inclusion of additional concepts with loose ends.

In command 5, the analyst defines a library to be a kind of (i.e., a specialization of) a repository that contains books. The RA knows what the general concept of a repository is, but does not know what a book is. This command answers two of the pending issues mentioned above. As well as defining the word library, it specifies what the state inside the UL is (namely the set of books contained in it).

```
5: (Define Library :Ako Repository
                   :Defaults (:Collection-Type Book))
Ul.Collection-Type Has-Value "Book".
...
```

Command 6 defines a book to be a physical object with certain roles (slots or properties). Command 7 specifies that the ISBN of a book (the Library of Congress number) is a role that can only contain a single integer value and that this value uniquely identifies a book. (The syntax "X.Y" is used to refer to the Y role of X.)

```
6: (Define Book :Ako Physical-Object
                :Member-Roles (Title Author Isbn))
...
7: (Define Book.Isbn
            :Integer :Card Single :Unique-Id T)
...
```

Having defined the basic environment of the library system, the analyst uses command 8 to begin the definition of the functional requirements. Interpreting this command presents a significant challenge to the RA because no type is specified and, while the words 'records' and 'remove' are both in the requirements library, neither one has a unique definition. This problem is resolved by attempting to locate something that can 'record' 'remove' and is meaningful in the context of a tracking system. This triggers a further specialization of the ULDB as a tracking information system in which check-out is a tracking operation. The information in this cliché, along with the current requirements knowledge-base, permits the RA to deduce a significant amount of information about check-out. For example, since the ULDB tracks the UL, and since the UL is a library that stores books, check-out must keep track of objects of type book. A default constraint in the tracking operation cliché specifies that, in the absence of anything else being said, the input of check-out should be a unique identifier for the kind of object being tracked and that the object being tracked is the object corresponding to this identifier. Finally, the word remove can be understood because it corresponds to one of the fundamental operations that can alter the state of a repository.

```
8: (Define Check-Out :Roles (:Records Remove))
Uldb Is-An-Instance-Of Tracking-Information-System.
Check-Out is-An-Instance-Of Tracking-Operation
Check-Out.Object-Type Has-Value Book.
Check-Out.Objects Has-Value
 (!The (?O) Such-That (= (Isbn ?O) $Input)).
Check-Out.Records Has-Value Remove-Repository.
...
```

In command 9, the analyst gives a quick definition of the check-in operation by specifying that it is the inverse of the check-out transaction (i.e., it tracks the inverse state change). From this statement, the RA is able to derive quite complete information about check-in. Starting with command 8, the amount of knowledge in the requirements knowledge-base has reached a critical mass where the RA can draw much more extensive conclusions from each statement of the analyst.

```
9: (Inverse Check-In Check-Out)
...
```

Next, the analyst defines an acquisition transaction that tracks the addition of an entirely new book to the library. The RA is again able to determine significant amounts of information about this transaction and deduces that there is a problem with the requirement. From what has been said so far, the acquisition and check-in transactions appear identical. They both record the addition (the inverse of removal) of a book to the library. The RA has a built-in expectation that terms should not be synonymous unless they are explicitly defined to be synonyms. This bias was introduced on the theory that an accidental alignment of this kind indicates that the analyst has likely left out some critical information, or is using some term in an incorrect way.

```
10: (Define Acquisition :Roles (:Records Add))
...
Conflict #1
Colliding-Definitions-Of "Check-In" And Acquisition;
Explanation:
 1.1 (Equal-Defs Check-In Acquisition)
     is True by Modus Ponens from
  2.1 Internal Premise:
      (Implies (And (Tracking-Operation Check-In)
                    (Tracking-Operation Acquisition)
                    (= Frame-I2 Frame-I3))
         (Equal-Defs Check-In Acquisition))
  2.2 (And (Tracking-Operation Check-In)
           (Tracking-Operation Acquisition)
           (= Frame-I2 Frame-I3))
      is True by Conjunction from
   3.1 (= Frame-I2 Frame-I3) is True by Equality from
...
```

The RA reports the problem and, by way of explanation, exhibits a proof of the equality of definitions. An unfortunate aspect of this proof is that, like many machine generated proofs, it is quite large and not particularly easy to understand (most of the proof is elided above). A significant area where additional work on the RA has to be done is developing better ways to present such explanations. It may be useful to provide a browser that can be used to explore the proof tree in an incremental fashion.

The output below illustrates two ways the RA can assist the analyst in resolving a conflict. First, the RA prints a list of premises underlying the conflict. The premises corresponding to statements made by the analyst are printed first, followed by information that comes from the cliché library. Although there can be a large number of these premises, it is often easier to grasp the problem by looking at the premise list than by looking at the proof. Note that the conflict cannot be resolved without retracting or changing one of the premises.

```
Premises:
1. (= (Records Check-Out) Remove)
2. (= (Records Acquisition) Add)
3. (Inverse Check-Out Check-In)
4. (Need (!Logic (Tracks University-Library-Database
                         University-Library)))
5. (Default 7 (= (Objects Check-In)
     (!The (?O) Such-That (= (Isbn ?O) $Input)))
...
Would you like to retract a premise?(Y or N) N
Would you like suggestions for alternate
premises?(N or #s) (1)
In the premise (= (Records Check-Out) Remove) you can
substitute for the term #<Term Remove-Repository>
the term #<Term Add-Repository>.
Would you like to make a substitution?(Y or N) N
```

It might be the case that one of the premises is totally wrong and should be discarded. However, more typically, all of the premises are at least partially correct. The RA can be helpful in this situation by providing suggestions for how a premise might be altered. This is done based on a number of heuristics. For example, if an equality premise specifies that something is equal to a particular value X, it might be the case that what is really desired is a some value X' that is a close relative of X. In the first premise, instead of remove, the analyst might have really meant some other operation on repositories. The only other operation on a simple repository is add, which the RA suggests as an alternative. Unfortunately, changing remove to add is certainly not the correct way to fix the conflict since this would cause acquisition and check-out to have the same definition.

The analyst decides to ignore the conflict for the time being—it goes onto the list of pending issues—and starts defining some reports the ULDB needs to support. This delay in dealing with Conflict 1 illustrates that the RA always allows the analyst to be in control of what is dealt with and when. It is often a good idea to ignore something for a while until clarifying information comes in.

The key content of commands 11 and 12 is the logical expression that is used to fill the query role of the report. This describes the essential information content of the report. This is the heart of a high-level requirement for a report. Detailed information about layout and the like belongs in more detailed specifications, or perhaps in some appendix of the requirement.

```
11: (Define Books-By-Topic :Report :Roles
      (:Data-In (!Decl ((?Topic Topic)))
       :Data-Out (!Decl ((?Titles (!Set-Of Title))))
       :Query (!Logic
        (= ?Titles
         (!The-Set-Of-All (?T Title) Such-That
           (!There-Exists (?B Book) Such-That
            (And (Mem ?B Ul)
                 (= ?T ?B.Title)
                 (= ?Topic ?B.Topic))))))))
Book Has-A :Property Called "Topic".
...
```

```
12: (Define Books-By-Borrower :Report :Roles
      (:Data-In (!Decl ((?B Borrower)))
       :Data-Out (!Decl ((?Books (!Set-Of Book))))
       :Query (!Logic
       (= ?Books
        (!The-Set-Of-All (?A-Book Book) Such-That
          (Borrower ?A-Book Ul ?B))))))
Ul is a Lending-Repository.
...
```

An interesting aspect of command 11 is that it refers to a previously undefined property of a book (its "topic"). The requirements cliché library does not contain any mention of the term topic. However, the context "?B.Topic" indicates that topic can be applied to an arbitrary book. As a result, the RA assumes that topic must be a property of books in general.

Similarly, command 12 mentions a word ('borrower') not used previously. However, unlike topic, borrower is referred to in the requirements cliché library. In particular, it is defined in conjunction with cliché lending-repository (a specialization of repository). Assuming that UL is not just a repository, but a lending repository allows a meaning to be assigned to the relation borrower.

In the initial response to Conflict 1, the analyst asked for suggestions on how to alter Premise 1. As a result, any new information regarding these suggestions is displayed to the analyst. Since lending repositories support two additional operations not supported by simple repositories, new choices become available.

```
Additional choices exist for substitution in premises
for Conflict #1.
In the premise (= (Records Check-Out) Remove) you can
substitute for the term #<Term Remove-Repository>
one of (#<Term Add-Repository>
#<Term Return-Lending-Repository>
#<Term Borrow-Lending-Repository>).
```

Prompted with the additional information above, the analyst decides to resolve Conflict 1. In response to command 13, the RA redisplays an explanation of the conflict (not shown) and enters a dialog about ways to fix the problem. The analyst chooses to have check-out record borrow instead of remove. Since check-out is the inverse of check-in, this causes check-in to no longer record add (the inverse of remove) and the problem is resolved.

```
13: (Resolve-Conflict 1)
...
Would you like to retract a premise?(Y or N) N
Would you like suggestions for alternate
premises?(N or #s) (1)
In the premise (= (Records Check-Out) Remove) you can
substitute for the term #<Term Remove-Repository>
one of (#<Term Add-Repository>
#<Term Return-Lending-Repository>
#<Term Borrow-Lending-Repository>).
Would you like to make a substitution?(N or #) 3
Check-Out.Records Has-Value Borrow-Lending-Repository.
...
Resolved-Conflict #1.
```

In command 14, the analyst specifies a transaction unshelf that records the permanent removal of a book. Command 15 then specifies a transaction unshelf-all that records the removal of every book with a given ISBN number. In this command, the analyst overrides the default logical expression that specifies the objects being tracked.

```
14: (Define Unshelf :Roles (:Records Remove))
...
15: (Define Unshelf-All :Roles
      (:Records Remove
       :Objects
       (!The-Set-Of-All (?B) Such-That
        (= (Isbn ?B) $Input))))
...
```

As above, the RA is able to deduce the basic features of both of these transactions. Also as above, the RA is able to detect a problem. Since the ISBN number is a unique identifier for books, there can never be two books with the same ISBN. As a result, the kind of removal recorded by unshelf-all is no different from the removal recorded by unshelf.

```
Conflict #2
Colliding-Definitions-Of Unshelf And Unshelf-All;
Explanation:
 1.1 (Equal-Defs Unshelf Unshelf-All)
     is True by Modus Ponens from
...
Premises:
1. (= (Records Unshelf-All) Remove)
2. (= (Objects Unshelf-All)
      (!The-Set-Of-All (?B) Such-That
        (= (Isbn ?B) $Input)))
3. (= (Records Unshelf) Remove)
4. (Default 23 (= (Objects Unshelf)
                  (!The (?O) Such-That
                   (= (Isbn ?O) $Input)))
...
Would you like to retract a premise?(Y or N) N
Would you like suggestions for alternate
premises?(N or #s) N
```

On seeing this conflict, the analyst realizes that the commands to this point reflect a type/token confusion between a physical copy of a book, and the logical notion of a book as a class of copies of books with some particular title, author, and ISBN.

(By this time it may seem that the errors made by the analyst in the scenario are a bit implausible. However, most errors look dumb after you have found them. In addition, the type/token confusion above was not merely fabricated as part of this scenario. Although the original problem statement maintains a general distinction between a book and a copy of a book, several parts of the problem statement suffer from type/token confusion and use the terms incorrectly (see [1]).)

To fix the problem, a new term corresponding to a copy of a book must be introduced. In addition, something has to be done about the fact that only some uses of the term book in the commands above refer to the concept of a book. The rest refer to the concept of a copy of a book. The RA provides a special command that can assist with this kind of conceptual realignment. The rename command displays all of the commands that contain the term to be split and asks the analyst to specify where renaming should occur. As shown below, libraries actually contain copies of books and the basic definition of a book really applies to copies of books. However, the ISBN is the unique identifier of a book, not a copy of a book. Further, the report books-by-topic does indeed want to refer to books. (Otherwise, you would see the same title ten times if the library contained ten copies of a relevant book.)

```
16: (Rename Book Copy-Of-Book)
 (Define Library :Ako Repository
                 :Defaults (:Collection-Type Book))
=Rename=>?(Y or N) Y
 (Define Book :Ako Physical-Object
              :Member-Roles (Title Author Isbn))
=Rename=>?(Y or N) Y
 (Define Book.Isbn
         :Integer :Card Single :Unique-Id T)
=Rename=>?(Y or N) N
 (Define Books-By-Topic :Report :Roles
   (:Data-In (!Decl ((?Topic Topic)))
    :Data-Out (!Decl ((?Titles (!Set-Of Title))))
    :Query (!Logic
    (= ?Titles
     (!The-Set-Of-All (?T Title) Such-That
      (!There-Exists (?B Book) Such-That
       (And (Mem ?B U1)
            (= ?T ?B.Title)
            (= ?Topic ?B.Topic))))))))
=Rename=>?(Y or N) N
...
U1.Collection-Type Has-Value Copy-Of-Book.
Check-Out.Object-Type Has-Value Copy-Of-Book.
Check-In.Object-Type Has-Value Copy-Of-Book.
...
```

Once the analyst has identified the commands to be altered, the RA retracts the old commands and asserts the new ones. The changes that result are presented to the analyst for review. The retraction and assertion is done in an incremental way so that the new state of the requirements knowledge-base can be determined with a minimum of rederivation. The underlying reasoning system makes sure that the rederivation is carried out completely and that every aspect of the requirements knowledge-base is rechecked for consistency. This kind of comprehensive support for change is a particularly important aspect of the RA.

In the interest of brevity the trace is truncated at this point. A number of additional commands are necessary to communicate the full content of the library database example to the RA.

3 The Next Steps

The next step in developing the RA will be to support the automatic production of requirements documents based on the content of the requirements knowledge-base. After that, work will begin on a more realistic interface. This will be followed by experimentation on requirements other than the library example.

An interesting additional area of research is suggested by the RA's abilities to make suggestions about how a conflict can be fixed. In principle, the RA's reasoning abilities are capable of going a long way toward evaluating which of these suggests are the best. In particular, it could straightforwardly prune them by eliminating any suggestions that are not actually capable of solving the immediate problem. In addition, the RA could look farther afield in the requirements cliché library for suggestions.

To date, support for this kind of processing has not been pursued, because it would undoubtedly require too much computation time to be practical in an interactive system. (The RA already requires a few minutes to process each command whereas a fully practical system would have to complete this processing in only a few seconds.) However, this kind of computation is an ideal candidate for background processing. It is plausible that the RA could carry out such investigations over night and greet the analyst in the morning with an improved set of suggestions.

4 Conclusion

Research on the RA addresses an important gap in much of the work on tools to support requirements analysis. Whereas the requirements process almost inevitably begins with only a vague and informal statement of what is desired, most requirements analysis tools need some sort of relatively formal requirement statement as their input. The RA attacks head-on the problem of fleshing out and cleaning up a vague and informal requirement statement.

Although research on the RA is still in progress, the current version of the system already demonstrates a number of capabilities that can be used to bridge the gap between informal and formal specifications. The RA has a knowledge-base of requirements clichés that allows it to infer large amounts of information from the analyst's statements. The analyst is able to talk in terms of high-level terms leaving the task of disambiguating these terms to the RA. The RA continually checks the requirement for consistency (searching for contradictions) and completeness (based on expectations set up by various clichés). The RA includes specific support for evolutionary modification of the requirement, using the facilities of the underlying reasoning system to ensure that each change is carried out in a consistent way throughout the requirement.

The partnership between the RA and an analyst embodies an effective division of labor where the analyst is responsible for communicating with the end user and entering the core information in the requirement and the RA takes care of the details making sure that the requirement is always in a consistent state even after numerous modifications.

Acknowledgments

This work is supported in part by the National Science Foundation under grant IRI-8616644, in part by IBM, in part by NYNEX, in part by Siemens, and in part by the Advanced Research Projects Agency of the Department of Defense under Office of Naval Research contract N00014-88-K-0487.

5 References

[1] R. Babb, *et al.*, "Workshop on Models and Languages for Software Specification and Design," *IEEE Computer*, 18(3):103–108, March 1985.

[2] R. Balzer, N. Goldman, and D. Wile, "Informality in Program Specifications," *IEEE Transactions on Software Engineering*, 4(2):94–103, March 1978.

[3] D.R. Barstow, "Domain-Specific Automatic Programming," *IEEE Transactions on Software Engineering*, 11(11):1321–1336, November 1985.

[4] T. Bell, D. Bixler, and M. Dyer, "An Extendable Approach to Computer-Aided Software Requirements Engineering," *IEEE Transactions on Software Engineering*, 3(1):49–59, January 1977.

[5] J.S. Bennett, "A Knowledge-Based System for Acquiring the Conceptual Structure of a Diagnostic Expert System," *Journal of Automated Reasoning*, 1(1), 1985.

[6] A. Borgida, S. Greenspan, and J. Mylopoulos, "Knowledge Representation as the Basis for Requirements Specifications," *IEEE Computer*, pp. 82-90, April 1985.

[7] M.S. Feather and P.E. London, "Implementing Specification Freedoms," *Science of Computer Programming*, 2:91–131, 1982.

[8] S. Fickas, "Automating Analysis: An Example," in *Proc. 4th International Workshop on Software Specification and Design*, IEEE Computer Society Press, April 1987.

[9] S. Fickas and P. Nagarajan, "Being Suspicious: Critiquing Problem Specifications," *AAAI88*, pp. 19–24, August 1988.

[10] N. Haas and G.G. Hendrix, "Learning by Being Told: Acquiring Knowledge for Information Management," *Chapter 13 in Machine Learning an Artificial Intelligence Approach*, R. Michalski, *et al.* editors, pp. 405–421, 1983.

[11] R.A. Kemmerer, "Testing Formal Specifications to Detect Design Errors," *IEEE Transactions on Software Engineering*, 11(1), January, 1985.

[12] J.M. Neighbors, "The Draco Approach to Constructing Software from Reusable Components," *IEEE Transactions on Software Engineering*, 10(5):564–574, September 1984.

[13] C. Rich, "The Layered Architecture of a System for Reasoning about Programs," *IJCAI85*, pp. 540-546, August 1985.

[14] C. Rich, R. Waters, and H. Reubenstein, "Toward a Requirements Apprentice," in *Proc. 4th International Workshop on Software Specification and Design*, pp. 79-86, IEEE Computer Society Press, April 1987.

[15] W. Swartout, "The GIST Behavior Explainer," *AAAI83*, pp. 402–407, August 1983.

Integrating Multiple Specifications Using Domain Goals

William N. Robinson

Department of Computer and Information Science, University of Oregon, Eugene, OR, 97403, U.S.A.

ABSTRACT

Design is a process which inherently involves tradeoffs. We are currently pursuing a model of specification design which advocates the integration of multiple perspectives of a system. We have mapped the integration problem onto the negotiation problem of many issues between many agents in order to apply known resolution techniques. Part of that mapping requires the modeling of domain goals which serve as issues for negotiation. Herein, we describe the use of domain goals in our conflict resolution process which is applied during the integration of specifications.

1. Introduction

Consider the problem of integrating two databases which (1) have constraints governing their form, (2) represent rich semantic entities, and (3) are the result of a large design effort—possibly conducted by multiple agents. Problems arise immediately: how does one determine (1) the correspondence between database entities, (2) the identification of conflicts, and (3) the resolution of those conflicts? Each of these problems in turn consists of subproblems: determining correspondences is a labeling problem that involves aspects of graph isomorphism[10] and concept learning[4]; identification of conflicts requires a theory of goals and plans[29]; finally, a theory of compromise and negotiation is necessary for the resolution of conflicts[22].

Instances of this integration problem may be found in the merging of database versions, program versions[14], software designs[12], and the area we are exploring—specification designs[25]. In this paper we will consider a model which uses the general notion of plan integration as part of its specification integration knowledge.

Viewed as an integration element, plans consist of rich semantic entities (i.e., operators), organized in a particular partial order, generated by a complex problem solving process. Commonly, the planning process involves the maintenance of a goal tree which records the derivation of subgoals and plan operators from the root goals of a plan. Our extended goal tree, termed the *development record*, plays a significant role in the characterization and resolution of integration interactions. In section 3, we describe the model around which we are constructing a computer-based system which automates integration via the maintenance and analysis of the development record. Section 4 traces the integration algorithm as two types of integrations are carried out. As a precursor, we describe the methodology by which we construct parallel designs and allow for their subsequent integration.

2. Parallel Elaboration of Specifications

Functional decomposition is a methodology in which software components can be independently designed under the constraints of common interfaces. Recognizing the benefits of such a methodology, Feather melded this approach with that of the transformational implementation paradigm[1] with the added twist that interface constraints need not be consistent across development lines[8]. Such an approach benefits from incremental development, i.e., (1) ease of understanding via a record of gradual refinement, (2) automation of specification editing operators, (3) reuse of (intermediate) specifications rather than code, and (4) maintenance of the specification by altering elaborations and then "replaying" them to a create a new specification (cf. [21, 28]). It also benefits from parallel development, i.e., (1) reduction in the number of concerns along lines of development, and (2) explicit consideration of compromises during the integration of independently developed specification components.

We are are currently formalizing Feather's model to allow for automation. Consider figure 1 as we describe our version of the Parallel Elaboration of Specifications (PES) methodology. At the top of the

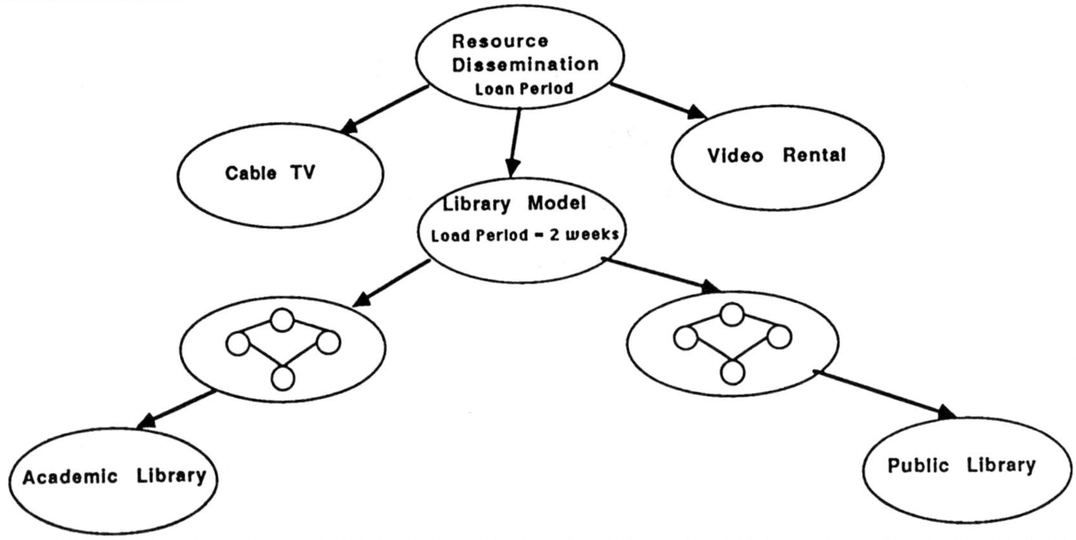

Figure 1. Abstract PES Domain Model Elaboration.

graph is the base model from which all other models are derived via the instantiation of domain goal attributes and the creation of specification components which support domain goals. The domain goal Loan Period is depicted within the **Resource Dissemination** model. Below, in the **Library Model**, this goal's ***proposed value*** attribute has been set to "2 weeks". This elaboration process is incremental, can be non-monotonic, and allows for parallel development of both domain models and specification components. (Figure 3 illustrates the linkage between specification components and the domain goals they support.)

Parallel development is unconstrained, e.g., functional decomposition may take place alongside ***multi-perspective design***. Multi-perspective design calls for the development of whole specifications from the desires of a subset of system agents[6, 9]. For example, with the design of an academic library, one may first develop a system description from the perspective of the staff, e.g., to reduce paperwork they may allow for only two types of users: staff and non-staff patrons. Another perspective could be library users who want a large "working set" of books and long loan periods. Due to the egocentrincity of such perspectives, we call them "selfish views."[1]

The integration of these two selfish views may require compromises of domain goals. Such integrations can be accomplished in a rational fashion with the use of negotiation techniques. Despite the difficulty of applying such techniques, recorded goal conflicts and their resolution provide a foundation for rationalizing designs. We suspect that such compromises are commonly done prior to implementation, but go unrecorded. By allowing for (in fact pushing for) explicit negotiation of domain goals, we make explicit the intents of the specifier and link those intents to the specification. Hence, we prefer multi-perspective design over functional decomposition due to its predilection to force negotiation of issues.

[1] Although the term *perspective* is preferred, *view* is often used interchangably, e.g., "selfish view".

3. Integration Architecture

As mentioned above, our use of parallel development is unconstrained. However, we tend to use it three standard ways: (1) within a single perspective for functional decomposition, (2) to describe alternative perspectives of a single system, i.e., multi-perspective design, and (3) as parallel development of different systems, e.g., designs of video rental and cable TV systems in parallel. This last case, combined with the use of our integration operator which reconciles multiple perspectives, allows for reuse via integration of two (or more) nearly "correct" systems, i.e., specifications which nearly satisfy the requirements.

We have subdivided section 4 into two examples which illustrate points (2) and (3) from above. But before their presentation, we describe the architecture and algorithms which will be used to assist analysts with the integration process.

3.1. Domain Goals

In the base domain model, the goal/subgoal structure is presented, and the direction of subgoal support is indicated (e.g., "+" associated with a subgoal indicates that an increase in satisfaction of that subgoal will contribute an increase in satisfication of its parent goal). A "-" direction indicates a reverse correlation between satisfaction of the

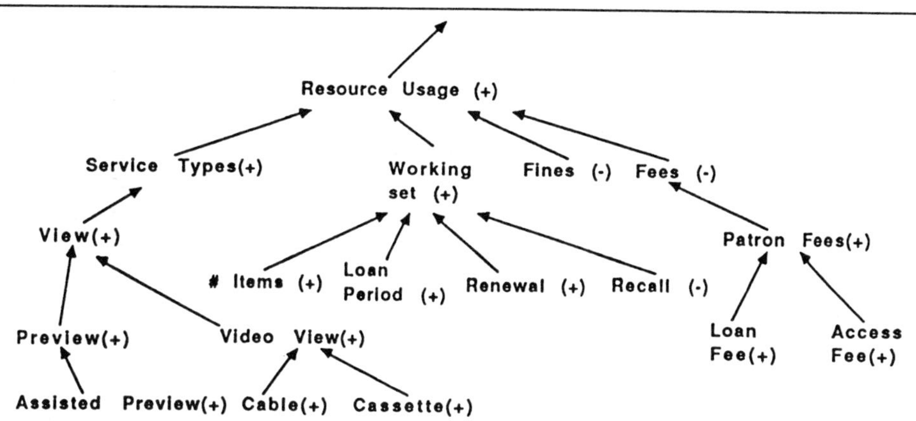

Figure 2. A Portion of the Domain Goal Relationships Graph.

subgoal and its contribution to the satisfaction of its parent goal. The integration algorithm uses these directional indicators to determine which way domain goal values should be moved to increase goal satisfaction and thus the acceptability of a resolution. An example of such a structure for resource usage is given in figure 2. Attributes may be associated with goals to capture ***importance***, relative ***subgoal contributions***, numeric or discrete ranges of ***utility***, ***feasibility***, and ***proposed values***. In the base domain model all goal attribute values are null. Elaborations of the base model (***perspectives***) set goal attributes based on the context of the application.

A utility curve can be represented as function $U(x)=y$, where x represents different possible values of a goal and y represents the satisfaction, 0 to 100%, that a goal achieves from attaining a value of x. Analytic decision techniques use such utility functions to resolve goal conflicts. Utility analysis can be combined with cased-based techniques to create a robust resolution algorithm as was done in Sycara's work on labor negotiation[27].

3.2. Elaboration Linkages

Once a perspective is created, the actual construction of the specification can take place. Domain goal perspectives are operationalized by applying a sequence of specification editing commands which create the specification language description of the sought behavior. Such ***elaborations*** are recorded with links between specification components, editing operators, and goal perspectives. These links will be used below to trace specification level conflicts to goal level conflicts during the process of integration. This process is conceptually similar to debugging software at the source language level rather than at the compiled code level.

Figure 3 shows how Oz, our automated PES environment, can highlight such linkages. The top pane contains domain goals. The goals highlighted were operationalized into the specification using the highlighted operators of the middle pane. Those operators added the highlighted components of the bottom pane. Such linkages can be traced upwards to find goal justification for specification components. Attempting to trace downward from an important goal may determine that the specification does not describe the desired behavior.

As a result of elaborations linkages, one can answer the following queries:

- Which domain goals are ***supported*** by a set of specification components?
- Which specification components are ***justified*** by a set of domain goals?

Such queries are generated during the integration process in order to determine which domain goals will be involved in negotiation.

3.3. The Four Steps of Integration

After two specifications have been created in the Oz environment, one may apply the following 4 step process to obtain their integration. Basically, the algorithm detects differences at the specification level and characterizes them as differences in goal attribute evaluations. Once the domain goals can be agreed upon, then the specification components can be merged.

Step 1: Correspondence Identification
Components of the two specifications must be identified as equivalent or non-equivalent. Since this is a difficult problem involving aspects of concept learning[4] and graph isomorphism[10], we currently rely on the analyst to carry out this process.[2]

Step 2: Conflict Detection and Characterization
Conflict detection attempts to map syntactic differences to differences of domain goal

[2]We do provide a tool which creates correspondences between components with the same name. The analyst may then edit this structure.

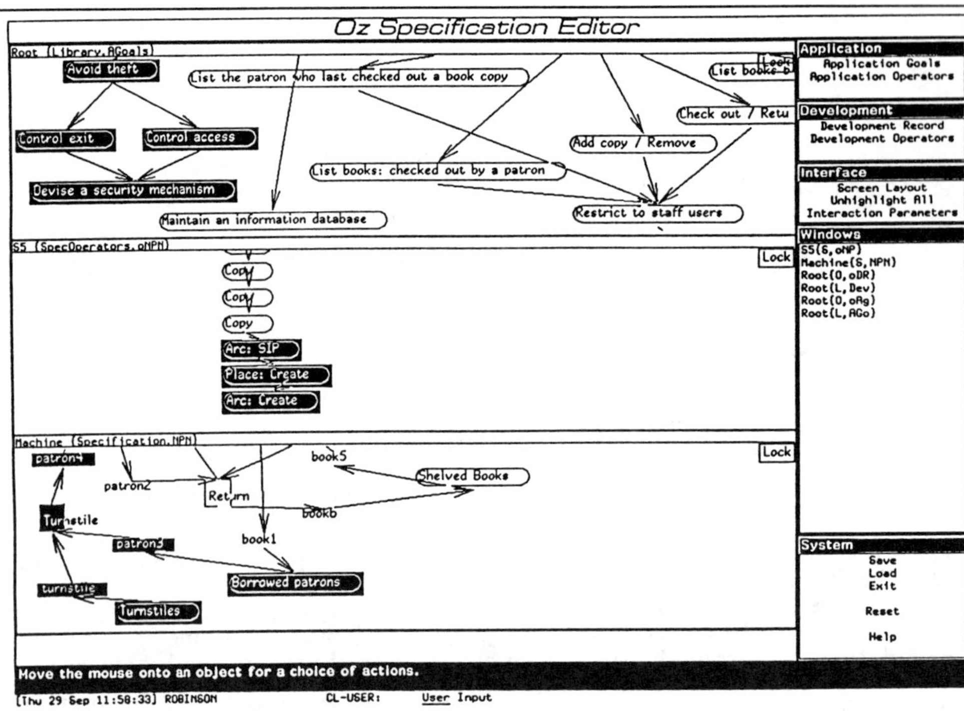

Figure 3. An Oz Depiction of Domain Goal Linkages

attribute evaluations.[3] First, one must identify which corresponding components conflict based on their structural differences. Next, conflicting components of each specification are placed into conceptually related groups. Components are grouped based on the common domain goals from which they were derived. For example, if components 'preview' and 'clerk' were found only in one specification and they were both derived from the domain goal Assisted Preview, then they would be grouped together.

Step 3: Conflict Resolution

Conflict resolution attempts to remove differences in conflicting specification components by appealing to compromises or goal substitutions within the domain goal perspectives. When a component conflict is detected, one traces up the elaboration links to find the particular domain goals from which the conflict stems. These goals and their attributes are then involved in (1) attribute utility analysis as applied in negotiation[16, 22], (2) goal substitution as applied in planning systems[27, 29], and (3) heuristic methods, either in rule form or as modification of previous case-based solutions[27].

[3]Step 2 is the only step of the four that has been significantly automated; the other three steps are carried out manually.

Step 4: Resolution Implementation

Once the conflicts have been resolved at the goal level, their resolution must be mapped back to the specification component level. It is assumed that difficult interaction problems will have been resolved and the remaining step involves simple merging and patching of specification components as illustrated in section 4.2.

4. Integration: Two Illustrative Examples

In this section two examples are presented, each emphasising a different aspect of integration. First, two perspectives of a single library system are integrated. In resolving a loan period conflict, this example emphasizes conflict resolution. The second example illustrates the integration of two different systems to form a third. Conflict characterization and resolution implementation are the emphasis as a hotel cable TV system is derived from the integration of systems describing video rental and cable TV viewing.

4.1. Integrating Parallel Designs

Figure 4 illustrates the notion that system perspectives may value domain goals differently. Both **circulation** and **user** are perspectives that have been independently derived from the **academic library** perspective. However, each places a different utility function over the range of loan periods:

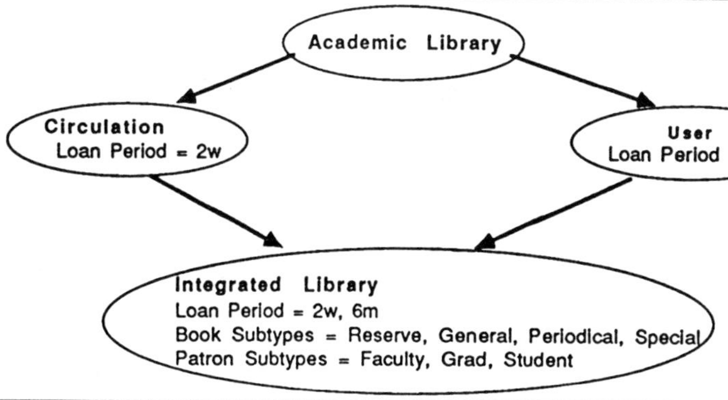

Figure 4. Issues Involved in the Integration of **circulation** and **user**.

circulation perceives a short loan length as beneficial to resource turnover, whereas, user's perceive a long loan period as a necessity for their research. Without dealing with the actual specification descriptions, below we describe the process of integrating these two perspectives. Not only do we show several resolutions of the loan conflict, we note how seemingly unrelated issues can become part of the resolution process.

Step 1: Correspondence Identification
The analyst carries out the process of correspondence identification.

Step 2: Conflict Detection and Characterization
From this contrived example, only one conflict is detected:

CF-1: circulation(Loan Period=2w) ≠ **user**(Loan Period=6m)

Since there is only one conflict, there is only one conflict group. Next, **CF-1** is traced directly to the loan period goal of figure 2. The conflict concerning the Loan Period's proposed value is identified as an ***issue*** requiring conflict resolution.

Step 3: Conflict Resolution
One resolution is to apply a compromise between the two goal perspectives based on their utility and importance values. A loan period of 14 weeks could result. Another compensatory solution is to maintain the value of one perspective but change some other values in favor of the other perspective. For example, maintain the two week loan period of the **circulation** perspective but in compensation do some combination of increasing the number of items, reducing recall, and increasing renewals. These items are found by examining the goal relationships graph (figure 2) to find siblings of the conflicting goal. However ultimately, it is the satisfaction of each complete perspective that we want to maximize. Hence, increasing local goal satisfaction (e.g., sibling goals) is a heuristic which gives way to searching up the goal relationships graph in case of an impasse. For example, if a satisfactory adjustment of Working Set subgoals could not be obtained, one might consider reducing user Fees or Fines.

A more novel solution can be had by the application of heuristic methods. One could subdivide the inputs of the loan process and distribute the loan periods over subclasses of inputs, i.e., based on patron subtypes and book subtypes. Our ***Predicate Input*** rule suggests just this third type of resolution. It is not specific to the loan issue, rather it uses the I/O behavior described in the specification to construct a resolution. Note how this last resolution lead us to consider another issue: resource and patron subtypes. Moreover, its inclusion into the design will be recorded with a specific justification for its existence, i.e., reconciliation of multiple loan periods.

Above we did not specify the controlling mechanism behind the generation of resolutions. This is a difficult and unresolved part of our algorithm. However, negotiators often employ an iterative strategy of generation followed by evaluation[22]. Sycara employed just this method of search in her labor mediation system[27].

Step 4: Resolution Implementation
After the analyst chooses a resolution in step 3, the system merges the components into a single specification. The next example will address this issue.

4.2. Integrating Previous Designs

The previous example illustrated the mechanisms of conflict detection and resolution of a one issue integration. It is more likely that an integration will involve a number of issues due to the size and complexity of specifications. Our next example illustrates the integration of specifications that conflict across a number of issues. Emphasis will be placed on the grouping of conflicting specification components into issues and the creation of an integrated specification from the resolved issues.

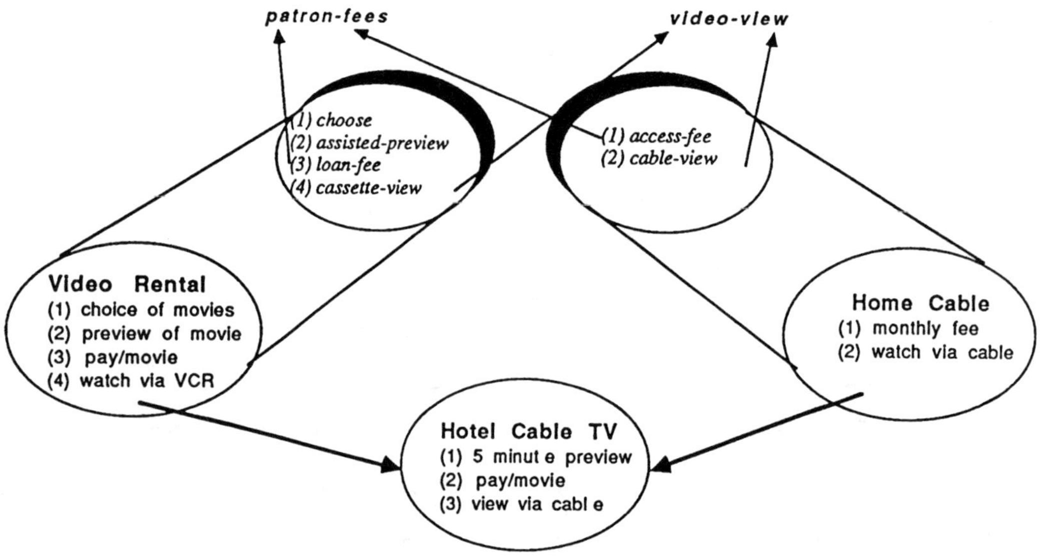

Figure 5. Issues Involved in the Integration of **video rental** and **home cable**.

Figure 5 shows the attributes of the two systems to be integrated. A **video rental** system allows patrons to: (1) choose their movies, (2) preview them with the assistance of a store clerk on a store monitor, (3) pay according to the number of movies rented, and (4) watch movies with the assistance of a VCR. A **home cable** system allows patrons to: (1) pay a monthly fee, and (2) view movies via a cable outlet. Each of these domain goals support more ubiquitous goals such as (1) choosing, (2) previewing, (3) patron fees, and (4) viewing video material. But, in figure 5 the italicized domain goals are more specific to the perspectives shown. It is the task of the Oz system to detect specification conflicts, map those conflicts to the intermediate goals of figure 5, and then find a common ancestral goal from which a resolution may be generated.

Note the disparity in the domains of **video rental** and **home cable**. Nevertheless, aspects of both are found in **hotel cable** systems. By combining two related specifications one can (1) reuse previous analysis, (2) explicate relevant issues, and (3) resolve differences rationally using negotiation techniques.

Below we show some of the component analysis created during the integration process to aid an intuitive understanding. However, one can follow the example entirely at the domain goal level.

Step 1: Correspondence Identification
Both the **video rental** and **home cable** specifications model 'patron-at-home', 'watch', and 'patron-money'. Pairs of these components are marked as corresponding.

Step 2: Conflict Detection and Characterization
Figure 6 shows the interaction between domain goals of the two specifications. A Most Specific Common Goal (MSCG) is a domain goal supported in all specifications, but whose support of its immediate subgoals varies across some specifications. A domain goal is said to be ***supported*** if a set of specification components have been linked to it, or a descendant of it. Domain goal support ***varies*** through differing support of subgoals or differing specification components across perspectives. For example, *Video View* is a MSCG because both **video rental** and **home cable** support it, but in different ways (e.g., by Cassette View in **video rental** vs. by Cable View in **home-cable**). Such domain goals are said to have ***direct interaction*** because of their shared MSCG and the resulting differences between their specifications. Specification components are placed into groups according to the domain goals they support as determined by the elaboration links of the development record (see figure 3).[4] Figure 6 also shows some domain goals that do not have direct interaction. Such goals (Choose and Assisted Preview) and the MSCGs are the ***issues*** for negotiation.

Step 3: Conflict Resolution
A resolution of the issues is: Cable View, Loan Fee, **home cable**(Environment), and Assisted Preview (modified). This resolution reflects a **hotel cable** system where one may preview scheduled movies for 5 minutes without charge, after which a per movie fee is assessed. For brevity, we will not consider alternative resolutions.

[4]There are also subgroupings according to which editing operators were used to modify components.

Specification	MSCG	Subgoal	Components
video rental		Choose	pick,picked-vid.,video
		Assisted Preview	preview,clerk
	Video View	Cassette View	watch,vcr,homevids.
	Patron Fees	Loan Fee	check-out,vid-fee,patron-money,store
	Environment	Environment	patron-at-home,patron-at-store,enter,exit
home cable	*Video View*	Cable View	watch,cable-access,clock,schedule
	Patron Fees	Access Fee	pay,cable-fee,patron-money,cable-co.
	Environment	Environment	patron-at-home

Figure 6. Table of Differences and their Interacting Issues.

Step 4: Resolution Implementation

Once the domain goals are reconciled, we place their supportive specification components into the integrated specification. During the integration process components are copied from input specifications to the integrated specification, e.g., Cable View's supportive components of figure 6. However, some copied components may depend on other components which are not included in the integrated specification due to the exclusion of their domain goals from the resolution. For example, components supporting the Loan Fee goal in **video rental** depend on 'patron-at-store' which is not copied into the integration. At this point some process (the analyst in Oz) must step in and provide a mapping from the missing components to those included. This last process of integration remains a manual task.

5. Summary

Oz is a specification environment which currently provides automated support of the bookkeeping aspects of parallel design and integration. One may create domain goal graphs, perspectives, elaboration linkages, specifications, and integrations[24]. However, the integration process is a complex knowledge intensive task that requires automated support. While currently we have little to offer in this regard, based on our experience from manual integrations and the results of related research, we believe that a useful portion of this process can be automated.

6. Related Research

Sycara's model of an automated labor mediator appears directly transferable to multi-perspective design[27]. In fact, we are currently involved in the construction of analytic and case-based techniques which we will apply to the integration of specifications.

Klein[17] and Lander[18] are also attempting to automate the resolution of conflicts. Klein is developing a hierarchy of conflicts and associated resolutions in mechanical design. Lander models conflict resolution as cooperation between expert systems.

Horwitz et. al. [14] analysis of integrating non-interfering programs has proven valuable as an interference detection mechanism. Unfortunately, it provides few clues as to how one can characterize the interference of designs or alleviate such interactions.

There are various projects which address specification design[19, 23] or parallel development from a language standpoint[2, 3, 7, 11, 13, 15, 26]. However, they do not deal explicitly with the negotiation of design issues that is inherent in multi-perspective design.

7. Conclusions

The integration of multiple designs must consider the process by which designs are constructed. Part of the specification design process entails the operationalization of goals into procedures[20]. When multiple designers construct specifications in this fashion they often assign different evaluations to the goals involved. These differences are observed as disparities between alternative designs[5]. To resolve such disparities rationally, one must engage in negotiating behavior. Automating portions of this process necessitates the representation of:

- domain goal relationships
- domain goal elaborations
- negotiation theory

The Oz specification environment represents our initial effort to capture such knowledge and facilitate its use during the design process.

ACKNOWLEDGEMENT

We would like to thank Stephen Fickas and the anonymous reviewers for their helpful comments on this paper. We would also like to thank the National Science Foundation for their support via grant DCR-8603893.

REFERENCES

1. R. Balzer, "Transformational implementation: an example," *Transactions on Software Engineering* **SE-7** (January 1981) 4-13.
2. R. Balzer, "Automated enhancement of knowledge representations," *Proceedings of the Ninth International Joint Conference on Artificial Intelligence* **2** (August 1985) 203-207.
3. R.M. Burstall and J.A. Goguen, "Putting theories together to make specifications," *Proc. 5th Int. Joint Conf. on AI,* (1977) 1045-1058.
4. T. Dietterich and R. Michalski, "A comparative review of selected methods for learning from examples," in: *Machine learning: an artificial intelligence approach,* Tioga Publishing (1983) 41-82.
5. T. Dietterich and D. Ulman, "Artificial intelligence approaches to design," *Artificial Intelligence in the Northwest,* (October 22-24 1985) 8/3.
6. M. Feather, S. Fickas, and W. Robinson, "Design as elaboration and compromise," in: *Automating Software Design Workshop,* AAAI-88 (1988) To appear.
7. M.S. Feather, "Language support for the specification and development of composite systems," *Transactions on Programming Languages and Systems* **9** (April 1987) 198-234.
8. M. S. Feather, "Constructing specifications by combining parallel elaborations," *Transactions on Software Engineering* **15** (February 1989) To appear (Also available as Tech. Report RS-88-216 from ISI).
9. S. Fickas and P. Nagarajan, "Being suspicious: critiquing problem specifications," *Proc. of the 7th National Conf. on Artificial Intelligence,* (August 1988) 19-24.
10. M.R. Garey and D.S. Johnson, *Computer and intractability: a guide to the theory of NP-completeness,* W.H. Freeman, New York (1979).
11. J.A. Goguen, "Reusing and interconnecting software components," *Computer* **19** (February 1986) 16-28.
12. I. P. Goldstein and D. G. Bobrow, "A layered approach to software design," in: Eds. E. Sandewall, *Interactive programming environments,* McGraw-Hill (1984) 387-413.
13. R. Greiner and D.B. Lenat, "A representation language language," *Proceedings,* (1980) 165-169.
14. S. Horwitz, J. Prins, and T. Reps, "Integrating non-interfering versions of programs," #690, University of Wisconsin-Madison (March 1987).
15. G. Kaiser, "Composing software systems from reusable building blocks," *Twentieth Hawaii International Conf. on Systems Sciences,* (January 1987)
16. R.L. Keeney and H. Raiffa, *Decisions with multiple objectives,* John Wiley and Sons, New York (1976).
17. M. Klein and S. C-Y Lu, "Run-time conflict resolution in cooperative design," in: *AI and Design Workshop,* AAAI-88 (1988) To appear.
18. Susan Lander and Victor Lesser, "Negotiation among cooperating experts," in: *AI and Design Workshop,* AAAI-88 (1988) To appear.
19. M.D. Lubars, "Schematic techniques for high-level support of software specification and design," *4th IWSSD,* (April 3-4, 1987) 68-75.
20. Jack Mostow, "A problem-solver for making advice operational," *AAAI-83,* (1983) 279-283.
21. J. Mostow and M. Barley, "Aumotated reuse of design plans," *ICED,* (August 17-20 1987)
22. Howard Raiffa, *The art and science of negotiation,* Harvard University Press (1982).
23. C. Rich, R.C. Waters, and H.B. Reubenstein, "Toward a requirements apprentice," *4th IWSSD,* (April 3-4, 1987) 79-86.
24. W.N. Robinson, *Towards formalization of specifciation design,* Masters thesis, University of Oregon (June 1987).
25. W.N. Robinson, "Automating the parallel elaboration of specifications: preliminary findings," Technial Report CIS-TR-89-02, University of Oregon (February 1989).
26. D.T. Ross and K.E. Schoman Jr., "Structured analysis for requirements definition," *Transactions on Software Engineering* **SE-3** (January 1977) 6-15.
27. K.P. Sycara, "Resolving adversarial conflicts: an approach integrating case-based and analytic methods," GIT-ICS-87/26, Georgia Insitute of Technology (1987).
28. Dave S. Wile, "Program developments: formal explanations of implementations," *CACM* **26** (1983) 902-911.
29. R. Wilensky, *Planning and understanding,* Addison-Wesley (1983).

Human Factors: Its Place in System Development Methods

R. Summersgill and D. P. Browne

Data Logic Limited
Queens House, Greenhill Way, Harrow, Middlesex, HA1 1YR, England

ABSTRACT

Interest in the needs of end-users has been growing for some years, leading to a host of notations, tools and approaches for the design of user interfaces. Unfortunately such techniques have remained isolated from traditional system development methods. The latter concentrating on functionality concerns. Thus, there remains a void between the approaches available for the specification and development of the two main components of any interactive information system. Namely, the application software that provides the storage, manipulation and dissemination of information and the user interface software that makes this functionality accessible to the end-user. This paper discusses the distinction between functionality centred and user centred approaches and makes a first pass attempt at reconciliation.

INTRODUCTION

As part of a software engineering research project, aiming to provide tools to support systems analysts during requirements capture and system specification, a task analysis of the job of systems analysis was conducted. The findings of this study made it clear that little attention is given to end-user requirements, except with respect to functionality. Analysts did not concern themselves with such issues as the semantics of command languages, preferred screen layouts or help facilities during requirements analysis. System specifications paid only scant attention to user interface requirements and as a result user interfaces were always implemented as adjuncts to application software. In addition, practices such as prototyping, constraints imposed by usability, and approaches such as end-user involvement were never considered during system development.

The advent of widely accepted system development methods provided an opportunity for human factors techniques to become an integral part of interactive system building. The 'best' techniques in terms of notations [5, 11, 9], tools [13, 6], and approaches [2, 7, 12] could have been integrated and utilised during system development. Unfortunately this has not happened.

There appear to be real problems in integrating human factors into system development. Two possible routes to improving this situation seem to exist. Firstly, the HCI community can pressurise system developers into allowing them to be involved from the earliest stages of systems analysis. This has been the main thrust of human factors practitioning for many years. Unfortunately, the approach has borne little fruit. The reason for this is not that all systems analysts are dismissive of the importance of user interface design nor that system procurers do not appreciate the value of good user interfaces. The evidence strongly suggests that more likely reasons include the perception that user interface design is expensive and that its place in system development is poorly established.

When considering user interface design, 'task analysis', 'prototyping', 'end-user involvement' and 'interface evaluation' are specific activities that are required over and above those normally carried out during system development. Obviously each of these does have an associated cost. What needs to be borne in mind is that user interfaces do get built. Every system has one, however poor it may be. There already exists a cost of building user interfaces and this rises dramatically both for the vendor and procurer as maintenance of this software is required and system productivity fails to meet anticipated levels. Thus there is a trade-off between the cost of performing user interface design in an organised and apposite fashion during systems analysis and development [10], and the cost of producing bolt-on interfaces and performing remedial maintenance both of which are unlikely to attain the desired usability.

This trade-off can never be adequately reconciled on the basis of following both approaches and costing each. No system is likely to be built twice by simultaneously following both approaches. Even if one were, there would be too many uncontrollable factors to prove conclusively the superiority of one approach over another. It would seem, therefore, that for some time to come, HCI design will have a battle to prove itself on cost grounds.

Another major reason why HCI design lacks acceptance by system developers appears to be its perceived lack of integration with existing development methods. Traditionally, and for good reasons, the management of a system development requires the acceptance of a structured development method with prescribed deliverables that can be agreed and 'signed-off'. At present, human factors specialists would find it difficult to identify where their work fits into an existing method [1] and to cost their contribution within such a framework. If these problems could be rectified then possibly human factors endeavours could be properly targetted and budgetted to the mutual satisfaction of systems analysts, system purchasers and project managers. The authors directed their attention to the need for integration in response to this problem.

To this end a number of presentations were made to systems analysts illustrating the virtues of task analysis, structured interface design methods and prototyping. The positive response received from these presentations was then capitalised upon so that further discussions between system analysts and ourselves could be arranged. In addition, attempts were made to identify those development methods which were amenable to having human factors deliverables integrated within them.

This led to a number of conclusions and confirmed some of our assumptions. Firstly, analysts were more than willing to accept the value of Human Factors (HF) although not without reservations. In general, they requested demonstration of how, for instance, the results of a task analysis could be integrated with a development method and who, in terms of skills, would undertake such work. With regard to existing methods, we found little to persuade us that any system development method catered adequately for human factors based findings.

Advocates of some system development methods [8, 3, 4] maintain that they can be used for the specification of at least certain aspects of user interface design, for instance, the sequencing of events at the user interface and task descriptions.

Nonetheless, consideration of a system as comprising user, task, and environment is beyond the remit of all currently used notations. Irrespective of the inherent capability of system development methods to represent interface specifications or not, a study of various methods shows that analysts are neither obliged nor encouraged to record facts pertinent to user interfacing decisions. The fault lies with system development methods themselves. If a method does not explicitly require something to be done then generally it will not be done. There is no place, we believe, in any existing method, where an analyst is required to question prospective users about acceptable performance times for completing a task, for instance. When would an analyst investigate the need for tailorability of an interface and if he did, how and where would the findings be recorded? On what basis would the designer/implementor of an interface decide on the naming of commands without end-user intervention?

In approaching the problems of integrating HF into system development, the traditional line has been that it is the responsibility of human factors experts to consider the requirements of software engineers, and contribute to the development cycle appropriately. While we agree with this sentiment, we have found that analysts can also provide a valuable contribution by familiarising themselves with the methods advocated by human factors specialists. Our attempt to bring these two apparently different skills together is discussed below.

INTEGRATION

Through discussion with an exponent of SSADM (Structured System Analysis and Design Method) [4], a first attempt at integration has been drafted. SSADM is the UK Government's standard method for performing the systems analysis and design stages of an Information Technology development project. It was developed by Learmonth and Burchett Management Systems (LBMS) in conjunction with the Central Computer and Telecommunications Agency (CCTA). It was formally accepted in 1981, became mandatory for all central government contracts in 1983 and is now in its third version.

It is not possible within this paper to give a complete overview of SSADM. The reader is referred to Downs et al 1988. Suffice it to say that SSADM comprises three phases which subdivide into two optional and six mandatory stages, each of which are further divided into steps. The phases and stages are shown in Figure 1. Each phase and stage will now be briefly discussed and a first attempt at integrating human factors activities and deliverables will be presented.

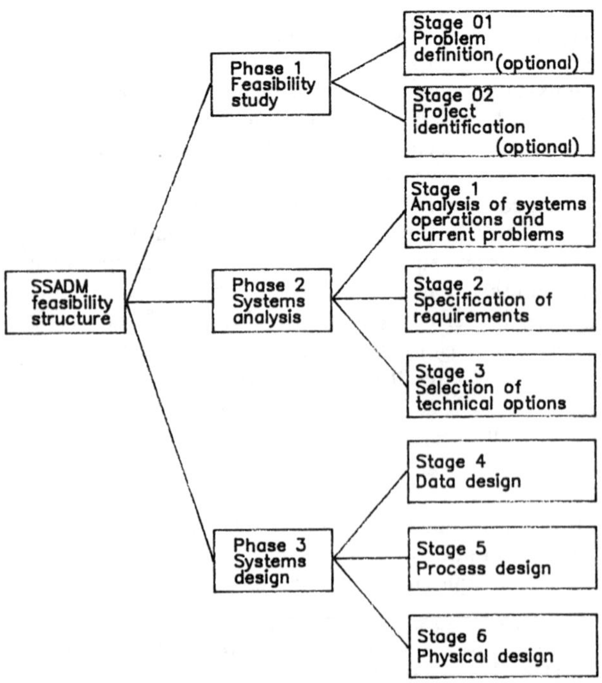

Figure 1 Breakdown of SSADM Phases into Stages

Feasibility Study

Stage 01 - Problem Definition. The problem definition derived during stage 01 is intended to provide an accurate description of the problem to be addressed. In this optional stage, 'system boundaries' must be agreed and a plan of work drawn up. One of the major problems in any system development method is the allocation of functions between system and user. This of course will depend on what users have a real need for, the limitations of human cognitive processing and what it is practically possible to provide, given resource availability. It has traditionally been the aim of task analysis, particularly when carried out by human factors practitioners with a behavioural science background, to provide the necessary information to address the first two of these dependencies. However, the output of a task analysis is seldom in a form which is consonant with system development methods.

In order to overcome this problem we have found it useful to generate a scoping chart placing tasks on a number of a dichotomies. For convenience these DIchotomy Scoping Charts will be referred to as DISCs. Obviously the dichotomies selected are context dependent but those we have found useful are whether the task:

- can actually be aided by computer support or not;
- needs interaction with people or systems external to the system under consideration or not;
- support of the task would require extensive research or not;
- should be in the scope of the project or is simply desirable.

For clarity and ease of assimilation, this information can be presented diagramatically as shown in Figure 2. The centre circle of Figure 2 encloses tasks that should be supported by the system as essential functionality. The larger circle encloses all tasks that it is felt could be automated. Tasks above the horizontal line are those which have to be performed by users in carrying out their jobs, while those below this line may be done and, if they could be supported by some automatic mechanism, would be of value. Tasks within elipses are performed with people or systems external to the system under consideration. Tasks in the outer area of an elipse bisected by an arc are very unlikely to be automatable and will remain off-line tasks for the users to perform. Tasks to the right of the vertical line are considered as straightforward but this does not mean that they are easy to support. It simply means the mechanisms or procedures for performing these tasks are well understood. Tasks to the left of the vertical line are not well understood and would require research before they could be supported.

DISCs afford the possibility of discussing the boundaries of the system. The feasibility phase of SSADM, or more par-

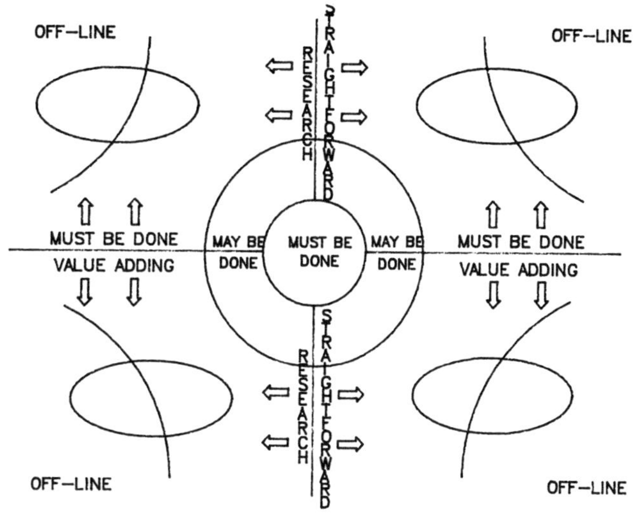

Figure 2 DISC (Scoping Chart)

ticularly stage 01, should encompass the generation of a scoping chart derived from a task analysis. How this might integrate with the steps of Stage 01 is shown in Figure 3, (additions to SSADM are shown using dashed lines).

The scope of a project should not be determined simply by the production of dataflow diagrams and logical data structures derived from the terms of reference. An analysis of the actual tasks to be addressed should help drive the scoping of the project. It is likely to be the case that the terms of reference reflect someone's perception of the problem areas, but these may not concur with the end-users' problems or requirements. Thus, a first pass task analysis would provide a useful break down of the tasks undertaken in a manner that would facilitate the decision making to be undertaken at stage 02. By first pass, or level 1 task analysis, is meant a short analysis performed with a limited number of end-users or their representatives. This is shown in Figure 4 in the format used by Downs et al [4].

Stage 02 - Project Identification. This stage essentially creates a series of options and aims to help the customer choose a suitable one. No human factors endeavours need to be undertaken at this stage.

Systems Analysis

Stage 1 - Analysis of Systems Operations and Current Problems. One of the important deliverables from this stage is the problem/requirements list. At present, SSADM does not capture adequately this list to the satisfaction of human factors practitioners. For instance, the users' requirements for naming conventions for data items and commands, and pure user interface functionality are not well catered for. Thus we propose at this stage to incorporate a full Task Analysis (TA) exercise, see Figure 5. This analysis will produce task catalogues and hierarchies in addition to contextual and organisational data as deduced from end-user investigation.

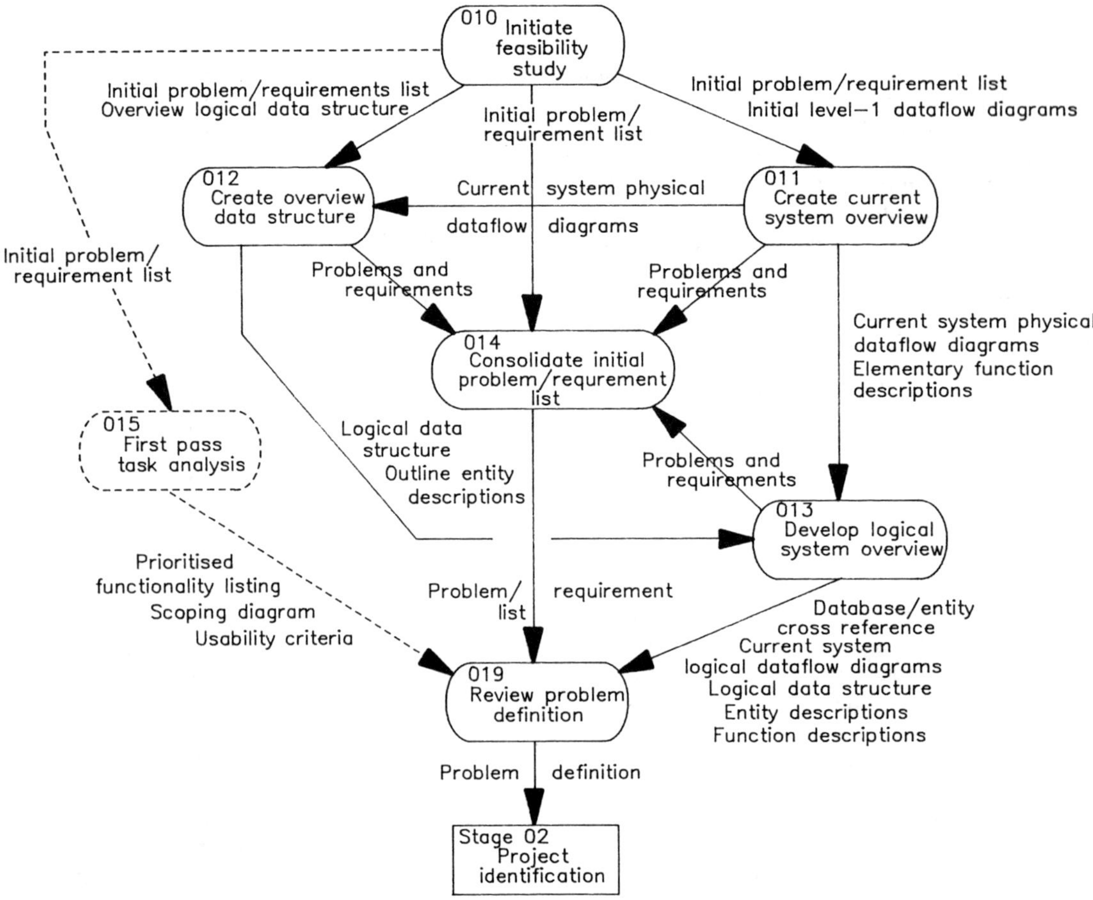

Figure 3 Stage 01 - Problem Definition

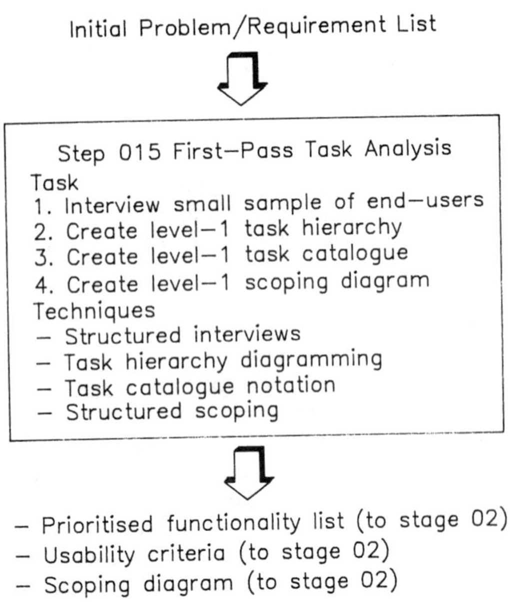

Figure 4 Step 015 - First Pass Task Analysis

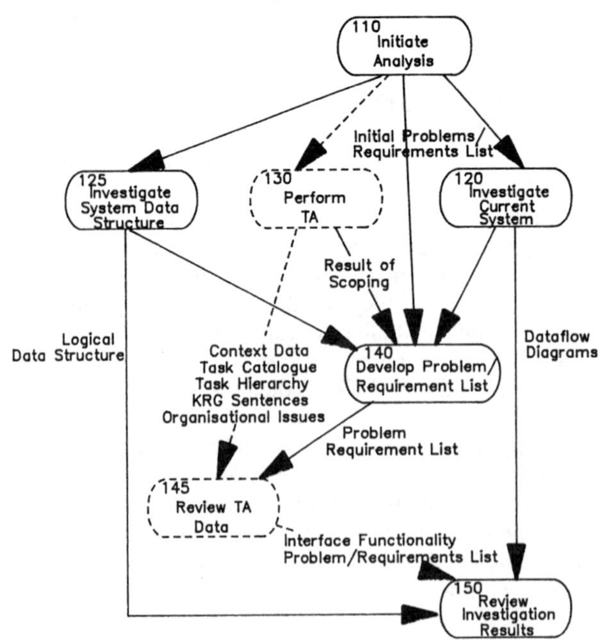

Figure 5 Stage 1 - Analysis of Systems Operations and Current Problems

Techniques which behavioural scientists are well trained for such as interviewing, observation and questionnaire production will be the mainstays of this work.

As can be seen, two extra steps have been added to stage 1. These being 'Perform Task Analysis (130)' and 'Review Task Analysis Data (145)'. Steps 130 and 145 are outlined in Figures 6 and 7. The major impact of these steps will be on the problem/requirements list which is a major deliverable from stage 1. An additional deliverable from stage 1 will now be an outline of the interface functionality. This will include required dialogue styles, error messaging, availability of help, dialogue sequencing, and defaulting behaviour. Such requirements will be reviewed with end-users using rapid prototyping techniques and screen walk-throughs.

- Usability Criteria (from stage 01)
- Prioritised Functionality List (from stage 01)

STEP 130 – PERFORM TASK ANALYSIS

Tasks
1. Produce task hierarchy
2. Produce task catalogue
3. Perform scoping exercise
4. Document organisational constraints

Techniques
1. Structured interviews
2. Direct observation
3. Protocol analysis
4. Questionnaires

- KRG sentences (to 145)
- Task hierarchies (to 145)
- Task catalogue (to 145)
- Context data (to 145)
- Organisational data (to stage 2, step 220)
- Scoping output (to 140)

Figure 6 Step 130 - Perform Task Analysis

- Task Catalogue (from 130)
- Task Hierarchy (from 130)
- KRG Sentences (from 130)
- Context Data (from 130)

STEP 145 – REVIEW TASK ANALYSIS DATA

Task
1. Agree dialogue style with users (errors/help/sequencing/defaulting)
2. Agree naming conventions with users
3. Agree acceptable system response times with users

Techniques
- Prototype finite set of screens
- Perform dialogue walk throughs

Level–1
- Interface functionality (to 256)

Figure 7 Step 145 - Review Task Analysis Data

Stage 2 - Specification of Requirements. Building on the problem/requirements list and other deliverables from stage 1, this stage derives a system specification. Following the human factors exercises conducted in stage 1, it is now necessary to consider the user interface logic and ensure its integration with the system logic. To this end it is proposed that two new steps be added at this stage as shown in Figure 8. Step 255 (Figure 9) takes the task catalogue, hierarchies, and descriptions applicable within the determined system boundary and validates them against the event catalogues and dataflow diagrams created within SSADM. The deliverable from this step is a Task/Event mapping for use in stage 4 and a task/DFD mapping, collectively known as a 'Task and Object-Oriented Event Specification' (TOES), as a basis for the second new step. Step 256 (Figure 10) uses TOES and the interface functionality from stage 1 to produce logical dialogue outlines (LDOs) and logical design controls (LDCs). LDOs and LDCs will go beyond those catered for by SSADM. This will be necessary given the inadequacy of LDOs and LDCs for describing user interface techniques and styles that can be supported by workstation/PC capabilities. For instance, LDOs and LDCs cannot adequately describe interfaces that support multi-tasking. If it is anticipated that transaction processing dialogues provided on dumb terminals will provide the user interface then the limitations this creates should obviously be considered. Rapid prototyping should again be utilised where at all possible during this step in order to validate the LDOs and LDCs. Organisational issues such as the impact of legislation, social communication requirements etc. as identified in stage 1 should also be taken into account. They should directly impact step 220 the identification and selection from business system options.

Stage 3 - Selection of Technical Option. The objective is to help users to choose a technical option for implementation of the required logical system. Given the selected business option, there is likely to be scope for choosing a technical option for the physical interface. For instance, choosing between personal computer options and input devices. Thus the findings of the task analysis, particularly organisational issues, user profiles and interface usage, should impact the choice of option. To this end step 325, 'Choose Physical Interface Option', shown on Figure 11 and detailed in Figure 12 has been added. The inputs to this step emanate from stage 2 and the output is a system specification for the user interface technology.

Although the user interface technology would necessarily be specified during step 330 of SSADM, it is unlikely that it would be made solely on the basis of end-user requirements, and without due consideration of contextual and organisational constraints. Thus step 325 is seen as a necessary and distinct step, replacing aspects of steps 310 and 330. The performance objectives specified in step 340 should now be extended to incorporate usability criteria explicitly. For instance, acceptable error rate, time to learn, and time to perform a representative set of tasks.

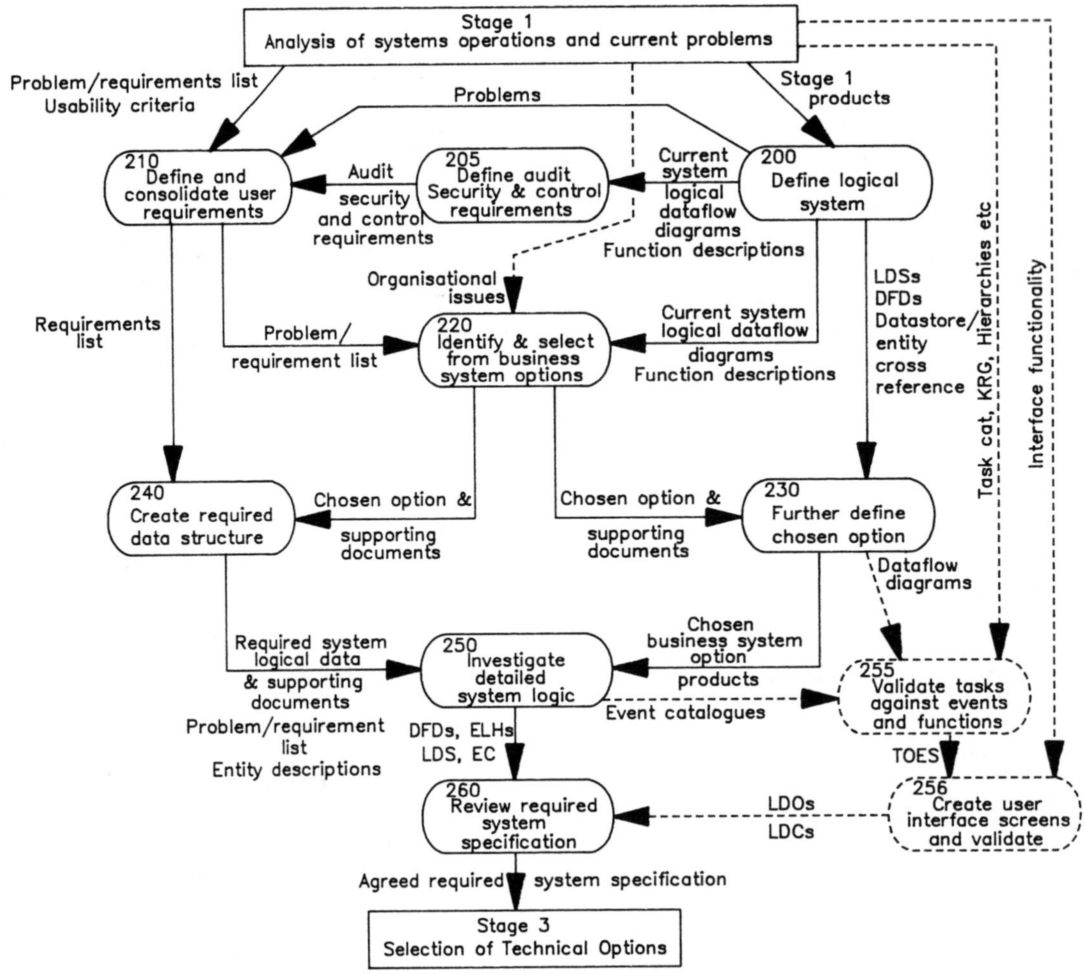

Figure 8 Stage 2 - Specification of Requirements

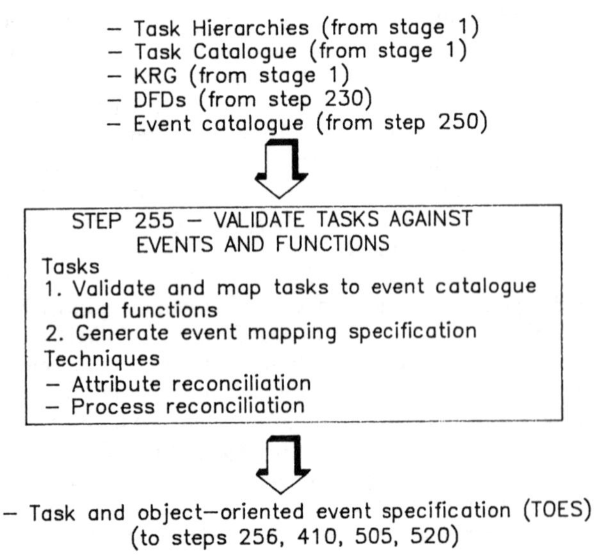

Figure 9 Step 255 - Validate Tasks against Events and Functions

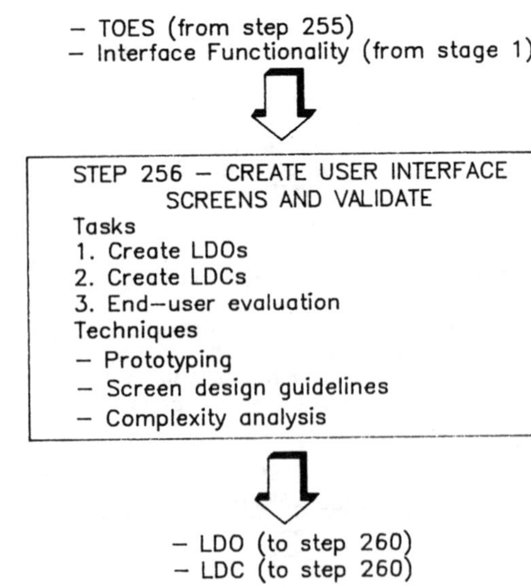

Figure 10 Step 256 - Create User Interface Screens and Validate

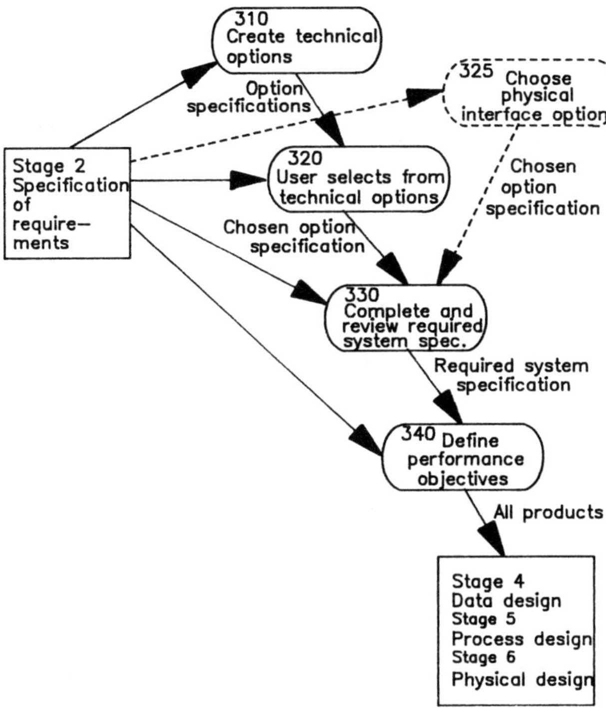

Figure 11 Stage 3 - Selection of Technical Option

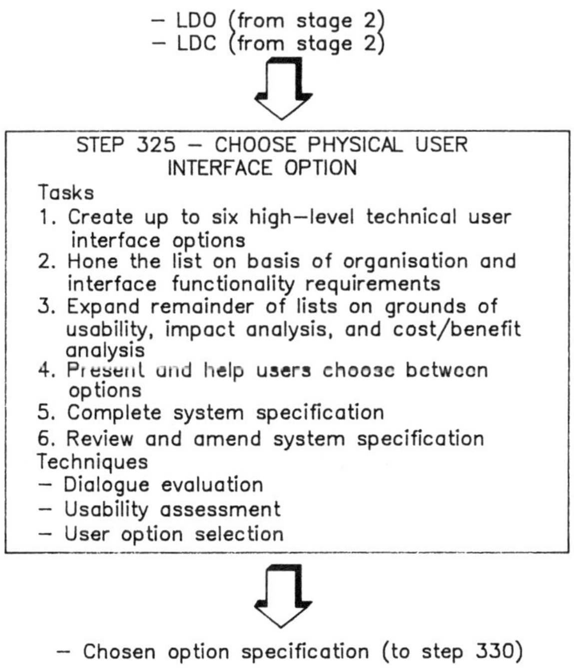

Figure 12 Step 325 - Choose Physical User Interface Option

System Design

Stage 4 - Data Design. This is the data modelling stage as conducted in conjunction with the process design (stage 5), the latter possibly requiring changes to the data model. Human factors steps may well impact data modelling, for instance because of the aggregation of data objects for purposes of screen presentation. Thus, step 410 'Conduct Relational Data Analyis' should take account of the object-oriented specification (TOES) generated in stage 2 (Figure13). That is, the tasks or user actions and task attributes or parameters that need to be supported.

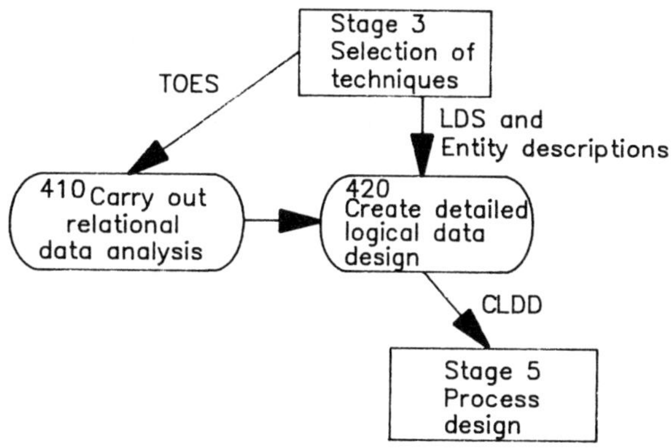

Figure 13 Stage 4 - Data Design

Stage 5 - Process Design. Where the technical option being followed does not include local PC capability for the user interface then this stage does not require extra steps. Nonetheless, steps 510 and 520 (Figure 14) should incorporate the prototyping of screens for the purposes of creating output formats and updating LDOs.

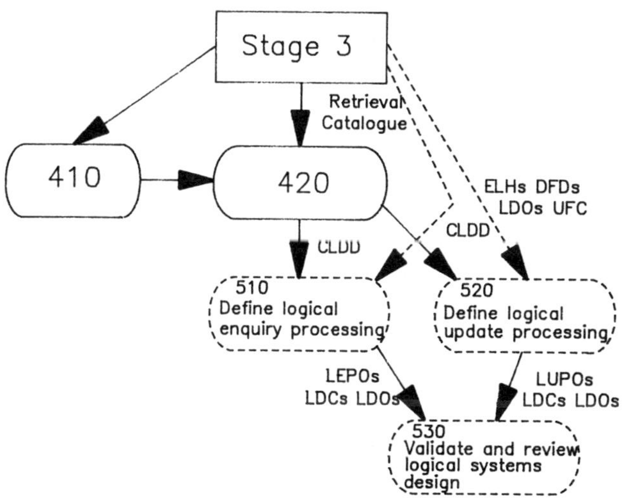

Figure 14 Stages 4 and 5 - Data Design and Process Design (Dumb Terminal)

If a PC option has been chosen then design of the user interface will be a powerful determinant of logical update and enquiry processing (LUPOs and LEPOs). Thus step 505 'Complete User Interface Design' provides LDOs, LDCs and confirms the TOES (Figure 15). At this point, the update function catalogues and retrieval catalogues will have to be verified against the TOES. Thus ensuring that they fulfill all of the users' task requirements.

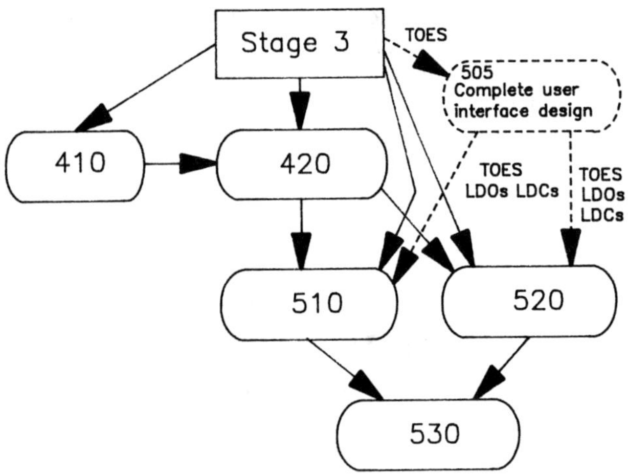

Figure 15 Stages 4 and 5 - Data Design and Process Design (PC Option)

Stage 6 - Physical Design. All human factors deliverables will have been documented and prototyped by this stage. Their final implementation will still require evaluation according to quality assurance practices in order to ensure that usability criteria have been met. In addition, necessary training packages, system documentation and workplace designs will have to be completed and implemented.

CONCLUSIONS

A task analysis confirmed the suspicion, held by many human factors practitioners, that systems analysts have an extremely simplistic view of what constitutes Human Computer Interface design: that it is simply screen layout design carried out late in the development cycle. This appears to be partly the fault of human factors practitioners themselves, in the scant attention paid to integrating human factors methods into current system development practices.

The work discussed in this paper makes it clear that there is scope, within at least one current system development method, for the integration of good human factors practices. In addition, it indicates that this can be carried out without either radically restructuring the original method or diluting the central human factors tenet of taking a user centred approach. Furthermore, such integration appears to blur traditional lines of demarcation between the two disciplines. Computer science has now grown to a stage where no single person can fully understand all aspects of system development. As has been the case within other scientific fields, specialisation has become the main method of handling the growing complexity. By integrating human factors and system development methods, it should be possible for each to draw on the skills available within the other in a far more flexible manner than can occur at the present time. Following such an integrated approach may finally address the problem of user dissatisfaction in software and result in functionally sound, robust, maintainable software which is easy to learn and productive to use.

REFERENCES

[1] D.E. Avison and A.T. Wood-Harper, "Multiview - An exploration in Information Systems Development," The Australian Computer Journal 18 (4), pp 174-179, 1986.

[2] R. Budde, K. Kuhlenkamp, L. Mathiassen, and H. Zullinghoven, "Approaches to Prototyping," Springer Verlag, 1984.

[3] J.R. Cameron, "An overview of JSD," IEEE Transactions on Software Engineering, 12(2), pp 222-240, 1986.

[4] E. Downs, P. Clare, and I. Coe, "Structured Systems Analysis and Design Method: Application and Content," PrenticeHall, 1988.

[5] D.Harel, "On Visual Formalisms," Communications of the ACM, 31(5), pp 514-530, 1988.

[6] D.A. Henderson, "The Trillium User Interface Design Environment," CHI'86, Proceedings of Human Factors in Computing Systems, pp 221-227, 1986.

[7] R.A. Hirscheim, "Participative Systems Design: User Experiences, Evaluation and Conclusions," The Australian Computer Journal, 18 (4),pp 166-173, 1986.

[8] M.A. Jackson, "Systems Development," Englewood Cliffs, NJ: Prentice Hall, 1982.

[9] P. Johnson, "Toward a task model of messaging: an example of the application of TAKD to user interface design," "People and Computers: Designing the Interface," Cambridge University Press, 1985.

[10] M.M. Mantei, and J. Teorey, "Cost/Benefit Analysis for Incorporating Human Factors in the Software Lifecycle". Communications of the ACM 31(4), pp 428-439.1988.

[11] T.P. Moran, "The Command Language Grammar: a representation for the user interface of interactive computer systems," International Journal of Man-Machine Studies, 15(1), pp 3-50, 1981.

[12] B. Myers, and W. Buxton, "Creating Highly-Interactive and Graphical User Interfaces by Demonstration," ACM Computer Graphics, 20(4), pp 249-258, 1986.

[13] D.R. Olsen, and J.R. Dance, "Macros by Example in a Graphical UIMS," IEEE Computer Graphics and Applications, 8(1), pp 68-78, 1988.

Specifying Coordinators: Guidelines For Groupware Developers

David A. Marca

Digital Equipment Corporation
110 Spit Brook Road Nashua, NH 03062 USA

Abstract

There is a growing trend to develop software that supports the work of groups, as opposed to individuals. Such software is currently being termed *groupware* (Tazelaar 1988), and the technical field is being called *computer-supported cooperative work* (Greif 1988). One aspect of supporting group work involves coordinating the speaking and actions of teams. A *coordinator* is software which supports team conversations (Winograd 1988). Coordinators are distinguished from traditional software applications because they contain embedded protocols which describe group work (Holt & Cashman 1981). This position paper presents guidelines for specifying coordinators.

1. Adaptable Specifications

In the past, software engineers interpreted group work as tasks which require coordination. Early coordinators like Monster (Holt & Cashman 1981) and XCP (Sluzier & Cashman 1984) took the approach of specifying group work as a set of rules which define the work tasks and their interrelationships. Such rule-based specifications have difficulty adapting to particular group work situations. To explain, these specifications sequence work tasks, and so it is difficult to specify rules without also considering their execution sequence. Not surprisingly, it is sometimes impossible to reliably modify these rules when a work process quickly changes.

Group work is plastic -- groups continually redesign they way they work. In fact, the work process of a group is always in a state of flux (Ehn 1988). In order for software to operate effectively in this domain, adaptable specifications must be written. A more flexible approach to specifying coordinators is to define rules for those work tasks that are independent of time. Task sequencing is left up to the group while they do their work. Coordinators like COSMOS (Buckley 1988) have adopted this approach, using a declarative specification language to describe "timeless" work tasks.

2. Specifications Of Conversation

Another interpretation of group work is to consider *conversation* being common to all work activity (Searle 1969, Winograd & Flores 1986). This interpretation sees work as language which generates action, and action which generates work products. Specifications written from this perspective define how to manage the commitments people make to each other during their work. Examples of these kinds of coordinators are: CHAOS (DeMichelis 1988), CONTRACT (Marcà et. al. May 1987), and The Coordinator (Winograd 1986).

Specifications that define structured conversations have the advantage of being less dependent on the actual work being done and being totally independent of time. This is possible because the specification defines the conversation, as opposed to the work tasks, which can vary in context, content, and complexity. The conversation is straightforward by comparison, and thus the specification is greatly simplified.

3. The CONTRACT System

The CONTRACT project (Marca et. al. April 1987), successfully developed a coordinator for a small manufacturing team. The day-to-day operation of the system returned significant savings to several organizations within the company. The process used to specify CONTRACT emphasized understanding the conversations underlying the work of the group. Before discussing the specification in detail, the value engineering work setting is summarized:

The mission of a value engineering enterprise is to improve the value of an existing product or product line (Mudge 1971). For the CONTRACT project, cost avoidance was the value goal. To achieve this goal, re-engineering is first done to particular parts in order to reduce their cost of manufacture. These changes are then introduced somewhere in the life of a product, realizing savings over the remaining life of the product (i.e. multiplying the cost reduction per part, the number of parts per product, and the expected product volume, yields an estimate of the savings returned from the part change).

4. The CONTRACT Specification

The specification of the CONTRACT coordinator was developed using a paradigm that stresses multiple, interconnected models (Marca & McGowan 1982). Applying this paradigm results in the *specification architecture* shown in Figure 1. The architecture encapsulates three major aspects of coordinating group work: the work tasks and information flow, the structured conversation types, and negotiation. Models lower in the architecture rely on the model above for context.

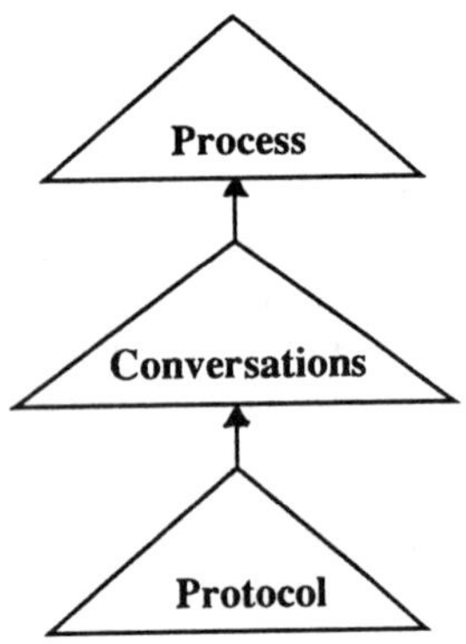

Figure 1: Specification Architecture

The first model in the CONTRACT specification defines the context in which the group works. The work process, specified as a user *experience* (Whiteside et. al. 1988), is the grounding for the remainder of the specification. For CONTRACT, developers worked along side users in order to specify the typical value engineering scenario shown in Figure 2. The scenario then became the source for the rest of the specification: The boxes represent more detailed work contexts, and the arrows represent the information shared during conversations.

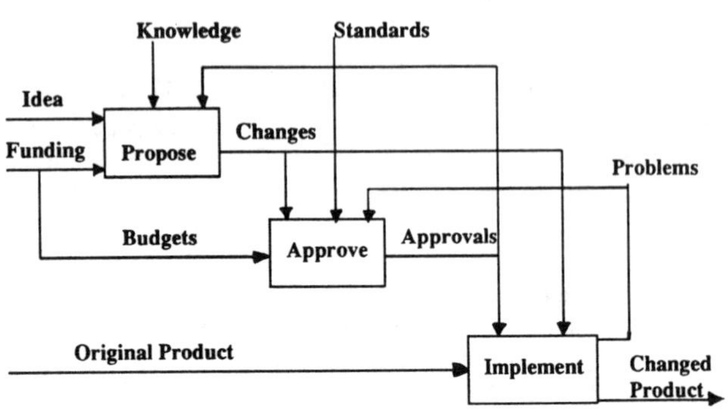

Figure 2: Work Process

The second model in the CONTRACT specification defines the kinds of conversations people have during value engineering. The simplicity of this model depends on how well the work process is synthesized into a set of well-defined *conversation types*, and how well these conversation types are consistently described from a given *viewpoint* (Marca & McGowan 1988). The value engineering group is the viewpoint for the model in Figure 3. This viewpoint sees some conversations as negotiable and others as "givens": Part is a promise to re-engineer a part, while Product is a fact about future product sales.

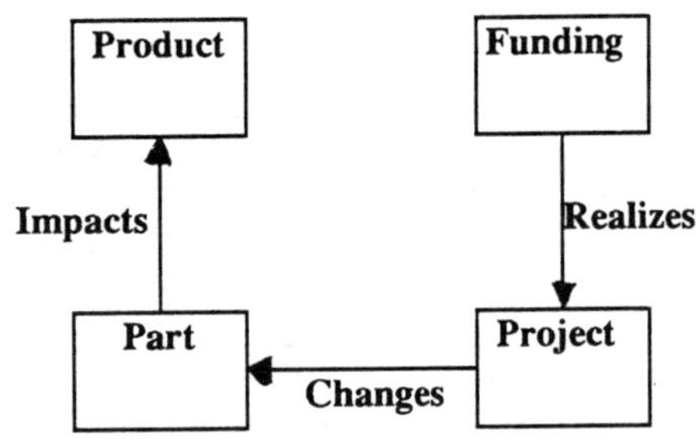

Figure 3: Conversation Types

The third model in the CONTRACT specification is a *protocol* for those conversation types that require negotiation, sometimes called conversations for action (Searle 1969). Specifications of negotiation take the form of a state-transition map that defines the speaking that occurs between an asker and a doer (Winograd 1987). The CONTRACT specification defines one protocol (see Figure 4) for all conversation types. The overall specification is optimal and extensible because a change to the protocol model simultaneously affects all conversation types.

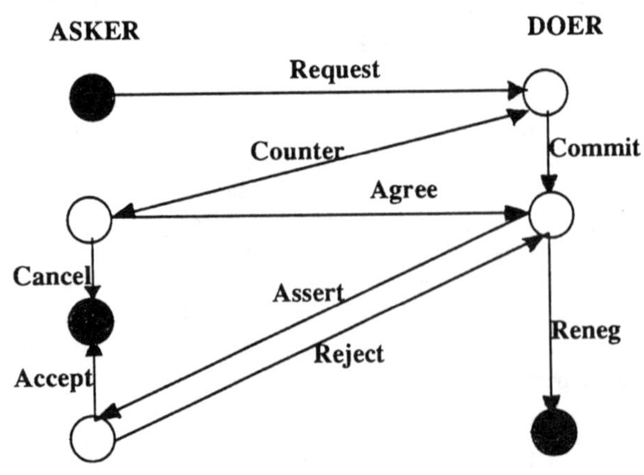

Figure 4: Negotiation Protocol

5. Complete Specifications

Completeness for the specification of a coordinator means that users of the resulting software can: 1) compute the business value of a commitment, 2) close commitments, 3) renegotiate, and 4) make consistent commitments. Completeness issues for the CONTRACT system are described below.

Computing Business Value: The product sales assumptions form the fact base from which the expected savings of a part change can be computed and compared against the cost of that change. The ability to compute business value at any step in a part change negotiation allows CONTRACT users to evaluate alternative proposals in minutes.

Closing And Renegotiating: The specification of two-party negotiation of Figure 4 contains distinctions for closing and renegotiating conversations. For closure, the doer asserting finished work is distinguished from the asker accepting or rejecting that work. For renegotiation, reneging a promise is distinguished from making a counter offer.

Granularity: Experience with earlier CONTRACT prototypes showed that there is a point of diminishing returns with regard to the granularity of recorded commitments. So, only the high-level commitment types given in Figure 3 are recorded. Doing so preserves a sufficient context for the more detailed offers, requests, and promises made on a moment-by-moment basis during a value engineering project.

Consistency: The specification guarantees that any change made to the commitment network leaves that network in a consistent state. Consistency for the CONTRACT database means that the savings promised for a particular part change actually pays back the required re-engineering costs. To accomplish this, the specification is organized and written so each commitment, regardless of its negotiation status, can always have its business value computed.

Acknowledgements

The CONTRACT coordinator program was developed within Digital Equipment Corporation by the Intelligent Systems Technology Group, and was usability engineered by the Software Usability Engineering Group. The CONTRACT project was sponsored in part by the Engineering & Technology Group of Computer Systems Manufacturing. The author would like to thank John Whiteside for his very valuable coaching during early writings which lead to this paper.

Notes

The views expressed in this paper are those of the author, and do not necessarily represent the views of Digital Equipment Corporation.

References

Buckley, P. "A Conceptual Model for COSMOS" COSMOS News Letter, Number 4; November 1988

DeMichelis, G. "Groups In A Language/Action Perspective" COSMOS News Letter, Number 3; July 1988

Ehn, P. "Work Oriented Design Of Computer Artifacts" Arbetslivscentrum; 1988

Flores, C.F., Ludlow, J. "Doing and Speaking in the Office" G. Fick and R. Sprague (ed) DSS. Issues and Challanges, Pergamon Press, London; 1981

Greif, I. "Computer-Supported Cooperative Work: A Book Of Readings" Morgan Kaufmann Publishers; 1988

Holt, A., Cashman, P. "Designing Systems To Support Cooperative Work" 5th International Conference on Computer Software and Applications Proceedings; November 1981

Marca, D., McGowan, C. "SADT: Structured Analysis And Design Technique" McGraw-Hill; 1988

Marca, D., McKenna, N., White, S. "Computer-Aided Support For Coordination Tecnology CASE'87 Proceedings; May 1987

Marca, D., Schwartz, S., Casaday, G. "A Specification Method For Coordinated Work" 4th International Workshop On Software Specification; April 1987

Marca, D., McGowan, C. "Static And Dynamic Data Modeling For Information Systems Design" 6th International Conference On Software Engineering; September 1982

Mudge, A. "Value Engineering: A Systematic Approach" Library of Congress number 70-145618; 1971

Searle, J.R. "Speech Acts" Cambridge University Press, Cambridge; 1969

Tazelaar, J. "In Depth: Groupware" BYTE; December 1988

Whiteside, J., Bennett, J., Holtzblatt, K. "Usability Engineering: Our Experience And Evolution" Handbook Of Human-Computer Interaction (ed) North-Holland; 1988

Winograd, T. "Where The Action Is" BYTE; December 1988

Winograd, T. "A language/action perspective on the design of cooperative work" Journal Of Human-Computer Interaction, Volume 3; 1987

Winograd, T. "A Language Perspective on the Design of Cooperative Work" CSCW'86 Proceedings; December 1986

Winograd, T., Flores, F. "Understanding Computers and Cognition" Ablex Publishing Company, Norwood, NJ; 1986

Software Design Issues: A Very Large Information Systems Perspective*

Gerald B. Williams, Chunka Mui, Vairam Alagappan, Bruce B. Johnson

Andersen Consulting
Center for Strategic Technology Research
100 South Wacker Dr.
Chicago, Illinois 60606

Abstract

Research in software engineering is concerned with the enhancement and automation of the processes of building computer application systems. While there is a broad consensus on the problems associated with software development, a specific understanding of the software engineering problem and the appropriate solutions are inevitably driven by the target application domain. Much of the current software engineering research is driven by the development of large scale embedded software systems. Our understanding of the problems is based on a different domain: that of very large information systems (VLIS). In this paper, we identify some significant software engineering problems from the context of developing very large information systems.

1. Introduction

The ultimate goal of research in software engineering (SE) is to improve the productivity and quality associated with both the processes and products of software development. The foreseen benefits are improvements in the management of the development process, increases in user satisfaction, and the delivery of greater functionality to the marketplace in the form of software and related products. As a means to this end, software engineering research is aimed at reducing costs and improving time in production by automating portions of the development process.

Some of the major problems associated with the automation of software development occur with respect to requirements specification, design, maintenance, reusability, validation, verification, and testing. While there is a broad consensus on the existence of these problems in general, a specific understanding of the software engineering problems and their appropriate solutions is inevitably driven by and is sensitive to the target application domain. *Software engineering solution methods are dependent on the application domain.*

* The full version of this short paper is available from the authors.

Much of the current software engineering research is being driven by the development of large scale embedded software systems. The nature of an embedded system can be characterized by asynchronous parallelism and urgent performance requirements [1]. The concentration of effort in this domain has resulted in attempts to develop formal, high level specification languages, methods of specification validation, and methods of transforming specifications into executable code.

Our approach to research on the problems of software engineering is founded on a different class of application domains; namely that of very large information systems (VLIS). In the following sections we briefly define and characterize VLIS and the problems associated with VLIS development. The intent is to contrast the nature of the software development problems related to large information systems with the development problems of the commonly investigated domain of embedded systems. As a result we hope to illuminate new perspectives on the software engineering problem and construct a foundation from which an integrated, productive research program can be launched for software engineering issues in VLIS.

2. VLIS Viewpoint

An information system is not a single monolithic structure. VLIS are federations of subsystems developed according to a system wide design plan to provide information to support the operational, managerial, analytical and decision-making functions of an organization. These subsystems are integrated and evolved over time for the purpose of supporting these organizational functions.

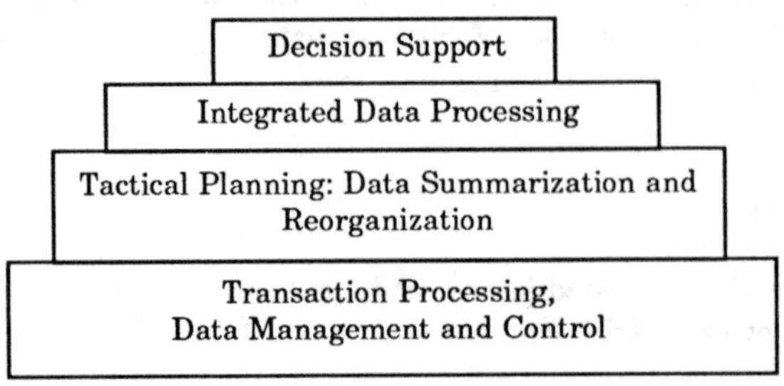

Figure 1: Information Systems Pyramid

The operational scope of VLIS across different levels of business activities can characterized as a pyramid structure similar to that shown in Figure 1. Each layer of the pyramid represents a class of information processing activities and provides a processing foundation for the levels above it. As one ascends through the layers of the pyramid the complexity of the business problem being addressed increases, additional use of business specific knowledge is required, the degree of integration across the activities increases, the accumulation of information increases and the form of the information being processed becomes more complex.

As is the case with embedded systems, VLIS development is certainly concerned with the functional complexity and the performance of software. However, in contrast to embedded systems, VLIS are more strongly characterized by relatively simple functional demands, massive size, enormous volumes of data, continuous use and constant evolution. In essence, the complexity of a VLIS is rooted in the size of the system and the demographic complexity of the application environment.

Base upon our experiences in developing very large information systems, we believe a significant amount of progress can be made to enhance and automate software development methods for VLIS by exploiting the unique properties of those systems. These properties place a set of real-world constraints on the systems development process and will allow problems which, in the general case, seem intractable to be addressed.

SE research therefore needs to contain a strong empirical component and be grounded by data generated from industrial experiences. The formulation of research problems and the strengths and weaknesses of the alternative approaches need to be subjected to the test of industrial practices, time constraints, resource limitations and economic pressures.

3. Software Development Issues

This section describes some of the issues associated with the software development process in the VLIS context. In each case we define the issue, identify the sources of its existence, and discuss the implications of what needs to be done. We see these issues as highly interdependent and regard the approach to an overall solution as necessarily dependent on concurrent development in each area.

3.1 System Evolution

In current practice, the process of maintenance is too often thought of as the patching of software bugs. Software maintainability is wrongly assumed to be a natural by-product of good initial systems development. These perceptions are faulty and contribute to the maintenance crisis being experienced today. In order to support the full scope of maintenance, it must be recognized that software systems need to *evolve* and that this evolution cannot be treated in the same manner as initial development.

The ability to continually evolve is crucial for VLIS. Information systems are typically a critical arm of the business and must adapt continually to the changing business environment. *Change is not the exception for these systems, it is the norm.* Unless they can effectively adapt to the needs of the company, the stability and competitive position of the company will be jeopardized.

In order to support system evolution, processes which directly support maintenance must be developed and information required during maintenance (design rationale) must be available. Taken together, design rationale and the maintenance processes must help the designer (1) understand the functionality, structure, and behavior of a system (2) assess the impact of alternative changes, and (3) control the impact of necessary changes. Of course, the integrity and maintainability of the system must be preserved.

Supporting system evolution must be viewed as a major driving factor in shaping an approach to formalizing the design process. Maintenance requires more information because an existing system represents a larger set of constraints that does not exist during initial design and the design tradeoffs made during maintenance differ from those in the initial design process. For example, data structure decisions may be driven by efficiency during initial development but by minimization of impact during maintenance.

3.2 Leveraging Expertise and Experience

The necessarily large size of VLIS development teams coupled with the relative scarcity of highly experienced systems builders mandate the judicious use of less experienced personnel in most phases of the development effort. Leveraging expertise and experience is concerned with the ability to manage and successfully complete large software development projects with a relatively small amount of highly experienced, proven resources. This is a critical issue given that the success of a development project is directly correlated with the levels of experience and talent across members of the project team [2].

The focus of SE research should be on supporting the high level design activities where the decomposition of high level problems into relatively independent components take place. The simple functional demands of individual programs allows for their construction by less experienced personnel.

3.3 The Design Process

The design process is the task of creating or generating design artifacts and subsequently evaluating, refining, integrating, and modifying these artifacts until the result satisfies the requirements of the problem definition. In essence, the design process is the task of mapping problem requirements into design solutions. The design process should be guided by a productive, economic, and controllable methodology that will ensure a high quality product.

The reasons why the design problem is important are fairly obvious. Good design decisions made early have a positive effect on the quality of the ultimate product as well as the efficiency of the development process. Poor design decisions play havoc with the quality, efficiency and cost of the development process and the design products.

Design is characterized by a necessity to deal simultaneously with a large number of diverse constraints that are highly intertwined. In general the design problem is intractable. However, we believe that the combination of the restricted domain of VLIS development, the simplicity of its algorithmic requirements, and the knowledge accumulated from the experience of building a large number of VLIS provides good insights into the available expertise, known solutions and alternatives. Our intention is to exploit the natural structure of the domain in ways that allow us to reduce the complexity of the problem to manageable levels. We cite several issues that help focus some of the design process concerns.

The Paradigm Problem: The paradigm problem refers to the failure to recognize and develop a manageable, productive, economically feasible process model for SE. Much attention has been focused on the development of new software engineering paradigms [3, 4] but no results have proven completely satisfactory for VLIS development. Any successful model must deal with the interdependent facets of making design decisions while recognizing the need for adequate leverage and project management.

Bridging the Functional to Technical Gap: A significant portion of the design process occurs during the creative process of translating the business problem description to a high level systems design. Presently techniques at this level of the development process are not adequately understood. The result is an inability to adequately map problem requirements to technical solutions. No good "language" has been developed in which the requirements of the problem can be expressed and ultimately transformed to technical solutions.

Design Evaluation: In order to make good design decisions, one must have the ability to assess the validity of a particular design decision or weigh the relative merits of competing design alternatives. The lack of evaluation ability leads to inadequacies in assessing the impacts of a design decision on all levels of the design process. Under the umbrella title of evaluation we include testing, validation, verification and, as a specific instance, prototyping.

The Representation Problem: The representation problem is a fundamental requirement for advancement in each of the areas mentioned above. The issue is the ability to express, manipulate and make inferences about design objects and processes. In current practice, major development takes place at very low levels of design for at least two reasons. First, current methods of software engineering encourage designers to think in terms of low level issues such as databases, data structures, performance measures, screens, and interfaces because low level representations are the only mechanisms that provide feasibility measures and evaluation feedback. As a result designers move quickly to lower levels without adequately investigating alternative early design decisions. Second, the nature of the business is that cost pressures often do not allow for an adequate investigation of high level design alternatives. As a result projects designs are often inadequate and brittle.

3.3 Large Scale Integration

The problem of large scale integration is concerned with the understanding, use and exploitation of the functionalities, standards, protocols, and communication interfaces of a heterogeneous set of technologies in developing large systems. Integration of component systems differing both in functionality and platform is important because systems within the commercial environment can no longer be treated as isolated entities. In fact there is great disincentive to do so.

The large scale integration problem points out the need to understand the interrelationships of all systems within a company. Efforts need to be concentrated on large scale design at the *enterprise*, or company wide, level before detail design and implementation of a particular component is undertaken. Understanding the enterprise level connectivity and integration issues is extremely important and will have tremendous impact upon the design process.

4. Conclusions

The intent of this paper is to discuss the implications that the process of developing very large information systems (VLIS) has on the approach to the software engineering problem. Although the same SE problems are found in many domains, they take on a unique set of constraints when considered in the context of developing VLIS. It is our position that possibilities for enhancing the software development process are functions of the domain in which one participates.

Acknowledgements

We wish to thank Mehdi Harandi, Wojtek Kozaczynski, and Bill Sasso for their contributions to the ideas presented in this paper.

References

[1] Pamela Zave, "An Operational Approach to Requirements Specification for Embedded Systems," in New Paradigms for Software Development, (ed. William W. Agresti), IEEE Society, Los Angeles, Ca., 1986, 159 -178.

[2] Bill Curtis, Herb Krasner, Vincent Shen, & Neil Iscoe, "On Building Software Process Models Under the Lamppost," in the Proceedings of the 9th International Conference on Software Engineering, Monterrey, CA., 1987, 96-103.

[3] Barry W. Boehm, "A Spiral Model of Software Development and Enhancement," *IEEE Computer*, May 1988, 61- 72.

[4] Cordell Green, David Luckham, Robert Balzer, Thomas Cheatham, and Charles Rich. "Report on a Knowledge-Based Software Assistant," Kestrel Institute, 1983.

FORMAL TECHNIQUES AND OPERATIONAL SPECIFICATION

Formally Specifying Electronic Instruments

Norman Delisle
David Garlan

Computer Research Laboratory
Tektronix Laboratories
Tektronix, Inc. 50-662
P.O. Box 500
Beaverton, OR 97077

Abstract

This paper shows how formal specification techniques can be beneficially applied in the development of electronic instrumentation. As an example of our approach we present a specification of a simple electronic instrument, written in the Z specification language. We argue that such specifications can be used to gain insight into software/hardware systems and to clarify the resulting design. A consequence is that formal specifications can assume a pivotal role in system design as non-executable prototypes and lead to a cost-effect application of formal techniques in industrial settings.

1 Introduction

Recently there has been renewed interest in applying formal specification to industrial software development [3,6,7,10] and there is starting to emerge a body of evidence that demonstrates that formal methods can have a substantial positive impact on industrial software development [4,5,8].

This paper outlines an approach for formally specifying electronic instrumentation. This approach makes both technical and methodological contributions. On the technical side it shows how one can blend functional and state-based specification styles to provide a framework for an important class of real-time, embedded systems. On the methodological side — in contrast to most formal specification efforts, which tend to emphasize issues of correctness and formal refinement — our focus has been on the use of specifications to gain *insight* into the system and to clarify the resulting design. A consequence of this focus has been that specifications take on a pivotal role in system design as *non-executable prototypes* and lead to a cost-effect application of formal techniques in real industrial settings.

2 Specification of a Simple Instrument

Before presenting the details of the specification it will help to outline our plan of attack. Our goal is to provide a *users' abstract model* of an electronic instrument. Such a model aims to clarify the user-accessible functions of an instrument. It is *abstract* in two ways: first, it suppresses details concerning *how* those functions are implemented; and second, it is independent of any *particular* user interface. For example, the model does not indicate which of the instrument functions are implemented in hardware and which in software, nor does it attempt to explain how those functions are controlled by specific knobs, menus, or buttons. This is an important level of abstraction to model since it supports not only multiple implementations of the same instrument functionality, but also different user interfaces to this functionality.

Examples of electronic instruments that could benefit from this approach range from oscilloscopes and spectrum analyzers through simple multimeters. For purposes of illustration, in this paper we specify a simple electronic counter/timer, an instrument for measuring the frequency or period of an electronic signal applied at its input. The user of the counter timer has several parameters available to ensure that the measurement is reliable.

Our approach in this specification will be to adopt a simple functional view; we describe the instrument as a mathematical function that can be applied to a *Signal* to produce a *Measurement*. The intrinsic complexity of that function will be handled by treating the overall function as a composition of simpler functions, each component function describing some portion of the measurement process. To account for a user's ability to configure the instrument we will, in fact, treat the instrument components as higher order functions. Thus given a set of user-provided parameters an instrument component produces a new function that performs some transformation on its input data. The use of higher-order functions nicely captures both the user's intuition of configuring an instrument and also the actual operating behavior of typical instrument implementations. The user typically sets up values for input parameters and then the instrument repeatedly applies the resultant functions in real-time to produce a series of measurements.

The notation used in this specification is Z [1,2]. For those not familiar with Z the accompanying discussion of the specification should provide enough context to get an intuitive idea of what is going on. We also include a glossary of the symbols used in this paper.

2.1 Domains

In Z, types of objects are defined as sets of values. We model our notions of time, voltage and measurements in terms of integers ($\mathbb{Z}$) and natural numbers ($\mathbb{N}$), which are predefined in Z. We then define signals as mathematical functions over those domains.

$$AbsTime \mathrel{\widehat{=}} \mathbb{N}$$
$$RelTime \mathrel{\widehat{=}} \mathbb{N}$$
$$Volts \mathrel{\widehat{=}} \mathbb{Z}$$
$$Measurement \mathrel{\widehat{=}} \mathbb{R}$$

The choice of discrete values for the first three definitions (as opposed to real numbers) deserves some explanation. Because an instrument has a finite bandwidth, it has finite time resolution. It makes sense, therefore, to base domains representing time on natural numbers. Intuitively, one can think of of *AbsTime* is as the number of time ticks since some absolute reference time (say, nanoseconds since the invention of the instrument). *RelTime* represents a time duration. A similar argument can be made for a discrete definition of *Volts* since there is finite voltage resolution due to thermal noise of electrical components. The *Measurement* represents either a frequency or time-period.

$$Signal \mathrel{\widehat{=}} AbsTime \rightarrow Volts$$

A *Signal* is modeled as a function from time to voltage. Note how this definition abstracts away from the passage of time; at any point in 'real time' we can observe the entire past and future of the signal. For example, the *Signal* function allows us to 'observe' a voltage value that occurred ten years ago, or five years in the future. We will return to the issue of abstracting away from real-time in section 3.

2.2 Components

We now turn to the specification of the behavior of the instrument. The path along which a *Signal* is converted to a *Measurement* is modeled as a function from *Signal* to *Measurement*. As indicated earlier, we will define this behavior as the composition of (higher-order) functional components. Figure 1 provides a overview of the specification.

A signal entering a typical counter/timer undergoes certain processing before measurements are made. As an illustration of this kind of function we define an operation that can be used to subtract a DC offset from a signal. Typically a user does this by selecting a choice of (what is referred to as) 'coupling'. In this specification there are two choices: Direct or Filter. If coupling is Direct, the signal is passed along unaltered; if it

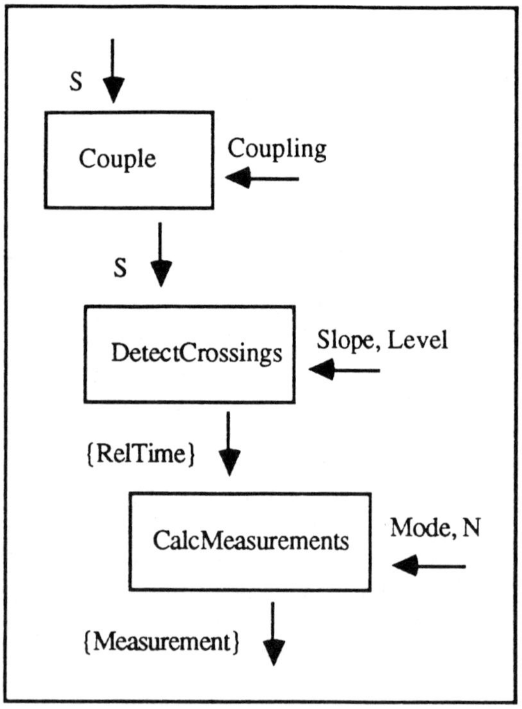

Figure 1: An Electronic Counter/Timer

is Filter, the DC voltage component is subtracted out. (We assume the existence of a function *dc* that computes the DC component of a Signal — details of this function are not given here.)

$$\mathit{Coupling} ::= \mathit{Direct} \mid \mathit{Filter}$$

$$\begin{array}{|l} \mathit{Couple} : \mathit{Coupling} \rightarrow \mathit{Signal} \rightarrow \mathit{Signal} \\ \mathit{dc} : \mathit{Signal} \rightarrow \mathit{Volts} \\ \hline \mathit{Couple\ Direct}\ s = s \\ \mathit{Couple\ Filter}\ s = \lambda\, t \bullet s(t) - dc(s) \end{array}$$

The above Z fragments define *Coupling* as a disjoint union of constants *Direct* or *Filter*. *Couple* and *dc* are defined as global functions, constrained by the predicates listed below the middle line, which effectively defines the function for each of the coupling options.

A signal entering a typical counter/timer undergoes certain processing before measurements are made. As an illustration of this kind of function we define an operation that can be used to subtract a DC offset from a signal. In this specification there are two choices: he can leave the signal unaltered or he can cause the DC voltage component of a signal to be subtracted out. (We assume the existence of a function *dc* that computes the DC component of a Signal - details of this function are not defined here).

Having conditioned the input signal, we are now in a position to look for a repetitive feature of the signal. In this simple counter/timer, a repetitive signal event is defined as one for which the signal crosses a specific voltage level along a positive or negative slope. To specify this we first introduce the types *Slope* and *Level*, and then define the function *DetectCrossings*, which produces a *set* of time values representing the detected periodic events.

$$\begin{array}{l} \mathit{Slope} ::= \mathit{POS} \mid \mathit{NEG} \\ \mathit{Level} \ \widehat{=}\ \mathit{Volts} \end{array}$$

$$\begin{array}{|l} \mathit{DetectCrossings} : \mathit{Level} \times \mathit{Slope} \rightarrow \mathit{Signal} \\ \qquad\qquad \rightarrow \mathbb{P}\, \mathit{AbsTime} \\ \hline \mathit{DetectCrossings}\ (l, \mathit{POS})\ s = \\ \qquad \{t \mid s(t-1) \leq l \leq s(t)\} \\ \mathit{DetectCrossings}\ (l, \mathit{NEG})\ s = \\ \qquad \{t \mid s(t) \leq l \leq s(t-1)\} \end{array}$$

We allow the user to select whether the measurement will be displayed as a frequency or a time-period. We also allow the user to select the number of digits of accuracy needed for the measurement. *CalcMeasurements* calculates the measurement as time-period or frequency values. The actual computation is defined by *CalcPeriods*, a function that calculates a time period by counting the number of crossings that occur within a known time-window. To ensure the required accuracy, the time window is adjusted to obtain a minimal number of crossings. This definition makes it clear to the user that the greater the accuracy required, the longer it takes to compute the measurement.

$$\mathit{Mode} ::= \mathit{FREQ} \mid \mathit{PER}$$

$$\begin{array}{|l} \mathit{CalcMeasurements} : \mathit{Mode} \times \mathbb{N} \rightarrow \mathbb{P}\, \mathit{AbsTime} \\ \qquad\qquad \rightarrow \mathbb{P}\, \mathit{Measurement} \\ \hline \mathit{CalcMeasurements}(\mathit{PER}, \mathit{accuracy})\mathit{crossings} = \\ \qquad \mathit{CalcPeriod\ accuracy\ crossings} \\ \mathit{CalcMeasurements}(\mathit{FREQ}, \mathit{accuracy})\mathit{crossings} = \\ \qquad \{1/t \mid t \in \mathit{CalcPeriods\ accuracy\ crossings}\} \end{array}$$

$$
\begin{array}{|l}
CalcPeriods : \mathbb{N} \rightarrow \mathbb{P}\ AbsTime \rightarrow \mathbb{P}\ RelTime \\
\hline
\forall m : CalcPeriods\ accuracy\ crossings \bullet \\
\quad \exists start : AbsTime, delta : RelTime, count : \mathbb{N} \\
\qquad | \ count = \#\{t \mid t \in crossings \\
\qquad\qquad \land start \leq t \leq start + delta\} \\
\qquad \land count \geq accuracy * 10 \\
\qquad \land m = delta / count
\end{array}
$$

Note that this definition does not say that every detected crossing is used in the computation of measurement values reported, but only that every measurement value that is actually reported has certain properties. Such non-deterministic functions are particularly useful for leaving details of the model open for future refinements. It turns out that for typical timer/counters there may be time 'gaps' between successive sampling time-windows. During these gaps crossings are ignored, so the predicate on *CalcPeriods* is just what we want.

We are now ready put all the pieces together. The instrument state is made explicit as a collection of user-supplied parameters. This is done by encapsulating those parameters in a Z schema, *UserParameters*. To describe the measurement configuration we curry the operations onto their user-supplied parameters and compose the component functions.

$$
\begin{array}{|l}
\text{--- } UserParameters \text{ ---} \\
c : Coupling \\
l : Level \\
sl : Slope \\
m : Mode \\
a : \mathbb{N} \\
\hline
\end{array}
$$

$$
\begin{array}{|l}
Configuration : UserParameters \rightarrow Signal \\
\qquad\qquad \rightarrow \mathbb{P}\ Measurement \\
\hline
Configuration\ p\ s = \\
\quad CalcMeasurements(p.m, p.a) \\
\quad \circ DetectCrossings\ (p.l, p.sl) \\
\quad \circ Preprocess\ p.c
\end{array}
$$

The simple counter/timer has one signal input and one measurement readout. The schema defining the instrument says how each measurement value displayed is related to the input signal and the user-defined parameters.

$$
\begin{array}{|l}
\text{--- } Instrument \text{ ---} \\
p : UserParameters \\
s : Signal \\
m : \mathbb{P}\ Measurement \\
\hline
\forall v : m \bullet \\
\quad v \in Configuration\ p\ s \\
\hline
\end{array}
$$

3 Discussion

Success in writing a specification comes from knowing what to include and what to ignore. Abstracting away from the passing of time is the key to the elegance and simplicity of this specification. The simplified view of time makes an electronic instrument specification much more manageable intellectually. However, it also limits the kinds of questions the formal specification can answer. One such issue concerns the dynamics of changing user-defined parameters. In our model parameters are changed via an operation such as *ModifyParameters*, shown below.

$$
\begin{array}{|l}
\text{--- } ModifyParameters \text{ ---} \\
newP : UserParameters \\
\Delta Instrument \\
\hline
p' = newP \\
s' = s \\
\hline
\end{array}
$$

This operation gives the illusion that the effect of modifying the parameters is as if the instrument had always had the new parameter values. In reality, of course, we cannot measure with new parameter settings the signals whose acquisition window has already past. There seems to be no obvious way to add this extra level of dynamics our the abstract specification without adding a great deal of complexity. This is a consequence of the approach we have taken in specifying instruments — namely, abstracting away from the passage of time. For the purposes of this specification this is, however, not a serious limitation since here is a great deal of insight to be gained from such a steady-state description of instrument behavior. Moreover, we have used this abstract specification as a basis for a more detailed design specification also written in Z. This refinement allows us to deal directly with time related issues.

This specification presents a user's model of the internal operations of the instrument. There were two primary reasons that we chose to model the user's perspective. First, an instrument is an interactive system that needs a simple, clean conceptual model. Second, we wanted to transcend the biases that arise from intimate knowledge of how instruments are implemented. All too early engineers tend to start thinking about concrete issues such as hardware/software tradeoffs and concrete data representations. We maintained a high level of abstraction by constantly asking the question: "Does the user need to know about that?". Because we chose the user's perspective, the specification can be used both as a basis for design and for user-level descriptions such as user manuals.

One of the distinguishing aspects of our work with formal specifications has been its methodological focus. Rather than emphasize the use of formal methods for proving 'correctness', we have concentrated on the use of formal notations for gaining insight into systems. In other words we have used mathematical tools and models as a way to clarify the working of a system, so that we could then produce better system designs. This orientation has resulted in a number of significant benefits. First, it has made our use of formal methods generally accessible to industrial engineers. These engineers can understand, question, and often create formal specifications such as the one illustrated in this paper, but they would have had difficulty carrying out numerous verification-style proofs that more traditional approaches would require. Second, it allowed us to concentrate our efforts at achieving system clarity in those areas where it mattered most. We were able to ignore many aspects of the system, which although complex in their own right, had existing well-understood models. An example in this specification is the use of the function dc, which we didn't bother to define. This in turn made the use of formal methods particularly cost-effective. Third, it allowed us to view a formal specification more as a process than as an artifact. Since formality was used to gain insight, we found we used formal models more as interactive tools for posing questions and suggesting solutions, than as a way to document a polished product. In this respect, formal specifications functioned as a conceptual prototype, for which the analogue of 'playing' with the prototype is asking formal questions of and reasoning about the specification.

This is, of course, not meant to argue that formal proofs have no place in the use of formal specifications. Indeed, the process of answering questions of a specification usually boils down to some form of proof (albeit often informal). What we *are* arguing is that formal reasoning and proofs of correctness should be subservient to the overall goal of clarity, rather than the other way around. Proofs are certainly useful insofar as they elucidate important properities of a specification and provide some indication of their complexity.

4 Evaluation

Having argued that it is possible to formally specify an electronic instrument, the question arises: is the cost of writing the formal specification worth the benefits? The benefits of formal specifications have been described in detail [9] and others. A formal specification provides a precise, concise description of a system which then forms a basis for both formal and informal reasoning. The formal specification is both a document for communication and it is a tool that leads to increased insight and understanding of the behavior of the system. Let's take a more detailed look at the costs of formally specifying instruments.

In the case of electronic instrumentation the cost/benefit analysis enjoys an economy of scale. Tektronix builds a wide variety of instrument models each of which provides functionality, price and performance suited for a specific segment of the overall market. The cost of developing a reusable 'framework' for specifying instruments can be amortized over many models. Such a framework provides the additional benefit of helping to ensure there is a high degree of compatibility across the variety of diverse instruments models. Frequently, a family of instruments are developed from a common hardware and software base. In this case the formal abstract specification framework can be followed by a formal design specification framework. This approach leads to a high level of reusability in design and code. Notice that because our abstract specification does not make a distinction between hardware and software, it is possible to develop a design framework that allows either hardware or software realization for a specific operation.

Finally, the cost of formal techniques can be reduced by providing a computer-based collection of support tools called a specification environment. A specification environment supports developing, maintaining, reasoning about, and refining the formal specification. We have developed a minimal Z specification environment which provides tools for editing the Z notation and producing documents, and parsing and type checking tools to help find errors. Additional automated support can include formal reasoning tools to assist in proofs, and tools aimed at refining the specification into executable simulations or implementations of the specification.

References

[1] J.M. Spivey *The Z Notation: A Reference Manual.* Prentice-Hall International, Englewood Cliffs, NJ, 1989.

[2] J.M. Spivey *Understanding Z: A specification language and its formal semantics.* Cambridge University Press, 1988.

[3] I. Hayes (editor) *Specification Case Studies.* Prentice-Hall International, Englewood Cliffs, NJ, 1987.

[4] G. Barrett *Formal Methods Applied to a Floating Point Number System.* Oxford University Computing Laboratory, Programming Research Group. Technical Monograph PRG-58, January 1987.

[5] I. Hayes *Specifying the CICS Application Programmer's Interface.* Oxford University Computing Laboratory, Programming Research Group. Technical Monograph PRG-47, July 1985.

[6] M. Nielsen, *et al.* The RAISE Language, Method and Tools. In R. Bloomfeld, L. Marshall, R. Jones (editors), *VDM – The Way Ahead.* Lecture Notes in Computer Science 328. Springer-Verlag.

[7] J.V. Guttag, J.J Horning, J.M. Wing The Larch Family of Specification Languages. *IEEE Software*, 2(5):24-36, September 1985.

[8] *VDM – The Way Ahead. Proceedings of the Second VDM-Europe Symposium.* Dublin, Ireland, September 1988. Lecture Notes in Computer Science 328. Springer-Verlag.

[9] B. Meyer On Formalism in Specifications. *IEEE Software* 2(1):6-26, January 1985.

[10] C.B. Jones *Systematic Software Development Using VDM.* Prentice Hall International, Englewood Cliffs, NJ, 1986.

A Glossary of Symbols

Z is a specification language developed at Oxford University. References for Z include the Z Reference Manual [1], a collection of case studies [3], and (for more serious readers) the formal semantics for Z [2]. This appendix gives brief definitions of the Z symbols used in the paper.

Z is based on typed set-theory with first-order logic. A *schema* is used to define functions and types. The schema groups definitions of variables together with predicates that constrain the possible values for those variables. Two forms of schemas are used in the instrument specification. The schema for defining a function uses the form:

declaration(s)
predicate(s)

The schema for defining a type X uses the form:

X
declaration(s)
predicate(s)

We used two additional kinds of type definitions. When there are no predicates we can abbreviate a definition:

$$X \mathrel{\widehat=} Y$$

An 'enumerated' type X is defined in a BNF-like form:

$$X ::= C1 \mid C2 \mid C3$$

A glossary of Z symbols used in the instrument specification follows. In it S, X, Y, and Z are sets; $x : X$, $y : Y$; and f and g are functions $f : X \rightarrow Y$, $g : Y \rightarrow Z$.

$\mathbb{Z}$	the set of integers
$\mathbb{N}$	the set of natural numbers
$\mathbb{R}$	the set of real numbers
$X \rightarrow Y$	the set of total functions from X to Y
$X \nrightarrow Y$	the set of partial functions from X to Y
$\lambda\, x \bullet f(x)$	the function that, given an argument x, the result is $f(x)$
$X \times Y$	cartesian product
$x \mapsto y$	x maps to y
$\mathbb{P}\, S$	power set, set of all subsets of S
$\# S$	size of the set S
$f \circ g$	function composition
$\{x : T \mid P\}$	the set of all x's of type T such that P holds
$\forall\, x : T \bullet P$	for all x of type T P holds
$\exists\, x : T \bullet P$	there exists an x of type T such that P holds

LCD-Reification: A Formal Method for Developing Prolog Programs*

Fuyau Lin *Frances E. Hunt*

Computer Engineering and Science
Case Western Reserve University
Cleveland, Ohio 44106

Abstract

The logic programming paradigm has emerged as an alternative to the traditional imperative style of software development. Modern development methods suggest the structure of the data and the program should be considered as important as the algorithm aspects of the computation. Kowalski's "Algorithm = Logic + Control" needs to be enriched by logic reification and control enhancement. The notion of data reification is also introduced. This paper describes our design methodology to develop Prolog programs by reifying logical specifications. We will look at Prolog as a design language. Our primary goal is to study a model for the design process.

1 Introduction

The need for precision in a specification is accepted in most engineering disciplines. In order to achieve precision, a specification must be written in a notation which has a formal basis. Formal development methods [34, 8, 17] are those based upon underlying mathematical theories which allow the properties of systems to be unambiguously expressed and deduced by formal methods [15]. A declarative specification gives us a clear portrayal of relations without giving methods to calculate them. An operational specification gives primitives and rules of composition and describes effective ways to calculate relations and objects. Prolog is a logic language that has both declarative and procedural meanings.

The logic programming paradigm [11, 27, 19] , as a pragmatic approach to software engineering, has emerged as alternative to the traditional imperative style of software development. Research on Prolog has not been lacking, but it has concentrated on languages and on implementation [7, 4, 30]. Kowalski used the pseudo-equation "Algorithm = Logic + Control" [18] to introduce logic programming to the world. This leads to the people a deception that programmers can describe their problems in the language of predicate logic, without regard to "how-to" knowledge, and then a system will execute the logic description as an algorithm to deliver the results.

Unfortunately, this is not the case in real world software development. We believe that programmers should be permitted to use the full power of logic when constructing logic programs. One way to meet this is to treat *logic as specifications* and to reify them into Prolog programs before executing them. Thus, we need algorithm reification by reified logic and control enhancement.

Modern development methods suggest *the structure of the data and the program should be considered as important as the algorithm aspects of the computation* [31, 8, 14] . In formal specification, there will be a class of manipulable data objects to form new data objects. The natural tendency is to define new operations as mathematical compositions of already defined operations. Expressing the representations of data objects has been the weakness of Prolog (may be a strength). Therefore, apart from the logic (relation) reification, we need to adopt data reification in our design process.

In this paper, we focus more on single unit specification and pay less attention to structuring issues, such as modules. The paper is organized as follows: Section 2 briefly describes some relevant work. Section 3 and section 4 describe data reification and algorithm reification, respectively. These two sections are conceptual, then section 5 shows the reification in action. The final section contains concluding remarks.

2 LCD-Reification: Logic, Control, and Data

We prefer to use the term "reification" instead of the more widely-used "refinement." The Concise Oxford Dictionary defines the word "reification" as "convert abstract concept into thing, materialize." Our development method is related to the notion of stepwise refinement. The early work on stepwise refinement [9, 33, 17] set guidelines for programmers and system developers to use in deciding what kind of refinement step to select in a given situation, and in what sequence to apply the refinement steps to achieve the desired effect.

Reification seems to refer to any activity which results in an increase of the closeness of a design to the ultimate implementation. It is appropriate to point out why the reification concept is critical to future progress in software engineering, and why the exercise of precisely defining and formalizing "reification" should not be underestimated.

Essentially, stepwise refinement is an iterative procedure: each step starts with a specification of the software and produces a new one, which is in some way more concrete (materialize) than the original. Reification typically involves both algorithms and data objects, since an alteration in one normally involves a change in the other. The following notions will be introduced in our specification reification:

- **Data reification**: involves the transition from abstract to concrete data types and the justification of the transition [17]. At the end of this process the data types are logical terms in Prolog.
- **Algorithm reification**: comprises the transformation from highly declarative logic to first-order logic and the enhancement of the control mechanism for efficiency. The final descriptions will be expressed in Horn Clause Logic as a *normal program* [19].

Styles and notations for one specification may be metamorphosed into the other [26, 8, 25] both in its algorithms and data representations. Program transformations [3], deductive synthesis [5, 21], declarative error diagnosis [19] and the "retrieve" function of VDM [17] have similar objectives for reification.

Synthesis and Transformation

Deductive synthesis[12, 5, 21] regards program synthesis as a theorem-proving task, it changes the mechanism of theorem proving by combin-

*Work supported in part by IBM Shared University Research Grant.

ing unification techniques, induction, and transformation rules within a single deductive system. This work has led to the development of the TABLOG[22] logic language.

Another approach, NUPRL [2], is based on Martin-Löf Intuitionistic Type Theory. Constructive logic proof simplifies the job of extracting the program from the inductive proof. Most of the guidance of the proof must come from the user. Therefore, the system can be treated as semi-automatic tool for program synthesis.

Feather provides a fairly complete survey of transformational research [10]. The use of transformation to support program development is an active area of automatic programming research. Most transformation research [3, 9, 29] has been conducted towards producing correct and efficient programs from their specifications. Two major transformations are widely used:

- **Vertical transformations** define an expression at one level of abstraction in terms of an expression at a lower level of abstraction.
- **Lateral transformations** specify an equivalence between two expressions at a similar level of abstraction.

The ideas of synthesis and transformations have been adopted to specification reifications. **Data structure mapping** [13] shares some common basis with program transformation.

This paper is not intended to sketch a system for developing programs. Instead, we investigate a formal method that will encourage us to construct better Prolog programs. Frequently, one specification might present a cogent presentation of the problem. It might be necessary to adopt different styles when working on program development. Using various reification schemes raises the problem of determining behavioral equivalence between two representations of the developments.

3 Data Types in Prolog

The data objects manipulated by Prolog[1], logical terms, correspond to record structures in conventional languages. Prolog is a declaration free, typeless language. Though it offers a flexible way to handle data objects, the user must be careful to use this feature wisely.

3.1 Data Objects in Prolog

Prolog recognizes the type of an object by its syntactic form. Data objects in Prolog include:

Simple Object

The basic elements of logical terms are constants and variables. **Constants** name specific objects or specific relationships; **atoms** include identifiers, sequences of special characters, and character strings; **numbers** include integer numbers and real numbers. **Variables** stand for anonymous objects.

Structures

Structure objects are objects that have several components. The components themselves can be structures. A compound term comprises a **functor** (to name that structure) and a sequence of one or more arguments, which are terms.

3.2 Types in Prolog

Logical terms can be classified into types. Analogous to the notion that a "type is a set of values", a type is a set of terms in Prolog. Some types are defined by relations or represented by compound terms. More complex recursive types can be defined by recursive logic programs. A program defining a type is called a type definition [27]. Recursive data types, such as integers, lists, and binary trees, all can be defined by simple recursive logic programs. We will specify types and associated predicates in the *algebraic style* (property-oriented specification) of many other specification languages. For example, to define a list,

```
%% list * ::= empty | cons * (list *)
list(empty).
list(cons(X,Y)) :- list(Y).
```

Like many languages, Prolog provides list as a built-in construct. Thus, `[X|Y]` replaces `cons(X,Y)` and `[]` denotes `empty`. Moreover, the **operator notation** allows Prolog to handle data representation in a very flexible way. For instance, if we wish to program a topological sort, then a data object to denote a graph is needed. A graph can be defined as a set of nodes and a set of edges, where each set can be represented as a list; each edge is a pair of nodes.

We use a functor **g** to combine both sets into a pair, and a functor e for edges. Yet another alternative graph represention is to associate with each node a list of nodes that are adjacent to the node. Then the graph is a list of pairs, each consisting of a node plus its adjacency list.

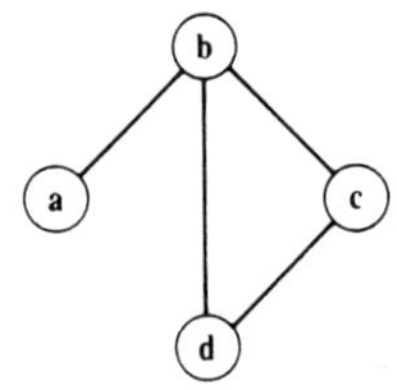


```
%% nodes   ==  [ node ]
%% edge    ::= e node node
%% edges   ==  [ edge ]
%% graph2  ::= g nodes edges
G1 = g([a,b,c,d], [e(a,b), e(b,d), e(b,c), e(c,d)]).

?- op(500, xfx, ->).
%% graph2  ==  [ node -> [node] ]
G2 = [a->[b], b->[a,c,d], c->[b,d], d->[b,c]]
```

In the second case, `findall(X, member(X -> Y, G2), L)` will give us the list of nodes for the graph. Data representation is a creative process in Prolog, and the better suited data objects can only be justified by the problems themselves. In the examples above, the transformation techniques can ideally be applied in a semi-automatic manner to get Prolog programs. To reify sets into lists we leave to the readers as an exercise.

4 Data Reification in Prolog

The structure of the data and the program should be considered as important as the algorithm aspects of the computation. Data abstraction makes use of complex data structures easier, and contributes to the clarity of programs. Data reification is a way to reify abstract objects to chosen (more concrete) representations in the early stages of software design. Hence, data reification is usually the first approach taken in program development.

4.1 Data Reification

Conventionally, a data type is a set of values and a set of operations on the set of values. In Prolog, a type is a set of terms and a set of relations that manipulate those terms. It is possible, in a mathematical sense, to define arbitrary relations among them. In discussing the *reification* relation between data objects, we are interested only in the kind of relations that capture our intuitive notion of compatible representation.

The idea of data reification is to reify abstract models into more concrete models, i.e. Prolog oriented representations. The key to reasoning about data reification is a total function, called a *retrieve function* in VDM terms, and an *adequacy proof obligation*. The retrieve function can be seen to impose an equivalence relation on the represen-

[1] We use SICStus Prolog which is developed by Swedish Institute of Computer Science.

tations. Sometimes, we want a function to be total by eliminating the unwanted values and properties from the domain. Hence, reification of models must comprise **cutout** and **confinement** of models. We define "reify" and "represent" as follows:

- Let D_1 and D_2 be two models, then $D_2 \rhd_d D_1 \Leftrightarrow \exists R : D_1 \times D_2$, where R is a total relation. We say that D_2 represents D_1.
- We have reification, $\gg_d$, then $D_2 \gg_d D_1 \Leftrightarrow \exists f : D_1 \rightarrow D_2, \ni \forall x \in D_1, \exists y \in D_2, f(y) = x$. Therefore, $D_2 \gg_d D_1 \Leftrightarrow D_2 \rhd_d D_1$.

In the same way, we can define $\ll_d$ as "is reified by" and $\lhd_d$ as " is represented by." In many cases, the adequacy proof obligation can be discharged by an informal, constructive argument. Also, this total function can be seen as providing an interpretation of representation.

4.2 Performing Data Reifications

Two cases are given to explain data reifications: "lists $\gg_d$ binary trees" and "relations $\gg_d$ graphs."

Example 1: Reify Binary Trees into Lists

A binary tree is either empty or it consists of three components: a root, a left subtree, and a right subtree. First, we need a special symbol to represent the empty tree, and need a functor, e.g. **bt** to construct a non-empty tree from its components.

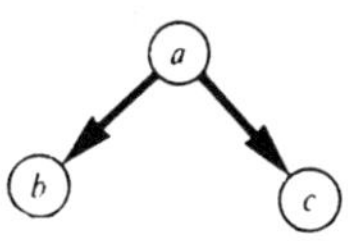


```
%% btree * ::= nil | bt (btree *) * (btree *)
btree(nil).
btree(bt(L, _, R)) :- btree(L), btree(R).

?- Bin_tree = bt(bt(nil, b, nil), a, bt(nil, c, nil)).

%% bseq * ::= nil | [(bseq *) * (bseq *)]
bseq(nil).
bseq([L, _, R]) :- bseq(L), bseq(R).

?- Bin_seq = [[nil,b,nil], a, [nil,c,nil]].
```

We can show that **bseq** and **btree** are compatible. Through a relation ">>" defined by `>> : (btree *) x (bseq *)`, we can demonstrate `(bseq *)` $\rhd_d$ `(btree *)`, because we can construct a total function f, derived from >>, to show that `(bseq *)` $\gg_d$ `(btree *)`.

```
%% f :: (bseq *) x (btree *)
?- op(600, xfx, >>).
nil  >> nil.
Bseq >> Btree :- Bseq = [Lseq, X, Rseq],
                 Btree = bt(Ltree, X, Rtree),
                 Lseq >> Ltree, Rseq >> Rtree.
```

Example 2: Reify a Graph into Relations

A non-deterministic finite automaton can be modeled by a digraph.

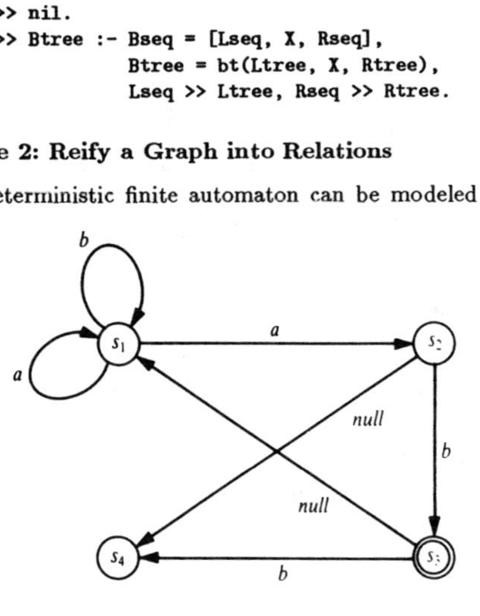

To present the digraph with labeled arcs we select the relation **dg** and functor **a**.

```
%% nodes   ==  [ * ]
%% arc     ::= a node node label
%% arcs    ==  [ arc ]
%%
%% graph   ::  dg nodes arcs
%% final   ::  node
%% accept  ::  node x [ label ]
dg([s1,s2,s3,s3],
   [a(s1,s1,a), a(s1,s2,a), a(s1,s1,b),
    a(s2,s3,b), a(s3,s4,b), a(s2,s4,null),
    a(s3,s1,null)]).
final(s3).
accept(S, []) :- final(S).
accept(S, [Car|Cdr]) :- dg(Nodes, Arcs),
                        member(a(S,D,Car), Arcs),
                        accept(D, Cdr).
accept(S, Sequence)  :- dg(Nodes, Arcs),
                        member(a(S,D,null), Arcs),
                        accept(D, Sequence).
```

Since we don't access the set of nodes, it is pointless to formulate the transition table represented by the digraph. By **cutout** nodes from digraph, "arcs $\lhd_d$ relation."

```
?- op(600, xfy, &).
%% trans       state  state  input
%% arc      :: node & node & label
s1 & s1 & a.   s2 & s3 & b.    s3 & s4 & b.
s1 & s2 & a.   s2 & s4 & null. s3 & s1 & null.
s1 & s1 & b.

final(s3).
accept(S, []) :- final(S).
accept(S, [Car|Cdr]) :- S & D & Car, accept(D, Cdr).
accept(S, Sequence)  :- S & D & null, accept(D, Sequence).

%% 4 step transitions from s1
?- Path = [_,_,_,_], accept(s1, Path).
```

The better performance of this program is predictable. This also points out that reification typically involves both algorithm and data.

The data types to be used in the specifications, and the feasible representations in Prolog are summarized below:

- **Set**: $\lhd_d$ binary tree $\lhd_d$ list
- **Sequence**: $\lhd_d$ list
- **Tuple**: $\lhd_d$ functor $\lhd_d \rhd_d$ list
- **Enumerated Type**: $\lhd_d$ functor & fact
- **Union Type**: $\lhd_d$ atom & functor.

5 Algorithm Reifications in Prolog

One of the strengths of logic programming is its declarative nature. Programmers need only concern themselves with a declarative specification of their problems, leaving the procedural aspect to the logic programming system itself. However, the ideal of pure logic programming is far from being achieved. We apply **logic reification** and **control enhancement** to support program development.

5.1 Logic Reifications

We feel that programmers should not be restricted to first-order Horn clauses, but must be free to use quantification, disjunction, negation, higher-order predicates, higher-order functions, set abstractions, etc, as needed. Of course, using this full cut logic, we can make logical specifications more declarative and stay away from operational descriptions.

The transition from these two classes is a reification of logic. The idea is to reify declarative, non-deterministic logic into operational, more-deterministic Horn clauses. The idea of logic reification is based on interpretation mapping.

- Let J be a pre-interpretation of a program P and I an interpretation based on J. Then $T_P^J(I) = \{A_{J,V} : A \leftarrow W \in P, V$ is a variable assignment wrt J, and W is true wrt I and $V\}$.
- $I \models P \Leftrightarrow T_P^J(I) \subseteq I$.
- Suppose I is a model for the equality theory. Then I with the identity function, "=". $I_= \models \text{comp}(P) \Leftrightarrow T_P^J(I) = I_=$.

The logic reification justifies the normalization of goals and programs. Suppose P is a program and G is a goal. Let G have the form, $\leftarrow W$, where W has free variable $x_1, \ldots, x_k$, for some k. The transformation tries to contradict G, then replaces G by a normal goal and adds a program statement, as in rule (j). Lloyd gives 10 rules to transform a program P into a *normal program* of P [19]. The first 9 rules, (a)–(i) belong to **lateral** reification, and (j) is the only **vertical** reification.

(a) $\neg(V \wedge W) \lhd_l \neg V; \neg W$
(b) $\forall W \lhd_l \neg\exists\neg W$
(c) $\neg\forall W \lhd_l \exists W$
(d) $V \leftarrow W \lhd_l V; \neg W$
(e) $\neg(V \leftarrow W) \lhd_l W \wedge \neg V$
(f) $V \vee W \lhd_l V; W$
(g) $\neg(V \vee W) \lhd_l \neg V \wedge \neg W$
(h) $\neg\neg W \lhd_l W$
(i) $\exists W \lhd_l W$
(j) $\neg\exists W \lhd_l \neg p(x_1, \ldots, x_k); p(x_1, \ldots, x_k) \leftarrow W$

Let P and Q be the programs which result from a single reification, $\lhd_l$. Then $Q \lhd_l P \Leftrightarrow Q \equiv P$, futhermore, $\text{comp}(Q) \equiv \text{comp}(P)$.

5.2 Performing Logic Reification

Example 1: Reify Logic by Rules

Lateral rules make logic more concrete. The vertical rule removes the universal quantifier. The subset, $\subseteq$, relation can be defined by the statement, S_1,

- $A \subseteq B \leftarrow \forall x(x \in A \rightarrow x \in B)$

A normal program of this relation can be derived by lateral (b), (e), and vertical (j) rules. Every derivation is a reification.

- By rule (b): $A \subseteq B \leftarrow \neg\exists x \neg(x \in B \leftarrow x \in A)$
- By rule (e): $A \subseteq B \leftarrow \neg\exists x(x \in A) \wedge \neg(x \in B)$

Finally, by rule (j), we lift the quantifier and reify the program into normal program.

- $A \subseteq B \leftarrow \neg p(A, B)$.
- $p(A, B) \leftarrow (x \in A) \wedge \neg(x \in B)$

Therefore, A is not a subset of $B, p(A, B)$, if $\exists x \in A$ for which $\neg(x \in B)$ holds. Unfortunately, Clark shows that "negation as failure" can stand only in front of atomic formulae [6]. The subset relation can be redefined by the statement, S_2, which is more operational than S_1.

- $\forall B, \{\} \subseteq B$, and
- $\forall x, \{x\} \cup A \subseteq B \leftrightarrow x \in B \wedge A \subseteq B$

We can apply membership and subset relations and make S_1 more deterministic than S_2. Since we can use "lists $\rhd_d$ sets," the union, $\cup$, is subsumed by list operations. Thus, we have "$S_1 \lhd_l S_2$."

```
%% complexity: O(n)
subset([], B).
subset([X|A], B) :- member(X, B), subset(A, B).
```

Example 2: Alpine Club Puzzle

Tony, Mike and John belong to the Alpine Club. Every member of the Alpine Club is either a skier or a mountain climber or both. No mountain climber likes rain, and all skiers like snow. Mike dislikes whatever Tony likes and likes whatever Tony dislikes. Tonly likes rain and snow.

(1) { John, Tony, Mike } $\subseteq A$, Alpine Club.
(2) $\forall x \in A \rightarrow x \in S \vee x \in C$, where $S \equiv$ skiers and $C \equiv$ climbers.
(3) $\forall x, x$ **likes** rain $\rightarrow \neg x \in C$.
(4) $\forall x, x \in S \rightarrow x$ **likes** snow.
(5) Tony **likes** rain and snow.
(6) $\forall x$, Tony **likes** $x \rightarrow \neg$ Mike **likes** x; $\neg$ Tony **likes** $x \rightarrow$ Mike **likes** x.

Query: *Is there a member of Alpine Club who is a mountain climber but not a skier*, $\exists x, x \in A, x \in C, \neg x \in S$? Applying the logic reification, we derive 5 relations from the description above as following:

- (2) $(A \rightarrow S \vee C) \ll_l (\neg A \vee S \vee C) \ll_l (\neg A \vee \neg\neg S \vee C) \ll_l (\neg(A \wedge \neg S) \vee C) \ll_l (A \wedge \neg S \rightarrow C) \ll_l (C \leftarrow A \wedge \neg S)$

  $\lhd_l$ `climber(X) :- alpinist(X), nonskier(X).`
- (3) $(L_r \rightarrow \neg C) \ll_l (\neg L_r \vee \neg C) \ll_l (\neg C \vee \neg L_r) \ll_l (C \rightarrow \neg L_r) \ll_l (\neg L_r \leftarrow C)$

  $\lhd_l$ `dislikes(X, rain) :- climber(X).`
- (4) $(S \rightarrow L_s) \ll_l (\neg S \vee L_s) \ll_l (\neg\neg L_s \vee \neg S) \ll_l (\neg L_s \rightarrow \neg S) \ll_l (\neg S \leftarrow \neg L_s)$

  $\lhd_l$ `nonskier(X) :- dislikes(X, snow).`
- (1) & (5) $\lhd_l$ relation, see program.
- (6) $\lhd_l$ `dislikes(mike, X) :- likes(tony, X).` and `likes(mike, X) :- dislikes(tony, X).`

```
%% member, object << atom
%% alpinist << facts
alpinist(tony).
alpinist(mike).
alpinist(john).

%% like, dislike  :: member x object
likes(tony, rain).
likes(tony, snow).
likes(mike, X) :- dislikes(tony, X).
dislikes(mike, X) :- likes(tony, X).
dislikes(X, rain) :- climber(X).

%% climber, nonskier :: member
nonskier(X) :- dislikes(X, snow).
climber(X) :- alpinist(X), nonskier(X).

?- alpinist(X), climber(X), nonskier(X).
```

5.3 Control Enhancements

Apart from the logic, the control mechanisms of the Prolog program affect the performance critically. Some program enhancements have been discussed in composing meta-interpreters [28]. Essentially, those improvements contribute mainly to the program controls (in their case, meta-level control).

Informally, we view control enhancements as programming techniques. In order to derive efficient or flexible programs, we would like to retrieve more flexible information from the program execution, e.g. meta-level reasoning. In general, we can classify three basic control enhancements:

- **Search guidance** improves search efficiency by rearranging and composing logical terms (clauses, goals, arguments) or controlling backtracking using cuts.
- **Addendum** offers efficiency by adding extra elements to programs, for instance asserting derived facts.
- **Data integration** employs better data structures, so that oper-

ations on data objects can be implemented more efficiently.

5.4 Performing Control Enhancement

We give three examples to show how problems can be enhanced in different ways. Though the problems are not very complex, the program developments do follow the guidelines and lead to the programs that are more efficient to execute.

Example 1: Search Guidance by Rearrangement

We disregard controlling the search using "cut" because there are some reservations against cut. It is part of good programming style: *to use cut with care and not to use cut without reason.* Non-deterministic programs can be easy to write, while they cannot always be executed efficiently using the standard control mechanisms. We borrow the peak detection problem [16] to illustrate these points. We want to decide if there is a peak in a sequence of numbers?

```
%% peak, up, down :: [ num ]
up([]).
up([X]).
up([A,B|Z])    :- A < B, up([B|Z]).
peak(L)        :- append(X, Y, L),
                  up(X), down(Y).
down([]).
down([X]).
down([A,B|Z]) :- A > B, down([B|Z]).
```

This program is declarative, but naive, with complexity $O(N^2)$. Requesting peak detection is only deciding whether or not there exists a peak. It is perfectly all right to scan the list once. By composing **peak(X)** and **up(X)** together[2], we obtain a more efficient program with complexity $O(N)$.

```
peak([]).
peak([X]).
peak([A,B|Z]) :- A < B, peak([B|Z]).
peak([A,B|Z]) :- A > B, down([B|Z]).
down([]).
down([X]).
down([A,B|Z]) :- A > B, down([B|Z]).
```

Example 2: Addendum Enhancement by Asserta

Keepinhg a "memo" of intermediate results is a technique for avoiding repeated computations. The idea is to use **asserta** and to add these results as facts.

```
?- op(600, xfx, =>).
%% fib :: num => num
1 => 1.   2 => 1.
N => F :- N > 2,
          N1 is N-1, N1 => F1,
          N2 is N-2, N2 => F2,
          F is F1+F2.
%%        F is F1+F2, asserta(N => F).
```

The variant addendum introduces new arguments for accumulating data to avoid recomputations. Fibonacci number computation can be rewritten in this way. Normally, it will make the programs more complicated and hard to understand, but more efficient to execute.

Example 3: Data Integration using Difference-Lists

Difference-lists [13, 27] are alternative data structures to lists for representing a sequence of elements. Recall the traditional definition of reverse list, which is inefficient when the list is long. Using difference-lists will simplify and increase the efficiency of list oriented processing.

```
%% reverse    :: (list *) x (list *)
%% reverse_dl :: (d_list *) x (d_list *)
```

[2] In Sterling's terms, it is Clause Join.

```
reverse(X, Y) :- reverse_dl(X, Y\[]).
reverse_dl([X|Xs], Y\Z) :- reverse_dl(Xs, Y\[X|Z]).
reverse_dl([], X\X).
```

Obviously, we can reify the "append" predicate to concatenate two sequences in a more elegant way. The task is done just by *matching* the goal with the clause. It gives constant time concatenation operation.

```
%% apnd_d     :: (d_list *) x (d_list *) x (d_list *)

apnd_dl(X\L, L\Y, X\Y).
```

6 Reification in Action

6.1 A Simple FP Interpreter

We show a definitional interpreter for FP [1]. In this model, the interpreting job is done by a serial connection of three phases called **lex**, **parser**, and **exec**. We sketch each one briefly.

- **lex**: The lexical phase is concerned with transforming the input sequence of characters into the sequence of tokens they represent. For example, `eqzero := = @ [id, $ 0]`.

```
 eqzero        :=      =       @        [        id
[id('eqzero'), defsy, eqsy, compsy, lbksy, idsy,
        ,          $           0          ]       .
          commasy, constsy, isnum(0), rbksy]
```

- **parse**: This phase converts the sequence of tokens constructed by "lex" into internal forms that more closely reflect the operations which the FP expression is to perform. For example, to continue the same example:

```
[id('eqzero'), defsy, eqsy, compsy, lbksy,
               idsy, commasy, constsy, isnum(0), rbksy]

def("eqzero", comp(pr(eqsy), cons([pr(idsy,const(num(0))])))
```

- **exec**: The evaluator is concerned with reducing the internal forms of FP applications into the results represented by a sequence of characters. For example, apply **eqzero** to a sequence,

```
& eqzero : [0, 1, 0].
result = [true, true, true]
```

The translation of an FP program can be expressed by the following clauses in SICStus Prolog:

```
%% p_fp :: [ char ] x [ char ]

p_fp(SourceText, Result) :-
        p_lex(SourceText, TokenList),
              p_parse(TokenList, IntForm),
                    p_exec(IntForm, Result).
```

Lex and the Token Set

We need to specify a data type that goes between "lex" and "parse." Each token represents a *class* of symbols and may be followed by a *value* part. First, the "token" is defined as follows:

```
%% token ::= (isnum num) | (isbool bool) | (id [char])
%%          | error | ifsy  | compsy | whilesy | constsy
%%          | lbksy | rbksy | lbrsy  | rbrsy   | lsssy
%%          | ...
%% tokens == [ token ]
%% tokens << atom & functor
```

In Prolog, we apply a *tokenizer* plus some transformations to convert the source text character into a list of tokens. The union type **tokens** is reified by *atoms* and *functors* implicitly, i.e. "tokens $\lhd_d$ atom & functor." New atoms, **gesy**, **lesy**, **ifsy**, and **nesy**, etc., are presented in the transformations. Cuts are used to reduce the search space of Prolog computations.

```
%% p_lex      :: [ char ] x [ token ]
%% transform :: [ char ] x [ token ]

p_lex(SourceText, TokenList) :-
        tokenize(SourceText, Temp),
                transform(Temp, TokenList).
transform([],[]).
transform(['>','='|Xs],[gesy|Ss]) :- !, transform(Xs,Ss).
transform(['<','='|Xs],[lesy|Ss]) :- !, transform(Xs,Ss).
transform(['-','>'|Xs],[ifsy|Ss]) :- !, transform(Xs,Ss).
transform(['~','='|Xs],[nesy|Ss]) :- !, transform(Xs,Ss).
...
transform([X|Xs],[X|Ss]) :- transform(Xs,Ss).
```

Parser and Internal Forms

We examine the syntax rules of FP programs to choose the data objects for representing FP expressions and objects. The syntax of FP is shown as below:

```
%% fp_def   --> ident ':=' fp_exp '.'
%% fp_app   --> fp_exp ':' fP-obj '.'
%%
%% fp_exp   --> fp_term '@' fp_exp | fp_term(T).
%% fp_term  --> '(' whbuif | '[' constr | fp_fact
%% fp_fact  --> num 'r' | num | prim | ident
%%              | '/' fp_exp | '%' fp_obj
%%              | '&' fp_exp
%% whbuif   --> 'while' fp_exp fp_exp ')'
%%              | ...
```

Naturally, our data abstractions fall into tree structures. We introduce three new data types. These data types play a central role in the entire development. The more we encapsulate the data types we choose, the more practically we can transform them into other languages.

```
%% ids   ::= nop | if ids ids ids | while ids ids
%%           | const obj | pr token | comp ids ids
%%           | cons [ids] | ...
%% obj   ::= num int | bool boolean | str [char]
%%           | seq obj | bottom
%% defs ::= def ident ids | app ids obj
%%
%% seq << list
%% ids, defs, obj << list & atoms & functor
```

Several functors will be used in the data representations, e.g. def, comp, pr. These functors can be viewed as a text representation of the FP syntax tree. Here we give two examples, one is a sequence of objects, the other is a inner product function.

```
[ 1, [2,3], [['abc']] ]

[ num(1),     .    ,    .  ]
             /           \
  [ num(2), num(3) ]     [ . ]
                            \
                       [ str('abc') ]
```

Since Prolog does allow dissimilar types in a list, we can map an FP sequence into a list directly. Thus, "sequences $\lhd_d$ lists" and "ids, defs, obj $\lhd_d$ list & atom & functor."

```
ip := / + @ & * @ trans.

def ('ip' , comp( . , . ))
                 /      \
          lins .    comp( . , . )
              /          /      \
        pr(+)   toall .     pr('trans')
                      |
                    pr(*)
```

The parser follows the rules shown above to construct the internal form of each FP function definition and application. A very useful subset of M-Grammars are Definite Clause Grammars (DCGs), which are based on Chomsky's contex-free grammars [32]. *DCGs are translated directly into Prolog clauses which involve a recursive descent parser using difference lists.* The Prolog DCG specifying the parser is fairly straightforward:

```
%% p_parse  :: [token] x [defs]
%% fp_def   :: defs
%% fp_exp   :: ids
%% fp_term  :: ...
p_parse([], []).
p_parse(TokenList, IntForm) :-
                        fp_def(TokenList, IntForm, []).
fp_def(def(N,B))     --> fp_id(N), [defsy], fp_exp(B), ['.'].

fp_exp(comp(T,C))    --> fp_term(T), ['@'], fp_exp(C).
fp_exp(T)            --> fp_term(T).
fp_term(while(F,G))--> ['(', while], fp_exp(F),
                                          fp_exp(G), [')'].
fp_term(bu(F,G))     --> ...
%% complete parser not shown here
%% p_exec: trivial, omitted
```

There is a close correspondence between the DCG program and the grammar that it parses. This means that less effort is needed to explain the program and modification is easier. After we have completely parsed the FP program, the evaluator takes the FP syntax trees and objects, and performs graph reduction to get the resulting object. This phase is merely an operational approach to constructing a reduction machine.

6.2 What a Wonderful FP in Prolog!

Operator definitions can alter the syntax of Prolog terms for the input predicates. The expressions that use operator definitions are treated exactly like other Prolog terms[3].

Reifying Data Abstraction

Prolog subsumes most of the FP objects, except the sequence notation `<1,2,3>` which is replaced by **`[1,2,3]`**. Operators are normally used, as functors, only to combine objects into structures and do not invoke actions on data. Actually, the operators resemble **constructors** in Miranda [4].

```
?- op(550, xfy, @).
?- op(600, xfy, :).
?- op(500, fy,  /).
?- op(500, fy,  &).
?- op(600, xfy, :=).
...
%% token << atom
%% ids   << operator & term = ids'
%% obj   << list & constant
%% defs  << functor & ids'
```

The operators replace the functors, as mentioned in the previous section, and change the Prolog "reader." There is no need for a lexical scanner and parser, because Prolog already has them. Then, FP programs can be embedded in Prolog without translation, because we can represent the FP programs by reified data representations, such as

(1) tokens $\lhd_d$ atom & functor,
(2) ids $\lhd_d$ operator & term,
(3) obj $\lhd_d$ list & constant,
(4) defs $\lhd_d$ functor & ids.

Reifying Logic and Control

Although, no operation on data is associated with an operator, there is no restriction to do so. We give rules to the operators, then the eval-

[3] Conventionally, operator definitions do not specify any operation or action, they are merely a data representation.

[4] Miranda is a trademark of Research Software Ltd.

uation of FP programs becomes enforcing the **laws of data types**[5]. Therefore, the FP programs become data types with implicit computation rules, i.e. the data object "`/ sqr : [1,2,3]`" represents the value "`[1,4,9]`."

Since FP expressions can be a sequence of applications, we need to keep the evaluated result somewhere for later use. The trick to passing the result of the application is to use **addendum**. We can retrieve a value by a fact, `fp(X)`, and store the result using assert, `update(X)`. Through this "single channel" we can achieve the functional behavior of the FP programs.

```
F := Exp :- asserta(def(F,Exp)).

F : X     :- def(F, Exp), Exp : X.
F : nil   :- update(nil).
+ : [X,Y] :- Res is +(X,Y), update(Res).
- : [X,Y] :- Res is -(X,Y), update(Res).
* : [X,Y] :- Res is *(X,Y), update(Res).
/ : [X,Y] :- Res is /(X,Y), update(Res).

L @ R : X :- R : X, fp(T), L : T.
& A : nil :- update(nil).
& A : []  :- update([]).
& A : [B|C] :- A : B, fp(E),
               & A : C, fp(F), update([E|F]).
/ F : nil :- update(nil).
/ F : [X] :- update(X).
/ F : [nil|R] :- update(nil).
/ F : [X|R] :- / F : R, fp(Vr), F : [X,Vr].

[] : X    :- update([]).
[A|B] : X :- A : X, fp(Xa), B : X, fp(Xb), update([Xa|Xb]).

N : L     :- number(N), select(N, L).
   select(N, []) :- update(nil).
   select(1, [X|Y]) :- update(X).
   select(N, [X|Y]) :- N1 is N-1, select(N1, Y).
   select(N, _) :- update(nil).

% use 'switch' to control trace
update(A) :- notrace(yes), retract(fp(_)), asserta(fp(A)).
update(A) :- notrace(no), write(A), nl,
             retract(fp(_)), asserta(fp(A)).

%% primitives
distl : [A, []] :- update([]).
distl : [A, [X|Y]] :- distl : [A, Y], fp(L),
                      update([[A,X]|L]).
distr : [[], A] :- update([]).
distr : [[X|Y], A] :- distr : [Y, A], fp(L),
                      update([[X,A]|L]).
id : X :- update(X).
trans : [[]|_] :- update([]).
trans : Op :- hdtl : Op, fp([A, B]),
             trans : B, fp(T), update([A|T]).
   hdtl : [] :- update([[],[]]).
   hdtl : [[A|B]|T] :- hdtl : T, fp([L, R]),
                      update([[A|L], [B|R]]).
fp(nil).
def(nil,nil).
notrace(no).

a :- fp(X), write('result = '), write(X).

defs :- setof([X,Y], def(X,Y), L), showdef(L).
   showdef([[F,E]|Y]) :- write(F), write(' := '), write(E),
                         write('.'), nl, showdef(Y).

traceon :- retract(notrace(yes)), asserta(notrace(no)).
traceoff :- retract(notrace(no)), asserta(notrace(yes)).

?- ip := / + @ & * @ trans.
?- mm := & & ip @ & distl @ distr @ [1, trans @ 2].
```

[5]Please refer to the law in Miranda [31].

This Prolog program is not a complete FP system, but it shows no problem in handling the higher-order functions, such as left-insert (/) and apply-to-all (&). The program itself is an integration of FP and Prolog, more or less, "FP $\triangleleft$ Prolog." An example session is listed in the appendix.

7 Final Remarks

We have presented concepts and methods for developing Prolog programs. The FP system described in section 5 was implemented based on reification. Our approach is mainly from the software engineering point of view. Abstract models with LCD-reifications are the basis of practical software systems being implemented at Case. We have constructed several FP interpreters [20] based on similar methods but using different target languages, such as Pascal, C, and Miranda. It took less than six hours to finish the FP prototype in the Prolog language. So far, the results are very encouraging in the sense of program quality and speed of development. our current research is to develop a more complete formal theory to support our design methodology.

We conclude our paper by summarizing our points:

- Define data *models* by deciding the abstract data objects and operations required to describe the structure and behavior of the proposed software.
- Use mathematical formalism, specifically recursion equations and data abstractions to specify the objects and operations precisely and state their exact meaning. Reify the data objects by **confinement** or **cutout** whenever it is necessary.
- Justify the logic aspects by vertical or lateral transformations Further, improve the execution efficiency through **search guidance, addendum**, and **data integration** enhancements.
- Use the fact that the specification is executable written in Prolog to validate the design as a prototype.

One of the problems of the current version of Prolog is the lack of facilities, like modules, for structuring large programs. There has been a proposal to add some additional features to extended languages, such as λProlog [23], that allow for the structuring of large specifications.

Software engineering concerns are equally relevant for programming in Prolog as in conventional languages. Prolog is no different from any other language in its need for a methodology to build and maintain large programs [27]. We support this view point, moreover, this paper confirms the standpoint that systematic software development methods are applicable and necessary for Prolog programming.

References

[1] J. W. Backus, "Can Programming be Liberated from the von Neumann Style? A Functional Style and its Algebra of Programs," *Communications of the ACM*, Vol. 21, pp. 931–935, (1978).

[2] A. Bundy, "A Broader Interpretation of Logic in Logic Programming," Proceedings of the 1988 International Conference and Symposium on Logic Programming, pp. 1624–1648, Seattle, Washington, (August 1988).

[3] R. M. Burstall, J. Darlington, "A Transformation System for Developing recursive Programs," JACM, Vol. 24, No. 1, pp. 44–67, (January 1977).

[4] edited by J. A. Campbell, Implementations of Prolog, Halsted Press, Ellis Horwood Limited, (1984).

[5] C. L. Chang, R. C. T. Lee, Symbolic Logic and Mechanical Theorem Proving, Academic Press, Inc., New York, (1973).

[6] K. L. Clark, "Negation as Failure," in Logic and Data Bases, edited by H. Gallaire, J. Minker, Plenum Press, New York, pp.

293–322, (1978).

[7] edited by K. L. Clark, S. Tarnlund, Logic Programming, Academic Press, (1982).

[8] B. Cohen, W. T. Harwood, M. I. Jackson, The Specification of Complex Systems, Addison-Wesley Publishing Company, (1986).

[9] E. W. Dijkstra, Selected Writings on Computing: A Personal Perspective, Spring-Verlag, (1982).

[10] M. Feather, "A Survey and Classification of Some Program Transformation Approaches and Techniques," IFIP Working Conference on Program Specification and Transformation, Bad Tolv, Germany, (April 1986).

[11] J. H. Gallier, Logic for Computer Science-Foundations of Automatic Theorem Proving, Harper & Row, Publishers, (1986).

[12] C. Green, "Application of Theorem Proving to Problem Solving," IJCAI-69, Washington, D. C., pp. 219–239, (1969).

[13] A. Hansson, S. Tarnlund, "Program Transformation by Data Structure Mapping," in Logic Programming, edited by K. L. Clark, S. Tarnlund, pp. 117–122, Academic Press, (1982).

[14] P. Henderson, "Functional Programming, Formal Specification, and Rapid Prototyping," IEEE T-SE, Vol. SE-12, No. 2, pp. 241–250, (1986).

[15] C. A. R. Hoare, J. C. Shepherdson, eds, Mathematical Logic and Programming Languages, Prentice-Hall International, (1985).

[16] C. J. Hogger, Introduction to Logic Programming, Academic Press, Inc., (1984).

[17] C. B. Jones, Systematic Software Development Using VDM, Prentice-Hall International, 1986.

[18] R. Kowalski, Logic for Problem Solving, North Holland, (1979).

[19] J.W. Lloyd, Foundations of Logic Programming, 2nd edition, Springer-Verlag, (1987).

[20] F. Lin, F. Hunt, "Executable Specification using Miranda: An Example," Proceedings of International Computer Symposium 1988, Taipei, (December 1988).

[21] Z. Manna, R. Waldinger, "A Deductive Approach to Program Synthesis," in Artificial Intelligence and Software Engineering, edited by C. Rich, R. C. Waters, pp. 3–34, Morgan Kaufmann, CA, (1986).

[22] Y. Malachi, Z. Manna, R. Waldinger, TABLOG: A New Approach to Logic Programming, Report No., STAN-CS-86-1110, Stanford University, (1986).

[23] G. Nadathur, "Higher-Order Logic Programming ans Applications," Ph. D. Thesis, Department of Computer and Information Science, University of Pennsylvania, (December 1986).

[24] D. O'Neill, "VDM Development with Ada as the Target Language," Proceedings of VDM'88, LNCS 328, pp. 116–123, Dublin, Ireland, (September 1988).

[25] C. Rich, R. C. Waters, Artificial Intelligence and Software Engineering, edited by C. Rich, R. C. Waters, Morgan Kaufmann, CA, (1986).

[26] W. Scherlis, "Expression Procedures and Program Derivation," Stanford AI Lab., Memo AIM-341, (August 1980).

[27] L. Sterling, The Art of Prolog, The MIT Press, (1986).

[28] L. Sterling, A. Lakhotia, "Composing Prolog Meta-Interpreters," Workshop on Meta-Programming in Logic Programming, Bristol, (June 1988).

[29] H. Tamaki, T. Sato, "Unfold/Fold Transformations of Logic Programs," Proceeding of 2nd ICLP, pp. 127–138, Sweden, (1984).

[30] S. Tarnlund, "Logic Programming-from a Logic Point of View," in Proceeding of the 1986 Symposium on Logic Programming, pp. 96–103, Salt Lake City, Utah, (August 1986).

[31] D. A. Turner, "Functional Programs as Executable Specifications," in Mathematical Logic and Programming Languages, (ed. C.A.R. Hoare and J.C. Shepherdson), Prentice-Hall International, pp. 29–54, (1985).

[32] D. H. D. Warren, "Logic Programming and Compiler Writing," Software–Practice and Experience, Vol. 10, pp. 97–125, (1980).

[33] N. Wirth, Systematic Programming: An Introduction, Prentice-Hall, (1973).

[34] P. Zave, R. T. Yeh, "Executable Requirements for Embedded Systems," in Proceeding of 5th ICSE, pp. 1037–1042, San Diego, CA., (March 1981).

Appendix: An Example Session

```
% sp
SICStus 0.6 #5: Sat Jan. 7 17:56:05 EDT 1989
Copyright (C) 1987, Swedish Institute of Computer Science.
All rights reserved.
| ?-
| ?- [fp].
{consulting /u/lin/prolog/fp...}
{fp consulted, 940 msec 5058 bytes}
yes
| ?- traceoff.
yes
| ?- ip := / + @ & * @ trans.
yes
| ?- mm := & & ip @ & distl @ distr @ [1,trans @ 2].
yes
| ?- trans : [[1,2,3,4],[5,6,7,8]], a.
result = [[1,5],[2,6],[3,7],[4,8]]
yes
| ?- ip : [[1,2,3,4],[5,6,7,8]], a.
result = 70
yes
| ?- mm : [ [[1,2], [3,4]], [[5,6], [7,8]] ], a.
result = [[19,22],[43,50]]
yes
| ?- append(X, Y, [1,2,3,4,5]), / + : X, a.
result = 1
X = [1],
Y = [2,3,4,5] ? ;
result = 3
X = [1,2],
Y = [3,4,5] ? ;
result = 6
X = [1,2,3],
Y = [4,5] ? ;
result = 10
X = [1,2,3,4],
Y = [5] ? ;
result = 15
X = [1,2,3,4,5],
Y = [] ? ;

no
| ?-
{ End of SICStus execution, user time 1.700 }
%
```

Developing Formally Verified Ada Programs*

Norman Ramsey[†]

Odyssey Research Associates

Abstract

Odyssey Research Associates has undertaken a study of the feasibility of developing formally verified Ada programs. We have designed a specification language for sequential Ada programs. It is a member of the Larch family of specification languages. We have built a prototype program editor that is intended to help programmers develop programs and proofs from specifications, as advocated by Dijkstra and Gries [1,2]. It contains predicate transformers, which compute *wp* (an approximation to the weakest precondition of a program), and it generates verification conditions.

The semantics of the specification language and the definition of the predicate transformers are derivable from a denotational definition of sequential Ada. The predicate transformers can be proved sound with respect to these definitions by structural induction on programs. The denotational-style definition of the predicate transformers is well suited to an implementation as an attribute grammar.

The program editor is designed to be used on program fragments, not just complete programs. The next step in improving the prototype editor is to find ways to simplify the intermediate values of *wp* so they can be used to guide the development of fragments into programs.

Introduction

Writing formal specifications of programs and proving that programs meet those specifications should help programmers develop more reliable software. Edsger Dijkstra and David Gries have stressed that a program should not face verification as a hurdle after development, but should be developed in such a way as to ensure its correctness [1,2]. One should begin with a formal specification, and the development of the program and its proof should follow from that specification. Gries, in his *Science of Programming*, suggests ways to use a specification to guide the development of a program and its proof.

We have undertaken to build software that will help programmers apply the methods of formal development advocated by Gries and Dijkstra. The software is designed to lead to formal verification tools with three properties:

- The tools should not just help to verify finished programs or to check proofs of such programs, but should help programmers to develop verified programs.
- The tools should be based on sound, explicitly stated mathematics.
- The tools should support programming in a subset of Ada, since there is a need for reliable software written in Ada.

Overview of results

We have designed a specification language, Larch/Ada-88, for sequential Ada programs. We have implemented a prototype of an editor, Penelope, which will help programmers develop and verify programs specified with Larch/Ada-88. The prototype implementation supports a subset of Ada that is roughly "PASCAL with exceptions." We have completed some of the mathematics that supports the Larch/Ada-88 definition and the Penelope implementation.

Specification language The Larch/Ada-88 specification language is part of the Larch family of two-tiered specification languages [3,4].[1] The two-tiered approach separates the specification of individual program modules from the specification of underlying abstractions. The Larch Shared Language is used to specify the underlying abstractions; for example, it can be used to define the notions of array, list, set, bag, and so on. A Larch Shared Language specification defines a set of terms (and some theorems about

*This research has been sponsored by the USAF, Rome Air Development Center, under contract number F30602–86–C–0071.

[†]Current address: Department of Computer Science, Princeton University, Princeton, New Jersey 08544

[1]We use "specification" in the traditional sense of a statement of requirements. What the Ada Language Reference calls "specifications" should be thought of as like "declarations" in other programming languages.

the terms); this set becomes the *assertion language* used in Larch/Ada-88 specifications.

Larch/Ada-88 (henceforth Larch/Ada) is a Larch *interface language*; it is used to specify Ada programs by attaching assertions at certain points, like the entry and exit points of subprograms. The specification constructs of Larch/Ada are called *annotations*, since most of them are derived from similar constructs in Anna [5].

Implementation Most verification sofware works in batch mode [6,7]. The user writes a program, supplies a specification and appropriate assertions, and then submits it all to a *verification condition generator*. The resulting verification conditions must be shown to hold. A verification condition for a program is an assertion whose truth guarantees that the program satisfies its specification.

When a programmer using a batch system makes a refinement or discovers a mistake, the whole job must be resubmitted, and correct work may have to be redone. Moreover, most batch systems cannot verify program fragments. As practiced by Gries and Dijkstra, program development consists largely in building up correct fragments by accretion, and in refining existing fragments. Batch verification fits poorly with these techniques.

We have replaced the traditional batch verification system with a program editor, which we call Penelope. Using Penelope, programmers can examine weakest preconditions as they are computed and can use them to guide program development. Program fragments can be proved correct, then picked up and placed in larger contexts.

We have built the Penelope editor by using the Cornell Synthesizer Generator [8,9]. Penelope can be used to create and edit abstract syntax trees that represent parts of an annotated Ada program. The interface is that of a traditional syntax-directed editor in which the user may use a mouse or an EMACS-like command set to manipulate trees. Penelope computes weakest preconditions as attributes of the nodes of the syntax tree.[1] Attribute evaluation is incremental; that is, every time the user changes the tree, weakest preconditions are recomputed where necessary, and the new preconditions are available for display. When certain Ada constructs are used, Penelope generates a verification condition; typically one verification condition is generated for each subprogram and one for each loop.

A user of Penelope begins by writing down a formal specification of an Ada subprogram using Larch/Ada. (The formal specification takes the form of an Ada "specification" augmented with *subprogram annotations*.) He or she then builds the subprogram body, working backwards as described by Gries [2]. Penelope can be instructed to display weakest preconditions at any point, and also to display any verification conditions that may be generated. The user can alter the program and immediately observe the effects on preconditions and verification conditions, since the recomputation of *wp* and of verification conditions is incremental and automatic. (The preconditions and verification conditions are simplified somewhat before being presented to the user.)

The verification conditions are sentences in pure logic; their statement is independent of program context. If they can be shown to hold, the program containing them satisfies its specification. Penelope contains a proving component that can be used to prove facts about integers, Booleans, and Ada types like arrays and records. The proving component is primitive; the proof of a program like binary search takes up many pages.

Formal foundations The formal foundation of Larch/Ada has two parts, one dealing with assertions and another dealing with annotations. The assertion part covers the semantics of the Larch/Ada assertion language as defined using Larch Shared Language specifications. This semantics is determined entirely by the semantics of the Larch Shared Language, and is therefore independent of Ada. The assertion part also covers the formal specification (using the Larch Shared Language) of Ada's data types.

The annotation part connects the execution semantics of sequential Ada with the annotations of Ada programs defined by Larch/Ada. The Penelope editor's weakest precondition computations are based on a formal statement of *predicate transformers*. The predicate transformers define a function from a Larch/Ada specification and an annotated Ada program to a set of verification conditions. The transformers are based on a continuation semantics for the sequential part of Ada. As part of this work, Polak [10] has shown how to establish a formal connection between a continuation semantics and predicate transformers. To define the predicate transformers, he lets the denotation of a program be a function on terms of the Larch/Ada assertion language.

Larch/Ada

Two-tiered specifications In the two-tiered system of specification, the *shared language* component is used to define all the abstractions used in specification and verification. For example, in an arbitrary-precision arithmetic package, the shared language part of the specification would define what we mean by integer and by addition. One might implement arbitrary-precision arithmetic using the idea of registers of arbitrary length. The shared language would be used to define what we mean by a register and its length.

[1] Actually, as in Gries [2], the system works with an *approximation* to the weakest precondition, called *wp*.

The *interface language* part of a specification is used to state what a program does in terms of the abstractions defined in the shared language part. The interface language part of the arbitrary-precision arithmetic package would show which subprograms perform what operations on the data, and would state that overflow never occurs.

Using the two-tiered system, a designer can keep the unpleasant details introduced by the programming language isolated in the interface language component, while doing the real intellectual work of specification in the shared language component. It is possible to use the shared language to say exactly what is meant by, for example, a stack or a directed graph, without getting bogged down in details of exceptional conditions or of representation.

The shared language part of a specification defines the assertion language used in the interface language part of the specification. Formulas in this assertion language are formulas in first-order predicate logic. When we attempt to prove that an implementation satisfies its specification, we first apply the predicate transformers, which are based on the definition of Ada, to a program and its specification. The predicate transformers produce a verification condition, which is a sentence in the assertion language. The proof of the verification condition needs to refer only to the shared language part of the specification; no further reference to the definition of Ada is required. Since the assertion language is really a particular formulation of first-order logic, checking the correctness of the proofs of verification conditions is straightforward.

Languages in the two-tiered system Three languages are important in the two-tiered system of specification. The Larch Shared Language enables users to write formal specifications of useful abstractions. It is a single language, used to write specifications. The Larch Shared Language part of a specification consists of one or more *traits*, each one of which may specify several abstractions. The shared language part of a specification defines an *assertion language*, which is the language used to refer to the abstractions. (A sentence stating that a stack is not empty would be a Boolean term in the assertion language.) In general, every shared language specification defines a different assertion language, although the different assertion languages have much in common, since they are just different formulations of first-order logic.

Larch/Ada is the language in which we write the *interface language* part of a specification. This part uses *annotations* to specify the behavior of a program. The annotations contain assertions, which are formulas in the assertion language defined by the shared language part of the same specification.

Description of Larch/Ada The assertion language defined by a particular shared-language specification is essentially a particular predicate calculus. We will describe the features of the Larch/Ada interface language, then give an example.

The simplest Larch/Ada annotation is the *embedded assertion*. The assertion is a formula in the current assertion language (defined by the shared language part of the current specification). Free variables in the assertion refer to program variables. Embedded assertions may be inserted at certain control points in an implementation (i.e. between statements or between declarations); they constrain the implementation to satisfy the assertion whenever control reaches that point. In other words, the embedded assertion says that, whenever control reaches it, if we substitute the actual values of program variables into the assertion, it must denote truth. The embedded assertion can be used only in an implementation, as a guide to the predicate transformers; it cannot be used in specifications.

Larch/Ada's *subprogram annotations* are used both to constrain subprogram implementations, and to specify subprograms. The entry/exit kinds are the *in annotation*, the *out annotation*, and the *result annotation*. Each of these contains a single assertion. They are used to constrain states on entry to a subprogram, to constrain states on exit from a subprogram, and to constrain the values a function might return.

Also among the subprogram annotations are several *exception propagation annotations*, which are used to say when exceptions may and may not be raised, when exceptions must be raised, and what conditions must hold when exceptions are raised. Finally there is the *side effect annotation*, which is used to document side effects on or dependence on global variables.

Larch/Ada has two features which help make the annotation mechanism more powerful. The first is the "`IN` variable." Within a subprogram, parameter names can be modified by `IN` to denote the value of the parameter on entry to the subprogram. `IN` variables are essential in subprogram specifications, because we almost always need to refer to the initial values of parameters. For example, here are specifications for some of the familiar stack operations:

```
PROCEDURE push(s: IN OUT stack; x: element);
--| WHERE
--|     OUT s = push(IN s,x);
--| END WHERE;

PROCEDURE pop(s: IN OUT stack);
--| WHERE
--|     IN NOT is_empty(s);
--|     OUT s = pop(IN s);
--| END WHERE;
```

The other enriching feature of Larch/Ada is a way to introduce "virtual variables."[1] These variables are not used in writing specifications, but are defined within implementations to help in proofs of correctness. Their values don't actually affect the results of a computation. Larch/Ada allows the user to declare virtual variables, to assign to them, and to use them in annotations.

Finally, in support of data abstraction (packages with private types), Larch/Ada enables the user to define *abstraction functions* using the Larch Shared Language, and to associate these abstraction functions with Ada types, using the `based on` annotation. Thus, a user writing an arbitrary-precision arithmetic package might implement registers using arrays, and would then define an abstraction function from arrays to registers. The proofs of correctness of implementations of abstract data types are as described by Hoare [11]; the abstraction function is used to rewrite a specification that was in terms of an abstract type to a new specification in terms of a concrete type.

Using Larch/Ada As an example, here is a Larch/Ada specification for some set operations. Jeannette Wing used these operators in her presentation of a Larch interface language for CLU [4]. As she did, we will use a Larch Shared Language description of sets and set operations. The trait describing these operations, called `SetOfE`, is shown in Figure 1.

We begin our example with the specification of a "choose" procedure that selects a member of a set, removes it from the set, and returns it. Since Ada functions may not have side effects on their parameters, we will formulate the returned member as an `OUT` parameter:

```
--| WITH SetOfE WITH [set FOR si, integer FOR e];
PROCEDURE choose (IN OUT s: set; i: OUT integer);
--| WHERE
--|     IN NOT IsEmpty(s);
--|     OUT has(IN s, i) AND s = remove(IN s, i);
--| END WHERE;
```

The `--| WITH` annotation specifies that `SetOfE` is the trait that defines the notion of set and the operations `IsEmpty`, `has`, and `remove`. The `IN` annotation states that `choose` may be called only on nonempty sets. The `OUT` annotation gives the relation between the initial and final values of the set `s` and the final value of the integer `i`. (Notice that the final values are specified by giving just the variable name, while the initial values are specified by modifying the name by `IN`. In the `IN` annotation, all variables are implicitly modified by `IN`.) Because no side effect annotation is present, `choose` may not modify or read any global variables.

[1] These are called "ghost variables" by Gries and Dijkstra; the name "virtual variable" is from Luckham [5].

Figure 1: Shared language specification of set operations (Wing [4])

```
SetOfE: trait
  includes Integer
  introduces
    empty: → SI
    add: SI, E → SI
    remove: SI, E → SI
    has: SI, E → Bool
    isEmpty: SI → Bool
    card: SI → Int
  constrains empty, add, remove,
             has, isEmpty, card so that
    SI generated by [empty, add]
    for all [s: SI, e, e1: E]
      remove(empty, e) = empty
      remove(add(s, e), e1) =
        if e = e1 then remove(s, e1)
                  else add(remove(s, e1), e)
      has(empty, e) = false
      has(add(s, e), e1) =
        if e = e1 then true else has(s, e1)
      isEmpty(empty) = true
      isEmpty(add(s, e)) = false
      card(empty) = 0
      card(add(s,e)) =
        if has(s, e) then card(s)
                     else 1 + card(s)
```

Figure 2 shows a Larch/Ada specification for a set package. This package specifies the same operators as the similar example in Wing [4].

Formal foundation of Larch/Ada and Penelope

Connecting Ada to a denotational model Formal verification of Ada programs must be based on a formal definition of the Ada language itself, but at this time there is no official formal definition of Ada. We circumvent this difficulty by providing a denotational model of a computing language Ada′, and by considering Larch/Ada to be a specification language for Ada′. Ada and Ada′ have the same syntax, and we argue informally that for a restricted class of programs and computations they have the same observable behavior.

We restrict Ada most by omitting from Ada′ all features involving concurrency. While there is widespread consensus on what are good methods to model and specify sequential imperative languages, there is no similar consensus on the

Figure 2: Larch/Ada specification for a set package

```
--| WITH SetOfE WITH [integer FOR e];
PACKAGE sets IS
  TYPE set IS PRIVATE; --| based on si;

  FUNCTION pair(i, j: integer) RETURN set;
    --| WHERE
    --|   RETURN 'add(add(empty, i), j);
    --| END WHERE;

  PROCEDURE union(s1: set; s2: IN OUT set);
    --| WHERE
    --|   OUT (FORALL j::
    --|         ((has(s2, j) = has(IN s1, j))
    --|                        OR has(IN s2, j)));
    --| END WHERE;

  PROCEDURE intersect(s1: set; s2: IN OUT set);
    --| WHERE
    --|   OUT (FORALL j::
    --|         ((has(s2, j) = has(IN s1, j))
    --|                        AND has(IN s2, j)));
    --| END WHERE;

  FUNCTION member(s: set; i: integer) RETURN boolean;
    --| WHERE
    --|   RETURN has(s, i);
    --| END WHERE;

  FUNCTION size(s: set) RETURN integer;
    --| WHERE
    --|   RETURN card(s);
    --| END WHERE;
END sets;
```

utility of the various proposed methods of modeling and specifying concurrent programs. We have omitted other features from Ada′ because they are machine-dependent (e.g. representation clauses) or because it is not feasible to formalize them (e.g. the exact circumstances under which `storage_error` is raised). Here is a partial list of omitted features:

- Concurrency
- Real number types
- Representation specifications and other features that are machine-dependent or implementation-dependent
- Unchecked conversion and unchecked deallocation
- The predefined exceptions `storage_error` and `numeric_error` (i.e. we consider that no execution of an Ada′ program ever raises these exceptions), and computations that result in "undetected numeric overflow"
- Optimizations that cause execution of Ada statements in other than the canonical order
- Parameter aliasing in procedure calls
- Any program called *erroneous* by the Ada reference manual

Some of these restrictions (e.g. that forbidding aliasing) can be enforced by suitable static checks.

Although Ada′ is not Ada, they are intended to be equivalent within our area of interest, and we will not distinguish them in what follows.

Connecting the denotational model to Larch/Ada and the predicate transformers The predicate transformers implemented in Penelope are derived from a continuation semantics for Ada. The task of defining a continuation semantics for Ada has been considerably simplified by two expedients. First, the static semantics of Ada is not part of the definition; the definition assumes a suitably checked and attributed abstract syntax representation of programs. Second, the semantics of the Ada types is not part of the definition; instead, the semantics of Ada types is defined by Larch Shared Language specifications. The technique used for deriving predicate transformers from a denotational semantics is one developed by Polak [12,10]. The current definition of the predicate transformers used in Penelope does not provide for proofs of termination.

Here we give an example that shows what we mean when we say that Larch/Ada and Penelope are formally based. The example suggests how we define the semantics of Larch/Ada and how we show that the VC generation implemented in Penelope is sound.

Generating verification conditions involves manipulating a number of different languages. Since a VC generator takes as input a program and a specification, and produces as output an assertion (the verification condition), the fundamental languages are the programming language P, the specification language S, and the assertion language A. For simplicity, we take the assertion language as fixed, although it is actually determined using the shared language part of the specification.

The actual input to Penelope is a specification together with an *annotated* implementation; we will call that conglomerate V, and we define projection functions that extract the relevant parts:

$\pi : V \to P$	The implementation *without* annotations
$\sigma : V \to S$	The specification

Then the VC generator is a function $vcgen : V \to A$, and we wish to show that $vcgen$ is sound, i.e. whenever the verification condition $vcgen(v)$ holds, the program πv satisfies its specification σv.

We need to consider the denotations of the various syntactic objects we have been discussing. For simplicity, we'll let the denotation of a program be a mapping from states to states (this makes sense even for a continuation semantics if one considers whole programs). We'll call B the special Boolean domain consisting of the two elements truth and falsehood (which we'll write as **t** and **f**). If the set of states is X, we have

$M_P : P \rightarrow (X \rightarrow X)$
A program denotes a state changer.

$M_S : S \rightarrow ((X \rightarrow X) \rightarrow B)$
A specification denotes a predicate on state changers.

$M_A : A \rightarrow (X \rightarrow B)$
An assertion denotes a predicate on states.

Intuitively, a program is a function from states to states, a specification defines a predicate ("satisfaction") on programs, and an assertion defines a predicate on states (also called "satisfaction"). A program $p \in P$ satisfies a specification $s \in S$ if

$$(M_S s)(M_P p) = \mathbf{t}.$$

The semantics of the specification language can be defined in terms of the semantics of the programming and assertion languages, M_P and M_A, provided we have a fixed (not necessarily finite) set of states X. If the specification language is a simple one that gives only entry and exit assertions, i.e. $S = A \times A$, then we can define

$$M_S \langle a_1, a_2 \rangle \rho = \forall x \in X. M_a a_1 x \Rightarrow M_a a_2(\rho x),$$

where $\rho = M_P(p)$ is a state transformer. The definition says that a program satisfies its specification if, whenever the entry condition a_1 holds on entry to the program, the exit condition a_2 holds on exit from the program. (We are using $\Rightarrow$ to denote mathematical implication.)

The semantics of Larch/Ada is defined in two steps: first, we define a mapping from Larch/Ada to a simpler language in which a specification consists of an entry condition, an exit condition for normal termination, and exit conditions for termination by raising exceptions. In the second step we define the semantics of the simpler language; this language is essentially $S = A \times \textbf{list}\ A$, and the definition of its semantics is very similar to that just shown.

As the discussion above suggests, V is not really fundamental; we introduced V to stand for the input to *vcgen*. If we have an (annotated program, specification) pair $v \in V$, we are really only interested in the projections πv and σv. The program satisfies its specification when

$$M_S(\sigma v)(M_P(\pi v)) = \textbf{true}.$$

VC generation is sound if the truth of the verification condition guarantees that the program satisfies its specification. The truth of a verification condition must be independent of state, so the function *vcgen* is sound if, for any $v \in V$,

$$\forall x \in X(M_A(vcgen(v))) \Rightarrow M_S(\sigma v)(M_P(\pi v)).$$

Polak [10] goes into more detail, giving a complete definition of *vcgen* for a small programming language P. He describes a way of deriving *vcgen* from the semantics of P and sketches a proof of soundness that uses structural induction on programs. The techniques he describes are the same ones used to define the semantics of Larch/Ada and to prove the soundness of the predicate transformers implemented in Penelope.

The Penelope implementation

We are implementing tools that support research in formal verification using Larch/Ada. Of these, the most important is the Penelope editor, which helps users develop verified programs. In the prototype, there is no support for writing traits; every specification has the same shared language part, and there is a fixed assertion language used for all specifications. The prototype can be used to specify and prove Ada subprograms, provided those subprograms use no global variables. We plan to extend the Penelope prototype to read definitions of extensions to the assertion language. We plan to supplement it with a tool that will help prove Penelope verification conditions.

Status of the implementation

Penelope is implemented using the Cornell synthesizer generator [8]. The Cornell synthesizer generator accepts as input a description of an attribute grammar and compiles this description into a syntax-directed editor which can compute and display the values of attributes. The heart of this editor is an algorithm which, when the edited tree is changed, computes and propagates the changes in attribute values [9].

We think of Penelope as having three components: predicate transformation, proving, and simplification. Predicate transformation is central. That component reads and interprets the Larch/Ada annotations, computes *wp*, and generates verification conditions. The user controls which intermediate values of *wp* are displayed and which verification conditions are displayed. The displayed values are updated every time the user changes his or her program or specification.

The proving component is a sub-editor that enables the user to construct proofs of the verification conditions, using a sequent calculus. The editor presents a list of hypotheses and a goal, and the user designates an inference rule to apply. The application may generate subgoals, and the process continues until the subgoals are reduced to axioms, which are automatically recognized by the editor. The editor has built in a small number of proof tactics; the user can designate one of these tactics instead of designating a rule.

The simplification component is a set of functions that can be called by the other two components. These functions make the preconditions and verification conditions more readable. One function does this by rewriting; terms like $P \wedge$ **true** are rewritten to P, and so on. Another function attempts to find ways to substitute simpler terms for terms that are especially complex or hard to read. Another performs arithmetic operations on integer literals. Several functions manipulate the forms of terms in order to make other operations easy; depending on circumstances, one may prefer $P \supset (Q \supset (R \supset S))$ to $P \wedge Q \wedge R \supset S$, or vice versa. (We are using $\supset$ to represent the implication symbol in the assertion language.) Collectively, these functions reduce the size of the verification conditions Penelope generates by about a factor of five.

The currently supported subset of Ada We have imposed a number of restrictions on programs editable with Penelope, as described earlier. Concurrency, real number types, parameter aliasing, `storage_error`, and some other features are forbidden. Here are the highlights of what Penelope does with those programs it accepts:

- Subprograms may call predefined or user-defined subprograms; recursion is supported.
- Arbitrary user-defined exceptions, `raise` statements, and exception handlers are supported.
- Integer, Boolean, enumeration, array, and record types are supported. The predefined Ada operators for these types are supported. (Subtyping is not supported.)
- All of the Ada control structures are supported except `goto` statements, `case` statements, and `for` loops.
- Some static semantic checking is performed, including type checking and overload resolution.

The current Penelope is limited in what it can prove. Many capabilities which might be considered difficult have been investigated mathematically but have not yet been implemented. These include:

- Proving that a program never raises the predefined exceptions `constraint_error` and `program_error`
- Proving that programs terminate
- Proving that programs are not erroneous
- Detecting potential aliasing and illegal order dependencies by suitable static semantic checking
- Proving programs that define subtypes whose bounds are set dynamically
- Proving programs that raise or handle the predefined exceptions `constraint_error` and `program_error`

The currently supported subset of Larch/Ada The current implementation of the Penelope editor supports most of Larch/Ada. The major features that are missing are those associated with termination, global variables and side effects, and data abstraction. As noted earlier, there is no support for writing traits in the Larch Shared Language. This means that the shared language part of every specification is the same, and that there is a single assertion language used for all Larch/Ada specifications. That assertion language is restricted to terms describing integers, Booleans, arrays, and records. (Enumeration literals are converted to integers during predicate transformation.)

Future plans

Simplification The greatest weakness of the current Penelope editor is that weakest preconditions and verification conditions are too hard to read. The simplification component is good at reducing the bulk and complexity of Boolean terms; most of the complexity in verification conditions comes from arithmetic terms. Simplifying such terms is the next step in improving our implementation. Rather than build an arithmetic simplifier from scratch, we plan to connect an existing simplifier to the Penelope editor. The simplifier that we plan to use is based on the Nelson-Oppen procedure for combining decision procedures [13,14].

Extending Penelope In order to support data abstraction, we intend to add packages and private types to Penelope's Ada subset. (Adding these constructs is straightforward; the major difficulties involved in supporting data abstraction arise in extending the assertion language, as discussed below.) We may also add new control structures, in particular the `case` statement and the `for` loop.

In the longer term, we plan to add support for proofs of termination and for proofs of subprograms that have side effects on global variables.

Data Abstraction It is not possible to write readable formal specifications of large programs without taking advantage of data abstraction. Generating verification conditions for programs that use abstract data types is not hard, but generating sound verification conditions for implementations of abstract data types can be tricky. This is especially true in Ada, where the abstraction constructs do not completely hide the representation.

It is also hard to simplify and prove verification conditions when specifications refer to abstract data types. The essence of the difficulty is that, when using data abstraction, the user must add new terms to the assertion language. (These terms describe the new abstractions, like stacks, buffers, registers, or whatever may be needed to specify a particular application. They are introduced and defined by traits written in the Larch Shared Language.) To be able to make effective use of the new terms, we must be able to show that their introduction does not lead to any logical inconsistency. We must also be able to extend the proving and simplification components of Penelope to be able to handle the new terms.

We will begin studying data abstraction by making our assertion language extensible. We will use a tiny subset of the Larch Shared Language, a subset which will enable us to add to the assertion language new sort and operator symbols. In particular, it will be possible to add abstract sorts and abstraction functions to the assertion language. We will then allow users to make assertions (without proof) involving the new symbols they have introduced. In proofs of programs, these assertions will be treated like axioms. We hope that, by studying the kinds of assertions users make, we will be able to learn what methods of proof might help users prove programs that use data abstraction.

Conclusions

Our efforts have been concentrated on defining Larch/Ada-88 and on building the Penelope prototype. Evaluation of Larch/Ada and Penelope must await the completion of the prototype and experience with its use, but we can draw some conclusions about the methods we have applied and about the difficulty of the problems that remain.

We have developed a useful technique for deriving predicate transformers, and we have developed a method for implementing the transformers using an attribute grammar. We have some preliminary observations about the results of attempting to mechanize Gries's and Dijkstra's methods of program development. Finally, we believe we have learned what problems need to be solved before a useful verification system can be built.

Implementing predicate transformers The denotational style of writing predicate transformers lends itself to a natural and efficient implementation of the transformers as an attribute grammar. Values in the transformer definition map to attributes of the grammar, and meaning functions map to the semantic equations that define the relationships among the attributes. We can avoid implementing lambda-abstraction and beta-reduction for the language of terms by using pairs of attributes to represent values of arrow types.

Mechanizing formal development The biggest obstacle to learning Gries's method of program development is the drudgery of computing *wp*. This difficulty increases as the complexity of the programming language increases; it would be unrealistic to expect to compute *wp* by hand for a language like Ada. Fortunately, it is easy to mechanize the computation of *wp*, provided a denotational-style definition of *wp* is available.

The problem with a mechanized computation of *wp* is that the resulting preconditions quickly become too complicated to be understood by a human being, at which point they can no longer be used to guide program development, which is the whole point of Gries's method. We have yet to learn whether mechanical simplifiers like the one described by Nelson and Oppen can make the preconditions understandably simple. The problem doesn't arise when *wp* is computed by hand, because in that case the programmer constantly applies his or her knowledge of integers, sequences, Booleans, and so forth, so that computation and simplification proceed simultaneously.

Open problems The Larch/Ada specifications we can write using Penelope are limited by the fixed, nonextensible assertion language. (It is a severe limit; for example, at this time we cannot introduce the factorial function for use in a specification.) The programs we can prove using Penelope are limited by the size of the weakest preconditions Penelope computes. We believe that the most important problem remaining to be solved is the one of being able to introduce new terms into an assertion language, while simultaneously introducing methods of simplification and proof for those terms. The Larch Shared Language provides a way of writing formal definitions of new terms. We need to develop a formal representation of methods of proof and simplification. Finally, we need to develop ways of showing that the addition of new definitions introduces no logical inconsistency, and ways of showing that the proof and simplification methods are consistent with the definitions.

Related work

Researchers at MIT and DEC SRC have developed several tools that manipulate Larch Shared Language traits. The Larch prover, LP, can read a description of an equational theory and attempt to prove sentences in that theory, primarily by term rewriting [15]. The Larch checker, LC, reads a trait and writes two files for input to LP: an axiomatization of the trait and a command script for discharging the proof obligations associated with that trait. (Not all of the proof obligations described in the reference manual for the shared language have been implemented yet.) LC supports the shared language's mixfix and overloaded operators [16].

AFFIRM, built at USC-ISI, was the first verification system to use both algebraic specifications and a rewrite rule prover [17]. The Gypsy system was the first verification system to handle a form of concurrency [6]. The Stanford

Pascal Verifier was the first verification system to handle a real programming language [18]. The most important contribution of the Stanford Pascal Verifier project was probably the Nelson-Oppen method of combining decision procedures [13].

The Anna project is an effort to introduce formal specification to Ada programmers by providing specification constructs which can be checked at run time [5]. The aim of AVA project is to define a verifiable subset of Ada and to give it a formal semantics using Boyer-Moore logic [19,20]. The AVA language is essentially a subset of that implemented in the Penelope prototype; it omits exception handlers and `raise` statements.

Acknowledgements

The work described herein was done at Odyssey Research Associates with Wolfgang Polak, Carla Marceau, David Guaspari, C. Douglas Harper, and Doug Weber. Anna provided large repository of specification constructs, on which we drew heavily when designing Larch/Ada. The Anna group at Stanford was forthcoming with suggestions about how formal verification of Ada programs might proceed. John Guttag helped us to understand Larch and to explore how we might adapt Larch to Ada. In particular, he helped us elucidate the issues that needed to be addressed in defining the semantics of a Larch interface language. John Guttag and Steve Garland lent us LP, which we used in our study of verification conditions generated by Penelope.

David Guaspari and Wolfgang Polak helped me understand the formal foundations of Larch/Ada and Penelope, and they corrected many errors in earlier drafts of this paper. Of course, they are not responsible for any errors that may remain.

References

[1] E. W. Dijsktra, *A Discipline of Programming.* Prentice-Hall, 1976.

[2] D. Gries, *The Science of Programming.* Springer-Verlag, 1981.

[3] J. V. Guttag, J. J. Horning, and J. M. Wing, "Larch in five easy pieces," Tech. Rep. TR 5, DEC/SRC, July 1985.

[4] J. M. Wing, "Writing Larch interface language specifications," *ACM Transactions on Programming Languages and Systems*, vol. 9, pp. 1–24, Jan. 1987.

[5] D. C. Luckham *et al.*, "Anna: A language for annotating Ada programs," tech. rep., Stanford University, 1986. The Anna reference manual.

[6] D. I. Good, R. L. Akers, and L. M. Smith, "Report on Gypsy 2.05," tech. rep., Computational Logic Inc., 1986.

[7] J. Crow, S. Jefferson, R. Lee, M. Melliar-Smith, J. Rushby, R. Schwartz, R. Shostak, and F. von Henke, "Preliminary definition of the revised SPECIAL specification language," tech. rep., SRI International, 1986.

[8] T. Reps and T. Teitelbaum, *The Synthesizer Generator Reference Manual.* Department of Computer Science, Cornell University, 1987.

[9] T. Reps, *Generating Language-Based Environments.* MIT Press, 1984.

[10] W. Polak, "A technique for writing predicate transformers." Unpublished manuscript.

[11] C. A. R. Hoare, "Proof of correctness of data representations," *Acta Informatica*, vol. 1, pp. 271–281, 1972.

[12] W. Polak, "Program verification based on denotational semantics," in *Principles of Programming Languages*, 1981.

[13] G. Nelson and D. C. Oppen, "Simplification by cooperating decision procedures," *ACM Transactions on Programming Languages and Systems*, vol. 1, pp. 245–257, Oct. 1979.

[14] T. Redmond, "Simplifier description," Tech. Rep. ATR-85 (8354)-8, Aerospace, Nov. 1985.

[15] S. Garland and J. V. Guttag, "An overview of LP, the Larch prover," in *Third International Conference on Rewriting Techniques and Applications*, 1988.

[16] S. Garland. Private communication.

[17] D. R. Musser, "Abstract data type specifications in the AFFIRM system," in *Proceedings of the Specifications of Reliable Software*, pp. 47–57, IEEE Computer Society, Apr. 1979.

[18] D. C. Luckham *et al.*, "Stanford Pascal Verifier user manual," Tech. Rep. STAN-CS-79-731, Stanford University, Mar. 1979.

[19] M. K. Smith, "A verifiable Ada," *Ada Letters*, vol. 8, pp. 136–142, July/August 1988. In the Formal Methods Committee report.

[20] R. S. Boyer and J. S. Moore, "Proving theorems about LISP functions," *Journal of the ACM*, vol. 22, no. 1, pp. 129–144, 1975.

An Example of Formal Specification as an Aid to Design and Development

Robert B. Terwilliger
Mark J. Maybee†
Leon J. Osterweil†

Department of Computer Science,
University of Colorado,
Boulder, CO 80309-0430

ABSTRACT

In this paper we describe an experiment which supports the hypothesis that formally specifying a system after a prototype has been created can enhance the development process. We conjectured that describing an existing system using a small number of well understood concepts could increase understanding and enhance communication between project members. We performed an experiment to verify this conjecture using software constructed by the Arcadia project: a consortium developing software environment technologies including "process programming" [10]. At the beginning of the experiment, a prototype requirements building system had been developed and was undergoing redesign and extension. Over the course of three months, the developers met with a specification expert and a formal description was written using PLEASE [11], an Ada®-based executable specification and design language which supports formal methods similar to VDM. Formal specification enhanced the development process by helping the developers to clarify the architecture of the system, separate their concerns, and discuss possible modifications.

1. Introduction

Traditional methods do not ensure the production of correct software. It has been suggested that formal specification can enhance the software development process [4]. Typically, it is proposed that such specifications should either be written before the production of a prototype, or should be executable and also serve as an initial implementation. We believe that formal specifications can enhance the development process in a number of ways. Specifically, we believe that further development can be enhanced by creating a formal specification after a prototype has already been constructed using traditional techniques. We believe that the purpose of prototype development should be to facilitate the acquisition of knowledge about the nature of a problem domain or solution approach. That being the case, it seems clear to us that describing the prototype and the nature of experiences with it more precisely should yield correspondingly more precise and valuable knowledge and insight. It should also increase understanding and enhance communication between project members. Post-prototype formal specification can in this way enhance the remainder of the development process by helping to clarify system architecture, separate concerns, and provide an "intellectual test bed" for the discussion of changes. In this paper, we describe an experiment performed in the context of the Arcadia project which supports these hypotheses.

Ada ® is a trademark of the US Government, Ada Joint Program Office.

This research was supported by NSF grants CCR-8705162 and CCR-8809418.

† Author's current address: Dept. of Information and Computer Science, University of California, Irvine, CA 92717.

The goal of the Arcadia project is to experimentally develop superior software environment technologies, one of which is *process programming* [10]. Advocates of process programming claim that software processes such as requirements specification, design, and testing are themselves software; therefore, they should be specified, designed, and coded. They further believe that process programs should be interpretable by software environments. Thus the Arcadia project is attempting to develop process programs and devise environment architectures capable of interpreting them. Towards this end, Arcadia is developing a series of process programs and supporting environments using a cycle of prototype development, evaluation, and migration. The first phase of this activity is the creation of a prototype process program for the entire software lifecycle called BOPEEP (But One Prototype End to End Process-program). The initial phase of BOPEEP has focussed on the creation of REBUS, a prototype REquirements BUilding System. These prototypes are intended to be used as vehicles for providing important early knowledge about key software processes and languages in which they might be programmed. Hence we conjectured that the use of formalization to describe these prototypes and their components would increase the knowledge acquisition effect of the prototyping activities.

In explaining REBUS and process programming in general, we found informal descriptions to be inadequate. While natural language facilitates the formulation and transfer of general concepts, its ambiguity makes precise communication difficult. We felt we could better analyze the complex issues involved in process programming with the aid of formal descriptions. For systems already constructed, programming language code might serve as a complete, formal description. However, such descriptions often lack abstraction and rigor. Code is written to efficiently utilize machine resources rather than to communicate new ideas. We believe that rigorous higher level descriptions of these systems can increase our understanding of the issues involved. With this in mind, we have attempted to describe some of our key activities using formal methods similar to VDM.

VDM (the Vienna Development Method) supports the top-down development of software specified in a notation suitable for formal verification [7]. In this method, components are first written using a combination of conventional programming languages and predicate logic. A procedure or function may be specified using a *pre-condition*, which states the properties that the inputs must satisfy, and a *post-condition*, which states the relationship of inputs to outputs. Similarly, an abstract data type may be specified with an *invariant* defining the acceptable states and pre- and post-conditions for the operations. To increase the expressive power of specifications, the high-level types *set*, *list*, and *map* are added to the language. In VDM, specifications are incrementally refined into programs in an implementation language. VDM is used in industrial

©1989 ACM 0-89791-305-1/89/0500/0266$00.75

environments [2] and seems to prove useful in practice; environments to support the method are now being constructed [1].

In one sense, VDM-style specifications can be written in any language which supports predicate logic annotations. For example, ANNA [8] is an annotated version of Ada. PLEASE [11] is a subset of ANNA specifically designed to support formal methods similar to VDM. In PLEASE, the types set, list, and map are pre-defined and annotations are restricted to Horn clauses: a subset of predicate logic which is also the basis for Prolog [3]. PLEASE specifications can be used in proofs of correctness; they can also be transformed into prototypes which use Prolog to "execute" pre- and post-conditions. PLEASE specifications are effectively exploited by ENCOMPASS [12], an environment which extends VDM with executable specifications, knowledge-based tools, and testing-based verification methods. At present, ENCOMPASS is not robust enough to be used in major development efforts. However, the PLEASE language is stable, and can be used independently of the tools developed for its support.

In the fall of 1987, we performed an experiment in which a high-level design for REBUS was written in PLEASE. At the beginning of the experiment, a prototype version of REBUS had been developed and was undergoing evaluation aimed at redesign and extension. We conjectured that describing the system using a small number of formally defined concepts could increase understanding, enhance communication between project members, and maximize the knowledge acquired though the prototyping activity. Over the course of three months, the developers met with a specification expert and the formal description was created. We found that formal specification enhanced the development process by helping the developers to clarify the architecture of the system, separate their concerns, and discuss possible modifications.

In the rest of this paper we describe this experiment in more detail. In section two we describe the experimental process more completely, including an overview of the original REBUS prototype and the issues raised during the specification process. The discussion centers around the *whiteboard*, a mechanism for controlling the interactions between multiple programmers. In section three we describe the formal specification of REBUS; it contains four parts: the object manager, the whiteboard, REBUS itself, and a skeleton of the entire specification process. Finally, in section five we summarize and draw some conclusions from our experience.

2. An Experiment in Formal Specification

In the Fall of 1987 at the University of Colorado, a prototype version of REBUS had been under construction since the preceding summer by a team of three graduate students. The prototype served as a focal point for integrating a number of pre-existing research efforts. It encorporated both an object-oriented database system [6] and a relational language [5] among its major components. Its major objectives included improved understanding of the nature of the requirement specification process and of the linguistic mechanisms needed to support its effective description by executable code. After a four month period of very rapid prototyping, it was decided that a review of the design would enhance further development; we believed that the developers' current perspectives might have been too heavily influenced by implementation considerations. It was suggested that the construction of a formal specification/design could prove to be interesting as well as an aid in future development. By creating an abstract representation of the system, we believed that the underlying issues and concepts would be separated from the implementation. Therefore, over a period of three months, formal specifications of REBUS were written in PLEASE.

During the experiment, weekly meetings were held between a senior graduate student and a faculty member serving as the specification expert. In these meetings, the student presented the goals and design of REBUS to the expert, who questioned the student in order to clarify concepts and devise formal representations for the design. The development of the specifications did not proceed at a uniform rate. Periods of discussion and thought would result in important insights and new formal representations; these would be followed by the rapid generation of specifications. At the beginning of the process a month passed before the specification expert's knowledge of the project was sufficient that any formal representations could be generated. During the second month many insights were reached and the bulk of the specifications were written. An initial version of the specifications were presented to the Arcadia group at the University of Colorado as soon as they were completed. During the third month the specifications were carefully reviewed, discussed, and put into their present form.

To better understand the issues raised and resolved during the experiment, we will consider the REBUS prototype in more detail.

2.1. The REBUS Prototype

REBUS is a requirements building system developed by the Arcadia group as part of BOPEEP, a prototype process program implementation. REBUS attempts to show that requirements specification development can be viewed as a programming activity by developing a system that implements a process program for requirements specification. In REBUS, a requirements specification is viewed as a DAG composed of requirements specification *nodes*, each of which may have *attributes* of various types. Nodes may have *relations* between them, and both nodes and relations may have to satisfy certain *constraints*. In REBUS, the requirements specification process consists of creating and modifying nodes, relating nodes to one another and forming larger aggregates, analyzing groups of nodes to see if they satisfy constraints, and coordinating the efforts of multiple developers.

More specifically, in REBUS a requirements specification is an instance of the type *Reqts_Spec*, which is a DAG of nodes, each of which is of type *Reqts_Elt*. Objects of type *Reqts_Elt* are records whose fields (attributes) are of various types, some of which are more familiar (for example, string or integer) and some of which are more esoteric (for example, predicate or dataflow sequence specification). *Reqts_Elt* objects may have relations between them which are specified in the language APPL/A [5]. APPL/A relations specify constraints that *Reqts_Elt* objects must satisfy and provide mechanisms to trigger appropriate actions when these constraints are violated. Development of an object of type *Reqts_Spec* is therefore a process of creating, evaluating, relating, and altering *Reqts_Elt* objects.

The REBUS prototype, then, implements a process program for requirements specification; this program consists of a number of concurrent sub-processes. For example, each person on a project is expected to specify different sub-requirements, and thus may have a different path of execution through REBUS. This requires different bindings for different sub-processes. The main REBUS process describes the various requirements software objects, attributes, and relations, as well as controlling the ways in which sub-processes can interact. Tasks such as creation, analysis and modification of nodes are represented by coordinated sub-processes; these tasks are concurrent, but may require synchronization at certain points. For example, analysis of a node should be suspended or disallowed while it is undergoing modification. High level direction of these tasks, and the coordination of the people to whom their execution is bound, is effected by the highest level of REBUS, which is viewed as the actual process program, while the lowest-level sub-processes, or possibly their operations, are considered to be the analogs of conventional tools.

In REBUS, the actions of independent sub-processes are coordinated using the *whiteboard*, a communication and coordination mechanism derived from the *blackboard* concept [9]. The REBUS whiteboard was designed specifically to coordinate multiple developers are engaged in the parallel creation of a software object whose partitions may be inter-dependent; requirements development for example. In our concept, a whiteboard holds a group of objects, each of which is in a particular *state*. The state of an object summarizes much of the information available about it; for example its consistency, stage in the lifecycle, work status, and completeness. Objects are moved from state to state to reflect changes in their underlying status. The whiteboard provides access to the objects it holds only through certain operations, the most notable of which modify the object or change its state on the whiteboard. Access and modification permissions may vary with the object, state and user.

To gain a deeper understanding of the whiteboard concept and how it evolved during our experiment, we now describe the whiteboard as it was originally implemented in the REBUS prototype.

2.1.1. The Original Whiteboard Model

Figure 1 shows a simplified version of the *Whiteboard* package specification as it appeared at the beginning of our experiment. The package implements an *abstract data type* (ADT), instances of which are whiteboards with persistent states. Thus, the package provides an interface to a persistent data store, the elements of which are whiteboards. A whiteboard stores and manipulates objects called *items*, each of which represents the state of a unit of a requirements specification object. whiteboard items can be thought of as messages for communicating the state of objects amongst independent processes. In this implementation, there are only three states of interest; therefore, a whiteboard consists of three lists of items: the items currently *posted*, and thus requiring attention; the items presently *locked* by a user; and the list of *completed* items. Posted items are indications of work remaining to be done. As new work is generated, corresponding items are "posted" to the whiteboard. Users select items on which to work by examining the posted items and "locking" them. The list of locked items is actually a list of lists: one for each user working on the project. Locked items represent work in progress. Locks are exclusive so there is no possibility of conflicting changes to the same item. The list of completed items represents work that has reached some reasonable standard of thoroughness and consistency. REBUS automatically subjects items on the completed list to checks for internal consistency and, if the appropriate conditions are not met, automatically re-posts the incorrect items.

The *Whiteboard* package provides four types of operations: operations to create, open and close a whiteboard; operations to access items on the whiteboard; operations which manipulate lists of items; and operations to move items between lists on the whiteboard. The second and third groups of operations are distinguished because it is possible to access items without manipulating lists of items. All operations take parameters of two basic types: *names*, text strings used to refer to objects; and *handles*, which provide more direct and machine-efficient access to objects For example, consider the operations to create, open and close whiteboards. The procedure *create_whiteboard* causes a new whiteboard to be created in the persistent data store with a specified unique name. The function *open_whiteboard* returns a handle to the pre-existing named whiteboard. The procedure *close_whiteboard* notifies REBUS that the user is done with the whiteboard accessed by the indicated handle.

Other operations manipulate lists of items. The function *itemlist* returns a handle to the list of posted items on the whiteboard referenced by *Ident*, while the functions *locked_itemlist* and *completed_itemlist* return handles to the lists of locked and completed items respectively. The procedure *get_item* updates the itemlist handle, returning copies of successive items on an itemlist when called repeatedly, and the function *end_of_items* returns true when the itemlist handle references an empty itemlist. The function

```
package Whiteboard is

--
--  create, open or close a whiteboard
--
procedure create_whiteboard( Name   : in string    );
function  open_whiteboard  ( Name   : in string
                           ) return  WB_handle    ;
procedure close_whiteboard ( Ident  : in WB_handle);

--
--  access an item on the whiteboard
--
function item   ( Board : in WB_handle ;
                  Id    : in item_id
                ) return  WB_item      ;
--
--  get an itemlist off a whiteboard
--
function itemlist           ( Ident  : in WB_handle
                            ) return   IL_handle  ;
function locked_itemlist    ( Ident  : in WB_handle
                            ) return   IL_handle  ;
function completed_itemlist ( Ident  : in WB_handle
                            ) return   IL_handle  ;
--
--  manipulate an itemlist
--
procedure get_item     ( Index : in out IL_handle ;
                         Item  : out    WB_item ) ;
function end_of_items( Index : in       IL_handle
                     ) return  Boolean            ;
--
--  post, lock, delete or complete an item
--
procedure post_item     ( Board     : in WB_handle ;
                          Contents  : in string  ) ;
procedure repost_item   ( Board     : in WB_handle ;
                          Id        : in item_id ) ;
procedure lock_item     ( Board     : in WB_handle ;
                          Id        : in item_id ) ;
procedure unlock_item   ( Board     : in WB_handle ;
                          Id        : in item_id ) ;
procedure delete_item   ( Board     : in WB_handle ;
                          Id        : in item_id ) ;
procedure complete_item ( Board     : in WB_handle ;
                          Id        : in item_id ) ;

end Whiteboard;
```

Figure 1. Simplified Version of Original Whiteboard Header

item provides random access to the items on a whiteboard; given a handle to a whiteboard and a unique identifier for an item it returns a copy of the item. Finally, consider the operations to move items between lists on the whiteboard. The procedure *post_item* creates a new whiteboard item containing *Contents*, and places it on the posted list, while the procedure *repost_item* transfers an item from the completed list to the posted list. The procedure *lock_item* locks the specified item by moving it from the posted list to the locked list, and the procedure *unlock_item* unlocks an item by moving it from the locked to the posted list. Lastly, the procedure *complete_item* takes a locked item and places it in the completed list, while the procedure *delete_item* removes an item from the whiteboard.

After the senior student had presented and explained these

operations to the specification expert, discussion of the underlying issues began in earnest.

2.2. Issues Raised by the Specification Process

The first question to arise was how to specify the persistent data store using PLEASE. One solution was suggested by the original package specification; persistence could be specified by declaring the stored objects as static variables local to the *Whiteboard* package. As in the original specification, the package would provide operations to create, access, and modify the whiteboards in the store. Unfortunately, we found that this solution makes the specification of concurrency constraints difficult; the effective unit for concurrency control is a single whiteboard, not the entire collection. The concurrency constraints can be specified simply if all operations on a whiteboard are *serializable* [14]. The serializability of operations can be easily modeled if each whiteboard is represented as a Unix process, or Ada *task*, with local variables used to store items. Each whiteboard must be able to accept requests to access or modify its contents. We found it easy to model this as message passing; other processes interact with a whiteboard by sending a request message and waiting for a reply. Since a process has only one thread of execution, only one message can be processed at a time.

While this representation makes serialization of whiteboard operations, and thereby specification of concurrency constraints, simple, it leaves some unanswered questions regarding the persistence of whiteboards. If each whiteboard is a process with local variables for its state, then persistence is determined by the lifetimes of processes. To create a new whiteboard a process must be invoked and to destroy a whiteboard a process must be terminated. Fortunately, these situations can be provided for by defining a *manager* for the whiteboard type. The whiteboard manager is itself a process, which controls a sub-process for each whiteboard in existence. Requests to create, open, or close whiteboards are handled by the manager.

The next issued to arise was the meaning of a name, and how it differed formally from a handle. In the prototype version of REBUS, the meanings of these two things were driven by implementation concerns. Handles were implemented as actual pointers to linked lists of items, and *item_ids* were implemented as indices into an array of items. Arbitrary items could be accessed by using the *item* function. An item could be on two whiteboards simultaneously, requiring concurrency control on the item level. Names were not unique identifiers for whiteboards, merely convenient labels which could be bound to new whiteboards as needed. There was no control over the circumstances under which the binding of a name to a whiteboard could change. The same name could refer to different whiteboards at the same time but for different users, and to different whiteboards at different times for the same user.

These characteristics had not been specified or even contemplated. Rather, they emerged from the implementation. Understanding of these characteristics came as the result of grappling with the need to formalize what had been implemented. This understanding caused some dismay and a strong desire to specify and build a conceptually cleaner version of REBUS. In the formal specification, names and handles are both unique identifiers for whiteboards. Each whiteboard has only one name, and the same name refers to the same whiteboard for all users in all situations. Handles are issued by the appropriate manager on an *open* and are necessary to invoke operations on an object. To make the efficiency aspects of handles explicit, they are formally specified as pointers.

Once these issues had been raised and resolved, formal specifications of REBUS were quickly generated. We also noted that REBUS was then easier to understand and explain. We believe this is leading to a cleaner notion of the requirements specification process.

3. Formal Specification of REBUS

The formal specification of REBUS centers on four components: an object manager, the whiteboard, the REBUS interface, and a top-level showing how the components are combined and interact. The specification does not completely define the objects created and used by REBUS or the policies used to control their development; however, it does define certain minimal characteristics of these objects and the mechanism used to implement these policies. Thus the specification is intended to be sufficiently general that it is reusable. Parts of it are fixed while others are parameters. While REBUS mandates certain methods and mechanisms, such as the use

```
type object_rec is record
    Name   : name_type  ;
    Object : obj_handle ;
    Info   : info_type  ;
end record ;

type operation_type is (create,destroy,open,close);

        •
        •
        •

generic

    type obj_handle is access object_type ;
    --: with predicate is_initial_object(
    --:                 Object : in out obj_handle ) ;

    type info_type  is private ;
    --: no_info : constant info_type ;
    --: with predicate is_okinfo (
    --:             Old_info : in out info_type      ;
    --:             User     : in out user_type      ;
    --:             Op       : in out operation_type ;
    --:             New_info : in out info_type    ) ;

    --: with predicate can_create (
    --:                 User   : in out user_type    ;
    --:                 Name   : in out name_type  ) ;
    --: with predicate can_destroy(
    --:                 User   : in out user_type    ;
    --:                 Object : in out object_rec ) ;
    --: with predicate can_open    (
    --:                 User   : in out user_type    ;
    --:                 Object : in out object_rec ) ;
    --: with predicate can_close   (
    --:                 User   : in out user_type    ;
    --:                 Object : in out object_rec ) ;

package manager_pkg is

    task type manager is

        •
        •
        •

    end manager ;
    type manager_handle is access manager ;

end manager_pkg ;
```

Figure 2. Specification of generic manager package

of a whiteboard, instances of REBUS can be created to support different policies and object types. For example, the object manager is defined in such a way that it may be instantiated to manage objects of any type. In REBUS, we instantiate a manager for requirements objects. The whiteboard is also generic in that a whiteboard may be created for any kind of item. REBUS itself is generic in that instances can be created for different types of objects and to implement different management policies. To better understand the specification, we will first examine the object manager package in detail.

3.1. The Object Manager

Figure 2 and Figure 3 show the PLEASE specification for the object manager. Its specified as a generic package with parameters to specify the type of objects to be managed, the history information to be kept for each object, and the policies to be used for management. The specification exploits Ada generic packages, which is particularly appropriate as REBUS is written in Ada, but was also found to be semantically appropriate as well. In Ada, a generic construct is instantiated with an actual set of parameters to produce a usable component. In our specification, an instance of *manager_pkg* implements an object manager using a task called *manager*. In Ada, tasks have independent threads of execution and may contain variables private to the task. Inter-task communication is accomplished with *rendezvous* at entry points. When one task calls an entry point and another task accepts the call a rendezvous occurs and the two threads of execution are merged until the call completes. In our specification, the object manager task has an entry for each operation it provides; other tasks can call the manager to *create* a new object, *destroy* a pre-existing object, *open* an object for further manipulation, or *close* an open object.

For the purpose of specification, the manager task has a *virtual state* consisting of a set of object records. Each item of type *object_rec* has three fields: the name of the object, a pointer to the object, and the information on the object's history being kept by the manager. The specification of the set of object records incorporates an invariant stating that no two names refer to the same object, and no two objects have the same name. The invariant makes use of *predicates* which are defined elsewhere. In PLEASE, predicates are similar to Boolean functions and are used to specify logical properties. For example, the predicate *member(Elmt,Set)* is true if *Elmt* is currently a member of *Set*. In PLEASE, a *predicate* definition syntactically resembles a procedure and may contain local type, variable, function or predicate definitions. Predicate definitions describe acceptable tuples in a format which has a simple translation into Prolog procedures.

The parameters used to instantiate *manager_pkg* define the properties of the resultant manager. The types *object_handle* and *object_type* and the predicate *is_initial_object* define the objects to be manipulated by the manager. For example, *is_initial_object*

```
task type manager is

     --: Objects : set of object_rec ;
     --|           where for all Obj1,Obj2 : object_rec =>
     --|                  member(Obj1,Objects) and member(Obj2,Objects) and
     --|                  ( Obj1.Name = Obj2.Name or Obj1.Object = Obj2.Object )
     --|                      -> Obj1 = Obj2  ;

     --: Obj0 : constant object_rec ;

     entry create( User : in user_type ; Name : in name_type ) ;
         --| where in ( cnot member((Name,_,_),Objects) and can_create(User,Name) ),
         --|        out( is_okinfo(no_info,User,create,(Info:info_type))
         --|             and is_initial_object((Obj:object_handle)) and
         --|             Objects = insert((Name,Obj,Info),in(Objects)) ) ;

     entry destroy( User : in user_type ; Name : in name_type ) ;
         --| where in ( Obj0.Name = Name and member(Obj0,Objects) and
         --|             can_destroy(User,Obj0) ),
         --|        out( Objects = delete(Obj0,in(Objects)) ) ;

     entry open( User : in user_type ; Name : in name_type ; Handle : out obj_handle ) ;
         --| where in ( Obj0.Name = Name and member(Obj0,Objects) and
         --|             can_open(User,Obj0) ),
         --|        out( (Obj:object_rec).Name = Name and
         --|             Obj.Object = Obj0.Object = Handle and
         --|             is_okinfo(Obj0.Info,User,open,Obj.Info) and
         --|             Objects = insert(Obj,(delete(Obj0,in(Objects)))) ) ;

     entry close( User : in user_type ; Name : in name_type ) ;
         --| where in ( Obj0.Name = Name and member(Obj0,Objects) and
         --|             can_close(User,Obj0) ),
         --|        out( (Obj:object_rec).Name = Name and Obj.Object = Obj0.Object and
         --|             is_okinfo(Obj0.Info,User,close,Obj.Info) and
         --|             Objects = insert(Obj,(delete(Obj0,in(Objects)))) );

end manager ;
```

Figure 3. Specification of generic manager

defines the initial or "empty" instance of *object_type*; *is_initial_object(Object)* is true only if *Object* is "empty". The type *info_type*, the constant *no_info*, and the predicate *is_okinfo* define the history information to be kept for each object. For example, *is_okinfo(Oldinfo,User,Op,Newinfo)* is true only if *Newinfo* is the correct history information for an object which had history *Oldinfo* before *User* performed *Op*. The predicates *can_create*, *can_destroy*, *can_open*, and *can_close* define the policy implemented by the manager.

The manager uses a simple mechanism to implement the policy: each entry has a pre-condition, which must be true for a rendezvous to begin, and a post-condition, which states the conditions which must hold when the rendezvous is complete. In the specification, the state before execution begins is denoted by *in(...)*, while the state after execution has completed is denoted by *out(...)*. For example, the pre-condition for *create* states that there is no record for an object called *Name* and that *User* has the proper permissions (note that *cnot* is a closed world not, which in this case is acceptable). The post condition for *create* states that an initialized object called *Name* has been created with the proper history information. Similarly, the pre-condition for *destroy* states that there is an object with the specified name and *User* is authorized to destroy it. The post-condition for *destroy* states that the object has been deleted from the set of object records (note that since *Obj0* is a constant, it must be the same in the input and output states). As *manager_pkg* is generic, managers can be created which implement different policies using the same mechanism.

The object manager ultimately controls the objects produced and used in the requirements specification process; however, users must access these objects through a whiteboard.

3.2. The Whiteboard

The PLEASE specification of the whiteboard is given in a longer version of this paper [13]. Like the object manager, the whiteboard is specified as a generic package. Parameters to the package define the type of objects to be manipulated using the whiteboard, the states these objects move between, the history information to be kept for the objects, and the management policies to be followed. As in the case of the object manager, an instance of the whiteboard package implements a whiteboard as an Ada task with an entry for each operation provided. In the specification, the whiteboard task has a virtual state consisting of a set of items. Each item contains a pointer to an object, the current state of the object and some history information. An invariant specifies that there can be only one item for any object. The whiteboard task provides four entries: *add*, *move*, *remove* and *getobjects*. Each entry has a pre-condition stating the conditions necessary for the operation to be invoked and a post condition stating the requirements for successful execution. The operation *add* puts a pre-existing object onto the whiteboard while *remove* takes an object off. The operation *move* puts on object already on the whiteboard into a different state while *getobjects* allows the user to examine all the objects in a certain state.

To be precise, users do not access the whiteboard directly, but only interact with the system through the REBUS interface.

3.3. REBUS Interface

The PLEASE specification of the REBUS interface is given in [13]. Like the object manager and whiteboard, the REBUS interface is specified as a generic package. Parameters to the interface package specify the type of objects to be manipulated, the states these objects move between, the history information to be kept by REBUS, the management policies to be followed, and the analyses that can be performed by the user. Like the object manager and whiteboard, an instance of the REBUS interface package implements REBUS as a task containing an entry for each operation provided to the user. In the specification, the REBUS task has a virtual state consisting of a set of records, each of which contains a pointer to an object as well as history information. An invariant specifies that there can be only one record for each object. In the specification, the interface provides five operations: *create*, *edit*, *move*, *getobjects* and *analyze*. The operation *create* allows the user to create a new object while *edit* allows objects to be modified. The *move* command transfers an object to the specified state; when an object is created its state is not defined, so *move* must be used to initialize the state. The *get_objects* operation allows the user to examine all the objects in a particular state, while the *analyze* command may be used to invoke an analyzer on a set of objects.

The object manager, whiteboard, and REBUS interface (as well as the users) are the principal elements in the specification process. We can now examine how these elements are combined and interact.

3.4. The Specification Process

Figure 4 shows a skeletal specification of the requirements specification process. The process contains multiple users who create, modify and combine objects to construct complete specifications. The objects are controlled by an object manager and the users interact via the whiteboard. The objects used by, as well as the policies used to control, the process are specified separately from the structure of the process and the mechanism used to implement the policies. To describe the specification process we must first define the type of objects from which the specification is to be created, the states that these objects can be in, and the history information to be kept for objects at each level of the system. This is accomplished by the types *object_type*, *state_type*, *obj_info*, *whiteboard_info*, and *rebus_info* respectively. Next, we specify the policies to be followed during the specification process. These policies are defined by the predicates *can_create_node*, *can_destroy_node*, *can_open_node*, *can_close_node*, etc. These predicates are then used in the instantiation of the object manager, whiteboard and REBUS interface. It is interesting that some policies can be conveniently described at any of the three levels (object manager, whiteboard or REBUS interface), while others may be easily specified only at a particular level. Finally we describe what actions the users can perform and when. This is accomplished by the task type *user*.

The formal specification of REBUS is now concluded. We have not completely defined all of the objects created and used by REBUS or the policies used to control their development. However, we have defined certain minimal characteristics of these objects and the mechanisms used to implement these policies, as well as showing how they could be completely defined. We can view the specification as a process program specification: parts of the process are fixed while other aspects are parameters. We can see this as static process programming: while REBUS mandates certain methods and mechanisms, such as the use of a whiteboard, instances of the system can be created to support different policies and object types. We feel the creation of this specification has greatly increased our understanding of REBUS and the requirements specification process.

4. Summary and Conclusions

We believe that formal specification can enhance the software development process in a number of ways. Specifically, we believe that software development can be enhanced by creating a formal specification after a prototype has already been constructed using traditional techniques. We have performed an experiment which supports this hypothesis in the context of the Arcadia project, an effort to experimentally develop superior software environment tech-

```
task body specification is

    -- Specification of types

    type object_type      is ... ;
    type state_type       is ... ;
    type obj_info         is ... ;
    type whiteboard_info  is ... ;
    type rebus_info       is ... ;

          • • •

    -- Specification of policy predicates

    predicate can_create_node ( ... ) ;
    predicate can_destroy_node( ... ) ;
    predicate can_open_node   ( ... ) ;
    predicate can_close_node  ( ... ) ;

          • • •

    -- Specification of users (who invoke rebus)

    task type user is

          • • •

    end user ;
    Users : array( user_names ) of user ;

    package obj_pkg is new manager_pkg     ( ... ) ;
    package wb_pkg  is new whiteboard_pkg( ... ) ;
    package rbs_pkg is new rebus_pkg       ( ... ) ;

    object_manager : obj_pkg.manager    ;
    whiteboard     : wb_pkg.whiteboard ;

begin

    whiteboard     ;          -- start the whiteboard,
    object_manager ;          --    object manager,

    for I in user_names loop
         User(I) ;            --    and users
    end loop ;

end specification ;
```

Figure 4. The specification process

nologies. One of Arcadia's current goals is the creation of REBUS, a REquirements BUilding System. In REBUS, a requirements specification is viewed as an attributed DAG which may have to satisfy certain constraints. In REBUS, multiple developers interact via objects stored on the whiteboard, a communications and coordination mechanism.

In the Fall of 1987, a prototype version of REBUS had been constructed and was undergoing redesign and extension. We conjectured that describing the system using a small number of formally defined concepts could increase understanding and enhance communication between project members. Over the course of three months, the developers met with a specification expert and a formal description was written in PLEASE, an Ada-based, wide-spectrum, executable specification and design language which supports formal methods similar to VDM. Several issues surfaced during construction of the specification, including persistence and concurrency control for whiteboards, as well as the meanings of names and handles. Construction of the formal specification enhanced further development by helping the developers to clarify the architecture of the system, separate their concerns, and discuss possible modifications. We feel the use of similar methods can enhance other software development efforts.

5. References

1. Bjorner, D., T. Denvir, E. Meiling and J. S. Pedersen, "The RAISE Project - Fundamental Issues and Requirements", RAISE/DDC/EM/1, Dansk Datamatik Center, 1985.
2. Bloomfield, R. E. and P. K. D. Froome, "The Application of Formal Methods to the Assessment of High Integrity Software", *IEEE Transactions on Software Engineering SE-12, 9* (September 1986), 988-993.
3. Clocksin, W. F. and C. S. Mellish, *Programming in Prolog*, Springer-Verlag, New York, 1981.
4. Gehani, N. and A. D. McGettrick, eds., *Software Specification Techniques*, Addison Wesley, Reading, Massachusetts, 1986.
5. Heimbigner, D., Stanley Sutton, Jr. and L. J. Osterweil, "APPL/A: A Language for Managing Relations", Report No. CU-CS-374-87, Department of Computer Science, University of Colorado at Boulder, 1987.
6. Hudson, S. and R. King, "The Cactis Project: Database Support for Software Engineering", *IEEE Transactions on Software Engineering*,, June 1988.
7. Jones, C. B., *Systematic Software Development Using VDM*, Prentice-Hall, Englewood Cliffs, New Jersey, 1986.
8. Luckham, D. C. and F. W. Henke, "An Overview of Anna, a Specification Language for Ada", *IEEE Software 2, 2* (March 1985), 9-22.
9. Nii, H. P., "Blackboard Systems: The Blackboard Model of Problem Solving and the Evolution of Blackboard Architectures", *The AI Magazine* 7, 2 (Summer 1986), 38-53.
10. Osterweil, L. J., "Software Processes Are Software Too", *Proceedings of the 9th International Conference on Software Engineering*, 1987, 2-13.
11. Terwilliger, R. B. and R. H. Campbell, "PLEASE: a Language for Incremental Software Development", *Proceedings of the 4th International Workshop on Software Specification and Design*, April 1987, 249-256.
12. Terwilliger, R. B. and R. H. Campbell, "An Early Report on ENCOMPASS", *Proceedings of the 10th International Conference on Software Engineering*, April 1988, 344-354.
13. Terwilliger, R. B., M. J. Maybee and L. J. Osterweil, "An Example of Formal Specification as an Aid to Design and Development", Report No. CU-CS-399-88, Dept. of Computer Science, University of Colorado at Boulder, May 1988.
14. Ullman, J. D., *Principles of Database Systems*, Computer Science Press, Rockville, Maryland, 1980.

Formal Specification of Fault-Tolerance and its Relation to Computer Security

D. G. Weber

Odyssey Research Associates, Inc.
301A Harris B. Dates Drive
Ithaca, New York 14850-1313
oravax!dgw@cu-arpa.cs.cornell.edu

Abstract

The techniques of formal verification are one means for gaining greater assurance of the correctness of software. These techniques require precise specification of the properties to be assured. This paper formulates precise specifications corresponding to the intuitive notions of "fault tolerance" and of "graceful degradation". An analogy is constructed between these fault-tolerance specifications and a particular class of specifications for computer security. On the basis of this analogy, it is argued that formal verification of fault-tolerance will face some of the same problems, and benefit from some of the same solutions, as verification of security.

1 Introduction

In this paper, we will be concerned with specification and verification of fault-tolerance properties. We will be seeking precise definitions of the term "fault-tolerance", and asking what steps must be taken to prove that a system design in fact is fault-tolerant according to the definition. We will only be minimally concerned with strategies, designs, and algorithms used to implement fault-tolerant systems, and only then as examples to show why a particular definition of "fault-tolerance" is relevant.

One previous effort toward verifying fault-tolerance can be found in the SIFT project (Software Implemented Fault Tolerance) [W+78]. SIFT was an ultra-reliable fault-tolerant computer designed for aircraft flight control. A precise model of this system was developed, and constraints (specifications) on the model which implied the correctness of the system were written down. However, the SIFT approach differs from ours, in that the property of "fault-tolerance" was never considered in isolation, but was always implicitly subsumed in the other system specifications. One could not prove, or even state, that SIFT was fault-tolerant without additionally stating and proving that it satisfied many other correctness properties as well. We intend to find a definition of fault-tolerance which can stand by itself.

The remainder of this Section discusses factors that should be excluded from a formal specification of computer system properties. Section 2 develops specifications for fault-tolerance and graceful degradation. In Section 3 we consider verification of systems against these specifications. The following discussion is condensed from [Web88]. A more complete discussion, development of formal fault-tolerance properties, and examples, can be found there.

1.1 Fault Scenarios and MTTF

A system's fault-tolerance is often expressed as a mean time to failure (MTTF). One goal of a verification methodology for fault-tolerant systems might be to prove that a system's MTTF exceeds some value. However, the MTTF is not just a property of a computer system, but involves the environment of that system as well. A measure of fault-tolerance which depends only on the system design, and not on its environment, would be preferred.

A **fault scenario** is a history of a system's interaction with its environment which includes not only its inputs and outputs, but also a description of faults, including which com-

[1]This work was supported by the Air Force Systems Command at Rome Air Development Center under Contract No. F30602-86-C-0263. The views and conclusions contained in this paper are those of the authors and should not be interpreted as necessarily representing the official policies, either expressed or implied, of the Air Force or the U.S. Government.

©1989 ACM 0-89791-305-1/89/0500/0273$00.75

ponents failed, when they failed, and how each failure is expected to manifest itself in the future. We suppose that a system's environment determines the likelihood of each fault scenario.

If we can now decide, for each scenario, whether the system design will fail, and at what time it fails, then we can (in principle) calculate the MTTF by averaging over all the fault scenarios. This average, however, is usually quite complicated and involves many approximations and assumptions about the environment.

Instead of calculating MTTF, we will consider verification of fault-tolerance to be proof that a system design will not fail for a given fault scenario or set of fault scenarios. For example, one might verify that failure does not happen in any fault scenario in which at most one fault occurs. This meaning of "fault-tolerance" depends only on the system design, and is independent of environmental factors.

2 Formal Specification of Fault-Tolerance

2.1 Specifying Faults

Before defining "fault-tolerance", it is first necessary to define "fault". Abstractly, a system or system component is faulty when it no longer performs according to its specification.

The literature of fault-tolerance identifies various "specifications" for components after they have failed. These include: Byzantine (a failed component exhibits arbitrary behavior), fail-stop (a failed component halts and its failure can be detected), and others.

2.2 Non-Interference

The simplest way to define "fault-tolerance" is converse to our previous definition of "fault": a system is fault-tolerant if it meets its specification. Thus, it must behave as though it were non-faulty, even in the presence of faulty behavior of its components.

Denote by N the set of fault scenarios under which no faults occur. Let C be a set of fault scenarios under which we desire fault-tolerance; no loss of generality will result if we require that $N \subseteq C$. Suppose that D is a design of an algorithm which exhibits the behavior desired, and that FTD is a fault-tolerant version of D. There are now three methods by which we may show that FTD is fault-tolerant under the given set of fault scenarios, C.

1. We may show that the behavior of D, under scenarios N, is identical to the behavior of FTD under C.
2. We may characterize the behavior of D under N by some specification, S. Then we may show that FTD implements S under C.
3. We may show that the behavior of FTD under N is equivalent to the behavior of FTD under C.

The first of these methods is impractical. We would need to construct two separate implementations for one system.

The second method is the one used in the SIFT project. The specification S describes the correct behavior both of D and of FTD. We would then require simply that FTD behave correctly.

The third method captures the notion of fault-tolerance as a comparison of behaviors with and without occurrences of faults. However, it does so without referring either to design D or to its specification S. The relevant aspects of each can be derived from FTD alone. The behavior of FTD under scenarios with no faults should be equivalent to behavior of D under the same scenarios. Therefore, the third method has a clear advantage over the others: the property of fault tolerance becomes entirely a property of the behavior of FTD, and does not involve extra correctness constraints that may be required by S. It is this third method we will proceed to develop.

Our statement of fault-tolerance is now a relation on the behavior of the system under different sets of fault scenarios. Let the possible ways a system may interact with its environment be called "events". Sequences of events will be called "histories", and a history that is possible for a system will be called a "trace" of that system. One way to characterize a design is to give the set of its traces. This is a simplification of the approach of CSP [BHR84]. "Behavior" wil be defined by the sequence of events of a trace that are visible to a system's users.

Simple fault-tolerance is then: allowing certain fault scenarios does not change the visible aspects of the set of traces of a fault-tolerant system. We may say that the occurrence of fault events does not *interfere* with a system's behavior.

2.2.1 Formal Definition

Let a system be characterized by a tuple $\langle E, F, T \rangle$, where E is the set of possible events, $F \subseteq E$ the set of possible fault events, and T is the set of traces of events chosen from E.

For any sequence h and set of events S, the notation $h \uparrow S$ will denote the sequence derived from h but with all events not in S removed, and the ordering of the remaining events retained. For any trace h, what was called "behavior" above will now be denoted by the sequence of non-fault events, $h \uparrow \overline{F}$, where $\overline{F} = (E - F)$ is the complement of F with respect to E. Two sets of traces exhibit the same behavior if, for any trace in one, there is a trace in the other which has the same sequence of events in $\overline{F}$.

We characterize fault scenarios as a sequences of events. Each scenario is simply a history, whether or not it is a possible history for a given system.

We will now formalize the above definition of fault-tolerance for the system $A = \langle E, F, T \rangle$. Let C be the set of fault scenarios for which A is to be fault-tolerant. The definition says that adding fault scenarios in C will not enlarge the set of behaviors. This is equivalent to the following statement in our notation:

$$(FT1) \qquad \forall \beta \in T, \beta \in C \rightarrow \beta \uparrow \overline{F} \in T$$

This says that from any given possible history that is also a fault scenario in C, we can construct a second possible history simply by removing all fault events from the first. This definition of simple fault-tolerance can be augmented in various ways.

2.2.2 Example: File System

As an example, consider a fault-tolerant file system. An external user or other client of the file system interacts with it through operations such as "read-file", "write-file", and so on. These operations, along with any of their associated parameters and return values, will be taken as the events from which system histories are constructed. Certain observable behaviors, or traces, are expected, e.g., if a user writes a file and then reads the same file, the contents returned should be the same as the contents written. So the history h_1 = ⟨ write-file 'contents', read-file 'contents' ⟩ should be a trace, while the history h_2 = ⟨ write-file 'contents', read-file 'garbage' ⟩ where 'contents' and 'garbage' are different, should not be.

Fault events in the hardware supporting the file system may make various bizarre behaviors possible. For example, if the sequence h_3 = ⟨ write-file 'contents', fault, read-file 'garbage' ⟩ is a trace, then the system may appear as though it had actually executed the illegal history h_2. If, however, the file system is to be fault-tolerant with respect to fault scenarios including h_3, then our property $(FT1)$ demands that h_3 won't exist if h_2 doesn't.

Why isn't property $(FT1)$ equivalent to requiring that the file system work correctly? In fact, $(FT1)$ is weaker. Suppose, for some reason, that when each file is written, the file system alters the contents with some arbitrary function *Mod*; when a file is read, the altered contents are returned. The traces of this new file system, if it is fault-tolerant, will include:

⟨ write-file 'contents', read-file Mod('contents') ⟩

⟨ write-file 'contents', fault, read-file Mod('contents') ⟩

and possibly many others. Like our previous file system that did not alter the content of files, this one meets $(FT1)$ since the alterations are made regardless of the presence of a fault. But, if we have specified a file system that does not modify the content of files, this implementation is incorrect even though it is fault-tolerant.

2.3 Analogy with Multi-Level Security

Property $(FT1)$ is often called a "non-interference" property. Non-interference properties have been explored and used extensively in the context of multi-level computer security (MLS) [GM82] [H+86] [McC87] [V+88]. It is reasonable to ask, then, what is the relation between fault-tolerance and multi-level security? We begin with a brief description of MLS.

In a secure computer system, it is desirable to prevent sensitive information from flowing to users who are not authorized access to it. In military systems, the sensitivity of information and the authorizations of users can be labeled by a partially ordered set of levels. Highly sensitive information is brought into the system by the inputs of users of the system with high levels of authorization. The multi-level security problem is the prevention of information transfer from those inputs to outputs which can be seen by users who are not so highly authorized.

The key to defining security in this way is the definition of "information flow". We suppose that the system's traces are known. One definition of information flow is then the ability of a particular user to use the observed behavior of the system, plus knowledge of its traces, to make deductions about its unseen behavior. Information will flow from unseen inputs to observed behavior if more can be deduced about those inputs than could be deduced if the system's behavior were not observed.

Non-interference can be taken (loosely) to mean that high-level inputs do not interfere with or influence processing, and hence outputs, on lower levels. Stated more precisely, the existence of high-level inputs cannot be deduced from observing a particular history of lower-level inputs and outputs.

An analogy between fault-tolerance and multi-level security properties can now be drawn. A non-interference property for multi-level security can be converted to a non-interference property for fault-tolerance by translating from "highly sensitive" inputs to "fault events", and from "less sensitive inputs and outputs" to "non-fault events", i.e., ordinary system behavior. A fault event is thus considered a type of input, although not from any user. The non-interference property for MLS can then be translated into the language of fault-tolerance: the existence of fault events cannot be deduced from particular histories of ordinary system behavior. This is the property $(FT1)$.

The analogy can be posed in another way if we consider the work of Biba [Bib77] in extending MLS to handle some concerns over information integrity. His work added integrity levels to the security levels already used for marking the sensitivity of information and the authorizations of users. The Biba property, in effect, allows information to flow only from inputs to outputs of the same or lower integrity level. Given this property, high-integrity users would be prohibited from deducing (and hence from being corrupted by) information about inputs at lower integrity levels. The analogy between fault-tolerance and MLS can be recast in terms of integrity, in which case a fault-event is seen to be analogous to an input of low integrity level. This becomes an appropriate analogy if we consider that fault events are not usually a high-integrity source of information.

The analogy between fault-tolerance properties and multi-level security properties is not perfect, and breaks down in several ways.

- Unlike the inputs from users, which are the ultimate source of information in MLS systems, fault events are often not external.
- Systems are never, in practice, tolerant to all fault scenarios. Some possible sequence of faults will cause the system to fail. This differs from the analogous multi-level security case, in which one desires to build systems that are secure under all possible histories of sensitive inputs. Users of an insecure system may conspire to transmit information by concocting unusual or unlikely sequences of inputs; fault events are assumed not to do this.

Since fault-tolerance non-interference properties and MLS non-interference properties are formally similar, can the same kinds of implementation mechanisms be used for both? The differences given above indicate why this will not work. Faults are not external events, and therefore it is not possible for a system to decide, without further processing, whether they are fault events or not. A fault detection mechanism may be needed. In secure systems, however, inputs are associated with the authorization level of the user who causes them. Thus, even though there is a formal similarity between fault-tolerance and MLS properties, the designs used to implement them must be different.

While fault-tolerance and MLS need different strategies for implementation, the methods used to *verify* an implementation either fault-tolerant or secure should be similar. See Section 3.

2.4 Graceful Degradation

The problem of specifying graceful degradation will have much in common with the previous discussion of specifying fault-tolerance. We expect that many systems will be fault-tolerant for some fault scenarios, gracefully degrade for others, and be chaotic for the rest. As a result, specifications for graceful degradation may be merely modifications or generalizations which weaken those we have already discussed for pure fault-tolerance. In fact, the specifications we will arrive at can be seen simply as a more comprehensive way to define fault-tolerance itself.

2.4.1 Limited Interference

If fault-tolerance is to be expressed as a non-interference property, as discussed in section 2.2, then graceful degradation may be expressible as some limited interference of faults with external behavior. A specification of limited interference should be a generalization of a specification for non-interference. The form of the specification must then show the way in which interference of fault events with normal behavior is limited.

When we developed property $(FT1)$, we required that system behavior with and without faults be *identical*. This prevents deducibility that *any* faults have occurred. Unlike the MLS case, though, it may not be a problem that one can deduce the existence of faults, so long as the system behavior in response to those faults is "good enough". Thus, we need not demand that behaviors be identical, but only that they be *acceptably equivalent*. If α and β are behaviors (sequences in which no fault events occur) then let $\alpha \equiv \beta$ mean that the two behaviors are acceptably similar. The relation '$\equiv$', called the **tolerance relation**, will be an equivalence relation on behaviors.

Adding fault scenarios to a system satifying $(FT1)$ will not enlarge the set of behaviors. We now want a second property, $(FT2)$, such that adding fault scenarios will not enlarge the set of possible equivalence classes of behaviors, where a "possible equivalence class" is one that contains at least one possible behavior. Repeating the analysis that led to $(FT1)$, but demanding only equivalent instead of identical behavior, we find that

$$(FT2) \qquad \forall \beta \in T,\ \beta \in C \rightarrow \\ \exists \gamma \in T,\ \gamma \uparrow F = \langle\rangle \ and\ \gamma \equiv \beta \uparrow \overline{F}$$

is the generalized fault-tolerance, or graceful degradation, property that results. This property says: for any fault scenario, we must be able to find an alternate possible history that is fault-free and is acceptably equivalent. If, for some reason, an observer of the system could not distinguish the behavior γ from $\beta \uparrow \overline{F}$, then, just as for $(FT1)$, the existence of faults could not be deduced.

As an example, consider a system which must perform two tasks, A and B. Suppose that fail-stop processors A_1 and A_2 are dedicated to simultaneous execution of task A, while fail-stop processors B_1 and B_2 are dedicated to task B. Ignoring the amounts of time needed for processors to compare final results, this system will be perfectly fault-tolerant $(FT1)$ for a fault scenario in which processors A_1 and B_1 fail: both tasks will complete, and they will complete in the same amount of time they would have taken if no faults had occurred. However, it will not be fault-tolerant for a fault scenario in which processor A_2 fails in addition to A_1 and B_1. In this case, processing of task A is interrupted, and will not be completed unless further steps are taken.

In this case we would like "graceful degradation" to mean that for any fault scenario in which three or fewer processors fail, both tasks A and B will eventually complete. To implement this specification will require some reconfiguration of the system: interrupted processing of task A will need to be continued or restarted on a processor originally dedicated to task B, or vice-versa. The processing power of the system will then be degraded, since a single processor will take longer to complete both tasks than either one separately, but the response to faults is graceful since at least both tasks will be finished. To describe this type of graceful degradation, we would choose a tolerance relation that ignores timing: two histories are equivalent if they involve the same *sequence* of events, but at possibly different times.

Note that ($FT2$) reduces to ($FT1$) in the case that the tolerance relation is equality. It is the choice of tolerance relation that determines how faults interfere with behavior, and therefore the meaning of "graceful degradation". As one chooses larger sets of fault scenarios, C, the tolerance relation must be chosen to treat more behaviours as equivalent.

This form of limited interference can be viewed in terms of the analogy with multi-level security. Systems that meet ($FT2$) but not ($FT1$) are analogous to systems that leak some information from high security levels to lower ones, and are thus not perfectly secure.

3 Verification of Fault-Tolerance

We have argued that non-interference specifications can be used to capture the intuitive notion of fault-tolerance. How can a system be verified, in practice, to implement this sort of specification?

Once the constructs of "event" and "trace" are related to features of the implementation, one might appeal directly to the definition in constructing a proof. However, for all but the simplest system, this approach becomes very complicated.

Many of existing verification tools [S+79] [G+78] provide little help either. Typically, these are designed for proof of invariants, or more generally, of *embedded assertions*: conditions that hold at a particular point in an execution history. Unfortunately, an embedded assertion expresses a condition that applies to each history independently, whereas a non-interference specification applies to the entire set of possible histories at once. The help provided by these tools is not sufficient.

Because fault-tolerance specifications are formally similar to specifications for multi-level security, this same problem occurs in the verification of MLS. In that domain, specialized techniques can be applied to analyze special cases. For example, the technique of [WL87] is one in which the existence of some traces is shown by modifying others in appropriate ways. Demonstrating the existence of one trace, given another trace, is exactly what is needed in both ($FT1$) and ($FT2$), and this technique is in fact one that can be applied either to designs in the MLS or fault-tolerance domains.

4 References

[BHR84] S.D. Brookes, C.A.R. Hoare, and A.W. Roscoe. A theory of communicating sequential processes. *Journal of the ACM*, 31(3), 1984.

[Bib77] K.J. Biba. Integrity considerations for secure computer systems. Technical Report MTR-3153, MITRE Corp., Bedford MA, April 1977.

[G+78] D.I. Good et al. Report on the Gypsy language, version 2.0. Technical Report TR ICSCA-CMP-10, Institute of Computer Science, Univ. of Texas, Austin, September 1978.

[GM82] J.A. Goguen and J. Meseguer. Security policy and security models. In *Proceedings of the Symposium on Security and Privacy*. IEEE, 1982.

[H+86] J.T. Haigh et al. An experience using two covert channel analysis techniques on a real system design. In *Proceedings of the Symposium on Security and Privacy*. IEEE, 1986.

[McC87] D. McCullough. Specifications for multi-level security and a hook-up property. In *Proceedings of the Symposium on Security and Privacy*, pages 161–166. IEEE, 1987.

[S+79] B.A. Silverberg et al. The HDM handbook, vol. II. Technical Report Deliverable A006, project 4828, SRI, Menlo Park, CA, June 1979.

[V+88] S. Vinter et al. The secure distributed operating system project. Technical Report 6144, BBN Labs and Odyssey Research Associates, February 1988.

[W+78] J.H. Wensley et al. SIFT: Design and analysis of a fault-tolerant computer for aircraft control. *Proceedings of the IEEE*, 66(10), October 1978.

[Web88] D.G. Weber. Specifications for fault-tolerance. Technical Report 19-3, Odyssey Research Associates, January 1988.

[WL87] D.G. Weber and Bob Lubarsky. The SDOS project – verifying hook-up security. In *Third Aerospace Computer Security Conference*, pages 7–15. AIAA/ASIS/IEEE, 1987.

Systematic Design of Algebraic Specifications

Sergio Antoy

Virginia Tech
Northern Virginia Graduate Center
2990 Telestar Ct.
Falls Church, VA 22042

Abstract: *Under-* and *over-specification* of abstract data types are conditions resulting from "flawed" equations in algebraic specifications. Two design strategies, the *binary choice* method and the notion of *recursive reduction*, are introduced for designing specifications which satisfy desirable properties of *completeness*, *parsimony*, and *termination* through which we address the above conditions. A number of results concerning these strategies are presented. Several examples are discussed and an implementation of these ideas is outlined.

Keywords: Algebraic specification, Binary choice, Recursive reduction, Term rewriting, Completeness, Parsimony, Termination.

1. Introduction

We define sorts through their constructors—see Figure 1. Each constructor is an element of the signature. The arity of a constructor, with the omission of the range which is obvious from the context, is typed following the constructor. Thus, *false* and *true* are the constant constructors of *Boolean*, *zero* and *succ* are the constructors of *nat*. *succ* takes an argument of sort *nat*.

sort *Boolean*	(1)
constructors	(2)
false, *true*.	(3)
sort *nat*	(4)
constructors	(5)
zero;	(6)
succ : *nat*.	(7)

Figure 1. Specifications of the sorts *Boolean* and *nat*, the natural numbers.

2. Completeness

The first half of Figure 2 defines the predicate "less than or equal" on natural numbers. The defining axioms are "directed equations"—the direction being denoted by $\to$. Variables in the equations are denoted by capital letters at the end of the alphabet. The problem with the specification of *le* is that from the term $le(zero, succ(zero))$ neither *true* or *false* can be derived. This is in contradiction with the arity of *le*, which claims that for each pair of natural numbers a *Boolean* value must be derived, and with the specifications in Figure 1, which defines how natural numbers and *Boolean* values are constructed. The culprit

operation $le : nat \times nat \to Boolean$	(1)
axioms	(2)
$le(zero, zero) \to true$;	(3)
$le(succ(X), zero) \to false$;	(4)
$le(succ(X), succ(Y)) \to le(X, Y)$.	(5)
operation $max : nat \times nat \to nat$	(6)
axioms	(7)
$max(zero, Y) \to Y$;	(8)
$max(X, zero) \to X$;	(9)
$max(succ(X), succ(Y)) \to succ(max(X, Y))$.	(10)

Figure 2. Examples of under- and over-specified operations.

is that *le*'s defining axioms are either poorly designed or are not "enough".

We denote with $\mathcal{C}$ the signature's constructors, with $\mathcal{X}$ a set of variables, and with $T(\bullet)$ the set of terms built over the object denoted by $\bullet$. *Under-specification* is the impossibility of equating some ground term $t = f(t_1, \ldots, t_k)$, where f is not in $\mathcal{C}$, to a term in $T(\mathcal{C})$. In the example, the condition occurs because $le(zero, succ(zero))$ is a normal form. Our first result is a necessary condition for avoiding under-specification.

> **Result 1.** If a specification is not under-specified, then for each term t of the form $f(t_1, \ldots, t_k)$, where f is not in $\mathcal{C}$ and each t_i is in $T(\mathcal{C} \cup \mathcal{X})$, there is an axiom for f of the form $l \to r$ such that t is an instance of l.

The above conditions can be addressed through the notion of *completeness* of a set of tuples of terms—see also [HUET82].

Definition. A set S of k-tuples of terms in $T(\mathcal{C} \cup \mathcal{X})$ is *complete* for a set of constructors $\mathcal{C}$ if every k-tuple of terms in $T(\mathcal{C})$ is an instance of an element of S.

Completeness is a useful concept for addressing the consequent of Result 1. We will call complete an operation satisfying the antecedent of Result 2.

> **Result 2.** If the set of the arguments in the left sides of the axioms of an operation f is complete for $\mathcal{C}$, then the consequent of Result 1 holds.

3. Parsimony

Over-specification is the opposite of under-specification—the situation in which a term can be rewritten by more than one axiom. The second half of Figure 2 shows this problem. The term $max(zero, zero)$ can be rewritten using both axioms 8 and 9. Here, the problem is a minor one, since both axioms lead to the same result (the term rewriting system associated to the specification is confluent [KNUT70, HUET80].) However, if we were to change the first axioms to, say, $max(zero, Y) \rightarrow succ(succ(Y))$, an unwanted consequence would be collapsing the sort *nat* into the integers modulo 2. We address over-specification through the notion of *parsimony* in the same way that completeness addresses under-specification.

Definition. A set $S = \{S_1, \ldots, S_p\}$ of k-tuples of terms is *parsimonious* if, for all i and j $(1 \leq i,j \leq p)$, S_i unifies with S_j only if $i = j$.

Our next result is a sufficient condition for avoiding over-specification.

> **Result 3.** If f is an operation of a specification, S is the set of k-tuples of terms consisting of the arguments of the left sides of the axioms for f, and S is parsimonious, then f is not over-specified.

Before applying these results to obtain high-level properties of specifications through simpler properties of sets of tuples of terms, two issues need to be discussed. Partial operations, which are known to present considerable difficulties, do not affect our treatment. We simply relax our notion of under-specification by allowing the reduction of a term to a distinguished symbol with the meaning of "undefined". The second issue concerns quotient sorts, i.e. sorts in which there are non-trivial equations, called quotient axioms, among terms in $T(\mathcal{C} \cup \mathcal{X})$. Sorts of this kind, which include *integer* and *set*, are common. The notion of parsimony seems too strong for them and should be weakened. No satisfactory solution to this problem is offered in this note.

4. Binary Choices

Complete and parsimonious sets can be generated in an algorithmic way. The procedure we are going to describe is non-deterministic and possibly non-terminating. In the applications, arbitrary selections and choices correspond to design decisions and the termination of the procedure is an expected consequence of the designer's strategy. $\mathcal{C} = \{c_j\}$ is the set of constructors, $|\mathcal{C}|$ is its cardinality, and $d(c_j)$ is the number of arguments of c_j. $\Box$ is a distinguished symbol, called *place*. In the procedure we adopt the notation and terminology of [HUET80].

Binary Choice Procedure.

1. [Initialization] $S := \{\langle\Box, \ldots, \Box\rangle\}$. S is initialized to a set consisting of a single k-tuple whose components are all places.
2. [Termination test] If there are no occurrences of places anywhere in S, then halt with output S.
3. [Selection] Select a k-tuple of S, say S_i, a component index n in S_i, and an occurrence u in S_i^n such that $S_i^n/u = \Box$, i.e. the subterm of S_i^n at u is a place.
4. [Binary choice] Chose either "variable" or "inductive" for S_i^n/u.
5. [Construction] Build the set T as follows: If the binary choice is "variable", then $T = \{\langle S_i^1, \ldots, S_i^n[u \leftarrow X], \ldots, S_i^k\rangle\}$ where X is a variable not occurring anywhere in S, else $T = \{T_1, \ldots, T_{|\mathcal{C}|}\}$ where $T_j \in T$ if and only if $T_j = \langle S_i^1, \ldots, S_i^n[u \leftarrow c_j(\Box, \ldots, \Box)], \ldots, S_i^k\rangle$, $c_j \in \mathcal{C}$, and there are exactly $d(c_j)$ places in $c_j(\Box, \ldots, \Box)$.
6. [Replacement] $S := (S - \{S_i\}) \cup T$. Replace S_i with T in S.
7. [Iteration] Go to step 2.

The following results justify the use of the binary choice procedure for defining the left sides of the axioms of operations.

> **Result 4.** The binary choice procedure terminates if the number of "inductive" choices is bounded.

The initial template, 1, results from the arity of *le*.

$$le(\blacksquare, \Box) \tag{1}$$

Templates 2 and 3 come from 1 with choice "inductive".

$$le(zero, \blacksquare) \tag{2}$$
$$le(succ(\Box), \Box) \tag{3}$$

Template 4 comes from 2 with choice "variable".

$$le(zero, X) \tag{4}$$
$$le(succ(\blacksquare), \Box) \tag{5}$$

Template 7 comes from 5 with choice "variable".

$$le(zero, X) \tag{6}$$
$$le(succ(X), \blacksquare) \tag{7}$$

Templates 9 and 10 come from 7 with choice "inductive".

$$le(zero, X) \tag{8}$$
$$le(succ(X), zero) \tag{9}$$
$$le(succ(X), succ(\blacksquare)) \tag{10}$$

Template 13 comes from 10 with choice "variable".

$$le(zero, X) \tag{11}$$
$$le(succ(X), zero) \tag{12}$$
$$le(succ(X), succ(Y)) \tag{13}$$

Figure 3. Application of the *binary choice* procedure to the design of the axioms specifying the predicate "less than or equal to" on natural numbers. At every iteration of the procedure the current state of the (left sides of the) axioms is diplayed. The place to which the binary choice applies is denoted by the symbol $\blacksquare$, called *cursor*. Places become cursors in lexicographic order by default, but the designer may override this strategy. The design is completed with five choices (which correspond to just five keystrokes in the implementation) and neither under- nor over-specification may occur. For clarity, the definition of the right sides is omitted.

The number of occurrences of places in S is decremented by every "variable" choice, and finitely incremented by "inductive" choices.

> **Result 5.** If the binary choice procedure terminates, then its output is a complete set.

The output of the binary choice procedure satisfies Huet's inductive definition of completeness [HUET82], hence, his Lemma 3 guarantees our completeness.

> **Result 6.** If the binary choice procedure terminates and there are no quotient axioms, then its output is a parsimonious set.

Any two distinct elements in S differ in at least one component. The leading symbols at the differing occurrences are different constructors. If there are no quotient axioms they cannot unify.

5. Recursive reductions

A second cause of under-specification is the absence of any normal form for a ground term not belonging to $T(\mathcal{C})$. We relate this condition *non-termination* [DERS85], a consequence of an improper use of recursion.

A sort S is *recursive* if at least one of its constructors has at least one argument of sort S. The sort *nat* of Figure 1 is recursive—*succ* is the recursive constructor of *nat*. Two conditions are necessary for applying recursion in an axiom defining an operation f: 1) the sort of at least one argument of f is recursive, and 2) in the left side of the axiom some argument has a recursive constructor as its leading symbol. For purposes of discussion and notation, we impose the additional condition that each recursive constructor of sort S has only one argument of sort S.

Definition. Let t be a term in $T(\mathcal{C} \cup \mathcal{X})$ (the kind of terms generated as arguments by the binary choice method.) The *recursive reduction* of t is defined as follows:

$$RR(t) = \begin{cases} RR(t'), & \text{if } t = c(\ldots,t',\ldots), \text{ where} \\ & c \text{ is a recursive constructor and} \\ & t' \text{ is its recursive argument;} \\ t, & \text{otherwise.} \end{cases}$$

We now extend the notion of recursive reduction to the left side of an axiom. If $l = f(x_1, \ldots, x_n)$ is the left side of an axiom, then the recursive reduction of l is $f(RR(x_1), \ldots, RR(x_n))$. We extend our notation with this concept. The symbol "!" on the right side of an axiom denotes the recursive reduction of the left side—see Figure 4. The next result provides sufficient conditions to avoid under-specification.

> **Result 7.** If f is a complete operation, and the terms on the right sides of its axioms are built using terminating operations and/or recursive reductions, then f terminates.

The proof is a structural induction [BURS69] over the "inductive" arguments of f.

The initial template, 1, results from $half : nat \rightarrow nat$.

$$half(\blacksquare) \tag{1}$$

Templates 2 and 3 come from 1 with choice "inductive".

$$half(zero) \rightarrow zero \tag{2}$$
$$half(succ(\blacksquare)) \tag{3}$$

Templates 5 and 6 come from 3 with choice "inductive".

$$half(zero) \rightarrow zero \tag{4}$$
$$half(succ(zero)) \rightarrow\, ! \tag{5}$$
$$half(succ(succ(\blacksquare))) \tag{6}$$

Template 9 comes from 6 with choice "variable".

$$half(zero) \rightarrow zero \tag{7}$$
$$half(succ(zero)) \rightarrow\, ! \tag{8}$$
$$half(succ(succ(X))) \rightarrow succ(!) \tag{9}$$

Figure 4. Design of the operation "integer division by 2" on natural numbers. In this examples the right sides of axioms are defined as soon as there are no places in their corresponding left sides. The left sides of the axioms are defined with the *binary choice* method. Two of the three right sides are obtained by *recursive reduction* of the corresponding left sides. The "!" in line 5 stands for $half(zero)$ which by line 2 is $zero$. The "!" in line 9 stands for $half(X)$.

6. Concluding Remarks

The idea of completeness has been proposed in [HUET82] as a condition for a *Principle of definition* required for an "inductionless" technique of proof by induction. The notion of parsimony is irrelevant for that treatment. Algorithms for testing the completeness of a set of axioms and possibly suggesting corrections are presented in [THIE84,KOUN85]. The emphasis of our work, through the binary choice procedure, is on a design strategy to obtain some desirable properties, including completeness, *a priori* rather than testing them *a posteriori*.

The aim of this investigation is to better understand the difficulties of designing defect-free algebraic specifications of abstract data types. We have shown that, when suitable conceptual tools are employed, this activity may require less creativity and effort than initially thought. The binary choice procedure has been implemented using the *GNU Emacs* text editor [STAL87]. The implementation, which is a *major mode*, provides syntax editing, abbreviations, and automatic generation of the templates and positioning of the cursor. Simple specifications including arithmetical operations, Boolean predicates, relational operators, and list, tree, and set manipulation are designed with a few keystrokes only and many conceptual and clerical errors become impossible to make.

A most important aspect of our approach, worth further investigation, is the ability of capturing *design decisions* rather than presenting their consequences. For this reason we prefer to keep the symbols "!" unexpanded. This feature makes manifest the decision of employing recursion rather than inferring it from the relation between two or more, possibly complicated terms. Finding a convenient notation for capturing the flow of binary choices would be equally beneficial.

7. Acknowledgments

Thanks go to John Gannon and Lee Erman for revising and commenting an earlier draft and to Chris Gordon for proofreading. Research support for this work was partially provided by Teknowledge, Inc.

References

[BURS69] Burstall R., "Proving Properties of Programs by Structural Induction", *Computer J.*, **21**-1, 1969, 41-48.

[DERS85] Dershowitz N., "Termination", Proc. Rewriting Techniques and Applications, Dijon, France, Springer-Verlag, May 1985, 180-223.

[GOGU78] Goguen J.A., J.W. Thatcher, and E.G. Wagner, "An Initial Algebra Approach to the Specification, Correctness, and Implementation of Abstract Data Types", in Current Trends in Programming Methodology **4**, 80-149 (Ed. R.T. Yeh), Prentice-Hall, Englewood Cliff, NJ, 1978.

[GUTT78] Guttag J.V., E. Horowitz, and D. Musser, "The Design of Data Type Specifications", in Current Trends in Programming Methodology **4**, 60-79 (Ed. R.T. Yeh), Prentice-Hall, Englewood Cliff, NJ, 1978.

[HUET80] Huet G., "Confluent Reductions: Abstract Properties and Applications to Term-Rewriting Systems", *JACM*, **27**, 1980, 797-821.

[HUET82] Huet G. and J.-M. Hullot, "Proofs by Induction in Equational Theories with Constructors", *JCSS* **25**, 1982, 239-266.

[KNUT70] Knuth D.E. and P.B. Bendix, "Simple Word Problems in Universal Algebras", in Computational Problems in Abstract Algebras, (J. Leech, ed.), Pergamon Press, New York, 1970, 263-297.

[KOUN85] Kounalis E., "Completeness in Data Type Specifications", LNCS **204**, 1985, 348-362.

[STAL87] Stallman R., *GNU Emacs Manual*, Sixth ed., Version 18, Free Software Foundation, Cambridge, MA, 1987.

[THIE84] Thiel J.J., "Stop Losing Sleep over Incomplete Data Type Specifications", in 11th Annual Symp. on Principles of Prog. Languages, 76-82, ACM, 1984.

Data-Flow Design as a Visual Programming Language

Susan Eisenbach and Lee McLoughlin

Department of Computing,
Imperial College of
Science, Technology, and Medicine
180 Queen's Gate, London SW7 2BZ.
Great Britain

Chris Sadler

Department of Computing
Mathematics and Statistics,
Polytechnic of North London,
Holloway Road, London. N78DB
Great Britain

Abstract

Data-flow design techniques and the functional programming style both decompose problems in a data-driven fashion. We propose a method based on data-flow diagrams which yields designs which can be mechanically translated into code written in a functional programming language. Users who specify or design systems with data-flow techniques can effectively execute their specifications or designs with a minimum of additional design decisions and without recourse to a programming language. Data-flow diagram elements behave as programming constructs in a "visual programming" language. The paper solves a single problem to illustrate the methodology and show the kind of code produced.

1. A Functional Design Methodology

The potential which a functional programming language has for producing programs capable of running on parallel hardware is beginning to be exploited by hardware designers looking to produce experimental parallel machines[1]. Ultimately these promise to turn into extremely fast, widely available computing engines on which many of the substantial processing tasks of the future will be performed. However most programmers would agree that a language like Hope[2] imposes a "functional programming style" which may not very closely match the types of problems which they are trying to solve. The software crisis is happening in the commercial and industrial arenas[3], not in research laboratories, and academics and researchers must be careful not to provide solutions to problems which people don't actually have. What we thought was needed was a functional *design* methodology which decomposed typical problems in such a way that the functional programming style would suggest itself at the implementation stage. We were attracted to the family of data driven design methodologies because there appear to be some similarities between the data driven design philosophy and the functional programming philosophy.

A data driven design technique decomposes a problem into a network of *processes* linked by *data flows*, this arrangement being represented pictorially as a "data-flow diagram"", or more usually, a hierarchy of data-flow diagrams. In constructing these designs, no consideration is given to the flow of "control". Likewise, functional programming languages are characterized by an absence of control-flow constructs dictated by the requirement for referential transparency[4]. Instead *functions* are invoked by the existence of their *arguments* (incoming flows) rather than by programmer initiation, and the evaluation model envisages the functional components of a program executing in parallel on a network of processors. A data-flow diagram can be thought of therefore as a circuit diagram for a configuration of processors built to execute the corresponding (functional) program.

The problem is that a set of data-flow diagrams is an informal representation of one particular aspect of a program's design while the ultimate program is formal at least in the sense that there can be no semantic ambiguity in the source-code whatever language it is written in. Traditional methodologies solve this problem by introducing more and more refined representations of other design decisions via, for instance, entity-relationship diagrams or structure charts[5]. Eventually, if enough detail is supplied it is possible to transform the design into a program mechanically[6][7]. However the effort which must go into this, and the potential for introducing error, makes following the methodology practically indistinguishable from actual programming and many programmers prefer to follow their inclinations and plunge straight into code.

If the target language is low-level the amount of detail required is correspondingly greater. By contrast, a very high-level language should meet the designer half-way and the transition to code could occur much earlier in the design process. We set out to find how early in the process coding could begin. We found that once the data-flow diagram stage is complete, the functions which it identifies must be specified and the structure of the data in flows and stores must be defined. We do the former in pseudocode and the latter in a data dictionary. Together these provide enough information to generate code mechanically *without any further design decisions.*

To reap the benefits of automatic code generation some of the informality must be given up. For example we found it necessary to eliminate all consideration of input/output operations from the data-flow part of the design. We need to do further theoretical work to link data-flow semantics with programming constructs more formally before judging how crucial the loss of informality will be. In this paper we omit discussion of our approach to data stores which is currently rather *ad hoc* pending the development of facilities for persistent data in Hope. Finally, we have not yet applied our method to as wide a range of problems as we plan to prior to refining our prototype tool.

2. Finding the Day of the Week

A worked example is presented here to illustrate the application of the design technique and to show how Hope code can be mechanically derived.

The problem is to read any date from (1800-2000) in the form dd/mm/yyyy and to compute the day of the week on which that date fell (or will fall). There is a concise algorithm which provides a solution to this problem[8]. The day on which January 1 falls for any given year in the indicated range can be calculated from the formula:

```
(4+Y+(Y+3)/4-(Y-1701/100+(Y-1601)/400+3)) MOD 7
```

where Y is the year and where Sunday corresponds to 0. The day of any date after January 1 is computed by brute force, adding up the days of the intervening months and date in the current month. This is not a complex problem but it is rich enough to demonstrate the different aspects of design and the underlying algorithm gives a fair illustration of the functional programming style.

2.1. Data-flow Design

Design begins with a data-flow diagram which shows the *context* - external inputs and outputs - within which the program operates. The whole program is represented as a single process (a circle in the diagram - see Figure 1) with the input "flowing" in from its *source* (Keyboard) and output data flowing to the *sink* (Screen). Decomposition consists of elaborating the functions (processes) which transform inputs into outputs in a hierarchy of diagrams. All flows and processes are named.

Diagrams are constructed with the aid of a Design Editor. As a diagram is constructed simple consistency checks are applied to ensure the integrity of the diagram set.

©1989 ACM 0-89791-305-1/89/0500/0281$00.75

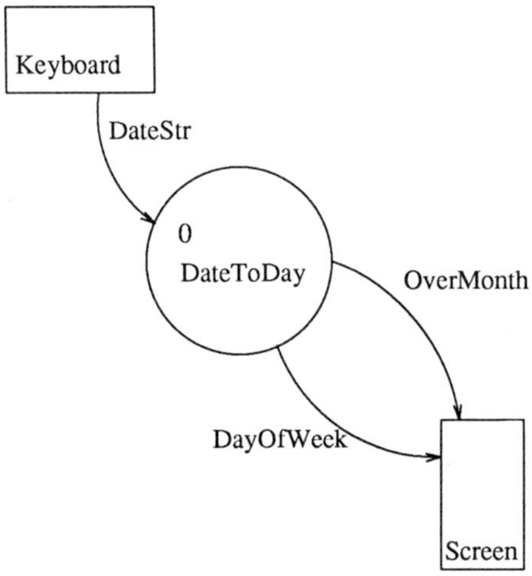

Figure 1 : The Context Diagram

Input/output is something of a problem in functional programming languages[9]. This is because input/output, especially interactive input/output, implies some synchronization between prompt and response. In a functional program when input and output are separate processes, the programmer has no control over the sequencing of processes and so cannot dictate the order in which the prompt and response functions will occur. In Hope this problem is primarily solved by a *continuation*[10] mechanism whereby the program terminates returning a continuation (a data object) and control is passed to the operating system to perform the input/output operation. In addition to the arguments necessary to perform the input/output operation one of the parameters to the continuation is a function which consists of the remainder of the program. On completion of the input/output operation this function is invoked and the program resumes[11]. Our methodology exploits this feature by associating a number of input/output related activities with the data type itself.

This strategy manifests itself in the following ways:

(1) a *prompt string* is associated with each input datum identified in the design.

(2) validation occurs, as far as possible, during the input operation and a user defined *error message* can be associated with any data element, otherwise a *default* message "<Pattern> expected" will be used. <Pattern> is the definition in the data dictionary. The input operation is not complete until a valid value is input.

(3) correspondingly, a *format* is associated with each output data element.

These constitute the major additions to the conventional data driven design methodology but they are sufficiently far-reaching to alter the direction of the design, even at this early stage. For instance the flow DatePrompt is actually the prompt associated with DateStr and so may be omitted from the diagram. Secondly, since the primary validation occurs during input, any validation steps in the program need only concern secondary validation. In this problem, the only secondary validation involves checking "short" months - especially February during leap year.

The context diagram therefore decomposes as follows:

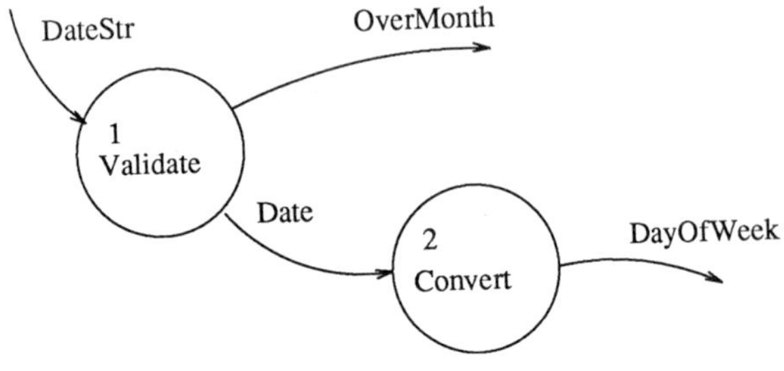

Figure 2 : Diagram 0

For the sake of robustness, input to the program is in the form of a string (DateStr). Because the algorithm requires integer values, the string will have to be converted (into Date) within Validate. This task is performed by a low-level function StrToInt which is not shown in the data flow diagram.

2.2. The Data Dictionary

Every identifier in the data-flow diagrams corresponds to a design decision. The purpose of the data dictionary is to catalogue each of these identifiers and any others which may crop up in subsequent design, together with definitions for all the flows. This phase of the design process is termed *data design*. The structure of all data structures must be shown and the nature of any data types must be established. In the case of input and output flows, the Error, Prompt and Format values must be given.

For the problem at hand the current state of design appears as follows:

```
Convert = PROC (* takes a valid date and returns the day it falls on *);
Date = Day, Month, Year;
DateStr = DayStr, "/", MonthStr, "/", YearStr
        &Error("Not in appropriate date format")
        &Prompt("Please type in your date in the form dd/mm/yyyy" );
DateToDay = PROC (* validates a date until successful then returns the
            day of the week this falls on *);
            &Format("It's a", DayOfWeek)
Day = 1..31;
DayOfWeek = "Sunday"|"Monday"|"Tuesday"|"Wednesday"|
            "Thursday"| "Friday"|"Saturday";
DayStr = "0", Digit-"0" | ("1"|"2"), Digit | "3", ("0"|"1")
        &Error("Not a day" );
Digit = "0"|"1"|"2"|"3"|"4"|"5"|"6"|"7"|"8"|"9"
        &Error("Non-numeric character where number was expected );
Month = 1..12;
MonthStr = "0", (Digit-"0") | "1", ("0"|"1"|"2")
        &Error("Not a month");
OverMonth = "Day not in Month";
Validate = PROC (* to check whether DayStr could be in MonthStr *)
        &Error(OverMonth);
Year = 1800..2000;
YearStr = "1", ("8"|"9"), Digit, Digit | "2","0","0","0"
        &Error("Not a year");
```

The syntax of data dictionary entries follows that laid down in BS6154: British Standard Syntactic Metalanguage[12]. The punctuation symbols used are similar to those found in Extended Backus Naur Form with the exception of "," which stands for "followed by". The symbol "&" is not part of BS6154 but marks an *annotation* to the entry. For each annotation, the keyword Error, Prompt or Format designates the role played by the subsequent item. These are used, when the code is generated, to construct the input/output operations mentioned in the previous section. Some entries (e.g. Day) do not appear in the data-flow diagrams but represent subsidiary items which arise out of the definitions of items which are (in this case Date).

Processes are identified by the keyword PROC together with an explanatory comment. Before code can be generated for the processes it will be necessary to show their algorithmic structure via mini-specs. However it is possible to generate data declarations directly from the data dictionary as follows:

```
type Date == (Day # Month # Year);
type DateStr ==
     (DayStr # char # MonthStr # char # YearStr);
type Day == num;
type DayOfWeek == string;
type DayStr == string;
type Digit == char;
type Month == num;
type MonthStr == string;
type OverMonth == string;
type Year == num;
type YearStr == string;
```

Note the structures Date and DateStr. These are known as *tuples* in Hope; "num" and "char" are standard data types while "string" is predeclared as "list(char)" where "list" is a standard Hope data structure.

2.3. Mini-Specs

The next stage is to produce a mini-spec for each process identified in the dictionary. In the course of algorithmic design further decomposition can be expected to occur so new functions and data will be identified. Although these do not appear in a data-flow diagram, it is necessary to enter them in the data dictionary.

```
DateToDay
= Convert(Validiate(DateStr))

Convert
= NumToName(NumOfDay(Date));

Validate
= let Date be Conv(DateStr) in
  if Day <= MaxOfMonth(MaxDays, Month)
  then Date
  else if (Month = 2) and (Day = 29) and LeapYear(Year)
     then Date
     else Error, Validate;
```

Note that Error is a standard function which outputs the error annotation associated with the enclosing process, after which Validate calls itself again. New functions which must be specified are NumToName, NumOfDay, Conv, MaxOfMonth and LeapYear, while MaxDays is a new data structure.

The functions specified above are generated as follows:

```
dec DateToDay : DateStr -> DayOfWeek;
--- DateToDay(_DateStr) <=
                Convert(Validate(_DateStr));
```

Note the _DateStr parameter identifier derived from the declared type DateStr.

```
dec Convert :  Date -> DayOfWeek;
--- Convert(_Date) <= NumToName(NumOfDay(_Date));

dec Validate : DateStr -> Date;
--- Validate(_DateStr) <=
     let (_Date) == Conv(_DateStr) in
     let (_Day, _Month, _Year) ==
       _Date_Split(_Date) in
     if Day <= MaxMonth(MaxDays, Month)
     then _Date
     else if (_Month = 2) and (_Day = 29) and
          LeapYear(_Year)
        then _Date
        else Error(OverMonth, Validate_In);
```

Note that for any tuple X the function X_split is automatically generated to enable the extraction of individual components.

The parameter to Validate needs to come from the keyboard. A continuation function Validate_In is generated which uses the rules in the data dictionary to perform both input and syntactic validation. Validate_In is the first function actually called in the execution of this program and upon completion it calls Validate providing its required argument.

The subsidiary functions specified below can be translated using the same or similar principles. Because these functions are not identified on data-flow diagrams, it is necessary to include formal parameters and return types in the mini-spec headers.

```
LeapYear(Yr) : TruthValue
= (Yr mod 400 = 0) or (Yr mod 4 = 0 and Yr mod 100 # 0);

Conv(D) : Date
= (StrToInt(DayStr),StrToInt(MonthStr),StrToInt(YearStr));
```

Note that StrToInt is a 'built-in' function.

```
MaxOfMonth(MaxDays, Month) : Day
= if Month = 1
  then Head(MaxDays)
  else MaxOfMonth(Tail(MaxDays), Month-1);

NumOfDay(NDate) : DayNum
= if not LeapYear(Year) or Month < 3
  then SumOfDays(NDate) mod 7
  else (SumOfDays(NDate) + 1) mod 7;

SumOfDays(NDate) : Number
= Jan1(Year) + PartialSum(MaxDays, Month-1) + Day;

PartialSum(Lst, HowMany) : Number
= if HowMany = 0 or Lst = Nil
  then 0
  else Head(Lst) + PartialSum(Tail(Lst), HowMany-1);

Jan1(Yr) : Number
= (4 + Yr + (Yr + 3)/4) - (Yr - 1701)/100 + (Yr-1601)/400 + 3;

NumToName(WhichDay) : DayOfWeek
= Case WhichDay Of
  0 : "Sunday"
  1 : "Monday"
  2 : "Tuesday"
  3 : "Wednesday"
  4 : "Thursday"
  5 : "Friday"
  6 : "Saturday" ;
```

Any new identifiers, together with their definitions which arise here must be added to the data dictionary.

3. Acknowledgements

We would like to thank Chris Condon and Anthony Heritage of the Forward Technology Unit at British Telecom who funded some of this work, and provided us with feedback from the "real world".

4. References

1. I. Watson, J. Sargeant, P. Watson and V. Woods, Flagship Computational Models and Machine Architecture, *ICL Technical Journal Volume 5 Issue 3*, (May 1987), 555-574, Oxford University Press.
2. R. M. Burstall, D. MacQueen and D. Sannella, Hope: an Experimental Applicative Language, *Proc. First International LISP Conference*, Stanford, 1980.
3. I. Sommerville, Software Engineering: Perspectives and Directions, in *Proc. SEAS Software Engineering Conference Edinburgh* , September 1987.
4. J. Darlington, Software Development in Declarative Languages, in *Functional Programming: Languages, Tools and Architectures*, S. Eisenbach (ed.), Ellis Horwood , 1987.
5. E. Yourdin and L. L. Constantine, *Structered Design: Fundamentals of a Discipline of Computer Program and Systems Design*, Yourdon Press, 1978.
6. *Software through Pictures Manual*, Interactive Developement Environments Inc., 1987.
7. T. Docker and G. Tate, Executable Data Flow Diagrams, in *Proceedings of BSC-IEE Conference: Software Engineering 86*, P. J. Brown and D. J. Brown (ed.), Peter Peregrinus, September 1986.
8. B. W. Kernighan and D. M. Ritchie, *The C Programming Language*, Prentice-Hall Software Series, 1978.
9. Arvind and J. D. Brock, Resource Managers in Functional Programming, *Journal of Parallel and Distributed Computing Volume 1*, (1984), 5-21, Academic Press.
10. A. J. Field and P. G. Harrison, *Functional Programming*, Addison-Wesley Publishing Company, 1988.
11. K. Karlsson, *Nebula: A Functional Operating System*, Chalmers University, Goteborg, 1981.
12. R. S. Scowen, *An Introduction and Handbook for the Standard Syntatic Metalanguage: BS6154*, NPL, 1983.

A FORMAL FRAMEWORK FOR THE DESIGN OF DEVELOPMENT ENVIRONMENTS

M. M. Pett

Institute for Defense Analyses
1801 N. Beauregard Street
Alexandria, Virginia 22311

M. D. Rice S. B. Seidman

Center for Parallel Computation
Department of Computer Science
George Mason University
Fairfax, Virginia 22030

ABSTRACT

This paper describes a new formalism for specifying development environments for general hierarchical, modular systems. The formal framework is based on a restricted collection of sets and partial functions. Two applications of the formalism are described.

In recent years, development environments have been built for many software and hardware systems. The essential similarity of these systems has been concealed by the wide variety of formal techniques that have been used in their description. In this paper, a new formalism is introduced for specifying development environments. The formalism emphasizes *hierarchy* and *modularity*, two features that are common to most application areas for which development environments have been constructed.

A development environment based on our formalism will include operations that construct and modify systems by selecting components from a library and specifying interfaces between these components. The formalism provides a logically consistent framework for the environment designer which can be adapted to a particular situation by choosing relevant framework attributes.

The formal framework is based on a restricted collection of sets and partial functions which are used to define a *construction setting*, and a collection of basic operations on construction settings. The framework is described using the set-theoretic specification language Z [3]. Two specific applications will be discussed below: a programming development environment for coarse-grain dataflow graphs [1, 2], and the STILE development environment [4].

In the framework, the lowest level of system components consists of *templates*, which reside in a common library Lib, which in turn is a finite subset of the basic set Temp. New templates can be added to the library using the *EXT* operation, described below. Each template has a unique non-empty set of *ports*, drawn from the basic set Port, which represent potential interfaces to other templates. The association between templates and ports is defined by the following Z schema: (Note that the symbol --|--> is used in Z to denote a *partial* function, while $\mathbf{F}_1$S denotes the set of *finite* subsets of a set S. The domain and range of a function f are denoted by dom f and ran f.)

Template_Association
interfaces : Temp --|--> $\mathbf{F}_1$Port
disjoint {interfaces(t) : t $\in$ dom interfaces}

The common library Lib is precisely the domain of the function *interfaces*. The following Z schema defines the *owner* function from ports to templates:

Port_Association
Template_Association owner : Port --|--> Temp
dom owner = $\cup${interfaces(t) : t $\in$ dom interfaces} $\forall$t : dom interfaces • interfaces(t) = owner^{-1}(t)

Notice that the specification of Template_Association is included in that of Port_Association. Each port has an associated set of *attributes*, which are referenced by the members of an index set AttrIndex, which is the disjoint union of the basic sets Struct and NonStruct. Struct will be used to reference attributes referring to relationships between components in a system, while NonStruct will be used to reference attributes referring to such consistency issues as type checking. The set of attributes indexed by i$\in$AttrIndex is denoted Attr(i), and the set of all attributes is the disjoint union of the Attr(i).

Every template port has a set of attributes, based on an *attribute function* specified by the following schema :

Port_Attribute
Port_Association attr : Port --|--> (AttrIndex ---> Attr)
dom attr = dom owner

The function attr can also be regarded as a partial function from the Cartesian product Port $\times$ AttrIndex to Attr.

The templates and ports defined above are used in a construction setting to create larger, more complex objects in a modular fashion. All system components are based on templates selected from the template library. When a template is to be used in a construction setting, it is instantiated by creating a module or *node* (from the basic set Node) based on the underlying template. The resulting relationship is described by the following Z schema:

©1989 ACM 0-89791-305-1/89/0500/0284$00.75

```
Node/Template_Association
---------------------------------------------
Template_Association
node_parent : Node --|--> Temp
---------------------------------------------
dom node_parent ∈ FNode
ran node_parent ⊆ dom interfaces
```

The domain of node_parent is the collection of all currently instantiated nodes.

For each instantiated node, its interfaces or *slots* are derived from the ports of the underlying template. These interfaces will be used in the construction setting to create relationships with other nodes or with the external environment. Formally, Slot is defined as the subset {(n,p)} of Node × Port whose members simultaneously satisfy the following conditions: n ∈ dom node_parent and p ∈ interfaces (node_parent(n)).

The following schema describes the relationships between slots, nodes, and ports:

```
Slot_Association
---------------------------------------------
slot_parent    : Slot ----> Port
owner*         : Slot ----> Node
---------------------------------------------
slot_parent(n,p) = p
owner*(n,p) = n
```

The following commutative diagram summarizes the relationships between slots, nodes, ports, and templates:

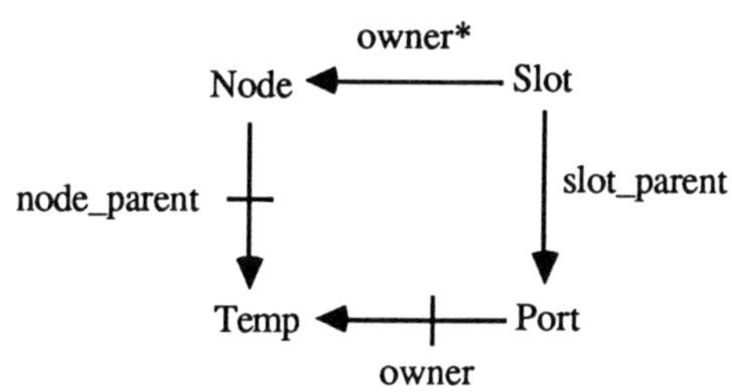

Using the diagram, properties of ports and templates can be lifted to become properties of slots and nodes. In particular, slots inherit attributes from their antecedent ports, as in the following specification:

```
Slot_Attribute
---------------------------------------------
Port_Attribute
Slot_Association
attr* : Slot ----> (Attr_Index --->Attr)
---------------------------------------------
attr* = attr ∘ slot_parent
```

After two or more nodes have been instantiated in the construction setting, they can be linked by associating a *label* (from the basic set Label) with a collection of slots associated with these nodes. To ensure that these slots are compatible, each label is given a set of non-structural attributes, corresponding to the index set NonStruct. The attributes shared by a slot and a label must match. This is accomplished by the following schema, which completes the formal definition of a construction setting:

```
Constr_Setting
---------------------------------------------
Node/Template Association
Slot_Attribute
label : Slot --|--> Label
type :  Label --|--> (NonStruct ---> Attr)
---------------------------------------------
ran label   dom type
∀a:NonStruct, s:dom label • type(label(s))(a) = attr*(s)(a)
```

The following five operations can be used to alter a construction setting: assign a label, update a label, delete a label, add a node to the construction setting, and create a template from the construction setting. The *Assign Label* operation requires an unlabeled slot s? and a label b? whose attributes from NonStruct match. The label b? may or may not have previously been used by the label function. The following Z schema specifies *Assign Label* . The appearance of ΔConstr_Setting in the schema indicates the existence of a Constr_Setting as both a precondition and a postcondition of the operation. The aspects of the Constr_Setting that are changed by Assign_Label are *primed*, as with label'. The Z operator ⊕ adds an ordered pair to a function definition, overriding any current pair with a matching first element.

```
Assign_Label
---------------------------------------------
ΔConstr_Setting
s? : Slot
b? : Label
---------------------------------------------
s? ∉ dom label
b? ∈ dom type
∀a:NonStruct • type(b?)(a) = attr*(s?)(a)
label' = label ⊕{s? |---> b?}
```

The *Update Label* and *Delete Label* operations are specified similarly. The *BUILD* operation is used to instantiate a new node n? in the construction setting, based on a library template t?.

```
BUILD
---------------------------------------------
ΔConstr_Setting
t? : Template
n? : Node
---------------------------------------------
t? ∈ dom interfaces
n? ∉ dom node_parent
node_parent' = node_parent ⊕{n? |---> t?}
Slot' = Slot ∪ {{n?} × interfaces(t?)}
```

The labels which are currently in use in a construction setting are called *Channels*. This set can be divided into two disjoint subsets: *External Channels* and *Internal Channels*. External Channels are labels which have been used only once, and are therefore assumed to be intended for communication with the external environment. Internal Channels are labels which have been used two or more times in a construction setting.

The EXT operation is used to transform the current construction setting into a library template. This operation supports hierarchy and modularity by allowing those subsystems which are used repeatedly in a system to be treated as a single entity. They can be stored as one template in the template library, and then brought into the construction setting as a single node. The External Channels of the current construction setting become the ports of the new template, and the attributes of these channels become the attributes of the ports. Note that Z uses the symbol >--->> to represent a one-to-one, onto function.

```
EXT
---------------------------------------------
ΔConstr_Setting
t? : Template
P? : F1Port
---------------------------------------------
t? ∉ dom interfaces
∀t : dom interfaces • P? ∩ interfaces(t) = ∅
∃h : p? >--->> ExternalChannels
interfaces' = interfaces ⊕{t? |---> P?}
attr' = attr ⊕ {p |---> attr*(x) | (p∈P? ∧ label(x) = h(p)}
```

The framework presented here has been used as the basis for a programming development environment for coarse-grain dataflow graphs [1, 2]. In this application, templates represent algorithms that are stored in a primitive library, and ports represent the formal parameters of the algorithms. Special index sets and attributes are also defined that respond to specific needs of this environment. For example, NonStruct contains the index TYPE, with corresponding attributes EDGE and VAR, while STRUCT contains the index DIR, with corresponding attributes IN and OUT. Restrictions are added to certain schemas to ensure that only certain kinds of attribute values may be used in combination. For example, in order to specify that variables have only the direction IN, the Port_Attribute schema is modified by adding the following constraint: $attr(p)(TYPE) = VAR \Rightarrow attr(p)(DIR) = IN$. Similarly, in order to specify that two identically labeled EDGE slots must have different directions, the following constraint is added to the Constr_Setting schema: $\forall\, r,s : dom\ label \mid r \neq s \bullet\ (label(r) = label(s) \wedge attr^*(r)(TYPE) = attr^*(s)(TYPE) = EDGE\ ) \Rightarrow attr^*(r)(DIR) \neq attr^*(s)(DIR)$.

When nodes are instantiated in the environment and their slots are created, the label assigned to a slot will be the name of an actual parameter defined in the environment. Assigning the same name to two slots creates a data queue between the corresponding nodes. The BUILD operation brings a new node, based on an existing primitive in the library, into the development environment. The EXT operation is used to transform a graph into a single primitive in the library, which can then be brought into the current construction setting with a single BUILD operation.

The framework can also be applied to the graphical design and development system STILE [4]. STILE describes the logical relationships among the components of a system, and allows modular components to be defined and hierarchically assembled into complex systems. Much of the terminology used by STILE maps naturally into our framework. A STILE system component, called a *part*, is specified by a *catalog page*, which tells what the part does, and a *blueprint*, which tells how the part is constructed. A blueprint is in turn divided into *external* and *internal* sections, which describe the part's external interfaces and implementation, respectively. The external section of a STILE blueprint corresponds to a template.

In STILE, a blueprint for a composite system is constructed by instantiating blueprints for the system components. An instantiated blueprint is called a *box*, and STILE boxes correspond naturally to template-derived nodes. When a box is constructed from a blueprint, the implementation contained in the blueprint's internal section is hidden from the user, just as a node inherits only the external interfaces from its underlying template. Blueprints for component parts are added to the blueprint of a composite part that is under construction, just as the BUILD operation takes a node that is modeled on a template from the template library and adds it to a construction setting. A blueprint's external interface is specified by its *ports*, just as we have done for templates. These ports are then carried over to ports that represent the external interface of a box. In our framework, node slots correspond naturally to STILE's box ports. STILE makes an important distinction between *data* ports and *control* ports, as well as between input and output ports. Since port attributes are defined for blueprint ports, and are carried over automatically to box ports, these attributes can be modeled straightforwardly in our framework by port attributes. Two ports with opposite orientation attributes and identical data/control attributes can be joined in STILE by attaching a *link* to each port. This can be modeled by assigning the same label to each of the corresponding node slots. STILE's requirement that the data/control attributes of ports joined by a link must be identical is enforced in our framework by modifying the Constr_Setting schema in a way similar to the modification described above for the dataflow graph programming development environment. Once a composite part has been defined, the corresponding blueprint can be used in the construction of other, more complex parts. The external portion of the blueprint is obtained from the external portions of the component blueprints, much as is done by the EXT operation.

The ease with which the dataflow graph programming development and the STILE system can be represented within our framework suggests that it can provide a common representation for a wide variety of systems that are intended to describe or construct hierarchical and modular software systems. The particularly good fit between our framework and these systems is due in part to the fact that these systems employ a bottom-up system design methodology. Since the attributes of composite templates are derived from the attributes of their components, consistency between composite and component attributes is obtained automatically, and our framework can therefore easily be made to model virtually any bottom-up system.

REFERENCES

[1] T. A. Gerasch, M. D. Rice, and S. B. Seidman, "A Programming Support Environment Based on a Formal Model for Coarse-Grained Dataflow Computation", Technical Report TR-6-86, Department of Computer and Information Science, George Mason University.

[2] T. A. Gerasch, M. D. Rice, and S. B. Seidman, "Graphical Programming Languages for MIMD Computation", Technical Report TR-10-87, Department of Computer Science, George Mason University.

[3] J. M. Spivey, *Understanding Z : A Specification Language and its Formal Semantics*, Cambridge University Press, Cambridge, 1988.

[4] M. P. Stovsky and B. W. Weide, "Building Interprocess Communication Methods with STILE", Proceedings of the 21st Annual Hawaii International Conference on System Sciences, v.2, pp. 639-647, 1988.

Functional Programming:
Executable Specifications and Program Transformation

Simon Thompson
Computing Laboratory, University of Kent, Canterbury, CT2 7NF, U.K.

Abstract

In this paper we give an example of the use of functional programming language in the specification and development of a program to solve a non-trivial problem. In particular, we show how we can give a direct implementation of a constructive specification (an *executable* specification, in other words) and then show how program *transformation* can be used to turn this specification into an efficient version of the program, using techniques from a standard library of transformations. We introduce the paper with a short review of functional programming.

1 Functional Programming

In this section we introduce the major ideas of functional programming, as exemplified by Miranda [1][4], (pure) ML [5] and various other languages ([3]). The language which we use here is Miranda, in fact.

The process underlying functional programming is one which we learn in elementary school, before we are exposed to micros, BASIC *et al.*. This is the process of *calculation*. Given an expression like $(2+3)/(7-2)$ we learn that we first have to *evaluate* the sub-expressions $(2+3)$ and $(7-2)$, and then *apply* the operator '/'. This is exactly what we do when we run a functional program — we calculate the value of an expression, which may involve operators or *functions* which are defined by the user.

Consider an example. To work out the sum of squares of the first hundred positive integers, we calculate the value of `sum_of_squares 100`where

```
sum_of_squares n
       = n*n + sum_of_squares (n-1) , n>1
       = 1      , otherwise
```


This operator describes *what* the sum is, in a natural way — if `n` is greater than one, we square it and add it to the sum up to `n-1`, if not, the answer is immediate — one.

Observe that we can read the above not only as a definition, but also a *property* of the function `sum_of_squares`. Function definitions are their own descriptions. This is not true of imperative languages, in which a program description has to be written in a logic separate from the language itself.

Take an example of evaluation, in which we abbreviate `sum_of_squares` by `sos`:

```
sos 3 = 3*3 + (sos 2)
      = 9 + (2*2 + sos 1)
      = 9 + (4 + 1)
      = 9 + 5
      = 14
```

we can see that the process is exactly that we used in the 'elementary school' example above, and shows that the mechanism underlying functional languages is simpler than that underlying imperative languages.

Functional programs contain no notion of machine state or assignment. We simply calculate values which are the result of combining operators and data in various ways. The language is therefore *referentially transparent* — every occurrence of a name (within a fixed scope) *has the same meaning*, with the consequence that we can read the defining equations as true mathematical statements, which in turn makes formal reasoning much simpler than for imperative languages.

The language we have described so far is not particularly powerful, indeed it might form a (small) subset of Pascal or even Basic. We go on now to look at some more advanced features, together with some applications.

The `sos` function takes numbers to numbers — a function is *higher order* if one of its arguments or its result is a function itself. For example:

```
twice f x = f (f x)
```

`twice f x` is the result of applying `f` to `x` twice, so if `succ` adds one to its argument,

[1] Miranda is a trademark of Research Software Ltd.

©1989 ACM 0-89791-305-1/89/0500/0287$00.75

```
  twice succ
```
will add two, and if `not` is the negation function over the Boolean type,
```
  twice not
```
will return its argument unchanged. Not only is the `twice` function higher order, but its definition is *generic*. We saw above that we could apply it to any function (returning a result of the same type as its argument). This feature of *polymorphism* combines with higher order functions to give powerful new ways of developing programs (and proofs about them).

Our examples thus far have been on atomic types. We now consider *lists* of objects from a fixed type. Formally, a list is an *ordered collection of objects*. For instance, `[]` is the empty list, `[2,3]` consists of two numbers 2 and 3, and the list `[[True,False,True]]` consists of one member which is itself a list with three members, `True`, `False` and `True`, in that order.

Lists are built from the empty list by repeated application of the operator '`:`' (or '*cons*'), so, for example,
```
  [2,3] = 2 : [3] = 2 : (3 : [])
```
Consider a function computing the *length* of a list:
```
  length []     = 0
  length (a:x) = 1 + length x
```
In a definition we use *pattern matching*, replacing formal variables with *patterns* built up from variables (`a,x`), constants (`[]`) and constructors (`:`). The patterns distinguish between cases, and allow for composite items to be decomposed into their components. We see this in the example evaluation:
```
  length [2,3]
    = length (2:[3])
    = 1 + length [3]
    = 1 + (1 + length [])
    = 1 + (1 + 0)
    = 2
```
What type has the operator? It takes a list and returns its length, independently of the type of objects in the list. It has a *polymorphic* type
```
  length :: [*] -> num
```
the type of functions (`->`) from lists of any type (`[*]`) to numbers (`num`).

Two functions which we use heavily are `map` and `foldr`. These are powerful and natural, and are both higher order and generic. The `map` function takes a function and applies it to every member of a list. For instance, if `sq` denotes the squaring function, then
```
  map sq [1,2,3] = [1,4,9]
```
which returns the result `[1,4,9]`. Similarly,
```
  map even [1,2,3] = [False,True,False]
```
Now, suppose we want to square every number in a list, and then test for evenness; we can *compose* these functions directly thus
```
  (map even).(map sq)
```
and if we call the result `g` then
```
  g [1,2,3] = (map even) [1,4,9] =
[False,True,False]
```

The second general function we define is `foldr`. This operation combines (or *folds together*) the components of a list, using an operator. For instance, the sum of a list is got by "folding in" the operator '+',
```
  sum [1,4,9] = 1 + 4 + 9
```
The formal definition of `foldr` incorporates two refinements. First, we have to choose which way to associate the applications of the operator — we choose to associate to the right, hence the 'r' of the definition. Second, we include a parameter which gives the *starting value* for the fold, or the value given to an empty list. We therefore have
```
  foldr op st [x1,x2,...,xn]
      = x1 op (x2 op ... (xn op st) ... )
```
So that `sum = foldr (+) 0`

To conclude the section, we give a different treatment of the sum of squares problem, which we call a *data directed* solution.

How could we define the sum of squares function in a completely explicit way, without recursion? We could, using only `map` and `foldr`, and starting from the list `[1..n]`, form the list of the squares
```
  map sq [1..n]
```
and then find the sum of the result, using
```
  foldr (+) 0 (map sq [1..n])
```
We have defined the function as a composition of three functions, thus:
```
  new_sos = (foldr (+) 0) . (map sq) . mklist
```
(where `mklist n = [1..n]`). The definition is *explicit*, using `map` and `foldr` rather than recursion. In our case study we shall see that this means we can transform and verify the definitions much more easily.

2 Formal Methods

The informal specification of our example problem is

> Given a finite list of numbers, find the maximum value for the sum of a (contiguous) sublist of the list.

Such calculations are used in pattern recognition problems in visual analysis amongst other areas. I first came across this problem in the fascinating collection [1].

We can formalise this specification in Miranda immediately; using a *data-directed* (c.f. above) style, we

> generate all sublists, find the sum of each sublist and find the maximum of the sums.

```
maxsub = (fold bimax).(map sum).sublists
```

where bimax is the binary maximum function, map and sum were defined above and fold is similar to foldr, except that it is only applied to non-empty lists, and so takes no starting value. For instance,

```
fold (*) [2,1,5,4] = 2*(1*(5*4))
```

Now, we have defined everything except the function sublists, which when given a list, returns the list of all its sublists. Looking at the sublists of a list (take [2,3,5] as an example) they are of two sorts. First, there are those like [2,3], which consist of the first item, 2, followed by a sublist of [3,5] which starts at the *front* of [3,5]. Secondly, there are the sublists of [3,5]. This is sufficient to describe the sublists:

```
sublists (a:x) = map ((:) a) (frontlists x)
                 ++ sublists x
sublists []    = [[]]
```

This is the formalisation of the definition above. Note that we join two lists with the operator ++, and the operator (:) is a prefix version of the list constructor :. The function frontlists is defined similarly.

Our program can be seen as an *executable* specification of the given problem. We can use it as a prototype implementation, but, equally importantly, we can use it as the starting point of a sequence of program *transformations*, which will lead us to a more efficient program.

Program transformation and verification go hand-in-hand. Transformation is the process of changing or transforming one program to another, in such a way as to preserve the meaning of the program. On the other hand, verification is the process of proving, formally, that a program has a property; often this property is a specification of the behaviour required. If we accept an *executable* specification as a starting point and develop another program by transformation from it, then if our transformations preserve meaning, the result of transformation is *guaranteed* to meet the specification.

How do we transform the program into efficient form? We use a number of laws, like the laws of arithmetic or trigonometry. The laws can be proved from the definitions of the functions using standard techniques of induction, but we can *use* them without proof, just as we do the trigonometric identities. Indeed, their informal justification is much easier. The laws we need for our example are:

```
map f (l ++ m) = map f l ++ map f m     [Law 1]
```

"The result of applying f to every member of the concatenation of l and m is the same as joining the results of applying f to each member of each list separately."

```
(map f).(map g) = map (f.g)             [Law 2]
```

"The effect of applying g to every member of a list, and then applying f to every member of the result is the same as applying (f.g), i. e. g then f to each member of the list."

If f is an associative function, then

```
fold f (l1++l2)
  = f (fold f l1) (fold f l2)           [Law 3]
```

Informally, "we can bracket repeated applications of an associative operator however we like". This law allows us, for instance, to take a maximum of a list in two portions, and it is in such a form that we use it in the program development.

Our final law concerns the interaction of fold and map. Consider an example:

```
(fold bimax).(map add1) [2,5,1]
  = fold bimax [add1 2,add1 5,add1 1]
  = fold bimax [3,6,2]
```

The result is 6, of course. This is the same as add1 5, where 5 is the maximum of [2,5,1]. In words, we get the same result whether we take the maximum and add one, or add one to each element before taking the maximum. This is no coincidence, and is a consequence of the fact that

```
bimax (add1 a) (add1 b) = add1 (bimax a b)
```

So, if f (g a) (g b) = g (f a b) then

```
(fold f).(map g) = g.(fold f)           [Law 4]
```

Law 4 contributes towards efficiency. The application of g to *every* member of a list by map g is replaced by a *single* application of the function.

What is the final result of the transformation?

```
maxsub (a:x)   = bimax (a + maxfront x)
                       (maxsub x)
maxsub []      = 0
maxfront (a:x) = bimax (a + maxfront x)
                       0
maxfront []    = 0
```

What does this algorithm do? It states that the maximal sublist will either contain the head element (a), in which case it will have its sum given by adding a to the maximal *front* sublist of x, or it will simply be given by the maximal sublist of x. We choose the appropriate value by taking the maximum of the two. This "scanning" algorithm is an efficient one, which we might discover after some thought. *Because we found it by transformation, we can be certain that it meets its specification, and so we have no need to prove anything about it — it is manifestly correct.*

The material in this section goes to emphasise the importance of using higher order operations like map and foldr in our specifications and proofs. Because we used these we were able to use some of the general laws about them — if we use recursion we have to start proving properties *from scratch* and there can be no reuse of proofs, or verified code.

3 The transformation

In this section we present the details of the program transformation discussed in section 2, using the laws introduced there. Recall that we defined

```
maxsub = (fold bimax).(map sum).sublists
```

where `sublists` was defined above and

```
frontlists (a:x) = map ((:) a) (frontlists x)
                   ++ [[]]
frontlists []    = [[]]
```

Clearly, we can compute `maxsub []` directly — it is `0`. What is `maxsub (a:x)`?

```
maxsub (a:x)
  = ((fold bimax).(map sum).sublists) (a:x)
  = fold bimax ( map sum (sublists (a:x)))
  = fold bimax ( map sum (l1 ++ l2))
```

where

```
l1 = map ((:) a) (frontlists x)
l2 = sublists x
```

Using law 1, this last value is equal to

```
fold bimax ((map sum l1) ++ (map sum l2))
```

which by law 3, gives

```
bimax (fold bimax (map sum l1))            (†)
      (fold bimax (map sum (sublists x)))
```

In (†), the second argument to `bimax` is in fact

```
maxsub x
```

We concentrate our attention on the first argument of (†), which is, if we write out `l1` in full,

```
fold bimax (map sum (map ((:)a) (frontlists x)))
```

Looking at the argument to `fold`, we have a composition of maps, so using law 2, this inner expression will be

```
map (sum.((:) a)) (frontlists x)           (‡)
```

By the definition of `sum`, (which uses `foldr`),

```
sum.((:) a) = ((+) a) . sum
```

This means that (‡) is equal to

```
map ((+) a).sum) (frontlists x)
  = ((map ((+) a)) . (map sum)) (frontlists x)
```

Recall that this was a subexpression of the first argument of (†), which itself becomes

```
( (fold bimax).(map ((+) a)).(map sum) )
                          (frontlists x)
```

Here we see `fold` interacting with `map`, and indeed we have the condition for applying law 4, since

```
bimax (a+b) (a+c) = a + bimax b c
```

This means that we can rewrite it as

```
a + ( (fold bimax).(map sum).frontlists x )
```

If we write the definition

```
maxfront x = (fold bimax).(map sum).frontlists
x
```

then (†) will be

```
bimax (a + maxfront x)
      maxsub x
```

which was the value we gave for `maxsub (a:x)` in the previous section. A similar process of transformation yields the definition of `maxfront`.

We have shown how a series of transformations can turn an executable specification into an efficient implementation — because each of the transformations can be shown to be sound, we can be sure that the final implementation implements the specification. The transformations themselves will be used over and over again, provided that we write our programs in terms of the general higher order operations which they describe, and not simply in terms of recursion. Often we write our first attempts using explicit recursion, only to find that we could replace the recursion with a suitable higher order operation. We can do this for our final versions of `maxsub` and `maxfront` — readers might like to try this for themselves.

Common objections to such formal developments suggest that they are both lengthy and difficult. This must be the case to some extent, but things are not as difficult as we might think. Given sufficient thought we would probably reach the final algorithm for `maxsub` informally. If we reflect on the process by which we found the algorithm, we find that we have gone through processes and proofs similar to those in the derivation above — *all that our formal derivation does is to make explicit insights we already have.*

What are the prospects for such techniques in larger-scale practical applications? The techniques we have discussed will scale up, but clearly machine assistance for transformations will be essential. We would envisage this taking the form of an "assistant" which would be able to perform the book-keeping operations necessary, giving support to the programmer, rather than a fully automated system. What we want is usefully to harness the programmer's intelligence, rather than to replace it.

Space limits prevent a survey of the literature in this area: an important reference related to the work of this paper is [2].

References

[1] Jon Bentley. *Programming Pearls.* Addison Wesley, 1986.

[2] Richard Bird. *Introduction to the theory of lists.* Technical Report, PRG, Oxford University, 1987.

[3] Richard Bird and Philip Wadler. *An Introduction to Functional Programming.* Prentice-Hall, 1988.

[4] David A. Turner. An overview of Miranda. *SIGPLAN Notices*, December 1986.

[5] Ake Wikstrom. *Functional Programming in Standard ML.* Prentice-Hall, 1987.

Representing First Order Logic-Based Specifications in Petri-net-like Graphs

Kaizhi Yue
USC Information Sciences Institute
4676 Admiralty Way,
Marina del Rey, CA 90292
U.S.A.

Topics:

Specification and validation of system properties;
Knowledge representation of specification;
Petri nets;

Abstract:

We describe a formalism that maps a first order logic-based specification into a graph representation (Influence Graph). The graph can be shown to be a representation scheme equivalent to ordinary Petri nets, with an emphasis on general causal implications instead of resource usage. By making the procedural aspects of a system explicit, the graph helps users in validating specifications of system behaviors. A program has been implemented to construct, simplify and analyze influence graphs.

Extended Abstract:

1. Motivations

A declarative style is proper for describing systems in a modular and reusable way. However, a description in such a style can be difficult to understand if the interactions of system components are considered. Extracting behavior patterns, i.e., the procedural aspects of systems, e.g., cycles, nested cycles and other characteristics of behaviors, from declarative descriptions thus is important for validating system specifications. ([Cohen 84], [Kemmerer 85], [Kuipers 86], [Weld 86])

We introduce a method and a formalism for extracting behavior patterns, which generates a graph by linking logically related relations, called an *influence graph*. Unlike symbolic executions or simulations, the method works on behavior classes rather than instances, so it stays at the proper abstraction level. It deals with local (component) state rather than system states, so it will not lose information about causality. The resulting graph is equivalent to a Petri net ([Peterson 81], [Genrich 81], [Reisig 85]). But the formalism is stronger than Petri nets since it provides the basis for connections among nodes in the nets.

2. Constructing Influence Graph

2.1. Modeling primitives

The modeling primitives in the first order logic-based specifications are *objects, relations* and *transitions*. ([Cohen 84]) Transitions are defined in terms of preconditions and consequences (postconditions). A precondition is a logic formula. A consequence can be a logic formula or an update. An update defines the new value of a variable in terms of the previous state. As such, it can be converted into a logic formula (to be explained shortly).

By definition, after a transition occurs any transition whose preconditions are true can occur. However, the duration of the transition may be indefinitely long in order to model delays and other non-deterministic behaviors.

We can specify a frog trying to jump out of a well watched by a cat (see [Weld 86]), in the following specification in the language DAO (see [Yue 86]):

```
(object frog (variable-attribute frog.height))

(object cat)

(relation (asleep cat))

(relation (ready frog))

(relation (tired frog))

(axiom (∀ frog (≡ (tired frog)(not (ready frog)))))

(Constant top : integer)

(Transition (jump frog)
        (let((height-previous frog.height))
          (preconditions (> frog.height 0) (< frog.height top)
                    (ready frog)(asleep cat))
          (consequences (= frog.height (+ height-previous 3))
                    ; "frog.height increase by 3"
                    (tired frog)))))

(Transition (slide frog)
        (let((height-previous frog.height))
          (preconditions (> frog.height 2) (< frog.height top)
                    (tired frog))
          (consequences (ready frog)
                    (= frog.height (- height-previous 2))
```

```
        ; "frog.height decrease by 2"
        )))

(Transition (fall-asleep cat)
        (preconditions (not(asleep cat)))
        (consequences (asleep cat)))

(Transition (awaken cat)
        (preconditions (> frog.height 0) (asleep cat))
        (consequences (not(asleep cat))))
```

2.2. Influence Graphs

Influence graphs have two kinds of nodes, transitions and relations (graphically ovals and rectangles), and two kinds of arcs (*influences*), *enablements* and *disablements* (graphically directed arcs and arcs with circles. Conjunctions of enablements are indicated by spanning arcs.). Each transition is enabled by its preconditions and enables its consequences. Any *consequence node* P can be connected to a *precondition node* Q, if their formulae are logically linked. The arc is

(1) an enablement if $P \rightarrow Q$;

(2) a disablement if $P \rightarrow \neg Q$;

(3) a conditional enablement or disablement (graphically an arc with a diamond, but usually only the enablement is shown if there are both conditional enablement and disablement), if P and Q are n-ary formulae, and the influences only hold for a subset of the domains, i.e.,

$$\exists x, y, ... [P(x, y, ...) \rightarrow Q(x, y, ...)] \quad (1)$$

or

$$\exists x, y, ... [P(x, y, ...) \rightarrow \neg Q(x, y, ...)]. \quad (2)$$

An influence graph for the frog-cat example is in Fig. 2-1 Note that some arcs, such as 1, 2, 3, 4, 5, etc. are directly from the definition. The arcs 10 and 11 are derived because of implications.

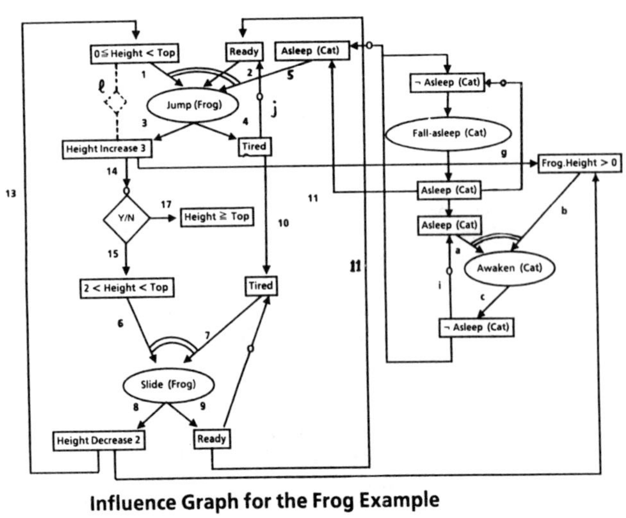

Figure 2-1: The Influence Graph for the Frog Example

A consequence can influence the preconditions of its own transition, so we have arcs like i and j. The update form "frog.height decreasing 2" can be converted into "$0 <$ frog.height $<$ top -2" on the basis of the precondition "$2 <$ frog.height $<$ top" and then we can infer arcs such as 13. The arc 14 indicates a conditional influence.

The influence arcs are inferred on the basis of logic but may not have actual effects if they are redundant or can be overwritten. This is the basis for simplifying influence graphs. The simplification can be independent of the order of occurrence of transitions and be only based on the their realizability. For example, if transition T has two preconditions P and Q, T1 is the only transition enabling P and T1 and T2 both enable Q, then the influence (here, enablement) of T2 can be ignored. The simplification may depend on the ordering of occurrence of transitions. For example, as shown in figure 2-2, if (1) transition T has two preconditions P and Q, (2) T1, T2, T3, T4 occur sequentially, (3) T3 is the only transition enabling Q and T4 disables Q, and (4) T1 and T2 influence P, then the influence of T1 can be ignored. Note that I and I' can be any influences and T1, T2, T3, and T4 need not immediately follow one another. The influence graph for the frog has been simplified, e.g., there is no arcs from node 3 to node 1. The simplification of influence graphs makes them easier to be analyzed by human or machines. Moreover, it provides insights into the system behaviors.

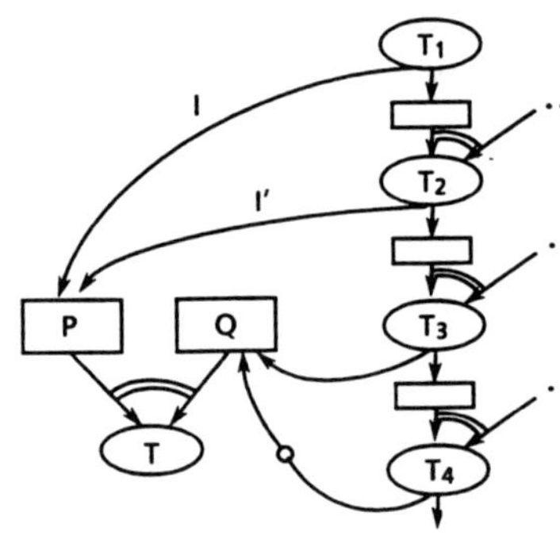

Figure 2-2: A removable arc in an influence graph

Influence graphs can be further simplified for understandability. We introduce *transition influence graphs*, in which a transition-transition arc exists from a transition T1 to a transition T, if (1) T1 enables P and P enables T , and (2) no disablement of P is parallel to T1, and (3) there is a disablement to P after the occurrence of T. The enablements and disablements corresponding to the transition-transition arc are removed from the graph. A transition influence graph is in Fig. 2-3.

3. Comparison with Ordinary Petri Nets

Influence graphs without quantifications are equivalent to ordinary Petri nets, e.g., predicate/transition-nets. (if the domains are finite.) As an example, in figure 3-1, we show how the disablement arcs are handled. Here, a relation node P enabling T, with disablements, D, D', and enablements, E, E', is converted into a Petri net unit containing a relation-node place, P+, the place for its negation, P-, and several auxiliary transitions and places. In the figure, T disables P. Other cases, e.g., T enabling P, [illegible] be handled similarly

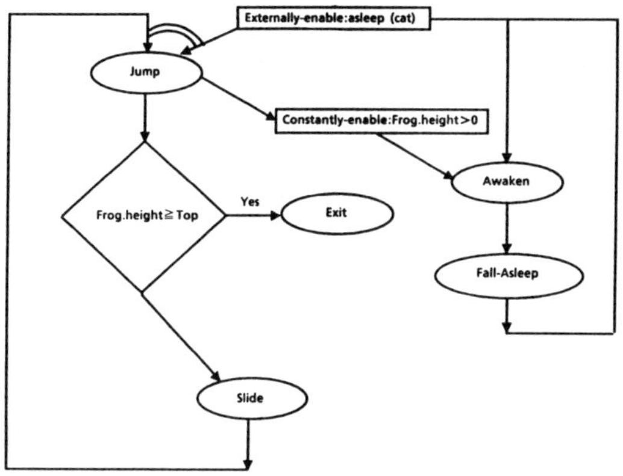

Figure 2-3: Transition Influence Graph for the Frog Example

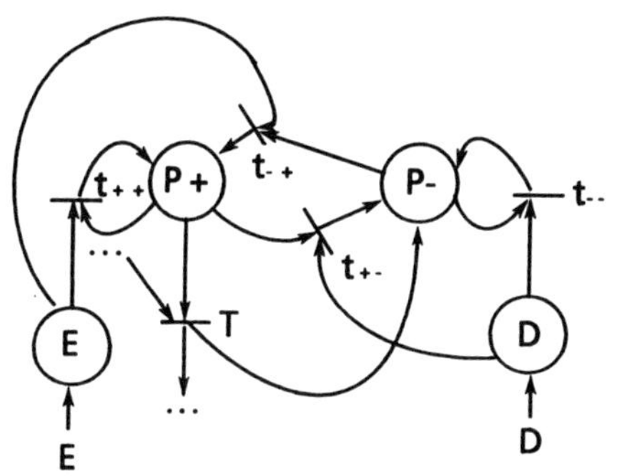

Figure 3-1: The equivalent Petri net unit for a node with disablement

However, There is a fundamental difference between the two formalisms. Unlike Petri nets, in influence graphs, the inter-transition connections (from consequences to preconditions) are distinguished from intra-transition connections and they are deducible on the basis of logic. As such, influence graphs make it possible to directly reason about behaviors defined in first order logic.

There are also minor differences in terms of processing conveniences between the two representation schemes. For example, an individualized token can be used in a Petri net for the holding of a relation, whereas the absence of a token will implicitly indicate the negation of the relation. In influence graphs, a formula and its negation have to be represented separately and explicitly. If the tokens are used for denoting physical objects, specifically resources, and if absences of tokens are not preconditions (i.e., no inhibitor arcs), a Petri net is concise and intuitive. However, in more general cases, the token representation loses its simplicity and the formulae in influence graphs are more uniform and direct.

4. Validating Specifications by Analyzing Influence Graph

Influence graphs, being graphs and equivalent to Petri nets, can benefit from all the concepts and algorithms developed in graph theory and Petri net theory. For example, in analyzing systems we wonder if certain designated component states, specifically "goal states" (see [Yue 89]), can be achieved in the system behaviors. The answer can be reduced to investigating the reachability problem for some case containing the goal states, where *reachability* is the same as in Petri net theory. ([Reisig 85]) For another example, in a cycle of transitions, some transitions contribute to make the cycle repeat, i.e, they both enable and are enabled, some other transitions are in the cycle only because they are enabled. A normal simulation or symbolic execution do not distinguish them since information are lost when putting all local interactions together to infer new system states. The analysis of influence graph, however, can indicate to the user what kind of contribution a transition makes.

5. Concluding Remarks

The formalism of influence graphs maps a first order logic-based specification into a graph representation. It can be shown that for a large class of specifications, the decidability problem of the existence of influences (between two nodes) is solvable (see [Yue 88]). It can be also shown that the graphs are a representation scheme equivalent to Petri nets. The program for constructing, analyzing and displaying influence graphs has been implemented in Common Lisp and applied to a dozen of examples.

Acknowledgment: The author has benefited from discussions in the Software Science Division of ISI.

References

[Cohen 84] Donald Cohen, "A forward inference engine to aid in understanding specifications," in *Proceedings of National Conference on Artificial Intelligence*, August 1984.

[Genrich 81] H.J.Genrich and K. Lautenbach, "System Modelling with High Level Petri Nets," *Theoretical Computer Science* 13, 1981.

[Kemmerer 85] Richard Kemmerer, "Testing Formal Specifications to Detect Design Errors," *IEEE transactions on software engineering* 11, (1), 1985.

[Kuipers 86] Kuipers, B., "Qualitative Simulation," *Artificial Intelligence* 29, (3), 1986.

[Peterson 81] James L. Peterson, *Petri Net Theory and the Modeling of Systems,* Prentice-Hall Inc., Englewood Cliffs, New Jersy, 1981.

[Reisig 85] Wolfgang Reisig, *Petri Nets,* Springer-Verlag, 1985.

[Weld 86] Weld, D., "The Use of Aggregation in Causal Simulation," *Artificial Intelligence* 30, (1), 1986.

[Yue 86] K. Yue, *Constructing and Analyzing Specifications of Real World Systems, STAN-CS-86-1090, Ph.D. Thesis,* Stanford University Computer Science Department, Technical Report, 1986.

[Yue 88] Yue, Kaizhi, Reasoning on the Basis of Component Conditions Instead of System States. Unpublished manuscript, available from the author upon request.

[Yue 89] Yue, Kaizhi, "Validating System Requirements by Functional Decomposition and Dynamic Analysis," in *To appear in Proceedings of The Eleventh Conference on Software Engineering,* Pittsburgh, Pennsylvania, May 1989.

Calculating of Z Specification

J.C.P. Woodcock

This paper will appear in the July 1989 issue (Volume 14, Number 5)
of *ACM SIGSOFT Software Engineering Notes.*

Author Index

Published by

IEEE Computer Society Press
1730 Massachusetts Avenue, N.W.
Washington, D.C. 20036-1903

IEEE Computer Society Order Number 1942
Library of Congress Number 89-80097
ISBN 0-8186-1942-2
IEEE Catalog Number 89CH2717-7
ACM Order Number 592891
ISBN 0-89791-305-1
SAN 264-620X